CW00816339

"A real masterwork from one of the most creative of contemporary New Testament scholars. Anyone who feels nervous about exploring a fully theological reading of the Gospels will take heart from this comprehensive, sophisticated, and profoundly nourishing account of how the Gospels themselves use Scripture theologically and invite us to do the same."

—**Rowan Williams**, Master, Magdalene College,
University of Cambridge

"In *Echoes of Scripture in the Gospels*, Richard Hays reads the four Gospels with an acuity of perception that is unmatched. His attention to scriptural subtexts allows each of the evangelists' visions to emerge from behind centuries' worth of obscuring and false assumptions, and to seize one's imagination afresh. Hays' prose is elegant and his arguments are utterly persuasive. Are we really prepared to hear the evangelists speak with this kind of clarity and power?"

—**Susan Garrett**, Dean and Professor of New Testament,
Louisville Presbyterian Theological Seminary

"Richard Hays has written another wonderful book. Exhibiting the extraordinary literary sensitivity and erudition of his *Echoes of Scripture in the Letters of Paul*, Hays produces here an even more important argument than in that previous, now-classic work. By tracing carefully the underpinnings of Hebrew biblical allusions in the Gospels, Hays shows how tightly these works are bound up with Israel, the God of Israel, and the Scripture of Israel. The theological implications of this work are astounding. Hays expresses it all in clear and limpid prose that makes the exegesis and the stakes clear as a bell."

—**Daniel Boyarin**, author of *The Jewish Gospels: The Story of the Jewish Christ* (2012), University of California, Berkeley

"This exceptional book combines thoroughness and elegance in equal measure, and also conjoins scholarly rigor with bold Christian conviction in its conclusions. Richard Hays has produced here a gripping account of the diverse approaches of the Evangelists to the Old Testament, and it is a volume to which I can confidently predict I will return again and again."

—**Simon Gathercole**, Reader in New Testament Studies and Fellow,
Fitzwilliam College, University of Cambridge

"Roughly a quarter of a century after his groundbreaking monograph *Echoes of Scripture in the Letters of Paul*, Richard Hays stimulates the ongoing discussion of intertextuality in New Testament writings with an impressive analysis of Scripture's polyphonic resonance in the four canonical stories of Jesus and how these intertextual semantic effects contribute substantially to the meaning and rhetorical cogency of the narratives. Richard Hays' ability to survey broad fields of knowledge and to synthesize complex textual phenomena makes *Echoes of Scripture in the Gospels* essential reading for everyone who is interested in the relevance of Scripture for understanding New Testament texts."

—**Matthias Konradt**, Lehrstuhl für Neutestamentliche Theologie,
Theologische Fakultät, Universität Heidelberg

"Every time Richard Hays has written a major book, he has opened our eyes to previously unimagined possibilities. This new book will do that too, only this time the view is an even more breathtaking invitation to fresh exegesis and theology. *Echoes of Scripture in the Gospels* challenges us to think differently about the way we read each of the four gospels—and therefore, by implication, about the traditions and early communities that stand behind them, and ultimately the elusive but powerful figure of the master exegete whose scripture-laden story these documents are telling."

—**N. T. Wright**, Research Professor of New Testament and
Early Christianity, University of St Andrews

"In this stimulating volume, Hays aims at a conversion of our imagination. By thoroughly discussing how the four Gospels adopt Scripture and create their stories of Jesus by use of numerous Scriptural echoes, Hays lays the foundations for a biblical theology of the Four Gospels."

—**Jörg Frey**, Chair of New Testament Studies, University of Zürich

"Richard Hays' *Echoes of Scripture in the Gospels* allows us to hear a rich chorus of voices in Scripture long silent. Like his *Echoes in the Letters of Paul*, Hays has performed nothing less than a *Copernican revolution* in turning the whole discipline of literary parallels and influences *upon an author* 'inside out': instead of New Testament authors like Mark or Matthew reaching back to pluck some citation to fit their need in presenting the gospel, Hays demonstrates that it was Scripture itself pressing and prodding and pushing its way into the formative thoughts and sermons and teachings about Jesus. Instead of a *monotone* word of the Evangelists' redaction, now suddenly a *mixed* chorale of melodies, a heavenly polyphony of scriptural songs burst through brightly, brilliantly to illuminate the 'good news' of God's reign. In Hays' *Echoes of Scripture in the Gospels*, God is anything but silent."

—**David P. Moessner**, A. A. Bradford Chair and Professor of Religion,
Texas Christian University

"A masterful achievement by a great scholar at the peak of his powers, *Echoes of Scripture in the Gospels* is a book that I expect to be revisiting for the rest of my life. Richard Hays traces with both depth and clarity the diverse uses the Evangelists make of the Hebrew Scriptures. His conclusion draws its title from the Emmaus Road story: 'Did not our hearts burn within us?' Indeed they did, and do."

—**Alan Jacobs**, Distinguished Professor of Humanities
in the Honors Program, Baylor University

ECHOES OF SCRIPTURE IN THE GOSPELS

Richard B. Hays

BAYLOR UNIVERSITY PRESS

If a Scripture quotation deviates from the New Revised Standard Version Bible, ©1989, it is the author's modification.

Cover design by Hannah Feldmeier
Cover art by Hannah Feldmeier, based on a photograph of the Four Evangelists scene within the Lamentation Window, Cologne Cathedral, Cologne, Germany. Photograph courtesy of Father Dave Dwyer.
Book design by Diane Smith

Library of Congress Cataloging-in-Publication Data

Names: Hays, Richard B., author.
Title: Echoes of scripture in the gospels / Richard B. Hays.
Description: Waco : Baylor University Press, 2016. | Includes bibliographical references and index.
Identifiers: LCCN 2015041443 | ISBN 9781481304917 (hardback : alk. paper) | ISBN 9781481305129 (ePub) | ISBN 9781481305136 (mobi) | ISBN 9781481305143 (web pdf)
Subjects: LCSH: Bible. Gospels—Criticism, interpretation, etc. | Bible. Gospels—Relation to the Old Testament. | Bible. Old Testament—Relation to the Gospels.
Classification: LCC BS2555.52 .H385 2016 | DDC 226/.066—dc23
LC record available at http://lccn.loc.gov/2015041443

For Judy,
my true companion.

This is the day that the Lord has made;
let us rejoice and be glad in it.

Psalm 118:24

CONTENTS

Preface

The unusual circumstances under which this book has been brought to publication obligate me to offer the reader a few words of explanation. And the extraordinary help I have received in completing the manuscript also calls for much more than the conventional expressions of thanks. To explain what I mean, a brief autobiographical narrative is necessary.

For the first twenty years of my academic career, I focused my attention chiefly on the theology of Paul the Apostle. Among the topics I explored was Paul's subtle and many-faceted engagement with Israel's Scripture. My studies of this question eventually resulted in two books: *Echoes of Scripture in the Letters of Paul* (1989) and *The Conversion of the Imagination* (published in 2005, but incorporating chiefly essays originally written before 2000). Starting during a sabbatical leave in 2001–2002, I began to think about how the hermeneutical observations I had made about Paul might open up fruitful lines of inquiry about the Gospels. Of course, the secondary literature on the Gospels is vast, and in order to move seriously into this field of study, I had a lot of homework to do. And so, during the years from 2001 to 2008, I began to focus my research and teaching on the canonical Gospels, and I turned out a few articles that offered preliminary probes into the question of how the four Evangelists interpreted Scripture.

It was during another sabbatical leave year in 2008–2009 that I began in earnest the work of writing the present book. I spent the first part of that sabbatical in Cambridge, where I was in residence as a Visiting Fellow at Clare Hall and enjoyed the use of the Tyndale House library; the latter part of the sabbatical was spent at the Center of Theological Inquiry in Princeton. By the end of that year, I had completed rough drafts of the major chapters on the three Synoptic Gospels and had begun work on John.

After I returned home to Duke, my progress on the book was brought nearly to a standstill early in 2010, when I was unexpectedly asked to step into the position of Dean of the Divinity School. From 2010 until the summer of 2015, my time was chiefly devoted to the multiple administrative responsibilities of the deanship, and the unfinished book manuscript languished most of the time in my file cabinet. I was able to do a little polishing occasionally, but little more.

There was a significant step forward, however, when I was asked to deliver the Hulsean Lectures in Cambridge during 2013–2014. For the meat of those lectures, I excerpted some bits of my much larger unfinished manuscript, focusing particularly on the question of "divine identity Christology" in the Gospels. These lectures afforded me the opportunity to sharpen my arguments and to write introductory and concluding lectures to frame the project. In light of the enthusiastic reception of the lectures—and the strong encouragement of my wife Judy, who urged me to go ahead and publish the lectures for the benefit of the church—I decided to shape the Hulseans into a little book, which appeared in 2014 as *Reading Backwards: Figural Christology and the Fourfold Gospel Witness*. Dr. Carey Newman of Baylor University Press played a key role in supporting the project and facilitating its publication.

In the spring of 2015, I announced my intention to conclude my term as Dean in the summer of 2016, hoping and intending to take another sabbatical in 2016–2017 to finish up work on the long-delayed book. But just a few months later, unforeseen circumstances intervened. In July 2015 I was suddenly diagnosed with pancreatic cancer. In light of this shattering diagnosis, I stepped down from the deanship immediately and went on medical leave. As I write these words in early October 2015, I have been through two months of chemotherapy and radiation treatments, and it is still unknown whether the treatments will have been sufficiently effective to make it possible for me to undergo surgery. If so, my prognosis will be uncertain. If not, my life expectancy will be short.

The awkward task of relating this personal background story is necessary in order for me to explain the remarkable events of the past two months. The prospect of impending death has the effect, as Samuel Johnson famously remarked, of concentrating the mind wonderfully. (I believe Johnson was referring to someone who was going to be hanged, but the point is pertinent nonetheless.) In addition to setting personal affairs in order and devoting all possible time to my family, the one large outstanding academic task for me in this moment of crisis was to attempt if possible to finish "The Book." In the midst of our personal grappling with anticipatory grief, Judy urged that we invite Carey Newman to come for a visit to discuss what could be done. And so in August, Carey came to spend a couple of days with us in Durham for brainstorming and strategizing.

The outcome of those conversations was an urgent and ambitious plan for completing the work and setting the book on a fast track to publication. We agreed that while I was finishing my chemo and radiation treatments, I would plunge into the task of finishing the John chapter, which was less than half written, and composing the introduction and conclusion. Carey then recruited a team of four of my friends and colleagues who graciously agreed to work on completing, updating, and fine-tuning the footnotes for my drafts of each of the four Gospel chapters. (I will name and thank each of them below.) They turned this work around in an astonishingly short time. Carey himself took up the task of what he described as "light copyediting" and handed the manuscript off to his editorial staff at Baylor, who started producing page proofs in a matter of days and sending them back, chapter by chapter, for me to read even before I had finished my own work on the introduction and conclusion. The astonishing result is that within less than two months, the substantive content of the book is finished. The arduous tasks of extracting a bibliography from the book's footnotes, compiling indices, final proofreading, and production are all being undertaken by the staff at Baylor.

Readers of this book are entitled to some account of how its content is related to the content of *Reading Backwards.* As I have explained, the Hulsean Lectures were in large part extracted from the larger unfinished manuscript. Consequently, it would be misleading to think of the present book as an expansion or development of *Reading Backwards.* The situation is, rather, the reverse: *Echoes of Scripture in the Gospels* is the parent or precursor work. Consequently, readers already familiar with *Reading Backwards* will find that *Echoes of Scripture in the Gospels* includes extended chunks of material that are substantially identical with, though in some cases slightly revised from, parts of the previously published work. I would estimate that about a quarter of the content of the present book was included in the Hulseans and/or first published in *Reading Backwards*. But here those chunks of material are set into the context of a wider examination of the Evangelists' reading of Israel's Scripture. The focus of *Echoes of Scripture in the Gospels* is not limited exclusively to the question of divine identity Christology; instead, this book seeks to shed light on the whole range of scriptural interpretation and hermeneutics in each of the four Gospels.

Inevitably, the rapid production of this book has some disadvantages. Careful readers may find a few places in which there is some redundancy, places where I have adduced the same evidence or explained the same phenomenon more than once. Given world enough and time, I would have subjected the text to more careful scrutiny to iron out such repetitions. Perhaps in a book this long, however, the occasional bit of repetition might prove more helpful than unhelpful. Likewise, if it had been possible for me to devote a year, rather than just a few weeks, to completing the writing of the book, I would have developed a much fuller theoretical account of my methodology. I would have engaged in more extended critical discussion with other studies of intertexuality and figural exegesis. But perhaps it is a mercy to the reader not to be subjected to too many pages of secondary theoretical discourse. The thing that matters in the end is the actual *reading* and interpretation of the primary texts. That is where my interpretations will stand or fall.

As in *Reading Backwards*, I want to acknowledge several journals and publishers for permission to reproduce and/or adapt material from some of my earlier published attempts to explore aspects of the Evangelists' use of Israel's Scripture. I would like to thank the journal *Pro Ecclesia* for permission to include and adapt some material that originally appeared in my essay "Can the Gospels Teach Us to Read the Old Testament?" *Pro Ecclesia* 11 (2002): 402–18. Likewise, I offer thanks to Cambridge University Press for permission to incorporate some material from my article "The Canonical Matrix of the Gospels," in *The Cambridge Companion to the Gospels* (ed. Stephen C. Barton; Cambridge: Cambridge University Press, 2006), 53–75. Portions of my Matthew chapter were adapted from my article in the South African journal *HTS Teologiese Studies/Theological Studies:* "The Gospel of Matthew: Reconfigured Torah," *HTS Theological Studies* 61, nos. 1–2 (2005): 165–90. My chapter on the Gospel of Luke has adapted a few paragraphs from my essay "Reading the Bible with Eyes of Faith: The Practice of Theological

Exegesis," *Journal of Theological Interpretation* 1 (2007): 5–21. And my John chapter has adapted short passages from my essay "The Materiality of John's Symbolic World," in *Preaching John's Gospel: The World It Imagines* (ed. David Fleer and David Bland; St. Louis: Chalice, 2008), 5–12. I have also drawn from "Reading Scripture in Light of the Resurrection," in *The Art of Reading Scripture* (ed. Ellen F. Davis and Richard B. Hays; Grand Rapids: Eerdmans, 2003), 216–38; "The Liberation of Israel in Luke–Acts: Intertextual Narration as Countercultural Practice," in *Reading the Bible Intertextually* (ed. Richard B. Hays, Stefan Alkier, and Leroy A. Huizenga; Waco, Tex.: Baylor University Press, 2009), 101–17; "Intertextuality, Narrative, and the Problem of Unity of the Biblical Canon," in *Kanon und Intertextualität* (ed. Stefan Alkier and Richard B. Hays; Kleine Schriften des Fachbereichs Evangelische Theologie der Goethe-Universität Frankfurt/Main, Band 1; Frankfurt am Main: Otto Lembeck, 2010), 53–70; "The Future of Scripture," *Wesleyan Theological Journal* 46 (2011): 24–38.

The important task that remains for me in this preface is to extend my deepest thanks to those who have contributed to bringing my work to fruition in this book. In the preface of *Reading Backwards*, I compiled a lengthy list of acknowledgments, both indicating my intellectual debts to other scholars and expressing thanks to many persons and institutions that had helped and encouraged me in one way or another in the thinking-through and writing of that book. I will not repeat that lengthy roll call here, but I draw the reader's attention to it, because all those intellectual debts and words of thanks remain no less significant with regard to the development of this larger book. Here, however, I simply want to offer thanks to a short list of people without whom *Echoes of Scripture in the Gospels* could never have come to completion in such a remarkably short time.

First of all, Carey Newman: conversation partner, visionary, impresario, cheerleader, captain of a team of "special forces" that has accomplished a feat I would have thought impossible within the time frame. I can say unequivocally that without Carey's encouragement and organizational skill, this book would still be sitting sadly in my file drawer as an unrealized dream.

Second, my gratitude goes to all of the staff at Baylor University Press who seemingly waved a magic wand to turn my detailed manuscript into page proofs with breathtaking speed. Diane Smith, the Director of Production and Design at the Press, was the chief magician who conjured the book into existence, but many others there—especially

Jenny Hunt and Cade Jarrell—performed Herculean service behind the scenes to help the finished book appear in the blink of an eye.

Third, my research assistant Chris Blumhofer played a crucial role in tracking down material I needed, proofreading all the Greek and Hebrew in the book and converting it into the right set of fonts for the press, catching a number of errors in the text, and handling numerous liaison duties with the press.

Fourth: words fail me to express the depth of my gratitude to the four friends who accepted the thankless task of filling in gaps in my endnotes. Many of the notes in the Synoptic Gospels chapters were already complete and fully documented in my manuscript, and most of the notes with lengthy comments and references to primary biblical texts are entirely my work. But in many more places I had written placeholder notes to myself saying something like "See what Luz says about this" or "Wright, *NT and the People of God*—find reference." And in still other places, I had not incorporated references to important secondary literature, especially literature that appeared after 2009. And so Carey Newman very quickly mobilized a team of four colleagues to bring the notes up to date and up to snuff for publication. They did so skillfully and speedily, making substantive contributions to the book's engagement with other relevant scholarship. I therefore want to acknowledge that the documentation found in the endnotes is truly the result of a collaborative effort. Each of the contributors to this team effort receives my profound gratitude for undertaking this work. Here are the members of the team:

> Notes on the Gospel of Mark: Dr. David Moffitt, the University of St Andrews, Scotland
> Notes on the Gospel of Matthew: Dr. Joshua Leim, Whitworth College
> Notes on the Gospel of Luke: Prof. C. Kavin Rowe, Duke Divinity School
> Notes on the Gospel of John: Prof. Marianne Meye Thompson, Fuller Theological Seminary

David, Josh, and Kavin all did their doctoral studies in New Testament here at Duke during my time on the faculty. I am now glad to count all three of them as colleagues and friends. And Marianne is a long-time friend and fellow-worker in the vineyard of New Testament studies. Her work calls for special recognition, because the documentation in my chapter on John was much thinner than in the Synoptic Gospels chapters. Having just completed her commentary on John for the New Testament Library series (Westminster John Knox), she volunteered her services to help with the notes on John. Her comprehensive knowledge of the literature has made the documentation for that chapter far more complete and useful to readers than it would have been had I been left to my own limited devices and limited time. In a very real sense, then, this book is not just mine; it is the product of a community of friends and scholars called to a common task.

Through all of this process, my wife, Judy, has played an indispensable role. She has consulted closely with Carey and me about the design of the cover and the interior look and layout of the book. She has continued to ask me probing questions about my arguments, and she has encouraged me in my dark moments of doubt about whether I could finish this work. She has continued to sacrifice her own priorities and desires for precious time together while I labored at my desk. Only she understands the persistent sense of vocation that has driven my academic work over the years. And only I have some inkling of what that vocation has cost her, and cost us both. Judy has been my true companion through our daily walk of putting one foot in front of the other, often reminding me that we should make each day shine, for "This is the day that the Lord has made; let us rejoice and be glad in it." This word laid upon her heart comes from Psalm 118, a psalm that prefigures resurrection. For all these reasons and a thousand more, this book is dedicated to her, in hope.

Richard B. Hays
Durham, North Carolina
7 October 2015

INTRODUCTION
Figural Interpretation of Israel's Scripture

Reading Scripture through the eyes of the Evangelists?

When Martin Luther published his German translation of the Pentateuch in 1523, he composed a preface explaining why his German readers
should value the Old Testament. Presumably then, as now, there was
some tendency in the churches to denigrate or disregard Israel's Scripture in favor of the allegedly more pure and spiritual New Testament.
Here is what Luther wrote:

> There are some who have little regard for the Old Testament. They think
> of it as a book that was given to the Jewish people only and is now out of
> date, containing only stories of past times. . . . But Christ says in John 5,
> "Search the Scriptures, for it is they that bear witness to me." . . . [T]he
> Scriptures of the Old Testament are not to be despised but diligently
> read. . . . Therefore dismiss your own opinions and feelings and think of
> the Scriptures as the loftiest and noblest of holy things, as the richest of
> mines which can never be sufficiently explored, in order that you may find
> that divine wisdom which God here lays before you in such simple guise
> as to quench all pride. Here you will find the swaddling cloths and the
> manger in which Christ lies. . . . Simple and lowly are these swaddling
> cloths, but dear is the treasure, Christ, who lies in them.[1]

1

"The manger in which Christ lies": it is a striking image, a vivid trope of the sort that Luther relished. What is Luther doing here? He is reading the Lukan birth story *figurally*, employing the manger as a metaphor for the manner in which the Old Testament contains Jesus Christ. Just as Jesus was wrapped in humble swaddling cloths in the manger, so too is he wrapped in the swaddling cloths of the Law, the Prophets, and the Writings.

We might put it this way: Luther is reading the New Testament figurally in order to proclaim the legitimacy of a figural reading of the Old. Only if we frame the question this way, only if we embrace figural interpretation, can we make sense of the Gospel of John's assertion that the Scriptures bear witness to Jesus Christ. He is the treasure who lies metaphorically wrapped in the folds of the Old Testament. But if he is wrapped, that suggests he is not only contained but also partly concealed within the manger. The interpreter of Christian Scripture must first enter the humble surroundings of the stable, as did the shepherds in Bethlehem, and then *"search the Scriptures"* by reading backwards to unwind the swaddling cloths and to disclose the Christ who lies there.

All four of the four canonical Evangelists, in interestingly distinct ways, embody and enact the sort of figural christological reading that Luther commends. Indeed, it would seem that Luther learned this hermeneutical strategy precisely from the Evangelists; he dares to proclaim that the Old Testament is "the manger in which Christ lies" precisely because Matthew, Mark, Luke, and John have taught him to read Scripture metaphorically.

But what is meant by "figural interpretation"? Here is Erich Auerbach's classic definition:

> Figural interpretation establishes a connection between two events or persons in such a way that the first signifies not only itself but also the second, while the second involves or fulfills the first. The two poles of a figure are separated in time, but both, being real events or persons, are within temporality. They are both contained in the flowing stream which is historical life, and only the comprehension, the *intellectus spiritualis*, of their interdependence is a spiritual act.[2]

There is consequently a significant difference between *prediction* and *prefiguration*. Figural reading of the Bible need not presume that the Old Testament authors—or the characters they narrate—were conscious of predicting or anticipating Christ. Rather, the discernment of a figural correspondence is necessarily retrospective rather than prospective.[3] The act of retrospective recognition is the *intellectus spiritualis*. Because the two poles of a figure are events within "the flowing stream" of time, the correspondence can be discerned only after the second event has occurred and imparted a new pattern of significance to the first. But once the pattern of correspondence has been grasped, the semantic force of the figure flows both ways, as the second event receives deeper significance from the first.[4] For that reason, a hermeneutical strategy that relies on figural interpretation of the Bible creates deep theological coherence within the biblical narrative; it "sets forth the unity of the canon as a single cumulative and complex pattern of meaning."[5]

This sort of figural reading—proclaiming that the events of Jesus' life, death, and resurrection took place "according to the Scriptures"—stands at the heart of the New Testament's message. All four canonical Gospels declare that the Torah and the Prophets and the Psalms mysteriously prefigure Jesus. The author of the Fourth Gospel puts the claim succinctly: in the same passage in John 5 to which Luther pointed, Jesus declares, "If you believed Moses, you would believe me, for he wrote about me" (John 5:46).

But, of course, this kind of reading has been distinctly out of fashion since the advent of modern historical criticism. Indeed, one reason for modernity's incredulity toward the Christian faith is the charge that Christian proclamation rests on twisted and tendentious misreadings of the Hebrew Scriptures. Historical criticism, of the sort commonly practiced in the academic guild for the past two centuries, characteristically judges that the New Testament's christological readings of Israel's Scripture are simply a big mistake: they twist and misrepresent the original sense of the texts.

To cite a single example, consider the following quotation from the distinguished German New Testament scholar Udo Schnelle, in his *Theology of the New Testament*: "A 'biblical theology' is not possible because: (1) the Old Testament is *silent* about Jesus Christ, [and] (2) the resurrection from the dead *of one who was crucified* cannot be integrated into any ancient system of meaning formation."[6] Notice that both of these reasons adduced by Schnelle for the impossibility of a biblical theology directly contradict the explicit testimony of the New Testament writers themselves. They emphatically do not think the Old Testament is silent about Jesus Christ, and they assert that the resurrection of Jesus from the dead actually provides the hermeneutical clue that decisively integrates Israel's entire "system of meaning formation."[7] It is a particularly poignant irony that Schnelle holds the chair as Professor of New Testament at the University of Halle-Wittenberg: the geographical proximity of Professor Schnelle to Luther's home base accentuates the hermeneutical distance traveled by biblical scholarship since the sixteenth century.[8]

Schnelle's views are hardly idiosyncratic. His forthright statements simply bring into clear focus a set of issues that require careful attention and theological reflection. The reading strategies of historical criticism—strategies that are themselves historically contingent—have created a cluster of quandaries for Christian theology. Why do the Gospel writers read Scripture in such surprising ways? Does Christian faith require the illegitimate theft of someone else's sacred texts? The full depth of these problems is too rarely explored in our theology.

In this book, I will propose that the Gospel writers summon us to a conversion of the imagination. We will learn to read Scripture rightly only if our minds and imaginations are opened by seeing the scriptural text—and therefore the world—through the Evangelists' eyes. In order to explore that hermeneutical possibility, we must give close consideration to the revisionary figural ways that the four Gospel writers actually read Israel's Scripture. How does each one draw upon the Old Testament to depict the identity of Jesus and to interpret his significance? Are their readings intelligible as coherent or persuasive interpretations of the Scriptures?

Our familiarity with the Gospels may actually blind us to the extraordinary hermeneutical revolution wrought by their performances of scriptural interpretation. In the opening chapter of *The Wound of Knowledge*, Rowan Williams incisively characterizes that revolution: "Christian faith has its beginnings in an experience of profound contradictoriness, an experience which so questioned the religious categories of its time that the resulting reorganization of religious language was a centuries-long task."[9] The "experience of profound contradictoriness" is, of course, the crucifixion of Jesus as the event that somehow brought God's salvation to the world: "the paradox of God's purpose made flesh in a dead and condemned man."[10] Of course, the testimony of the Gospel writers is that the dead and condemned man Jesus was also raised triumphant from the dead. Williams' formulation, however, highlights the troubling, counter-intuitive character of the early Christian proclamation of Jesus' death as a saving event—as well as the hermeneutical complexity of the community's efforts to understand that event's meaning.

The "reorganization of religious language" to which Williams refers is the subsequent process of *retrospective reinterpretation* of Israel's traditions and of the earliest stories about Jesus, in dialogue with one another, and in light of the events of the cross and resurrection. It is, in other words, a process of *reading backwards* in light of new revelatory events. We see the beginnings of this "reorganization" within the New Testament itself in the New Testament writers' reinterpretations of Israel's Scripture.

Even if the Gospel writers were questioning and reorganizing their inherited "religious categories," there is nonetheless a certain obvious sense in which the Gospels arose out of the religious and cultural matrix of the Old Testament. Jesus and his first followers were Jews whose symbolic world was shaped by Israel's Scripture: their ways of interpreting the world and their hopes for God's saving action were fundamentally conditioned by the biblical stories of God's dealings with the people Israel. Therefore, it is not surprising that as the earliest Christian communities began to tell and retell stories about Jesus, they interpreted his life, death, and resurrection in relation to those biblical stories (i.e., the texts that Christians later came to call the Old Testament). The authors of our four canonical Gospels were the heirs of this tradition of storytelling, and they shared the early Christian community's passionate concern—a concern that, as far as we can tell, goes back to Jesus himself—to show that Jesus' teachings and actions, as well as his violent death and ultimate vindication, constituted the continuation and climax of the ancient biblical story.

Difficulties for contemporary Christian theology, however, arise wherever this acute awareness of narrative continuity with Israel's Scripture is lost—whether unwittingly forfeited or deliberately rejected. Many Christian congregations today are in fact naively Marcionite in their theology and practice: in their worship services they have no Old Testament reading, or if the Old Testament is read it is rarely preached upon. Judaism is regarded as a legalistic foil from which Jesus has delivered us. I once had a Divinity student say to me in class: "Judaism was a harsh religion that taught people to *fear* God's judgment, but Jesus came to teach us to *love* God with all our heart and soul and strength." Sadly, this earnest student was completely unaware that the command to love God with all your heart and soul and strength, quoted by Jesus in Mark 12:29-30 and parallels, comes from Deuteronomy 6:5 and that it stands at the heart of daily prayer in the Jewish tradition.

The unconscious Marcionite bias reflected in this student's words has had a disastrous effect on the theological imagination of many churches, and indeed on certain sectors of New Testament scholarship: everything in the Gospels that looks too much like the Old Testament is screened out as "inauthentic" and theologically dangerous—teachings about the election of a particular people, the mandate for holiness and purity, the expectation of God's ultimate judgment of the world. All this is excluded from the authentic red-letter material of what Jesus "really" taught.

This is the sort of thing Dietrich Bonhoeffer had in mind when he wrote, near the end of his life, about the crucial importance of having our lives and our understanding grounded in the Old Testament: "Whoever would too quickly and too directly be and feel in accordance with the New Testament is, in my opinion, no Christian."[11] In Bonhoeffer's historical setting, he was locked in a life-and-death struggle with a heretical and malevolent "German Christianity" that sought to cut Christianity loose from its Jewish roots. Although in the early twenty-first century we face different cultural and political challenges, the task of maintaining the rootage of Christian faith in the Old Testament is no less urgent. In the spirit of Bonhoeffer's admonition, this book will seek to trace the ways in which the Gospel writers themselves articulated their message through deep engagement with Israel's Scripture.

The design of this book: Scope, structure, and method

Anyone who has explored this area of study realizes how impossible is the task of accounting fully for the vast intertextual network of scriptural citations, allusions, and echoes in the four canonical Gospels. Furthermore, the historical and theological issues that ripple outward from such a study are numerous and complex. The reader of this book may therefore be assisted by a few preliminary pointers about what the book will and will not seek to accomplish.

Scope. First of all, *this is not a book about "the historical Jesus,"* or an attempt to reconstruct how Jesus of Nazareth interpreted Scripture or understood his own vocation and identity.[12] That sort of reconstructive work is fascinating and perhaps important for some purposes, but it necessarily entails a series of complex hypothetical judgments about facts and events "behind" the Gospel texts and about the processes of evolution and transmission that generated these texts.[13] The present book seeks more modestly to study the *literary* shape and texture of the Gospels that the Evangelists wrote, with attention to their evocations of Israel's Scripture and with the aim of clearly distinguishing their voices. This project is still very much a *historical* task, but it entails the description and analysis of extant texts rather than conjectural reconstruction of events predating the texts that are our primary sources for knowledge of Jesus.

Second, *this is not a book about the social context of the communities that produced, received, and transmitted the traditions found in the Gospels*; nor does the book attempt to argue for any particular hypothesis about a scribal school or about the social or geographical location of the authors of the Gospel texts.

Third, *this is not a book that seeks to explain how the early Christian communities came to develop their remarkable beliefs about Jesus as the embodiment of the God of Israel.* In this way, the present book differs in its aims from other recent studies that have argued—in my judgment, rightly—for a fresh consideration of the development of a "high" Christology at a very early stage of the history of the earliest church.[14]

Instead, *this is a book that offers an account of the narrative representation of Israel, Jesus, and the church in the canonical Gospels, with particular attention to the ways in which the four Evangelists reread Israel's Scripture—as well as the ways in which Israel's Scripture prefigures and illuminates the central character in the Gospel stories.* It is, in short, an exercise in intertextual close reading. Such a reading may offer fresh perspectives that might prove helpful in exploring the difficult historical questions outlined in the previous paragraphs, but that is not the aim of the present study.

One possible critique of the approach taken in this book might go something like this: Does this approach to the Evangelists as authors engaged in intertextual narration presuppose an anachronistic view of the Gospel writers as creative literary geniuses? Were the Evangelists consciously manipulating snippets of preexisting traditions to craft their own clever imaginative fictions? A concern of this kind was articulated by Markus Bockmuehl in an incisive private communication responding to some of the ideas found in the present book:

> I wonder if there may not be an equally important dynamic whose force operates the other way. It seems both a matter of fact and part of the biblical authors' intent that their engagement with the Old Testament is at least as much a function of the text's own agency in terms of its (divine) *claim and impact on them*, rather than merely of their "use" of it. Could one say that that they speak as they do because they are thunderstruck by the pressure that Scripture *as a hermeneutical Other* exerts on their own view of things? In other words, perhaps what seems to the critic as a device or strategy of manipulation may have seemed to the authors mere faithfulness

to the divine word's strong naming of the fresh reality God had worked in their midst.[15]

I cite Bockmuehl's cautionary counterpoint chiefly in order to endorse it and to clarify that I do not want to be understood as suggesting that the Evangelists were engaged in fanciful Promethean poetic creativity. Indeed, as Bockmuehl proposes, they may indeed have been "thunderstruck" by the paradigm-shattering implications of their fresh encounter with Israel's Scripture in light of the story of Jesus.

As long ago as my book *Echoes of Scripture in the Letters of Paul,* I was fumbling toward articulating something like this by arguing that Paul's interpretation of the Old Testament was an instance of "dialectical," rather than "heuristic," intertextuality:

> The difference between these modes of imitation lies in the extent to which the subtext is finally allowed by the poet to retain its own voice, to answer back, to challenge the poet's own attempt at integration. . . . [T]he precursor goes on speaking in the derivative text. . . . Paul's proclamation needs the blessing of Scripture, and Scripture's witness . . . stands in judgment of all formulations of the gospel. On the other hand, Scripture's witness gains its eschatological coherence only in light of the gospel.[16]

Just this same sort of dialectical interaction is hardwired into the practice of figural interpretation that is characteristic of the hermeneutics of the Evangelists. It will be the burden of the present book to illustrate how this dialectic operates in the Gospel narratives.

Another way of putting this point is to say that the Gospel narratives are not simply artful edifying fictions; rather, they are *testimony.* Our primary task as readers is to listen carefully to the four Evangelists' acts of narrative witness-bearing and to discern the ways in which *their testimony is the product of a catalytic fusion of Israel's Scripture and the story of Jesus.*

Structure. The structural plan of the book is simple. Following this introductory chapter, there will be one chapter on each of the four Gospels, seeking to listen to the distinctive voice of each and delineating the ways in which they draw upon Scripture—both explicitly and implicitly—in their narratives.

Each of these four chapters will have five sections, following the same fivefold heuristic pattern, as follows:

- The Evangelist as interpreter of Israel's Scripture: overview.
- How does the Evangelist invoke/evoke Scripture to re-narrate Israel's story?
- How does the Evangelist invoke/evoke Scripture to narrate the identity of Jesus?
- How does the Evangelist invoke/evoke Scripture to narrate the church's role in relation to the world?
- Summary conclusion: findings about the distinctive scriptural hermeneutics of the Evangelist.

A final chapter will then reflect on the similarities and differences in the Gospels' hermeneutical approaches to the task of telling the Gospel story. What are the benefits and potential pitfalls of each of the four strategies of narration? What do they share in common, and what tensions might distinguish them? Finally, can we read Israel's Scripture in the same ways they did? And, if so, what theological consequences might follow?

The decision to treat all four canonical Evangelists together as readers of Scripture requires some comment and justification. It has become a commonplace of Gospel studies in modernity to set the Gospel of John apart as a late text that reflects a more advanced stage of doctrinal development and a "higher" Christology. Because of this critical convention, the question naturally arises whether to focus a study of this kind on the Synoptic Gospels only and to leave John out of the mix, perhaps reserving the Fourth Gospel for a subsequent study. But the more deeply one explores the ways the synoptic Evangelists evoke Israel's Scripture, the more steadily the recognition grows that their common witness to the latent import of Israel's Scripture belongs closely together with John's witness. To be sure, John has his own distinctive narrative idiom and style—as indeed do all four of the Evangelists—but, at the end of day, John joins in chorus with the testimony of Mark, Matthew, and Luke that Jesus was not only the Son of God but actually the embodiment of the divine presence in the world. For that reason, to exclude John from consideration would be to occlude an important aspect of the fourfold Gospel witness and to perpetuate a critical convention that, theologically considered, obscures more than it reveals. The present study, therefore, follows the lead of the early church fathers, Irenaeus above all, in affirming both the legitimacy of figural interpretation of Israel's Scripture and the complementarity of the four Evangelists. Indeed, these two affirmations are hermeneutically intertwined as one unbreakable cord.

Method. If the structural design of the book is straightforward, its inter-pretative methodology is only slightly less so. This study presupposes that all four canonical Gospels are deeply embedded in a symbolic world shaped by the Old Testament—or, to put the point in a modern critical idiom, that their "encyclopedia of production" is constituted in large mea-sure by Israel's Scripture. This does not mean that the symbolic world of Greco-Roman pagan antiquity is insignificant for the Gospels, but that it is secondary; the Evangelists' constructive christological affirmations are derived chiefly from hermeneutical appropriation and transformation of Israel's sacred texts and traditions. Therefore, within the frame of cul-tural knowledge provided by the stories and prayers of Israel's Scripture, the Gospels insistently gesture toward the meaning of Jesus' life, death, and resurrection by quoting or evoking scriptural texts. This means that a discerning interpretation of a Gospel text will often require recovery and exploration of these precursor texts.

Some of the Evangelists' evocations of Scripture are indirect in char-acter, referring or alluding to biblical texts, events, or characters with-out an explicit quotation formula or extended verbatim citation. There is nothing surprising about this fact; all literature—indeed, all human discourse—includes elements of intertextuality.[17]

We can roughly categorize the scriptural intertextual references in the Gospels by employing the terms "quotation," "allusion," and "echo." These terms are approximate markers on the spectrum of intertextual linkage, moving from the most to the least explicit forms of reference. Generally speaking, a "quotation" is introduced by a citation formula (e.g., "as it is written"), or it features the verbatim reproduction of an extended chain of words, often a sentence or more, from the source text. An "allusion" usually imbeds several words from the precursor text, or it at least in some way explicitly mentions notable characters or events that signal the reader to make the intertextual connection. It is difficult to separate the concept of allusion from notions of authorial intentionality; the meaning of a text in which an allusion occurs would be opaque or severely diminished if the reader failed to recognize the implied reference to the earlier text. "Echo" is the least distinct, and therefore always the most disputable, form of intertextual reference; it may involve the inclusion of only a word or phrase that evokes, for the alert reader, a reminiscence of an earlier text. Readers who hear the echo will discern some semantic nuance that carries a surplus of significance beyond the literal sense of the text in which the echo occurs; ordinarily, however, the surface meaning of the text would be intelligible to readers who fail to hear the echoed language.[18]

In all three of these forms of intertextual reference in the Gospels, readers should be on the alert for the possibility that any particular intertextual connection may create a poetic effect known as "metalepsis." Metalepsis is a literary technique of citing or echoing a small bit of a precursor text in such a way that the reader can grasp the significance of the echo only by recalling or recovering the original context from which the fragmentary echo came and then reading the two texts in dialogical juxtaposition. The figurative effect of such an intertextual linkage lies in the unstated or suppressed points of correspondence between the two texts.[19] As our study of the Gospels unfolds, we will discover many such instances in which the Evangelists, writing within the "cave of resonant signification"[20] created by Israel's Scripture, create allusive narratives that beckon the reader to hear and activate recollections of their biblical precursors.

This is not some arcane theory-driven methodology. It is a matter of simple attention to the way that human language and storytelling ordinarily work.[21] I offer by way of illustration a single elegant contemporary example.

In his eloquent victory speech on the night of his initial election to the presidency of the United States in 2008, Barack Obama declared that his hearers could put their hands "on the arc of history and bend it once more toward the hope of a better day." The phrase echoed a maxim from the speeches of Martin Luther King Jr.: "The arc of the moral universe is long, but it bends toward justice." Certainly Obama's declaration was not a direct quotation of King; the verbal link between the two utterances depends on just two words, *arc* and *bend*. But just as certainly, Obama's sentence was an audible echo that summoned his audience to take up once again the moral legacy of the American civil rights struggle and to renew their efforts to work for a just society.[22]

This example illustrates the way that literary echo can create subtle semantic transformations. King's dictum functioned as a word of *assurance* to his hearers that their struggle belonged to a larger providential purpose ("the moral arc of the universe") that would inevitably prevail; by contrast, Obama's evocation of King's words functioned as a word of *exhortation* to his listeners to recommit their energies to building a better world. There is no explicit appeal here to an insuperable transcendent design; instead, there is an emphasis on the necessity of human agency. Yet the echo of King's legacy perhaps did lend an aura of transcendence to the political actions Obama was championing.

For any hearer seeking confirmation that Obama's fleeting echo was indeed a gesture pointing to the history of Rev. Dr. King and the civil rights movement, that confirmation arrived just a bit later in Obama's speech when he warned his hearers that the road to a better day would be long and that "we may not get there in one year or even one term, but America . . . I promise you—we as a people will get there." Here, there is an unmistakable echo of King's prophetic final speech in Memphis that fateful day in 1968: "I've seen the promised land. I may not get there with you." Obama's audience would have to be hard of hearing indeed not to hear this loud echo and grasp its import: Obama was metaphorically assuming the mantle of Joshua in relation to King's figural assumption of the role of Moses. King/Moses had led the people out of bondage to the brink of the promised land, and Obama/Joshua was now kindling hope that, under his leadership, the (American) people as a whole were about to enter the promised land of milk, honey, and justice. As I write these words in 2015, that promise of entering the land of Canaan seems no less eschatologically remote than it did in 2008. But perhaps even that not-yet-fulfilled eschatology could be interpreted as one more appropriate sign of a figural correspondence between the story of Exodus and the yearning for justice in American political history.

Regardless of what readers may think of the rhetoric and politics of this particular evocative example, my point is simply to indicate how intertextual echo works *poetically*. Examples of this kind could be multiplied endlessly because our discourse is inherently intertextual and allusive. In order to catch the full semantic force of the language in the example just given, readers have to hear the echoes of earlier texts and think backwards—from Obama to King to Exodus—to grasp the relevant and illuminating parallels. The language of the Gospels works in the same way. A careful interpretation of the Gospel stories will require patient attention to their evocation of intertexts from Israel's Scripture.[23]

As we examine the intrabiblical intertextuality of the Gospels, we will frequently find that the language of the Evangelists resonates most strongly with the language of the Old Greek versions of Israel's Scripture, commonly referred to as the Septuagint (LXX), rather than with the Masoretic Hebrew texts (MT). This is hardly surprising, since the Evangelists were writing in Greek for Greek-reading audiences. In the present book, I have therefore referred with some frequency to the Greek, rather than the Hebrew, text of the Old Testament. Readers should be aware, however, that the translation of Israel's scriptural texts into Greek, along with the collection by Christians of these Greek versions into codex form as a Greek "Old Testament," was a complex historical process over time. The question of the exact textual forms accessible to the Evangelists is therefore a complicated one.[24] The present book is not intended as an in-depth study of this phenomenon or as a contribution to the highly specialized debates surrounding it.[25] For the sake of simplicity, I have continued the traditional practice of referring to the various Old Greek textual forms that appear in the New Testament's citations of Scripture as coming from "the Septuagint," even while being aware of the textual complexities concealed by this general designation.

Another methodological issue that receives only glancing attention in these pages is the question of the possible literary dependence among the Gospels themselves—a different sort of intertextuality. This complex problem is not the chief topic of the present study, but readers may desire at least a cursory explanation of my working understanding of the matter.

I share the consensus position of the majority of New Testament scholars that the Gospel of Mark is the earliest of the four canonical Gospels and that both Matthew and Luke drew upon Mark as a source. I do not, however, place any weight on the hypothesis that Matthew and Luke independently made use of a hypothetical common source, designated as "Q." There is no extant manuscript of such a source, nor is there any reference to it in the surviving documents of earliest Christianity. It seems to me equally probable—indeed more probable—that Luke knew Matthew and that the verbal agreements between these two Gospels can be explained in this fashion rather than through positing a hypothetical Q source.[26] But the interpretations developed in the present book do not depend on a resolution of this classic problem in New Testament studies. Instead, the chapters that follow will seek to read each of the four Gospels with a view to the Old Testament intertexts that it evokes and to ask how these intertexts function within the literary and theological construction of that individual Gospel. If we knew for certain that Luke used Matthew as a source, we could draw more specific conclusions on some points. But the nature of the evidence does not permit certainty, and we can go a long way in reading Luke and Matthew without appealing to any particular theory of their sources, beyond the recognition of their use of Mark and of the Old Testament.

Finally, one concern that arises naturally in any study of the Evangelists' interpretation of Israel's Scripture is whether their christologically centered exegesis in fact invalidates Judaism and generates a hostile supersessionist understanding of the relationship between Israel and the church. The question is both important and complicated. It is beyond the scope of the present study to solve the thorny theological problems surrounding Jewish-Christian dialogue. But it is my hope that the exegetical observations contained in this book might actually promote constructive dialogue by clarifying how deep are the roots of these early Christian narratives in Israel's Scripture. *It is particularly important to see that the sort of figural interpretation practiced by the canonical Evangelists is not a rejection but a retrospective hermeneutical transformation of Israel's sacred texts.* Figural readings do not annihilate the earlier pole of the figural correspondence; to the contrary, they affirm its reality and find in it a significance beyond that which anyone could previously have grasped. This recognition will not dissolve disagreements between Jews and Christians over the interpretation of Israel's Scripture, but it will at least clarify what is at issue and, in the best of cases, encourage respectful controversy between divided communities that both seek to serve the one God proclaimed in the *Shema*.

Mapping the road ahead

Having offered these preliminary observations, we are ready to begin a journey of exploration. Our goal is not to offer a comprehensive account of the theology of each of the Evangelists. Still less is it our aim to harmonize their texts and smooth over their differences. Rather, we are seeking to listen carefully to the ways in which each of them draws upon Israel's Scriptures in constructing a distinctive narrative testimony to Jesus.

In order to listen well, we will pose three heuristic questions to each Gospel. (1) We will be asking how each Evangelist carries forward and renarrates the story of *Israel* through intertextual references to Scripture. (2) We will listen carefully for the ways in which each Evangelist draws on scriptural stories and images to interpret the world-changing significance of *Jesus*. And finally, (3) we will ask how each of the Evangelists begins to shape the story of the *church* (i.e., the community of Jesus' followers) through evoking texts from Israel's Scripture.

The expository movement from Israel to Jesus to the church already hints at a common narrative substructure, but the ways in which the four Evangelists shape this narrative are strikingly different. Each one brings a particular literary and theological sensibility to the interpretation of Israel's Scripture, and each one speaks with a distinctive poetic voice. We will seek to listen carefully to each of those voices in turn.

As we listen, we will find that all four Evangelists are deeply engaged in the task of *reading backwards*, discovering figural fusions between the story of Jesus and the older and longer story of Israel's journey with God. We turn now to the task of exploring those fusions.

Chapter 1

The Gospel of Mark
Herald of Mystery

"To you has been given the mystery of the kingdom of God,
but for those outside, everything comes in parables."

§1 "TAKE HEED WHAT YOU HEAR"
Mark as Interpreter of Scripture

The Gospel of Mark tells a mysterious story enveloped in apocalyptic urgency, a story that focuses relentlessly on the cross and ends on a note of hushed, enigmatic hope. Many of the key images in this mysterious narrative are drawn from Israel's Scripture; indeed, a reader who fails to discern the significance of these images can hardly grasp Mark's message. Yet, unlike Matthew, Mark rarely points explicitly to correspondences between Israel's Scripture and the story of Jesus. Readers are left to make the connections for themselves. Just for that reason, many readers have underestimated the importance of the Old Testament in Mark's narrative.[1] It is as though, in his deft but allusive use of Scripture, Mark is whispering to his readers the same admonition that Jesus delivers to his disciples as they puzzle over his enigmatic parables: "Pay attention to what you hear; the measure you give will be the measure you get, and still more will be given you. For to those who have, more will be given; and from those who have nothing, even what they have will be taken away" (Mark 4:24-25).

As we seek to pay attention to what we hear in Mark's Gospel, we shall focus on Mark's interpretation of Scripture by posing the three heuristic questions outlined in the introductory chapter of this book: How does Mark employ Scripture to re-narrate the story of Israel? How does Mark draw on Israel's Scripture to narrate the identity of Jesus? How does Mark evoke Israel's Scripture to narrate the church's role in relation to the world? Our discussion will be anchored in the passages that Mark explicitly cites; yet these explicit citations repeatedly gesture toward wider contexts and implications that remain not quite overtly stated—just as the risen Lord remains absent in the Gospel's final scene (Mark 16:1-8). To read Mark faithfully, we must follow the pointers offstage.

§2 APOCALYPTIC JUDGMENT AND EXPECTANCY
Israel's Story in Mark's Narrative

The narrative context

In order to see how Mark continues Israel's story, we must first consider his understanding of the shape of the story prior to Jesus' appearance on the scene. Although Mark, in contrast to Matthew and Luke, provides little introductory framing for his narrative, his account presupposes that Israel has reached a moment of crisis. When the curtain rises on Mark's drama, we find Israel still in exile—at least metaphorically—still under the thumb of Gentile powers.[2] Despite God's past favor, the people are now in a state of powerlessness, confusion, and need; they are "like sheep without a shepherd" (Mark 6:34). There is an ill-formed but widespread hope for God to send a "Messiah" (Χριστός: Mark 8:29, 14:61) who will restore the kingdom of David and put an end to Israel's suffering (Mark 10:46, 11:9-10). The situation has become so terrible that only drastic divine intervention can bring deliverance.

Such a diagnosis of Israel's dire need is by no means unprecedented; Mark finds precursors in Israel's Scripture, particularly in the Psalms and prophetic literature. Near the end of the book of Isaiah, for example, the prophet appeals fervently to God to "tear open the heavens and come down," to bring deliverance to his people.[3]

Look down from heaven and see,
from your holy and glorious habitation.
Where are your zeal and your might?

The yearning of your heart and your compassion?
They are withheld from me.
For you are our father,
though Abraham does not know us
and Israel does not acknowledge us;
you, O LORD, are our father;
our Redeemer from of old is your name.
Why, O LORD, do you make us stray from your ways
and harden our heart, so that we do not fear you?
Turn back for the sake of your servants,
for the sake of the tribes that are your heritage.
Your holy people took possession for a little while;
but now our adversaries have trampled down your sanctuary.
We have long been like those whom you do not rule,
like those not called by your name.
O that you would tear open the heavens and come down,
so that the mountains would quake at your presence—
as when fire kindles brushwood
and the fire causes water to boil—
to make your name known to your adversaries,
so that the nations might tremble at your presence!
When you did awesome deeds that we did not expect,
you came down, the mountains quaked at your presence.
From ages past no one has heard, no ear has perceived,
no eye has seen any God besides you,
who works for those who wait for him.

(Isa 63:15–64:4)

Why this urgent cry? The prophet looks around and sees a people with hardened hearts, who stray from the Lord's ways (63:17). He sees the holy city Jerusalem trampled down by foreign powers (63:18). Despite memories of God's glorious deliverance of Israel in the past (63:7-14), it seems as though God no longer rules (63:19). God seems to have withdrawn and sealed up the heavens, hiding his face from his people (64:7). In this time of need, Isaiah cries out to God to remember his love for Israel and to act, to break open the silent heavens and manifest his saving power once more.

This apocalyptic prayer sets the stage for the narrative of Mark's Gospel. Although Mark does not explicitly quote this passage from Isaiah, the story of Jesus' baptism (Mark 1:9-11) alludes to it: "And immediately as he was coming up out of the water, he saw *the heavens torn open* and the Spirit *descending* like a dove into him" (1:10). Only Mark, of the three synoptic Evangelists, uses the violent participle "torn" (σχιζομένους); Matthew and Luke, in their parallel accounts of the baptism of Jesus, use the more colorless expression "the heavens were opened" (Matt 3:16: ἠνεῴχθησαν; Luke 3:21: ἀνεῳχθῆναι), which reflects the language of the Septuagint. Mark's more vivid verb offers a stronger allusion to the Hebrew text tradition of Isaiah 64:1 (63:19 MT), the only passage in the Old Testament that uses the verb קרע ("tear") in relation to the heavens.[4] This allusion gives us cause to suppose that Mark has Isaiah specifically in mind.[5] The gospel, according to Mark, is God's answer to Isaiah's intercessory cry: the tearing of the heavens and the descent of the Spirit upon Jesus signifies that God's eschatological work of deliverance is beginning. *God is coming to rule over Israel once again.*

Many other passages from Israel's Scripture, especially the Psalms, could have been adduced to evoke a similar sense of yearning for deliverance. In first-century Judaism, there was a widespread sense that the time was out of joint, that God's promises to Israel remained unfulfilled, that God must somehow act dramatically to set things right.[6] That is to say that Israel was awaiting the coming "kingdom of God," not some sort of otherworldly postmortem existence, but a concrete historical reality in which God would reassert kingly sovereignty over Israel in order to bring healing and justice.[7] Mark does not pause, however, to explain all of this—or to explain the analogies between the time of Jesus and his own time of writing, some forty years later—for he assumes his readers will be well acquainted with Israel's grief and longing. Mark writes either in the immediate aftermath of the Roman army's destruction of the Jerusalem temple or in the time of unrest leading up to that cataclysmic event.[8] Either way, the story presupposes readers who need little briefing.

The coming of God's kingdom, however, is not necessarily good news for everyone. One prominent theme of Israel's prophetic books is that the coming "day of the LORD" is a day of God's judgment upon human unrighteousness.

> Alas for the day!
> For the day of the LORD is near,
> and as destruction from the Almighty it comes.

> (Joel 1:15)

For that reason, "prepare to meet your God, O Israel!" (Amos 4:12) should be heard not as a word of comfort but as a terrifying word of warning. The prophet Amos declares God's solemn warning to a complacent nation that tramples on the poor:

> Alas for you who desire the day of the LORD!
> Why do you want the day of the LORD?
> It is darkness, not light.

> (Amos 5:18)

God, who abhors injustice and oppression, will come to set things right—as even the gloomy book of Amos affirms[9]—but that setting-right necessarily entails a day of reckoning for those who have violated God's covenant and abused his creation. That is why John the Baptist, the preliminary herald of God's kingdom, proclaims a message of repentance (Mark 1:4): Israel must turn from its evil ways in preparation for God's coming. Consequently, the theme of *eschatological restoration* is inextricably interwoven with the theme of *inbreaking judgment*, both in Israel's Scripture and in Mark's Gospel.

As we shall see, Mark draws upon Old Testament texts to craft a fresh interweaving of these themes. *Mark re-narrates the story of Israel by seeking to show that, in the events of Jesus' life and death, God has at last torn open the heavens and come down and that in Jesus the Christ both judgment and restoration have come upon Israel in a way prefigured in Scripture.* The announcement of God's powerful setting-right of things is the keynote of Jesus' own apocalyptic message, which Mark describes as τὸ εὐαγγέλιον τοῦ θεοῦ ("the good news of God"): "The time is fulfilled and the kingdom of God has come near" (Mark 1:14b-15a). Mark is declaring that Israel's story has reached, in Jesus, its divinely ordained climax.

Yet this climax is also a moment of dramatic complexity, for neither judgment nor restoration has reached completion. The judgment and restoration adumbrated in Scripture are enacted in Jesus' teaching and actions, yet the story remains unfinished. Mark writes with a sense of eschatological urgency, still looking forward to the future coming of the Son of Man in power (Mark 13:24-27, 14:62). Because Mark and his readers continue to await the full unveiling of the coming kingdom of God, they stand under the imperative to repent and receive the kingdom message, the same imperative that confronted the generation of Jesus' original hearers. Therefore, those who have eyes to see and ears to hear (Mark 8:18) will understand the proleptic revelation of God's kingdom in the story of Jesus, while others remain blind and deaf to the good news.

Here we encounter a grave narrative complication. Even in the face of God's inbreaking power, many of the people, especially the religious leaders, remain blind and resistant.[10] And so Jesus' proclamation of the kingdom comes into conflict with the authorities, the "wicked tenants" who are the keepers of God's vineyard, Israel (Mark 12:1-12). We might expect the outcome of this clash to be the annihilation of those who resist God's kingdom, Jewish leaders and Gentile rulers alike. Instead, Mark's story leads astonishingly to the violent death of Jesus, the "beloved son," the bearer of the kingdom message. How is such an event "good news"? To ask that question is to draw near to the heart of the mystery of the kingdom.

Our task, then, is to explore the subtle ways in which Mark employs Israel's Scripture to carry forward the four narrative strands we have identified: inbreaking judgment, eschatological restoration, the strange continuing resistance of Israel, and the shocking death of God's son. Mark finds each of these strands prefigured in Scripture and finds in Scripture the language and imagery necessary to tell the story.

Inbreaking judgment

The harbinger of judgment and the new exodus (Mark 1:1-3). A few deft strokes in the opening lines of the Gospel evoke the time of crisis and trigger a rush of hope that at last God's promised deliverance is at hand:

> The beginning of the good news of Jesus Christ, the Son of God, as it is written in the prophet Isaiah:
>   "See, I am sending my messenger ahead of you
>   who will prepare your way;
>   the voice of one crying out in the wilderness:
>   'Prepare the way of the Lord,
>   make his paths straight.'"
>
>   (Mark 1:1-3)

The quotation, of course, is derived not from Isaiah alone; it begins with a fusion of words from Exodus and Malachi. Why then does Mark attribute the citation to Isaiah? Is he simply confused? The apparent mistake has sometimes been taken as evidence that Mark is actually quoting from a primitive collection of messianic testimonies rather than directly from the Old Testament passages.[11] It is more likely, however, that Mark's attribution of the mixed citation to "the prophet Isaiah" reflects not ignorance but theological intentionality.[12] Mark's use of the Isaiah ascription here signals that the conceptual framework for his Gospel is the Isaianic new exodus.[13] By naming Isaiah in particular—and by bringing the citation to its climax with words taken from Isaiah 40, Isaiah's pivotal declaration of hope for the end of exile—Mark signals his readers that the *euangelion* of Jesus Christ is to be read within the matrix of Isaiah's prophetic vision: God will return to Zion and restore Israel.

At the same time, however, these opening lines of the Gospel also sound the theme of God's purifying judgment. The quotation ascribed in Mark 1:2 to "the prophet Isaiah" begins with words reminiscent of the somber warning of the prophet Malachi:

> See, *I am sending my messenger to prepare the way before me*, and the Lord whom you seek will suddenly come to his temple. The messenger of the covenant in whom you delight—indeed, he is coming, says the LORD of hosts. *But who can endure the day of his coming, and who can stand when he appears?* For he is like a refiner's fire and like fullers' soap; he will sit as a refiner and purifier of silver, and he will purify the descendants of Levi and refine them like gold and silver, until they present offerings to the LORD in righteousness. Then the offering of Judah and Jerusalem will be pleasing to the LORD as in the days of old and as in former years. *Then I will draw near to you for judgment*; I will be swift to bear witness against the sorcerers, against the adulterers, against those who swear falsely, against those who oppress the hired workers in their wages, the widow and the orphan, against those who thrust aside the alien, and do not fear me, says the LORD of hosts.
>
> (Mal 3:1-5)

In Malachi, the messenger sent to prepare the way for God's coming is identified with the returning prophet Elijah, whose mission will be to bring about repentance so that the coming of the Lord will not result in the cursing of the land (Mal 4:5-6). Mark subliminally reinforces the identification of John with Elijah by reporting that John was "clothed with camel's hair, with a leather belt around his waist," an image strongly reminiscent of Elijah (2 Kgs 1:8).[14] Thus, for Mark the appearance of this rough prophet in the wilderness is, first of all, a sign of God's approaching judgment. Furthermore, the allusion to Malachi 3 suggests a critique of the temple establishment in Jerusalem, which stands in need of purification to present righteous offerings—a foreshadowing of things to come in Mark's narrative (see especially Mark 11:12-25, 13:1-2). Any reader who hears the echo of Malachi in this opening citation will understand that Mark is warning that the fire of God's purifying judgment is at hand.

It is no accident that when Christians eventually configured the Old Testament, they placed the Prophets at the end of the book, with Malachi, the last of the minor prophets, as the final word spoken: in Malachi's message of judgment and of Elijah's coming to prepare the hearts of the people for the coming of the Lord, they saw a prefiguration of John the Baptist's preaching as the prolegomenon to the story of Jesus. Although Mark wrote long before this decision about canonical ordering, he anticipates its hermeneutical logic: he opens his narrative with a deft segue linking the beginning of his narrative seamlessly to Malachi, the end of the prophetic canon.[15] Early Christian interpreters such as Origen and Jerome were fully aware that Mark's opening citation was a conflation, not a verbatim quotation of Isaiah, and they consistently understood Malachi's oracle of warning as the other source, alongside Isaiah, for Mark's material.[16]

In fact, however, despite patristic emphasis on Malachi as the background to the opening of Mark's Gospel, the wording of Mark 1:2 is closer to Exodus 23:20 LXX than to Malachi 3:1 LXX, as the following comparison illustrates (boldface indicates verbatim agreement):

Mark 1:2 **ἰδοὺ ἀποστέλλω τὸν ἄγγελόν μου πρὸ προσώπου σου**,
ὃς κατασκευάσει τὴν ὁδόν σου·

Exod 23:20 καὶ **ἰδοὺ** ἐγὼ **ἀποστέλλω τὸν ἄγγελόν μου πρὸ προσώπου σου**
ἵνα φυλάξῃ σε ἐν τῇ ὁδῷ ὅπως εἰσαγάγῃ σε εἰς τὴν γῆν
ἣν ἡτοίμασά σοι

Mal 3:1 **ἰδοὺ** ἐγὼ ἐξαποστέλλω **τὸν ἄγγελόν μου**
καὶ ἐπιβλέψεται ὁδὸν **πρὸ προσώπου μου**

The linkage of Mark 1:2 to the Exodus passage is also hermeneutically significant, for it evokes the other side, the positive side, of the dialectic of judgment and restoration. It is taken from a passage in which God, speaking with Moses on Mount Sinai, promises to send an angel/messenger (ἄγγελος) to lead Israel into the promised land of Canaan:

I am going to send an angel in front of you (LXX: ἐγὼ **ἀποστέλλω τὸν ἄγγελόν μου πρὸ προσώπου σου**), to guard you on the way and to bring you to the place that I have prepared. Be attentive to him and listen to his voice; do not rebel against him, for he will not pardon your transgression; for my

name is in him. But if you listen attentively to his voice and do all that I
say, then I will be an enemy to your enemies and a foe to your foes.

(Exod 23:20-22)

By echoing this passage Mark artfully hints that the Baptist is not
only a voice of judgment (as the Malachi allusion would suggest) but
also the forerunner of a new entry into the land of promise.[17] "I will send
my angel before your face" is a word of promise, signifying protection,
victory, and the end of wilderness wandering. It also suggests, however,
that the progress of the "gospel of God" into the world may be, like
the occupation of Canaan, the beginning of a campaign against hostile forces now in possession of the land. This suggestion is amply confirmed by the narrative that follows, in which Jesus launches an offensive
against demonic powers, who perceive immediately that Jesus has come
to destroy them (e.g., Mark 1:24; cf. 3:23-27, 5:1-20).

A reader who senses the echo of the exodus/conquest[18] language in
Mark 1:2 will find the intuition immediately reinforced by what follows.
The messenger sent by God is also "the voice of one crying out in the wilderness: 'Prepare the way of the Lord, make his paths straight'" (Mark
1:3; quoting Isa 40:3). The prophet's cry, in Isaiah, announces the end
of exile, symbolically portrayed as a second exodus in which the power
of God leads Israel through the wilderness and back to Zion.[19] Isaiah's
poetic image of the return from exile as a "new exodus" becomes a central
organizing image for Mark's Gospel.[20] Just as Isaiah employed the earlier exodus imagery to depict God's deliverance of Israel from the later
Babylonian exile, so Mark draws on Exodus 23:20 and Isaiah 40:3, texts
that evoke both of these past acts of God's deliverance of Israel, to introduce God's coming again in power through Jesus. The imagery is apocalyptic in character, emphasizing the inbreaking salvific power of God.
For Isaiah "'the way of the LORD' means Yahweh's *own* way through
the wilderness, his victory march," which carries along Israel and is a
demonstration of God's power to save.[21] Likewise, in Mark "prepare the
way of the Lord" means far more than "be on your best behavior"; rather,
it means "acknowledge that God's power is once more on the march to
save Israel."[22]

Thus, in his abrupt and forceful opening, Mark quickly frames the
events of his story with allusions to God's promise to lead Israel into the
land (Exod 23), God's intention to send a messenger warning Israel of
impending judgment (Mal 3), and God's comforting word that promises redemption and a new exodus (Isa 40). This is one of the few places

where Mark explicitly clues the reader to look for the Old Testament context for the story of Jesus. Yet these clues are so explicit and so fraught with theological significance that the reader of this Gospel is invited or—to speak more consonantly with Mark's narrative world—*driven* to interpret everything that follows in relation to the narrative matrix adumbrated by these opening verses.[23] Once we have understood this, we recognize that *Mark is prompting his readers to read Israel's story figurally*: Mark 1:1-3 suggests that Israel's story contains multiple prefigurations of the saving action of God climactically revealed in Jesus. From this point forward, if anyone has ears to hear, let him hear.

Other resonances of eschatological judgment. The theme of God's eschatological judgment continues to sound through Mark's narrative, often evoking Old Testament resonances. One such resonance often missed by later Christian readers is found in Jesus' initial call to Simon and Andrew to become his disciples: "Come after me, and I will make you to become fishers (ἁλιεῖς) of people" (Mark 1:17). Christian preachers have usually understood this passage as a call to evangelism: the disciples are to "catch" outsiders and bring them into the church. Against the background of the Old Testament prophetic use of fishing imagery, however, Jesus' call has a very different ring to it. Indeed, for Jeremiah the imagery is used for judgment against Israel:

> I am now sending for many fishermen (LXX: ἁλεεῖς), says the LORD, and they shall catch them; and afterward I will send for many hunters, and they shall hunt them from every mountain and every hill, and out of the clefts of the rocks. For my eyes are on all their ways; they are not hidden from my presence, nor is their iniquity concealed from my sight. And I will doubly repay their iniquity and their sin, because they have polluted my land with the carcasses of their detestable idols, and have filled my inheritance with their abominations.
>
> (Jer 16:16-18)

Here again, the original context of Jeremiah's oracle blends restoration and judgment in a complex manner; the immediately preceding verses (Jer 16:14-15) speak of God's bringing Israel back from places of exile into Israel's own land. Nonetheless, the "fishermen" whom God is summoning are agents of judgment, hauling people in so that God can "repay their iniquity and their sin." A similar connotation of "fishing" imagery appears in Amos' scathing indictment of the wealthy women of Samaria:

> Hear this word, you cows of Bashan who are on Mount Samaria, who oppress the poor, who crush the needy, who say to their husbands, "Bring something to drink!" The Lord GOD has sworn by his holiness: The time is surely coming upon you, when they shall take you away with hooks, even the last of you with fishhooks.
>
> (Amos 4:1-2)

These unforgettable metaphors create the cultural and poetic tradition within which the phrase ἁλιεῖς ἀνθρώπων ("fishers of people") must be heard. Against this background, Jesus' call of Simon and Andrew should be understood as a call to participate—like John the Baptist—in declaring the imminence of judgment. Indeed, Jesus' later instructions to the disciples suggest precisely such a mission of warning of God's judgment and shaking off the dust of their feet against those who fail to receive the message (Mark 6:10-12). If in fact the mission of the disciples ultimately turns out also to include healing and caring for the abused flock (Mark 6:13, 6:37a; cf. 10:42-45), the transformation of their task from condemnation to mercy is made the more striking if we hear the overtones of judgment associated with the fishing metaphor in the opening call narrative.

In other Markan passages the Old Testament images of judgment are more overt. For example, the parabolic image of the farmer putting in the sickle for the harvest (ἀποστέλλει τὸ δρέπανον, Mark 4:29) echoes Joel's imagery of God's judgment of the nations on the day of the Lord in the "valley of decision": "*Put in the sickle* (LXX: ἐξαποστείλατε δρέπανα), for the harvest is ripe. Go in, tread, for the wine press is full. The vats overflow, for their wickedness is great" (Joel 3:13 [4:13 LXX]). Or again, Jesus' dire warning that it is better "to enter the kingdom of God with one eye than to have two eyes and be thrown into Gehenna, where *their worm never dies and the fire is never quenched*" (Mark 9:47-48) takes its gruesome imagery directly from the final sentence of the book of Isaiah, which describes the eschatological fate of those who have rebelled against God (Isa 66:24). Or, to cite one more example, Jesus' warning against preening scribes who "devour widows' houses" (Mark 12:38-40) derives its force from the Torah's portrayal of God's passionate wrath against those who abuse widows and orphans (Exod 22:22-24). Perhaps particularly important as background to this Markan judgment passage is an oracle of Isaiah against those who manipulate *the law* to oppress the needy:

> Ah, you who make iniquitous decrees,
> who write oppressive statutes,
> to turn aside the needy from justice
> and to rob the poor of my people of their right,
> *that widows may be your spoil,*
> and that you may make the orphans your prey!
> What will you do on the day of punishment,
> in the calamity that will come from far away?
> To whom will you flee for help,
> and where will you leave your wealth,
> so as not to crouch among the prisoners
> or fall among the slain?
> For all this his anger has not turned away;
> his hand is stretched out still.

(Isa 10:1-4)

In all these passages, then, Mark evokes images of divine wrath and judgment from the Old Testament to address his own first-century setting, warning that the time is fulfilled and the judgment pronounced in Scripture at hand.

Prophetic action in the temple (Mark 11:15-19). Perhaps the single most illuminating instance of Mark's figural use of Old Testament prophetic judgment material, however, occurs in the climactic scene in the temple where Jesus, in an act of prophetic street theater, overturns the tables of the money changers (Mark 11:15-19).[24] It is widely recognized that Mark, by intercalating this story with the story of Jesus' cursing of the fig tree (Mark 11:12-14, 20-25),[25] presents the temple action as a prophetic sign of God's judgment on the temple and its authorities.[26] A full reading of the event requires careful attention to the commentary provided by Jesus' words in the temple after driving out the merchants and money changers, commentary in which we find another fusion of Old Testament texts, this time from Isaiah and Jeremiah.

> "Is it not written,
>> '*My house shall be called a house of prayer for all nations*'?
>> But you have made it *a den of robbers*."

(Mark 11:17)

The explicit quotation, from Isaiah 56:7, belongs originally to Isaiah's vision of an eschatologically restored Jerusalem in which God's deliverance has been revealed (Isa 56:1). One salient feature of this redeemed order is that *Gentiles* will come to Mount Zion to worship alongside God's people:

> These [foreigners] I will bring to my holy mountain,
> and make them joyful in my house of prayer;
> their burnt offerings and sacrifices will be accepted on my altar;
> *for my house shall be called a house of prayer for all nations.*
> Thus says the Lord GOD,
> who gathers the outcasts of Israel,
> I will gather others to them
> besides those already gathered.
>
> (Isa 56:7-8)

By citing this passage, Mark portrays Jesus' protest action as an indictment of the temple authorities for turning the temple into a bazaar, cluttering the outer "court of the Gentiles" and making it unsuitable as a place of worship for the Gentile "others" who might want to gather there to pray. By driving out the merchants, Mark's Jesus clears the way, figuratively, for the restored worship of the kingdom of God, in which all nations will participate along with the returning exiles of Israel. Thus, while Jesus' action is a sign of God's judgment on the temple, it is also at the same time a sign that looks forward to the eschatological redemption of Jerusalem.[27] Jesus' prophetic denunciation of the money changers and traders presupposes this eschatological vision.

We may also interpret Jesus' expulsion of the merchants in light of a similar vision that appears in the closing chapters of Zechariah. This late prophetic book anticipates the gathering of the nations to worship in Jerusalem and concludes with the prophecy that when all Jerusalem is at last made holy by God, "there shall no longer be traders in the house of the LORD of hosts on that day" (Zech 14:21).[28] The fact that this is the concluding sentence of the book of Zechariah gives it a special rhetorical force. Thus, while Mark's account of the expulsion of sellers and buyers (τοὺς πωλοῦντας καὶ τοὺς ἀγοράζοντας ἐν τῷ ἱερῷ) contains no direct verbal echo of this passage, Zechariah 14 may well provide, along with Isaiah 56, the conceptual matrix within which we should interpret the symbolism of Jesus' prophetic action: it signals the coming eschatological restoration of Jerusalem.

At the same time, Jesus' accusation that, in contrast to the eschatological vision, the temple authorities have made God's house "a den of robbers" (σπήλαιον λῃστῶν) alludes forcefully to Jeremiah's temple sermon (Jer 7:1–8:3). In this well-known passage, God instructs Jeremiah to "stand in the gate of the LORD's house" and deliver a scathing denunciation and prophecy of destruction. In order to appreciate the force of Mark's "den of robbers" allusion, we must recall the context in which Jeremiah first used this arresting phrase:

> Thus says the LORD of hosts, the God of Israel: Amend your ways and your doings, and let me dwell with you in this place. Do not trust in these deceptive words: "This is the temple of the LORD, the temple of the LORD, the temple of the LORD." For if you truly amend your ways and your doings, if you truly act justly one with another, if you do not oppress the alien, the orphan, and the widow, or shed innocent blood in this place, and if you do not go after other gods to your own hurt, then I will dwell with you in this place, in the land that I gave of old to your ancestors forever and ever. Here you are, trusting in deceptive words to no avail. Will you steal, murder, commit adultery, swear falsely, make offerings to Baal, and go after other gods that you have not known, and then come and stand before me in this house, which is called by my name, and say, "We are safe!"—only to go on doing all these abominations? Has this house, which is called by my name, become *a den of robbers* (LXX: σπήλαιον λῃστῶν) in your sight? You know, I too am watching, says the LORD.
>
> (Jer 7:3-11)

Jeremiah's judgment oracle concludes with a declaration that the Lord intends to destroy the temple (Jer 7:13-15). Consequently, when Jesus storms into the temple, overturns the tables of the money changers, and invokes Jeremiah's image of the temple as *a den of robbers*, there can be no doubt that the allusion is meant to recall the wider context of Jeremiah's prophetic tirade, and that the action foreshadows the temple destruction that is later specifically prophesied in Mark 13:1-2. Indeed, this section of Mark's narrative (Mark 11–13) focuses relentlessly on Jesus' prophetic critique of the temple and its authorities: Jesus enters Jerusalem as the returning Davidic king and performs an act of prophetic symbolism foreshadowing the temple's demise (11:1-25); this action triggers a series of controversies with various Jewish authorities in Jerusalem (11:27–12:44); Jesus prophesies the destruction of the temple as part of the birth pangs of the coming kingdom (13:1-37). The correspondence between Jesus and Jeremiah is far from fortuitous; it is essential to the dramatic logic of the narrative.[29]

Just in case we might miss the allusion, however, Mark provides one more telling clue that links Jesus' jeremiad with the Jeremiah passage. The cursing of the fig tree (11:12-14, 20-21) frames Jesus' temple action with an enacted parable of destruction for the unfaithful, unfruitful nation. While the meaning of this parable might be self-evident even without an Old Testament precursor, the story of the withered fig tree explicitly echoes the judgment oracle of Jeremiah 8:13:

> When I wanted to gather them, says the LORD,
>   there are no grapes on the vine,
>   nor figs on the fig tree;
>   even the leaves are withered,
>   and what I gave them has passed away from them.

Thus, Mark's narrative casts Jesus in figural relation to Jeremiah. Just as Jeremiah had spoken of Israel as an unfruitful, withered fig tree, Jesus performs a symbolic tree-withering act that prefigures the fate of Israel—or, at least, of the temple. Just as Jeremiah condemned the prophets and priests who spoke false deceptive words of peace and comfort while practicing injustice and idolatry, so Jesus takes up the mantle of Jeremiah to condemn the temple establishment once again. The phrase "den of robbers" and the image of the barren fig tree provide the imaginative links; for the reader who grasps the connection, the outward-rippling implications are clear. As judgment fell upon Israel in Jeremiah's time, so it looms once again over the temple in the time of Jesus.[30]

Prefigurations of Israel's eschatological restoration

Yet, as we have seen, the threat of judgment and destruction can never be sounded apart from the more fundamental promise of God's ultimate design to bring about Israel's deliverance and restoration. We have already noted a number of passages where these hopeful themes appear, even in connection with the proclamation of coming judgment (e.g., Mark 1:2-3, 1:10, 11:17). Mark's story sets out from the beginning, after all, to narrate "good news." Let us survey a few of the many passages in which Mark's account of the good news draws upon Old Testament language and imagery.

After the arrest of John the Baptist, Jesus comes into Galilee pro-claiming "the good news (τὸ εὐαγγέλιον) of God" (Mark 1:14). Although the noun εὐαγγέλιον is never found in the LXX, the related verb εὐαγγελίζω appears repeatedly, primarily in contexts describing the announcement of a military victory. For instance: "Good tidings for my lord the king (εὐαγγελισθήτω ὁ κύριός μου ὁ βασιλεύς)! For the LORD has vindicated you this day, delivering you from the power of all who rose up against you" (2 Kgdms 18:31 = 2 Sam 18:31).[31] The LXX rendering of Isaiah 52:7 employs participial forms of the verb εὐαγγελίζω in a similar way to describe the proclamation of God's victorious return to Zion and restoration of Jerusalem:

> . . . like the feet of a herald (εὐαγγελιζομένου) of a message of peace, like a herald (εὐαγγελιζόμενος) of good things, [announcing] that I will make your salvation known, saying to Zion, "Your God will reign."

Here God is portrayed as the victorious king whose triumph is pro-claimed to the previously captive city of Jerusalem. The *euangelion* is the announcement of "the return of the LORD to Zion" (Isa 52:8).[32] Isaiah's use of this terminology provides the background against which Mark's *euangelion* is to be understood.[33]

In Mark 1, where Isaiah 40:3 has already been given prominent play, the twofold reference to Jesus' proclamation of the *euangelion* (Mark 1:14-15) echoes the repeated use of εὐαγγελίζω in Isaiah 40:9:

> Go up to a high mountain, O herald of good tidings (ὁ εὐαγγελιζό-
>   μενος) to Zion;
> lift up your voice with strength, O herald of good tidings
>   (ὁ εὐαγγελιζόμενος) to Jerusalem.
> Lift it up, do not fear; say to the cities of Judah, "Behold, your God!"
>
>   (Isa 40:9)[34]

As we have noted, Mark has primed his readers to expect that his story will focus on the fulfillment of Isaiah's prophecy of a new exodus and the establishment of God's kingly rule in Jerusalem (Mark 1:3). When, therefore, Jesus appears proclaiming τὸ εὐαγγέλιον τοῦ θεοῦ, which takes the form of proclaiming "the kingdom of God," this is a sure sign that his message is to be heard in chorus with Isaiah 40's prophecy of resto-ration. Any reader steeped in Isaiah's language would understand Jesus to be proclaiming the consummation of Isaiah's long-deferred hope.

The message that Jesus announces, according to Mark, has a strongly apocalyptic content: "The time is fulfilled (πεπλήρωται ὁ καιρός) and the kingdom of God has drawn near. Repent and believe the good news." The image of time being (literally) "filled up" is an apocalyptic image, reflecting the thought world of texts such as Daniel 7:22: ". . . then judgment was given for the holy ones of the Most High, *and the time* (LXX: ὁ καιρός) *arrived* when the holy ones gained possession of *the kingdom*." In the Jewish apocalyptic imagination, history is foreordained by God, so that pivotal events occur in accordance with a providentially allotted timetable.[35] Jesus' words in Mark 1:15 tap into this apocalyptic understanding of history and arouse keen hope that the moment of God's destined intervention is at last at hand.[36] In any case, Jesus' keynote proclamation that the time was fulfilled and the kingdom at hand certainly arouses expectations of God's radical renewal of Israel.

These expectations are reinforced by Jesus' action of appointing *twelve* disciples to proclaim his message and exercise authority in his name (Mark 3:13-19a, 6:7-13). In the context of Jesus' announcement of the kingdom of God, this gesture should be understood as a symbolic reconstitution of the twelve tribes of Israel.[37] Interestingly, Mark makes no direct allusion to any specific Old Testament texts to underscore this symbolism. Given his emphasis on the symbolic value of the number twelve, however (6:42, 8:19), he can hardly suppose that his readers will overlook the significance of the number. Once again, those who have ears will hear.

Indeed, Mark peppers his narrative with other symbolic pointers to Israel's eschatological destiny. For example, in the parable of the mustard seed (Mark 4:30-32), the climactic story in Mark's parable chapter, the seed sown grows up and "puts forth large branches, so that the birds of the air can make nests in its shade." This is a transparent allusion to Ezekiel 17:23-24, in which the restoration of the Davidic kingdom is symbolized by God's planting of a cedar twig "on a high and lofty mountain":

On the mountain height of Israel I will plant it,
in order that it may produce boughs and bear fruit,
and become a noble cedar.
Under it every kind of bird will live:
in the shade of its branches will nest
winged creatures of every kind.

All the trees of the field shall know
that I am the LORD.

By echoing Ezekiel's image, Mark implies that the kingdom of
which Jesus continues to speak metaphorically must be understood as
the fulfillment of the prophetic vision. To be sure, the manner in which
the fulfillment occurs is surprising, as suggested by the transformative
metaphorical substitution of an inauspicious mustard seed for Ezekiel's
noble cedar. That is why Jesus' hearers continue to be baffled and the
message of the kingdom remains mysterious. Nonetheless, any unraveling of the mystery must take account of this symbolic claim that the
kingdom proclaimed by Jesus stands in continuity with the restored
Israel prophesied by Ezekiel.

Again, in an important passage offering an editorial summary of
Jesus' healing ministry, Mark symbolically links Jesus' activity to the
Isaianic expectation of a new exodus and return from exile: "They were
astounded beyond measure, saying, 'He has done everything well: he
even makes the deaf to hear and the mute to speak'" (Mark 7:37). The
full force of this popular acclamation of Jesus can be heard properly only
when we read it in counterpoint with Isaiah 35:5: "Then the eyes of the
blind shall be opened, and the ears of the deaf shall be unstopped." In
Mark's narrative, we have just witnessed the healing of a deaf and mute
man (Mark 7:32-35), and we are about to encounter the first of two stories
about opening the eyes of the blind (8:22-26; cf. 10:46-52). The allusion to
Isaiah 35 suggests that all of these healing stories are to be read as hints
that in Jesus' mighty acts we are meant to see the fulfillment—or at least
the beginnings of fulfillment—of Isaiah's hope of the return of the exiles
on a highway through the desert:

And the ransomed of the LORD shall return,
and come to Zion with singing;
everlasting joy shall be on their heads;
they shall obtain joy and gladness,
and sorrow and sighing shall flee away.

(Isa 35:10)

Mark does not tell us explicitly that the healing stories are to be linked
in this way with Isaiah's promise of an eschatological new exodus. But
the broad hint given in Mark 1:1-3 ought to serve as a sufficient indicator

for the attentive reader. After that, where we hear other allusions to Isaiah's prophecies of national redemption, we should prick up our ears.

On the other hand, Mark is under no illusion that the kingdom of God proclaimed by Jesus has arrived in its fullness. Of all the Evangelists, Mark is the most reticent about claims of fulfillment and the most sensitive to the "not yet" side of the eschatological dialectic. Surely that is one of the reasons for his remarkable decision not to narrate any resurrection appearances of Jesus: by ending his story with an announcement of the resurrection but without a narrated appearance of the risen Lord, Mark suggests that the community of his readers remains in the same posture of expectant waiting enjoined by the conclusion of the eschatological discourse in chapter 13, where Jesus' words to the disciples become a general admonition to all readers of the Gospel: "And what I say to you I say to all: keep awake!"[38] Therefore, it remains clear that the consummation promised in the eschatological discourse of Mark 13 is still a future hope:

> "But in those days, after that suffering, the sun will be darkened, and the moon will not give its light, and the stars will be falling from heaven, and the powers in the heavens will be shaken. Then they will see 'the Son of Man coming in clouds' with great power and glory. Then he will send out the angels, and gather his elect from the four winds, from the ends of the earth to the ends of heaven."
>
> (Mark 13:24-27)

The description of cosmic portents in Mark 24–25 echoes prophetic imagery for the day of the Lord's judgment, particularly Isaiah 13:10 and 34:4 and Joel 2:10. More important, however, is the way in which the images of the coming Son of Man and the gathering of the elect (Mark 13:26-27) are drawn directly from Old Testament antecedents. Daniel's visionary picture of the Son of Man coming with the clouds of heaven is a text of great significance for Mark's narrative:

> As I watched in the night visions,
> *I saw one like a son of man*
> *coming with the clouds of heaven.*
> And he came to the Ancient of Days
> and was presented before him.
> To him was given dominion
> and glory and kingship,
> that all peoples, nations, and languages

should serve him.
His dominion is an everlasting dominion
that shall not pass away,
and his kingship is one
that shall never be destroyed.

(Dan 7:13-14)

In its original context in Daniel, this is a vision of the vindication of Israel. In contrast to the four strange beasts in Daniel's dream, each of which represents a Gentile empire (Dan 7:1-8), the human figure ("one like a son of man") in Daniel 7:13-14 symbolizes Israel, at last vindicated and exalted by God[39]—in accordance, we might note, with the promises of 2 Samuel 7:12-16 and Psalm 89:19-37 that the Davidic kingdom would be established forever, "as long as the heavens endure" (89:29). Mark 13:24-27 fuses this Danielic image of Israel's eschatological vindication with another persistent biblical image of Israel's hope, the image of the scattered exiles being brought back from all over the earth to reinhabit the promised land.

> . . . Then the Lord your God will restore your fortunes and have compassion on you, *gathering you again from all the peoples among whom the Lord your God has scattered you. Even if you are exiled to the ends of the world, from there the Lord your God will gather you*, and from there he will bring you back. The Lord your God will bring you into the land that your ancestors possessed, and you will possess it; he will make you more prosperous and numerous than your ancestors.
>
> (Deut 30:3-5)

> Up, up! Flee from the land of the north, says the Lord; for *I have spread you abroad like the four winds of heaven*, says the Lord. Up! Escape to Zion, you that live with daughter Babylon. For thus said the Lord of hosts (after his glory sent me) regarding the nations that plundered you: Truly, one who touches you touches the apple of my eye.
>
> (Zech 2:6-8)

> On that day the Lord will extend his hand yet a second time to recover the remnant that is left of his people, from Assyria, from Egypt, from Pathros, from Ethiopia, from Elam, from Shinar, from Hamath, and from the coastlands of the sea. *He will raise a signal for the nations, and will assemble the outcasts of Israel, and gather the dispersed of Judah from the four corners of the earth.*
>
> (Isa 11:11-12)

Against this background of Old Testament texts—and more could be added—two things are clear. First, the apocalyptic vision of Mark 13 is one not of cosmic annihilation but rather of *the restoration of Israel*.[40] Second, Jesus prophesies dramatic events that have *not yet* occurred within Mark's narrative world; consequently, the story teaches readers to look forward expectantly to these events, with patient endurance (Mark 13:28-37). The resurrection of Jesus is a confirming sign of the truth of these prophecies, and the community that trusts in the resurrection therefore trusts also in the eschatological restoration of community that is promised throughout Mark's story.

Nowhere in Mark (in contrast to the Gospel of John) is there any sign that these hopes have become spiritualized into some sort of otherworldly expectation. How, then, does Mark deal with the tension between eschatological hope and present suffering? He preserves the tension and urges his readers to trust while remaining in a posture of watchfulness. The reality of the coming restoration is assured above all, paradoxically, by the death of Jesus. In the story of Jesus' last meal with his disciples, he interprets his impending death as a kind of sacrifice that reconfirms God's covenant promise: "This is my blood of the covenant, which is poured out for many. Truly I tell you, I will never again drink of the fruit of the vine until that day when I drink it anew in the kingdom of God" (Mark 14:24-25). The portentous phrase "my blood of the covenant" echoes two crucial Old Testament texts. The first is Exodus 24:8, in which Moses solemnizes the Sinai covenant between God and the people of Israel by dashing sacrificial blood on the people and declaring, "See *the blood of the covenant* that the LORD has made with you in accordance with all these words." The blood symbolically binds Israel to God and God to Israel. The second, and equally significant, text is Zechariah 9:11, which carries the ancient covenant language forward into a promise of restoration and end of exile:

As for you also, because of *the blood of my covenant with you*,
I will set your prisoners free from the waterless pit.

Mark, like Zechariah, interprets the covenant as a promise that assures God's ultimate deliverance of Israel, even in the face of changed historical circumstances. In the last supper scene, however, this motif is given a hermeneutical twist: Jesus' *own* blood now becomes the covenant-sealing sign. Mark's text does not speak of a "new covenant"; those manuscripts that include the word "new" in Mark 14:24 represent later harmonizations with Luke 22:20. Mark certainly thinks that something new has come about through Jesus (cf. Mark 2:21-22), but the effect of his last supper story is something quite different: it affirms that Jesus' death stands in direct continuity with God's covenant with Israel, first enacted by Moses (Exod 24:8). Jesus' blood *is* the blood of the covenant, the blood that binds Israel to God; therefore, it carries a promise of liberation for those who are now imprisoned, in accordance with Zechariah's prophecy. All who are sealed by that blood are taught to *wait expectantly* for the coming kingdom in which they will once again drink wine with the king whose blood was shed for them. Thus, for Mark, Jesus' death both *hermeneutically redefines* and *reconfirms* God's covenant with Israel.

In all these passages, we see that Mark has drawn on Old Testament imagery to project a vision of eschatological hope for the restoration of Israel. To be sure, it is an Israel reconfigured by allegiance to Jesus; yet it remains recognizably and concretely a historical people. Mark's story carries forward the prophetic message of judgment and promise in surprising ways, bringing Israel to a definitive indictment and offering hope in ways unforeseeable to those who had come before him. Yet the contours of Mark's message are unintelligible apart from the Old Testament texts that provide both background and content to Jesus' proclamation of the kingdom of God.

Israel's blindness and resistance

It is a characteristic theme of Jewish apocalyptic thought that God's elect people are granted a privileged knowledge of God's eschatological purposes. Outsiders, blind to God's saving action, live as though the world were not ruled by God and as though the present oppressive order will continue indefinitely into the future. The elect, however, consoled by the knowledge of the truth, eagerly await the disclosure of God's coming justice. One function of apocalyptic writings is to reveal knowledge of God's redemptive purposes, often in a mysterious or symbolically coded form. Although the Gospel of Mark does not belong to the literary genre of "apocalypse," it shares significant elements of this worldview, including the motif of human blindness to God's eschatological activity, a motif rooted in the writings of the Old Testament prophets. In Mark's hands, however, this motif undergoes theologically significant modification.[41]

As the plot of Mark's Gospel unfolds, we read of an escalating conflict between Jesus and the Jewish religious leaders of his day, particularly the scribes and Pharisees. Jesus grieves at their hardness of heart

(Mark 3:4) and castigates them (in 7:6-7) by citing Isaiah 29:13—a passage whose wider context deplores the blindness and stupor of Judah (see Isa 29:9-12). This is not an incidental echo for Mark, who is pervasively concerned with the theme of Israel's mysterious incomprehension of the gospel, including the failure of Jesus' own disciples to comprehend the good news. Even though Jesus announces the kingdom of God and does mighty works that signify the inbreaking of God's restorative power, most of the human characters in the story, including the disciples, remain puzzled and uncomprehending of his message.

The purpose of parables (Mark 4:11-12). Mark brings this problem sharply into focus in Mark 4, which assembles a collection of Jesus' parables, primarily parables of seed and harvest. After Jesus teaches a large crowd by telling the parable of the sower (Mark 4:1-9), his disciples interrogate him in private about his method of teaching in indirect, parabolic speech. Jesus' reply, which has baffled generations of New Testament interpreters, indicates that he is speaking in parables deliberately in order to veil his message:

> And he said to them, "To you has been given the μυστήριον of the kingdom of God, but for those outside, everything comes in parables, in order that
>
> 'they may indeed look, but not perceive,
> and may indeed listen, but not understand;
> so that they may not turn again and be forgiven.'"
>
> (Mark 4:11-12; quoting Isa 6:9-10)

The term μυστήριον ("mystery" or "secret") appears often in apocalyptic texts as a designation for the hidden truth revealed to the seer. For example, when Daniel goes before King Nebuchadnezzar to decode the king's symbolic dream, he prefaces his interpretation with these words: "No wise men, enchanters, magicians, or diviners can show to the king the *mystery* that the king is asking, but there is a God in heaven who reveals *mysteries*, and he has disclosed to King Nebuchadnezzar what will happen at the end of days" (Dan 2:27-28; cf. 2:47). In the context of Mark's Gospel, however, it seems odd that the disciples are described as recipients of the mystery of the kingdom of God, since they repeatedly demonstrate their failure to understand what Jesus is trying to tell them. The saying must be understood proleptically, as a promissory indication of a secret vouchsafed to the disciples, whose meaning will be understood only later, after the crucifixion and resurrection of Jesus.[42]

We shall return later to consider how Mark understands the content of this "mystery." For the present, we note merely that Jesus' message, rather than being stated in obvious user-friendly terms, is cloaked in mysterious ambiguity. His teaching in parables produces a concealment of his message.

The reason for this strategy of indirection is explained by a citation of Isaiah, drawn from the account of Isaiah's prophetic call (Isa 6:1-13). Just as Jesus' prophetic condemnation of the temple was modeled on Jeremiah, here we find Jesus aligning his mission with Isaiah's divinely given commission to "make the mind of this people dull, and stop their ears, and shut their eyes" (6:10). It is important to recognize that God's appointment of Isaiah to harden the people's senses is not an arbitrary act of divine spite; rather, it is a specific punishment for Israel's injustice and idolatry, as detailed in the previous chapter of the book of Isaiah: ". . . they have rejected the instruction (תורה) of the Lord of hosts, and have despised the word of the Holy One of Israel" (5:24c). Because they refused to listen, God inflicts deafness and blindness upon them. This is a punishment particularly appropriate for the sin of idolatry, as suggested by the Old Testament's recurrent critique of lifeless idols:

> The idols of the nations are silver and gold,
> the work of human hands.
> They have mouths, but they do not speak;
> They have ears, but they do not hear,
> and there is no breath in their mouths.
> Those who make them
> and all who trust in them
> shall become like them.
>
> (Ps 135:15-18)[43]

The placement of Mark's parable chapter, with its strange saying about the obscuring effect of the parables, follows the same logic of judgmental blinding that appears in Isaiah 5 and 6.[44] The Beelzebul controversy in Mark 3:20-35 demonstrates that the scribes from Jerusalem (3:22) have closed their eyes to the healing and restoring work of the kingdom,[45] attributing Jesus' exorcisms to "the ruler of demons." For that reason, they have become "outsiders" to the kingdom;[46] thus, Jesus' parables have the effect of further blinding them to the truth.[47] In this structural comparison between Isaiah 5–6 and Mark 3–4, the parable of the unfruitful vineyard in Isaiah 5:1-7 is balanced by the parable of the sower in Mark 4:3-9; the latter parable announces judgment on those in whom the word bears no fruit, while promising eschatological blessing for the seed that falls on good soil.

That is why for Mark everything depends on listening carefully to the word of the kingdom proclaimed by Jesus. Mark stitches together traditional sayings that are scattered about in other contexts in Matthew (see Matt 7:2, 13:12) to create an urgent summons to hear Jesus' teaching:

> And he said to them, "Pay attention to what you hear; the measure you give will be the measure you get, and still more will be given you. For to those who have, more will be given; and from those who have nothing, even what they have will be taken away."
>
> (Mark 4:24-25)

That divine action of "taking away" is precisely what is described in Isaiah 6:9-10 and in Mark 4:11-12, and Mark's use of Isaiah 6:9-10 emphasizes judgment upon those who have already refused Jesus' message, marking them as outsiders.[48] Yet, though this reading helps us to understand the narrative movement from Mark 3 to Mark 4, it does not fully account for the irony of Mark's plot. Mark's narrative constantly destabilizes the distinction between insiders and outsiders—and thereby marks a certain distance from conventional apocalyptic discourse. Even the disciples, to whom the mystery of the kingdom is said to be given, remain uncomprehending fools.

Just before the hinge point of the narrative (Mark 8:27–9:13), Jesus finally becomes exasperated with their obtuseness. Speaking metaphorically, Jesus has warned them to "beware of the leaven of the Pharisees and the leaven of Herod" (8:15). The discerning reader of the Gospel will recall that the Pharisees and Herodians are conspiring together to kill Jesus (3:6); the disciples, however, being less than adept at interpreting Jesus' figurative speech, begin to fret that Jesus is chastising them for failing to bring enough bread along on their boat trip. Since this episode immediately follows the second account of Jesus' miraculous feeding of a crowd (8:1-10), their literalistic anxiety on this point seems especially stupid. Jesus at last loses patience and upbraids them in language that explicitly recalls his earlier description of the condition of the hardened outsiders: "Why are you still talking about having no bread? Do you still not perceive or understand? Are your hearts hardened? Do you have eyes, and fail to see? Do you have ears, and fail to hear?" (8:17-18). Despite the clear echo of Isaiah in Mark 4:12, the language of Jesus' questions corresponds more closely to Jeremiah 5:21 and Ezekiel 12:2—both passages that prophesy exile and judgment on the unfaithful people. Thus, the befuddled disciples have become outsiders to the kingdom, no less than the scribes and Pharisees of Mark 3. Mark ends the first half of his Gospel with an open, plaintive question that invites his readers, no less than the disciples, to take heed and answer: "Do you not yet understand?" (Mark 8:21).

In these passages that draw upon Old Testament accounts of Israel's failure to see and hear, Mark never argues that the blinding of the people is necessary in order to complete a scenario predicted by the prophets. In contrast to John's use of the same text (Isa 6:10) to explain the divinely ordered necessity of the people's unbelief (John 12:37-41), Mark 4:11-12 does *not* say, "everything comes in parables in order that what was spoken by the prophet might be fulfilled."[49] Instead, Mark describes Jesus' parabolic teaching as *parallel* and *analogous* to Isaiah's prophetic activity, producing the same result in the hearers. In other words, in the parable chapter, Mark does not press a claim that the resistance Jesus encountered was pre-scripted by God; rather, the resistance seems to be part of the contingent unfolding of the story of Israel, and the scriptural citations demonstrate the figural correspondence between the Israel of Isaiah's day and the Israel to whom Jesus speaks in parables. In both historical settings, Israel has turned a deaf ear to God's word.

The parable of the wicked tenants (Mark 12:1-12). As the action of the narrative moves toward its climax in Jerusalem, Jesus tells a parable that encapsulates the plot of Israel's story. For those with eyes to see and ears to hear, it foreshadows the climax of that plot in the fate of Jesus himself.

The full significance of this parable comes into view only when we see its intertextual relationship with Isaiah's song of the unfruitful vineyard (Isa 5:1-7). As soon as Jesus begins his description of the vineyard owner's action, echoes of the Isaiah passage sound audibly: "A man *planted a vineyard, put a fence around it, dug a pit for the wine press, and built a watchtower.*" Each of these details is drawn directly from Isaiah 5:2, though the order varies slightly. The Greek words in Mark 12:1 correspond almost exactly to the LXX.[50] Because of the close verbal correspondence, we expect the parable to recapitulate the message of Isaiah's song. Instead, however, there is a striking revision in Jesus' telling of the tale. In Isaiah, the vineyard owner expresses wrath toward the unfruitful vineyard; despite his careful, loving tending of the vineyard, it has not produced the sought-for harvest: "he expected it to yield grapes, but it yielded wild grapes" (Isa 5:2c). Therefore, the owner lodges a complaint against the vineyard and expresses his intention to remove his protection so that it will be destroyed. The final verse of the song (5:7) leaves no ambiguity about the meaning of its images:[51]

> For the vineyard of the LORD of hosts
> is the house of Israel
> and the people of Judah
> are his pleasant planting;
> he expected justice
> but saw bloodshed;
> righteousness,
> but heard a cry.

In Jesus' telling, however, the vineyard image mutates into quite a different application. We are still to understand that the vineyard is Israel, but the problem is different. The problem is no longer that the vineyard fails to produce grapes but rather that it is cared for by unscrupulous tenant farmers who refuse to give the vineyard owner his rightful share of the fruit; indeed, they repeatedly resort to violence against the owner's emissaries (Mark 12:2-5).

The meaning of all this is thoroughly transparent, even to Jesus' hard-hearted adversaries. The parable is addressed to "the chief priests, the scribes, and the elders" who had challenged Jesus' authority to overturn the tables of the money changers and merchants in the temple court (Mark 11:27). These leaders immediately recognize that Jesus' improvisational riff on Isaiah's song has now targeted them—the caretakers of the people—as scoundrels who are not rendering to God his due (Mark 12:12). Since Jesus has just reminded them of Jeremiah's prophecy of the destruction of the temple by accusing them of turning it into a "den of robbers" (Mark 11:17/Jer 7:11), they may also remember, in light of Jesus' parable, Jeremiah's further accusation against the disobedient priests and people of his day:

> From the day that your ancestors came out of the land of Egypt until this day, *I have persistently sent all my servants the prophets to them, day after day*; yet they did not listen to me, or pay attention, but they stiffened their necks. They did worse than their ancestors did.
>
> (Jer 7:25-26)[52]

The "many" slaves sent by the vineyard owner in Jesus' parable correspond to "all my servants the prophets" in Jeremiah's judgment oracle. Thus, Jesus' rendition of the story follows Jeremiah's lead in accusing Israel of a long history of rejecting God's servants, while at the same time focusing the accusation on the religious authorities of Jesus' own time as murderous villains whose unfaithfulness is about to bring destruction on the nation. The shift in emphasis here is striking, for the brunt of the accusation falls upon the chief priests, scribes, and elders, rather than upon the people as a whole, as in Isaiah's song. It is the leaders who bear culpability for their resistance to God. That is why the climax of the parable pronounces judgment on the *tenants*, not on the vineyard as in Isaiah: "What then will the owner of the vineyard do? He will come and destroy the tenants and give the vineyard to others" (Mark 12:9). There will be judgment on the leaders, and care of Israel will be entrusted to new tenants. This outcome is entirely consistent with the programmatic emphasis we have seen elsewhere in Mark on the themes of judgment and restoration of Israel.

Jesus' parable, however, carries one more distinctive element. Whereas Jeremiah spoke of an extended sequence of rejected prophets, the sequence in Jesus' story builds to a singular climax:

> "He had still one other, *a beloved son*. Finally he sent him to them, saying, 'They will respect my son.' But those tenants said to one another, 'This is the heir; come, let us kill him, and the inheritance will be ours.' So they seized him, killed him, and threw him out of the vineyard."
>
> (Mark 12:6-8)

Readers of Mark's Gospel have encountered references to a "beloved son" twice already at pivotal moments in the narrative: the baptism of Jesus and the transfiguration. On both occasions a heavenly voice identifies Jesus as "my Son, the Beloved" (Mark 1:11, 9:7). Accordingly, Mark's reference to a "beloved son" (12:6) inescapably evokes a christological interpretation of the parable: the beloved son is Jesus himself, the one on whom the Spirit has descended (1:10), the one in whom the kingdom of God has come with power (9:1). After the long series of rejected prophets, God finally sends Jesus, as his beloved son, to reclaim authority over the vineyard. The fate that will befall him, however, is a violent one, as Jesus has already prophesied repeatedly (Mark 8:31, 9:31, 10:32-34, 10:45). That is to say, the parable of the wicked tenants foreshadows the passion narrative.

This strange fate of the beloved son would hardly seem surprising for readers steeped in Israel's heritage.[53] With eerie regularity, the beloved son in Israel's scriptural stories becomes the victim of violence, either intended or accomplished. The archetypal account is the story of Abraham's sacrifice of Isaac, in which God's command comes to Abraham: "Take your son, your only son Isaac, *whom you love*, and go to the land of Moriah, and offer him there as a burnt offering on one of the mountains that I shall show you" (Gen 22:2). The language of the LXX prefigures Mark's christological turn even more tellingly: λαβὲ τὸν υἱόν σου τὸν ἀγαπητόν ὃν ἠγάπησας τὸν Ισαακ ("Take your son *the beloved, whom you love*, Isaac . . ."). When Jesus tells a story, then, about the owner (God) sending a *beloved son* into harm's way, the story resonates with the longer and older story of Israel.

Though Genesis 22 seems horrifying, Jewish interpreters had long understood it as a story of redemption: the obedience of Abraham and the submission of Isaac become salvific for the nation. God, recognizing Abraham's faithful compliance, sends an angel at the last moment to stay his hand; nonetheless, soteriologically speaking, it is as though God regards the sacrifice as having been completed. Consequently, the *Akedah*, the "binding" of Isaac, becomes the ground of Israel's future confidence in God's mercy.[54] By employing the loaded epithet "beloved son," Mark causes the story of the sacrifice of Isaac to echo in the background of Jesus' parable, with the effect that the murder of the vineyard owner's son is not necessarily only a grim ending to the tale—death is not necessarily the final word.

Just as importantly, the story of Joseph also echoes in counterpoint with the parable. When the wicked tenants say, "come, let us kill him (δεῦτε ἀποκτείνωμεν αὐτόν), and the inheritance will be ours" (Mark 12:7), they repeat exactly the words used by Joseph's envious brothers plotting to do away with him (Gen 37:20 LXX). This specific formulation, "come, let us kill him," occurs nowhere else in the Old Testament. A reader who hears this fleeting echo might recall that Joseph was thrown into a pit by his brothers but later rose to rule over all the land of Egypt and to provide saving aid for his family in a time of famine. This figurative "resurrection" of Joseph also foreshadows Jesus' fate.[55] For that reason, the parable of the tenants does not end with the threat of judgment in Mark 12:9; instead, it continues with the celebratory citation of Psalm 118, which—in the context of Mark's story—points to the resurrection and vindication of the crucified Son of God:

> The stone that the builders rejected
> has become the cornerstone;
> this was the Lord's doing,
> and it is amazing in our eyes.
>
> (Mark 12:10-11; quoting Ps 118:22-23)[56]

Without the resurrection, this is an unintelligible conclusion to the parable. In fact, Mark 12:10-11 is often taken to be an incongruous secondary addition to the parable; however, the echo of the Joseph story provides the subliminal typological link between parable and *kerygma*. In light of the resurrection, the killing of the beloved son becomes a part of the larger drama of human rejection and divine vindication, a drama already prefigured in the Joseph story and in Psalm 118. The parable of the wicked tenants, then, functions as an allegorical representation of Mark's larger story of God's redemptive action. At the same time, it gives the reader a key to understanding the identity of Jesus.

How, then, does Mark use Scripture to re-narrate the story of Israel? We have seen that the continuation of the story is a complex matter. Israel has long been in a state of oppression and captivity, but Mark draws upon prophetic texts, especially Isaiah, to proclaim that God's longed-for deliverance of Israel is finally at hand. The coming of God's kingdom, presaged by John the Baptist and proclaimed by Jesus, is an apocalyptic event, fulfilling Isaiah's vision of a new exodus in which God will lead the people on a way through the desert to return in power to Zion. This powerful coming of the divine presence entails judgment on Israel's sin and idolatry, as well as restoration of God's just and benevolent order. Because the leaders of Israel, the priests and scribes, resist Jesus' announcement of the kingdom and his revision of the law, they grow hardened and blind in their opposition. Thus they act under the shadow of God's judgment while opposing Jesus. Their opposition to Jesus, the Beloved Son, leads finally to the climax of Israel's story, the crucifixion of Jesus. Yet Mark hints, by citing Psalm 118:22-23, that the story will not end in violence, death, and futility. The vineyard, under care of different hands, may yet flourish again and yield fruit to its rightful owner.

§3 JESUS AS THE CRUCIFIED MESSIAH

As we examined Mark's continuation of the story of Israel, we found ourselves focusing repeatedly on Jesus as the key figure who carries forward the story. It is Jesus who announces the inbreaking of the kingdom of God, Jesus who enacts the signs of judgment and restoration, Jesus who bears the brunt of Israel's resistance to God. This is not a surprising finding, for Mark's story from its first sentence onward highlights the identity and action of "Jesus Messiah, the Son of God" (Mark 1:1). Thus far, we have attended chiefly to Jesus' instrumental role in transforming the story of Israel. We turn our attention now to the character of Jesus himself within the narrative. How do Mark's scriptural citations and allusions function to illumine the identity of this commanding figure who stands at the climax of Israel's story?

At the pivot point of the story, Jesus asks his disciples the crucial question: "But you—who do you say that I am?" (Mark 8:29). Others have said that he might be John the Baptist *redivivus* or that he might be the Elijah figure awaited as the forerunner of God's triumphant return or that he is another in the ongoing sequence of prophets sent by God (8:28). For Mark, these answers are insufficient and wrong. Jesus' question pointedly seeks to elicit from the disciples an answer that will be adequate to the wonders they have witnessed throughout the first half of the Gospel. Peter's answer, "You are the Messiah," is certainly on the right track, for it corresponds to Mark's own designation of Jesus as *Christos* in the story's opening words (1:1).[57] Yet Jesus abruptly commands the disciples not to tell anyone about him.

This strange injunction to silence was the basis for William Wrede's theory about the "messianic secret" in Mark. According to Wrede's hypothesis, the Jesus of history made no claim to be the Messiah and was confessed as such only later by the church. Therefore, Mark was faced with an embarrassing disjunction between the church's kerygmatic confession of Jesus as Messiah and a body of nonmessianic Palestinian Jesus-traditions. Mark solved the problem by fabricating an apologetic construct, the messianic secret: Jesus had deliberately hidden his identity as Messiah from his contemporaries, demanding that his disciples keep silence about it during his lifetime.[58] For a variety of reasons, Wrede's theory cannot be accepted in the form he proposed it—not least because, apart from Mark 8:30, most of Jesus' injunctions to silence have nothing to do with the title "Messiah" or with expectations connected to it.[59] Nonetheless, Wrede rightly draws attention to a major motif in Mark's Gospel: the mysterious elusiveness of Jesus' true identity. If we attend carefully to Mark's use of the Old Testament to characterize Jesus, we will discover reasons other than the one Wrede proposed for this elusiveness.

As we examine the way that Mark draws upon Israel's Scripture to define the identity of Jesus, four themes emerge as the most salient:

Jesus as the Davidic king, Jesus as the Son of Man, Jesus as the God of Israel, and Jesus as the crucified Messiah.[60] Three of these four images have been widely recognized as key components of Markan Christology. But the suggestion that Mark actually depicts the man Jesus as *the embodied presence of the God of Israel* has rarely been considered; indeed, this suggestion may sound as bizarre and off-putting today as it must have sounded to first-century audiences encountering such claims for the first time. In the following pages, I will contend that inattention to this dimension of Mark's message has been, in large part, a consequence of deafness to Mark's subtle and mysterious manner of deploying Old Testament echoes to intimate, with reverent indirectness, the divine identity of Jesus. Further, I will argue that the four christological motifs I have named do not dangle separately in the narrative as unintegrated remnants of earlier traditions; Mark has woven them together into a startling but cohesive portrayal of the figure of Jesus. To isolate any one of the four is to misconstrue Mark's gospel message. The four images must be read together as aspects of Mark's narrative representation of his central character.

For example—to take the easiest illustration—to interpret Jesus as the Davidic king-Messiah is seriously misleading unless the meaning of that ascription is understood in dialectical relation to his death on a cross. While we shall examine each of the four images individually in turn, to read the images in isolation is an exercise analogous to plunking out the individual vocal parts of a chorale, for purposes of rehearsal. The effect of the musical composition is to be perceived only when all four parts are heard together. That perceptual act of hearing-together will be attempted in the conclusion of this section on Mark's christological narration.

Jesus as Davidic king

Royal allusions in the superscription and baptism story. The identification of Jesus in the Gospel's opening sentence predisposes the reader to expect an account of Jesus as bearer of the Davidic legacy: "The beginning of the good news of Jesus Christ, the Son of God." The term "Christ" (Χριστός) is not a proper name but a role designation; it means "anointed one." Mark uses the term six more times in his Gospel, and in five of them he clearly understands it as a title, "*the* Messiah" (Mark 8:29, 12:35, 13:21, 14:61, 15:32).[61] The royal significance of this title is shown especially by the taunt of the passersby in 15:32: "Let *the Messiah, the King of Israel* (ὁ Χριστός ὁ βασιλεὺς Ἰσραὴλ), come down from the cross now." This use of *Christos* as a designation for the Davidic ruler is no Christian innovation; it is illustrated, for example, by Psalm 18:50 (17:51 LXX):

> Great triumphs he gives *to his king*,
> And shows steadfast love *to his anointed* (τῷ Χριστῷ αὐτοῦ),
> to David and his descendants forever.

The synonymous parallelism of these lines shows that—in this passage, at least—*Christos* is an epithet for the Davidic king.[62] After the demise of the Davidic monarchy, such texts came to be read eschatologically, as prefigurations of the coming anointed king who would restore the kingdom to Israel.[63] The expectation of such a king was rooted in the scriptural promise that David's kingdom would be established eternally, as can be seen in the word of the prophet Nathan to King David:

> When your days are fulfilled and you lie down with your ancestors, I will raise up your offspring after you, who shall come forth from your body, and I will establish his kingdom. He shall build a house for my name, and I will establish the throne of his kingdom forever. I will be a father to him and he shall be a son to me.
>
> (2 Sam 7:12-14a)[64]

In its original narrative setting, of course, this prophecy applies to Solomon; but, after Israel's experience of exile, it was reappropriated as a prophecy of the coming Messiah, as demonstrated in a florilegium of messianic texts discovered among the Dead Sea Scrolls:

> And "YHWH de[clares] to you that he will build you a house. I will raise up your seed after you and establish the throne of his kingdom [forev]er. I will be a father to him and he will be a son to me." This (refers to the) "branch of David" who will arise with the Interpreter of the law who [will rise up] in Zi[on in] the last days, as it is written, "I will raise up the hut of David which has fallen." This (refers to) "the hut of David which has fallen," who will arise to save Israel.[65]

The opening words of Mark's Gospel, then, evoke this same expectation for a future king who will reclaim the throne of David and set things right.

The title "Son of God," if it belongs to the original text of Mark 1:1, reinforces the identification of Jesus as a kingly figure.[66] In the Psalms, the king is acclaimed as God's "son," not because of a belief about his supernatural origin but as a way of expressing the special status of election and divine favor into which the king was embraced, as in the enthronement acclamation of Psalm 2:6-8:

> "I have set my king on Zion, my holy hill."
> I will tell of the decree of the LORD:
> He said to me, "*You are my son*;
> today I have begotten you.
> Ask of me, and I will make the nations your heritage,
> and the ends of the earth your possession."

This passage echoes loudly in the voice that speaks from heaven on the occasion of Jesus' baptism: "*You are my Son*, the Beloved; with you I am well pleased" (Mark 1:11). Thus, whether the appellation "Son of God" was in Mark's original text in 1:1 or not, the subsequent baptismal account implicitly links Jesus with the royal Davidic "son" of Psalm 2. Furthermore, in view of the prominence given to Isaiah 40 in Mark 1:2-3, we should perhaps also hear fainter overtones here of Isaiah 42:1: "Here is my servant, whom I uphold, *my chosen, in whom my soul delights*; I have put my spirit upon him; he will bring forth justice to the nations."[67] If the heavenly voice in Mark 1:11 is echoing this passage, the implied fusion between the anointed Davidic king of Psalm 2:7 and the servant of Isaiah 42:1 is significant for understanding Markan Christology.[68] The same fusion occurs again in the words of the voice that speaks from the clouds in the transfiguration story: "This is my Son the Beloved (ὁ υἱός μου ὁ ἀγαπητός); listen to him!" (Mark 9:7). Thus Mark doubly reinforces the application of this royal title to Jesus. In the baptismal story, the heavenly voice addresses Jesus himself; in the transfiguration account, the awestruck disciples.

In any case, within a few lines of the opening of the Gospel, Mark has tipped off the reader that Jesus is to be understood in relation to the figure of the anointed Davidic king. Consequently, when we hear Jesus announcing that "the kingdom of God has come near" (Mark 1:15), this appears to be, among other things, a veiled announcement of his own claim to the throne. The echo of Psalm 2 in Mark 1:11 turns the baptism of Jesus into a *disguised* royal anointing, and Jesus' proclamation of the kingdom follows, implicitly, as the assertion of his own claim to sovereignty. It is, however, characteristic of Mark's narrative strategy that none of this is said explicitly in Mark 1. Only the reader who hears the echoes of Psalm 2 and Isaiah 42 will perceive the royal Davidic significations imbedded in these crisply told opening episodes.

Davidic typology in Jesus' actions. Subsequently, in the first of Mark's two Sabbath controversy stories, Jesus justifies his own authority to permit the disciples' plucking of grain by appealing to the example of David (Mark 2:23-28). The implicit Davidic typology supports Jesus' claim in the halakhic controversy because Jesus' status parallels that of David in 1 Samuel 21: like David, he is the anointed king (cf. 1 Sam 16:1-13) whose authority has not yet been recognized within Israel, save by his fugitive band of followers.

Even more illuminating is the first of Mark's two miraculous feeding stories (Mark 6:30-44). Jesus, seeing the hungry crowd, "had compassion for them, because they were *like sheep without a shepherd*" (6:34). This authorial comment metaleptically evokes two key passages from Israel's Scripture. The first is Moses' plea to God to appoint a successor to him as leader of the people, "so that the congregation of the LORD may not be *like sheep without a shepherd*" (Num 27:17). The successor whom God commissions turns out to be Joshua (Greek: Ἰησοῦς, *Iēsous*). The echo of this passage in Mark 6:34 might suggest a Moses/Joshua typology, which would depict Jesus as Moses' successor. This reading is apparently confirmed by the event that follows, a miraculous feeding of a multitude in the wilderness (Mark 6:35-44). On the whole, however, Mark does not develop a sustained picture of Jesus as a new Moses.

In this case, a second echo turns out to be more integrally related to Mark's distinctive Christology, for the reference to "sheep without a shepherd" also recalls Ezekiel's prophetic indictment of the false shepherds of Israel:

> Ah, you shepherds of Israel who have been feeding yourselves! Should not shepherds feed the sheep? You eat the fat, you clothe yourselves with the wool, you slaughter the fatlings; but you do not feed the sheep. You have not strengthened the weak, you have not healed the sick, you have not bound up the injured, you have not brought back the strayed, you have not sought the lost, but with force and harshness you have ruled them. *So they were scattered, because there was no shepherd*; and scattered, they became food for all the wild animals. My sheep were scattered, they wandered over all the mountains and on every high hill; my sheep were scattered over all the face of the earth, with no one to search or seek for them.

> (Ezek 34:2b-6)

This allusion is significant for understanding Mark's portrayal of Jesus as the Davidic king because of the solution that Ezekiel's oracle finally promises for the plight of Israel's scattered flock:

> I will set up over them *one shepherd, my servant David, and he shall feed them*: he shall feed them and be their shepherd. And I, the LORD, will be their God, and my servant David shall be prince among them; I, the LORD, have spoken.
>
> (Ezek 34:23-24)

Thus, when Jesus feeds the multitude in Mark 6, he is not only symbolically reenacting Moses' manna miracle of the exodus but also prefiguring the restored Davidic kingship promised by Ezekiel's prophecy. Assuming the role of "my servant David," Jesus not only feeds the flock but also accomplishes what the false shepherds did not: he heals the sick and seeks the lost (cf. Ezek 34:4). The two motifs (exodus and Davidic kingship) should be seen as complementary rather than as competing alternatives, precisely because the new exodus envisioned in the Old Testament, especially in Isaiah, has as its *telos* the restoration of God's rulership over Israel. Consequently, the Old Testament allusions in Mark 6 lead us to perceive Jesus as a kingly figure who integrates the exodus typology with Ezekiel's vision of a restored kingdom.[69]

Once again, however, these associations are perceptible only for readers with ears to hear the subtexts of Mark's narrative; it is not Mark's way to make the connections overt. Indeed, because the Old Testament links are enacted but unspoken, the figural identification of Jesus as messianic king remains hidden not only from the uninformed reader but also from the characters in the story—that is, up until Peter's confession at Caesarea Philippi.

Bartimaeus' acclamation. In keeping with Mark's fondness for dramatic irony, it is a blind man who most clearly sees and blurts out Jesus' identity as the Davidic heir. At the conclusion of the Gospel's central section on discipleship, the final episode that occurs as Jesus approaches Jerusalem is an encounter with Bartimaeus, a blind beggar (Mark 10:46-52). Being told that Jesus is coming, Bartimaeus begins to shout out "Jesus, Son of David, have mercy on me!" The crowd tries to silence him, but he cries even more loudly, repeating the acclamation of Jesus as Son of David. The narrative effect of this repetition is to cast the resistant crowd in an unsympathetic light while creating readerly sympathy for Bartimaeus and validating his manner of addressing Jesus. Jesus reinforces this effect by singling out Bartimaeus, healing him,[70] and commending him for his faith. The final sentence of the account is fraught with symbolic significance: "Immediately he regained his sight and followed him on the way" (10:52). Mark's central discipleship section is bracketed by stories about the healing of blind men (8:22-26, 10:46-52). The first is partial and gradual, corresponding figuratively to the disciples' halting grasp of Jesus' identity and mission, while the second is immediate and complete, signaling the completion of Jesus' instruction on discipleship. Bartimaeus becomes a paradigmatic disciple, doing what the rich seeker had refused to do (10:21-22) by *following Jesus on the way*. Though he was blind, he now sees truly, and he acts accordingly, joining Jesus on the road.

An unresolved question nags at us, however: Does Bartimaeus' identification of Jesus as "Son of David" belong to the era of his blindness, or is it a prescient manifestation of the faith that Jesus praises? Is this title an appropriate one for a disciple of Jesus to use? Is the title "Son of David" wrong or inadequate, and one Jesus actually rejects in Mark 12:35-37?[71] Mark 12 demands careful treatment in its own place, but at the end of Mark 10 we are given no indication whatever that Bartimaeus' acclamation is misguided. His calling out to Jesus fits into a familiar Markan pattern: the marginalized outsider rightly recognizes Jesus and responds to him in faith. We have already encountered similar patterns in the stories of the leper (1:40-44), the woman suffering from hemorrhages (5:25-34), the Syrophoenician woman (7:24-30), the father of the boy with an unclean spirit (9:14-29), and the people who bring little children for Jesus' blessing (10:13-16).[72] The climactic event in this series—a climactic event still to come in Mark's narrative—is the confession of the centurion at the foot of the cross (15:39). In none of these cases does Mark hint that the outsider's perception of Jesus requires correction. Instead, in each case the audacious words and actions of the outsiders serve as correctives to the perspective of the "insider" characters in the story. Mark has taught his readers to pay respectful attention to what such outsiders say. Thus, after the persistently foolish misunderstandings of Jesus' disciples (e.g., Mark 10:35-45), when we hear Bartimaeus cry to Jesus as "Son of David," we should take heed what we hear.

Jesus' triumphal entry to Jerusalem. The story that follows immediately in Mark's Gospel chronicles Jesus' entry to Jerusalem (Mark 11:1-11) and dramatically reinforces Bartimaeus' identification of Jesus as the Davidic king. By executing a plan to enter Jerusalem riding on a colt, Jesus sub-liminally evokes the messianic prophecy of Zechariah 9:9:

> Rejoice greatly, O daughter Zion!
> Shout aloud, O daughter Jerusalem!
> Lo, your king comes to you;
> triumphant and victorious is he,
> humble and riding on a donkey,
> on a colt, the foal of a donkey.

Having walked all the way from Galilee, Jesus now commandeers the colt only when he arrives at Bethany, just two miles over the hill from Jerusalem. Thus, surely, his riding into the city in this manner is a staged symbolic gesture. Unlike Matthew, however, who quotes the passage from Zechariah, Mark offers no explicit interpretation of the gesture; those who have eyes to see will understand. They will recall Zechariah 9 and discern that this figure riding into Jerusalem on a donkey is the one who will "cut off the chariot from Ephraim and the war horse from Jerusalem" and "command peace to the nations" (Zech 9:10).

As the story unfolds, Jesus' symbolic gesture is not lost on "those who followed him"—still, we presume, including Bartimaeus—who begin a chant based on Psalm 118:25-26:

> Hosanna!
> Blessed is the one who comes in the name of the Lord!
> *Blessed is the coming kingdom of our father David!*
> Hosanna in the highest!

The sentence *"Blessed is the coming kingdom of our father David!"* does not appear in Psalm 118, but it interprets the drama being played out in Jesus' entry to the city. Jesus is not (yet) explicitly named as king, but he is acclaimed as the one who heralds the "coming kingdom" of David, an eschatological hope that challenges the powers now ruling Jerusalem. At a minimum, the crowd's chant is merely part of a larger celebration of the festival,[73] not an acclamation of Jesus specifically, and "the one who comes in the name of the Lord" could apply to any pilgrim arriving in the city.[74] This reading, however, fails to account for the details of Mark's narrative, which portrays the crowd as spreading their cloaks and palm branches on the road in front of Jesus (Mark 11:8), a gesture acknowledg-ing his royal status. Nonetheless, Mark's description of the event remains muted, and it requires the reader to listen for Old Testament texts that remain just below the surface of the narrative. The hints have become stronger, but it remains possible for readers of the story to have ears and yet somehow to miss the significance of what the crowd is chanting. Jesus' kingship is adumbrated rather than proclaimed.

Jesus' riddle about David's son. In light of the many pointers in Mark's Gospel to Jesus' identity as the Davidic king, how then are we to understand 12:35-37, in which Jesus apparently refutes the scribal opinion that the Messiah (*Christos*) is the Son of David? The passage is sometimes taken to be an outright repudiation of Davidic messianism. Is Jesus now refusing the same title that he praised Bartimaeus for shouting out? Here we must read with the alert subtlety that, as we have by now learned, Mark demands of his readers.

Jesus' enigmatic question comes at the conclusion of an extended series of controversy discourses in the temple (Mark 11:27–12:34), in which Jesus matches wits with various Jewish authorities: the chief priests, scribes and elders (11:27–12:12), Pharisees and Herodians (12:13-17), Sadducees (12:18-27), and finally a single sympathetic scribe (12:28-34). He confounds all those who challenge him and finally elicits the approval of the scribe, who recognizes his teaching as a truthful exposition of the Torah. At the conclusion of this cycle of material, Mark tells us, "After that, no one dared to ask him any question" (12:34). Jesus' question in 12:35-37 initiates a new narrative movement, in which Jesus becomes the interrogator:

> While Jesus was teaching in the temple, he said, "How can the scribes say that the Messiah is the son of David? David himself, by the Holy Spirit, declared, 'The Lord said to my Lord, "Sit at my right hand, until I put your enemies under your feet."' David himself calls him Lord; so how can he be his son?" And the large crowd was listening to him with delight.

The first thing to recognize is that this passage takes the form of a riddle, not a categorical denial. Jesus asks a question, quotes Psalm 110:1, then asks another question. The second question is literally, "Whence (πόθεν) [comes it that] he is *his* son?" The unusual Greek word order (πόθεν αὐτοῦ ἐστιν υἱός) places emphasis on the possessive pronoun. Matthew and Luke, finding the question awkward, change Mark's πόθεν to πῶς ("how," Matt 22:45; Luke 20:44). The question, as Mark has stated it, could be understood as a request for another text to prove that the Messiah is to be Son of David. But such a question would hardly be baffling to the scribes, since many good prooftexts were readily at hand.[75] More likely, Jesus' question should be heard as a challenge to explicate the logic of Psalm 110:1 itself: "Where *in this text* do you see the idea that the Messiah is David's son? Doesn't the text say that the Messiah is David's Lord?"

The crowd's approval derives from seeing Jesus get the upper hand over the scribes—the tweaking of authority figures is a timeless source of readerly delight—just as he had stumped the Pharisees and Herodians by his response to their question about paying taxes to Caesar (Mark 12:13-17). There is no reason for the crowd to take particular pleasure in a denial of a lineal connection between David and the Messiah. Rather, they are savoring Jesus' outsmarting the experts: he has come up with a text, a very impressive one, that problematizes conventional scribal teaching.

But Jesus' query also poses a conundrum. The way forward may not be to deny flat-footedly that the Messiah is to be David's son; rather, the solution may lie in rethinking the categories that create the conundrum in the first place. Mark challenges his readers to recognize that the Messiah is much more than simply the Son of David.[76] The title "Son of David" was often associated with nationalistic hopes for a military ruler to drive out the foreign powers that controlled Jerusalem and to restore the sovereignty of Israel. An early attestation of this title in such militaristic messianic expectation is found in the *Psalms of Solomon*, composed in the century before Jesus' lifetime:

> See, Lord, and raise up for them their King,
> *the son of David*, to rule over your servant Israel
> in the time known to you, O God.
> Undergird him with the strength to destroy the unrighteous rulers,
> to purge Jerusalem from Gentiles who trample her to destruction . . .
> in wisdom and righteousness to drive out
> the sinners from the inheritance;
> to smash the arrogance of sinners like a potter's jar;
> to shatter all their substance with an iron rod;
> to destroy the unlawful nations with the word of his mouth. . . .
> He will gather a holy people
> whom he will lead in righteousness;
> and he will judge the tribes of the people
> that have been made holy by the Lord their God. . . .
> And he will be a righteous king over them, taught by God.
> There will be no unrighteousness among them in his days,

for all shall be holy,
and their king shall be the Lord Messiah.

(*Pss. Sol.* 17:21-24, 26, 32)[77]

If that is what "Son of David" means, Jesus has already given his disciples—and the reader of Mark's Gospel—ample cause to doubt the suitability of this title as a description for his own vocation. He has repeatedly prophesied his own rejection and violent death (Mark 8:31, 9:30-32, 10:32-34), and he has insisted that those who follow him are not to lord it over others but to become slaves, following the example of his own self-surrender for others (10:42-45). Clearly, these teachings do not fit the usual pattern of messianic expectation. Yet the psalm that Jesus cites (Ps 110) does speak of a subjugation of the Messiah's enemies: "until I put your enemies under your feet." The script presupposed by Psalm 110, however, does not involve the Messiah's leading a revolutionary army; rather, he is to be seated at God's right hand, there to await God's defeat of the enemies.

In light of these observations, a better reading of Jesus' riddle would see it not as a rejection of Davidic messiahship but as a *redefinition* of the same.[78] David himself, speaking by the inspiration of the Holy Spirit (Mark 12:36), had foreseen a different sort of Messiah, one greater than himself in being exalted to heavenly glory, one who would not fight with weapons of war but who would trust God to vindicate him and give the victory. Of course, this interpretation of the riddle makes sense only in the retrospective light of the cross and resurrection. A suffering *Christos* who is enthroned at the right hand of God? No one in the world of Second Temple Judaism expected such a thing. Thus, like the parable of the wicked tenants (12:1-12), Jesus' riddle about David's Son comes into focus only when it is read retrospectively within the larger story that Mark tells.

At this point, as at so many others, Mark affirms continuity with Israel's tradition while also simultaneously insisting on transforming innovation. Jesus *is* the Son of David, the Messiah, as Bartimaeus had perceived and as the title *Christos* asserts. But the meaning of *Christos* is transposed to a new key and subjected to an inversion. The Messiah is more than a new military leader and pretender to the throne; he is the Son of God who is to be enthroned in the heavens and recognized as David's Lord. The Davidic image, it turns out, is "both too triumphant and not triumphant enough." It is not triumphant enough because it fails to suggest the cosmic, apocalyptic scope of the Messiah's victory over supernatural foes; at the same time, it is too triumphant because it fails to reckon with suffering and death as the means of winning the victory.[79] The crucial point, though, is that Mark's narrative does not reject the royal Davidic identification of Jesus; rather, through this mysterious riddle, it presses the reader to a transformative re-imagination of the larger significance of that identification.

It is for that reason that the most explicit royal imagery in Mark's gospel appears in the passion narrative.[80] Jesus is flogged and mocked as "King of the Jews" (Mark 15:16-20), and the inscription on the cross identifies him by that title (15:26). The chief priests and scribes taunt him by calling out, "Let the Messiah, the King of Israel, come down from the cross now, so that we may see and believe" (15:32). Yet, in the midst of the mocking, the reader of the Gospel discerns that the taunts are ironically true. Jesus really is the King of Israel, but he will demonstrate his kingship not by coming down from the cross but by enduring it. Jesus' death redefines kingship—but does not renounce it. Indeed, in his stunning reply to the high priest's interrogation, Jesus explicitly affirms that he *is* the *Christos* (14:61-62), as readers of the Gospel have known from its first sentence. As Rowan Williams writes:

> Jesus before the High Priest has no leverage in the world. He is denuded of whatever power he might have had. Stripped and bound before the court, he has no stake in how the world organizes itself. . . . It is at this moment and this moment only that he speaks plainly about who he is. . . . God's "I am" can only be heard for what it is when it has no trace of human power left to it; when it appears as something utterly different from human authority, even human liberty; when it is spoken by a captive under sentence of death.[81]

Thus, to reiterate, the motif of Davidic kingship is not rejected but transformed by Jesus' story—the "Davidic typology is both constructed and disrupted."[82] It would be more accurate to say, however, that the typology is not so much disrupted as reshaped by the story of Jesus. The eschatological reality that the Messiah's enemies are to be made a footstool for his feet (Ps 110:1) has already been proleptically enacted in Jesus' decisive silencing of his interlocutors in the temple in the controversies of Mark 11:27–12:34. Indeed, there is a sense in which the riddle of 12:35-37 is Jesus' real answer to the questions posed by the temple authorities at the beginning of this long narrative: "By what authority are you doing these things? Who gave you this authority to do them?"

(11:28). After parrying all their objections, Jesus finally hints that it is God who has given him the authority, an authority premised upon his own eschatological place at the right hand of God. The enemies who will at last be put under his feet are prefigured by the feckless adversaries in the controversy discourses, who end up with their mouths stopped.

Jesus as the glorified Son of Man

By alluding obliquely to Jesus' eschatological enthronement alongside God, Mark 12:35-37 suggests that Jesus is not just the anointed king awaited by Israel; he enjoys a still higher dignity. Though there have been various hints of this higher status earlier in the narrative (most especially the transfiguration in 9:2-8), Jesus' explicit self-interpretations have focused repeatedly, by contrast, on his impending suffering and death (e.g., Mark 8:31–9:1, 9:12, 9:30-32, 10:32-34, 10:42-45). In Mark 12, however, Jesus' interactions with the Jerusalem authorities begin to pull back the veil and to disclose glimpses of eschatological glory through the citations of Psalm 118:22-23 (12:10-11) and Psalm 110:1 (12:35-37). The glory intimated in these passages is still more fully disclosed, in the subsequent chapters, through Mark's identification of Jesus with the figure of the glorified Son of Man.

In each of the earlier prophecies of suffering, Jesus refers to himself by using the cryptic appellation "the Son of Man." Endless debates have raged about the derivation of this title, whether Jesus in fact used it of himself, and if so what he meant by it.[83] It is impossible and unnecessary to pursue these debates here, for our concern is not with questions of sources but with the significance of the title within Mark's Gospel. In that context, the meaning of "Son of Man" is clearly illuminated by two passages that appear as the story nears its climax in Jerusalem (Mark 13:24-27, 14:62); in each instance, "the Son of Man" is linked to the glorified figure who appears in Daniel 7:13-14 as the symbol of Israel's eschatological vindication. Because these passages appear in such crucial positions in Mark's plot, they must weigh heavily in any attempt to understand how Mark employs Scripture to narrate the identity of Jesus.

The first of these references to Daniel's glorified Son of Man appears at the dramatic climax of Jesus' apocalyptic discourse in Mark 13. After Jesus predicts the destruction of the temple, he is asked by Peter, James, John, and Andrew to explain when this cataclysmic event will occur and what the warning signs will be (13:1-4). Seated on the Mount of Olives, overlooking the city and the temple, Jesus begins a lengthy speech (13:5-37) about the "birth pangs" of the new age, in which he warns of many trials and persecutions, the desecration of the temple, and the emergence of false messiahs and false prophets. The portentous phrase "abomination of desolation" (13:14) alludes directly to Daniel's picture of the defiling of the temple by a pagan ruler (Dan 8:11-13, 9:27, 11:31, 12:11).[84] Winking at the reader, Mark expects the allusion to be grasped without need for explanation: "But when you see the abomination of desolation set up where it ought not to be (let the reader understand), then those in Judea must flee to the mountains." The distinctive expression "abomination of desolation" unmistakably links Jesus' discourse to Daniel's apocalyptic picture of history and prepares the way for Mark's introduction of the triumphant Danielic Son of Man in Mark 13:24-27. The linkage to Daniel's apocalyptic scenario is strengthened still more by the echo of Daniel 12:1 in Mark 13:19:

> Dan 12:1 LXX—That day will be a day of suffering (θλῖψις), such as has
>   not been since they first came into existence until that day.

> Mark 13:19—For in those days there will be suffering (θλῖψις), such as has
>   not been from the beginning of the creation that God created until
>   now, no, and never will be.

Against this backdrop, Jesus prophesies an end to the suffering in language borrowed from several prophetic texts:

> But in those days, after that suffering (θλῖψις),
>
>> the sun will be darkened,
>> and the moon will not give its light,
>> and the stars will be falling from heaven,
>> and the powers in the heavens will be shaken.
>
> Then they will see *the Son of Man coming in clouds* with great power and
> glory. Then he will send out the angels, and gather his elect from the four
> winds, from the ends of the earth to the ends of heaven.
>
> (Mark 13:24-27)

The images of cosmic signs in Mark 13:24 and 25 (sun and moon darkened and stars falling) are derived from Isaiah 13:10, Joel 2:10, 3:15, and Isaiah 34:4 LXX.[85] These cosmic portents signify "the day of the Lord," and, in Isaiah, they are specifically associated with God's judgment on Babylon and on the pagan nations that have oppressed Israel. Mark's language echoes these passages, without citing them directly. The reference to the Son of Man coming in clouds, however, is an overt allusion to Daniel 7:13-14:

> As I watched in the night visions,
> I saw *one like a son of man* (LXX: ὡς υἱὸς ἀνθρώπου)
> *coming with the clouds of heaven.*
> And he came to the Ancient One
> and was presented before him.
> To him was given dominion and glory and kingship,
> that all peoples, nations, and languages should serve him.
> His dominion is an everlasting dominion
> that shall not pass away,
> and his kingship is one that shall never be destroyed.

The NRSV renders the key phrase in Daniel 7:13 as "one like a human being," rightly conveying the original sense of the text. The final figure to appear in Daniel's vision has a human aspect, in contrast to the four horrible beasts that have preceded, beasts who symbolize the pagan empires that have ruled over Israel. The "one like a Son of Man" who is finally exalted to the heavenly throne room symbolizes Israel, "the people of the holy ones of the Most High; their kingdom shall be an everlasting kingdom, and all dominions shall serve and obey them" (7:27).

In light of this background one might suppose that "the Son of Man" in Mark 13:26 could be interpreted purely as a symbol for the people Israel who will emerge vindicated after their troubles. Throughout this Gospel, however, Mark has given us ample reason to think of the Son of Man as an individual figure—indeed, as Jesus himself, who has the authority to forgive sins on earth (2:10), who will suffer and be rejected, who will ultimately mete out judgment (8:38) and, as we now learn, be enthroned in heavenly glory (13:26). In all these roles, to be sure, the Son of Man stands as Israel's representative; his destiny prefigures and embodies theirs. Nonetheless, he has a distinct individual identity. As 13:27 indicates, the Son of Man does not simply *symbolize* the elect; rather, he is an exalted figure who *sends out* the angels to gather the elect.

If the reader has followed Mark's intertextual hints, the message of the apocalyptic discourse in chapter 13 is clear. Jesus has pronounced judgment on the temple (11:12-21) and prophesied that not one of its stones will be left upon another (13:1-2). The destruction of the temple—the demolition of the sacred locus of Israel's cultic relationship to God—will be one of the traumatic events within the series of eschatological sufferings of God's people. Nonetheless, the destruction of the temple will not be the end of God's mercy toward Israel; after his own suffering and violent death, Jesus will ultimately appear as the Son of Man in glory and power and regather the people into the promised kingdom. Mark 13:27 recalls the covenant promise of Deuteronomy 30:3-4:

> The LORD your God will restore your fortunes and have compassion on you, gathering you again from all the peoples among whom the LORD your God has scattered you. Even if you are exiled to the ends of the world, from there the LORD your God will gather you, and from there he will bring you back.

Thus, in the midst of exhortations to endure suffering (e.g., Mark 13:7-13), Jesus promises his own eschatological triumph and, with it, the restoration of the covenant people Israel.

But is "the Son of Man" in Mark 13:26-27 Jesus? The text does not say so explicitly. Like Mark 8:38, the saying remains oblique. Taken out of its narrative context, it could refer to some future figure different from Jesus. Indeed, some have hypothesized that the future coming Son of Man sayings, if they are to be traced to the historical Jesus, were originally used by Jesus to prophesy about the coming figure.[86] But such a reading is possible only if the sayings are artificially extracted from the narrative in which they appear. As we have seen, Mark's Gospel encourages another interpretation. For Mark, the "Son of Man" title has been exclusively linked with Jesus (2:10, 28; 8:31; 9:12, 31; 10:33, 45; see also 14:21, 41). The slight evasiveness or indirection of these references, however, is characteristic of Mark's manner: he leaves it to the reader to understand, to connect the clues and perceive the identity of Jesus.

This pattern of indirection is finally broken at the climax of Jesus' interrogation before the high priest and the council of priests, elders, and scribes (Mark 14:53-65). Frustrated by the false and inconclusive testimony brought against Jesus, and by his inscrutable silence, the high priest finally poses the blunt question, "Are you the Messiah, the Son of the Blessed One?" And at last, after all the hints, veiling, and mysterious evasion, Jesus shatters the silence: "I am."[87] This text is the decisive confirmation of the evidence that has previously pointed to Jesus as the Davidic Messiah. Of course, there is nothing ipso facto illegal or blasphemous about claiming to be the Messiah. Indeed, a century later, Rabbi Akiba proclaimed that Bar Kokhba, the leader of the second revolt against Rome, was the Messiah.[88] If Jesus had merely said "I am," it would be a daring claim but not cause for judicial condemnation. Jesus, however, presses the point further: "I am; and *'you will see the Son of Man seated at the right hand of the Power,'* and *'coming with the clouds of heaven.'"* The high priest's reaction—accusing Jesus of having committed public blasphemy—shows that here the reference to Daniel's exalted Son of Man must be understood as directly applying to Jesus himself. Jesus' declaration does not interpret Daniel 7:13-14 as a prophecy that the Son of Man will *descend* on the clouds from heaven to earth; rather, the passage is presented, consistently with its original contextual sense, as a portrayal of the *ascent* of the Son of Man to a heavenly enthronement.[89] This explains why the high priest regards the saying as blasphemy: Jesus is claiming that he will be exalted to heaven and enthroned alongside God (cf. also the earlier citation of Ps 110:1 in Mark 12:35-37).[90]

The story moves on swiftly to Jesus' condemnation and crucifixion, but the reader who understands the force of the Daniel citation is left with a stunning revelation: this prisoner being led away to execution is the eschatological Son of Man who will be revealed in his full glory in due course—or, at least, the reader is forced to decide whether this is true. Is this Jesus, the Messiah of Israel, also a transhuman figure of greater glory and dignity than any merely human king? Will he receive an everlasting dominion that shall not pass away?

Jesus as the God of Israel?

Mark's carefully layered plot gradually elaborates the mystery surrounding the identity of Jesus. In the early moments of Mark's Gospel, Jesus is a powerful wonder-working figure who seems comparable to Elijah or one of the prophets of old (e.g., Mark 6:15). At other points in the tale, his words and actions seem to correspond typologically to the words and actions of Moses or Joshua or Jeremiah. As the plot moves toward its climax in Jerusalem, there are abundant hints that Jesus is the bearer of David's legacy as king of Israel. Each of these images of Jesus illumines some facet of his mission and identity, yet the images all remain tentative, partial, and inadequate. Jesus remains elusive and avoids direct speech about the secret of his own personhood, except in his cryptic declarations about the Son of Man.

The revelatory declaration in Mark 14:62, the capstone of these Son of Man sayings, seems to divulge the secret at last. After so much evasion and deferral, Jesus finally unambiguously declares that he is "the Messiah, the Son of the Blessed One" and that he will ascend to heavenly eschatological dignity as the Son of Man, exercising dominion over the world. This astounding claim explains much, if not all, that has gone before. If Jesus is ultimately to rule alongside God, we now understand more fully, for example, how he can presume to reinterpret Torah with sovereign freedom (e.g, Mark 2:23-28: ". . . the Son of Man is Lord even of the sabbath"; cf. 7:1-23). We can understand the mysterious event of the transfiguration (9:2-8) as a prefiguration of Jesus' heavenly glory. We can understand why it is not sufficient to interpret Jesus as a great prophet or even as the expected Davidic king, for he is one who is still greater. The categories of prophet and messiah are not wrong; they are simply incomplete and fail to do full justice to his glory.

Yet even the title "Son of Man," understood in its full Danielic context, does not exhaust the mystery. Mark's characterization of Jesus is still more complex and elusive, and there are several hints scattered through the story that lead us to press the inquiry forward. If Jesus is identified, through Mark's references to Daniel 7, as the eschatological Son of Man enthroned in heavenly glory, the question inevitably arises of how to understand his relation to the "Ancient One," the God of Israel. If Israel's God is a jealous God who brooks no other gods before his face (Exod 20:1-3; Deut 5:6-7), who then is this figure who exercises everlasting dominion, with whom the heavenly throne room is to be shared?[91] In light of Jesus' breathtaking self-disclosure in the trial scene (Mark 14:62), we are compelled to remember and reread the whole story to see whether there are further clues to Jesus' identity that we might have missed along the way.

And upon rereading, we discover numerous passages scattered through this Gospel that offer intimations of a disturbing truth—*Jesus' identity with the one God of Israel*. Unlike the Gospel of John, which explicitly declares that Jesus is the *Logos* who is one with the Father, Mark shies away from overt ontological declarations. Nonetheless, Mark's Gospel suggests that Jesus is, in some way that defies comprehension, the embodiment of God's presence.[92] Mark never quite dares to articulate this claim explicitly; it is too scandalous for direct speech. Indeed, to speak unguardedly of "Jesus as the God of Israel"—as I am doing here—is to betray Mark's circumspect narrative strategy. For Mark, the character of God's presence in Jesus is a mystery that can be approached only by indirection, through riddle-like allusions to the Old Testament, as several passages prior to the passion narrative indicate.

Mark 1:2-3: Who is the Kyrios? Mark's opening mixed citation already contains a major clue about the divine identity of Jesus. Mark weaves together citations of Malachi 3:1, Exodus 23:20, and Isaiah 40:3 to portray John the baptizer as God's harbinger of the new exodus and the restoration of Israel. The Baptist's message prepares the way for "one more powerful" who is soon to come (Mark 1:7-8). But who is this more powerful one? Jesus' mysterious identity is strongly suggested by the language of Isaiah that Mark cites: "Prepare the way of *the Lord* (κυρίου), make his paths straight" (1:3b; quoting Isa 40:3).

In Isaiah 40, there can be no question that "the Lord" is the LORD God of Israel (in the Hebrew text, יהוה), who will return to Zion to set things right, and "the way of the LORD" refers to the path that God will make through the desert, leading the triumphant procession of returning exiles. The full citation from Isaiah 40:3 reads, "In the wilderness prepare the way of the LORD, make straight in the desert a highway *for our God.*" The emphasis in Isaiah's prophetic vision points to "the return of Yahweh's actual presence" as the cause of deliverance.[93] The connection is made abundantly clear a few verses later:

> Get you up to a high mountain,
> O Zion, herald of good tidings;
> lift up your voice with strength,
> O Jerusalem, herald of good tidings,
> lift it up, do not fear;
> say to the cities of Judah,
> *"Here is your God!"*
> *See, the* LORD *God* (κύριος) *comes with might,*
> and his arm rules for him;
> his reward is with him,
> and his recompense before him.
>
>   (Isa 40:9-10)

Two points, then, are unmistakably clear: Isaiah 40 prophesies the coming of the *Kyrios* (the LORD God) to reign, and Mark appropriates this prophecy to characterize John's preparation of the way for the coming of *Jesus.* The only question is whether we should draw the obvious inference that, for Mark, Jesus is in fact to be identified with the *kyrios* of whom Isaiah speaks. Although *Kyrios* is not a common Markan epithet for Jesus (in contrast to Luke), several passages in Mark do connect this title to Jesus: 2:28, 11:3, and 12:36-37.[94] Mark 5:19 should also be added to this. There Jesus says to the formerly demon-possessed man, "Go home to your friends, and tell them how much *the Lord* has done for you." Mark adds in 5:20 that the man went and told how much *Jesus* had done for him. Thus, the opening lines of Mark seem to encourage us to understand Jesus' appearing as the fulfillment of Isaiah's prophecy of the return of the Lord to Zion.

An objection to this reading of Mark 1:3 lies readily at hand: If Mark means to portray Jesus as the *Kyrios*, why does he alter the last line of his citation of Isaiah 40:3?

> Isaiah 40:3 LXX: εὐθείας ποιεῖτε τὰς τρίβους τοῦ θεοῦ ἡμῶν.
>   ("Make straight the paths of our God.")
>
> Mark 1:3c: εὐθείας ποιεῖτε τὰς τρίβους αὐτοῦ.
>   ("Make straight his paths.")

Mark's abbreviation of the citation might suggest a certain reserve about referring to Jesus as "our God."[95] Yet, the parallelism of the two lines "prepare the way of the Lord" and "make straight his paths" would ordinarily be understood as synonymous. Therefore, to the extent that Mark's citation of Isaiah 40 carries forward the substance of its original sense,[96] there is an implicit claim about Jesus' divine status in the opening lines of this Gospel.[97]

It would be hasty to conclude on the basis of this one citation that Mark unequivocally identifies Jesus with the *Kyrios* of the Old Testament. Yet we would be heedless readers indeed if we failed to wonder why Mark selects Isaiah 40:3 as the keynote of his account of Jesus' activity. The verse hardly closes or determines our understanding of Jesus' identity, but it provocatively opens up the question of how the figure of Jesus Christ (Mark 1:1) is related to the liberating and comforting *Kyrios* of Isaiah 40. A certain ambiguity hovers about these opening verses of Mark's story. Should we see in Jesus' arrival on the scene the veiled but palpable fulfillment of Isaiah's fervent expectation? Mark's suggestive citation of Isaiah creates the possibility of such a reading and heightens the suspense, causing us to keep searching for further clues in the story.

Mark 2:7: Who can forgive sins but God alone? The healing of the paralytic (Mark 2:1-12) provides a further clue about Jesus' divine identity and is the first unit of Mark's opening cycle of controversy discourses (2:1–3:6). In this form-critically complex story,[98] Jesus not only performs a dramatic healing but also asserts his authority to forgive sins. Here, there is no explicit Old Testament citation, but the question of the skeptical scribes sends out ripples of significance when it is read against the background of the Old Testament: "Why does this fellow speak in this way? It is blasphemy! Who can forgive sins but God alone?"[99]

In Israel's Scripture, as the scribes' incredulous protest implies, it is beyond doubt that the prerogative to forgive sins belongs to God alone. Since sin is offense against God, only God has the right to declare it cancelled. Several key passages may come to mind as the basis for the scribes' question, particularly Exodus 34:6-7, in which God, appearing to Moses on Mount Sinai on the occasion of the giving of the second set of tablets of the law, solemnly proclaims an account of his own identity in which forgiveness of sins plays a constitutive part:

> "The LORD, the LORD, a God merciful and gracious, slow to anger, and abounding in steadfast love and faithfulness, keeping steadfast love for the thousandth generation, *forgiving iniquity and transgression and sin*, yet by no means clearing the guilty, but visiting the iniquity of the parents upon the children and the children's children, to the third and the fourth generation."

We need not concern ourselves here with the vexing problem of how to understand the relationship between the assertions that God forgives sin yet does not clear the guilty; the pertinent point is that this central confession of Israel's faith posits forgiveness of sins as belonging to God's character. Similarly, the scribes in Mark 2 might be recalling Isaiah 43:35: "I, I am He who blots out your transgressions for my own sake, and I will not remember your sins."[100]

Jesus' response to the scribes' thoroughly understandable objection is to command the paralytic to stand up and walk, as a visible sign of his own authority as Son of Man to forgive sins on earth (Mark 2:8-11). The reference to the authority of the Son of Man foreshadows Mark's later explicit evocation of Daniel 7, with its emphasis on the Son of Man's dominion over the whole earth.[101] It may even be that the phrase "so that you may know" in Mark 2:10 echoes the wording of Moses' confrontational speeches to Pharaoh in Egypt. For example:

> "Thus says the LORD, the God of the Hebrews: Let my people go, so that they may worship me. For this time I will send all my plagues upon you

yourself, and upon your officials, and upon your people, *so that you may
know* that there is no one like me in all the earth."

(Exod 9:13b-14; cf. Exod 8:10, 22; 10:2)

Thus, the echo in Mark 2:10 suggests that it is now the scribes whose
hearts, like Pharaoh's, are hardened—as Mark 3:5 confirms—and that,
like Pharaoh, they will incur God's judgment for their resistance to
the power of God.

With regard to the question of Jesus' identity, however, their question lingers. Who can forgive sins but God alone? One might read Mark
2:10 to mean that Jesus, as Son of Man, is exercising on earth a delegated
authority from God to forgive sins,[102] but in light of the already noted
identification of Jesus as the *Kyrios* (1:3), the reader of Mark's Gospel may
ponder at least the possibility that his sovereign authority to forgive sins
is not just delegated.

Mark 4:35-41: Who then is this that even the wind and sea obey him? If the
first two chapters of Mark have kindled sparks of insight into Jesus'
divine identity, the story of Jesus' stilling of the storm in Mark 4:35-41
fans the sparks into a fire. While crossing the Sea of Galilee in a boat,
Jesus and his disciples are caught in a storm that threatens to swamp
the small craft. Jesus sleeps blissfully, but the terror-stricken disciples
awaken him, asking, "Teacher, do you not care that we are perishing?"
Jesus then rebukes the wind and orders the sea to be still. When his
commands prove immediately effective, he scolds the disciples for their
lack of faith. For their part, they ask each other, in awe, "Who then is
this, that even the wind and the sea obey him?"

Mark provocatively leaves the question unanswered. The words hang
suspended over the story—leaving the reader to supply the answer. For
any reader versed in Israel's Scripture, there can be only one possible
answer: it is the Lord God of Israel who has the power to command
wind and sea and to subdue the chaotic forces of nature. Resonating in
the background of Mark's story of Jesus' calming the sea is a vivid passage from Psalm 107:

> Some went down to the sea in ships,
> doing business on the mighty waters;
> they saw the deeds of the Lord,
> his wondrous works in the deep.
> For he commanded and raised the stormy wind,
> which lifted up the waves of the sea.

They mounted up to heaven, they went down to the depths;
their courage melted away in their calamity [cf. Mark 4:40];
they reeled and staggered like drunkards,
and were at their wits' end.
Then they cried to the LORD in their trouble,
and he brought them out from their distress;
he made the storm be still,
and the waves of the sea were hushed [cf. Mark 4:39].
Then they were glad because they had quiet,
and he brought them to their desired haven.
Let them thank the LORD for his steadfast love,
for his wonderful works to humankind.
Let them extol him in the congregation of the people,
and praise him in the assembly of the elders.

(Ps 107:23-32)

The resemblance between these two accounts is so striking that Mark 4:35-41 looks very much like a midrashic narrative based on the psalm. If so, then, what are we to conclude about the identity of Jesus, since his role in the story is precisely the role ascribed to the LORD in Psalm 107?

Psalm 107 is by no means the only Old Testament passage that speaks of God's authority over wind and waves.

Or who shut in the sea with doors
when it burst out from the womb?—
when I made the clouds its garment,
and thick darkness its swaddling band,
and prescribed bounds for it,
and set bars and doors,
and said, "Thus far shall you come, and no farther,
and here shall your proud waves be stopped"?

(Job 38:8-11)

You rule the raging of the sea;
when its waves rise, you still them.

(Ps 89:9; cf. also Ps 65:7)

The passage from Job shows that the theme of God's mastery over the sea can be understood as a creation motif, expressing the common ancient Near Eastern image of creation as God's triumph over the primordial chaos symbolized by the sea (cf. Gen 1:1-10). God's act of separating the water from the dry land can be described through the image of the

Lord's "rebuking" the sea, as in Job 26:10-12 and Psalm 104:5-9—an image explicitly recapitulated in Jesus' command in Mark 4:39.[103] Furthermore, in several biblical passages, the image of God's rebuking of the primal chaos is superimposed upon the events of the exodus, demonstrating that the creator God is the same God who delivered Israel from bondage in Egypt.

> Yet he saved them for his name's sake,
> so that he might make known his mighty power.
> *He rebuked the Red Sea*, and it became dry;
> he led them through the deep as through a desert.
> So he saved them from the hand of the foe,
> and delivered them from the hand of the enemy.
> The waters covered their adversaries;
> not one of them was left.
> Then they believed his words;
> they sang his praise.
>
>   (Ps 106:8-12)

Isaiah 51:9-11, which calls upon God to *awake from slumber* to save Israel, takes the further step of recalling the Lord's past actions of subduing the sea in creation and in the exodus in order to prophesy a similar new action of deliverance: God will lead Israel out of exile, causing "sorrow and sighing" to flee away, just as the sea had in the past fled at his command:[104]

> Awake, awake, put on strength,
> O arm of the Lord!
> Awake, as in days of old,
> the generations of long ago!
> Was it not you who cut Rahab in pieces,
> who pierced the dragon?
> Was it not you who dried up the sea,
> the waters of the great deep;
> who made the depths of the sea a way
> for the redeemed to cross over?
> So the ransomed of the Lord shall return,
> and come to Zion with singing;
> everlasting joy shall be upon their heads;

they shall obtain joy and gladness,
and sorrow and sighing shall flee away.

This passage from Isaiah—with its resonant Near Eastern antecedents—
may be in the background of Mark 4:35-41, and Mark's picture of Jesus
sleeping in the boat while the disciples appeal to him to wake up and do
something reinforces the symbolic likeness of Jesus to the God of the
Old Testament.[105] Of particular significance is the fact that Psalm 44:23
was recited regularly in the liturgy of the Second Temple:

Rouse yourself! Why do you sleep, O Lord?
Awake, do not cast us off forever![106]

It is not clear that the idea of an appeal to God to awake and deliver
Israel from exile should be read alongside Mark 4:35-41, although in light
of Mark's recurrent echoing of Isaiah's new exodus imagery, the possibility can hardly be dismissed out of hand. What is unmistakably clear,
however, is that Jesus' mastery over the wind and waves demonstrates
that he is the possessor of a power that the Old Testament consistently
assigns to the LORD God alone. It is God who rebuked the waters and
formed the dry land, God who parted the sea for Israel, God who made
the storm be still. Well might the disciples ask, "Who then is this . . . ?"

By the end of this story in the Gospel, then, Mark has firmly planted
the idea that Jesus somehow embodies the presence of Israel's God. The
attentive reader will be on the lookout for subsequent clues that might confirm this astounding claim. Such attentiveness will not go unrewarded.

Mark 6:34: Who is the shepherd of Israel? In the opening lines of Mark's
story of the miraculous feeding of the five thousand (Mark 6:30-44), we
are told that when Jesus saw the great crowd of people, "he had compassion on them, because they were like sheep without a shepherd, and he
began to teach them many things." The expression "like sheep without a
shepherd" was already a proverbial way of describing Israel's plight after
the demise of a king, or under inept or wicked rulers (e.g., 1 Kgs 22:17;
2 Chr 18:16; Zech 10:2; Jdt 11:19). We have already noted that this passage
echoes both Numbers 27:17 and Ezekiel 34 and thereby hints that Jesus
is to be the new messianic shepherd of the people who will "lead them
out and bring them in" and provide protection and sustenance. He thus
assumes a role typologically prefigured by Joshua (Ἰησοῦς) and David.

In light of Mark's insistent suggestions about the divine identity of Jesus, however, the image of "sheep without a shepherd" also evokes one further intertextual echo from Ezekiel's poignant portrayal of the scattered flock of Israel. The description of David as the shepherd/king over Israel (Ezek 34:23-24) is secondary to a more fundamental prophecy about the agency whereby the sheep are to be rescued:

> *For thus says the Lord God: I myself will search for my sheep, and will seek them out.* As shepherds seek out their flocks when they are among their scattered sheep, so I will seek out my sheep. I will rescue them from all the places to which they have been scattered on a day of clouds and thick darkness. I will bring them out from the peoples and gather them from the countries, and will bring them into their own land; and I will feed them on the mountains of Israel, by the watercourses, and in all the inhabited parts of the land. I will feed them with good pasture, and the mountain heights of Israel shall be their pasture; there they shall lie down in good grazing land, and they shall feed on rich pasture on the mountains of Israel. *I myself will be the shepherd of my sheep*, and I will make them lie down, says the Lord God.
>
> (Ezek 34:11-15)

Significantly, Ezekiel 34:15 LXX differs from the MT, attesting the additional clause καὶ γνώσονται ὅτι ἐγώ εἰμι κύριος ("and they shall know that I am the Lord"). The true shepherd in Ezekiel's prophecy—whose identity is revealed through his act of feeding the sheep—is the Lord God himself; presumably the Davidic king of 34:23-24 is an intermediary instrument through whom this divine shepherding function is to be performed.

What, then, shall we infer when Mark tells us that Jesus sees the people as sheep without a shepherd and that Jesus then makes them sit down on the green grass and feeds them? Is Jesus acting as an intermediary, fulfilling a role prefigured by Moses and prophesied for the coming Davidic Messiah? Or is he also symbolically declaring, "You are my sheep, the sheep of my pasture, and I am your God" (Ezek 34:31)? If the next story, the story of Jesus walking on the sea, is to be connected closely with the miraculous feeding (as their close connection in the Gospel traditions would suggest; cf. John 6:1-21), it may offer a hint of how such questions are to be answered.

Mark 6:45-52: Who walks on the sea? The very next narrative provides even more provocative food for thought, as we encounter another strange epiphany during a sea-crossing (see the discussion of 4:35-41): Jesus comes walking on the sea to the disciples. In response to their terror, he offers a word of reassurance: θαρσεῖτε, ἐγώ εἰμι· μὴ φοβεῖσθε ("Take heart, it is I; do not be afraid"). Should we read this as another revelatory disclosure of Jesus' divine identity?

There is no Old Testament citation in this story, and the image of God's walking on the sea is not so widely attested as the image of his commanding and stilling the waves. The possible connections of this story to an exodus typology can be seen in passages such as Psalm 77:19, Isaiah 43:16, and Isaiah 51:9-10.[107] But these are not really apposite, for they refer to the exodus sea-crossing in which God parted the waters to lead the people through *on dry ground* (Exod 14:21-22, 15:19). The image in these passages is not one of the deity walking *atop* the waters of the sea.

There is, however, at least one Old Testament passage that paints a picture prefiguring Mark's sea-walking story: a doxological passage in Job, portraying God as sovereign over all creation, acclaims him as the one "who alone stretched out the heavens and trampled the waves of the sea" (Job 9:8). In its original context, this text was probably meant as another reference to God's subduing the primordial watery chaos; but the LXX offers a rendering of Job 9:8 that may be of considerable importance for understanding Mark 6:45-52: ὁ τανύσας τὸν οὐρανὸν μόνος καὶ περιπατῶν ὡς ἐπ᾽ ἐδάφους ἐπὶ θαλάσσης ("who alone stretched out heaven *and walks upon the sea as upon dry ground*").[108]

If Mark had Job 9 in mind, it would help to explain another notoriously puzzling feature of the water-walking tale. In Mark's telling of the story, when Jesus comes walking on the sea, the narrator comments cryptically, "He intended to pass them by" (ἤθελεν παρελθεῖν αὐτούς, Mark 6:48). This remark has consistently baffled interpreters—beginning with the Evangelist Matthew, who deletes the clause (Matt 14:25)—and has generated labored explanations, such as Augustine's suggestion that "his intent in passing by them was to serve the purpose of eliciting those outcries in response to which he would then come to bring relief."[109] If we recognize the allusion to Job 9, however, we may glimpse a far more illuminating reading. In the same passage that speaks of the creator God walking upon the sea, Job goes on to marvel at the way in which God eludes his own limited understanding:

He is wise in heart, and mighty in strength—
who has resisted him, and succeeded?—
he who removes mountains, and they do not know it,

when he overturns them in his anger;
who shakes the earth out of its place,
and its pillars tremble;
who commands the sun, and it does not rise;
who seals up the stars;
who alone stretched out the heavens
and trampled the waves of the Sea (LXX: καὶ περιπατῶν ὡς ἐπ᾽ ἐδάφους
    ἐπὶ θαλάσσης ["*and walks upon the sea as upon dry ground*"]);
who made the Bear and Orion,
the Pleiades and the chambers of the south;
who does great things beyond understanding,
and marvelous things without number.
Look, he passes by me, and I do not see him;
he moves on (LXX: παρέλθη με, "*he passes me by*"), *but I do not*
    perceive him.[110]

(Job 9:4-11)

Thus, in Job 9 the image of God's walking on the sea is linked with a confession of God's mysterious transcendence of human comprehension: God's "passing by" is a metaphor for our inability to grasp his power.[111] This metaphor, as we surely realize by this time, accords deeply with Mark's emphasis on the elusiveness of the divine presence in Jesus. Thus, the story of Jesus' epiphanic walking on the sea, read against the background of Job 9, can be perceived as the signature image of Markan Christology.

To these observations should be added the insight that the verb παρελθεῖν almost surely alludes to Exodus 33:17-23 and 34:6, where God is said to "pass by" Moses in order to reveal his glory indirectly, for "no one shall see me and live."[112] The LXX repeatedly uses παρελθεῖν in this passage, with the result that it subsequently becomes almost a technical term for the appearance of God.[113] Thus, Mark's mysterious statement in Mark 6:48, read as an allusion to the Exodus theophany, suggests simultaneously that Jesus' walking on the water is a manifestation of divine glory and that it remains indirect and beyond full comprehension—as the disciples' uncomprehending response amply demonstrates (Mark 6:51-52).

In this narrative context, there is little doubt that we should also hear Jesus' comforting address to the disciples ("It is I [ἐγώ εἰμι]; do not be afraid," Mark 6:50) as an echo of the self-revelatory speech of the God of Abraham, of Isaac, and of Jacob speaking from the burning bush in Exodus 3:14: "I am who I am" (LXX: ἐγώ εἰμι ὁ ὤν). Several other Old Testament passages echo this fundamental Exodus revelation in divine self-disclosure speeches, employing (in the LXX) the phrase ἐγώ εἰμι (e.g., Deut 32:39; Isa 41:4, 51:12; cf. Isa 43:11). Thus, when Jesus speaks this same phrase, "I am," in his sea-crossing epiphany, it serves to underscore the claim of divine identity that is implicitly present in the story as a whole.

The obtuse disciples, who have failed to grasp the meaning of the miracle of the loaves, fail also to understand even a sign so dramatic as this one. Matthew, finding their dullness inexplicable, writes a different ending to the story: when Jesus gets into the boat, the disciples promptly worship him and declare, "Truly you are the Son of God" (Matt 14:33). In this way, they model the response to Jesus that Matthew seeks to encourage in the church. Mark, I suggest, seeks to elicit a response of a slightly different kind: those who have picked up the clues Mark has offered will perceive that God is strangely present in Jesus, but their response—at least at this point in the story—will be one of reverent reticence. By refusing to trumpet the secret of Jesus' identity, instead signifying it through mysterious symbol-laden narrative, Mark is teaching his readers to question, and to listen more deeply, before they start talking about things too wonderful for their understanding.

Mark 7:37: Who makes the deaf to hear and the mute to speak? In 7:31-37, Mark narrates a brief story of Jesus' healing of a deaf man with a speech impediment (μογιλάλος, 7:32). Since the healing occurs in "the region of the Decapolis" (7:31), it is usually supposed that the deaf man and the surrounding crowd are Gentiles rather than Jews, particularly since the immediately preceding story of Jesus' encounter with the Syrophoenician woman (7:24-30) has introduced Jesus' healing power for Gentiles as a thematic focus. The third-century interpreter Lactantius saw in the healing of the deaf man a sign of the future mission to the Gentiles: "But there was also contained in this display of power another meaning. It would shortly come to pass that those who were previously ignorant of heavenly things, having received the instruction of wisdom, might soon speak God's own truth."[114] Note that this formulation is general enough to describe the past historical event of the revelation of the gospel to the Gentiles while at the same time allowing the story to serve as a symbol for the enlightenment that is subsequently available to all through "the instruction of wisdom."

The motif of inclusion of the Gentiles in the sphere of God's healing power may indeed be part of the meaning of the story. Mark, however, gives the tale another spin by implicitly linking the healing of the deaf-mute with Isaiah's prophecy of the eschatological restoration of Israel.

The astonished crowd, speaking in chorus, declares, "He has done everything well; *he even makes the deaf to hear and the mute to speak*" (Mark
7:37). Though there is no explicit citation of Scripture here, their acclamation echoes Isaiah 35:5-6. The similarity to the LXX version of these
verses is especially noteworthy:

> Then the eyes of the blind shall be opened,
> and *the ears of the deaf shall hear*;
> then the lame shall leap like a deer,
> and *the tongue of the stammerers* (μογιλάλων; cf. Mark 7:32) will be clear.

This echo hints that Jesus' activity is a sign of the fulfillment of Isaiah's
promise.[115] Mark's allusion to Isaiah intimates that in Jesus' wonder-
working activity the new creation envisioned by Isaiah is now breaking
in and that the return from exile is underway. If the echo of Isaiah 35:5-6
evokes a memory of its wider context, the reader will recall that Isaiah's
oracle ends with the promise that

> . . . the ransomed of the Lord shall return,
> and come to Zion with singing;
> everlasting joy shall be upon their heads;
> they shall obtain joy and gladness,
> and sorrow and sighing shall flee away.

> (Isa 35:10)

Thus, Mark 7:37 exhibits a theme that we have observed throughout
Mark's narrative, the theme of Israel's restoration. The present passage,
by focusing God's eschatological healing activity on Gentile beneficiaries, also extends the story of redemption to include those who were
previously excluded from Israel.[116]

The link between Mark 7:37 and Isaiah 35 carries one further implication, however, that has been less often recognized. If the allusion to
Isaiah 35:5-6 has the metaleptic character we have just proposed, we
should not overlook the fact that the *agent* of the healing and restoring
action in Isaiah 35 is none other than God himself.[117] The verse immediately preceding Isaiah's reference to healing the deaf and the mute makes
the point forcefully:

> Say to those who are of a fearful heart,
> "Be strong, do not fear!
> *Here is your God.*

He will come with vengeance,
with terrible recompense.
He will come and save you."[118]

(Isa 35:4)

Once more, then, Mark has offered for the discerning reader a provocative hint that Jesus is more than a prophet or a wonder-worker or an
intermediary figure announcing God's salvation. The one who makes
the deaf to hear and the mute to speak, according to Isaiah, is the same
one who shepherds his people, the LORD God who comes with might to
bring redemption to Israel.[119] The acclamation of the crowd in Mark 7:37
ends the narrative unit and lingers resonantly in the air, evoking sympathetic harmonies from Isaiah 35. The reader who has ears to hear will
pause and whisper, in accord with Isaiah, "Here is our God."[120]

Mark 11:12-14: Who comes looking for figs on the fig tree? The passages we
have considered so far, spread over the first seven chapters of Mark's
Gospel, create more than a casual presumption that Jesus is somehow
directly identified with Israel's God: Jesus is the *Kyrios* whose way is
prepared by the voice of one crying in the wilderness; he has the authority to forgive sins; he has the power to command the wind and sea; he
is the true shepherd of Israel; he walks upon the sea; and he makes the
deaf hear and the mute speak. All these clues point to the mind-bending
claim that God is mysteriously but directly present in the figure of Jesus.
Yet, as we have seen, his own disciples fail to understand the clues, and
the religious leaders of the people meet him with hard-hearted rejection.
Therefore, as Jesus approaches Jerusalem the tension builds.

The conflict comes to a crisis point in Jesus' prophetic action of
judgment against the temple (Mark 11:12-25). As we have observed,
Jesus' words and actions are crafted to reenact Jeremiah's prophecy
of destruction (Jer 7–8). In light of the many hints we have seen that
Mark's Jesus somehow mysteriously embodies the presence of the God
of Israel, one further detail of Jeremiah's oracle now claims our attention. Jeremiah speaks prophetically in the persona of God, addressing
his unfaithful people:

When *I* wanted to gather them, *says the LORD,*
there are no grapes on the vine,
nor figs on the fig tree;

even the leaves are withered,
and what I gave them has passed away from them.

(Jer 8:13)

It is *God* who is represented as seeking unsuccessfully to gather grapes and figs. What, then, are we to think when Mark tells the ominous and obviously symbolic story of *Jesus'* fruitless search for figs on the fig tree, followed by the withering of the tree (Mark 11:12-14, 20-21)? What does this suggest about the identity of the one who searches for the fruit? This is yet another case in which Jesus steps, at least functionally, into a role given exclusively to the Lord God in the Old Testament. If this were an isolated instance, one would perhaps not make too much of it, but, in light of its correspondence to the foregoing texts, the conjunction of Mark 11:12-14 with Jeremiah 8:13 points subtly but inexorably toward the identity of Jesus with the Lord in whose name Jeremiah spoke. As before, however, this mysterious identity is suggested through narrative figuration rather than asserted by means of direct statement.[121]

Complicating the picture: Jesus' distinction from God. Alongside the passages we have surveyed, we must acknowledge that several passages in Mark's Gospel seem to distinguish Jesus from Israel's God. Mark's narrative does not posit a simple undifferentiated equivalence between Jesus and the God of Israel.

In Jesus' enigmatic challenge to the scribes' teaching about the Davidic sonship of the Messiah (Mark 12:35-37), a distinction is made between the Lord who summons and the Lord who is summoned to sit at the right hand of the throne. Likewise, Jesus later proclaims that the Son of Man is ultimately to be seated at the right hand of the Power (14:62). If, as we have argued above, Mark identifies Jesus as both Davidic Messiah and Son of Man (drawing on Ps 110:1 and Dan 7:13-14), it would seem that his exalted future status will place him *beside* the Ancient of Days. This is a position of extraordinary honor and power, to be sure, but exalted proximity is not quite the same thing as simple *identity* with the God of Israel.

A distinction between Jesus and God is also made with respect to Jesus' limitation of knowledge concerning the time of the end. Near the conclusion of the apocalyptic discourse in Mark 13, Jesus declares his own ignorance on this point: "But about that day or hour no one knows, neither the angels in heaven, nor the Son, but only the Father" (13:32). Nowhere else in Mark does Jesus refer to himself in just this way as "the Son." The terminology looks like a strange Johannine fragment in

Mark's Gospel, but the reader of the Gospel will not find it difficult to interpret, since Jesus has already been designated as God's Son by the heavenly voice at his baptism (1:11) and at the transfiguration (9:7)—as well as by the demons (3:11, 5:7). The transparently christological parable of the wicked tenants has also depicted him as the "beloved son" (12:6). Furthermore, the repeated references to Jesus as Son of Man—including the immediately preceding one in 13:26—also prepare the reader to understand Jesus' expression here as a form of self-reference. Apart from 13:32, there are only three references to God as "Father" in the Gospel of Mark (8:38, 11:25, 14:36), but the first of these anticipates and illuminates the Father/Son language in the eschatological discourse: "Those who are ashamed of me and of my words in this adulterous and sinful generation, of them *the Son of Man* will also be ashamed when he comes in the glory of *his Father* with the holy angels" (8:38). This saying shows that "the Son" in 13:32 can readily be understood to be the same figure as "the Son of Man" (8:38, 13:26, 14:62). All these eschatological references, then, identify Jesus as the Son and distinguish his role from that of the Father. The Father/Son language binds Jesus in the closest possible relationship with God, whose glory and authority Jesus shares, while maintaining a distinction of roles and persons.

This relationship is expressed also in Jesus' prayer in Gethsemane, in which he subordinates himself to the will of the Father: "Abba, Father, for you all things are possible; remove this cup from me; yet, not what I want, but what you want" (Mark 14:36). Here, Jesus seems to play the role of Israel rather than the role of God: in the midst of doubt and agony he submits and becomes obedient. His self-description in 14:34—"I am deeply grieved (περίλυπός ἐστιν ἡ ψυχή μου), even to death"—echoes the prayer of the psalmist who longs for God's help in a time of profound disquiet and need (Pss 42:5, 11; 43:5).

> I say to God, my rock,
> "Why have you forgotten me?
> Why must I walk about mournfully
> because the enemy oppresses me?"
> As with a deadly wound in my body,
> my adversaries taunt me,
> while they say to me continually,
> "Where is your God?"
> Why are you cast down, O my soul (LXX: ἵνα τί περίλυπος εἶ ψυχή),
> and why are you disquieted within me?

> Hope in God; for I shall again praise him,
> my help and my God.
>
> (Ps 42:9-11)

And yet, precisely in the midst of this grief-stricken struggle, Jesus identifies God as "Father" and thereby affirms the Father/Son relationship that has been constitutive of his identity from the very beginning of Mark's story, beginning at least with the account of Jesus' baptism.[122]

Finally, the cry of dereliction from the cross once again draws on the language of the Psalms to express not only a distinction between Jesus and God but also a stark separation: "My God, my God, why have you forsaken me?" (Mark 15:34; echoing Ps 22:1). Whatever we make of this cry, the Jesus of Mark's passion narrative is a human being who suffers and dies in obedience to God and who, in the last hour of his anguish, experiences abandonment by God.[123]

In light of these elements of Mark's story, how are we to understand the pervasive Markan indicators that Jesus is mysteriously the embodiment of God's presence? Mark offers us no conceptual solution to the problem. Rather, his narrative holds these truths in taut suspension. His central character, Jesus, seems to be at the same time—if we may put it crudely—*both the God of Israel and a human being not simply identical with the God of Israel.* Indeed, Mark's story already poses the riddles that the church's theologians later sought to solve in the christological controversies of the fourth and fifth centuries. The logical tensions are internal to Mark's account; they are not created only when we set the "divine" Jesus of the Fourth Gospel in contrast to the "human" Jesus of the synoptics—a caricature misleading in both its terms. Rather, Mark's story repeatedly draws upon Old Testament imagery to portray the human Jesus as the Lord whom wind and sea obey.

It is all the more shocking, then, that the story of this Lord moves inexorably toward his ignominious death on a cross. Our examination of Mark's use of Scripture to narrate the identity of Jesus will not be complete without attention to the way that Scripture sheds light upon the central paradox of Mark's Gospel: the identity of Jesus as the crucified Messiah.

Jesus as crucified Messiah

It is universally recognized that Mark's story of Jesus focuses relentlessly on the crucifixion as the central revelation of Jesus' identity. Only at the moment of Jesus' death does a human character at last perceive and confess the truth, as the Roman centurion declares, "Truly, this man was God's Son" (Mark 15:39).[124] Jesus is, for Mark, rightly known as "Jesus the Nazarene, the crucified One" (16:6). The purpose of the following remarks, then, will be not to establish (redundantly) that the cross is at the heart of Mark's message but rather to explore the ways in which Mark draws upon Israel's Scripture to narrate Jesus' death and explicate its significance.

Early in Mark's passion narrative, Jesus utters two mysterious declarations that, in light of the unfolding events of his suffering and death, are to be understood as the playing-out of a destiny foretold in Scripture. The first of these sayings appears in Mark's telling of Jesus' final supper with his disciples. Following his prophecy that one of them will betray him, Jesus intones this dark oracle: "For the Son of Man goes *as it is written of him*, but woe to that one by whom the Son of Man is betrayed!" (Mark 14:21). The second saying occurs at the climactic moment of Jesus' arrest in the Garden of Gethsemane; this time he speaks to his captors: "Have you come out with swords and clubs to apprehend me as though I were a robber? Day after day I was with you in the temple teaching, and you did not arrest me. *But let the Scriptures be fulfilled*" (14:48-49).

The striking thing about these two declarations is that neither of them specifies any particular *texts* that are to be read as prophecies of the passion.[125] The effect of this narrative technique is to rouse our curiosity and to put us on alert. Having been forewarned by the authoritative voice of Jesus to listen for scriptural resonances, we will be prepared to search carefully for them and to interpret the connections we find as especially crucial for interpreting the grim events played out before our eyes. *What* Scriptures are being fulfilled in Jesus' suffering and death?

Surprisingly, in Mark's Gospel there are only four quotations of Israel's Scripture that are linked by the narrative to Jesus' passion and death, and of these only two are marked explicitly as quotations. It is noteworthy that both marked quotations are found in direct speech of Jesus; *Jesus the central character of the drama provides the explicit hermeneutical clues, while Mark the narrator refrains from overt commentary, subtly weaving scriptural allusions into the fabric of the story.* The first marked quotation, already discussed above, comes at the conclusion of the parable of the wicked tenants (Mark 12:1-11). Having told the parable, Jesus directly addresses the chief priests and scribes and elders (cf. 11:27, 12:12):

"Have you not read this Scripture?

'The stone which the builders rejected (ἀπεδοκίμασαν).
This one has become the head of the corner.
This has come from the Lord,
And it is amazing in our eyes.'"

(Mark 12:10-11; quoting Ps 118:22-23)

As we have already seen, Psalm 118 plays a role in Jesus' triumphal entry into the city, as the crowd acclaims him as a coming royal figure, using the words of Psalm 118:25-26. The religious leaders of the people have of course read this Scripture many times, for it stands at the climax of the Hallel psalms, sung repeatedly at Passover; thus, Jesus' question is pointedly ironic.

We saw previously that the linkage of Psalm 118:22-23 with the parable of the wicked tenants foreshadows Jesus' resurrection and triumph over those who have opposed him. Imbedded within the psalm itself, however, is a reference to the *rejection* of the stone. Indeed, the verb "rejected" (ἀπεδοκίμασαν) is the very same word that Jesus used in his first prediction of his coming death: "And he began to teach them that it was necessary (δεῖ) for the Son of Man to suffer many things and to be *rejected* (ἀποδοκιμασθῆναι) *by the elders and the chief priests and scribes* and to be killed and after three days to rise" (Mark 8:31). The overlap between these two texts cannot be merely coincidental: in both passages, Jesus is speaking of his own rejection and death at the hands of the same three-fold grouping of Jerusalem religious authorities, and in both cases, there is a promise of resurrection (explicit in Mark 8:31, implicit in Mark 12:10-11). In Mark 12, all this is said to be foreshadowed by the words of Psalm 118; consequently, the verbal link created by the use of ἀποδοκιμάζω in both passages suggests that when we read Mark 8:31 *retrospectively*, we should understand that Jesus has already shaped the first prophecy of his passion with a view to the words of this psalm. This is a subtle echo we almost surely would have missed on a first reading of the Caesarea Philippi episode. Indeed, the expression "it was necessary" (δεῖ), in this retrospective reading, can be understood as an allusion to a *scripturally* foretold necessity of suffering and death. Thus, even within Psalm 118, a psalm of thanksgiving that celebrates triumph over Israel's enemies, Mark sees also an adumbration of the cross. This is of course all very subtle and can be understood only as we "read backwards" in the larger context of Mark's narrative, which climaxes in the story of cross and resurrection.[126]

The second explicitly marked quotation in Mark's passion story appears immediately following Jesus' final supper with his disciples.

> And after singing a hymn, they went out to the Mount of Olives. Jesus said to them, "You will all be caused to stumble, for it is written: 'I will strike the shepherd, and the sheep will be scattered.'"
>
> (Mark 14:26-27)

Coming close on the heels of Jesus' observation that "the Son of Man goes as it is written of him" (14:21), this scriptural citation surely fills in at least part of the meaning of Jesus' enigmatic saying. The text in view here is Zechariah 13:7. The wording of Mark's citation, though it is close to one manuscript of the Septuagint (LXX^Q), does not agree precisely with any known manuscript of Zechariah. In both the Hebrew and LXX traditions the saying is an imperative addressed in poetic apostrophe to the sword[127] that is summoned to strike the shepherd:

> "Awake, O sword, against my shepherd, against the man who is my associate," says the LORD of hosts. "Strike the shepherd, that the sheep may be scattered."

In Mark 14:27, however, the verb is a first-person singular future indicative, πατάξω ("*I will* strike"). This textual adjustment carries two significant implications. First, the change turns a command into a prophecy—or perhaps more precisely a declaration of intent; the death of Jesus is then portrayed as the fulfillment of this future-directed declaration.[128] And second, even more significantly, the agent doing the striking, it is implied, is God himself, who spoke beforehand through the prophet Zechariah to disclose what he planned to do to Jesus, "my shepherd." Characteristically, Mark offers no explanation of this somber divine purpose, except insofar as we might find an explanation figured forth symbolically in the immediately preceding supper account: "This is my blood of the covenant, which is poured out for many" (14:24), where the divine intent expressed in the πατάξω of 14:27 corresponds precisely to the δεῖ of 8:31. For reasons difficult to fathom, God has deemed it necessary to strike down the Son of Man who is also, as adumbrated in the feeding narrative of 6:30-44, the shepherd who rightly feeds God's people.

To elucidate this strange turn of events by pointing to Zechariah 13 is to explain the obscure by the still more obscure. The apocalyptic prophecy of Zechariah 9–14 is a notoriously difficult text, riddled with puzzling symbols and apparently odd internal tensions.[129] For example, is the shepherd who is struck down in Zechariah 13:7 the same figure as the "worthless shepherd who deserts the flock" and is therefore to be struck by the sword (Zech 11:15-17)? Or is this a different character in Zechariah's confusing scenario? Is the shepherd of 13:7 to be identified with the one whom the inhabitants of Jerusalem have "pierced" but for whom they then mourn bitterly, "as one mourns for an only child" (12:10)? Though Zechariah's prophetic visions are shrouded in mystery, they clearly lend themselves to reinterpretation by the followers of Jesus as a foreshadowing of the events of the crucifixion, as the explicit quotation of Zechariah 12:10 at John 19:37 equally, but independently, attests.

The fact of the matter is that, while Mark draws our attention pointedly to Zechariah 13:7, his narrative does not supply sufficient information to enable us to sort out precisely how he understood the wider context of Zechariah 9–14. But whatever we make of the details, this much is clear: the citation of this one ominous prophecy ("I will strike the shepherd . . .") encourages readers to understand the rapidly unfolding events of the passion narrative in the strongly *apocalyptic* context signaled by Zechariah's closing chapters. The arrest and violent death of Jesus are not merely ordinary events, random brutalities to be added to a seemingly endless litany of afflictions endured by Israel. Rather, these events are signs that the climactic days prophesied by Zechariah have at last arrived. Even though the shepherd is struck down and the sheep scattered (a prophecy fulfilled directly and literally in Mark 14:50 as Jesus' disciples flee for their lives), a day is coming soon when God will reaffirm and reestablish his covenant relation with his people (Zech 13:8-9) and subdue the nations that oppress Israel so that "the LORD will become king over all the earth; on that day the LORD will be one and his name one" (14:9). Indeed, it is precisely the impending death of Jesus that shows this moment is now at hand.[130]

Beyond this point in the narrative, Mark offers no further marked scriptural citations. As readers, having been given the hint to listen for echoes of Scripture and to see patterns of typological fulfillment in the passion, we are now left to our own interpretative devices as we move deeper into the gathering darkness. At two key points in the ensuing events, Mark's narration imbeds quotations of scriptural texts in the story, with no explicit flags to identify them as such. As we shall see, these two unmarked quotations are of particular importance for grasping Mark's account of the crucifixion.

Immediately after Mark's exceedingly spare narration of the cruci-fixion ("and they crucify him," 15:24a),[131] he adds this detail: "and *they divided* his *clothes among them, casting lots for them* to decide what each should take" (15:24b). Given the concise character of Mark's telling of the tale, we might wonder why he bothers to inform us about the seemingly trivial matter of the disposition of Jesus' garments at the moment of his execution. For the reader who knows the Psalter, the answer is not far to seek. The words italicized in the quotation above are taken directly from Psalm 22, an agonized psalm of lament. It is, perhaps not incidentally, a psalm of David, in which the voice of the psalmist includes among the catalogue of his sufferings the following:

> I can count all my bones.
> They stare and gloat over me;
> they divide my clothes among themselves
> and for my clothing they cast lots.

(Ps 22:18)

Thus, the apparently small narrative detail of Mark 15:24 not only signi-fies Jesus' state of being dispossessed and stripped utterly naked but also suggests that, as he had prophesied, his death is being played out accord-ing to the Scriptures. In particular, this citation of Psalm 22 intensifies the clues already scattered through Mark's story that lead us to see *the Psalms as particularly important intertexts for interpreting the shape of Jesus' life and death.*

And, of course, only a few sentences later, Jesus' last coherent words in Mark's Gospel are a direct citation of the opening words of this very same psalm: "My God, my God, why have you forsaken me?" (Mark 15:34; citing Ps 22:1). Mark strikingly recounts the words in Aramaic (*Eloi, Eloi, lema sabachtani?*) and then gives his reader a Greek transla-tion. The effect of the Aramaic citation is to enhance the raw immediacy of the moment and to enhance the narrative's historical verisimilitude. But why, in terms of Mark's story, does Jesus die with a cry of dereliction on his lips? The question has been endlessly discussed and debated by biblical scholars and theologians. This much, at least, may be affirmed: Jesus' expression of abandonment indicates the full depth of his suffer-ing and the radical character of his coming "not to be served but to serve, and to give his life as a ransom for many" (10:45). But in light of our investigation of the ways in which Mark draws upon Scripture to nar-rate the identity of Jesus, perhaps at least two more things can be added.

For one thing, in counterpoint to the previous scriptural evocations of Jesus' identity with the God of Israel, Jesus speaks here as a fully human figure who experiences the radical *absence* of God.[132] This confirms the enormous complexity of Mark's narrative rendering of Jesus. It is not difficult to understand how early docetic interpreters developed the notion that the divine spiritual "Christ" abandoned the earthly man Jesus before his death on the cross, leaving him bereft and bewildered by what was happening to him; such a reading cushions the divine from the scandal of suffering and leaves our categories of "divinity" and "humanity" comfortably distinct and intact. But such a reading is far too simple to do justice to the Gospel of Mark. Mark offers no such tidy explanation; rather, his Jesus maintains a unity of identity throughout. The one who has power over wind and sea, the one who is described by David as "Lord," the one who will be seated at the right hand of the Power and coming with the clouds of heaven is the *same* Jesus who cries out in dismay from the cross. And—here is the central point—*both aspects of his identity are prefigured by Scripture.* The paradoxical unity of his identity is grounded in a hermeneutical vision that discovers attestations of Jesus' suffering and his exalted status intertwined into God's mysterious revelatory word to Israel.

The second thing to note about Mark's use of Psalm 22 in narrating Jesus' death is this: we have seen in Mark a consistent pattern of *metaleptic* reference to Scripture. That is to say, Mark's intertextual references, more often than not, have an allusive character. They beckon the reader to examine the context and background of even the most fragmentary citations and to consider how that wider context might inform our reading of the story. Significant elements of the intertextual relations lie just under the surface, suggested but not explained by the narrative. Mark offers ample reason for us to assume a similar narrative technique here; indeed, he has given the reader more hints than usual. We have already seen that he explicitly cites Psalm 22's depiction of enemies dividing the sufferer's garments and casting lots for them (Mark 15:24). The parallels continue in 15:29-30: "those who passed by derided him, *shaking their heads* (κινοῦντες τὰς κεφαλάς) and saying, 'Aha! You who would destroy the temple and build it in three days, save yourself, and come down from the cross.'" Surely we are meant to hear an echo of Psalm 22:7-8:

> All who see me mock at me;
> they make mouths at me, they shake their heads (LXX: ἐκίνησαν κεφαλήν);

"Commit your cause to the LORD; let him deliver—
let him rescue the one in whom he delights!"

The single direct verbal echo is in the phrase "shaking their heads," but the cluster of intertextual references to Psalm 22 virtually compels us to see the crowd's mockery of Jesus as one more facet of the mysterious homology between the righteous sufferer of the psalm and the Messiah hanging shockingly on the cross.[133]

If all that is correct, it follows that we cannot stop reading the psalm with its opening cry, "My God, why have you forsaken me?" Mark has signaled his readers that the *whole* psalm is to be read as a prefiguration of Jesus' destiny. Consequently, as Christian interpreters have long recognized, Jesus' dying cry of desperation evokes the full sweep of Psalm 22's movement from desolate lament and complaint (Ps 22:1-8, 12-19) to passionate petition (22:9-11, 19-21a) to praise and thanksgiving (22:21b-31). If we read to the end of the psalm, we find an affirmation of the Lord's universal dominion over the nations (like the everlasting dominion of the Son of Man in Dan 7:14) and even, for the reader who knows Mark's full story, an adumbration of the resurrection in the glad affirmation that God "did not despise or abhor the affliction of the afflicted; he did not hide his face from me, but heard when I cried to him" (Ps 22:24-25).[134] Indeed, the psalmist sings, "before him shall bow all who go down to the dust, and I shall live for him" (22:29).

What I am suggesting is that to read Jesus' cry from the cross in Mark 15:34 as an intertextual evocation of Psalm 22's promise of hope is not simply an exegetical cop-out, a failure of nerve that refuses to accept Mark's bleak portrait of Jesus' death at face value. Rather, *it is a reading strategy that Mark himself has taught us* through his repeated allusive references to snatches of Scripture that point beyond themselves to their own original narrative settings and lead the reader to reevaluate the surface sense of the Jesus story. Such a reading strategy is an act of readerly responsiveness to Mark's admonition to take heed what we hear.

Precisely such a hermeneutical approach allows us to take with full seriousness the shape of the narrative that Mark actually tells, a narrative that proclaims the cross in the foreground but whispers in its subtexts that Jesus' death is not the end of the tale. The crucified One at the center of Mark's story is somehow the embodiment of Israel's God, and even though the risen Lord never appears in the story, we are given many pointers assuring us of his ultimate triumph. Precisely by perceiving the scriptural roots of his identity, we will be able to enter with the psalmist into the full depths of his agony and yet believe—even if we hardly dare breathe it in so many words—that he lives and rules over the nations.

Excursus: Where is the Suffering Servant?

The reader may be surprised to find no reference to the Suffering Servant figure of Isaiah 52:13–53:12 in the foregoing discussion. Is not this a key image for Mark's account of the identity of Jesus? Unexpectedly, an actual search for allusions to the Isaian servant in Mark's narration of the passion turns up very little evidence.

The strongest case for an allusion is found in Mark 10:45: "For the Son of Man came not to be served, but to serve and to give his life as a ransom for many." It is often suggested that this account of the Son of Man's vocation is dependent on Isaiah 53:12: ". . . he poured out himself to death, and was numbered with the transgressors; yet he bore the sin of many, and made intercession for the transgressors." Yet, on close examination, the only word shared by these two texts is πολλῶν ("many"), hardly a significant echo. The verbs translated as "serve" in Mark 10:45—διακονηθῆναι and διακονῆσαι—are not etymologically related to the terms (the noun παῖς and the participle δουλεύοντα) that refer to the Servant in the Greek versions of Isaiah 53. And the Isaiah passage nowhere uses Mark's key term λύτρον ("ransom").

Again, it is sometimes suggested that Jesus' silence before the high priest's interrogation (Mark 14:61) is a fulfillment of Isaiah 53:7 ("He was oppressed and afflicted, yet he did not open his mouth; like a lamb that is led to the slaughter, and like a sheep that before its shearers is silent, so he did not open his mouth"). If so, Mark gives us no clues to that effect; there is not a single verbal link between the two passages. Furthermore, any possible parallel is compromised by the fact that as the scene unfolds, Jesus *does* speak emphatically in the very next verse, declaring himself to be the Christ, the Son of the Blessed One and the Son of Man who will be seated in glory at the right hand of God (Mark 14:62).

Finally, some interpreters have heard an echo of Isaiah 53 in Jesus' words at the last supper with his disciples: "This is my blood of the covenant, poured out for many" (Mark 14:24). Once again, it is chiefly the expression ὑπὲρ πολλῶν ("for many") on which the case for an allusion hangs. But this is a very slender thread. The prepositional phrase does not appear in Isaiah 53 ("He bore the sins of many," v. 12), and there is no reference to "blood" or "covenant" anywhere in the context. Much clearer is the echo of Exodus 24:8, describing the ceremony initiating the covenant at Mount Sinai: "Moses took the blood and dashed it on the people, and said, 'See *the blood of the covenant* that the LORD has made with you in accordance with all these words.'" Also, because of several other allusions to Zechariah throughout the passion narrative, as noted above, we might well hear in Mark 14:24 a second echo of Zechariah 9:11: "As for you also, because of *the blood of my covenant* with you, I will set your prisoners free from the waterless pit." These two intertexts would suggest in Mark 14 an interpretation of Jesus' impending death as a recapitulation (or replacement?) of the Sinai covenant at which the Torah was given to the people *and* as a sign of the apocalyptic deliverance promised in Zechariah, in which the people are set free.

In sum, it is very difficult to make a case that Isaiah's Suffering Servant texts play any significant role in Mark's account of Jesus' death—at least at the level of Mark's text-production. There can be no doubt that, at the level of text-reception, subsequent Christian readers—placing Mark within a canonical framework that includes not only Isaiah but also texts in Paul, Luke, and John that point more explicitly to Isaiah 53—have heard faint but significant echoes of the Servant in Mark's Gospel. But *within the verbal texture of Mark's own narrative*, it is chiefly the psalms of the suffering righteous one, along with the apocalyptic visions of Zechariah and Daniel, that provide the hermeneutical framework for interpreting the death of Jesus, the crucified Messiah.

§4 WATCHFUL ENDURANCE
The Church's Suffering in Mark's Narrative

Our third heuristic question is how Mark evokes Israel's Scripture to narrate the church's role in relation to the world. This is not an easy question to answer for the Gospel of Mark, for at least two reasons. Mark never actually uses the word "church" (ἐκκλησία) anywhere in his narrative. The term thus as used here should be understood as a convenient shorthand for "the followers of Jesus" or "the community of readers for whom Mark writes."[135] Mark is also less explicitly concerned than are the other Evangelists with the church's relation to Roman government and pagan culture; the contrast with Luke on this point is particularly evident. Mark is primarily concerned to narrate his gospel as the climax of Israel's hopes, and the conflicts that emerge in the narrative are, as we have seen, chiefly internal family struggles between Jesus and Israel's own leaders. The broader Greco-Roman world and its authorities remain, for the most part, on the periphery of the story—at least up until the concluding portion of the passion narrative.

However, precisely because Mark situates his Gospel so firmly within a Jewish apocalyptic worldview, political questions are never far from view. Jewish apocalyptic thinkers looked forward to God's ultimate deliverance of Israel from foreign hegemony, and indeed expected a radical transformation of the political status quo. If Jesus is in fact the hoped-for Davidic king—even if in an entirely unexpected way—how does his message of "the kingdom of God" relate to the empire that held power in Mark's day? How does Mark's retelling of the story of Israel position his community of readers in relation to the nations? And what role does Mark's scriptural hermeneutic play in shaping answers to such questions? Let us explore the few hints that Mark gives about these matters.

The church under persecution

Although the narrated action of Mark's story is set firmly in the brief final years of the life of Jesus of Nazareth, at a few points we catch forward-looking glimpses of the narrator's own time, about forty years later. One of the salient features of the church's experience in that later time seems to be the prospect of persecution. This is already prefigured in Jesus' interpretation of the parable of the sower, where we are told that some hearers of the word are "the ones sown on rocky ground: when they hear the word, they immediately receive it with joy. But they have no root, and endure only for a while; then, *when trouble or persecution arises on account of the word*, immediately they *fall away* (σκανδαλίζονται)" (Mark 4:16-17). The verb σκανδαλίζω, here translated "fall away" but literally meaning "cause to stumble," is precisely the same word used in Jesus' later prophecy of the disciples' desertion: "You will all fall away/be caused to stumble (σκανδαλισθήσεσθε)" (14:27). When the shepherd is struck down—that is, when persecution comes from the brutal power of the empire that crucified Jesus—his followers will wither away like the seedlings on rocky ground.

It requires little imagination to see here a reflection of conditions for an embattled church in Mark's own time,[136] particularly since the parable's symbolic portrayal of a church under persecution "on account of the word" is vividly reinforced in Jesus' apocalyptic discourse in Mark 13. After prophesying the destruction of the temple and speaking of the beginnings of the "birth pangs" of the coming age, Jesus addresses the disciples directly with a stern warning:

"As for yourselves, beware; for they will hand you over to councils; and you will be beaten in synagogues; and you will stand before governors and kings because of me, as a testimony to them. And the gospel must first be proclaimed to all nations. When they bring you to trial and hand you over, do not worry beforehand about what you are to say; but say whatever is given you at that time, for it is not you who speak, but the Holy Spirit.[137] Brother will betray brother to death, and a father his child, and children will rise against parents and have them put to death; and you will be hated by all because of my name. But the one who endures to the end will be saved."

(Mark 13:9-13)

Here again we see, in much more explicit terms, the expectation that Jesus' followers will endure serious persecution, from authorities both Jewish (councils and synagogues) and Gentile (governors and kings), and even from their own families. The final promise of salvation for those who endure to the end is reminiscent of the ending of Daniel: "Happy are those who persevere and attain the thousand three hundred thirty-five days [i.e., the interval between the appearance of the "abomination of desolation" and the final resurrection and deliverance of Israel]. But you, go your way, and rest; you shall rise for your reward at the end of the days" (Dan 12:12-13).[138] This picture of a time of terrible tribulation for God's elect, followed by an end-time that brings vindication and salvation, is, by the time of Mark's writing, a standard aspect of Jewish apocalyptic thought, rooted particularly in the tradition represented by Daniel.

Indeed, allusions to Daniel play a major role in Jesus' dire words of warning throughout this apocalyptic discourse, the longest extended speech by Jesus anywhere in Mark's Gospel. The most obvious reference appears in Mark 13:14: "But when you see *the abomination of desolation* set up where it ought not to be (let the reader understand), then those in Judea must flee to the mountains." Jesus' prophetic warning echoes an unusual phrase (τὸ βδέλυγμα τῆς ἐρημώσεως) that occurs several times in the later chapters of Daniel's apocalyptic visions (Dan 9:27, 11:31, 12:11). In Daniel, this "abomination of desolation" almost surely refers to the provocative action of Antiochus IV Epiphanes, who in the second century B.C.E. profaned the temple in Jerusalem by placing in it an altar to Zeus (1 Macc 1:54-61). Mark now takes this event as a prophetic foreshadowing of some final desecration of the temple.[139] Mark then offers one of his rare authorial asides, nodding knowingly to the reader, who is expected to share the inside information required to decode the symbol. But the precise signification of this "abomination" within Mark's story-world remains somewhat unclear, and it has excited numerous speculations over centuries of interpretation—speculations that need not detain us here.[140] In any case, Mark remains consistent as a narrator by withholding overt explanation of his mysterious language.

Whatever is meant by "abomination of desolation," it signifies some horrific desecration of the temple that will trigger a time of destruction and suffering. The linkage between Daniel's apocalyptic scenario and Jesus' prophetic warning is strengthened still more by the strong echo of Daniel 12:1 in Mark 13:19:

> Dan 12:1 LXX—That day will be a day of suffering (θλῖψις), such as has not been since they first came into existence until that day.

> Mark 13:19—For in those days there will be suffering (θλῖψις), such as has not been from the beginning of the creation that God created until now, no, and never will be.

Through these insistent intertextual echoes of Daniel, Mark is positioning the church to understand itself in a role analogous to the nation of Israel portrayed in that prophetic book: a powerless, oppressed people suffering under oppressive foreign rule and experiencing the pain of frustrated hopes for deliverance.

At the same time, however, just as in Daniel, so in Mark's apocalyptic vision, there remains a confident hope for future deliverance by divine power:

> But in those days, after that suffering (θλῖψις),
>
>> the sun will be darkened,
>> and the moon will not give its light,
>> and the stars will be falling from heaven,
>> and the powers in the heavens will be shaken.
>
> Then they will see *the Son of Man coming in clouds* with great power and glory. Then he will send out the angels, and gather his elect from the four winds, from the ends of the earth to the ends of heaven.
>
> (Mark 13:24-27)

The images of cosmic signs in Mark 24 and 25 (sun and moon darkened and stars falling) are derived from Isaiah 13:10; Joel 2:10, 3:15; and Isaiah 34:4 LXX.[141] These portents signify "the day of the Lord," and it is very important to recognize that in Isaiah they are specifically associated with *God's judgment on Babylon and on the pagan nations that have oppressed Israel.*[142] The cosmic signs do not portend the end of the world; rather, they signify the punishment of evil powers and the downfall of "the insolence of tyrants" (Isa 13:11). In other words, they are the signs of the end of an oppressive political order and the establishment of a new one, in which the Lord "will again choose Israel and will set them in their own land" (14:1).

The language of Jesus' apocalyptic discourse echoes all these passages, without citing them directly. But the cumulative effect of these echoes is to reassure the community that its present experience of suffering is part of the great apocalyptic script. If the church is a persecuted minority now, this is to be expected as part of the tribulation that the chosen must endure in the time of crisis that precedes God's final saving action and restoration of justice. All this is prefigured in Scripture and strongly reinforced by Jesus' own prescient words, performed against the background chorus of Israel's prophets.

And, of course, the crucifixion of Jesus—prophesied both in Scripture (the Psalms and Zechariah) and in Jesus' own passion predictions and figured with special poignancy in his words and actions at the last supper—is the definitive embodiment of the agony of God's people in the last days. The prophecy that "the sun will be darkened" is explicitly fulfilled in Mark's narrative at precisely the time when Jesus is dying on the cross (Mark 15:33); Mark once again trusts his readers to observe the pattern of fulfillment without the aid of authorial comment. A community that follows Jesus can expect nothing other than the same suffering he endured ("If any want to become my followers, let them deny themselves and take up their cross and follow me"), while living in the hope of the future life of the resurrection ("For those who want to save their life will lose it, and those who lose their life for my sake and the sake of the gospel will save it").

Challenge to Caesar

As we have seen in our examination of the motif of Davidic kingship, Mark's Gospel presents Jesus as a royal figure, the rightful heir of the throne of Israel. His entry to the city of Jerusalem elicits a public demonstration that acclaims "the coming kingdom of our father David" (Mark 11:9-10; citing Ps 118:25-26). Further, as Son of Man, the risen Jesus will exercise cosmic lordship: "To him was given dominion and glory and kingship, that all peoples, nations, and languages should serve him" (Dan 7:14). Such claims can hardly be made without creating confrontation with the claims of imperial Rome, with its aspirations to universal rule. It is not insignificant that the inscription placed by Pilate on the cross read ironically, "The King of the Jews" (Mark 15:26): the humiliating public execution of Jesus was meant to mock the futility of Jewish pretensions to kingship and resistance to Rome's sovereignty.[143]

Yet Mark remains undeterred. The opening line of his book declares "the beginning of the gospel (εὐαγγέλιον) of Jesus Christ, God's Son." The term εὐαγγέλιον no doubt suggests a bold counterclaim to the propaganda of the *Pax Romana* and the emperor cult. An important inscription in honor of Augustus Caesar, found at Priene in Asia Minor and dating from 9 B.C.E., declares that "the birthday of the god Augustus was the beginning of the good news (εὐαγγελίων) for the world that came by reason of him."[144] For Mark to pick *this* term as the keynote of his narrative is already to set up a clash between the "gospel" of the empire and the gospel of the kingdom of God: "The time is fulfilled and the kingdom of God has drawn near; change your minds, and trust in the gospel" (Mark 1:15). Additionally, both *Christos* and "God's Son" are designations for the anointed king of Israel, a claim underscored by Mark's brief narration of the baptism of Jesus, where the heavenly voice addresses him in the words of the royal acclamation of Psalm 2:7: "You are my son" (Mark 1:11). And yet, at the same time, "son of God" is also a widely attested title for the Emperor.[145] At the heart of Mark's Gospel are these questions: Who really is the son of God—Caesar or Jesus—and which one of these divine sons is the true bearer of good news for the world?[146] We can hardly, then, read Mark's opening lines without recognizing that the Gospel's central character is on a collision course with Caesar. If the tearing open of the heavens at the baptism is, as we have argued, an allusion to Isaiah 64:1, we can hardly miss the implications of the following verse in Isaiah: the purpose of God's hoped-for tearing open of the heavens and coming down is "to make your name known to your adversaries, *so that the nations might tremble at your presence*" (64:2).

Similarly, if Mark's opening prophetic quotation (Mark 1:2-3) is programmatic for his entire narrative, and if indeed this quotation suggests that the story of Jesus is to be interpreted in terms of the vision of new exodus/end of exile that is found in Isaiah 40, it follows that the community of Jesus' followers would be encouraged by this imagery to understand themselves as set free from bondage to the rulers that previously held them captive.[147] If Jesus is the bearer of the authority of the God of

Israel, then the Roman Empire's power can only be a usurpation, a trivial interruption of the true order of things:

> Even the nations are like a drop from a bucket,
> and are accounted as dust on the scales. . . .
> All the nations are as nothing before him;
> they are accounted by him as less than nothing and emptiness.
>
> (Isa 40:15, 17)

Just in case we readers might begin to forget the conflict between the kingdom ruled by Rome and the kingdom of God proclaimed by Jesus, Mark includes a sly reference to Roman military power in his account of Jesus' exorcism of the Gerasene demoniac. When Jesus demands to know the name of the unclean spirit that is possessing and destroying his human host, the spirit replies, "My name is *Legion*, because we are many" (Mark 5:9). No first-century reader would need to be reminded that the Legions stationed throughout the Mediterranean world and ready to respond to rebellion and revolt belonged to Rome. When Jesus then powerfully dispatches the demons into a herd of unclean pigs who plunge to their death in the sea, Mark hardly needs to explain the joke. It is a kind of political cartoon, in which the Roman army is driven out by Israel's true king, sent back into the sea from which their invading ships had come.[148]

Of course, any reading of the Gospel of Mark that seeks to take the measure of its stance toward Caesar must reckon with the key pronouncement story in which Jesus answers whether paying taxes to Caesar is lawful (Mark 12:13-17). There is a long history of Christian interpretation that reads Jesus' answer as authorizing a "two kingdoms" solution in which Caesar's authority over material and commercial matters is acknowledged, while that which belongs to God is relegated to a separate "spiritual" realm. But this interpretation fails to make sense of the narrative dynamics of the text.

The question of the Pharisees and Herodians is explicitly described as a trap (Mark 12:13) that seeks to force Jesus either to declare rebellion against Rome or to discredit himself in the eyes of the people by endorsing passive acquiescence in Roman hegemony. If Jesus' answer to their question ("Give back to Caesar the things that belong to Caesar, and give back to God the things that belong to God") means simply, "Yes, pay the tax," then he has fallen into one side of the trap, the quietist/collaborationist side. In fact, however, Mark tells us that Jesus' interlocutors, far from gleefully celebrating his answer, are "utterly amazed" by it. Why so? His answer is a riddle that throws the task of discernment back on the questioners, forcing them to offer a discernment about what in fact belongs to God. The key to understanding the passage lies in the often overlooked fact that Jesus does not immediately respond to the question with a pithy aphorism; rather, he first challenges the questioners' motives ("Why do you put me to the test?") and then demands that the questioners bring him a denarius. When they comply, he puts a question to them: "Whose image (εἰκών) is this, and whose inscription?" Only after they have given the obvious answer does Jesus spring his own trap back on them by stating in a pointed imperative that the (unclean, idolatrous) object with Caesar's εἰκών on it should be summarily returned to its owner, while "the things that belong to God" should be truly rendered to him.

But what belongs to God? The full force of Jesus' reply sinks in only when we recognize that the word εἰκών echoes the creation story of Genesis, in which we learn that God created the human being *according to his own image* (κατ᾽ εἰκόνα θεοῦ, Gen 1:27 LXX). With this echo in our ears, we will understand Jesus' answer very differently: it summons all who hear this imperative to give back our created selves fully to the one whose image we bear. That is why Jesus' answer astonishes his questioners; by drawing on scriptural imagery it reminds us not only that everything belongs to God but that human beings in particular, who are made in his image, belong to him—and therefore *not* to Caesar.

All of this is fully consistent with the other elements we have seen in this Gospel. By alluding to the Genesis creation story, Mark offers still more scriptural shaping of the church's self-understanding as a community set apart from business as usual, a community that owes ultimate obedience to God, while rendering only the most provisional acknowledgment of Caesar's temporary grasp on power.

The gospel for all nations

If the kingdom of God claims sovereignty over all whom God has created in his image, it necessarily follows that the good news brought by Jesus cannot be restricted to the restoration of the nation of Israel alone. In contrast to Matthew and Luke, Mark develops no programmatic emphasis on a mission to the Gentiles. Nonetheless, he does seem to presuppose the existence of such a mission, and at a few key points he offers glimpses of a rationale for it that is rooted in Israel's Scripture.[149]

In Mark's story of Jesus' turning over the tables of the money chang-ers in the temple, we have seen that he invokes the prophecy of Isaiah: "My house shall be called a house of prayer for all the nations" (Mark 11:17; citing Isa 56:7). When we compare the passage to its synoptic par-allels, two distinctive features of Mark's account jump out at us. First, Mark introduces the quotation with this narrative framing: "And *he was teaching*, and he said to them. . . ." Of the synoptic Evangelists, only Mark specifies that Jesus' citation of Isaiah is specifically didactic in purpose. Second, and more significantly, only Mark includes in the Isaiah cita-tion the words πᾶσιν τοῖς ἔθνησιν ("for all the nations"). Assuming that Matthew and Luke were using Mark as a source, it seems that they have deliberately edited out this reference—presumably because it appears anachronistic on the lips of the pre-Easter Jesus. But whatever judgment may be made about the historical factuality of such a teaching, Mark clearly signals that the inclusion of Gentiles alongside Israel in prayer is actively taught by Jesus *precisely through appeal to Scripture*. And at this point, the appeal is hardly an idiosyncratic one; it is a straightforward reading of Isaiah's specific vision that the eschatologically restored Israel would embrace "foreigners who join themselves to the LORD, to minister to him, to love the name of the LORD, and to be his servants" (Isa 56:6).[150]

In light of this distinctive emphasis, we should not then be sur-prised that in Mark's later account of Jesus' apocalyptic discourse we find among the prophesied future events that "the gospel must (δεῖ) first be proclaimed to *all the Gentiles*" (Mark 13:10). Once again, Mark's form of the saying is far more explicit than the parallels in Matthew and Luke. Matthew simply says, "You will be brought before governors and kings for my sake as a witness to them and to the Gentiles" (Matt 24:18), and Luke omits reference to the Gentiles altogether. Mark's use of δεῖ sug-gests a scripturally determined necessity (as, e.g., in 8:31, 9:11, and 13:7). In this case, however, Mark does not specify the texts that are the basis for the necessity of this universal gospel proclamation. One suspects that Isaiah hovers somewhere in the background (passages such as Isa 2:2-4, 49:6, 57:6-8, 60:1-3; cf. Ps 22:27-28), but Mark keeps his own counsel about this rather than seeking to instruct the reader.

Mark's identification of Jesus with the figure of the glorified Son of Man would suggest a universal dimension to his reign: "all peoples, nations, and languages should serve him" (Dan 7:14). Mark foreshadows this eschatological sovereignty over the Gentile world in the earlier parts of his narrative. The most prominent instance during the period of Jesus' ministry of teaching and healing is the Syrophoenician woman who wittily prevails upon Jesus to cast a demon out of her daughter (Mark 7:24-30). Also possibly pertinent is the immediately following healing of a deaf man "in the region of the Decapolis" (a Gentile territory; 7:31-37) and the subsequent second miraculous feeding of a multitude (8:1-10), which is sometimes interpreted as the feeding of a Gentile crowd, though Mark does not say so explicitly.[151]

But Mark plays these notes with understated subtlety; stories such as these can perhaps be read as hints of the extension of the gospel to non-Israelites, but they are only hints. The decisive *peripeteia* comes only at the moment of Jesus' death, when the Roman centurion astonishingly blurts out, "Truly this man was God's Son" (Mark 15:39), a declaration reminding Mark's readers of a similar one at the beginning of the story—when the heavenly voice at Jesus' baptism declared, "You are my Son" (1:11). Thus, the centurion not only answers the question, "Who really is the Son of God?" but does so precisely by unwittingly echoing Psalm 2, the very psalm that proclaims the futility of the efforts of kings and nations to conspire "against the Lord and his anointed" (LXX: κατὰ τοῦ κυρίου καὶ κατὰ τοῦ χριστοῦ αὐτοῦ; Ps 2:2). The Gentile outsider, the soldier who had been the tool of "the kings of the earth" to plot the death of the Lord's anointed, now joins the heavenly voice in naming Jesus, the crucified Messiah, as God's true Son. The dramatic irony of this paradoxical reversal is exquisite, and its full impact is felt only by the reader who hears the reprise of the scriptural intertext from Psalm 2:7.

What does all this have to do with the way in which Mark draws upon Israel's Scripture to position the church in relation to the pagan world? It suggests that the church is not only a persecuted minority standing in tension with the systems of power in the pagan world but also a witness whose very suffering continues to embody the message of a crucified Messiah—a message that actually has the power to reach across national and ethnic boundaries and convert even the unlikeliest outsiders, even the oppressors who inflict violence upon the community. *The story of Jesus, when understood within its proper scriptural matrix, opens up the eschatological hope for all nations to join with Jesus' first Jewish followers in prayer, confession, and service to the crucified king.* Thus, the church, even though beset by persecution, never can become an inward-turning sectarian society. Its own defining story insists again and again that the strange gospel of the crucified Christ has a way of turning insiders into outsiders and mysteriously embracing outsiders with the good news of the kingdom of God.

The political posture required of the church, then, as it awaits the eschatological disclosure of Jesus' glory as the Son of Man, is one of *patient, watchful endurance.* That is the response repeatedly commended in the apocalyptic discourse of Mark 13, which ends with a word of direct exhortation from Jesus to the reader: "Therefore, keep awake—for you do not know when the master of the house will come, in the evening, or at midnight, or at cockcrow, or at dawn, or else he may find you asleep when he comes suddenly.[152] And what I say to you, I say to all: Keep awake" (13:35-37). The community's model for such watchfulness is Jesus in the Garden of Gethsemane, ardently praying while the disciples, unable to stay awake for even one hour, fall asleep (14:32-42). Jesus scolds but does not reject them, urging them one more time: "Keep awake and pray that you may not come into the time of trial."

The church then, is called neither to foment revolution against Caesar nor to withdraw into the wilderness like the Qumran sectarians to form a perfect society. Rather, they are simply to proclaim the good news of the kingdom, despite its paradoxical improbability, and to accept whatever suffering may come as a result. They are not to exclude Gentile outsiders but to remain critically open to those who somehow respond in faith to the gospel. Most of all, they are not to be seduced by the illusion of power projected by the empire. Instead, their radical reappraisal of power is grounded in the example of "the stone that the builders rejected," the Son of Man who came not to be served but to serve and to give his life as a ransom for many. Thus, their vision of community is shaped by the hermeneutical fusion of Israel's story with the story of Jesus.

§5 "HIDDEN IN ORDER TO BE REVEALED"
Mark's Scriptural Hermeneutics

Because Mark's use of Scripture is less overt than that of Matthew and Luke, there has been a tendency for New Testament scholars in modernity to overlook or downplay the importance of scriptural interpretation in this Gospel. For a long time, the most extensive study of the Old Testament in Mark was a monograph by Alfred Suhl, *Die Funktion der alttestamentliche Zitate und Anspielungen im Markusevangelium.* This study, under the influence of Suhl's mentor Willi Marxsen, was primarily a polemic against finding any conception of *Heilsgeschichte* or promise-fulfillment motifs in Mark.[153] As a constructive study of how Mark reads the Old Testament, the book is of little value. More recently, Richard

Horsley has challenged all attempts to treat scriptural interpretation as a significant feature of Mark's Gospel:

> Focusing on how isolated passages in Mark conflate and interpret isolated passages from "scripture" tends to abstract and divert attention from a dynamic sequential narrative full of multiple conflicts, subtleties, and ironies. . . . Further undermining the claim that Mark is "quoting" and interpreting scripture, the "quotations" usually turn out to be at most a few words of allusion. . . . And the hypothesis of Mark engaged in interpretation of scripture is based on what we now recognize as unwarranted assumptions that literacy was widespread and scrolls readily available and that a well-defined canon of scriptures existed already in Mark's historical situation.[154]

If the foregoing reading of Markan texts in this chapter has demonstrated anything, it has shown that Horsley badly underestimates the density and hermeneutical sophistication of scriptural citation in Mark. Precisely for that reason, Horsley also advocates an interpretation of the Gospel that minimizes Mark's Christology; if the scriptural intertexts in Mark are ignored, a diminished Christology inevitably follows.

At the same time, recent years have seen a number of more useful constructive studies of Mark's interpretation of Scripture.[155] The major studies of Joel Marcus and Rikki Watts are particularly important for understanding the complexities of Mark's hermeneutics, and the work of Thomas Hatina helpfully emphasizes the importance of understanding Mark's references to Scripture in the literary context of Mark's own narrative. The reading of Mark offered in the foregoing pages builds upon the exegetical work of these scholars but also seeks to unfold some christological implications that are not fully explored in their work. These christological implications can be discerned only when we attend to the poetics of allusion imbedded in Mark's distinctive narrative strategy.[156]

Mark's way of drawing upon Scripture, like his narrative style more generally, is indirect and allusive. Rather than placing overt theological claims on the table (in the manner of John's Gospel) and giving his reader explicit explanations of the scriptural background of the events he narrates (in the manner of Matthew's Gospel), Mark for the most part works his narrative magic through hints and allusions, giving just enough clues to tease the reader into further exploration and reflection. On rare occasions, he steps from behind the curtain of the stage to call the reader's attention to a particularly important intertextual allusion (e.g., "Let the reader understand," in Mark 13:14), but for the most part his scriptural references are woven seamlessly into the fabric of the story. The story is intelligible, at one level, for readers who do not hear the scriptural echoes. But for those who do have ears to hear, new levels of complexity and significance open up. To cite an obvious example, Mark tells the story of Jesus' entry into Jerusalem riding on a colt without any authorial comment whatever about scriptural fulfillment (11:1-11). But the reader who perceives the subliminal symbolism of Zechariah 9:9 imbedded in the action will more fully grasp the significance of the episode. In this case, readers who lack the requisite "encyclopedia of reception"[157] to "get" the allusion are helped out by one of Mark's earliest readers, Matthew, who eagerly supplies the quotation of Zechariah, along with an explanatory reassurance that this event took place in order to fulfill what was written by the prophet (Matt 21:4-5). But this example is merely the tip of an iceberg of intertextual allusion in Mark; we would be singularly inept readers if we confined our recognition of these intertexts, and their significance, to the few cases that Matthew has happened to elucidate.

One way of putting my point about Mark's use of Scripture is to say that his hermeneutical strategy for reading Israel's sacred texts is exactly analogous to his understanding of the function of parables, as disclosed in Jesus' answer to the disciples' question about his enigmatic manner of teaching in parables. As we have seen, Jesus' reply speaks of a "mystery of the kingdom of God" that is disclosed to some but hidden from others in the form of parables (Mark 4:11-12). Yet at the end of Mark's parable chapter, we find this authorial comment: "And with many such parables, he spoke to them the word, just as they were able to hear. He did not speak to them apart from a parable, but privately to his own disciples he explained all things" (4:33-34). There appears to be some tension between 4:11-12 and 4:33. In the former, the parables seem to have the function of hiding the message of the kingdom, but in the latter, they seem to be instruments of communication that allow Jesus' listeners to grasp the message at their own level of understanding. Is this an outright contradiction, a sign of Mark's incompetence and inconsistency as a storyteller? Or, on the other hand, does it communicate something essential about the character of the paradoxical veiled communication we find both in the parables and in the identity of Jesus himself throughout this Gospel?

Mark himself gives us a clue to the answer in a densely packed paragraph lodged in the midst of Jesus' parable discourse:

And he said to them, "A lamp doesn't come, does it, to be placed under a bushel-basket or under the bed? Does it not come in order to be placed on a lampstand? For there is not anything that is hidden except in order to be revealed, nor is anything secret except in order to be disclosed. If anyone has ears to hear, let him hear." And he said to them, "Watch what you hear! The measure with which you measure will be measured back to you, and still more will be added to you. Whoever has, it will be given to him; and as for the one who does not have, even what he has will be taken away from him."

(Mark 4:21-25)

In its context in Mark 4, as a direct continuation of Jesus' answer about teaching in parables, this is surely to be understood as a figurative discourse about the hermeneutics of hearing and understanding the word.

A comparison of Mark 4:22 to the parallels in Matthew 10:26 and Luke 8:17 reveals an interesting difference. The saying in its Matthean and Lukan forms draws a contrast between present concealment and future revelation. For Matthew, ". . . nothing is veiled that will not be revealed, and nothing is hidden that will not be known"; for Luke, ". . . nothing is hidden that will not be disclosed, nor is anything secret that will not be known." But Mark's form of the saying highlights the intentionality of the hiding: "For there is not anything that is hidden except in order to (ἵνα) be revealed, nor is anything secret except in order to (ἵνα) be disclosed."[158] As in apocalyptic, the hiddenness somehow belongs to the revelatory purpose, or even promotes the revelation. In view of all we have seen in Mark's Gospel, it would not be too much to suggest that the purpose implied here is the divine intent to offer veiled self-revelation in the person of Jesus, whose identity is finally fully disclosed only at the moment of greatest obscurity, his shameful death on a cross ("Truly this man was the Son of God").

The suggestion that Mark 4:21-22 speaks in a veiled manner of divine self-disclosure is also supported by the odd construction of the saying in 4:21, literally, "Does a lamp come (ἔρχεται) . . . ?" English translators characteristically find this formulation intolerable and render it with a passive voice construction of some different verb, such as "Is a lamp brought . . . ?" (NRSV).[159] But in fact, the sentence as Mark wrote it describes the lamp as an active agent that "comes." The nearly inescapable consequence of this observation is that Mark has shaped this saying as a christological parable about Jesus' coming into the world.[160] When it is joined to the paradoxical saying in Mark 4:22 about things hidden in order to be revealed, we are close to the heart of Mark's Christology and, I would suggest, to his hermeneutical approach to Israel's Scripture.

That is why the very next verses contain an urgent exhortation: "Pay careful attention to what you hear," says Jesus, "because if you 'measure' generously in interpreting the word, still more rewards will follow. But if you are a stingy hearer who hears only the literal surface sense, your reading of the Gospel—and of Israel's Scripture—will offer only diminishing returns, leading finally to nothing but impoverishment." That is of course a broad paraphrase of Mark 4:23-25, but we are compelled to understand this text as a teaching about how to hear the proclaimed word. Mark has shaped these sayings, even if they may have been in the earlier tradition a scattered group of logia,[161] into a cohesive exhortation about hermeneutics. Readers are called to listen closely to what might be hidden in the text in order to enter fully into the outpouring of signification that awaits the attentive interpreter.

Mark's hermeneutical directive, however uncongenial for modernist interpreters accustomed to seeking a single clear and explicit "original sense" in texts, is in fact precisely attuned to the way that figurative language actually works. Metaphors do not deal in direct statement; rather, they intensify meaning precisely by concealing it, by speaking in an indirect mode and saying something other than what is meant. Robert Frost phrased this insight simply: "Poetry is the one permissible way of saying one thing and meaning another."[162] And the literary critic Frank Kermode, in his penetrating study of the hermeneutics of Mark's Gospel, observed, "Parable, it seems, may proclaim a truth as a herald does, and at the same time conceal truth like an oracle."[163]

In light of these observations, the importance of Mark 4:21-25 as a hermeneutical directive for the Gospel as a whole can hardly be overstated. Mark is alerting his readers that christological signification may be hidden but that attentive listening can discern, within the Gospel's parabolic figuration, layers of meaning that point to "the mystery of the kingdom of God." It is no accident that in 4:11 Mark has the singular μυστήριον, rather than the plural μυστήρια, which occurs in the synoptic parallels, Matthew 13:11 and Luke 8:10. The singular mystery disclosed in and through the narrative is nothing other than the identity of Jesus himself, the Crucified Messiah who is also paradoxically the embodiment of the God of Israel.

And yet to state this claim bluntly in so many words, as I have just done, is to betray Mark's far more circumspect way of communicating the mystery. It is to blurt out crassly a secret so huge that its right expression must be concealed in figures, riddles, and whispers. In a discussion of Mark's trial narrative, Rowan Williams gets the delicate balance just right, in a way sympathetically responsive to Mark's manner of telling the story:

> Throughout [Mark's] Gospel, Jesus holds back from revealing who he is because, it seems, he cannot believe that there are words that will tell the truth about him in the mouths of others. What will be said of him is bound to be untrue—that he is master of all circumstances; that he can heal where he wills; that he is the expected triumphant deliverer, the Anointed. . . . "There is a kind of truth which, when it is said, becomes untrue." Remember, the world Mark depicts is not a reasonable one; it is full of demons and suffering and abused power. How, in such a world, could there be a language in which it could truly be said who Jesus is? . . . Jesus, described in the words of this world, would be a competitor for space in it, part of its untruth.[164]

But Mark is not reduced to simple silence. "How, in such a world, could there be a language in which it could truly be said who Jesus is?" Mark's answer is that there is such a language in the stories and symbols of Israel's Scripture, read in counterpoint with the stories about Jesus. If it is misleading, or careless of the mystery, to say "Jesus is the God of Israel"—just as it is not permitted to speak the ineffable name of God figured in the Tetragrammaton—there is still a way of *narrating* who Jesus is by telling stories in which he has the authority to forgive sins, to still storms, to walk on the sea, to feed the scattered sheep as the true shepherd, to make the deaf to hear and the mute to speak. There is a way to *narrate* who Jesus is by identifying John the Baptist as the voice in the wilderness who will proclaim Isaiah's gospel message of the end of exile by crying, "Prepare the way of the *Kyrios*." Through the poetics of allusion, Mark gestures toward the astounding truth. Those who have ears to hear will hear.

Even such indirect confessional claims, however, must be read within the larger context of Mark's story. The identity of Jesus as the mysterious embodiment of Israel's God can never be separated from his identity as the crucified One. And therein lies a still deeper layer of the mystery: If Jesus is the embodiment of Israel's God, and if the body in whom these figural correspondences to Israel's Scripture are enacted ends up nailed to a cross, what does that tell us about the identity of God?

Has Mark thought through such implications of his way of telling the story? We cannot say, because he does not say. But readers who listen carefully to the resonances of Israel's Scripture in Mark's Gospel and then see how the story drives toward the passion narrative may find themselves, like the women in Mark's artful dramatic ending, reduced, at least for a time, to silence. "They said nothing to anyone, for they were afraid."[165]

So, if we seek to read Scripture through Mark's eyes, what will we find? We will find ourselves drawn into the contemplation of a paradoxical revelation that shatters our categories and exceeds our understanding. We will learn to stand before the mystery in silence, to acknowledge the limitation of our understanding, and to wonder. The "meaning" of Mark's portrayal of the identity of Jesus cannot be rightly stated in flat propositional language; instead, it can be disclosed only gradually in the form of narrative, through hints and allusions that project the story of Jesus onto the background of Israel's story. As Mark superimposes the two stories on one another, remarkable new patterns emerge, patterns that lead us into a truth too overwhelming to be approached in any other way.

This reading of Mark as scriptural interpreter corresponds closely to an important stream of interpretation of Mark's Gospel in the Orthodox tradition. On the annual feast day of St. Mark the Evangelist, there is a prayer in the Greek Orthodox liturgy that invites the congregation to give honor to Mark for his distinctive, mysterious way of bearing witness: "Come, let us praise Mark, the herald of the heavenly mystagogy (τὸν τῆς ἐπουρανίου μυσταγωγίας κήρυκα), and the proclaimer of the gospel."[166] *Herald of the heavenly mystagogy*—that is, one who proclaims a message that leads us into the mystery.

Chapter 2

THE GOSPEL OF MATTHEW
Torah Transfigured

O come, O come, Emmanuel,
And ransom captive Israel,
That mourns in lonely exile here,
Until the Son of God appear.

§6 THE LAW AND THE PROPHETS FULFILLED
Matthew as Interpreter of Scripture

If the earliest Christian writers were seeking, as Rowan Williams suggests, to reorganize Israel's religious language,[1] what sort of hermeneutical reorganization will we find when we turn to the Gospel of Matthew? Matthew makes an ambitious attempt to advance the work of scriptural interpretation well beyond the mysterious frontiers so cautiously explored by Mark. Although he begins in territory charted by Mark's Gospel, Matthew shows little of Mark's restraint in pressing bold narrative claims about Jesus and linking them explicitly to numerous Old Testament texts. Indeed, in many passages we find him supplying overt explanations to Mark's hints and allusions.

A familiar example: Mark's account of Jesus' entry into Jerusalem alludes to Zechariah's prophetic vision of the city of Jerusalem shouting acclamation to a victorious king who rides humbly on a donkey, but Mark leaves the scriptural intertext entirely unvoiced (Mark 11:1-10;

gesturing covertly toward Zech 9:9). Matthew, on the other hand, is so eager to draw his readers' attention to the intertextual link that he quotes the Zechariah passage in full and explicitly points out that Jesus' action is a fulfillment of the prophecy. Furthermore, he reshapes the story to include *two* animals, a donkey and a colt, both mentioned in Zechariah 9:9 (Matt 21:1-9), thereby underscoring the fulfilled prophecy but also creating for his readers the notoriously baffling image of Jesus somehow astride both creatures: "they brought the donkey and the colt, and put their cloaks on *them*, and he sat on *them*" (Matt 21:7).

Another example that is no less illuminating of Matthew's concerns: Matthew's renarration of Jesus' apocalyptic discourse closely follows the script given by Mark, in which Jesus refers to a mysterious sign that should warn his followers to flee the city: "But when you see the abomination of desolation set up where it ought not to be (let the reader understand), then those in Judea must flee to the mountains" (Mark 13:14). This is one of the few places where Mark winks knowingly at the reader, signaling the presence of an allusion and trusting the reader to take the hint. Matthew repeats the saying, but he wants to make sure that the reader *will* understand, and so he glosses the text with additional information: but when you see the abomination of desolation—*the one spoken of by the prophet Daniel*—standing *in the holy place* (let the reader understand), then those in Judea must flee to the mountains (Matt 24:15). Ever the careful scribe, Matthew has specified the textual source for the reader who may need to look it up. He has also clarified the indefinite location of the event—not just "where it ought not to be" but specifically "in the holy place" (i.e., the temple). It is as though Matthew is producing an annotated study Bible, providing notes and references that will give the uninitiated reader enough information to perform the necessary act of scriptural interpretation.

Indeed, Matthew leaves nothing to chance: he repeatedly erects highway signs in large letters to direct his readers, making it unmistakably explicit that Jesus is the fulfillment of Israel's Scripture. Matthew has organized his material in a didactic, user-friendly fashion—a kind of "training manual for prophets."[2] It is therefore not without reason that, when the fourfold Gospel canon was later assembled, Matthew was placed first.[3] Nor was it without reason that Matthew became the Gospel most frequently cited by early Christian writers and that commentaries were written on it by Origen, Jerome, John Chrysostom, Theodore of Mopsuestia, and Cyril of Alexandria, to mention just some of the patristic authors who focused on this Gospel.[4] Matthew successfully organized the Jesus tradition in a form that made it clear, harmonious, and accessible.

When we consider Matthew's use of the Old Testament, the first thing that springs to mind is his distinctive manner of introducing prooftexts—as in the example of Jesus' triumphal but humble entrance into Jerusalem—through a repeated formula in which the Evangelist addresses the reader directly in an authorial voiceover: "This took place to fulfill what had been spoken through the prophet, saying. . . ." Ten quotations in Matthew appear under this rubric, with minor variations: 1:22-23, 2:15, 2:17-18, 2:23, 4:14-16, 8:17, 12:17-21, 13:35, 21:4-5, and 27:9.[5] Additionally, at least three other Old Testament quotations in the Gospel bear close affinities to this pattern of fulfillment citation: 2:5-6, 3:3, and 13:14-15.[6] Also closely related to the formula quotations are the words of Jesus at the time of his arrest in Gethsemane, affirming that "all this has taken place so that the Scriptures of the prophets may be fulfilled" (Matt 26:56; cf. 26:54), though in this case no specific quotation is adduced. This saying, alongside the Evangelist's thirteen authorial voiceovers, highlights Matthew's strong interest in the theme of fulfilled prophecy. Cumulatively, these passages frame Israel's Scripture as a *predictive* text pointing to events in the life of Jesus.

Matthew's emphasis on prediction and fulfillment has an evidently apologetic thrust:[7] this rhetorical tactic seeks to validate his affirmations about the identity of Jesus by grounding them in Israel's authoritative texts, presumably in opposition to other interpreters who would see Matthew's christological claims as incongruous with Israel's Scripture. For this reason, the reconstruction of the social setting in which Matthew's apologetic arguments should be understood has become a focus for research. If the interpretation of Scripture was a contested issue for Matthew, who were his opponents, and what was the specific historical context in which Matthew felt compelled to adduce these scriptural prooftexts in defense of the story of Jesus? Although it is impossible to be certain of the details, there is a strong consensus among recent scholars that the text must have been written in a setting (such as Antioch in Syria) where Jewish Christianity found itself in fierce competition with the synagogue and its scribal leadership in the period following the destruction of the Jerusalem temple.[8] Krister Stendahl's classic study *The School of St. Matthew* focused on the eclectic use of different Old Testament textual traditions in the formula quotations and argued that this practice was the product of a Jewish-Christian scribal "school" that combed through various ancient texts and versions to find passages that could be interpreted as messianic prooftexts.[9] It is, however, a speculative business to reconstruct a precise social history on the basis of the text's patterns of scriptural citation and argument. The best we can do is observe the combative character of Matthew's rhetoric and surmise that his exegesis took shape in a volatile, contested environment in the decades following the Roman army's destruction of the Jerusalem temple, as Jewish interpreters sought to interpret the troubling times in light of the Scriptures and vice versa.[10]

It has sometimes been suggested that the Matthean fulfillment quotations come from a preexisting collection of messianic prooftexts, and that Matthew has simply plugged them into his story, without regard to their original meaning or context.[11] However, careful study of Matthew's citation practices demonstrates that the same redactional tendencies at work in the formula quotations are to be found also in other scriptural citations in Matthew's Gospel. Indeed, Matthew himself should be seen as the controlling synthetic imagination responsible for assembling this material and giving it a focused christological interpretation.[12]

Matthew has front-loaded these formula quotations in the opening chapters of his Gospel. Four of the ten formula quotations appear in the birth and infancy narratives; if we add the fulfillment citations in Matthew 2:5-6 and 3:3, we find that nearly half of these weighty hermeneutical directives are placed in the plot structure even before the baptism of Jesus, and still another accompanies his initial proclamation of the kingdom in Galilee (4:14-16). This clustering of fulfillment quotations near the beginning of the Gospel conditions readers to expect that nearly everything in the story of Jesus will turn out to be the fulfillment of something prescribed by the prophets. Thus, Matthew presents Israel's sacred history as an elaborate figurative tapestry designed to point forward to Jesus and his activity.

The rhetorical impact of these formula quotations is so powerful that they have tended to dominate our understanding of how Matthew appropriates Scripture. Because of Matthew's eventual placement at the head of the New Testament canon, these quotations have exerted an even more sweeping influence: they dominate popular Christian understanding of how the Old Testament is to be read. But it is probably wise not to allow this one distinctive feature of Matthew's citation practice to monopolize the interpretation of Matthew.[13] The understanding of Matthew's use of Scripture will be far too narrow if we are enraptured by the formula quotations.[14]

These citations, to be sure, express a theological perspective that pervades Matthew's Gospel—as expressed in certain key programmatic statements such as Jesus' declaration in the Sermon on the Mount that he has come not to abolish the law but to fulfill it (Matt 5:17). Yet precisely this saying suggests that we must reckon with a Matthean hermeneutical program considerably more comprehensive than a collection of a dozen or so prooftexts. In what sense does Jesus fulfill the law? If Jesus has come to fulfill every jot and tittle of the law (5:18), we should expect Matthew to develop a far more wide-ranging account of the accordance between Scripture and his Gospel. And indeed, that is just what we find in this narrative: a diverse and complex use of Scripture. There are at least *sixty* explicit Old Testament quotations in the Gospel. That means that the formula quotations constitute, even by the most generous estimate, only about one-fifth of Matthew's total. And that does not even begin to reckon with the hundreds of more indirect Old Testament allusions in the story.[15]

Above and beyond the question of citations of particular texts, we must reckon also with Matthew's use of figuration, his deft narration of "shadow stories from the Old Testament."[16] Through this narrative device, with or without explicit citation, Matthew encourages the reader to see Jesus as the fulfillment of Old Testament precursors, particularly Moses, David, and Isaiah's Servant figure.[17] And at a level still deeper than these narrative figurations, Matthew's language and imagery are from start to finish soaked in Scripture; he constantly presupposes the social and symbolic world rendered by the stories, songs, prophecies, laws, and wisdom teachings of Israel's sacred texts. It is of course impossible to survey all this material, but we shall examine a few key passages that shed light on Matthew's strategies for reading Scripture. We will first trace the ways in which the story of Israel is renarrated in this Gospel. Then, in that context, we can consider the way in which Matthew employs scriptural interpretation to present the identity of Jesus and to portray the position of the church in relation to its cultural environment.

§7 THE END OF EXILE
Israel's Story in Matthew's Narrative

The genealogy (Matt 1:1-17). In contrast to Mark's strategy of plunging abruptly into the story at the point of Jesus' baptism, Matthew anchors the story of Jesus in Israel's history by opening his Gospel with a genealogy. This genealogy may strike many readers today as plodding, unedifying, or even clumsily comical in its repetitive formal structure.[18] Still, while Matthew's genealogy is hardly an electrifying way to begin a narrative—in contrast to the immediate dramatic action of Mark's opening paragraph—it actually performs several important hermeneutical functions.

First, the genealogy ensures *continuity* between Israel's story and the story that Matthew is about to narrate. Unlike Mark's Jesus, Matthew's Jesus does not burst on the scene out of nowhere; he is the heir of a familial line that stretches back through forty-two generations to Abraham.[19] This genealogy prepares the reader to interpret Jesus as the heir of the promises to Abraham, the consummation of Israel's epic story that began in the patriarchal narratives of Genesis. Even Matthew's opening words in 1:1, βίβλος γενέσεως Ἰησοῦ Χριστοῦ ("the book of the genesis of Jesus Christ"), reinforce this association with the Torah's first book.[20] Matthew's opening line may function as a title for the Gospel as a whole, suggesting that the story of Jesus is in fact a "new Genesis," the story of an eschatological redemption that begins the world anew.[21] The redeemer figure who accomplishes this redemption is, moreover, "Jesus Christ, son of David, son of Abraham." This identification links the new creation inextricably to the past of Israel, as signified by references to Abraham, the patriarchal *Urvater* of the nation, and David, its great iconic royal figure. Indeed, each name in the genealogy, particularly the more well-known ones, evokes the recollection of Israel's story. Matthew thus grounds Jesus' identity in Israel's story, and the detailed genealogy functions as a "call to remembrance," summoning the reader to locate the entire Gospel narrative within the history sketched in these opening lines.[22]

The genealogy also periodizes the story of Israel into three great chapters leading up to the birth of Jesus, each chapter encompassing fourteen generations:[23] chapter 1, from Abraham to David; chapter 2, from David to the exile; and chapter 3, from the exile to the Messiah (Matt 1:17). This way of charting Jesus' genealogy highlights Jesus' Davidic lineage—and therefore his messianic identity. Matthew underscores this point by referring to Jesus in the final phrase of the genealogy as "the Christ"; here Matthew's use of the definite article signals the titular sense of this term. Perhaps even more significantly, 1:17 unmistakably signals that the coming of Jesus portends the end of Israel's exile: "So all the generations from Abraham to David are fourteen generations; and from David to the deportation to Babylon, fourteen generations; and from the deportation to Babylon to the Messiah, fourteen generations." The periodization of the genealogy outlines the *plot* of Israel's story. From the founding

promise to Abraham there is an ascending movement to the Davidic
kingship (1:2-6a), then a decline into exile (1:6b-11), followed by a period
of obscurity awaiting the advent of the Messiah (1:12-16). It is very striking that *Moses* does not figure in this sketch of Israel's story; it is a story
about promise, kingship, exile, and return—a story in which the law of
Sinai plays no explicit part. This does not mean, of course, that Matthew has no interest in the Mosaic law. Quite the contrary. Nonetheless,
his narrative strategy of beginning with the genealogy has the effect of
highlighting Jesus' identity as messianic king rather than as lawgiver.

The strong emphasis given to Israel's exile in Matthew's genealogy imparts a particular shape to the history that the reader is asked to
remember: the story of Israel is a story that juxtaposes *God's covenant
faithfulness*—as signified by the promise to Abraham[24] and the promise
to David of an everlasting kingdom (2 Sam 7:12-14)—to *Israel's unfaithfulness,* as signified by David's sinful taking of the wife of Uriah (Matt 1:6;
alluding to 2 Sam 11–12) and by the checkered history of the kings that
followed David, leading up to the deportation to Babylon. The genealogy
functions, for the reader who remembers the complexity of the stories
evoked by Matthew's list of names, as a *Sündenspiegel*, a long and tortured
narrative in which Israel sees its corporate sins reflected.[25] Yet, at the same
time, the structure of the genealogy clearly points forward in hope, for
it leads finally to "the Messiah" Jesus, the one who "will save his people
from their sins" (1:21).[26] Here we see an example of the hermeneutical significance of the genealogy: it compels the reader to understand that the
"sins" from which God's people are saved are not merely petty individual
transgressions of a scrupulous legal code but rather the national sins of
injustice and idolatry that finally led to the collapse of the Davidic monarchy and the Babylonian captivity. The Messiah, in Matthew's narrative
world, is precisely the one who saves his people from the consequences
of their sins by closing the chapter of powerlessness and deprivation that
began with "the deportation to Babylon." The opening chapter of Matthew's Gospel is strongly consonant with interpretations of Jesus' work as
bringing about the end of Israel's exile.[27]

Matthew's genealogy equally introduces four anomalies into
the story, through the appearance of four women in the list of Jesus'
ancestors—Tamar (1:3), Rahab (1:5), Ruth (1:5), and Bathsheba, the wife
of Uriah (1:6). Since the names of women were not ordinarily included in
genealogical lists, the reader might well wonder why these four are singled out, particularly in view of the omission of well-known matriarchs
such as Sarah, Rebekah, and Leah. It is sometimes suggested that each

of the four women mentioned by Matthew was in some way involved in unusual or disreputable sexual activity that thus provides a backdrop for an apologetic reading of the story of Jesus' mother Mary (1:16), who was also suspected of sexual impropriety (1:18-25).[28] If the Abrahamic-Davidic line was carried forward to the Messiah through these women of questionable virtue, so the argument goes, then readers should not be surprised if doubt attends the reputation of the Messiah's mother as well. Yet, anyone who took offense at these women and their offspring would be "depreciating what God had chosen to bless."[29] It is by no means clear, however, that Ruth should be included in a list of women accused of sexual irregularities. Additionally, in the case of the story of David and Bathsheba, it is *David* who is singled out as a sinner; that is where all the emphasis is placed in the canonical narrative: "The thing that *David* had done displeased the LORD," and the LORD sent the prophet Nathan to tell the parable of the rich man who took the poor man's lamb, in order to lure David into pronouncing condemnation on himself and acknowledging his sin (2 Sam 11:27b–12:15).[30] The story places no blame on Bathsheba. Furthermore, we should not overlook the fact that three of these anomalous women (Tamar, Rahab, and Ruth) are heroines who are commended in the biblical stories for their daring and faithful actions (Gen 38:1-30; Josh 2:1-24, 6:22-25; Ruth passim). In other words, they are characterized in the stories not by their doubtful reputations but by their tenacious fidelity.[31]

More pertinent for Matthew's purposes is the fact that all four can be regarded as non-Israelites. Tamar was understood in some Jewish traditions as a Canaanite or a proselyte.[32] Rahab was a Canaanite, Ruth was a Moabite, and Bathsheba was the wife of Uriah the Hittite.[33] In each case, these foreigners were included within the story of Israel and indeed made part of the bloodline of David, the archetypal king of Israel. Thus, in the genealogy Matthew already hints at a major theme of his gospel: the story of Israel is open to the inclusion of Gentiles. These four women in the ancestry of the Messiah prefigure the mission to "all nations" (Matt 28:19) by demonstrating that God has woven ethnic outsiders into the story from start to finish. Matthew explains none of this, nor does he quote any of the Old Testament passages in which Tamar, Rahab, Ruth, and Bathsheba appear. Still, his inclusion of them in the genealogy of Jesus encourages the reader to recall their stories and ponder their significance for understanding the shape of Israel's story. They prefigure the mission to "all nations" that is announced in the Gospel's closing chapter.

Christological fulfillment: Jesus enacts Israel's destiny (Matt 2:13-18 and Matt 4:1-11). Another way that Matthew carries forward the story of Israel is through a typological identification of Jesus with Israel: Jesus becomes the one in whom the fate of Israel is embodied and enacted.[34] The story of Israel and the story of Jesus become one and the same. In this respect, Matthew's narrative differs notably from Mark's, in which the identification of Jesus as "Israel" plays very little, if any, role.

The motif of Jesus as Israel runs throughout Matthew's Gospel, but it is most vividly expressed in his compressed account of the Holy Family's flight into Egypt and return after the death of Herod (Matt 2:13-15)—a tale unparalleled in the other Gospels. Matthew, reading backwards, sees in this episode a figural fulfillment of Israel's sojourn in Egypt and return to the land of promise. The key prophetic text adduced in the formula quotation of Matthew 2:15 is drawn from Hosea 11:1: "When Israel was a child I loved him, and out of Egypt I called my son." The quotation of Hosea here is a celebrated case in which Matthew does not follow the LXX, which reads, "out of Egypt have I recalled his children (τὰ τέκνα αὐτοῦ)." Matthew's predictive christological reading depends on a Greek text (τὸν υἱόν μου) that corresponds to the MT.[35] In context in Hosea, the "son" is clearly the people Israel as a whole; the sentence is not a prediction of a future messiah but a reference to past events of the exodus. Thus, Hosea's metaphor, referring to Israel corporately as God's "son," evokes a tradition that goes all the way back to God's instructing Moses to tell Pharaoh that "Israel is my firstborn son" (Exod 4:22-23). Matthew, however, *trans*figures Hosea's text by seeing how it *pre*figures an event in the life of Jesus. Matthew now sees the fate of God's "son" Israel recapitulated in the story of God's Son, Jesus: in both cases, the son is brought out of exile in Egypt back to the land.[36]

This example suggests that Matthew's formula quotations may have more narrative resonance and allusive subtlety than is often credited to them. Matthew cannot be unaware of the original contextual meaning of Hosea 11:1 as an expression of God's love for Israel, a love that persists even through Israel's subsequent unfaithfulness (Hos 11:8-9). Indeed, Matthew's use of the quotation depends upon the reader's recognition of its original sense: if Hosea's words were severed from their reference to the original exodus story, the literary and theological effect of Matthew's reading would be stifled. *The fulfillment of the prophet's words can be discerned only through an act of imagination that perceives the figural correspondence between the two stories of the exodus and the gospel.* Through the lens of the figural imagination Matthew projects the two narrative patterns on top of one another, so that the story of Jesus acquires the resonances of the story of Israel's deliverance.

The effect of the juxtaposition is to hint that Jesus now will carry the destiny of the people Israel and that the outcome will be the rescue and vindication of Israel, as foreshadowed in the exodus story and brought to fulfillment in the resurrection of Jesus. The prophetic text from Hosea 11:1 functions as a middle term between the two stories, providing the hermeneutical clue that the exodus story is to be read as a narrative template for God's choosing and saving his people, a template that can be applied to subsequent historical circumstances, whether to God's mercy to disobedient Israel in Hosea's day or to God's climactic rescue of his people Israel in the person of the Messiah Jesus.[37]

It is also significant that Matthew's citation of Hosea has the effect of naming Jesus as God's Son in first-person divine discourse. Although the story of the miraculous conception of Jesus (Matt 1:18-25) has already disclosed to the reader that Mary's child is begotten "from the Holy Spirit," the first explicit identification of Jesus as God's "son" in Matthew's narrative is placed in the mouth of God himself, as the introduction to this formula citation emphasizes: the flight into Egypt was the fulfillment of "that which was spoken *by the Lord* through the prophet" (2:15).[38] This divine validation of Jesus' sonship anticipates the declarations of the divine voice at Jesus' baptism and transfiguration: "This is my Son, the Beloved, in whom I am well pleased" (3:17, 17:5).[39] Thus, 2:13-15 accomplishes at least two purposes at once: it articulates the identity of Jesus as God's Son, and it guarantees that the reader who knows the exodus tradition will understand his "sonship" precisely as a confirmation of his figural identity with Israel.

Alerted to this figural dimension of Israel's story, the reader of Matthew's Gospel may then also hear other resonances in the next brief unit of the birth narrative, the grim account of Herod's slaughter of the children of Bethlehem (2:16-18), which concludes with another formula quotation:

Then was fulfilled what had been spoken through the prophet Jeremiah:
> A voice was heard in Ramah,
> wailing and loud lamentation,
> Rachel weeping for her children;
> she refused to be consoled,
> because they are no more.

(Matt 2:17-18)

Here it appears that the story of Israel, as Matthew renarrates it, is a story of suffering and lament. Ramah, in the book of Jeremiah, appears as a staging ground for the deportation of the Judean captives to Babylon (cf. Jer 40:1).[40] Rachel, the wife of Jacob/Israel and therefore the figurative mother of the people as a whole,[41] mourns proleptically from the past over the exile—and, by implication, over the repeating pattern of violence against God's chosen. Herod's murder of the innocents takes its place alongside Pharaoh's decree against the Hebrew boy babies (Exod 1:15-22) and the defeat and exile of Judah in Jeremiah's time. Yet, recalling the latter story of exile, we may also hear an echo from the conclusion of Matthew's genealogy: ". . . from the deportation to Babylon to the Messiah, fourteen generations." Indeed, to recall Jeremiah's prophecy is necessarily to recall also its wider context:[42]

> Thus says the LORD:
> A voice is heard in Ramah,
>   lamentation and bitter weeping.
> Rachel is weeping for her children;
>   she refuses to be comforted for her children,
>   because they are no more.
> Thus says the LORD:
> Keep your voice from weeping,
>   and your eyes from tears;
> for there is a reward for your work,
>   says the LORD:
>   they shall come back from the land of the enemy;
> there is hope for your future,
>   says the LORD:
>   your children shall come back to their own country.
>
>   (Jer 31:15-17)

Thus, Jeremiah's image of Rachel weeping is a prelude to his bold prophecy of hope for the end of exile. Indeed, Jeremiah's oracle continues with an account of God's undying love for "Ephraim my dear son," promising that "I will surely have mercy on him" (Jer 31:18-20). That is the reason why there is hope for the future: *violence and exile do not have the final word*, for God's love for Israel will prevail and bring about restoration.

Surely it is not merely coincidental that in consecutive formula quotations (Matt 2:15 + Matt 2:17-18) Matthew has linked these two very similar passages from Hosea 11:1-11 and Jeremiah 31:15-20. Both prophetic texts speak of the exile and suffering of an unfaithful people, and both declare that God will reach out in mercy and bring the people back from exile. *By evoking these two prophetic passages in the infancy narrative, Matthew connects both the history and the future destiny of Israel to the figure of Jesus, and he hints that in Jesus the restoration of Israel is at hand.*

Matthew is not merely looking for random Old Testament prooftexts that Jesus might somehow fulfill (as is sometimes suggested); rather, he is thinking about the *specific shape* of Israel's story and linking Jesus' life with key passages that promise God's unbreakable redemptive love for his people.[43] That is why Matthew comments on Herod's slaughter of children by selecting a citation from the same chapter in Jeremiah that also promises "*a new covenant* with the house of Israel and the house of Judah" (Jer 31:31): Matthew's reference to Rachel works as a metaleptic trope, recalling the wider context of Jeremiah's prophecy. Herod's murderous acts, then, function within Matthew's tale as a metaphor for all the history of Israel's grief and exile. Yet even in the dark moment of Rachel's grief, the echo of Jeremiah 31 offers comfort, beckoning God's people to lean forward into the hope of the days that are surely coming when God will have mercy, bring back the exiles, and write the law on their hearts.

If Matthew's birth narratives suggest a typological link between Jesus and Israel, that linkage is confirmed in the story of Jesus' baptism (Matt 3:13-17) and subsequent temptation in the wilderness (4:1-11). In contrast to the accounts of the baptism in the other Gospels, only Matthew narrates John's hesitancy to baptize Jesus, and it is only Matthew who has Jesus reply enigmatically, in the first words he utters in Matthew's story, "Let it be for now; for thus it is fitting for us to fulfill all righteousness." In precisely what way does Jesus' submission to John's baptism of repentance serve "to fulfill all righteousness"? Many interpretations have been suggested, but whatever reading we give must accord full weight to Matthew's use of the verb πληρῶσαι, which elsewhere characteristically appears in statements about the fulfillment of *Scripture* (e.g., 5:17, 26:56, and all the formula quotations). In this case, Matthew cites no specific scriptural text that is said to have foreshadowed Jesus' baptism; however, I would propose that Jesus' acceptance of a baptism of repentance, performed at the Jordan River, is meant to signify his symbolic identification with sinful Israel (the people whom he will "save from their sins"), and the figurative beginning of that new Israel's entry into the land of promise.[44]

Taken in isolation, Matthew 3:15 is a mysterious utterance. In its Matthean narrative context, however, its meaning emerges compellingly from the unfolding plot. John the Baptist is directly identified as the "voice of one crying in the wilderness," as prophesied by Isaiah, the one who will herald the end of Israel's exile (Matt 3:1-3; quoting Isa 40:3). Remarkably, according to Matthew, "Jerusalem and all Judea and all the surrounding region of the Jordan" were responding to John's summons and going to be baptized by him, confessing their sins. It is precisely at this moment that the adult Jesus appears in the story, presenting himself also for baptism. We have just been told in the preceding birth narratives that this Jesus is "God's Son," who takes on the role of God's "son" Israel, called out of Egypt and out of exile; now, in a symbolically fraught act, he is to undergo repentance and, like Israel, pass through the waters. But before Jesus/Israel can enter the land, he must undergo a time of testing in the wilderness, just as unfaithful Israel had done once before—this time with dramatically different results.

And so, Jesus is led by the Spirit into the wilderness where "he fasted for forty days and forty nights." The motif of fasting and the explicit phrase "forty days and forty nights"—both Matthean editorial adaptations of Mark's understated temptation story[45]—clearly link Jesus to Moses, who also spent forty days and forty nights fasting in the presence of God on Mount Sinai (Exod 34:28; Deut 9:9).[46] Matthew does not tell us explicitly what Jesus was doing, besides fasting, during this forty-day period, but the strong allusion to the story of Moses suggests that perhaps he was interceding for Israel's sins, just as Moses did: "Throughout the forty days and forty nights that I lay prostrate before the LORD when the LORD intended to destroy you, I prayed to the LORD and said, 'Lord GOD, do not destroy the people who are your very own possession, whom you redeemed in your greatness, whom you brought out of Egypt with a mighty hand'" (Deut 9:25-26). If this inference is correct, then Matthew's allusion to the story of Moses would lead us to envision Jesus in the wilderness identifying with the people's plight and speaking to God on their behalf, as Moses did.

At another metaphorical level, the forty days and forty nights in the wilderness might be interpreted to correspond to the forty years of Israel's wandering in the desert. If so, then Jesus stands simultaneously in typological relation to Moses and to Israel as a whole. One of the properties of figurative language is to hold different, overlapping significations in simultaneous suspension, just as contrapuntal music allows us to hear more than one vocal line at once, within the same moment of time.[47] There is thus no need to exclude either of these interpretative options; the text gives intimations of both. The latter reading (Jesus as Israel) is reinforced by Jesus' ensuing dialogue with the devil, in which all of Jesus' lines are taken directly from Deuteronomy: he speaks the words that Israel was enjoined to learn and to speak, though they failed to do so, because they were a stubborn and stiff-necked people (Exod 34:9; Deut 9:13). Where Israel proved wayward and disobedient, Jesus now emerges from the temptation narrative as the obedient son who gives honor to God and embodies Israel's true destiny.[48]

All three of Jesus' responses to the tempter are direct scriptural quotations, each introduced by some variation of the formulaic γέγραπται ("it is written"). The first quotation, in response to the devil's bidding Jesus to turn stones into bread, is taken from Deuteronomy 8:3: "The man (ὁ ἄνθρωπος)[49] will not live on bread alone, but on every word that comes out through the mouth of God." A full understanding of this response requires the reader to recall the original context from which the citation comes. Moses is speaking to the people of Israel, near the end of their wilderness sojourn:

> Remember the long way that the LORD your God has *led* you these *forty* years *in the wilderness,* in order to humble you, *testing you* to know what was in your heart, whether or not you would keep his commandments. He humbled you by *letting you hunger,* then by *feeding you with manna,* with which neither you nor your ancestors were acquainted, in order to make you understand that *one does not live by bread alone, but by every word that comes from the mouth of God.*
>
> (Deut 8:2-3)

To recover the Deuteronomic context of Jesus' words is immediately to shed light on the significance of the temptation of Jesus. He stands, like Israel, at the end of his time in the wilderness; the devil's invitations will test him to see whether indeed he has been humbled and whether he will be obedient to God's commandments. If Jesus takes up the suggestion to turn stones into bread, he will thereby show his lack of trust in the God who can provide manna from heaven to those who hunger. But if he rejects the temptation, Jesus will show his trust in God's word, which is in fact perfectly enacted precisely by his quotation of what is written. So God's "son" passes the first test by obediently trusting God—just as Israel should have done, when so instructed by Moses.[50]

Then, in response to the devil's deceitful scripturally inflected encouragement (Ps 91:11-12) to throw himself down from the pinnacle of the temple in Jerusalem, Jesus responds a second time with a scriptural quotation: "Again it is written, 'You shall not put the LORD your God to the test'" (Deut 6:16). Once again, the specific context in Deuteronomy is pertinent: putting God to the test is identified specifically with Israel's rebellious complaints at Massah, when the people encamped in the wilderness were ready to stone Moses because they had no water to drink. In Moses' Deuteronomic oration, he reminds the people of their earlier lack of trust: "*Do not put the LORD your God to the test*, as you did at Massah."[51] In contrast, the Israelites are exhorted to keep God's commandments and to "do what is right and good in the sight of the LORD, so that it may go well with you, and so that you may go in and occupy the good land that the LORD swore to your ancestors to give you" (6:16-18). Given Matthew's presentation of Jesus as the Messiah who brings Israel's exile to an end, this is a highly significant passage: by resisting the temptation to aggrandize himself through a spectacular stunt, Jesus again reaffirms obedience and trust in God as the means whereby Israel is to be brought at last into the land of promise. And his response as obedient Son exemplifies the role Israel is meant to take in the world: not seeking to force God's hand through risky self-assertion but waiting faithfully and doing what is right. So God's Son passes the second test by responding obediently, typologically invoking Moses' instructions to Israel.

Finally, the devil's climactic temptation is to offer Jesus "all the kingdoms of the world and their splendor" if only Jesus will worship him. And for the first time, Jesus addresses the devil directly with a nonscriptural response: "Away with you, Satan!" The clinching final word, however, is once again drawn from Deuteronomy: "For it is written, 'The LORD your God you shall worship, and him only you shall serve'" (6:13).[52] In its immediate Deuteronomic context, this command is part of a larger warning against idolatry.[53] And it is immediately followed by another admonition: "Do not follow other gods, any of the gods of the peoples who are all around you, because the LORD your God who is present with you, is a jealous God" (6:14-15a). Thus, the Scripture that Jesus quotes, read in its context, is meant to secure Israel's exclusive covenantal relation to the one God and thereby to protect their distinctiveness against the surrounding pagan nations. Once again, by allowing this Scripture to answer the devil's temptation, Jesus identifies himself fully with/as Israel, heeding God's commandment. With this final decisive rejoinder, Jesus has named the fundamental issue: Who is God, and whom are we to serve? His answer, scripturally voiced, is to declare his own allegiance to the one God of Israel and to reject worship of any other. With that, the tempter is confounded and dismissed from the scene. And so

God's Son passes the third test by responding obediently, just as Moses instructed Israel to do.

Jesus' answers have been working their way subtly backwards through Moses' address to the people of Israel (Deut 8:3, 6:16, 6:13); this final reply moves very close to the most fundamental commandment of Israel's faith, the *Shema*: "Hear, O Israel: The LORD is our God, the LORD alone. You shall love the LORD your God with all your heart, and with all your soul, and with all your might" (6:4-5).[54] Much later in Matthew's Gospel, Jesus will finally quote this text, too, as "the greatest and first commandment" (Matt 22:36-38). But the attentive reader of Matthew's temptation narrative has already been alerted to the fundamental importance of the Deuteronomic commandments through Jesus' modeling of obedience to them. At the end of his time in the wilderness, Jesus has rightly embodied the covenant faithfulness Israel was meant to render to God—and he has done it, in Matthew's elegant narration, simply by reciting the very Scriptures through which that covenant faithfulness was originally defined and commanded.

Jesus demands a higher righteousness that includes obedience to Torah (Matt 5:17-48). If Matthew portrays Jesus as the typological fulfillment of Israel's true vocation, and if this vocation is articulated through direct appeals to Deuteronomy, the question inevitably arises whether Matthew's way of renarrating the story of Israel includes total obedience to the Torah as an ongoing requirement. A similar question is raised by Matthew's richly allusive citation of Jeremiah 31 in the birth narrative material. If the reader is meant to recall the context of "Rachel weeping for her children" in Jeremiah, the suggestion lies at hand that Jesus, the Messiah who will bring the end of Israel's exile, will also establish "a new covenant with the house of Israel and the house of Judah" (Jer 31:31-34; cf. Matt 26:28). One striking feature of Jeremiah's new covenant prophecy is the image of the law written on the hearts of the people (31:33). Matthew never employs this image directly, but in important ways it anticipates Matthew's treatment of the demands of Torah.

Distinctively among the Evangelists, Matthew insists that the commandments of the law remain fully in force (Matt 5:17-19). Jesus, rather than abolishing the law, calls his followers to a higher righteousness that *exceeds*, rather than negates, the righteousness of the scribes and Pharisees (5:20).[55] How does the righteousness for which Jesus calls exceed scribal and pharisaic righteousness? According to the programmatic antitheses of 5:21-48, the higher righteousness is a matter not only of outward actions but of inner dispositions and motivations. It is not sufficient, for example, to refrain from murder; the real problem is anger in one's heart. Jesus instructs his disciples to recognize such inner malformations of the self, to seek reconciliation with their brothers and sisters (5:23-24), and to pursue the goal of perfection (5:48). The startling demand "You shall be perfect (τέλειοι) as your heavenly Father is perfect (τέλειος)" echoes two of the Torah's radical admonitions to Israel: "You shall be holy, for I the LORD your God am holy" (Lev 19:2) and "You shall be perfect (τέλειος) before the LORD your God" (Deut 18:13 LXX). According to Matthew, such radical obedience, to which the Torah rightly understood points, is possible only through a transformation of character, enabling not merely outward obedience to the law's requirements but also an inner obedience from the heart. In light of such a vision Jesus summons his disciples to renounce not only murder but also anger, not only adultery but also lust (Matt 5:21-30).[56]

For Matthew the story of Israel is carried forward by a community of discipleship, as envisioned in the Sermon on the Mount, a community that *embodies* radical obedience to the Torah as authoritatively interpreted by Jesus. Apart from such obedience, confessional orthodoxy is useless: "Not everyone who says to me 'Lord, Lord,' will enter into the kingdom of heaven, but only the one who does the will of my father in heaven" (Matt 7:21). Matthew's vision of community is, if we may put it this way, thoroughly Deuteronomic. He would applaud the admonition of Deuteronomy 30:11: "Surely, this commandment that I am commanding you this day is not too hard for you, nor is it too far away." Jesus' answers to the devil's temptations in the wilderness exemplify this Deuteronomic vision of obedience and radical faithfulness.

That Matthew seriously believes that not a jot or tittle shall perish from the law (5:18) is nowhere made clearer than in Jesus' scathing attack on the scribes and Pharisees in Matthew 23. Matthew's Jesus here offers a hermeneutical refocusing of the law in terms of justice, mercy, and faith, but he takes care to specify that these virtues neither replace nor preempt the demand for meticulous observance of Torah's commandments: "Woe to you, scribes and Pharisees, hypocrites! For you tithe mint, dill, and cummin, and have neglected the weightier matters of the law: justice and mercy and faith. It is these you ought to have practiced *without neglecting the others*" (23:23). Even in this fierce polemic, Jesus nonetheless instructs his disciples and the crowds to follow whatever the scribes and Pharisees teach, abiding by what they say but not following the example of what they do. The major indictment against them is that they are hypocrites: pretenders who feign obedience to Torah but do not practice what they teach (23:1-3). Matthew is a good holiness theologian: he teaches that Jesus' followers must carry forward the story of Israel within a community of great moral stringency, in strict obedience to the commandments of Torah.[57]

And yet, for all his affirmation of the Torah, Matthew's account of what obedience to Torah actually entails has some distinctive features over against other contemporary forms of *halakhah*. Surprisingly, Matthew is silent about circumcision, and his position on purity laws is emphatically nonpharisaic, as shown by his account of Jesus' rejection of oral Torah—"Why do you break the commandment of God for the sake of your tradition?" (Matt 15:3)—and his casual stance on food and purity laws: "It is not what goes into the mouth that defiles a person, but it is what comes out of the mouth that defiles" (15:11). Again, here, we see the concern with purity of heart as the key issue for Matthew: ". . . what comes out of the mouth proceeds from the *heart*, and this is what defiles" (15:18).[58] Matthew's concern is not to advocate a program of rejecting Jewish food laws but rather to shift the emphasis to purity of heart as the Torah's chief concern. How are such teachings to be squared with the claim that Jesus has come not to abolish the Torah but to fulfill it? Clearly, Matthew is operating with a flexible theological notion of "fulfillment" that is not rigidly identified with literal performance of all of the law's commandments. Jesus' fulfillment of the law is partly related to his own embodied enactment of its meaning (as in the fulfillment quotations), but it is also connected to a particular *hermeneutical construal* of Torah.

This becomes clear especially in Matthew's handling of the lawyer's question about the greatest commandment (Matt 22:34-40). In Mark 12:28-34 the questioning scribe affirms Jesus' answer and then gives his own commentary that links the two great commandments to other confirming scriptural texts, thereby earning Jesus' blessing. In contrast to Mark's dramatic complexity, we find that Matthew has streamlined the account to turn it into a straightforward pronouncement story: the lawyer asks; Jesus answers. His answer, of course, is a fusion of the *Shema* of Deuteronomy 6:5 and Leviticus 19:18, commanding love of God and of neighbor.[59] In Matthew's narrative, this answer comes as no great surprise to the reader. In Jesus' response to the rich man's question about what he must do to gain eternal life, Jesus has already pointedly linked Leviticus 19:18 to the Ten Commandments (Matt 19:16-19). The temptation narrative, too, already establishes Deuteronomy as a foundational text for defining obedience to God. Thus, the emphasis placed on these two commandments is consonant with the general portrait of Jesus' teaching and example that Matthew has been drawing throughout the story. We might see Jesus' pronouncement in Matthew 22:37-39 as a neat summation of the teaching he has offered throughout the Gospel.

In Matthew 22, however, Jesus' quotation of the two great commandments is not yet the final punch line of the pronouncement story. The climax of the pronouncement in Matthew is this: "On these two commandments hang all the law and the prophets." These two commandments, in other words, are not merely the greatest or the most important, the ones at the top of the list; rather, they have a systemic, structural, and hermeneutical role. All the other commandments in Torah are *suspended from* these two pillars. It is a matter not just of priority but of *weight-bearing*. This claim is fully consistent with Matthew's insistence that in Jesus' teaching the law remains in force. Yet, at the same time, the passage inescapably proposes a particular *hermeneutical reconfiguration of Torah*, one in which *love* becomes the most determinative requirement.[60] As the history of interpretation amply demonstrates, where such a hermeneutical reconfiguration takes place, the other commandments tend over time to recede in importance.[61] Thus, in 22:34-40, we see the forces at work that produce—perhaps even contrary to Matthew's own intention—a reshaping of Torah into a new framework.

The hermeneutic of mercy. The distinctive character of that new framework is foregrounded in the Sermon on the Mount, where Jesus both affirms the Torah (Matt 5:17-20) and radicalizes it (5:21-48). Even in the midst of that radicalization, however, some of the Sermon's prescriptions very strongly echo the counsels of Torah as interpreted in the wisdom tradition. The most striking example is to be found in Jesus' admonitions to his disciples to renounce anger (5:21-26) and practice forgiveness (6:12, 14-15), which very closely parallel the wise counsel of Sirach 27:30–28:7. This remarkable passage is sometimes noted briefly in passing by commentators,[62] but it is far too little known among general Christian readers, who tend to assume that Jesus' prohibitions of anger and vengeance are anti-Jewish innovations. It will, therefore, perhaps be helpful to cite Sirach in full:

> Anger and wrath, these also are abominations,
>   yet a sinner holds on to them.
> The vengeful will face the LORD's vengeance,

for he keeps a strict account of their sins.
Forgive your neighbor the wrong he has done,
and then your sins will be pardoned when you pray.
Does anyone harbor anger against another,
and expect healing from the Lord?
If someone has no mercy (ἔλεος) towards another like himself,
can he then seek pardon for his own sins?
If a mere mortal harbors wrath,
who will make an atoning sacrifice for his sins?
Remember the end of your life, and set enmity aside;
remember corruption and death, and be true to the commandments.
Remember the commandments, and do not be angry with your neighbor;
remember the covenant of the Most High, and overlook faults.

In view of the close parallels between this Jewish wisdom text—written two hundred years before the time of Jesus—and the teachings of the Sermon on the Mount, commentary is nearly superfluous. But the following points of convergence may be noted. Jesus' teaching follows Sirach in calling for renunciation of anger and warning that a failure to forgive others will cause God to exact vengeance in the eschatological judgment. Both texts connect forgiveness of neighbors with prayer for forgiveness of one's own sins. And, tellingly, both texts present the practice of forgiveness as a matter of fulfillment of, or obedience to, the law: "Remember the commandments, and do not be angry with your neighbor." Matthew places Jesus within this established Jewish tradition of interpreting the law to require generous dealings with the neighbor's shortcomings. Jesus' teaching about forgiveness is to be read not as a reversal or rejection of Torah but rather as a particular hermeneutical focusing of Torah.

Matthew's strict exhortation to Torah-obedience (Matt 5:19-20) is modulated into another key by his equally firm insistence that the obedient community of disciples must also be a community animated by mercy, love, and forgiveness. The moral rigor of the Sermon on the Mount, to be rightly understood and practiced, must be framed both by the recognition that we are weak and fallible and by the willingness to forgive one another as freely as God forgives us, even seventy times seven (18:21-22). "Seventy times seven" (or "seventy-seven times"— whichever it is) should certainly be heard as an echoic reversal of the chest-thumping boast of Lamech: "I have killed a man for wounding me, a young man for striking me. If Cain is avenged sevenfold, truly Lamech seventy-sevenfold" (Gen 4:23b-24). This theme of merciful forgiveness appears repeatedly in the Gospel of Matthew—not only in Jesus' instruction about how to pray (6:9-15) but also in the parable of the unforgiving servant (18:23-35), which climaxes in the Lord's rebuke to his hard-hearted servant: "You wicked slave! I forgave you all that debt because you pleaded with me. Should you not have had *mercy* on your fellow slave, as I had *mercy* on you?" (18:32-33).

This key Matthean motif of *mercy* (ἔλεος; cf. Sir 28:4) is highlighted particularly through Matthew's use of Scripture. In two places Matthew tellingly inserts references to Hosea 6:6 into a narrative taken over from Mark, in order to emphasize the hermeneutical primacy of mercy.

The first instance appears in Matthew's account of Jesus' controversy with the Pharisees over his practice of eating with tax collectors and sinners (Matt 9:9-13). Matthew follows Mark's text closely through most of the passage;[63] in Jesus' climactic pronouncement Matthew reproduces Mark 10:17 almost word for word except that he adds the crucial citation of Hosea:

> "Those who are well have no need of a physician, but those who are sick.
> *Go and learn what this means, 'I desire mercy, not sacrifice.'*
> For I have come to call not the righteous but sinners."
>
> (Matt 9:12-13)

In the Markan form of the story, Jesus responds to the carping of his critics with a forceful aphorism that justifies his association with sinners on the grounds that he must go to those in need of healing and correction; the Markan saying offers no biblical warrant for this claim. Matthew, however, imbeds within the aphorism a scriptural quotation that produces further ripples of signification. The Pharisees, who protest Jesus' association with sinners, are chided for their failure to grasp the intention of God. Jesus directs them to a particular prophetic text for remedial education: if they learn what Hosea means, they will understand that God is a God of mercy (חסד, ἔλεος) who desires to bring back the erring, not to condemn them, not even to compel them to offer the proper sacrifice.

Once again, as in the formula quotations in the birth narrative, Matthew has focused on a prophetic text (Hos 6) that describes the plight of exilic Israel and figures forth the gracious mercy of God. This transformation of Israel's plight to a vocation of mercy suggests inter alia that Jesus' mission to the tax collectors and sinners aims not merely at individual moral reform but at the restoration of the nation. Furthermore, it is hardly accidental that Matthew links Jesus' saying about the need for a *physician* to a prophetic passage that depicts Ephraim and Judah as crying out, "Come, let us return to the Lord; for it is he who has torn, *and he will heal us*" (Hos 6:1; cf. 7:1).[64] The passage in Hosea deals with the hope that God will bring healing to Israel, a torn and broken nation. Thus, if the Pharisees go to learn what Hosea 6:6 means, they will need to read more than one verse. Once they search the wider context of God's scriptural intentions, they will find there, in the midst of a judgment oracle against the people, a call for repentance and a portrayal of a merciful God who wants his people to show mercy, not contempt, to those who have gone astray.

Matthew's second pointer to Hosea 6:6 appears in the controversy story about plucking grain on the sabbath (Matt 12:1-8). Once again Matthew, while following Mark's narrative framework very closely,[65] alters the content of Jesus' concluding pronouncement. This time, the alterations are quite substantial.[66] Most significantly, Matthew once again inserts a reference to Hosea 6:6: "But if you had known what this means, *I desire mercy and not sacrifice*, you would not have condemned the guiltless." Here the application of the Hosea citation to the situation of the grain-plucking disciples is less than obvious. It appears that "mercy" and "sacrifice" are used metonymically. They stand for, respectively, a form of piety that focuses on God's compassion toward human needs and a form of piety that focuses on ritual observances. The Pharisees are at fault because they demand punctilious observance of the law at the expense of basic human need, represented by the disciples' hunger. As the capstone of this unit, Matthew retains Mark's declaration that "the Son of Man is Lord of the sabbath" (Mark 2:28/Matt 12:8). While Mark 2:28—in which the declaration is introduced by ὥστε—can be read as Mark's authorial comment on the controversy story, Matthew's editing of the saying almost surely should be understood as placing this bold claim on the lips of Jesus himself. Thus, Jesus himself is asserting, as Lord of the sabbath, his right to declare the priority of merciful action over other construals of the sabbath that focus chiefly on the prohibition of work.

In both of these passages, Hosea 6:6, with its emphasis on mercy, is put forward as a hermeneutical lens through which the entire Torah is to be interpreted. The Pharisees go astray in their understanding of the law because they fail to realize that its central aim, as disclosed in Hosea, is mercy. Alongside these passages should be placed the Matthean beatitude "Blessed are the *merciful*, for they shall receive *mercy*" (Matt 5:7) and Jesus' pronouncement, noted above, that "the weightier

matters of the law" are "justice and *mercy* and faith" (23:23). Clearly, for
Matthew, mercy is a central theme. The important thing to recognize, in
all these passages, is that the quality of mercy is not set in opposition to
the Torah; rather, Matthew's Jesus discerns *within Scripture itself* the hermeneutical principle—expressed epigrammatically in Hosea 6:6—that
all the commandments are to be interpreted in such a way as to engender
and promote the practice of mercy among God's people.[67]

It may appear that there is a certain hermeneutical slippage here: Can
the meaning of the Torah (conceived as the books of the Pentateuch) be
determined by a citation from a *prophetic* book? Should a distinction be
made between Torah and the Prophets?[68] Can Hosea 6 rightly be used
as a lens to determine what Torah requires? The point is near the heart
of Matthew's controversy with the Judaism of his day. And yet, at this
point as at so many others, Matthew does not stand far away from the
emergent rabbinic tradition. An intriguing parallel to these Matthean
passages may be found in the later *'Abot de Rabbi Nathan* 4:

> Once as Rabbi Johanan ben Zakkai was coming forth from Jerusalem,
> Rabbi Joshua followed after him and beheld the Temple in ruins. "Woe
> unto us!" Rabbi Joshua cried, "that this, the place where the iniquities of
> Israel were atoned for, is laid waste!" "My son," Rabbi Johanan said to
> him, "be not grieved; we have another atonement as effective as this. And
> what is it? It is acts of loving-kindness, as it is said, *For I desire mercy and
> not sacrifice.*"[69]

Like Rabbi Johanan, Matthew lives in the immediate aftermath of the
destruction of the temple and seeks to interpret Israel's Scripture as a
word addressed to the needs of his time. It is perhaps no accident that
both of them focus on Hosea 6:6 as a clue to the rereading of Torah in
changed circumstances. The difference, of course, is that Matthew justifies this move on the basis of the authority of Jesus, whose death and
resurrection confirm his uniquely authoritative status as Lord of the sabbath and interpreter of the law. Matthew is not concerned about replacing temple sacrifices as a means of atonement, for he is confident that
another means of atonement has already been provided in Jesus' death.
But he does insist that Hosea's emphasis on mercy has always been a
pointer to the heart of Scripture's meaning.

Matthew's hermeneutical privileging of the Prophets is precisely
one of the key ways that he reconfigures Torah.[70] *Thus, for Matthew, the
story of Israel is carried forward through a particular, prophetically shaped,*

interpretation of Torah within a community called to embody the mercy of God. Such a community might also remember Psalm 24:10 LXX: "All the ways of the Lord are *mercy* (ἔλεος) and truth for those who seek his covenant and his testimonies."

Lost sheep and the resistance of Israel. Our reading of Matthew so far has drawn attention to his concern for the continuity of the story of Jesus with the story of Israel. But a serious reading of Matthew's Gospel must come to grips also with some gloomier aspects of Matthew's renarration of Israel's story. If Jesus has come "to save his people from their sins" (Matt 1:21), this implies both that they are in need of being saved and that their plight is, in some measure, a consequence of their own wrong choices and actions. Or to put the same point differently: if Matthew presents Jesus as the Messiah who will bring about the end of Israel's exile (1:17), anyone familiar with the Prophets will recall that the exile was God's judgment on Israel's infidelity to the covenant. Thus, Matthew sketches a complex plot in which the people of Israel have gone astray and stand in need of rescue. And, as we might expect, he interprets the people's plight through scriptural lenses.

Distinctively among the Evangelists, Matthew twice narrates scenes in which Jesus refers to "the lost sheep of the house of Israel" as the object of his mission.[71] Just as Matthew highlights the call of Hosea 6:6 for *mercy* by repeating it in his narrative, so also this double reference to "lost sheep" creates special emphasis through repetition. The first of these references appears in the great discourse in which Jesus sends the twelve disciples out to proclaim the gospel and to perform healings and exorcisms (Matt 10:5-42). Their mission is explicitly restricted, however, in its geographical and ethnic scope: "Go nowhere among the Gentiles, and enter no town of the Samaritans, but go rather *to the lost sheep of the house of Israel*" (10:5-6). The language of the charge echoes Jeremiah:

> My people have been *lost sheep*; their shepherds have led them astray, turning them away on the mountains; from mountain to hill they have gone, they have forgotten their fold. All who found them have devoured them, and their enemies have said, "We are not guilty, because they have sinned against the Lord, the true pasture, the Lord, the hope of their ancestors."
>
> (Jer 50:6-7)

In this oracle Jeremiah is portraying Israel during the Babylonian exile. As in Ezekiel 34, where the expression "lost sheep" does not occur explicitly, much blame for the predicament of the nation is laid at the feet of the incompetent "shepherds" (whether inadequate kings or religious leaders) who have led the sheep into danger and destruction. Interestingly, in Jeremiah 50 it is the *enemies* of Israel, not the prophet, who accuse the people of having "sinned against the LORD" and thus brought troubles upon themselves.

Matthew 10, however, shows no interest in pronouncing judgment on the people for straying from the fold. Rather, Jesus is portrayed as sending the disciples out to rescue and regather them, because "the kingdom of heaven has come near" (10:7). In this respect, Matthew's mission discourse accurately reflects the context in which the "lost sheep" phrase appears in Jeremiah: Jeremiah 50 is chiefly a judgment oracle portending the destruction of Babylon and the *return* of Israel from exile (see especially 50:4-5, immediately preceding Jeremiah's reference to lost sheep). Jesus' use of the phrase, then, evokes yet again the theme of the impending end of exile that has appeared in earlier chapters of the Gospel. At the same time, it subtly suggests that the responsibility for the people's plight lies with their own leaders, the authorities who have led them astray.

The second appearance of the phrase "lost sheep of the house of Israel" is in Matthew's story of Jesus' encounter with a "Canaanite woman" in the district of Tyre and Sidon (Matt 15:21-28). In a fairly lengthy expansion of the story told in Mark 7:24-30, Matthew tells us that Jesus initially ignored the woman's pleas for him to help her demon-possessed daughter and that the disciples pressed him to send her away. Finally, in response to *their* request, he remarks, "I was sent only *to the lost sheep of the house of Israel.*" This saying appears only in Matthew and has no parallel in any of the other Gospels. Again, as in Matthew 10:5-6, we see that Matthew portrays Jesus' concern as focused on Israel in particular rather than the Gentile world.[72] The chief point of interest here is that Matthew's repetition of the allusion to Jeremiah 50:6 underscores twin affirmations: the people of Israel have gone astray, and it is Jesus' purpose to rescue them.[73]

That rescue is made difficult, however, by the hard-heartedness and resistance of the people. Matthew brings this difficulty into sharp focus in his retelling of the story of Jesus' response to the disciples' question about why he teaches in parables. In the Markan account, Jesus replies that he speaks in parables *in order that* (ἵνα) the people might look but not perceive and hear but not understand (Mark 4:11-12; echoing Isa 6:9). For Mark, the figural obscurity of the parables belongs to the divine purpose of veiled self-disclosure. Matthew, seemingly finding this explanation too arcane, edits Jesus' reply to produce a somewhat different rationale for parabolic speech. He preserves Mark's reference to Isaiah but reinterprets it to cast blame upon the people for their obtuseness: *"For this reason* (διὰ τοῦτο) I speak to them in parables: *because* (ὅτι) 'while seeing they do not see and while hearing they neither hear nor understand'" (Matt 13:13). As Frank Kermode paraphrases the force of the saying in its Matthean form, "As Isaiah remarked, their stupidity is extremely tiresome; this seems the best way to get through to them."[74] This has the effect of making Jesus' parabolic teaching an act of gracious accommodation to the people's failure of perception (rather than a mysterious veiling of the truth), while simultaneously ratcheting up the element of moral condemnation for their lack of understanding.

While Mark evokes Isaiah 6:9 without any explicit quotation formula, Matthew, characteristically, identifies the source of the citation and recalls the theme of prophetic judgment that is present in its original Isaian context. He achieves this result simply by including an extended explicit quotation of Isaiah 6:9-10:[75]

> "Indeed, with them is fulfilled the prophecy of Isaiah that says:
>> 'You will listen and listen but never understand,
>> and you will look and look but never perceive.
>> For the heart of this people has grown fat,
>> and they hardly hear with their ears,
>> and they have shut their eyes,
>> so that they might not (μήποτε) perceive with their eyes
>> and hear with their ears
>> and understand with their heart and turn—
>> and I will heal them.'"

> (Matt 13:14-15)

The last clause is potentially ambiguous. Should we interpret it as the last in a series of verbs syntactically following upon μήποτε—giving the sense "so that they might not perceive . . . and hear . . . and understand . . . and turn . . . (so that I might not) heal them"? Or should we interpret it as a break with this series, expressing God's ultimate intent to heal them *despite* their failure of understanding? Thus: ". . . they have shut their eyes, so that they might not perceive . . . and hear . . . and understand . . . and turn. *But* I will (nonetheless) heal them." The latter interpretation is strongly encouraged by the LXX rendering, which Matthew follows here. The verb "heal" (ἰάσομαι) in the last clause is in the future indicative, breaking the pattern of aorist subjunctives in the preceding series. This syntactical nuance virtually requires the second interpretation: it was the fault of the people that they brought judgment upon themselves by closing their eyes and ears; nonetheless, in Matthew's renarration, God *will* bring deliverance and healing.

Not long afterward in Matthew's narrative, in the controversy about ritual handwashing (15:1-20), we find another quotation from Isaiah (this time, Isa 29:13) that similarly pronounces judgment on the people for their unfaithfulness.[76] In this case, however, Matthew's tale refocuses Isaiah's oracle so that it addresses not the people as a whole but specifically the Pharisees and scribes (Matt 15:1), who quibble delicately over handwashing practices but at the same time devise hermeneutical evasions that effectually circumvent the Mosaic Decalogue. Jesus accuses them of using "the tradition of the elders" to negate the commandment to honor father and mother, thereby making void the word of God.[77] He is presented here as the defender of the Mosaic law against its casuistic perversion and abuse. Thus, this controversy story is fully in accord with Matthew's earlier programmatic statement that Jesus has come to uphold the law in its fullness (5:17-20). His accusation against the scribal authorities is then underlined by a further scathing denunciation that characterizes their scholastic nitpicking as the embodiment of Isaiah's prophecy:

> You hypocrites! Well did Isaiah prophesy concerning you, saying: "This people honors me with their lips, but their heart stands off afar from me. In vain they worship me, while teaching human commandments as doctrines."
>
> (Matt 15:7-9; quoting Isa 29:13 LXX)[78]

Isaiah's judgment oracle against the nation is reinterpreted as an indictment of Israel's *leaders*. This is not entirely out of line with the wider context in Isaiah, with its sharply negative evaluations of priests, prophets, and seers (Isa 28:7, 29:10), as well as of the "scoffers who rule this people in Jerusalem" (28:14; cf. 29:20-21). But the Matthean citation of Isaiah seems to target Pharisees and scribes in a particular way for cloaking themselves in religious tradition in order to flout God's Torah. That their hypocrisy leads to disastrous consequences not just for the leaders themselves but for the people as a whole—as implied in the metaphor of the lost sheep of the house of Israel—is finally shown with devastating force in the passion narrative.

Earlier in the story, the crowds have played a mixed narrative role. Sometimes they flock to Jesus (Matt 4:25, 7:28-29, 8:1, 9:35-38, 13:1-2, 15:29-31, 19:1-2, 20:29) and acclaim him as a prophet or even as the Son of David (9:33, 16:14, 21:9-11). On other occasions, however, they are castigated as fickle (11:16-19), blind and deaf (13:13-15), and even hostile to the good news of the kingdom (10:14-25, 11:20-24). From the very beginning of Matthew's story, Jesus has been teaching his followers to expect rejection, abuse, and persecution (5:10-12). It is therefore no surprise that at the dramatic climax of the story, the Jerusalem authorities are able to persuade the crowd to turn against him, requesting the release of Barabbas and calling for the crucifixion of Jesus (27:22-23).

Just at this point in the narrative, Matthew introduces two distinctive episodes subtly evoking scriptural intertexts that shape our reading of the events he recounts. First, Pilate washes his hands publicly and declares, "I am innocent of this man's blood" (Matt 27:24). His action—which appears only in Matthew's Gospel—seems to be an ironically inverted mirror image of the ritual prescribed for Israel's elders to perform when a dead body is discovered and the murderer cannot be identified (Deut 21:1-9). The elders are to break the neck of a heifer and *wash their hands* over it, while declaring, "Our hands did not shed this blood, nor were we witnesses to it. Absolve, O LORD, your people Israel, whom you redeemed; do not let the guilt of innocent blood remain in the midst of your people Israel" (21:7-8). In the Deuteronomic narrative Moses then comments, "So you shall purge the guilt of innocent blood from your midst, because you must do what is right in the sight of the LORD" (21:9).[79] Thus, Pilate, the Gentile ruler, is portrayed, with great dramatic irony, as performing the act prescribed for Israel's leaders to "purge the guilt of innocent blood" at precisely the moment when the people of Jerusalem voluntarily take this guilt upon themselves. Within Matthew's narrative world, the significance of this action is not so much to exonerate Pilate, who after all remains responsible for ordering the crucifixion despite this lame attempt to deflect responsibility;[80] rather, the significance of the hand-washing story is that it illustrates vividly, by contrast, how far away Israel has come from heeding the Torah. Rather than doing "what is right in the sight of the Lord," they press ahead with murderous intent, as already foreshadowed in Jesus' passion predictions and in the parable of the wicked tenants (Matt 21:33-44).

And this is where Matthew adds a second distinctive feature of the story, once again echoing Israel's Scripture and heightening the dramatic irony of the scene. In response to Pilate's public hand-washing gesture, Matthew chillingly tells us that "*the people as a whole* (πᾶς ὁ λαός) answered, 'his blood be on us and on our children!'" (Matt 27:25). Resonating in the background of this terrible episode is the story (2 Sam 1:1-16) of David's wrathful response to the young Amalekite messenger who, perhaps expecting a reward, brings a report[81] that he himself has administered the fatal blow to the defeated King Saul, who had unsuccessfully attempted to commit suicide on the battlefield. David orders the Amalekite executed on the spot and declares, "Your blood be on your head; for your own mouth has testified against you, saying 'I have killed the Lord's anointed (LXX: τὸν χριστὸν κυρίου)'" (1:16). The reader who hears an echo of this story in the people's answer to Pilate will feel the awful foreshadowing of impending disaster for the people of Jerusalem. Their own mouths have testified against them in calling for the death of the Lord's *Christ*, and they have taken blood on their own heads.

In the history of interpretation, this Matthean story has had fateful and horrible consequences, as Christian readers have taken it upon themselves to assume, as it were, the role of David in executing wrath on those who are thought to have claimed responsibility for the blood of the Lord's Anointed. The scandal of Christian violence against the Jewish people is a shameful legacy of history.[82] Many reasons can be given for abhorring this history of anti-Jewish violence—not least the fact that the Jesus of Matthew's Gospel emphatically teaches his followers to put away the sword and choose reconciliation instead of retaliation against enemies.[83] But to the many other good reasons for rejecting such violence, we can add one more: violence rests on an incomplete and therefore faulty reading of Matthew's own narrative account of the blood of Jesus, God's covenant with Israel, and Israel's final destiny.

Covenant renewal and the ingathering of Israel. The pivotal text is Matthew's account of Jesus' last Passover supper with his disciples:

> While they were eating, Jesus took a loaf of bread, and after blessing it he broke it, gave it to his disciples, and said, "Take, eat; this is my body." Then he took a cup, and after giving thanks he gave it to them, saying, "Drink from it, all of you; for this is *my blood of the covenant*, which is poured out for many for the forgiveness of sins. I tell you, I will never again drink of this fruit of the vine until that day when I drink it new with you in my Father's kingdom."

> (Matt 26:26-29)

These words over the bread and cup interpret Jesus' impending death as an act of covenant initiation, recalling the inauguration of the Sinai covenant: after reading the book of the covenant to the people, "Moses took the blood and dashed it on the people, and said, 'See *the blood of the covenant* that the LORD has made with you in accordance with all these words'" (Exod 24:8). The intertextual resonance here suggests strongly that Jesus' death is a sacrificial offering and that his blood signifies the sealing of a new covenantal relationship between God and the people. The fact that these words of institution occur in the context of a *meal* is also directly reminiscent of Exodus 24:9-11: "Then Moses and Aaron, Nadab, and Abihu, and seventy of the elders of Israel went up, and they saw the God of Israel[!]. . . . God did not lay his hand on the chief men of the people of Israel; also they beheld God, *and they ate and drank*." Just as Moses and the chief men of the people ate and drank in the presence of God, so also the twelve disciples (Matt 26:20) eat and drink in the presence of God in order to celebrate and solemnize the covenant of which Jesus speaks—a covenant that foreshadows an eschatological future ("that day when I drink it new with you in my Father's kingdom") in which God's presence with Israel will be fully realized and celebrated.[84]

There is one further dimension of the figural correspondence that might be metaleptically evoked in Matthew's account of the last supper. Just before Moses dashes blood on the people of Israel, the narrator in Exodus offers this account: "Then [Moses] took the book of the covenant, and read it in the hearing of the people; and they said, 'All that the LORD has spoken we will do, and we will be obedient'" (Exod 24:7). In light of Matthew's special interest in portraying Jesus as a Moses-like teacher, as well as his special interest in the theme of *obedience* to all that God has commanded in the law and in Jesus' own teachings (e.g., Matt 5:17-20, 7:21-27, 28:20), the reader may well surmise that the covenant inaugurated by Jesus' blood in Matthew 26:28 must also be understood as the climax of the whole foregoing narrative, in which Matthew outlines in considerable detail what is required of those who will pledge obedience to "all that the LORD has spoken." This interpretation is of course not spelled out by Matthew but tellingly suggested by his story's echo of Exodus 24:8.

At the same time, the expression "my blood of the covenant" also carries with it a second highly significant intertextual association—an allusion to Zechariah's prophecy that God will bring eschatological deliverance to Jerusalem:

> As for you also, because of the blood of my covenant with you,
> I will set your prisoners free from the waterless pit.
>
> (Zech 9:11)

This allusion is particularly clear in view of the fact that Matthew previously quoted Zechariah 9:9 explicitly at the point of Jesus' triumphal entry to Jerusalem (Matt 21:5). This would suggest he is fully cognizant of Zechariah's expectation for a messianic king who will "command peace to the nations" and reign over a dominion "from sea to sea, and from the River to the ends of the earth" (Zech 9:10). This hope for eschatological liberation and peace is causatively linked in Zechariah to "the blood of my covenant with you." Consequently, Matthew's last supper scene creates a complex overlay of intertextual echoes, recalling both the blood-spattered covenantal banquet of Exodus 24 and the blood-secured messianic promise of deliverance found in Zechariah 9.[85]

In light of these observations, we can now return to the trial scene before Pilate with fresh perspective. When the people say, "His blood be on us and on our children!" they are responding to Pilate's hand-washing disclaimer of responsibility for "this man's blood" (Matt 27:24-25). At the surface level of the narrative, they appear to be bluntly assuming bloodguilt on themselves. But at a deeper level, Matthew's narrative has already tapped into subterranean exegetical currents running the other way, currents that associate outpoured *blood* not with guilt but rather with cleansing, binding commitment, and liberation. If the people of Israel were originally brought into membership in the Mosaic covenant by having blood dashed upon them, and if Jesus has already (in private with twelve disciples who symbolize a restored Israel) declared that the new (or renewed) covenant[86] is sealed by participation in his own blood—if these are the textual precursors of the scene before Pilate— what then can it mean for the people (πᾶς ὁ λαός) to say, "his blood be upon us"? They themselves, as characters in the unfolding narrative, certainly do not mean to place themselves under a covenant initiated by Jesus. But as readers we may wonder whether there is a deeper intentionality at work here, not the intentionality of the hostile, fickle crowd, but the intentionality of the God who has sent Jesus to the lost sheep of the house of Israel. If so, surely that intentionality is not to secure their eternal condemnation but rather to bring about the liberation promised by Zechariah and even earlier prefigured by that dreamlike banquet at the foot of Mount Sinai, where the elders of Israel beheld God standing on "something like a pavement of sapphire stone, like the very heaven for clearness" (Exod 24:10). Perhaps that is the God who, contrary to the intention of the crowd that has been agitated and deceived by false shepherds, will see the blood of Jesus figuratively on the heads of the people of Israel and regard it as blood "poured out for many for the forgiveness of sins"—that is, as a redeeming sign of the new covenant promised by Jeremiah, in which God will say, "I will forgive their iniquity, and remember their sins no more" (Jer 31:34).[87] If so, that would be the culmination of the promise foregrounded by Matthew in the very beginning of his Gospel: "He will save his people from their sins" (Matt 1:21).

Of course, this reading might be thought to require the supposition that Matthew has narrated the trial scene with consummate dramatic irony and that contrary to his earlier predilection for explaining all things clearly he has now shifted to a much subtler technique of narrative communication. Perhaps this is so: surprisingly, Matthew gives us relatively few explicit biblical quotations in the passion narrative. This can hardly mean that he has lost interest in the motif of scriptural fulfillment.[88] It is, rather, as though he has instructed his readers thoroughly in the earlier chapters to look for the fulfillment of scriptural texts and types, and he therefore now supposes that they can go on drawing the links themselves without overt authorial guidance. But with regard to Matthew 27:25, there is another possibility: Matthew himself may not fully perceive the hermeneutical potentiality of the allusions present in the last supper scene, and he may be oblivious to the ironic ambiguity of the crowd's grim assumption of responsibility for Jesus' blood on their heads.[89] If that were so, we would have before us a good illustration that the meaning of a text cannot be strictly delimited by the original intentions of the author. Precisely because the text participates in an intertextual field and activates different encyclopedias of reception in different reading communities, there is always the possibility of a fresh reading that discloses layers of significance of which the author was unaware. Even if the actual author of 27:25 was unaware of a possible double sense in the crowd's words, he has placed their self-incriminating sentence in a larger narrative matrix that almost inescapably intimates that Jesus' blood is redemptive for Israel.

What we can say with some confidence is that Matthew certainly does not regard the crucifixion of Jesus as signifying the final rejection of Israel or the end of God's concern for his people. One indicator of this is that Matthew leads his readers to understand the risen Jesus as "the Son of Man," the glorious figure from Daniel 7 who represents Israel's eschatological vindication and triumph over oppressive foreign powers (Matt 26:64; see also the use of imagery from Dan 7:13-14 in the Gospel's final resurrection appearance, 28:16-20). And in the great apocalyptic discourse of Matthew 24, Jesus tells the disciples that when the glorious Son of Man appears, coming on the clouds of heaven, "he will send out his angels with a great trumpet, and they will gather his elect from the four winds, from one end of heaven to the other" (24:30-31). As we have seen in our discussion of the parallel passage in Mark, this is an image of the eschatological regathering of Israel from its exilic dispersion. This interpretation of the image is made particularly clear by Matthew's addition of the phrase μετὰ σάλπιγγος μεγάλης, an allusion to the final and climactic sentences of the "Isaiah apocalypse" in Isaiah 24–27:

> On that day, the LORD will thresh from the channel of the Euphrates to the Wadi of Egypt, and you will be gathered one by one, *O people of Israel*. And on that day, *a great trumpet will be blown* (LXX: σαλπιοῦσιν τῇ σάλπιγγι τῇ μεγάλῃ), and those who were lost in the land of Assyria and those who were driven out to the land of Egypt will come and worship the LORD on the holy mountain at Jerusalem.
>
> (Isa 27:13)

Matthew's direct allusion to the trumpet of Isaiah 27 emphatically drives home the point that Jesus is prophesying a final regathering of the people of Israel who have previously been in exile, and the final restoration of right worship in Jerusalem.

In this restored Israel, also, "when the Son of Man is seated on the throne of his glory," the twelve disciples who have followed Jesus "will also sit on twelve thrones, judging the twelve tribes of Israel" (Matt 19:28). This is an image not of condemnation but of restoration: the twelve are the symbolic heads of the restored Israel, and "restoration includes judgment."[90] For a clear Jewish analogue, we may compare the messianic vision set forth in the *Psalms of Solomon*:

> He will gather a holy people
> whom he will lead in righteousness;
> and he will judge the tribes of the people
> that have been made holy by the LORD their God.
>
> (*Pss. Sol.* 17:26)

According to Matthew 19:28, this function of messianic judgment is to be delegated to the twelve rather than exercised solely by the Messiah himself; but in both of these examples the gathering and restoration of Israel are in view. Indeed, the role of "judging" probably refers not to the final determination of individuals' eschatological fate but to a role more closely related to governing, like the role of the ancient judges of Israel described in the book of Judges. The twelve disciples will be charged with administrative responsibility over the twelve tribes.

Even the distinctive Matthean conclusion of the parable of the vineyard (Matt 21:33-44) does not point, as sometimes thought, to a categorical supersessionist exclusion of Israel from the kingdom of God.[91] On the contrary, when Jesus says, "Therefore I tell you, the kingdom of God will be taken away from you and given to a people that produces the fruits of the kingdom" (21:43), he is quite explicitly addressing "the chief priests and Pharisees," who immediately recognize that "he was speaking about them" (21:45). This is yet another expression of Matthew's prophetic judgment against the leaders and authorities who have not been faithful stewards of their trust to care for the people.[92] The vineyard itself, as in Isaiah 5:1-7, represents Israel:

> For the vineyard of the LORD of hosts is the house of Israel,
> and the people of Judah are his pleasant planting.
>
> (Isa 5:7a)

But in distinction from Isaiah, who pronounces judgment and destruction on the unfruitful vineyard, Jesus' parable condemns the wicked *tenants* and declares that the vineyard will be given "to other tenants who will give [the Lord of the vineyard: κύριος in Matt 21:40] the produce at the harvest time" (Matt 21:41). Thus, even this passage looks forward to a time of eschatological fruitfulness for Israel.

At every point, then, Matthew's narrative suggests that Jesus' mission to the lost sheep of the house of Israel intends and prefigures the end of exile, the regathering of elect Israel, the restoration of a glorious and fruit-bearing kingdom under the rule of Jesus himself (as Son of Man) and those followers with whom he will share his reign. And at every point this image of Israel's identity and destiny is developed and sustained through evocative reinterpretation of Israel's Scripture.

In sum: Matthew's references to Israel's Scripture situate the story of Jesus within a comprehensive interpretation of the story of Israel. On Matthew's reading, it is the story of a people chosen and loved by God who have nonetheless tragically fallen into disobedience and exile. But it is also a story that contains prophetic anticipations of God's ultimate renewal of the covenant through sending a ruler who will save the people from their sins and bring the exile to an end. This messianic figure takes the destiny of Israel upon himself and embodies the radical covenant obedience that God has always desired of his people; further, he gathers around himself a new community within Israel, a community that also is called to embody the obedience, love, and mercy that are at the heart of Israel's Torah. Matthew's construal of Israel's scriptural story, then, is deftly encapsulated in John Mason Neale's 1851 translation of the ancient Advent carol "Veni, Veni, Emmanuel":

> O come, O come, Emmanuel,
> And ransom captive Israel,
> That mourns in lonely exile here,
> Until the Son of God appear.

But what of this "Son of God" who comes to ransom captive Israel? How does Israel's Scripture shed light upon his identity?

§8 JESUS AS EMMANUEL

In nearly every paragraph of his Gospel, Matthew seeks to show—whether explicitly or implicitly—that Jesus' life, teachings, death, and resurrection constitute the fulfillment of Scripture. As we explore Matthew's christological reading of Israel's Scripture, we will encounter frustration if we expect to find a single controlling image or motif as the key to Matthew's interpretation of Jesus. Matthew is not that sort of systematic thinker, and no one master concept controls his Christology; rather, he interweaves many different images and scriptural traditions to build up a multilayered portrait of Jesus as the one who fulfills and exceeds all of Israel's hopes. The result is a narrative account of the identity of Jesus that is irreducibly complex, bearing significations from many different strands of Israel's story.

Israel embodied. Matthew's retelling of the story of Israel's destiny finds its embodiment in the figure of Jesus, who takes on the role of "God's son" called out of Egypt (Matt 2:15) and enacts the restoration of Israel through his radical obedience. This means not only that Israel's story is given a christological fulfillment but also, conversely, that the identity of Jesus is given an "Israelogical" specification. By identifying fully with Israel in order to fulfill all righteousness, Jesus locates himself in a particular national history, with all its pain and ambiguity, and with its hope for final vindication by God. Thus, the "end of exile" motif that features so prominently in Matthew's narration of Israel's story illuminates Jesus' identity and mission as well: Jesus saves his people from their sins (1:21) by *representatively* overcoming their unfaithfulness—*proleptically* in his baptism (3:15) and the wilderness temptation (4:1-11), where he shows himself the obedient "Son of God" in a way that Israel had failed to be, and *definitively* in the passion/resurrection narrative.[93] Thus, as Messiah, he brings the exile to an end (1:17).

One often-overlooked clue to Jesus' identity as the obedient Son is to be found in Matthew's baptism and transfiguration narratives, where the divine voice from heaven twice identifies Jesus—in precisely the same wording—as "my Son, the beloved one (ὁ ἀγαπητός), in whom I am well pleased" (Matt 3:17, 17:5). While this epithet echoes the royal figure of Psalm 2:7 and the "servant" of Isaiah 42:1, Matthew's language corresponds more closely to the story of Abraham's near-sacrifice of Isaac, where is it *Isaac* who is repeatedly identified as the "beloved son" (τὸν υἱόν σου τὸν ἀγαπητόν; Gen 22:2, 12).[94] This Isaac typology, which is fully consistent with Matthew's repeated stress on Jesus' obedience, gives a far richer sense to Matthew's programmatic identification of Jesus as "son of Abraham" (1:1): Jesus is Abraham's son not only because of genealogical descent but also because he embodies the fulfillment figurally foreshadowed by Isaac.

From this point of view, the sufferings of Jesus—not only in the flight into Egypt (Matt 2:13-15), but also preeminently in the crucifixion—can be understood as expressions of solidarity with Israel's suffering. This solidarity is emphasized by the many resonances between Jesus' passion and Israel's psalms of lament. In his account of Jesus' arrest and death, Matthew not only preserves Mark's allusions to Psalm 22 and Psalm 69 but also turns up the volume of the allusions by introducing additional details. For example, Matthew recognizes in Mark 15:36 ("And someone ran, filled a sponge with *vinegar* [ὄξους], put it on a stick, and gave it to him to drink [ἐπότιζεν]") an echo of Psalm 68:22 LXX:

> And they gave (ἔδωκαν) me gall (χολὴν) for my food,
> And for my thirst they gave me vinegar (ἐπότισάν με ὄξος) to drink.

Consequently, he not only reproduces Mark's account (Matt 27:48) but also amplifies it by introducing an earlier statement, not found in Mark, that the soldiers who crucified him "gave (ἔδωκαν) him wine to drink, mixed with *gall* (χολῆς)."[95] The allusion is subtly underscored by the fact that Matthew carefully recapitulates not only the key nouns from Psalm 68:22 LXX (χολὴν and ὄξος) but also the verbs (ἔδωκαν and ἐπότισαν).

But why should we understand this connection with the psalm as an indication of Jesus' solidarity with *Israel*? The point is not just that the psalms were read in Jewish corporate worship but more importantly that *the suffering figure* in the psalms of lament is already presented as a representative of *Israel's national destiny*, so that his suffering is already interpreted as an expression of the suffering of the people as a whole. That is why this particular psalm (Ps 69 [68 LXX]) can end with an expectant celebration of impending *national* deliverance:

> Let the oppressed see it and be glad;
> you who seek God, let your hearts revive.
> For the LORD hears the needy,
> and does not despise his own that are in bonds.
> Let heaven and earth praise him,
> the seas and everything that moves in them.
> *For God will save Zion*
> *and rebuild the cities of Judah;*
> and his servants shall live there and possess it;
> the children of his servants shall inherit it,
> and those who love his name shall live in it.
>
> (Ps 69:32-36)

The reversal of the sufferer's fortunes is expressed not just in individual terms but in the specific hope for God's salvation of Zion and the cities of Judah.

A similar pattern of symbolic identification appears in Matthew 27:39: "And the passers-by (οἱ παραπορευόμενοι) blasphemed him, wagging their heads (κινοῦντες τὰς κεφαλὰς αὐτῶν). . . ." This passage is usually understood, with good reason, as an allusion to Psalm 22:7, particularly in view of the repeated allusions to this psalm in the passion tradition. The wording of Matthew's text, however, actually corresponds more closely to Lamentations 2:15 LXX: "All who pass by (οἱ παραπορευόμενοι) along the way clap their hands at you; they hiss and wag their heads (ἐκίνησαν τὴν κεφαλὴν αὐτῶν) at daughter Jerusalem."[96] This is no mere stray echo of Lamentations; rather, it belongs to a larger pattern of intertextual reference in which Matthew interprets the death of Jesus as the spilling of "righteous blood" (Matt 23:35; 27:4, 24; cf. Lam 4:13) which leads to the destruction of the city of Jerusalem. While this symbolism connects the crowd's mockery to Jesus' prophecy of the destruction of the temple (27:40), which is the central theme of Lamentations, many overlook yet another layer of implication in the echo of Lamentations 2:15. In that prophetic passage, the hostile mockery is directed precisely *"at daughter Jerusalem."* The head-wagging mockers say, "Is this the city that was called the perfection of beauty, the joy of all the earth?" And the prophet goes on to lament over the city in this way:

> All your enemies open their mouth against you;
> they hiss, they gnash their teeth,
> they cry, "We have devoured her!
> Ah, this is the day we longed for;
> at last we have seen it!"

(Lam 2:16)

Thus, if Matthew 27:39 reverberates with echoes of Lamentations 2:15-16, it subliminally suggests that the crucified Jesus paradoxically has become the embodiment of the scorned and destroyed city of Jerusalem. Here again, then, Matthew's Jesus assumes and recapitulates the destiny of Israel as portrayed in Scripture.

But of course, Lamentations is not the end of Israel's story. Within the wider canon of Israel's Scripture, God intends and promises that the final destiny of the people will be glorious, and it is precisely in Jesus' role as the glorified Son of Man that Israel's eschatological vindication is symbolized and foreshadowed.

In a series of prophetic sayings, Matthew's Jesus refers explicitly to the future glorious state of the Son of Man, building to a climax in the great judgment parable that concludes the Matthean discourse material: "When the Son of Man comes in his glory, and all the angels with him, then he will sit on the throne of his glory" (Matt 25:31; see also 16:27-28, 24:27, 24:30-31). All of these prophecies are couched in the third person, leaving their referent slightly uncertain. But in the trial scene before Caiaphas the high priest, Jesus at last responds to interrogation about his identity by declaring, "From now on you will see the Son of Man seated at the right hand of Power and coming on the clouds of heaven" (26:64). This stunning statement, which the high priest regards as definitive evidence of blasphemy, directly identifies Jesus himself as the Son of Man and, at the same time, interprets this mysterious title in light of Daniel 7:13-14:

I saw one like *a Son of Man coming with the clouds of heaven*.
And he came to the Ancient of Days and was presented before him.
To him was given dominion and glory and kingship,
that all peoples, nations, and languages should serve him.
His dominion is an everlasting dominion that shall not pass away,
and his kingship is one that shall never be destroyed.

It is, in short, a prophecy of Jesus' enthronement at the right hand of God.

On the one hand, such a claim surely sets Jesus apart from all other human beings (hence the high priest's horrified reaction); however, on the other hand, the glorified Son of Man figure, in its original setting in Daniel 7, must also be understood as a symbolic representation of the nation Israel.[97] In Daniel's dream vision, four great beasts come up out of the sea to exercise dominion for a time (Dan 7:1-8); these beasts symbolize pagan empires that have violently exercised sovereignty over Israel (see 7:17). Their dominion, however, is ultimately taken away by God (7:9-12), and the Son of Man who then will receive "everlasting dominion" is explicitly interpreted in Daniel's prophecy as symbolizing "the people of the holy ones of the Most High"—that is, Israel (7:27; cf. 7:18). Thus, the Daniel passage, taken as a whole, proclaims a vision of Israel's ultimate vindication. For that reason, when Jesus identifies himself with Daniel's triumphant Son of Man figure, he is linking himself and his destiny to God's promised deliverance of the people as a whole.

The narrative effect of this identification is complex. It continues the motif of Jesus' identification with Israel that we have seen woven into Matthew's narrative from the beginning, while signaling that this identification consists not only in Jesus' solidarity with Israel's *suffering* but also in his embodiment of Israel's *final hope*. Thus the Son of Man title has both individual and corporate dimensions. We cannot rightly understand Jesus' identity in Matthew without perceiving simultaneously that he bears an utterly unique eschatological authority *and* that he does so *on behalf of Israel* in such a way that his glorification somehow accomplishes theirs. All of this symbolic density is packed into the Son of Man figure.

Moses typology. Matthew's narrative also produces wide-ranging echoes of Israel's traditions about Moses. Like Moses, the infant Jesus is shielded from the murderous decree of a ruler who seeks to kill Hebrew children (Matt 2:13-18; Exod 1:8–2:11). Like Moses, Jesus is called out of Egypt (Matt 2:15). In the temptation narrative, Matthew adds to his Markan source the detail that Jesus fasted "for forty days and forty nights," just as Moses did at Mount Sinai (Matt 4:2; Exod 34:28; Deut 9:9). Jesus delivered his teaching from a mountain (Matt 5:1-2), just as Moses proclaimed the law received on Mount Sinai.[98] The great authority of Jesus' teaching parallels the authority of Moses rather than the derivative authority of the scribes (7:28-29). Jesus had pity on the people because he saw them as "like sheep without a shepherd" (9:36)—an expression that echoes Moses' request to God to send a successor to lead the people after his death (Num 27:16-23; the successor that God designates turns out to be Joshua, Ἰησοῦς in the LXX). The story of the transfiguration is full of narrative motifs that echo the Pentateuchal account of the revelation to Moses on Sinai: mountain, cloud, shining appearance of Jesus/Moses, a voice calling from the cloud, even the interval of "six days" (Matt 17:1-8; cf. Exod 24 and 34).

In addition to these clear narrative parallels, two slightly less obvious connections may be mentioned as significant links between Matthew's Jesus and the figure of Moses. First, each of Matthew's five great teaching discourses ends with a concluding transitional formula: "and it happened when Jesus finished these words . . ." or some closely related expression (7:28, 11:1, 13:53, 19:1, 26:1). In each of these passages, the first six words in the Greek are exactly the same (καὶ ἐγένετο ὅτε ἐτέλεσεν ὁ Ἰησοῦς), and the thing that Jesus is said to have "finished" is a particular body of teaching. A similar formulation appears three times in Deuteronomy at the conclusion of Moses' extended teaching to Israel—Deut 31:1: "When Moses had finished speaking all these words to all Israel" (LXX: καὶ συνετέλεσεν Μωυσῆς λαλῶν πάντας τοὺς λόγους τούτους πρὸς πάντας υἱοὺς Ισραηλ; see also Deut 31:24, 32:45). Matthew's wording in 7:28, 19:1, and 26:1 echoes the Deuteronomic language very closely indeed, and his addition of πάντας in 26:1 (all these words) provides an impressive concluding cadence that signals the end of Jesus' teaching ministry, just as the formula in Deuteronomy signals the conclusion of Moses' instruction of the people. It has of course been suggested that the five Matthean discourses are meant to correspond typologically to the five books of Moses; whether this suggestion is persuasive or not, it can hardly be denied that Matthew's formula for concluding the discourses sounds a loud echo of the ending of Deuteronomy.[99] The effect of this echo is to hint at a parallelism between Moses and Jesus as sources of authoritative revelatory teaching.

This parallelism is evoked one last time in the resurrection appearance scene that concludes Matthew's Gospel (28:16-20). While this text shares features with Daniel's vision of the enthroned Son of Man, it should not be overlooked that Matthew has scripted the scene in a way that reminds us also of the Mosaic motifs that we have already noted. Jesus' commissioning of his disciples on the mountain in Galilee is reminiscent of the commissioning of Joshua in Deuteronomy 31:23 and Joshua 1:1-9.[100] Joshua is instructed to be "careful to act in accordance with *all the law that my servant Moses commanded you*" (Josh 1:7), and he is given the promise of continuing divine presence ("I will be with you"; Deut 31:23).

It would be a mistake to suppose that the Son of Man typology somehow excludes these Mosaic echoes or that we must choose between one and the other. *It is precisely Matthew's narrative genius to fuse these elements together into a new story that evokes aspects of these and many other precursor texts in Israel's Scripture.* It is also important to recognize that figural parallels of this kind should not be interpreted in a wooden one-to-one manner. For example, while both Deuteronomy 31:23 and Matthew 28:20 speak of continuing divine presence, in one case the reference is to God's ongoing presence with Israel in the *absence of Moses*, whereas in the other the manner of God's presence is precisely through the continuing *presence of Jesus* to the end of the age. This does not mean there is no figural link between Jesus and Moses; rather, it means that readers are called upon to discern the similarities and dissimilarities at the same time. To put the point somewhat crudely, in Matthew's concluding commissioning scene, Jesus assumes the roles *both* of Moses (authoritative teacher departing) *and* of God (continuing divine presence). Both ranges of signification are triggered by the very same narrative typology.[101]

In the midst of Matthew's artful weaving of correspondences, however, he always reminds us that Jesus is more than a successor to Moses, more than a new Joshua, far more than a prophet like Moses who continues Moses' ministry in some derivative fashion. Jesus is, in a way that Moses never was, "Emmanuel," God with us. That is why Jesus can declare that he has come not merely to remind people of the law and the prophets but to fulfill them. That is why he can cite Moses and then add, "but I say to you," asserting his own authority as definitive source and interpreter of Torah. And that is why he can promise to be present to his followers to the end of the age, in a way that never could have been claimed for Moses. Moses, then, is a *foreshadowing* of Jesus, a forerunner who prefigures some facets of the identity of Jesus. Jesus takes up into his own story line all that Moses signified for Israel, while also surpassing his precursor.

"Great David's greater son." If Matthew's identification of Jesus with Moses operates chiefly at the level of implicit figuration, the situation is quite different with regard to the figure of David. The Gospel's opening superscription identifies Jesus as "the son of David" (Matt 1:1), and Jesus' Davidic lineage is further highlighted by the structure of the genealogy, which identifies David as one of the two pivot-points in Israel's history leading up to the coming of the Messiah (1:17). In Matthew's birth narrative, the angel who appears to Joseph in a dream addresses him as "Joseph, *son of David*" (1:20)—thereby making it clear that by accepting Mary as his wife, Joseph is adopting Jesus into the line of Davidic descent and legitimating Jesus' status as Davidic Messiah (1:16).

The same motif is underscored once again by Matthew's account of the birth of Jesus in Bethlehem, the city of David. When the magi come to King Herod looking for a child "who has been born king of the Jews," Herod suspiciously asks the chief priests and scribes "where the Messiah was to be born." They answer his question by citing a prophecy from Micah 5:1-3 that foretells the coming of a ruler out of Bethlehem (Matt 2:1-6).[102] The quotation as Matthew presents it, however, fuses the Micah passage with 2 Samuel 5:2, a key line in the account of David's accession to the throne. In this text, "all the tribes of Israel" come to David and say, "The LORD said to you: It is you who *shall be shepherd of my people Israel.*" The wording of the last clause in the prophecy as reported by Matthew agrees almost verbatim not with Micah but with the Greek text of the 2 Samuel passage:

> Matt 2:6: . . . ὅστις ποιμανεῖ τὸν λαόν μου τὸν Ἰσραήλ
>
> 2 Sam 5:2 LXX: σὺ ποιμανεῖς τὸν λαόν μου τὸν Ἰσραήλ

The full implications of this echo are rarely noticed, but it is hardly coincidental that in 2 Samuel the tribes of Israel are declaring their greater allegiance to David *in contrast to* the recently deceased Saul. They say, "For some time, while Saul was king over us, it was you who led out Israel and brought it in. The LORD said to you: It is you who shall be shepherd of my people Israel, you who shall be ruler over Israel." They are acclaiming David as true king and leader over against their previous ineffectual ruler and acknowledging a change of kingship. Their acclamation is immediately followed by the anointing of David as "king over Israel" (2 Sam 5:3). The effect of Matthew's splicing of this text together with Micah 5:1-3 is to foreshadow the supplanting and death of Herod

(Matt 2:15) and to hint, within the very words of the prophecy as reported by the chief priests and scribes, that Jesus is about to assume his rightful place as Israel's anointed king. Matthew's evocation of these interwoven texts serves to emphasize even more strongly the *Davidic* origin and vocation of the messianic child born in Bethlehem.

After this forward-pointing passage in the birth narrative, we hear no more of David until we are deep into Matthew's account of Jesus' Galilean ministry. Two blind men approach Jesus on the road and cry out, "Have mercy on us, Son of David!" (Matt 9:27). While the foregoing narrative (8:1–9:26) has thematized Jesus' authority and displayed his power to heal, it is not immediately clear why the two blind men ascribe this Davidic title to him. The episode in Matt 9:27-31 is of particular interest because this unit is a unique Matthean insertion into the Markan narrative structure; it appears to be a doublet of the later Matthew 20:29-34, which is closely adapted from Mark's story of the healing of blind Bartimaeus in Mark 10:46-52. But why has Matthew chosen to insert this story at this point, particularly since it overlaps so considerably with the later account? One possible explanation is that it allows him to reintroduce the title "Son of David" and to remind the reader that Jesus' wonder-working activity, highlighted just before and after, is related to his *messianic* role and identity. He is not just a powerful prophet but still, as prefigured in the genealogy and birth narrative, the rightful king of Israel.

Even so, the appearance of the title "Son of David" here is surprising. Does Matthew's telling of the story suggest that the anticipated Davidic Son-Messiah will have healing powers? This seems odd, because none of the scriptural stories about David depict him as a healer. He is a shepherd, victorious general, king, penitent sinner, and poet, but nowhere are miraculous healing powers ascribed to him.[103] Yet in addition to Matthew 9:27-31 and its twin in Matthew 20:29-34 there are several other passages in which Matthew seems to associate healing and/or exorcism with Jesus' messianic identity, and several of these are linked with the "Son of David" title. For example, Matthew introduces his version of the Beelzebul controversy (12:22-32) with a brief account of Jesus' curing of a blind and mute demoniac, to which the crowds respond by asking, "Can this be the Son of David?" (12:24). Or again, the Canaanite woman seeking Jesus' help for her daughter cries out, "Have mercy on me, Lord, Son of David; my daughter is tormented by a demon" (15:22).

Perhaps the most striking example of this Matthean redactional motif appears in chapter 21, immediately following Jesus' driving out of the money changers in the temple. Matthew adds a narrative element unparalleled in the other three Gospel accounts: "The blind and the lame (τυφλοὶ καὶ χωλοί) came to him in the temple, and he cured them" (21:14). Then, in the following sentence, Matthew links this healing activity to Jesus' Davidic identity: "But when the chief priests and the scribes saw the amazing things that he did, and heard the children crying out *in the temple,* 'Hosanna to the Son of David,' they became angry" (21:15). By placing the cry of the children in the temple itself (not just along the road from the Mount of Olives to Jerusalem, as in 21:1-11), Matthew links the Davidic acclamation directly to his distinctive account of Jesus' healing activity in the sacred precincts.

This linkage suggests a complex transformation of an Old Testament precursor. In the story of David's accession to the throne, we find an account of his capturing "the stronghold of Zion" from the native Jebusites in Jerusalem, who had contemptuously taunted him with these words: "You will not come in here; even the blind and the lame will turn you back" (2 Sam 5:6). In other words: "Our fortress is so strong that we can fend off your attack even with the feeblest soldiers." David had replied in kind with a sarcastic summons to his own troops: "Whoever wishes to strike down the Jebusites, let him get up the water shaft to attack 'the lame and the blind,' those whom David hates." In the midst of recounting David's successful assault on the city, the narrator then adds the following rather puzzling etiological comment: "Therefore it is said, 'The blind and the lame (LXX: τυφλοὶ καὶ χωλοί) shall not come into the house.'" (LXX reads εἰς οἶκον κυρίου: "into the LORD's house.")[104] If Matthew's abrupt and distinctive placement of "the blind and the lame" in the Lord's house in Matthew 21:14 is indeed a subtle echo of 2 Samuel 5:8, several interpretative possibilities unfold before our eyes. On the one hand, the reminiscence of "the blind and the lame" may suggest that Jesus' table-upsetting action in the temple is in fact a triumphant "capturing" of the holy site, reminiscent of David's victory over the Jebusites. In Matthew's story, however, the figuratively "blind" opponents are now the chief priests and scribes (cf. Jesus' charges against the "blind" scribes and Pharisees in Matt 15:14 and 23:16-19). But, at the same time, the literally blind and lame of Jesus' time, rather than being excluded from the Lord's house, are welcomed in and healed by Jesus. Thus we find once again a transformative surpassing of the scriptural precursor text: whereas David merely subdued "the blind and the lame," this new Son of David establishes his sovereignty in a way that embraces and heals them.

Readers who might find this transforming echo of 2 Samuel 5:8 a bit too subtle to be persuasive should recall that Matthew has already cited a closely related bit of text from 2 Samuel's narrative of David's ascent to kingship: in the birth narrative the infant Jesus was identified as one who "shall be shepherd of my people Israel" (Matt 2:6/2 Sam 5:2). Strictly from a literary point of view, the earlier specific quotation of this Davidic passage in Matthew 2:6 makes a subsequent allusion (in Matt 21:14-15) to the same original narrative context both more likely and more readily comprehensible—particularly since the passage itself is of pivotal importance in the plot of David's saga. Matthew is portraying Jesus, in ways both overt and indirect, as "great David's greater Son." The textual echoes both establish the link and, at the same time, hint at Jesus' peaceful reshaping of Israel's messianic hope.

A similar reshaping may be at work also in one other Matthean text that indirectly connects Davidic sonship/messianism with healing rather than conquest. In Matthew 11:2-6, we find the story of John the Baptist's question of Jesus: "Are you the Coming One, or are we to wait for another?" The answer given directs John's attention (and the reader's) to Jesus' powerful healing actions: "Go and tell John what you hear and see: the blind receive their sight, the lame walk, the lepers are cleansed, the deaf hear, the dead are raised, and the poor have good news brought to them" (11:4-5). Such actions are described by Matthew's narrative introduction as τὰ ἔργα τοῦ Χριστοῦ: "the works of the Messiah" (Matt 11:2). There is no specific reference to David here, but the titular use of "the Messiah" suggests that the reader should, here as in the other passages we have considered, reinterpret Israel's royal messianic expectation in light of Jesus' healing activity.

At this point, Matthew seems to be drawing on a tradition that finds a very close parallel in 4Q521, a fragmentary text discovered among the Dead Sea Scrolls:

> . . . heaven and earth will obey his messiah. . . . For the Lord will seek out the pious and call the righteous by name, and his spirit will hover over the poor and he will renew the faithful by his might. For he will glorify the pious on the throne of an eternal kingdom, releasing captives, giving sight to the blind and raising up those who are bo[wed down] . . . and the glorious things that have not taken place the Lord will do as he s[aid], for he will heal the wounded, give life to the dead and preach good news to the poor and he will satisfy the weak ones and lead those who have been cast out and enrich the hungry.[105]

Drawing upon the imagery of Psalm 146:5-9 and Isaiah 61:1 (see also Isa 35:5-6), this visionary passage imagines an eschatological age in which God will act to set all things right by bringing miraculous healing and even resurrection of the dead. Despite the reference to a messiah in the first extant line of the fragment, the text clearly attributes the works of healing and giving life to the dead to the agency of the Lord rather than to the messiah himself.[106] Particularly the power to "give life to the dead" is God's alone, as reflected in Jewish liturgical tradition in the second of the Eighteen Benedictions: "Blessed are you Lord, who makes the dead alive."[107]

If Matthew was aware of such traditions, he has performed two highly significant transformations: he has attributed these divine deeds to *Jesus*, and he has framed them not as future hopes but as actions already performed in recent time. Far more clearly than 4Q521, then, Matthew's narrative presents the eschatological healing actions not just as signs of a future "messianic age" but as "works of the Messiah," healing deeds performed by the Messiah himself. For that reason, Matthew 11:2-6 should be linked with the other passages we have surveyed in which healing belongs to Jesus' role as messianic Son of David. Matthew assimilates the eschatological hopes expressed in Isaiah 61 and in Psalm 146 to his picture of Jesus as Son of David, despite the fact that neither of these scriptural texts ascribes this sort of restorative power specifically to a royal Davidic figure.

In several other places, Matthew incorporates Markan traditions that associate Jesus with David. We might make particular mention of Matthew 12:1-4, in which Jesus justifies the action of his disciples in plucking grain on the sabbath by appealing to the example of David and his companions, who ate the holy bread of the Presence taken from the temple in a time of need (1 Sam 21:1-5).[108] The analogical argument suggests that Jesus is, like David, the Lord's anointed one whose mission and authority can override ordinary legal restraints. Matthew then adds to the Markan material an additional halakhic argument about the authority of priests in the temple to break the sabbath by performing actions that would ordinarily be understood as work, and he appends a further saying of Jesus: "I tell you, something greater than the temple is here" (Matt 12:5-6). In this context, we might well infer that Jesus is also greater than David. If so, this example would be analogous to what we have already observed in the case of Matthew's Moses typology: Jesus is like his scriptural precursor but also far greater.

Such a comparison is explicitly articulated in Matthew 22:41-46, the story in which Jesus confounds the Pharisees by quoting Psalm 110:1 and asking them how the Messiah can be David's son if David calls him Lord. Matthew makes a number of interesting minor redactional adjustments[109] to his precursor text in Mark, but the point of the pericope remains the same: David's own psalm, which has the status of scriptural authority, portrays another figure whom David calls "my Lord" as summoned to sit at God's right hand. Implicit in the argument is the assumption that this enthroned figure whose enemies will be placed under his feet is the Messiah. It is striking that in this case Matthew resists his usual tendency to explain riddles and that he leaves Jesus' rhetorical question ("If David thus calls him Lord, how can he be his son?") unanswered. Given Matthew's repeated emphasis on Jesus as Son of David, it is even clearer here than in Mark's Gospel that this question can hardly be read as a repudiation of Jesus' status as a Davidic messiah; rather, the function of the narrative is to emphasize yet again that Jesus both fulfills and transcends the expectation of a messianic Son of David.

One more passage in Matthew's Gospel merits particular attention for its prominent display of Davidic themes. In narrating Jesus' triumphal entry into the city of Jerusalem, Matthew elaborates the story with several noteworthy details. Matthew reedits the words of the exultant crowd to make Jesus' Davidic identity more explicit than it had been in his Markan source. Placing the two texts in synoptic parallel will demonstrate the relevant point:

Mark 11:9b-10	Matthew 21:9b
Hosanna!	Hosanna *to the Son of David!*
Blessed is the one who comes in the name of the Lord.	Blessed is the one who comes in the name of the Lord.
Blessed is *the coming kingdom of our father David.*	
Hosanna in the highest heavens!	Hosanna in the highest heavens!

Both texts echo Psalm 118:25-26, the climactic passage of the Hallel psalms, whose association with Passover and the Feast of Tabernacles rendered them fraught with eschatological hope. In Mark, the crowd celebrates Jesus' entry with words that anticipate the coming kingdom of David, and the inference lies at hand that Jesus—the figure acclaimed by their chants—is the Coming One, the one who comes in the name of the Lord. Nonetheless, in Mark this remains an inference rather than an affirmation. Matthew resolves any possible uncertainty by having the crowd explicitly identify Jesus as "the Son of David," precisely the appellation already conferred by the narrator upon Jesus from the very beginning of the story (Matt 1:1).

More complex, however, is the effect of the fulfillment citation that Matthew inserts into the story in Matthew 21:4-5. It is widely recognized that Matthew interprets the story of Jesus' entry into the city as the fulfillment of Zechariah 9:9, with its striking image of a victorious king riding humbly into the city of Jerusalem on a donkey. In this way, Mark's evocative allusion (not accompanied by any scriptural citation) is raised to the level of explicit commentary. It is perhaps less often observed, however, that Matthew's editorial handling of the quotation raises a number of interesting questions. Once again, let us place the passages side by side for comparison.

Zech 9:9	Matt 21:5
Rejoice greatly, O daughter Zion!	*Tell the daughter of Zion,*
Shout aloud, O daughter Jerusalem!	
Lo, your king comes to you;	Look, your king is coming to you,
triumphant and victorious is he,	
humble and riding on a donkey,	humble, and mounted on a donkey,
on a colt, the foal of a donkey.	and on a colt, the foal of a donkey.

The English translations (here following the NRSV) conceal a number of minor textual discrepancies between Zechariah 9:9 and the form in which Matthew quotes it,[110] but the most salient distinctions are apparent even in translation.

First, the opening words of Matthew's quotation differ slightly but significantly from Zechariah 9:9 in either the Hebrew text or the LXX. They agree instead verbatim with a phrase taken from Isaiah 62:11 LXX: εἴπατε τῇ θυγατρὶ Σιών ("Say to daughter Zion"). The difference from Zechariah is subtle, but Matthew's choice of wording can hardly be an accident. The passage in Isaiah is a dramatic oracle of salvation for the city of Jerusalem. Matthew would have found the surrounding context, particularly in its LXX form, laden with christological significance:

> For behold, *the LORD has made it heard to the end of the earth*:
> Say to daughter Sion,
> *Behold, your savior has come to you,*
> having his reward and his work before his face.
>
> (Isa 62:11 LXX)

By appending this introductory phrase from Isaiah, Matthew has fused together two scriptural texts (Isa 62:11 + Zech 9:9), as we have witnessed him do in other cases. The reader who hears the echo of Isaiah's oracle will perceive the metaleptic effect: the passing allusion to Isaiah universalizes the proclamation (Jesus' entry into the city is an act of revelation not only to Jerusalem but also "to the end of the earth") and draws attention to Jesus' identity as *sōtēr* ("savior").[111]

Second, and perhaps of equal significance, Matthew deletes from his quotation of Zechariah 9:9 the phrase "triumphant and victorious is he." In this case, we should probably not understand the omission as an instance of metalepsis. Since Matthew has cited the surrounding material in full, this can hardly be read as a case in which the reader is meant to recall the continuation or wider context of the quoted material; this looks more like a case of deliberate editing-out of a phrase. Perhaps Matthew's own narrative design requires him to regard ascriptions such as "victorious" as inappropriate to the pre-passion setting; only after the resurrection can Jesus rightly be regarded as victorious. The most striking effect of the omission is to focus attention on the description of the entering king as πραΰς ("humble" or "gentle"), a significant Matthean motif (cf. 5:5, 11:29).[112] "The Son of David" who enters Jerusalem riding on "a donkey, and on a colt, the foal of a donkey" is not a conquering military hero but a lowly, gentle figure who is reshaping Israel's messianic hope in a way that could hardly have been anticipated—a way, indeed, that will lead to the cross.

So far, our discussion of the title "Son of David" has paid scant attention to the fact that in the Old Testament story David's son and direct successor was Solomon, the king who built the temple and who was renowned especially for his great wisdom. Yet there is reason to suppose that Matthew also has a special interest in relating his portrayal of Jesus to scriptural wisdom traditions.

"Take my yoke upon you." A handful of passages in Matthew seem to suggest an identification of Jesus with the figure of divine Wisdom—an implication that lies particularly close to the surface in Matthew 11:28-30. Indeed, some recent readings of Matthew have taken the wisdom motif as the key to Matthean Christology.[113] Any attempt to consider Matthew's appropriation of scriptural traditions must therefore consider his allusions to this personified figure from Israel's Wisdom literature (as portrayed in Prov 8, Sir 24, Wis 7:22-27, and other similar sources) and to

the way that this motif figures in a larger reconstruction of the development of early Christianity's christological affirmations.

One popular scholarly approach is to propose that, for Matthew, Jesus is "Wisdom incarnate," a claim for which Matthew 11:28-30 is a central piece of evidence. This approach capitalizes on the long observed parallel between Matthew 11 and Sirach 51:23-27 to argue that Jesus does not speak as a sage summoning disciples to come under the yoke of *sophia*; rather, he speaks directly in the persona of *Sophia*.[114] This proposed Matthean identification of Jesus with personified Wisdom is alleged to stand on a developmental trajectory midway between the prophetic Christology of Q (Jesus as a prophetic sage) and later gnostic speculations about divine *sophia*.[115]

Other scholars, however, have emphasized the link between Wisdom and Torah and proposed that Matthew's allusions to the wisdom motif have the effect of presenting Jesus as "the functional equivalent of Torah."[116] And still other scholars have challenged the whole linkage between Matthew 11 and Sirach 51. How are we to assess this debate among interpreters?[117]

The first necessary observation is that the distance between Matthew 11 and Sirach 51 is not so great as critics of the wisdom Christology hypothesis would contend. To be sure, the saying of Jesus is not a direct *quotation* of the wisdom utterance, but there are manifest similarities that have struck many readers as impressive—surely one good test for the presence of an allusion:

Sir 51:23-27	Matt 11:28-30
Draw near to me,	Come to me,
you who are uneducated . . .	all you who labor (κοπιῶντες)
	and are heavily burdened,
Why do you say you are lacking in these things,	
and why do you endure such great thirst?	
	and I will give you rest (ἀναπαύσω).
I opened my mouth and said,	
Acquire wisdom for yourselves without money.	
Put your neck under her yoke (ζυγόν),	Take my yoke (ζυγόν) upon you,

and let your soul (ψυχή) receive instruction;	and learn from me,
it is to be found (εὑρεῖν) close by.	for I am gentle and lowly in heart.
See with your own eyes	
that I have labored (ἐκοπίασα) but little	
and found (εὗρον) for myself much rest (ἀνάπαυσιν).	and you will find rest (εὑρήσετε ἀνάπαυσιν)
	for your souls (ψυχαῖς).
	For my yoke (ζυγός) is easy, and my burden is light.

Both passages take the form of a direct call ("Draw near to me" / "Come to me") to hearers who are in some way needy or suffering (lacking and thirsting / laboring and burdened). The link is strengthened by observing that the same verb (κοπιάω) appears in both texts: in Matthew 11:28 to describe the labors of those to whom the offer is given and in Sirach 51:27 to describe the labors of the sage who offers himself as an example to be followed. In both passages, the addressees are exhorted to take on the *yoke* by *receiving instruction* or *learning*. In both passages the result of taking on this yoke of instruction is that the thirsting/laboring hearers will *find rest*. Furthermore, this rest is said in Matthew to be "for your *souls*," while in Sirach it is "your souls" that are called to receive instruction. Finally, the Sirach passage emphasizes the great disproportion between the minor toil required ("I have labored but little") and the great reward that follows; this is not far at all from the sense of Jesus' reference to taking up a light burden. And in both texts, the reward that ensues is named as "rest" (ἀνάπαυσιν). The words that are in common are key words (particularly "yoke" and "find rest"), thus increasing the volume of the echo, and they appear in passages with many striking structural parallels beyond simple verbal agreement.

Two more observations may be added. First, in Sirach 6:18-31, there is a similar passage in which the sage summons hearers to submit to discipline in order to find wisdom and finally receive rest. The verbal parallels to Matthew 11:28-30 are not as close as the links we have traced in Sirach 51, but Sirach 6 does feature the imagery of a heavy weight that fools cannot bear, while promising that those who do "bend your shoulders and carry her" will at last receive the rest (ἀνάπαυσιν, Sir 6:28) that wisdom gives. It seems more than probable that the two passages from Sirach flow together to create the wisdom imagery that is the intertextual precursor of the Matthean saying. Second, the possible allusion to the figure of Wisdom in Matthew 11:28-30 is greatly strengthened by the fact that Matthew has explicitly referred to the figure of personified Wisdom just a few verses previously, in 11:19: "Yet Wisdom is vindicated by her deeds"—perhaps a reference to the deeds of Jesus summarized in Matthew 11:4-6.[118] In light of this immediately preceding reference, a connection of Jesus the Son to the figure of Wisdom is less jarring.[119]

In sum, there is an overwhelmingly strong case for an intertextual link between Sirach and Matthew. The Matthew passage is not a quotation, but it is at the very least a loud echo of Sirach 51. Any interpretation that fails to discern this intertextaul connection will surely be a diminished interpretation, deaf to the text's resonance with an important older tradition.

But that still leaves open the question of what we are to make of the connection. Must the speaker of the promises in Matthew 11 *be* Wisdom, so that Matthew is portraying Jesus as Wisdom incarnate? In this regard, we must pay close attention to the Sirach passage in its own context. Sirach 51 is *not* a speech attributed to Lady Wisdom; on the contrary, it is an utterance of the sage who has sought wisdom and summons others to follow his example. In the most important LXX manuscripts, the whole chapter is given the title "Prayer of Jesus Son of Sirach." Whether or not this belongs to the original text, it is an apt description of the chapter's contents. The sage thanks God for protection and deliverance from harm, in a manner reminiscent of the Psalms (Sir 51:1-12), then reflects autobiographically on his own successful pilgrimage in search of wisdom (51:13-22), and concludes with an exhortation to others to follow his instruction by seeking wisdom for themselves (51:23-30). Throughout the chapter, Wisdom is consistently referred to in the third person ("I sought wisdom openly in my prayer. . . . I inclined my ear a little and received her, and I found for myself much instruction," and so forth). This is particularly evident in Sirach 51:26-27, the heart of Matthew's allusive link: "Put your neck under *her* yoke. . . . See with your own eyes that I have labored but little and found for myself much rest." The voice here is emphatically not that of *Sophia*: it is the voice of the sage who is her grateful beneficiary. To be sure, there are important passages in Wisdom literature that depict *Sophia* speaking in the first person and summoning hearers to heed her (e.g., Sir 24:1-22), but neither Sirach 51 nor Sirach 6 is among those texts. Thus, it is not the case that Matthew 11 has taken a first-person discourse of Wisdom and placed it in the mouth of Jesus. The relationship between the two passages is one not of form-critical transference but of *metaphorical transformation*. Jesus speaks in the way we might expect Wisdom to speak, but this does not mean that Jesus *is* Wisdom. It means, rather, that some of the attributes of wisdom are being *metaphorically* associated with Jesus.

Matthew 11:28-30 contains another prominent scriptural echo that is too rarely given its due in debates about this passage. The phrase εὑρήσετε ἀνάπαυσιν ταῖς ψυχαῖς ὑμῶν in Matthew 11:29 not only echoes Sirach but even more strikingly stands as an unmarked verbatim quotation of Jeremiah 6:16.[120] Despite the promissory character of the words cited here, the context in Jeremiah is actually a scathing judgment oracle. The Lord exhorts his people to walk in "the good way" and promises that if they do they will find rest for their souls. But the very next line expresses their disastrous rejection of the gracious offer of God: "But they said, 'We will not walk in it.'" The ensuing prophetic speech, then, is a thunderous declaration of God's judgment against "daughter Zion" and a warning of destruction of a rebellious and corrupt people (Jer 6:17-30). Indeed, this passage immediately precedes Jeremiah's temple sermon (7:1-15), which proclaims the impending downfall of the Jerusalem temple.

It is possible, of course, that Matthew has randomly lifted a phrase out of this setting in Jeremiah 6 without awareness of or concern for its original context. In light of all we have seen of his skillful and highly intentional uses of Scripture, however, this seems unlikely. In Matthew 11 Jesus' call to "those who labor and are heavily burdened" follows immediately upon his complaint that the people have rejected both John the Baptist and himself (Matt 11:16-19) and his bitter judgment oracle against Chorazin and Bethsaida as worse than "the land of Sodom" (11:20-24). In such a context, then, Jesus' *Jubelruf* in 11:25-27 should be heard as an exclamation of thanksgiving for the Father's revealing the truth to Jesus and his simple followers *while hiding it from Jesus' adversaries* (the wise and learned scribes and Pharisees, whose opposition continues and intensifies in chap. 12) *and thereby bringing them under judgment.*[121] If so, Jesus' gracious word about "rest for your souls" in Matthew 11:29 evokes the same ominous overtones found in Jeremiah 6: this is an offer of divine grace, but refusal of the offer leads to disaster. This same motif is also pervasive in the wisdom tradition: fools who turn away from Wisdom's instruction will suffer calamity and destruction (e.g., Prov 1:20-33, 8:35-36; cf. Matt 22:1-14). Recognizing this intertextual background helps us to see more clearly the logic of Matthew's placement of Jesus' striking sayings in Matthew 11:25-30 in their present narrative context.

The promise of comfort and rest takes on its special force against a background of rejection, persecution, and God's impending judgment of a disobedient people.

Where then have we come in our effort to discern the poetic effects of the intertextual echoes in Matthew 11:28-30? I would suggest, by way of summary, the following interpretation. A reading attuned to the Scriptures of Israel will perceive in Jesus' words at least two key intertexts, Sirach 51:23-27 and Jeremiah 6:16. These interwoven texts trigger a complex theological interaction.

First, by evoking the motif of the yoke of instruction and the rest promised to those who accept it, Matthew links Jesus metaphorically with *sophia*/Torah. Yet when Jesus speaks the words "Take *my* yoke upon you," he is speaking not merely as *Sophia*/Torah but as the person Jesus of Nazareth, whose identity is established in many and various ways throughout Matthew's narrative (for example, he is Son of David, Son of Man, Suffering Servant, Emmanuel; he is like Moses but greater than Moses). To take *Jesus'* yoke, therefore, is neither to become trained in the conventional practical maxims of the wisdom tradition nor to obey all the precepts and commandments of the Torah of Moses, as the scribes and Pharisees do. Rather, to take Jesus' yoke is to become *his* disciple, to embrace the radical teachings of the Sermon on the Mount, to imitate his gentleness and lowliness, and to embark on the way of the cross. The shape of such a life can hardly be explained fully by pointing to traditional Jewish understandings of the figure of Wisdom. To paraphrase the point in characteristically Matthean fashion, something greater than Wisdom is here. Jesus, who is "gentle and lowly in heart," transforms and redefines what is meant by "wisdom" by virtue of the specifically narrated character of his teachings, his life, and his death and resurrection.

At the same time, however, the metaphorical linkage with Sirach 51 does suggest a cosmic, divine aspect to Jesus' teaching. He is more than a sage, more than a prophet: he can speak authoritatively of "my yoke" as none of Israel's sages could ever do. He does not merely point the way to wisdom as a source of rest; rather, he is the one who can promise actually to *give* rest to all who come to him. Thus, even while redefining Wisdom, he takes up into himself not just her *functions* but also her personal *attributes*. This provocative metaphorical/theological identification opens up many possibilities for theological reflection that are hinted at, but not fully explicated, by Matthew. Just as Jesus reshapes our understanding of Wisdom, so also Wisdom reshapes our understanding of

Jesus the teacher. Something greater than a sage, something greater than Solomon, is here.

Finally, the Jeremiah allusion introduces a contrasting theme: the gracious divine offer of rest articulated by Wisdom as well as by the prophet Jeremiah repeatedly encounters rejection. Many of Jesus' hearers, especially the wise and learned, say, in effect, "We will not walk in it." Therefore, the promise of "rest for your souls" remains open to those who hear and obey Jesus, but those who refuse the summons will come under dire judgment. The allusion to Jeremiah would appear to be a dissonant note within the confines of Matthew 11:25-30, but within the larger polyphonic narrative context of Matthew 11–12 it harmonizes perfectly. Like John the Baptist, like Jeremiah, and like the figure of Wisdom herself, Jesus encounters rejection by God's chosen people, and disastrous consequences are to follow. This minor-key overtone should certainly be heard in the apparently "comfortable words" of Matthew 11:28-30. The promise of rest is real, but Matthew clearly teaches that the promise is precisely and only for those who do place their necks under Jesus' yoke and embrace the way of discipleship.[122]

The righteous sufferer. "He trusted in God; let God deliver him now if he wants to." The way of discipleship and obedience, as exemplified in the pattern of Jesus' own life, leads to suffering. Near the beginning of Jesus' public career in the Gospel of Matthew, the beatitudes already indicate that suffering and persecution will be the lot of the righteous and those who follow Jesus' teaching (Matt 5:10-12). And Matthew's plot, like Mark's, moves inexorably toward Gethsemane and Golgotha. There can be no doubt that for Matthew Jesus is a suffering Messiah—in stark contrast to many other forms of contemporary Jewish messianic expectation.

Yet if we ask about the way in which Matthew has drawn upon Israel's Scripture to interpret Jesus' identity as a sufferer, we find that Matthew has given surprisingly little attention to formulating a scriptural apologetic for the crucifixion of Jesus. As we have seen, his scriptural fulfillment quotations are clustered in the early part of his story. The only explicit fulfillment quotation anywhere in Matthew's passion narrative (27:9-10) seems badly garbled: it asserts that the chief priests' decision to use the "blood money" flung back at them by Judas to buy a field for burying foreigners took place as the fulfillment of something "spoken through the prophet Jeremiah," though, confusingly, the quotation is not from Jeremiah. It only very roughly approximates Zechariah

11:13, with perhaps an allusion to Jeremiah 32:6-15. In any case, while the citation serves to explain the conclusion of the subplot concerning Judas' fate, it remains tangential to the central narrative of Jesus' condemnation and death.

Matthew retains the scriptural allusions present in Mark's passion story and, as we have seen, sharpens and amplifies a few of the Markan allusions to the psalms of suffering, while also creating subtle links between Jesus' death and the destruction of Jerusalem, as mournfully recounted in Lamentations. On the whole, however, it is striking how little Matthew has done to create new correspondences between Jesus' death and its scriptural foreshadowing. To a later Christian reader, the most unexpected omission is the lack of strong intertextual references to Isaiah's portrayal of the Suffering Servant in Isaiah 52:13–53:12.[123] Matthew does quote Isaiah 53:4 in one of his fulfillment quotations: "He took our infirmities and bore our diseases" (Matt 8:17). But Matthew does not seem to link this citation in any way to his subsequent account of Jesus as a suffering figure: in the context of Matthew 8, the quotation serves simply to demonstrate that Jesus' activity of *healing* is the fulfillment of prophecy. Nothing in Matthew's narrative at this point corresponds to Isaiah's depiction of the Servant's vicarious bearing of afflictions. At best, we might take the citation as offering a foreshadowing of Jesus' role as sufferer, but if so, the foreshadowing is very indistinct.

A few other possible references or allusions to Isaian prophecies about the Servant are scattered through Matthew's narrative. The most explicit citation (in Matt 12:15-21; quoting Isa 42:1-4 in extenso) highlights Jesus' vocation to "proclaim justice to the Gentiles." The passage points to Matthew's consistent theme of Jesus' gentle, nonviolent character ("He will not break a bruised reed or quench a smoldering wick . . ."), but again it says nothing about suffering, nor is such a motif to be found in the wider context of Isaiah 42.[124]

In Matthew 20:28, Matthew reproduces verbatim Mark's wording of Jesus' saying about the Son of Man's giving his life "as a ransom for many" (λύτρον ἀντὶ πολλῶν; Mark 10:45), but he neither expands nor elaborates on the Markan formulation. As we have noted, it is at best doubtful whether the saying echoes Isaiah 53:10-12. Matthew, despite his general predilection for commenting on fulfillment of prophecy, makes no gesture here to relate the logion to Isaiah 53. Even more tenuous is the suggestion that Jesus' refusal to answer Pilate's question (Matt 27:13-14) should be understood as an allusion to Isaiah 53:7

("like a sheep that before its shearers is silent, so he did not open his mouth"): in this case, there is no verbal link at all between the passages. Only slightly more promising is the suggestion that Jesus' prayer in Gethsemane for "this cup" to pass from him (Matt 26:39) might allude obliquely to Isaiah 51:22: "See, I have taken from your hand the cup of staggering; you shall drink no more from the bowl of my wrath." In any case, this text does not appear in one of the Servant passages in Isaiah. It is not the Servant who speaks, but the Lord God, who is declaring his intention to take the "cup" of his wrath away from Jerusalem and give it to her enemies and tormentors. Any application of this text to Jesus' impending death would surely require more interpretation than Matthew provides.

Probably the likeliest allusion in Matthew's passion narrative to the suffering of the Isaian Servant appears in two passages that refer to Jesus' captors beating him and spitting in his face: 26:67-68 (at the interrogation before the high priest) and 27:30 (as the Roman soldiers prepare to crucify him). This might well be read as an allusion to Isaiah 50:6: "I gave my back to those who struck me, and my cheeks to those who pulled out the beard: I did not hide my face from insult and spitting." Particularly interesting is that Matthew makes an otherwise apparently unmotivated minor redactional alteration to Mark's text that has the effect of emphasizing that the tormentors were spitting on Jesus' *face*:

> Mark 14:65: Some began to spit on him and to wrap his face [i.e., in a blindfold] and to strike him.

> Matt 26:67: Then they spat on his face and struck him.

Matthew removes the blindfold and makes the face the explicit target of the spitting, perhaps to suggest correspondence to Isaiah's prophecy. But if so, he once again calls no attention to the link.

Far more salient than these faint echoes of Isaiah's Servant are several Matthean narrative devices that strengthen the connection of Jesus' death to the suffering figure of Psalm 22 and Psalm 69. We have discussed above the way in which Matthew, in comparison to Mark, binds his account of the crucifixion more closely to Psalm 69 by the addition of narrative details that allude to the wording of Ps 69:21 (68:22 LXX), the offering of gall as well as vinegar. And of course, Matthew, following Mark, recounts Jesus' dying cry of Psalm 22:1, "My God, my God, why have you forsaken me?" as the climactic moment of the crucifixion account (Matt 27:46). Just as strikingly, immediately preceding this terrible moment, Matthew has distinctively prepared the way for the cry by placing in the mouths of the mocking chief priests, scribes, and elders a taunt derived from another verse of the same psalm: "He trusted in God; let God deliver him now if he wants to" (27:43; cf. Ps 22:9 [21:9 LXX]; cf. Wis 2:13, 18). There can be no doubt that we are meant to recall these texts and read Matthew's account of Jesus' suffering and death against the background of these psalms of suffering, lament, and ultimate vindication.

In sum, Matthew gives scant evidence of an explicit apologetic for Jesus' passion and death. A few submerged echoes of the Suffering Servant figure of Isaiah may lie below the surface of Matthew's narrative, but it is difficult to be sure about this. More likely, the figure of the Isaian Suffering Servant belongs more prominently to the "encyclopedia of reception" of later Christian readers than to Matthew's own encyclopedia of production. This does not mean that intertextual readings that place Matthew's passion story in counterpoint with Isaiah 53 are theologically misguided; indeed, they may reflect a profound intracanonical insight. But such readings place the hermeneutical accents differently from Matthew's own composition; by contrast, Matthew lays the stress more clearly upon Jesus as the embodiment and figural fulfillment of the voice that speaks in the psalms of the righteous sufferer, with Psalm 22 as an especially crucial intertext for understanding Jesus' death. The effect of this hermeneutical shaping of the passion is to identify Jesus closely with Israel's suffering and lament, while also foreshadowing God's final deliverance. Yet Matthew does not deploy the Psalms in the passion story for the purposes of argument or assertion; rather, these texts belong to the presuppositional level of the narrative, its symbolic world. They are a constitutive aspect of the intertextual *matrix* within which the death of Jesus is retold and received.[125]

"They shall call his name Emmanuel." Finally, as we consider the ways in which Matthew draws upon Scripture to explicate the identity of Jesus, we come face to face with the most distinctive feature of Matthew's narrative Christology: its bold identification of Jesus as Emmanuel, "God with us." This motif establishes the structural framework on which the story is built, as signaled by its appearance at the beginning and end of the story (Matt 1:23, 28:20); these references create an *inclusio* that frames and supports everything in between. In contrast to Mark's circumspect

indirection in identifying Jesus with the God of Israel, Matthew explicitly presents Jesus as the embodiment of divine presence in the world.[126]

This astounding claim about Jesus bursts onto the scene in the first
of Matthew's fulfillment quotations. After a concise account of Mary's
unexpected pregnancy and Joseph's dream in which he is told by the
angel of the Lord that Mary's child is from the Holy Spirit, Matthew the
narrator steps forward to explain:

> All this took place to fulfill what had been spoken by the Lord
>   through the prophet:
> "Look, the virgin shall conceive and bear a son,
> and they shall name him Emmanuel,"
> which means "God is with us."
>
> (Matt 1:22-23; citing Isa 7:14)

The history of interpretation has witnessed vigorous debate about Matthew's citation of Isaiah 7:14. Most of the controversy has centered upon
the LXX's rendering of העלמה ("the young woman") as ἡ παρθένος ("the
virgin"): Matthew follows the LXX, thereby facilitating his interpretation of Isaiah's prophecy as a prediction of a virgin birth. Our present
concern, however, is not with the question of Mary's virginity or with
whether Matthew has illegitimately read the notion of a miraculous conception into Isaiah's prophecy. Rather, an intertextually attuned reading will focus attention on the way in which the Isaiah citation allows
Matthew to introduce his characterization of Jesus: he is not only the
one who "will save his people from their sins" (1:20) but also—because
his conception is "from the Holy Spirit"—the one in whom God will be
palpably present to his people (1:23).

The relation of this promise to the passage in Isaiah 7 is notoriously
obscure. There, the reluctant King Ahaz refuses to ask the Lord for
a sign, even when invited to do so. Presumably, he does not want to
heed the political counsel offered to him through Isaiah, so he makes
an empty theological excuse about not wanting to put God to the test
(Isa 7:10-12). In response, Isaiah impatiently declares that the Lord will
provide a sign whether Ahaz wants it or not. The sign is not presented in
Isaiah 7 as a miraculous birth; rather, the sign is given in the prophet's
declaration that a child soon to be born (a son of Ahaz?) is to be named
Immanuel. The name signifies that, despite Ahaz's lack of trust in God,
God is indeed present to Judah.[127] The confirmation of this claim will be
that "before the child knows how to refuse the evil and choose the good"

(i.e., while he is still a small child) the threat posed by the alliance of the hostile kings Rezin and Pekah will have dissipated altogether: "The land before whose two kings you are in dread will be deserted" (Isa 7:16).

But "God with us" is hardly an unambiguous promise of deliverance and prosperity. The passage in Isaiah 7 takes a swift turn to become an oracle of judgment: because Ahaz fails to believe the prophetic promise and trust God, a fate of destruction will come upon his kingdom (Isa 7:17-25). The king of Assyria is going to overrun Judah like a flood, and the catchword "God is with us" will become an ironic one, a reminder that all human counsel and opposition is futile against God (8:5-10; note the repetition of *Immanuel* in 8:8, 10).

In a similar way, in the Gospel of Matthew the presence of God in the person of Jesus may be seen as portending both salvation and judgment. Just as Isaiah's prophecy of Immanuel turns out to portend the coming destruction of the kingdom of Judah, so in Matthew we find that Jesus, the one in whom God is present, will announce the impending destruction of the temple at the hands of an invading imperial power (Matt 24:1-2). The failure of the people and their leaders to believe the prophetic word of grace and assurance offered by Jesus' proclamation of the kingdom of God will lead to their disastrous downfall (as signified particularly by 22:1-10, in which Matthew's redaction of the parable turns it into a transparent allegory depicting the destruction and burning of Jerusalem [22:7]). Later Christian readings of 1:22-23 have tended to read "God with us" as a univocal promise of salvation, but a recovery of its intertextual implications leads to a more complex interpretation. The themes of judgment and salvation are always dialectically interrelated in Israel's prophetic tradition; in this respect, Matthew's narrative continues the tradition faithfully.

Further, it is no accident that Matthew's opening fulfillment citation places Jesus' prophesied identity in connection with the precarious political situation of the people of God living under the shadow of a threatening empire. Isaiah's word about "Immanuel" was uttered in response to Judah's vulnerable position in the eighth century B.C.E., surrounded by ominous foreign powers. The reader who recalls the context of the prophet's words in Isaiah is drawn to recognize the analogy: Israel at the time of Jesus' birth also stands under foreign imperial domination. Matthew's identification of Jesus as Emmanuel signifies that his birth is a sign: those in Israel who trust God's promise will see in Jesus a harbinger of salvation (the heir who will restore the Davidic line), but those who reject the divine presence in Jesus will suffer the consequences—as indeed the city of Jerusalem had learned to its dismay, in the years immediately preceding Matthew's composition of his Gospel.[128]

The effect of both salvation and judgment being present in Jesus goes to the heart of Matthew's Gospel: readers must continue to search to discover who is saved and who is judged. The reader must also continue on to find out what it means to say of Jesus that he is Emmanuel, and *in what sense* God is made manifest in him. Whatever we make of the complexities of Matthew's appropriation of Isaiah 7:14, his placement of this scriptural citation at the beginning of his narrative sounds a major keynote for his Gospel: Israel's God is now present to his people precisely in the person of Jesus. The reader of Matthew's Gospel is thereby alerted to watch closely for the ways in which the story elaborates this central message about Jesus' identity through additional scriptural intertexts.

We have already observed that Matthew cites Hosea 11:1 ("Out of Egypt I have called my son") in order to identify Jesus figurally with the people of Israel, graciously called by God out of slavery (Matt 2:15). If we examine the context of the Hosea citation in light of the framing Emmanuel motif, however, another layer of possible significance emerges. The Hosea text contrasts God's persistent loving call of Israel to Israel's stubborn disobedience: "The more I called them, the more they went from me; they kept sacrificing to the Baals and offering incense to idols" (Hos 11:2). For this reason, an oracle of judgment is pronounced against Israel: they will fall prey to military destruction by Egypt and Assyria (11:5-7). But that is not the end of the story, for God remembers his tender compassion and resolves not to give up on Ephraim or abandon Israel finally to hostile powers.

> My heart recoils within me;
> my compassion grows warm and tender.
> I will not execute my fierce anger;
> I will not again destroy Ephraim;
> for I am God and no mortal,
> *The Holy One in your midst,*
> and I will not come in wrath.

(Hos 11:8-9)

It is precisely because God is present to the people—"the Holy One in your midst"—that his compassion trumps and transforms his wrath. The Lord will roar like a lion, but the roar will not be a harbinger of judgment and destruction; instead, it will be a summons to his children to return trembling to their homes (Hos 11:10-11). In short, Hosea 11:1-11, read as a whole, is a poetic foretelling of the end of exile.

Hosea 11:1-11 thus resonates richly with the Matthean Emmanuel theme: the God who called his Son out of Egypt is the same God who is present *in their midst*. And Matthew has already disclosed that the form of God's presence is to be found in Jesus. If we understand the formula quotation of Matthew 2:15 as a metaleptic evocation of its broader context in Hosea, we see that Matthew is beckoning his readers to interpret the homecoming of the Son out of Egypt as figuring forth the homecoming of Israel from exile (Hos 11:10-11), while *simultaneously* adumbrating the presence of Jesus as the presence of the God who calls them home and dwells in their midst (11:9).

Because Matthew closely follows Mark's narrative outline of Jesus' Galilean ministry, many of the same stories that in Mark imply Jesus' identity with God function similarly in Matthew. For example, Matthew retells the story of Jesus' stilling of the storm (Matt 8:23-27) in a way that closely parallels Mark (Mark 4:35-41). If anything, Matthew more strongly hints at Jesus' divine status in the words the disciples use to address him when they wake him up in the midst of the storm.

> Mark 4:38: "Teacher, do you not care that we are perishing?"
>
> Matt 8:25: "Lord, save us (κύριε, σῶσον)! We are perishing!"

The exclamation in Matthew takes on the form of an urgent prayer to Jesus as the Lord, a prayer for deliverance.

In the thematically related story of Jesus' walking on the sea (Mark 6:45-52/Matt 14:22-33), Matthew not only expands the tale to include an account of Peter's attempt to join Jesus in walking on the waves but, most tellingly, writes a different ending to the story. When Jesus finally gets into the boat, the astonished Markan disciples, the reader is told, fail to understand because their hearts are hardened (Mark 6:51-52); the Matthean disciples, on the other hand, *worship* him, saying, "Truly, you are the Son of God" (Matt 14:32-33).[129] It is difficult to imagine a clearer illustration of Matthew's didactic remolding of the tradition. Whereas Mark's enigmatic story summons readers to awe-filled meditation on the mystery of Jesus' identity, Matthew reimagines the water-crossing as a clear parable of Jesus' relation to the church: the worship of the disciples anticipates and represents the worship eventually to be given to the risen Lord, to whom all authority in heaven and on earth has been given. But both stories—the storm-stilling and the water-walking—rest on a common Old Testament substratum: there is only One who can command the wind and storm, only One who can stride across the waves. Matthew receives the scriptural message encoded in the Markan mystery and brings it to more explicit expression for the instruction of his readers. The worship of the disciples acknowledges and declares Jesus' identity with the one God of Israel, present in the midst of his people.

The action of the disciples in worshiping Jesus (προσεκύνησαν αὐτῷ) is only one of numerous incidents in this Gospel where various characters are depicted in the posture of worshiping him: the Magi (Matt 2:2, 11), a leper seeking healing (8:2), a ruler of the synagogue (9:18), the Canaanite woman (15:25), the mother of James and John (20:20), the two Marys who first encounter the risen Lord (28:9), and the disciples at the resurrection appearance on a mountain in Galilee (28:17). Now, to be sure, the verb προσκυνεῖν possesses a certain ambiguity. It can in some contexts mean "pay homage, bow down," without necessarily implying a divine status of the one who receives the gesture of homage. Several of these Matthean passages might be understood in such a sense, particularly in the cases of those who come to Jesus as postulants. Yet in view of Matthew's portrayal of Jesus as "God with us" and his use of the verb in settings where it unmistakably narrates an appropriate human response to Jesus' epiphanic self-manifestation (14:33, 28:9, 28:17), it is hard to deny that, in and through these references to worshiping Jesus, Matthew is identifying him as nothing less than the embodied presence of Israel's God, the one to whom alone worship is due, the one who jealously forbids the worship of any idols, images, or other gods.[130]

Indeed, the clinching argument for this reading is to be found in the story of the devil's temptation of Jesus in the wilderness. The devil offers Jesus all the kingdoms of the world if Jesus will only fall down and worship him (προσκυνήσεις), but Jesus repels this seduction by a ringing quotation of Deuteronomy 6:13 LXX: "The Lord your God you shall worship (προσκυνήσεις) and him alone you shall serve" (Matt 4:9-10). Once this commandment has been forcefully set forth in the narrative, readers have little choice but to interpret Jesus' acceptance of worship from other characters as an implicit acknowledgment of his divine identity.[131]

Matthew's accounts of various figures worshiping Jesus are all the more striking when we set his narrative alongside the other two synoptic Gospels. In Luke, the verb προσκυνεῖν appears only in the wilderness temptation narrative (Luke 4:7-8) and in the disciples' response immediately *after* the risen Jesus is taken up into heaven (24:52). In Mark, it occurs only as a description of the actions of the Gerasene demoniac who addresses Jesus as "Son of the Most High God" (Mark 5:6) and of the Roman soldiers who mock Jesus by offering satirical "worship" to the bloodied prisoner they are about to crucify (15:19). In other words, the Gospels of Mark and Luke pointedly avoid using προσκυνεῖν to describe ordinary deferential obeisance to a human authority figure. Its multiple narrative uses in Matthew, then, are to be understood by contrast as a reflex of Matthew's Emmanuel Christology.

A similar point is made in Matthew's supplementation of the Markan controversy story about plucking grain on the sabbath (Mark 2:23-28/Matt 12:1-8). To the argument about a Davidic precedent, Matthew's Jesus adds a halakhic argument about priests who work on the sabbath in the temple and yet are blameless (referring to the prescribed sabbath offerings, Num 28:9-10). But the punch line—the assertion that makes sense of this second argument—is that "something greater than the temple is here" (Matt 12:6). We are not told precisely what the "something greater" might be, but the inference lies readily at hand that it must be Jesus himself.[132] What could be greater than the temple other than the one to whom it is dedicated, the one who is worshiped in it? Matthew's argument is in effect this: if Jesus is "God with us," then his presence sanctifies the labors of those who work to serve him, even on the sabbath. Indeed, if Jesus is "God with us," then his personal presence now takes the place of the temple where the presence of God was formerly thought to dwell.[133] Writing his Gospel in the aftermath of the catastrophic destruction of the temple in Jerusalem, Matthew affirms that Jesus' presence is "greater than the temple" and thereby offers powerful reassurance for Jesus' followers as well as a provocative challenge to those who reject him.

The Emmanuel theme surfaces dramatically again in the fourth of the five great teaching discourses in Matthew's Gospel, Jesus' teaching on church discipline and forgiveness (18:1-35). After giving instruction about how the ἐκκλησία is to deal with offenders (18:15-17), Jesus promises to the community the authority to bind and loose both on earth and in heaven (18:18-19). The warrant for this extraordinary promise is given by Jesus in his pledge of continuing presence with the gathered community: "For where two or three are gathered in my name, I am there among them" (18:20). Commentators have long noted the close parallel between this word of Jesus and the reassuring promise about Torah study articulated by the rabbis: "But if two sit together and the words between them are of Torah, then the *Shekhinah* is in their midst" (*m.Aboth* 3:2).[134]

It is difficult to know whether one of these two claims is dependent upon or reactive against the other. If Matthew has modeled this Jesus saying (Matt 18:20) on an older rabbinic tradition about the Torah, then for his Gospel Jesus takes the place of the law, and his continuing presence in the community occupies the place previously accorded to the *Shekhinah*—the glorious presence of God that accompanied Israel in the wilderness, as manifested in the tabernacle. If, on the other hand, the Mishnah's saying postdates Matthew's Gospel, then perhaps the rabbis were seeking to counteract what they regarded as a blasphemous claim of the early Christians that Jesus could somehow embody God's presence, by asserting an alternative claim about the Torah as the effective agent mediating divine presence to the people of God.[135] In either case, both sayings, Matthean and Mishnaic, represent hermeneutical adaptations in the irrevocably changed situation after 70 C.E. Once the temple has been destroyed and the Holy of Holies no longer stands in a building made with hands, the community must seek to discern how the God of all the earth will be made known in the world. In this situation, Matthew emphatically locates the divine presence in the figure of Jesus himself, who promises (in a saying that anticipates the resurrection and the ending of the Gospel) to be forever present wherever his followers gather and invoke his name. *In short, in Matthew 18:20 Jesus now declares himself, for the first time, to be the Emmanuel promised in the narrator's opening fulfillment citation in 1:23.*

Precisely because Jesus is Emmanuel, in his subsequent discourse on the end of the age (Matt 24) he can offer the further remarkable assurance that his words will outlast all creation: "Heaven and earth will pass away, but my words will not pass away" (24:35). If we ask ourselves who might legitimately say such a thing, once again there can be only one answer: we find ourselves face to face with the God of the Old Testament. Isaiah gives definitive expression to this theological truth:

> The grass withers, the flower fades,
> when the breath of the LORD blows upon it;
> surely the people are grass.
> The grass withers, the flower fades;
> but *the word of our God will stand forever.*

> (Isa 40:7-8)

Christian interpreters lulled by familiarity with Matthew's Gospel may not fully appreciate the theological boldness of the christological assertions made at every turn by Matthew. But there can be no doubt that the word spoken by Jesus in Matthew 24:35 can be true only if it really is "the word of our God," only if the speaker who says "my words will not pass away" is in fact the God of Israel, God with us.

And yet, alongside these mind-boggling claims that portray Jesus as greater than the temple, worthy of the worship that belongs to God alone, able to speak a word that transcends time and space, Matthew also proclaims Jesus' presence among his people in the form of the poor and the suffering. In the climactic unit that concludes the teachings of Jesus in this Gospel, Matthew creates an *inclusio* with the Beatitudes of Matthew 5:3-12 by narrating an unsettling last judgment scene in which Jesus/Emmanuel turns out to have been present among us in the hungry and thirsty and naked and sick and imprisoned of this world (Matt 25:31-46). This, too, is an integral part of what "God with us" means in Matthew, as exemplified in the story of Jesus' own suffering, culminating in the cross. To recognize God's presence truly, then, Matthew's readers must serve the needs of the poor, for "just as you did it to one of the least of these my brothers, you did it to me" (25:40).

Where could such an idea originate, the notion that caring for the poor is somehow equivalent to encountering the presence of God? Just at this point, Israel's wisdom tradition once again provides an unexpected shaft of illumination upon the identity of Jesus: "Whoever is kind to the poor lends to the LORD, and will be repaid in full" (Prov 19:17; cf. 21:13). Matthew does not quote this text, and there is no obvious verbal echo of it in Matthew 25, though the LXX rendering of Proverbs 19:17 employs language characteristic of Matthew's concerns and emphases: ὁ ἐλεῶν πτωχόν ("the one who *has mercy* on the poor man"). Nonetheless, Matthew's account of the final judgment stands in continuity with this fundamental insight of Israel's sages, as articulated in the Proverbs text: we will be judged and recompensed in accordance with our treatment of the poor. But the most remarkable link here between Proverbs and Matthew lies in the former's affirmation that those who show mercy to the poor are in effect lending *to the LORD*. This is precisely what Matthew reaffirms and elaborates: it is the Lord Jesus who is the ultimate recipient of human acts of kindness.

If the connection between Proverbs 19:17 and Matthew 25:40 be granted, a crucial corollary follows: when Jesus says that mercy shown to the poor is really shown to him, he is placing himself directly into the role of the LORD referred to by Proverbs—that is, the LORD God of Israel. In the context of Matthew 25, this makes perfect sense, for the mysterious lowly figure to whom mercy was (or was not) shown is also portrayed as eschatological judge of the nations, the Son of Man (Matt 25:31-33) whose destiny is to sit at the right hand of Power, coming on the clouds of heaven as prophesied in Daniel 7:13-14 (cf. Matt 26:64). Thus, an intertextual reading of Matthew's last judgment scene alongside Proverbs 19:17 has the unexpected effect of underlining once again the identity of Jesus with the God of Israel.

All of Matthew's prior pointers to Jesus' identity with God come to their *telos* in the words of reassurance with which his Gospel ends: "And behold, I am with you all the days until the end of the age" (28:20). No merely human figure could offer such an extravagant promise of eternal presence; the very content of this comforting word implies the divine identity of the one who speaks it. But, beyond the simple logical implications of Jesus' parting promise, its significance is amplified by the extensive network of scriptural intertexts that it evokes. In the MT and LXX there are at least 114 instances of a formula declaring that God is "with" an individual, a group, or the nation Israel.[136] It is not possible to study all these examples here, but we may focus in particular on three passages whose verbal formulation most closely resembles the concluding words of Matthew, asking in each case what the resultant intertextual echo might contribute to our appreciation of Matthew's account of Jesus' identity.

First, hearers of Matthew's ending might well perceive reverberations of the promise spoken by God in Jacob's dream at Bethel in Genesis 28:12-17.[137]

> And he dreamed that there was a ladder set up on the earth, the top of it reaching to heaven; and the angels of God were ascending and descending on it. *And the* LORD *stood beside him* [cf. Matt 28:18a] and said, "I am the LORD, the God of Abraham your father and the God of Isaac; the land on which you lie I will give to you and to your offspring; and your offspring shall be like the dust of the earth, and you shall spread abroad to the west and to the east and to the north and to the south; and all the families of the earth (πᾶσαι αἱ φυλαὶ τῆς γῆς; cf. Matt 28:19: πάντα τὰ ἔθνη) shall be blessed in you and in your offspring. *Know that I am with you* (ἰδοὺ ἐγὼ μετὰ σοῦ) and will keep you wherever you go (ἐν τῇ ὁδῷ πάσῃ), and will bring you back to this land; for *I will not leave you* until I have done what I have promised you." Then Jacob woke from his sleep and said, "Surely the LORD is in this place—and I did not know it!" And he was afraid (ἐφοβήθη), and said, "How awesome is this place! This is none other than the house of God, and this is the gate of heaven."

The clearest link between this promissory passage and Jesus' final words in Matthew is found in their similar formulas announcing divine presence:

Gen 28:16: καὶ ἰδοὺ ἐγὼ μετὰ σοῦ

Matt 28:20: καὶ ἰδοὺ ἐγὼ μεθ' ὑμῶν εἰμι

The change from the singular σοῦ to the plural ὑμῶν is of course dictated by the different narrative settings, though in different ways both Jacob and the eleven disciples are to be understood as representing Israel corporately. But apart from the direct verbal parallel, there are other noteworthy similarities. In both texts, the Lord comes and stands in the presence of the hearers. Jacob is told that "all the tribes of the earth" will find blessing through him, while the eleven are told to go with good news to "all the nations/Gentiles." In both texts, the recipients of revelation greet it with fear and worship. The promise that the Lord will bring Jacob "back to this land" is closely bound together with the theme of the end of exile, which we have encountered throughout Matthew's story from the beginning. But most significantly, in both texts, the Lord speaks in the first person and promises continuing presence:

Gen 28: "Behold I am with you. . . . I will not leave you until I have done what I have promised you."

Matt 28: "Behold I am with you all the days until the end of the age."

The parallel cries out for readers to draw an obvious christological conclusion: in the ending of Matthew, Jesus now stands in the same role occupied by the Lord God in Jacob's dream.

A different emphasis emerges in our second example. At the beginning of the book of Jeremiah, we find a call/commissioning narrative, in which the youthful Jeremiah is appointed by God as "a prophet to the nations" (Jer 1:5; LXX: προφητὴν εἰς ἔθνη). He protests that he is only a boy and does not know what to say. And this is the response he receives from the Lord:

Do not say, "I am only a boy":
for you shall go to all to whom I send you,
and you shall speak whatever I command (πάντα ὅσα ἐὰν ἐντείλωμαί) you.
Do not be afraid of them,
for I am with you (μετὰ σοῦ ἐγώ εἰμι) to deliver you, says the Lord.

(Jer 1:8-9)

Whereas God's speech in Jacob's dream was chiefly a word of promise, this passage resembles the ending of Matthew in focusing on the *mission* of the one who receives the word of revelation. Like Jeremiah, the disciples in Matthew 28 (even those who hesitate, 28:17) are commissioned and sent *to the nations.* Like Jeremiah who is ordered to speak "whatever I command you," the disciples are to teach the nations to keep "all things, whatever I have commanded you" (πάντα ὅσα ἐνετειλάμην ὑμῖν). And in both texts, the ground for confidence in this ambitious mission is simply the promise "I am with you." Once again, Matthew's story seems to give Jesus the same line to speak that in the Old Testament belongs to God.

The final intertext to consider is found in the book of the prophet Haggai. The prophecies of this book are set in the period immediately following the end of the Babylonian exile. The returned exiles, though unsure of themselves, have tentatively begun the work of rebuilding the ruined temple. It is in this context that the word of the Lord comes to the people:

> Then Haggai, the messenger of the LORD, spoke to the people with the LORD's message, saying, I am with you (ἐγώ εἰμι μεθ᾽ ὑμῶν), says the LORD.
>
> (Hag 1:13)

A month later, Haggai goes on to repeat this same word of reassurance, encouraging the people to continue working on the building, "for I am with you, says the LORD of hosts" (Hag 2:4). This time the presence formula is supplemented by a reminder of the promise given to Israel "when you came up out of Egypt" and an additional promise: "My spirit abides among you; do not fear" (2:5). Here, the most interesting parallels have to do with Haggai's postexilic setting, corresponding analogically to the immediate postresurrection setting of Matthew's ending. Haggai's repeated assurance of God's presence in this moment of fragile hope serves to strengthen the resolve of the people for the work to which they are called—just as Jesus' final assurance provides a warrant for the disciples to proceed confidently to the mission on which Jesus is sending them. Indeed, Haggai's word of encouragement might have had special resonance for a late first-century community of Jesus' followers, living in the immediate aftermath of the destruction of the temple in Jerusalem. In this case, however, they are called not to rebuild an edifice to house the presence of God but rather to recognize the living presence of God in the one who stands before them and promises, just as God had promised more than five hundred years before, to be present and to sustain their labors. As in the other examples just reviewed, we see that once again it is *Jesus* who now utters the reassuring promise of divine presence, thereby embodying the divine role in his own person.

It would be possible to continue in this vein, but the instances surveyed here are sufficient to make the point clear. Jesus—who even before his birth was identified by Matthew the Evangelist as Emmanuel, God with us—now speaks after his resurrection in fulfillment of precisely that identity. He possesses all authority in heaven and on earth, and he promises his sustaining presence throughout all time in all places, as he sends his followers out to summon all nations to obey him. There is only One who can speak such things truthfully.

At just this point, however, David Kupp, whose wide-ranging and astute readings have done much to illuminate the central importance of the Emmanuel motif in Matthean Christology, begins to back away from the radical implications of his own analysis. He writes:

> [N]owhere in Matthew's portrayal are Jesus and God simply identified. Jesus' self-perception throughout the Gospel is clearly within the hierarchical relationship of the Son to his Father (even within the triadic baptismal formula in 28:19). . . . For Matthew, Yhwh is the only true God, and worship of Jesus his Son, the Emmanuel Messiah, is a christological window to his divine agency of his Father's will. Worship of Jesus in Matthew does not conflict with worship of God, but is his followers' way of recognizing Jesus' divine sonship and God's presence among them in Jesus, i.e., some kind of perceptual equivalence between them.[138]

Kupp is correct to say that Jesus and God are not *simply* identified; the identification is complex and worked out through the medium of narrative, particularly through the overlapping intertextual patterns we have traced, some overt and some subtle. By the same token, however, it is far too simple to say that the relation between the Father and the Son is "hierarchical" and subordinationist; Matthew's narrative offers, as we have seen, far too many clues of a richer unity in identity. And to speak of a "christological window" that relates Jesus to Yhwh merely in terms of "agency" or "perceptual equivalence" is at once to superimpose foreign categories upon Matthew's text and to subvert the explosive theological logic of the story. Indeed, if we may press the point, it is to suggest that the disciples who worship Jesus in Matthew 14:33, 28:9, and 28:17 are actually guilty not only of a category mistake but of idolatry.

Matthew highlights the worship of Jesus for one reason: he believes and proclaims that Jesus is the embodied presence of God and that to worship Jesus is to worship Yhwh—not merely an agent or a facsimile or an intermediary. If we read the story within the hermeneutical matrix of Israel's Scripture, we can draw no other conclusion.

§9 MAKING DISCIPLES OF ALL NATIONS
The Church's Mission in Matthew's Narrative

How does Scripture function in Matthew's story to locate the church's role in relation to the wider pagan world of the Roman Empire? The study of Matthew's use of the Old Testament to narrate the identity of Jesus has already foreshadowed many of the key themes. For example, we have seen that Matthew depicts Israel's recent history as a long period of exile that is at last coming to an end through the agency of Jesus, the Davidic messianic king. If so, then the Gentile rulers of the land can only be regarded as usurpers and oppressors, and we would expect Jesus' followers to regard themselves as the vanguard of a liberation movement for the people of Israel. Likewise, if Jesus is identified as Emmanuel, we would expect those who trust in him to reject alliances with any foreign powers and to live in the intense expectation that God will protect and deliver them from the scourge of occupation by a Gentile empire. These expectations are not entirely wrong, but Matthew's reading of Scripture also gives them an unexpected hermeneutical twist. As we have seen, the kingship of Jesus confounds and transforms expectations about Israel's coming messiah; correspondingly, the church, the community of Jesus' followers, finds itself standing also in a paradoxical and surprising relation to the powers and cultures of the world around it.

Light to the Gentiles. In contrast to any narrowly ethnocentric conception of Israel's destiny, Matthew's reading of Scripture opens the narrative of God's mercy to embrace the Gentiles. Indeed, Matthew intimates that it has always been Israel's special destiny to bear God's light to the nations and that this destiny has now come to fruition in the mission that Jesus has initiated. The Isaianic eschatological vision of the nations bringing tribute and coming to worship the God of Israel is adumbrated in Matthew's story of the magi from the East, who say to Herod, "We have seen his star at its rising, and we have come to worship him" (Matt 2:2). This artful story—without the direct quotation of any prooftexts about

Gentiles—already prefigures Jesus' sovereignty over all nations, which is explicitly declared in the conclusion of Matthew's narrative (28:16-20).

The church's subsequent interpretative tradition has well understood this figurative dimension of Matthew's story, as shown in the traditional lectionary readings for Epiphany, which connect Matthew 2:1-12 with Isaiah 60:1-6.[139] Though Matthew does not quote this text, he subliminally evokes it in his reference to the gifts brought by the magi: "On entering the house, they saw the child with Mary his mother; and falling down they worshiped (προσεκύνησαν) him. And opening their treasures, they offered him gifts: *gold and frankincense* and myrrh" (Matt 2:11). The specific gifts offered recall the Isaianic vision that when the nations come to Israel's light, "*They shall bring gold and frankincense*, and shall proclaim the praise of the LORD" (Isa 60:6b). Interestingly, the LXX reads ἥξουσιν φέροντες χρυσίον καὶ λίβανον οἴσουσιν καὶ τὸ σωτήριον κυρίου εὐαγγελιοῦνται: ". . . they will come bearing gold, and they will bring frankincense, and they will proclaim the LORD's salvation." By echoing this passage, Matthew associates Jesus with "the glory of the Lord" that "has risen upon you" in the ending of the exile (Isa 60:1), while at the same time prefiguring the Gentiles' acknowledgment of the Lord's sovereignty.

Matthew's interest in the Gentile mission is foreshadowed once again in the formula quotation that accompanies the beginning of Jesus' Galilean ministry.

> Now when Jesus heard that John had been arrested, he withdrew to Galilee. He left Nazareth and made his home in Capernaum by the sea, in the territory of Zebulun and Naphtali, so that what had been spoken through the prophet Isaiah might be fulfilled:
> "Land of Zebulun, land of Naphtali,
>   on the road by the sea, across the Jordan, *Galilee of the Gentiles*—
>   the people who sat in darkness have seen a great light,
>   and for those who sat in the region and shadow of death
>   light has dawned."
> From that time Jesus began to proclaim, "Repent, for the kingdom of heaven has come near."
>
> (Matt 4:12-17)

At the most literal level of discourse, this citation simply functions as a prooftext explaining why Jesus took up residence in Capernaum. To read the citation only at this level, however, is to truncate its sense and miss the figurative implications of the passage. The quotation of Isaiah 9:1-2 (8:23–9:1 MT), read metaphorically, suggests that the scope of Jesus' revelatory work will be wider than one limited geographical area.

In the original historical context of Isaiah 8:23–9:1, "the people who walked in darkness" were the Israelites living under Assyrian rule.[140] This foreign imperial occupation is poetically likened to a "thick darkness" that covered the people (cf. Isa 60:2). Carrying this historical sense forward analogically into the first century C.E., one could possibly read Matthew 4:12-17 as referring simply to Jesus' announcement of God's impending political liberation for the Jewish residents of this area of Galilee. Narratively, this makes sense on a first reading, and it would be consistent with Matthew's portrayal of Jesus' ministry as restricted to "the lost sheep of the house of Israel" (10:5-6).

Several features of the passage, however, lend themselves to the suggestion that Matthew also sees here a prefiguration of the extension of the gospel to the Gentiles. The most obvious indicator is the phrase "Galilee of the Gentiles" as a description of the place where the light appears.[141] More subtly, the following line of Matthew's quotation introduces an anomalous reading of Isaiah 9:1. Whereas both the MT and LXX read, "The people that walked in darkness," Matthew has ὁ λαὸς ὁ **καθήμενος** ἐν σκότει: "the people that *sat* in darkness." Why this reading? It seems that we see here another of Matthew's synthetically interwoven scriptural quotations. The reference to those who "sat in darkness" is derived from Isaiah 42:7, here melded into Isaiah 9:1. The significant point about this blending is that Isaiah 42:1-9—a passage from which Matthew will quote in extenso later in his Gospel—declares that God has commissioned his servant (Israel) to "bring forth justice *to the nations*" (Isa 42:1). This special vocation of Israel is further elaborated in Isaiah 42:6-7:

> I am the LORD, I have called you in righteousness,
> I have taken you by the hand and kept you;
> I have given you as a covenant to the people,
> *a light to the nations*,
> to open the eyes that are blind,
> to bring out the prisoners from the dungeon,
> from the prison *those who sit in darkness* (καθημένους ἐν σκότει).

The two passages, Isaiah 9:1-2 and Isaiah 42:6-7, are linked by the catchwords *light* and *darkness*. By conflating the wording of the two texts,

Matthew's formula quotation hints metaleptically that the "great light" appearing in Capernaum as Jesus inaugurates his mission of proclaiming the kingdom of heaven (Matt 4:17) is precisely the "light to the nations" of Isaiah 42:6.[142] The fulfillment citation is not only a promise of vindication for Israel (as in Isa 9:1) but also a prefiguration of salvation for the Gentiles who previously "sat in darkness" (as in Isa 42:7).

Equally significant is the reference in Matthew 4:16 to the *dawning* of the light (φῶς ἀνέτελειν αὐτοῖς). Once again, the wording of Matthew's quotation differs from both MT and LXX, which use verbs meaning to "shine" (MT: נגה; LXX: λάμψει—interestingly a future tense). Why does Matthew instead use the verb ἀνέτελειν ("has risen")? Is he simply working from a different scriptural *Vorlage*? Again, I would propose instead that Matthew's distinctive reading is better explained as a hermeneutically motivated interweaving of multiple texts. The verb ἀνατελεῖν appears in the LXX's rendering of the climactic sentence of the Servant passage we have just been considering:

> See, the former things have come to pass,
> and new things I now declare;
> before they spring forth (LXX: ἀνατεῖλαι),
> I tell you of them.
>
> (Isa 42:9)

Thus, by weaving ἀνέτελειν into his formula citation of Isaiah 9:1-2, Matthew creates yet another poetic link with Isaiah 42:1-9, this time suggesting that Jesus' appearing in "Zebulun and Naphtali" is the fulfillment of Isaiah's foretelling of "new things" that have now "arisen."

Additionally, and not coincidentally, the same verb appears in Isaiah 60:1, a text we have already noted as a significant intertext for Matthew's vision of Gentile inclusion: "Arise, shine, for your light has come, and the glory of the LORD has risen (ἀνατέταλκεν) upon you." In light of the connections we have already noted between Isaiah 60 and Matthew's telling of the story of the magi, it is likely that we should hear in Matthew 4:16 a complex harmonic fusion of *three* passages from Isaiah that associate the image of a rising light with the theme of revelation to the Gentiles: Isaiah 9:2, 42:7, and 60:1. The echo of Isaiah 60:1 (perhaps a rather faint one in Matt 4:16) is amplified by the earlier words of the magi in Matthew 2:2: εἴδομεν γὰρ αὐτοῦ τὸν ἀστέρα ἐν τῇ ἀνατολῇ (literally, "for we have seen his star in the *rising*"). The Greek ἀνατολή is of course the ordinary word for the directional term "east," and it is so rendered in many English translations of 2:2. But in light of the matrix of Isaian passages evoked by Matthew in the early chapters of his narrative, we might well glimpse here one more ray emanating from the complex image of Jesus as a *rising* light for Jews and Gentiles alike.[143]

Further, Matthew's description of the sphere of the people's confinement as "the region and *shadow of death*" (here closely following the LXX of Isa 9:1; MT has "a land of deep darkness") lends itself readily to metaphorical reinterpretation in a post-resurrection situation: the light revealed in Jesus overcomes the power of *death*. Thus, the saving power of Jesus is not limited to providing a solution for Israel's national predicament of oppression by a foreign empire; it also addresses the more fundamental human problem of bondage to death.

In consideration of all these factors, Matthew's narrative leads readers to see the beginning of Jesus' ministry as the dawning of light for the whole world, including Gentiles.[144] The linking of Messiah and the Gentiles in Matthew 4:14-16 effectively foreshadows the church's later mission to all nations. Even if Jesus must first and only seek the lost sheep of the house of Israel, his kingdom will eventually include the Gentiles as well.[145]

Justice to the Gentiles. This reading of Matthew 4:12-17 is confirmed by Matthew's handling of another passage from Isaiah near the midpoint of his narrative. We have already suggested that Matthew 4:16 echoes Isaiah 42:7. The echo of this Isaian prophecy is greatly amplified by Matthew's subsequent explicit quotation in 12:15-21 of four whole verses—the lengthiest Old Testament citation in this Gospel—from the immediately preceding material in Isaiah 42.[146] Isaiah 42:1-4 is an odd prooftext for Jesus' ordering the crowds not to make him known, and Matthew quotes much more of the text than he needs to make this point.[147] This surplus of cited material suggests that Matthew is seeking to draw the reader's attention to the broader literary and theological context in Isaiah.

> When Jesus became aware of this, he departed. Many crowds followed him, and he cured all of them, and he ordered them not to make him known. This was to fulfill what had been spoken through the prophet Isaiah:
>> "Here is my servant, whom I have chosen,
>> my beloved, with whom my soul is well pleased.
>> I will put my Spirit upon him,
>> and he will proclaim justice *to the Gentiles.*
>> He will not wrangle or cry aloud,

nor will anyone hear his voice in the streets.
He will not break a bruised reed
or quench a smoldering wick
until he brings justice to victory.
And in his name the Gentiles will hope."

(Matt 12:15-21; quoting Isa 42:1-4)

Once again here, Matthew has drawn the reader's attention to a prophetic text that proclaims the extension of salvation through Israel to the
nations. The form of Matthew's citation of the final line of the quotation
agrees significantly with the LXX against the MT:

Isa 42:4b MT: ולתורתו איים ייחילו
     And for his law the coastlands will wait.

Isa 42:4b LXX: καὶ ἐπὶ τῷ ὀνόματι αὐτοῦ ἔθνη ἐλπιοῦσιν
     And in his name *Gentiles* will hope.

Matthew follows the LXX verbatim, except for his omission of the prep-
osition ἐπί.[148] One result of Matthew's preference for the LXX text form
is to sharpen the focus on the christological significance of the prophecy.
It is "his name" rather than the Torah that is the object of expectation or
hope. And the reader of Matthew can hardly help wondering whether
that name is explicitly "Jesus" or "Emmanuel."[149] At the same time, the
LXX textual form specifies the identity of those who look to him: it is
"Gentiles" who will hope in his name. This aspect of the Isaiah quotation
is surprising at this point in Matthew's story, because the immediately
preceding narrative has given no indication that the crowds following
Jesus and being healed by him are anything other than Jewish people; in
Matthew 12:1-14 we see Jesus in controversy with the Pharisees, and the
healing of a man with a withered hand has taken place in a synagogue.
Why then does Matthew adduce a fulfillment citation about *Gentiles*
hoping in the name of the Servant?

This dimension of the citation makes sense only as a dramatic foreshadowing of the mission charge with which the Gospel concludes: "Go
and make disciples of all nations" (Matt 28:19a). In the immediate narrative context of Matthew 12, Matthew needs only a quotation to explain
why Jesus withdraws from confrontation with the Pharisees and tells
people not to make him known (12:15-16). But the Isaiah text that he

selects not only satisfies that narrative need but also points beyond itself to create the anticipation of events not yet narrated—indeed, events that belong to a future beyond the temporal bounds of Matthew's story. Matthew's concern here is not only to provide a scriptural warrant for the puzzling secrecy command but also to hint that Jesus' healing activity prefigures the Isaian Servant's larger mission of bringing healing and justice *to the nations*.

Matthew's handling of the quotation turns it into "a divine pronouncement on the person of Jesus" that functions programmatically for Matthew's Christology; further, a major emphasis of that christological presentation is to proclaim that "the justice inaugurated in Jesus will finally be brought to victory by Jesus."[150] Matthew's vision of ultimate justice includes, prominently, the embracing of Gentiles among God's people. The citation of Isaiah 42:4 in its LXX form—and the fact that Matthew ends the citation on this note—underscores that Jesus' spirit-empowered ministry of justice will become for Gentiles as well as Jews a source of eschatological hope.[151]

Gentiles in the eschatological judgment. A number of other passages in Matthew's Gospel point specifically to the vindication of Gentile believers in the eschatological judgment. Prominent among such passages is Matthew's account of Jesus' healing of the centurion's servant (Matt 8:5-13), which belongs to a cycle of stories in chapters 8–9 that emphasize the theme of Jesus' authority. The centurion's acknowledgment of Jesus' authority to command healing, even from a distance, is the pivot point of the tale, and it evokes Jesus' amazement: "Truly I tell you, in no one in Israel have I found such faith." And here, in contrast to the otherwise closely parallel Lukan account, the faith of the centurion becomes the occasion for a more general pronouncement from Jesus: "I tell you, many will come from east and west and will eat with Abraham and Isaac and Jacob in the kingdom of heaven, while the heirs of the kingdom will be thrown into the outer darkness, where there will be weeping and gnashing of teeth" (8:11-12). In the Matthean narrative context, this can only mean that the centurion exemplifies "many" *non-Israelites* who will be ultimately included in salvation and the great final eschatological feast—in contrast to at least some Jewish "sons of the kingdom" who will be excluded.[152] The language used to articulate this message enacts a particularly surprising reversal, because it echoes a number of scriptural passages that envision the final gathering of *Israel* out of exile and their restoration to the land.

> Let the redeemed of the LORD say so,
> those he redeemed from trouble
> and gathered in from the east and from the west,
> from the north and from the south.

> (Ps 107:2-3)

> Do not fear, for I am with you;
> I will bring your offspring from the east,
> and from the west I will gather you;
> I will say to the north, "Give them up,"
> and to the south, "Do not withhold;
> bring my sons from far away
> and my daughters from the end of the earth—
> everyone who is called by my name,
> whom I created for my glory,
> whom I formed and made."

> (Isa 43:5-7)

> Look toward the east, O Jerusalem,
> and see the joy that is coming to you from God.
> Look, your children are coming, whom you sent away;
> they are coming, gathered from east and west,
> at the word of the Holy One,
> rejoicing in the glory of God.

> (Bar 4:36-37)

The last of these examples makes explicit what is implicit in the others: it is the children of *Jerusalem*, the Jewish people in exile, who will be gathered from east and west. This is also suggested by Isaiah's reference to "everyone who is called by my name." Thus, when Matthew's Jesus speaks of many *Gentiles* coming from east and west to sit at the eschatological table with Abraham and Isaac and Jacob, he has dramatically transformed a standard Jewish apocalyptic *topos*. Now it is the Gentile outsiders being gathered to the feast.

A parallel reversal is performed in Matthew 12:38-42, where Jesus declares that, in contrast to the skeptical sign-seeking scribes and Pharisees, "the men of Nineveh" and "the Queen of the South" will "rise up [a reference to the resurrection][153] with this generation and condemn it," because they responded in faith to God's message, as brought by Jonah

and Solomon. These allusions to Jonah 3:1-10 and 1 Kings 10:1-13 once
again provide scriptural narrative precedents for Gentiles who embrace
opportunities to believe and are accepted and rewarded by God; the
saying of Jesus reported here by Matthew imagines that they will be
vindicated in the eschatological resurrection of the dead. Similarly, the
climactic passage of Jesus' teaching in Matthew, the great parable of the
final judgment (Matt 25:31-46), depicts "all the nations (πάντα τὰ ἔθνη)"
being gathered before the throne of the Son of Man—a transparent allusion to the scene of final enthronement in Daniel 7:13-14. But the pagan
nations are not simply summoned for judgment and destruction. Rather,
many people among these Gentile nations, Jesus teaches, will be welcomed and invited to "inherit the kingdom prepared for you from the
foundation of the world" (Matt 25:34) because of their acts of kindness
and mercy to the poor and needy.[154]

Making disciples of all the nations. The development of this theme comes
to its climax in the resurrection appearance story that concludes Matthew's narrative (Matt 28:16-20). Matthew brings his Gospel to its close
with Jesus' charge that his disciples should go and "make disciples of all
nations" (πάντα τὰ ἔθνη). This conclusion functions as both warrant and
motive for a mission that carries the preaching of the gospel beyond the
boundaries, both geographic and ethnic, of Israel. It is, in a very real
sense, the *telos* toward which Matthew's whole narrative has been driving.
The last sentence of the Gospel, in which Jesus promises his continuing
presence with the disciples in their work of baptizing and teaching the
nations to obey Jesus' commandments, functions as reassurance and support for this mission—no doubt a highly controversial mission in Jewish
communities in Matthew's time. All of this is widely recognized.

Perhaps less often recognized, however, is the crucial point that
Jesus' words in this concluding mission charge echo the description of
the everlasting authority over all nations given to the "one like a Son
of Man" in Daniel 7:14: "To him was given dominion and glory and
kingship, that all peoples, nations, and languages should serve him. His
dominion is an everlasting dominion that shall not pass away, and his
kingship is one that shall never be destroyed." The connection to Matthew 28:18-20 is most visible when one compares the LXX rendering of
Daniel 7:14 to Matthew's account of Jesus' final commissioning words,
particularly noting the thematic emphasis given to the Son of Man's
authority (ἐξουσία).

Dan 7:14 LXX	Matt 28:18b-20
καὶ ἐδόθη αὐτῷ ἐξουσία	ἐδόθη μοι πᾶσα ἐξουσία
	ἐν οὐρανῷ [cf. Dan 7:13] καὶ ἐπὶ [τῆς] γῆς.
καὶ πάντα τὰ ἔθνη τῆς γῆς κατὰ γένη	πορευθέντες οὖν μαθητεύσατε πάντα τὰ ἔθνη
	βαπτίζοντες αὐτοὺς εἰς τὸ ὄνομα τοῦ πατρὸς
	καὶ τοῦ υἱοῦ καὶ τοῦ ἁγίου πνεύματος,
καὶ πᾶσα δόξα αὐτῷ λατρεύουσα	διδάσκοντες αὐτοὺς τηρεῖν πάντα ὅσα ἐνετειλάμην ὑμῖν·
καὶ ἡ ἐξουσία αὐτοῦ ἐξουσία αἰώνιος	καὶ ἰδοὺ ἐγὼ μεθ* ὑμῶν εἰμι πάσας τὰς ἡμέρας
ἥτις οὐ μὴ ἀρθῇ	
καὶ ἡ βασιλεία αὐτοῦ ἥτις οὐ μὴ φθαρῇ.	ἕως τῆς συντελείας τοῦ αἰῶνος.

In this comparison, only words actually occurring in both texts are underlined, but even where precise verbal agreement is lacking, the conceptual parallels are significant. For example, in Daniel, all nations are said to serve the Son of Man, while in Matthew they are to be taught to obey all Jesus has commanded.[155] In Daniel, the Son of Man's authority will never pass away and his kingdom will never be destroyed, while in Matthew, Jesus, who possesses all authority, promises to be present always, until the end of the age.

When we read the ending of Matthew against this background, we recognize that Matthew is portraying the risen Jesus as the triumphant Son of Man figure—representing Israel—who exercises ἐξουσία over all the nations of the world in a kingdom that will not pass away.[156] Thus is fulfilled Jesus' declaration before the high priest during the passion narrative: "From now on (ἀπ' ἄρτι[!]) you will see the Son of Man seated at the right hand of Power and coming on the clouds of heaven" (Matt 26:64; again echoing Dan 7:13-14). Thus—and here is the crucial point for our present concerns—*the disciples' mission to the Gentiles actually constitutes the fulfillment of the triumph of the Son of Man.* Daniel's vision of Israel at last vindicated and ruling over the Gentile nations is to be enacted precisely through the disciples' work of preaching and teaching. Their mission will instantiate the triumph of Israel's God by extending his sovereignty over all the nations on earth. Integral to Matthew's vision, however, is his insistence that the sovereignty of God over the nations will become effectual through nonviolent means. The nations are "conquered," as it were, through baptism into the name of the Father and of the Son and of the Holy Spirit and through their instruction to obey the teachings of a master who has insisted that the meaning of the Torah is summed up in acts of love and mercy.

Summary. In view of this evidence, what can we say by way of summary about Matthew's use of Scripture to situate the church in relation to the surrounding world? The most salient finding is that Matthew presents the pagan world as a *mission field* for the disciples of Jesus. While several of Matthew's scriptural allusions (particularly the evocations of Isa 7–9 in the infancy narrative and the beginning of Jesus' Galilean ministry) might suggest that pagan empires are to be seen as threatening oppressive powers, Matthew does not develop this line of thought to any significant degree. To be sure, the church stands apart from such powers, with its distinct identity, but that identity is to be a light to the world (Matt 5:14), precisely the vocation given to Israel in Isaiah's prophecy (Isa 42:6-7). Rather than standing in hostile opposition to the surrounding pagan world, the church according to Matthew is called to bear hopeful witness to it. And Matthew provides many scripturally informed models of Gentiles who respond positively to the light: the magi, the centurion who recognizes Jesus' authority, the men of Nineveh, the Queen of the South, the "sheep" who unwittingly offer mercy to Jesus.[157]

To be sure, the church may suffer terribly at the hands of Gentile powers: "Then they will hand you over to be tortured and will put you to death, and you will be hated by all nations because of my name" (Matt 24:9). Yet despite any present experience of opposition and persecution (see also 5:10-12, 13:20-21), one chief function of *scriptural* citation in Matthew's narrative is to hold before the church a vision that Gentiles may in unforeseeable ways and places become receptive to the gospel. They will receive instruction, as Isaiah had foretold (Isa 2:2-3), and learn to hope in the name of Jesus—again, as Isaiah had foretold (Matt 12:21/Isa 42:4). The kingship of Jesus stands over against the kingdoms of the present world, but ultimately his authority will both conquer and embrace them all. This imparts to the community of the church a role of faithful and peaceful witness-bearing until the end of the age, embodying the message of Jesus by obeying him and letting the community of the faithful shine as a light to the world so that all may see and give glory to their Father in heaven (Matt 5:16).

§10 THE TRANSFIGURATION OF TORAH
Matthew's Scriptural Hermeneutics

Matthew imaginatively draws upon Scripture to retell the story of Israel, to narrate the story of Jesus, and to map the role of the church in relation to the pagan world. In view of our findings, what conclusions can we draw about the characteristic patterns and strategies of Matthean hermeneutics? Before addressing substantive thematic emphases, we should note three general observations about the form and method of Matthew's engagement with scriptural texts.

First, contrary to initial impressions, it is inaccurate to characterize Matthew's method as prooftexting or as fixated on a prediction/fulfillment model of interpretation. To be sure, Matthew does believe that the words of the prophets have come to fulfillment in and through the life of Jesus, and he takes pains to shine a spotlight on certain points where he discerns a providential correspondence between Jesus' career and the earlier mysterious prophetic oracles. Nonetheless, these instances of prediction and fulfillment are only highlights on a larger map, only fragmentary features of a much larger intertextual reality. For Matthew, Israel's Scripture constitutes the symbolic world in which both his characters and his readers live and move. The story of God's dealings with Israel is a comprehensive matrix out of which Matthew's Gospel narrative emerges. The fulfillment quotations, therefore, invite the reader to enter an ongoing exploration of the way in which the law and the prophets *in their entirety* find fulfillment (Matt 5:17) in Jesus and in the kingdom of heaven.

Second, we have observed that Matthew's scriptural citations sometimes *interweave* two or more Old Testament texts, imbedding wording from one text within another.[158] Our analysis has led to the conclusion that this is a matter neither of accidental misquotation from memory nor of simple dependence on some otherwise unknown textual tradition that differs from the MT and LXX. Rather, these blended quotations seem to function as allusive, hermeneutically constructive compositions; they beckon the reader to recall two different scriptural contexts simultaneously and to reflect upon the way in which each one illuminates the other, or to discern how both subtexts contribute to a nuanced interpretation of events narrated in the Gospel. For example, when Matthew's rendering of the text from Micah 5 about the birth of the Messiah in Bethlehem (Matt 2:16) subliminally interweaves wording from 2 Samuel 5:2, the reader who hears the echo is invited to perceive the challenge of the child Jesus to Herod's kingship against the narrative backdrop of David's succession to the throne, supplanting Saul. The following table lists several other examples discussed in the present chapter:

Passage in Matthew	Interwoven scriptural intertexts
Matt 2:6	Mic 5:1-3 + 2 Sam 5:2
Matt 4:14-16	Isa 9:1-2 + Isa 42:6-7
Matt 11:29	Sir 51:27 + Jer 6:16
Matt 21:5	Isa 62:11 + Zech 9:9
Matt 27:39	Ps 22:7 + Lam 2:15

Some instances of this technique in Matthew are more obvious than others, but many of them would surely require the reader-competence of a "scribe trained for the kingdom of heaven" (Matt 13:52).[159] Matthew does not lay out all the treasures of his intertextual narration in plain sight.

Third—and here we simply repeat a critical commonplace—Matthew seems to have a special affinity for prophetic texts, and for Isaiah in particular. Isaiah occupies a privileged place in Matthew's operative canon; it offers the key to recognizing Jesus as Emmanuel and understanding the church's vocation to spread the gospel to the nations. At the same time, however, we should not overlook the crucial hermeneutical role occupied in Matthew's story by other texts such as Deuteronomy 6:5 ("You shall love the LORD your God . . ."), Hosea 6:6 ("I desire mercy and not sacrifice"), and the psalms of the righteous sufferer. Likewise, a careful reading of Matthew discloses the slightly submerged but pervasive influence of Israel's Wisdom literature. Matthew's citations and allusions range across the entirety of the biblical canon and—partly because of the phenomenon of textual interweaving—encourage readers to see Israel's Scripture as a vast, complex, but cohesive cloud of witnesses prefiguring the reality that comes to expression with new clarity in Matthew's Gospel.

How, then, shall we characterize that reality? Rowan Williams has proposed that the death and resurrection of Jesus led to a prolonged process of "reorganization of religious language," a process to which the New Testament documents are our earliest witnesses. If anything, "reorganization" is too modest a word to describe Matthew's engagement with Israel's Scripture. We might more accurately speak of a "transfiguration," with emphasis on the *figural* dimension of Matthew's interpretative vision. What sort of shape is given to Israel's Scripture by Matthew's interpretations? Our findings may be summarized under four headings.

Scripture as Israel's story. Matthew reads Israel's Scripture, in the first instance, neither as a collection of rules and commandments nor as an anthology of isolated predictions about the Messiah but as a story that outlines a broad arc of God's dealings with Israel. It is a story whose plot may be summed up in the following narrative sequence: election, kingship, unfaithfulness, exile, messianic salvation. This is precisely the plot sketched in the opening genealogy and in the metaphorically prefigurative Scripture citations in the birth and infancy narrative. This sequence—with the pattern of exile and return at its center—creates the frame of reference within which we are then to interpret everything that follows in Matthew's story of Jesus. Even Matthew's predilection for reading prophetic texts as predictive oracles derives its theological intelligibility from his conviction that all of Scripture is a great coherent story in which the elements of Israel's past point toward a messianic consummation, in which God will at last be present with his people (cf. Matt 1:21-23, 28:20). This consummation transfigures the story that has gone before, and the *hermeneutically transfigured* story of Israel remains for Matthew a constitutive intertext, a *Grundgeschichte* that serves as the primary matrix for the story of Jesus.

Scripture as summons to transformation of heart, radical obedience, and mercy. Matthew's readers find themselves called into a community of rigorous, demanding discipleship, living under the radical interpretation of the law given by Jesus. They are addressed as a city set on a hill, meant to exemplify in their life together the meaning of radical obedience. In this respect, Matthew stands very close indeed to the pharisaic Judaism that is the target of so much of his polemic. The thing that sets Matthew's program apart from that of his Jewish contemporaries is not only the specific halakhic norms established by Jesus' teachings (e.g., on divorce or swearing oaths or the ethics of retaliation) but, even more fundamentally, his distinctive emphasis on the importance of inner transformation of motivations. The Torah is reconfigured into a call for transformation of the heart. Only in this way can the righteousness of Jesus' disciples exceed that of the scribes and Pharisees. Yet the call for radical obedience is given a distinctive spin by Matthew's emphasis on *mercy* as the hermeneutical key to the whole law. While insisting that the law's specific commandments remain in force (Matt 5:17-20, 23:1-3, 23:23), Matthew foregrounds mercy and forgiveness as the heart of the law's message. There remains an inevitable tension between these elements in Matthew's thought—not a contradiction, but a contrast in emphasis and sensibility. At the end of the day, if the call for rigorous obedience seems to clash sometimes with the call for forgiveness of sinners, how is the tension to be resolved? Matthew provides no systematic solution, but the tendency of his hermeneutical strategy is to valorize mercy (or, as in 22:34-40, love) as the deepest reality that provides the critical framework within which particular commandments are to be interpreted. Once again, here we find a significant reconfiguration of Torah, in contrast to other Jewish construals of Matthew's day.

Scripture as prefiguration of the Christ. This is perhaps the point at which our findings require the most substantial corrective of popular perceptions of the Gospel of Matthew. Matthew's christological hermeneutics cannot be understood as random cherry picking of a few juicy prophetic proof-texts. Instead, this Gospel creates a subtle and ever-shifting range of *figural* patterns that invite us to discern narrative correspondences between Jesus and many different Old Testament precursors: Isaac, Moses, David, Jeremiah, Wisdom, the Servant, the Righteous Sufferer, the Son of Man, and more. And underlying this kaleidoscopic variety of typologies, the most fundamental prefiguration is Matthew's astounding identification of Jesus as Emmanuel, God with us. How can the diverse stories of Israel's Scripture all point somehow to the single figure of Jesus? The answer implicit in the complex figural design of Matthew's Gospel is that the scriptural stories are all, in one way or another, designed to disclose something about the identity of God. When Jesus/Emmanuel appears on the narrative stage, we are enabled to recognize that he is "something greater" than all his predecessors in earlier chapters of the story, while he also gathers into himself the significations imbedded in their stories. He can do so because he is *simultaneously* the messianic bearer of Israel's destiny in whom "all righteousness" is at last fulfilled *and* the embodiment of Israel's God, the possessor of all authority who will be present to his people to the end of the age. Matthew's Gospel offers no evidence that its author has attempted to articulate this paradoxical reality in ontological or propositional terms. The Council of Chalcedon lies far in the future, and its conceptual categories lie outside Matthew's horizon. Nonetheless, the narrative typologies woven into Matthew's story help to create the theological puzzles that Chalcedon and its successors sought to solve. How can Jesus be both Israel and the embodiment of Israel's God? Matthew does not explain, but he affirms *narratively* that both descriptions are true of the central figure in his Gospel.

Scripture as call for mission to the nations. Matthew narrates a vision of the followers of Jesus as a community that is both loving and radically obedient to Jesus' transfigured Torah. One of the key purposes for the existence of such a community in the world is to bring Gentiles to the light, so that they too can become disciples. In the overall design of Matthew's narrative, Jesus' exhortation in the Sermon on the Mount to "let your light shine before [others], so that they may see your good works and give glory to your Father in heaven" (Matt 5:16) prefigures the "Great Commission" with which the Gospel ends (28:18-20). The outsiders who are to see the light surely must include those Gentiles who previously sat in darkness (4:16). The disciples' vocation to show this light is nothing other than an extension and fulfillment of the charge given by God to Israel in the prophecy of Isaiah: "I will give you as a light to the nations, that my salvation may reach to the end of the earth" (Isa 49:6). Further, as we have seen, by carrying out this mission the disciples will effect the fulfillment of Daniel's vision of the Son of Man's ἐξουσία over all nations. Thus, Matthew's reconfiguration of Israel's Scripture as a manifesto for mission provides the final, eschatological element in the narrative reading of Scripture. By making disciples of all nations, the followers of Jesus draw them into the final chapter of the story of Israel, a chapter in which God's people are sustained and guided by the presence of the risen Son of Man, until the end of the age.

All four of these elements are, arguably, organic developments of first-century Jewish thought and practice. Matthew envisions Israel redeemed and brought back from exile, living in radical obedience to God, under the leadership of a messianic deliverer who will rule benevolently over the nations. It is not difficult to find analogies to this vision in other Jewish texts of the later Second Temple era and its immediate aftermath: the *Psalms of Solomon*, the Qumran scrolls, and 1 Enoch immediately come to mind. Matthew fits recognizably within this landscape of Jewish eschatological expectations. Yet his narrative also constitutes a striking transformation of these expectations, for Matthew performs a hermeneutical transfiguration of Torah that depends at every point on his narrative presentation of the singular authority of the one man Jesus, Emmanuel. In the light of Jesus' rising, Israel, Torah, Messiah, and the nations all assume a new shape. All must be understood anew if all authority in heaven and on earth has been given to the Jesus whose story Matthew tells.

Chapter 3

The Gospel of Luke
The Liberation of Israel

"He has brought down the powerful from their thrones,
and lifted up the lowly;
he has filled the hungry with good things,
and sent the rich away empty.
He has helped his servant Israel,
in remembrance of his mercy,
according to the promise he made to our ancestors . . ."

§11 CONTINUING THE SCRIPTURAL STORY
Luke as Interpreter of Scripture

Of all the Evangelists, Luke is the most intentional, and the most skillful, in narrating the story of Jesus in a way that joins it seamlessly to Israel's story. As Nils Dahl aptly observed, Luke is seeking to write "the continuation of biblical history."[1] The overall design of Luke's two-volume work, accordingly, highlights God's purpose in fulfilling the promise of redemption for his people Israel.

From the opening words of his narrative, Luke seeks to provide assurance (τὴν ἀσφάλειαν, Luke 1:4) for his readers that Israel's story has come to its true consummation in the death and resurrection of Jesus and in the outpouring of the Spirit on the community of Jesus' followers. These events are characterized by Luke as "the things that have been *brought to fulfillment* (πεπληροφορημένων) among us" (Luke 1:1). His choice of language suggests the overflowing fullness of the saving power of God that has been poured out into the present time. It is no coincidence that forms and derivatives of πίμπλημι and πληρόω (both meaning "fill") and Πληροφορέω ("bring to fullness/fulfillment") appear no fewer than fifteen times in the first four chapters of this Gospel. Luke is seeking to reassure his implied readers—symbolized by "Theophilus," the probably fictive addressee[2]—that the story of Jesus constitutes the fulfillment of the story of Israel; therefore, he retells the story of Jesus "in good order" (καθεξῆς, 1:3) in order to highlight, with considerable narrative skill, the coherence of the epic story that runs from Adam (3:38) through Abraham to Jesus and on into the life of the church.

It is illuminating to compare Luke's practice of intertextual narration to Matthew's. Matthew's formula quotations—which appear in the form of "voiceovers," explicit authorial commentary on the story—appear to treat the Old Testament as a book of inspired oracles pointing to future events fulfilled in the singular person of Jesus. Luke's Gospel, by contrast, contains very few such overt interpretive directives from author to reader, and it conceives the relation between Israel's Scripture and Jesus' career in a subtly different manner. Luke sees the Old Testament not merely as a collection of *predictions* about a future Messiah but rather as a book of self-involving *promises* made by God to the people Israel: through his covenant promise, God has bound himself to this particular people and can therefore be trusted to rescue them from oppression. Further, Luke repeatedly highlights the *ecclesiological* implications of those promises: they find their fulfillment not only in the life of Jesus but also in the continuing history of a people prepared for the Lord.[3]

Luke's narrative design unfolds the pattern of promise and fulfillment with graceful skill. Scriptural intertexts appear chiefly in two ways. First, in Luke's Gospel direct quotations of Scripture are almost always found *in the mouths of characters* in the story, not in overt authorial commentary.[4] This narrative device imparts to Luke's intertextual citations a *dramatic* character; readers are required to interpret the intertextual relations in light of the narrative's unfolding plot. To take a leading example, to which we shall return later in our discussion, the meaning of Isaiah 61:1-2 in Luke's account is shaped by Luke's placement of the Isaian words in the mouth of Jesus at the inauguration of his activity in Galilee, as Jesus begins his ministry of healing and teaching with a public proclamation in the synagogue in Nazareth (Luke 4:16-21). The number of these explicit quotations, however, is surprisingly small, though many more are to be found in the second volume of the story, the Acts of the Apostles.

Second, most of the intertextual references in the Gospel itself are implicit correspondences, suggested through the literary devices of allusion and echo. To be sure, the opening two chapters of the Gospel create a vivid expectation of the fulfillment of scriptural promise, and the concluding resurrection appearance stories assert forthrightly that Moses and the Prophets and the Psalms are somehow fulfilled in Jesus (Luke 24:25-27, 44-47). Yet, in between these signposts, the narrative offers, for the most part, only elusive hints and reminiscences of Old Testament precursors. Luke "ripples with intertextuality" because it constantly folds Old Testament textual patterns into its story.[5] The effect of this narrative technique is to lure us into the work of close, retrospectively alert reading, seeking to discern and interpret the intertextual clues woven into the fabric of the story.

Luke's diction and imagery repeatedly evoke fragmentary Old Testament prefigurations of the story of Jesus. We might picture his narrative technique in the following way: it is as though the primary action of the Gospel is played out on center stage, in front of the footlights, while a scrim at the back of the stage displays a kaleidoscopic series of flickering sepia-toned images from Israel's Scripture. The images can flash by almost unnoticed; however, if the viewer pays careful attention, there are many moments in which the words or gestures of the characters onstage mirror something in the shifting backdrop—or, possibly, the other way around. At such moments of synchronicity, the viewer may experience a flash of hermeneutical insight, as the "live action" recapitulates a scene from the older story, allowing the two narrative moments to interpret one another. But it is not Luke's style to develop sustained sequences in which the patterns coincide and run parallel; rather, almost as soon as we recognize one such narrative convergence, the moment has passed, and a different image appears on the backdrop, perhaps suggesting an entirely different set of linkages. For purposes of analysis, we can freeze the action and study it slowly. But that is not the effect created for the reader or hearer of Luke's narrative. The story keeps moving and leaves us with a powerful but indistinct sense of analogy between God's saving acts for Israel in the past and the new liberating events coming to fulfillment in the story of Jesus.[6]

Thus, many of the Old Testament echoes in Luke do not function as direct typological prefigurations of events in the life of Jesus. Rather, they create a broader and subtler effect: they create a narrative world thick with scriptural memory. The Gospel scenes are played out on a stage with scenery familiar to the reader who remembers the biblical drama. The things that happen in Luke are the *kinds* of things that happened in the tales of the patriarchs and prophets, and the plotted action, while never simply identical to the Old Testament stories, is often suggestively reminiscent of Israel's sacred past. It is as though we are hearing, throughout Luke's Gospel, subtle musical variations on a theme. Most significantly, the character of God portrayed in this Gospel is consistent with his character as displayed throughout Israel's history: this God who elects the people of Israel, judges their faithlessness, and still acts in unexpected ways to redeem them is recognizably the same God the reader knows from previous episodes of the story.

The biblical coloration of Luke's narration creates one more important effect: a sense of *anticipation*. In a very early scene, we are told by a heavenly messenger, the angel Gabriel, that Jesus will be given the Davidic throne and that he will reign forever over the house of Jacob (Luke 1:30-33). In light of Luke's opening declaration that he plans to write a narrative about "the things that have been brought to fulfillment among us" (1:1), we expect to see the angelic word validated by Jesus' elevation to the throne and the establishment of his kingdom. Yet the events of the Gospel story do not obviously bear out this expectation, as indicated by the fact that the apostles are still asking, in the opening scene of Luke's second book, "Lord, is this the time when you will restore the kingdom to Israel?" (Acts 1:6). Thus, the biblical promises and allusions throughout the first book create a foreshadowing of things to come. Or, to return to the realm of musical metaphor, the allusions produce a suspension that awaits resolution. As the associations between Jesus and various Old Testament precursors accumulate throughout the Gospel, we find ourselves wondering ever more urgently when and how he will assume the role promised in the story's beginning and whether his finally disclosed identity will integrate and fulfill the wide range of typological roles suggested by the many tantalizing intertextual motifs sounded throughout the Gospel. In short, Luke's Gospel story sets up narrative expectations that are satisfied or brought to closure only in Acts. The Gospel—like Israel's Scripture—points beyond itself.

Because the aim of the present study is to survey and compare the four Gospels as interpretative engagements with Israel's Scripture, we cannot treat Acts in detail. But neither can we ignore it; precisely because Luke's Gospel contains anticipations of themes that become fully intelligible only in Luke's second book, our reading of the Gospel will sometimes

necessarily draw in material from Acts in order to shed light on the dangling expectations created by the story. Yet we do well to remember that,
whatever Luke's original literary intentions might have been, the Gospel
of Luke had a long history of transmission and reception as a constituent
element of the fourfold Gospel, apart from its continuation in the Acts
of the Apostles.[7] Even if Luke leaves some loose narrative threads in his
Gospel, the book can still be read in its own right as a coherent, if unfinished, telling of the story of Jesus.

§12 THE PROMISE OF ISRAEL'S LIBERATION
Israel's Story in Luke's Narrative

The story of Israel's liberation: Recollections of divine promise
and signs of hope

In the opening scenes of his Gospel, Luke signals that "the things
brought to fulfillment among us" (Luke 1:1) have to do with God's long-
awaited action to liberate Israel from captivity to oppressive powers—a
theme that sounds repeatedly in the first two chapters of the story. We
find here no direct explanation of Israel's plight or of how the nation
came to be in "the hands of our enemies" (1:74). Luke simply assumes
the reality of such a condition and picks up the story with the dawning
of signs of hope.

In Luke's annunciation story (1:26-38), the angel Gabriel appears to
Mary with a momentous proclamation about the child she is destined to
bear: "This one will be great, and he will be called the Son of the Most
High, and the Lord God will give to him the throne of his father David.
And he will reign over the house of Jacob forever, and of his kingdom
there will be no end" (1:32-33). In these words, the reader who knows Israel's story will hear a strong echo of the Lord's promise to David through
the prophet Nathan: "I will raise up your seed after you, who shall come
forth from your body, and I will establish *his kingdom*. He shall build a
house for my name, and I will establish *the throne of his kingdom forever.*
I will be a *father* to him, and he shall be a *son* to me" (2 Sam 7:12b-14a).
The effect, then, of Gabriel's words is to kindle the reader's expectation
that God's ancient promise to David will now find its fulfillment, despite
the intervening years of exile, in an everlasting kingdom ruled by a king
who is both son of David[8] and son of the One who gave the promise.
This interpretation assumes a reader whose "encyclopedia of reception"
includes knowledge of the story of God's promise to David, which is also

recalled and elaborated in Psalm 89.[9] Characteristically, Luke is content to *allude* to this well-known messianic promise[10] without any citation formula, without any overt cues to the reader to read intertextually.

The presence of the angelic figure Gabriel is another intertextual clue whose significance eludes many modern Christian readers. In Israel's Scripture, Gabriel appears only in the apocalyptic visions of Daniel (Dan 8:16, 9:21), where he brings a word of divine reassurance that the time of the people's persecution and suffering is near its end. His role in Daniel 9 is particularly significant, because there Gabriel appears in response to a fervent prayer in which Daniel confesses Israel's sin and begs God to forgive and to act for the sake of Jerusalem and the people who bear God's name. Gabriel, coming "in swift flight at the time of the evening sacrifice," declares that Daniel is "greatly beloved" and that after many catastrophic events there will be "a decreed end" to the power of the oppressive ruler who has desecrated the sanctuary. "Thus, Gabriel, in both Daniel and Luke, symbolizes the renewal of God's involvement among his people."[11] In both texts Gabriel announces their impending rescue; he is a harbinger of hope and liberation for Israel.

Luke's emphasis on the theme of divine promise appears even more clearly in the joyful songs and prophecies that dominate the remainder of his birth and infancy narrative. In Mary's *Magnificat* (Luke 1:46-55), she praises the Lord not just for the remarkable conceptions that she and her kinswoman Elizabeth have experienced but also—indeed, primarily—for the way in which these pregnancies portend God's saving action for the downtrodden nation:

> He has helped Israel his servant,
> in remembrance of his mercy,
> just as he spoke to our fathers,
> to Abraham and to his seed forever.

> (Luke 1:54-55)

The language and themes of Mary's song (bringing down the powerful and lifting up the lowly) are strongly reminiscent of the song of Hannah in 1 Samuel.[12]

> Hannah prayed and said,
> "My heart exults in the LORD;
> my strength is exalted in my God.
> My mouth derides my enemies,

because I rejoice in my victory.
There is no Holy One like the LORD,
no one besides you;
there is no Rock like our God.
Talk no more so very proudly,
let not arrogance come from your mouth;
for the LORD is a God of knowledge,
and by him actions are weighed.
The bows of the mighty are broken,
but the feeble gird on strength.
Those who were full have hired themselves out for bread,
but those who were hungry are fat with spoil.
The barren has borne seven,
but she who has many children is forlorn.
The LORD kills and brings to life;
he brings down to Sheol and raises up.
The LORD makes poor and makes rich;
he brings low, he also exalts.
He raises up the poor from the dust;
he lifts the needy from the ash heap,
to make them sit with princes
and inherit a seat of honor.
For the pillars of the earth are the LORD's,
and on them he has set the world.
He will guard the feet of his faithful ones,
but the wicked shall be cut off in darkness;
for not by might does one prevail.
The LORD! His adversaries shall be shattered;
the Most High will thunder in heaven.
The LORD will judge the ends of the earth;
he will give strength to his king,
and exalt the power of his anointed."

(1 Sam 2:1-10)

Once again, however, Luke does not directly quote the precursor text; rather, he subliminally evokes it, so that the reader who knows 1 Samuel will hear Mary singing a harmonious descant to Hannah's song of praise.

Both of these hymns expand their praises beyond the immediate occasion of childbirth to celebrate God's vindication of the people as a whole, symbolized in 1 Samuel 2:10 by images of the shattering of God's adversaries and the exaltation of God's anointed king (LXX: καὶ ὑψώσει κέρας χριστοῦ αὐτοῦ).[13] It is not merely coincidental that the language of Hannah's song reappears in Psalm 113, the first of the cycle of Hallel psalms sung before the Passover meal in Jewish tradition; the Passover celebrates God's powerful intervention to "raise the poor from the dust and lift the needy from the ash heap" (1 Sam 2:8; Ps 113:7) by bringing Israel out of Egypt.[14] If the hearers of Luke's Gospel understood this link between Hannah's hymn of deliverance and the Passover, they might well have understood that Mary's song, too, should be heard in this same tradition, as a song celebrating the impending deliverance of Israel, this time through Mary's own offspring.

Such an interpretation once again presupposes a reader whose encyclopedia of reception is formed by Israel's scriptural story and its interpretation within Jewish tradition. Readings of this kind recognize that Luke's scriptural allusions frequently depend upon the trope of *metalepsis*. In order to grasp the force of the intertextual reference, the reader must recover the unstated or suppressed correspondences between the two texts.

At the same time, Mary sings of God's promise "to Abraham and to his descendants forever" (Luke 1:55), alluding directly to the Genesis stories of God's election and call of Israel's forefather Abraham (e.g., Gen 12:1-3, 17:1-8, 18:18, 22:15-18).[15] Of course, the news of the pregnancy of the previously barren Elizabeth, who along with her husband Zechariah was "advanced in days" (Luke 1:7), has already summoned up echoes of the story of Abraham and Sarah, who were granted in old age the miraculous conception of Isaac, the heir through whom God's covenantal promise was realized.[16] Luke does not line up the stories in the directly typological fashion we might have expected: in Luke's birth narrative, it is the mother of John the Baptist, not the mother of Jesus, who conceives a child after long barrenness and disappointment. But the evocation of this easily recognizable scriptural pattern does alert the reader to expect connections between God's gracious saving actions for Israel in the past and in the present: the same God who fulfilled his promise to Abraham is now at work again in the events of Luke's story. That is why the stories "rhyme." Mary's song declares that the unexpected pregnancies given to her and to Elizabeth are a reminder and a sign that God has not forgotten his promises.

Further, in light of what we (and perhaps Luke's early readers?) know about Paul's exegesis of the story of Abraham and Sarah (Gal 3 and Rom 4), we may wonder whether Luke's reference to the Abrahamic promise also adumbrates the extension of the blessing to "all the nations of the earth" (Gen 22:18; cf. Gen 12:1-3). Certainly this theme would be consonant with the narrative program of the Acts of the Apostles: "For the promise is for you, for your children, and for all who are far away, everyone whom the Lord our God calls to him" (Acts 2:39). Indeed, Luke's inclusion of the Gentiles in the blessing promised to Israel is a major theme of his two-volume work, and it repeatedly influences his handling of biblical citations. A characteristic example is his citation of Isaiah 40 in the account of the preaching of John the Baptist: Luke finds the quotation of Isaiah 40:3 in his Markan source, but he expands the quoted material to include the entirety of Isaiah 40:3-5, so that it climaxes in the proclamation that *"all flesh* shall see the salvation of God" (Luke 3:3-6). By means of this deft stroke of intertextual narration, Luke's introduction of the Baptist's preaching evokes the universal thrust of Isaiah 40–55 and prefigures the Gentile mission described in Acts. While this reading of the tradition may represent a major bend in the river of Second Temple Jewish eschatological hope[17]—a case of giving people a new past to live with that would change their future indefinitely—it also highlights the deeper continuity of the epic story of God's election and redemption of Israel. In Luke's telling, God's intent to reveal salvation to all flesh was part of Israel's plotted role from the beginning.

The theme of God's promise to Israel is highlighted once again in the prophecy of Zechariah (Luke 1:67-79). After the birth of John, Zechariah finds his tongue loosed by the power of the Spirit (1:67) and declares that Israel's God

> spoke through the mouth of his holy prophets from of old,
> promising salvation from our enemies and from the hand of
>   all who hate us—
> to show us mercy along with our fathers,
> and to remember his holy covenant,
> the oath that he swore to Abraham our father,
> to grant us, that we, being rescued from the hands of our enemies,
> might serve him without fear, in holiness and righteousness
> before him all our days.
>
> (Luke 1:72-75)

Here again, Luke interprets Israel's Scripture as the medium of divine promise of Israel's deliverance. Zechariah's speech is specifically characterized as a word of prophecy (Luke 1:67), declaring in advance what will come to pass in the narrative that is to follow. Readers of the Acts of the Apostles will perceive retrospectively that, for Luke, the promise is

brought to fulfillment in a most unexpected way through the work of the
Holy Spirit in forming the church, a community that serves and glorifies
God in holiness and righteousness.

The figure of Abraham is once again invoked here (Luke 1:73),
reminding the reader a second time (cf. 1:55) to read Luke's story of Jesus
as the fruition of the Genesis tale of election and promise. Further, Zechariah's prophecy also invokes the image of "a horn of salvation for us in
the house of his servant David, as he spoke through the mouth of his
holy prophets from of old" (1:69-70). Thus, both of the two major effu-
sions of praise in Luke 1 (Mary's and Zechariah's) link God's new saving
work to the promises made to *Abraham* and *David* in Israel's Scripture.[18]
By the end of the first chapter of the Gospel, then, Luke has given the
reader abundant clues that his story of Jesus is to be read as the narrative
continuation of Israel's story and as the liberating climax toward which
that story had moved.

The conclusion of Zechariah's prophecy declares that the aim of
God's revelatory saving action will be "to guide our feet into the way of
peace" (Luke 1:79). Luke thus invokes the prophetic vision of *shalom* as the
goal of God's liberating action. As we shall see, in Luke's overall composition the emphasis on *peace* suggests a powerful implicit critique of other
contemporary Jewish hopes for Israel's liberation through violent means.

Remarkably, older redaction-critic studies of Luke were often blind
to these themes of liberation and the programmatic significance of the
story of Israel, perhaps because they tended to regard the Lukan birth
and infancy material as coming from a pre-Lukan source that could not
be assumed to represent Luke's own theology.[19] Of course Luke works
from sources, as he tells us in the Gospel's opening words (Luke 1:1-4).
But surely even if this material is derived from a source, we must ask why
Luke has given it such prominence in his composition and what narrative
effects are created by its placement at the beginning of the story. When
we attend in this way to the overall shape of Luke's narrative, it becomes
evident that these opening chapters play a crucial hermeneutical role:
they construct a bridge, effectively linking the story of Jesus to Israel's
past and setting the framework of expectation for all that follows.[20]

In many ways small and great, then, Luke weaves connecting threads
between his story and its scriptural antecedents. After the shepherds
report what the angels of the heavenly host have revealed concerning the
infant Jesus, Luke tells us that "Mary kept all these words (συνετήρει
τὰ ῥήματα ταῦτα) and pondered them in her heart (ἐν τῇ καρδίᾳ αὐτῆς)"
(Luke 2:19). A similar expression appears once again after the episode

of the boy Jesus' staying behind in the Jerusalem temple to talk with the teachers; following Jesus' unnerving reply to Mary's scolding ("Did you not know that I must be in my Father's house?"), Luke remarks that she "kept all these words in her heart (διετήρει πάντα τὰ ῥήματα ἐν τῇ καρδίᾳ αὐτῆς)" (2:51). In these passages, there is no scriptural quotation, or even anything that could be considered a clear allusion. But the reader steeped in Scripture might well hear an echo of Genesis 37:11, in which Jacob ponders the words of his similarly precocious son Joseph, who had reported prophetic dreams signifying his own future lordship over his parents and eleven brothers. Jacob scolds him for talking presumptuously; however, the narrator then remarks, "So his brothers were jealous of him, but his father *kept the word* (διετήρησεν τὸ ῥῆμα)" (Gen 37:11 LXX). Both in Genesis 37 and in Luke 2, we find a loving parent given pause by the apparently grandiose claims of a young son who will later undergo suffering but then in fact turn out to be vindicated as an elect bearer of God's special favor; in both texts the parent "keeps" the word/words and ponders them.[21] For the reader who hears it, this echo in Luke 2 creates a sense of anticipation: Will Jesus, like Joseph, rise to a position of authority and offer life-giving help even to those of his own people who have rejected him? The Lukan story can of course be read smoothly apart from any such intertextual connection. But for readers who perceive the ripple of Pentateuchal echo, the dramatic foreshadowing of the Lukan scene is intensified.

But there is perhaps still one more echo lingering in these Lukan passages. In Daniel 7, Daniel is given a revelatory interpretation of his vision of four terrible beasts that are ultimately supplanted by the "one like a Son of Man," who receives dominion over "all peoples, nations, and languages" (Dan 7:13-14). After hearing the interpretation, Daniel concludes his visionary account in this way: "I, Daniel, was seized by exceeding astonishment, and my face changed, and I fixed the word in my heart (τὸ ῥῆμα ἐν καρδίᾳ μου ἐστήριξα)" (7:28 LXX). Here the LXX's verb ἐστήριξα differs from the compounds of τηρεῖν found in Luke 2:19 and 2:51, but the pattern of a disturbing word "fixed/kept *in the heart*" (a phrase not present in Gen 37:11 but used in both Lukan texts) might evoke in the knowledgeable reader stirrings of reminiscence, particularly since, in both Daniel 7 and Luke 2, the word "kept in the heart" offers a prophetic foreshadowing of the deliverance and vindication of Israel through the person of an exalted messianic figure whose kingdom will have no end (cf. Luke 1:33; Dan 7:14).

The same sort of intertextual counterpoint illustrated by this example continues to play throughout Luke's story. One of the most commonly recognized instances of this narrative technique of intertextual echo appears in Luke's account of the transfiguration (Luke 9:28-36). This is a triple-tradition story, and Luke's account generally follows Mark fairly closely. But Luke distinctively adds the remark that Moses and Elijah "were discussing *his exodus* (τὴν ἔξοδον αὐτοῦ), which he was going to *fulfill* (πληροῦν again) in Jerusalem" (9:31). Of course, the Greek word ἔξοδος can mean simply "departure"—as it is rendered in modern English translations such as the NRSV and NIV. Such a translation, however, obscures Luke's subtle hint of a correspondence between Jesus' passion/resurrection and Israel's exodus from bondage in Egypt.[22]

On the other hand, one looks in vain for Luke to develop a consistent allegory or typology in which the whole Gospel story sequentially replays the exodus events.[23] Instead, he drops the hint, then moves on. And by the time we reach Luke 9:51-62, the intertextual references have to do not with Exodus but with the cycle of Elijah narratives: Jesus' being "taken up" (Luke 9:51/2 Kgs 2:9-12); fire from heaven (Luke 9:54/1 Kgs 18:20-40; 2 Kgs 1:9-13); followers warned not to look back from the plow to say farewell to family (Luke 9:59-62/1 Kgs 19:19-21).[24] Even here, the shifting patterns are complex. In Luke's story Jesus will indeed, like Elijah, be taken up to heaven (Luke 24:51; Acts 1:9-11), but Jesus emphatically rejects the disciples' call for Elijah-like vengeance of fire from heaven on those who fail to receive him, and his summons to discipleship is even more radically uncompromising than that of Elijah, who did, after all, grumpily allow Elisha to follow him after first returning and feasting with his own people. The intertextual linkage works not only as a positive parallelism but also as a *dissimile*, marking Jesus' distinctive identity by his simultaneous likeness to and difference from Elijah.[25]

It is no accident that Luke 9 contains fleeting reminiscences of the stories of both Moses and Elijah, the two great Old Testament figures who appear with Jesus on the mountain of transfiguration. But Luke does not permit his readers to linger over either one as a distinctively privileged precursor or typological pattern. Instead, they appear on the flickering backdrop, lending depth and resonance to the story of Jesus; then the images shift again, and the story moves on.

Passing intertextual echoes of this kind appear on virtually every page of Luke's Gospel. Luke 12 offers a collection of teaching material, mostly addressed to Jesus' disciples, counseling them to be prepared for opposition and persecution (Luke 12:4-12, 49-53) and to beware of entanglement in concern for material possessions (12:22-31). They are to sell their possessions and give alms, confident that it is the Father's pleasure to give them the kingdom (12:32-34). This confident counterintuitive counsel is framed by intense eschatological expectation that the day of judgment will reveal all hidden motives (12:1-3) and that the Son of Man will come at an unexpected hour (12:35-48). In the midst of this discourse, we come upon the admonition "Let your loins be girded (Ἔστωσαν ὑμῶν αἱ ὀσφύες περιεζωσμέναι) and your lamps lit" (12:35). Contextually in Luke 12, there is no reference to a specific time or place in which the disciples are to be prepared in this way; rather, the language is metaphorical, exhorting them to live in a state of constant readiness for the coming kingdom by giving generously and leading unencumbered lives. But the metaphor of girded loins is not simply a general admonition; instead, the language echoes very specifically the directive given to Israel concerning how to eat the Passover meal in preparation for the flight from Egypt:

> This is how you shall eat it: *your loins girded* (LXX: αἱ ὀσφύες ὑμῶν περιεζωσμέναι), your sandals on your feet, and your staff in your hand; and you shall eat it hurriedly. It is the passover of the LORD. For I will pass through the land of Egypt that night, and I will strike down every firstborn in the land of Egypt, both human beings and animals; on all the gods of Egypt I will execute judgments: I am the LORD.
>
> (Exod 12:11-12)

By evoking the language of the first Passover, Luke 12:35 suggests—in this distinctively Lukan passage—that Jesus' disciples are to interpret their own situation analogously: God's judgment is coming, so they must be prepared to be on the move at a moment's notice. Yet for those who are participants in this new time of Passover, the judgment of God is not something to fear; it is instead a moment of impending deliverance and freedom. The poignant fusion of warning and celebration that pervades Luke 12 is captured vividly in this fleeting intertextual echo of the exodus story.

This is a good illustration of the way in which the *volume* of intertextual echo is enhanced by the prominence or familiarity of the precursor text. Exodus 12 is not some obscure bit of scriptural narrative: it is a familiar story that Israel recalls year in and year out in its celebration of the Passover.[26] By using the phrase "your loins girded," we see that Luke deftly links the church's present identity to the foundational story of Israel's liberation.[27] Unfortunately, the NRSV's paraphrase of Luke 12:35 ("dressed for action") completely obscures its close verbal correspondence to Exodus 12:11. This sort of translation is both symptom and cause of the inability of readers of English translations to perceive the densely intertextual character of Luke's narrative.

In Luke 14:1-24, the Evangelist draws on a different part of the Pentateuchal narrative to highlight continuity between Jesus' teaching and Israel's traditions. The passage contains several units of distinctive Lukan material, linking meals and feasting to the coming kingdom of God. The scene opens with an account of Jesus, at a sabbath meal in the home of "a leader of the Pharisees," healing a man with dropsy (14:1-5). Staring down the disapproval of "the lawyers and Pharisees," Jesus defends his provocative action of healing on the sabbath: "If one of you has a child or an *ox* that has *fallen* into a well, will you not immediately pull it out on a sabbath day?" In part, this saying is merely an appeal to common sense, but it is also more than that. In the narrative context of a confrontation with expert interpreters of the Torah, Jesus' challenge derives its particular force by its implicit halakhic appeal to the logic of Deuteronomy 22:4: "You shall not see your neighbor's donkey or *ox fallen* on the road and ignore it; you shall help to lift it up." Jesus' act of healing on the sabbath, then, becomes a sign: Jesus is both performing and proclaiming the liberation of Israel in a way that draws hermeneutically on motifs already present in Israel's story. His mission stands in continuity with Torah, not in contradiction to it.[28]

Likewise, Jesus' counsel to the dinner guests to sit at the lowest place rather than seeking a place of honor (Luke 14:7-11) is a reprise of advice already given in Israel's Wisdom literature: "Do not put yourself forward in the king's presence or stand in the place of the great; for it is better to be told 'Come up here,' than to be put lower in the presence of a noble" (Prov 25:6-7). In the Lukan narrative context, however, this teaching becomes more than a pragmatic hint about court etiquette; it is implicitly a directive about how the coming kingdom should impinge already on the present, producing a reversal of values and status.[29] In the eschatological kingdom of God, the last will be first and the first last (Luke 13:30); therefore, those who are Jesus' followers should begin already to assume roles of lowliness (cf. Luke 22:24-27).[30]

In Luke 14:12-14, Jesus poses one more pointed challenge to his host: when you give a dinner party, Jesus proposes, you should not invite your affluent friends and relatives. Rather, you should invite "the poor, the crippled, the lame, and the blind" (14:13). While this advice may appear counterintuitive in light of ancient Mediterranean notions of friendship and reciprocity, it is thoroughly consistent with the Lukan vision of social reversal that surfaced already in Mary's programmatic song in the first chapter of the Gospel (1:51-53) and even more emphatically in Luke's version of the beatitudes and woes (6:20-26): God deflates the pretensions of the rich and fills the hungry with good things. This is precisely the kingdom-of-God vision articulated in Jesus' parable of the great dinner at which the guests will be "the poor, the crippled, the blind, and the lame" (14:15-24; note especially 15:21, where Luke inserts this same phrase again, an emphasis unparalleled in Matthew's similar parable, Matt 22:1-10). And yet this rebalancing of resources should not be perceived as a novelty in Israel; it is profoundly consistent with the commandments of Deuteronomy concerning the economic practices required of the people Israel when—after their liberation from bondage in Egypt and their long sojourn in the wilderness—they at last enter the land. Every third year, they are to store up "the full tithe of your produce for that year" to create resources not only for the Levites (who own no land) but also for "the resident aliens, the orphans, and the widows in your towns, that they may come and eat their fill so that the LORD God may bless you in all the work that you undertake" (Deut 14:28-29). The passage is not quoted in Luke 14; there is not even a direct verbal echo. Yet it is clear that Jesus is calling his Pharisaic host to a fuller and more radical vision of Israel's identity as a liberated people, living in realization of the Deuteronomic vision.

Our final example is one of Luke's most distinctive stories of reversal, the parable of the rich man and Lazarus (Luke 16:19-31). Once again, there is no direct quotation of Scripture here. Yet the teaching of Moses and the prophets is at the heart of the passage. In this powerful and familiar fable, a rich man who lives in ostentatious luxury and the poor beggar Lazarus undergo a dramatic change of fortunes in the afterlife: the poor man is comforted in the presence of Abraham, while the rich man is tormented in the flames of Hades.

The story has long disturbed interpreters because it gives no explicit explanation for the postmortem fates of its central characters. Lazarus is not described as particularly virtuous, nor is there any indication that the rich man's wealth was ill-gotten. For that reason, the tale might appear to suggest that wealth is evil in principle. Such a reading fails, however, to understand the story in the context of its scriptural background. The rich man receives condemnation not simply because he was wealthy but because he was ignoring his obligations to God under the covenant God made with Israel. How do we know that? There is one irrefutable piece of evidence: the poor man Lazarus starving on the ground outside his house, hoping to rummage through the rubbish to find something to eat (Luke 16:20-21).

Why is the presence of a starving beggar evidence of covenant violation? We should first recall the Deuteronomic directive noted above that Israel should store up resources within their towns so that the transients and orphans and widows might come and eat their fill (Deut 14:28-29). If we pick up the story at that point in Deuteronomy, we find that Moses goes on to give even more explicit instructions about the response to poverty that God desires:

> If there is among you anyone in need, a member of your community in any of your towns within the land that the LORD your God is giving you, do not be hard-hearted or tight-fisted towards your needy neighbor. You should rather open your hand, willingly lending enough to meet the need, whatever it may be.
>
> (Deut 15:7-8)

The presupposition of such teaching on sharing of wealth is that Israel is a covenant community of brothers and sisters who share a common history of deliverance from bondage in Egypt and a common call to manifest the righteous purpose of God in their life together by seeking to ensure that "there will be no one in need among you" (Deut 15:4).

The rich man in the parable was signally failing to heed this call. Lazarus languished "at his gate," and the rich man ignored him. That is why the judgment is so harsh on the rich man. Oblivious to Lazarus, he is not merely breaking some code of civic decency; he is despising the covenant with God and selfishly seeking his own private satisfaction. Thus, he is de facto denying his bond with the Israel that God has called.

That also explains, significantly, why *Abraham* appears as a central character in this parable. The text does not say that Lazarus was carried by the angels to *heaven*. Rather, it says he was carried to *the bosom of Abraham* (Luke 16:22).[31] This otherwise puzzling detail signifies that Lazarus is embraced by the father of the whole family of Israel. By contrast, when the rich man, in torment, belatedly appeals to Abraham as "Father" (16:24), he is claiming a link with the covenant community, hoping to get his share also of the family benefits. But this appeal to Father Abraham comes far too late. Readers of Luke's Gospel will recall the earlier warning of John the Baptist: "Bear fruits worthy of repentance. Do not begin to say to yourselves, 'We have Abraham as our father.' ... Every tree that does not bear good fruit is cut down and thrown into the fire" (3:8-9). By the time the rich man seeks to reclaim this family tie with Israel through Father Abraham, he discovers belatedly that he is such a tree that has not borne good fruit, and so he has been thrown into the fire. His own selfish choices have placed "a great chasm" between him and the place where Lazarus and Abraham feast together. Readers of the parable—within the literary framework of Luke's Gospel—should hear an echo from Mary's song: "He has put down the mighty from their thrones, and exalted those of low degree. He has filled the hungry with good things, and the rich he has sent empty away" (1:52-53).

That looks like it should be the end of the parable: the great reversal has occurred; Lazarus is comforted; the rich man is tormented. End of story. But it is not the end of the story. The parable goes on. Abraham pronounces that a great chasm has been fixed, and it is too late for the rich man to receive any comfort or help. Then, resigned to his fate, the rich man appeals to Abraham to send Lazarus back from the dead to warn his five brothers. Abraham—probably thinking of Deuteronomy 15—shrugs and comments that they have already received ample warning from Moses and the prophets. But the rich man, knowing his own family, realizes that they are not disposed to take the Bible too seriously. Ah, but if Lazarus could be sent to them like Dickens' ghosts of Christmas, perhaps even these Scrooges could repent. The biblical texts are too unimpressive; what is needed is a spectacular supernatural sign to get their attention. Then comes Abraham's chilling final reply: "*If they do not hear Moses and the prophets, neither will they be convinced if someone should rise from the dead.*" There is the twist in the second part of the parable: no sign will be given to this faithless generation. Those who hear the word of Scripture and respond with mercy and compassion for the poor will be welcomed into the kingdom of God. But for those who ignore the call of Moses and the prophets to share their goods with their poor brothers and sisters, *even Jesus' resurrection* will remain a mute, meaningless apparition.

Obedience to Torah exemplified

As the parable of the rich man and Lazarus suggests, Luke's narrative places a high value on obedience to God's law. While Luke lacks a programmatic pro-nomistic statement equivalent to Matthew 5:17-20, he nonetheless scatters many hints throughout the story that literal obedience to Torah is praiseworthy—and thereby creates another line of continuity between Israel's story in the past and the continuation of that story into the world of his readers. Luke valorizes Torah-obedience not through direct didactic statements, but through narratives that *exemplify* it.

The motif of law-observance emerges forcefully in the birth and infancy stories. Zechariah and Elizabeth are introduced, in strongly Deuteronomic language, as "righteous before God (δίκαιοι ἐναντίον τοῦ θεοῦ), walking blameless in all the commandments and ordinances of the Lord (πορευόμενοι ἐν πάσαις ταῖς ἐντολαῖς καὶ δικαιώμασιν τοῦ κυρίου ἄμεμπτοι)" (Luke 1:6; cf. Deut 4:40). Luke highlights Elizabeth's status as a "daughter of Aaron" and Zechariah's priestly role (1:5, 8-10). He also mentions that they observed the commandment to circumcise their son on the eighth day, in accordance with Genesis 17:12 and Leviticus 12:3. There is of course nothing unusual about this; it was normal Jewish practice. But it is Luke alone among the Evangelists who makes a point of narrating the circumcision of John the Baptist in accordance with provisions of Torah. And it is Luke alone who relates the divine command that John should not "drink wine or strong drink," in implicit accordance with the requirements for priests serving in the tent of meeting (Lev 10:9) or persons living under a Nazirite vow (Deut 6:3).

Similarly, Luke alone among the Evangelists goes out of his way to tell us that the parents of Jesus scrupulously obeyed the laws concerning circumcision of a male child (Gen 17:9-12); likewise, they brought the infant Jesus to be presented to the Lord in the Jerusalem temple and offered sacrifice for him as well as for the postpartum ritual purification for his mother Mary, in accordance with the prescriptions of Leviticus 12:2-8 and Exodus 13:1-2, 12, 15. Luke regards these acts of obedience to Torah as being of sufficient importance to merit explicit comment and citation of the relevant Pentateuchal passages—almost the only instances in his two-volume work of such direct authorial commentary (Luke 2:21-24).[32] (Interestingly, Luke's notation that they offered "a pair of turtle-doves or two young pigeons" indicates, in accordance with Lev 12:8, that they could not afford to offer a sheep; thus, we are subtly informed that Jesus' parents are not only law-observant but also poor.)[33] Further, Luke also mentions that Jesus' parents went up every year to celebrate the festival of the Passover in Jerusalem (2:41). The net effect of these narrated details is to show that Jesus was grounded from his birth in a devout, poor, but Torah-obedient family.[34]

Against this background, it comes as no surprise that, after his baptism by John, the adult Jesus resists the devil's temptations by quoting a sequence of three texts from Deuteronomy, texts that in their original narrative setting emphasize the vital importance of obedience to the Torah (Luke 4:1-12; quoting Deut 8:3, 6:13, and 6:16). In the opening chapters of the Gospel, then, Luke has set the scene for Jesus' subsequent ministry, preparing readers to interpret it in continuity rather than conflict with the law of Moses. Luke's Jesus is no renegade seeking to revise or reject God's commandments; to the contrary, Jesus is a radically obedient son living in harmony with the covenant given to Israel.

Reminders of this motif surface throughout the story. For instance, when Jesus heals a leper, he immediately commands him to go and show himself to the priest, making the offering commanded by Moses (Luke 5:12-14; alluding to Lev 14:1-32).[35] Or again, when Jesus is asked by a lawyer (νομικός) what is necessary to gain eternal life, he throws the question back on his interlocutor by asking, "What is *written in the law*? How do you read?" The clear implication is that Jesus regards the teaching of the Torah as giving a sufficient answer to such a question. And indeed, when the lawyer responds by formulating the double love command, quoting Deuteronomy 6:5 and Leviticus 19:18, Jesus endorses his answer: "You have answered rightly; do this, and you will live" (Luke 10:25-28). Here Luke's account differs interestingly from the parallels in Mark 12:28-34 and Matthew 22:24-40, where it is *Jesus* who first articulates the double love commandment. Luke's telling of the story has the effect of emphasizing that Jesus brings no new revelation; rather, Jesus simply reinforces what Israel's teachers of the law already knew well. In the tradition of Israel's prophets, he is simply summoning the leaders of the people to obey the law already given to them.

Later in the narrative, as Jesus draws closer to Jerusalem, he is asked exactly the same question again (Luke 18:18-25). The questioner is "a certain ruler," who inquires, "What must I do to inherit eternal life?" This time, Jesus answers the question directly by saying, "You know the commandments," and then citing five of them from the second table of the Decalogue (referring to Exod 20:12-16; Deut 5:16-20). When the man replies that he has kept all these commandments since his youth, Jesus imposes another requirement: he should sell all his possessions, distribute the money to the poor, and follow Jesus. Here we are left with some uncertainty about whether following Jesus should be understood as an additional commandment beyond the Torah or whether Jesus' demand for divestment of worldly goods is simply a radicalization of the tenth and final commandment against coveting (Exod 20:17; Deut 5:21)—the one commandment pointedly omitted from Jesus' initial summary of the commandments. Perhaps the rich ruler's attachment to his possessions indicates that he has *not* kept the commandment against coveting his neighbor's goods. But either way, Luke's narrative implies that following Jesus commits the disciple to a life of uncompromising obedience to God's law.

The demand for uncompromising obedience is expressed even more starkly in Jesus' earlier challenge to the crowds that were drawn to him: "If anyone comes to me and does not hate his own father and mother and wife and children and brothers and sisters, he is not able to be my disciple" (Luke 14:26). This daunting teaching echoes Deuteronomy 33:8-9, in which Moses pronounces a blessing on Levi because he "said of his father and mother, 'I regard them not'; he ignored his kin, and did not acknowledge his children. For they [i.e., the sons of Levi] observed your word, and kept your covenant."[36] That passage in turn refers to Exodus 32:25-29—part of the episode of the golden calf—in which the sons of Levi rally to Moses' call to take arms against those who have committed the sin of idolatry; they go back and forth through the camp killing their brothers, friends, and neighbors. By alluding obliquely to this grim episode, Jesus challenges the crowd of would-be followers to reckon with the radical implications of joining his movement. Yet at the same time, this Old Testament story of murdering one's own kin is given a significant metaphorical twist in Luke's narrative, for the summarizing climax of Jesus' challenge to the crowds is this: "So, therefore, none of you who do not say farewell to all your own *possessions* can be my disciple" (Luke 14:33). Hating one's family now becomes a matter of surrendering attachments by leaving home and relinquishing material security, rather than drawing the sword in violence.

For Luke, the meaning of radical obedience is exemplified most decisively in the passion narrative, where Jesus suffers violence rather than inflicting it on others. Luke shares this narrative pattern with the other Gospels, but he focuses attention on it even more clearly in his account of Jesus' arrest on the Mount of Olives. Distinctively among the Evangelists, Luke tells us that at the moment of the arrest, Jesus' followers ask him, "Lord, should we strike with the sword?" (Luke 22:49). Without waiting for an answer, one of them does strike the slave of the high priest and cuts off his ear, a narrative detail found in all four Gospels. But again distinctively among the Evangelists, Luke relates Jesus' response in this way: "But Jesus said, 'No more of this!' and, touching the ear, he healed him" (22:51). One could hardly imagine a clearer indication that the Lukan vision of covenant obedience eschews the violence of the sword and depicts Jesus' mission in terms of healing—even the healing of enemies.

At the same time, this radically nonviolent interpretation of Torah-obedience suggests that the characters in the story who seek Jesus' death, even if they imagine themselves to be defenders of the law, are actually violating it, a theme that later surfaces explicitly in the apostolic speeches in Acts, most pointedly in the dramatic climax of Stephen's speech that leads to his martyrdom:

> You stiff-necked people, uncircumcised in heart and ears, you are forever opposing the Holy Spirit, just as your ancestors used to do. Which of the prophets did your fathers not persecute? They even killed those who declared in advance the coming of the Righteous One, the one whose betrayers and murderers you have now become. *You are the ones that received the law as ordained by angels, and yet you have not kept it.*
>
> (Acts 7:51-53)

Stephen's accusation is itself rich in scriptural echoes of charges uttered against unfaithful Israel in the past by Moses and the prophets—for example, "stiff-necked people," Exodus 33:3, 5; "uncircumcised heart," Leviticus 26:41; "uncircumcised ears," Jeremiah 6:10; "opposing the Holy Spirit," Isaiah 63:10; persecuting and killing prophets, 1 Kings 19:10, 14, and Nehemiah 9:26. These biblical resonances not only strengthen the bill of indictment against those in Israel who reject Jesus but also reinforce Luke's positive depiction of Jesus and his followers as the ones who are truly faithful to God's covenant with Israel.

Yet, in Luke's story, Jesus' faithfulness also entails his clinging to hope for the ultimate forgiveness and deliverance of Israel. The theme of Torah-faithfulness is most powerfully exemplified in his intercessory prayer from the cross: "Father, forgive them, for they do not know what they are doing" (Luke 23:34). This prayer implicitly appeals to an important distinction in the Torah between two different kinds of sin. In Numbers 15:22-31 there is an extended discussion of the means of atonement for the people if they "unintentionally fail to observe all these commandments that the LORD has spoken to Moses." If violation of the law has occurred "unintentionally without the knowledge of the congregation," then a burnt offering may be offered to "make atonement for all the congregation of the Israelites, and they shall be forgiven; it was unintentional." On the other hand, "whoever acts high-handedly, whether a native or an alien, affronts the LORD, and shall be cut off from among the people. Because of having despised the word of the LORD and broken his commandment, such a person shall be utterly cut off and bear the guilt." It would appear, then, that the dying Jesus' prayer pleads a case for his own people by portraying their complicity in his execution as an act of ignorance and therefore a *forgivable* violation of God's will rather than a "high-handed" intentional defiance of God. Precisely this interpretation of the crucifixion of Jesus is repeated in the Acts of the Apostles, in speeches given by both Peter (Acts 3:17) and Paul (13:27): the people and their leaders "acted in ignorance" and can therefore be summoned to repent for what they did and to receive forgiveness. *Here again, then, we find a Lukan narrative detail that comes more clearly into focus when it is interpreted intertextually by readers whose cultural repertoire includes a detailed knowledge of Israel's law.* In Luke's story, Jesus not only remains obedient to God all the way to his death but also continues to appeal for the forgiveness of unfaithful Israel by invoking a defense based on specific knowledge of Torah.[37]

Throughout the concluding sequences of the Gospel, Luke continues to portray Jesus and his followers as devoutly observant Jews. Jesus' final meal with his disciples is repeatedly identified (in agreement with Mark and Matthew) as a Passover meal (Luke 22:1, 7-8), and Jesus tells them, "I have eagerly desired to eat this Passover with you before I suffer" (22:15). Jesus prepares for the ordeal he is to undergo by observing the traditional Passover ritual and thereby fervently recalling the great story of Israel's deliverance. Then, after Jesus' death, Joseph of Arimathea requests permission to take the body down from the cross, thereby adhering to the requirement of Deuteronomy 21:22-23 that the body of an executed man must be buried the same day, so as not to defile the land.[38] Further, after recounting that the women who saw where the body of Jesus was laid made burial preparations, Luke, distinctively among the Evangelists, tells us that "on the sabbath they rested *according to the commandment*" (23:56). These seemingly small narrative details provide, in effect, an *inclusio* with the similar passing notes of Torah observance in the birth and infancy narrative of the opening chapters. Just as Jesus' family prepared the way for his life by faithful obedience to the law, so also at the end of the story his followers prepare for his burial in a way that honors God's commandments.

God's kindness and mercy to Israel

Despite Luke's positive narration of faithfulness to Torah by various human characters in the story, it would be deeply misleading to suppose that this is his primary point of theological emphasis. The chief function of Luke's references to law-observance is to create a symbolic world, to situate the story in time, place, and culture, and thereby to align his tale with the dramatic arc of Israel's history with God. And it is *God* who is the chief actor in that story.[39] In the songs of the birth narrative, it is God who is the subject of the key verbs. The characters joyfully confess that it is *God* who has shown strength with his arm, *God* who has brought down the powerful and lifted up the lowly, *God* who has remembered his promises and helped his servant Israel. It is *God* who has redeemed his people and shown the mercy promised to the patriarchs in the past, in remembrance of his covenant. It is by the tender mercy of *God* that "the dawn from on high will break upon us" (Luke 1:78). This is neither the language of religious achievement nor the language of plodding submission to inexorable divine requirements. Rather, it is the language of praise and thanksgiving for God's gracious, incalculable life-giving power, which has shown itself particularly in acts of faithfulness toward Israel.

Much of what needs to be said about God and God's faithfulness shall be considered when we examine how Luke uses Scripture to narrate the identity of Jesus, in whom the divine faithfulness is decisively enacted. But even apart from the specific account of Jesus' actions, Luke's Gospel affirms the graciousness of God in language that draws upon Israel's scriptural traditions. Particularly telling is the passage in the Sermon on the Plain in which Jesus tells his audience to love their enemies and to lend without expecting to receive anything in return (Luke 6:27-38). Two reasons are given for following this counterintuitive counsel. First, those who act in this way will receive a great reward. But the second reason is even weightier: ". . . you will be children of the Most High; for he is kind (χρηστός) to the ungrateful and the wicked. Be merciful (οἰκτίρμονες), just as your Father is merciful (οἰκτίρμων)." Jesus' followers are called to be kind and merciful because they will thereby mirror the character of the God they serve—indeed, they will be his children, bearing his likeness in the world.

Although the passage is substantively parallel to a similar teaching in Matthew's Sermon on the Mount (Matt 5:43-48), the specific wording of Luke 6:35-36 is completely different from Matthew's[40] and unparalleled elsewhere in the Gospels. The two adjectives that Luke uses here to describe God, χρηστός and οἰκτίρμων, are not randomly chosen; both evoke rich scriptural resonances.

The confession that God is χρηστός sounds again and again throughout the LXX Psalms. To take a single example, Psalm 85:5 LXX addresses

God gratefully: "For you, LORD, are kind (χρηστός) and gentle and abounding in mercy to all who call upon you." Here, as typically elsewhere in the Psalms, χρηστός renders the Hebrew טוב. English versions often render it as "good." This is an accurate translation of the Hebrew, but it does not entirely capture the semantic nuance of the Greek word, which can carry the connotation of "kind" or "gracious," as the usual English translations of Luke 6:35 rightly indicate. But readers of English translations will miss the way in which Luke 6:35 echoes the confessional tradition of the Psalms in declaring that God is good/kind.[41] And upon closer examination of the context in which such language appears in the Psalms, we see that the description of God as χρηστός is not merely a vague character attribute: it refers specifically to God's gracious acts of covenant faithfulness toward Israel. For particularly telling examples, see Psalm 105:1 LXX and Psalm 106:1 LXX (106:1 MT/107:1 ET), where the confession that the Lord is good/kind (χρηστός) introduces lengthy recitations of the ways in which God has redeemed and delivered his people Israel despite their heedlessness and sinful ways.

Similarly, Luke's declaration that God the Father is merciful (οἰκτίρμων) is evocative of one of the most fundamental confessions of Israel's faith, the narrative of the epiphany to Moses on Mount Sinai:

> The LORD descended in the cloud and stood with him there, and proclaimed the name, "The LORD." The LORD passed before him, and proclaimed, "The LORD, the LORD, a God merciful (LXX: οἰκτίρμων) and gracious, slow to anger, and abounding in steadfast love and faithfulness, keeping steadfast love for the thousandth generation, forgiving iniquity and transgression and sin, yet by no means clearing the guilty, but visiting the iniquity of the parents upon the children and the children's children, to the third and the fourth generation."
>
> (Exod 34:5-7)

The characterization of God as "merciful and gracious, slow to anger and abounding in steadfast love" becomes a repeated formulaic element in Israel's language of confession and prayer, appearing in many texts verbatim, or with minor variations, once again including a number of Psalm texts.[42] Given the familiarity of this language, and its central importance in Israel's story, no one familiar with the LXX could miss hearing the scriptural echo in Luke 6:36. To say that God is "merciful" evokes a foundational element of the biblical story of Israel's God.

Interestingly, there is one psalm that links these two ascriptive adjectives together in close parallelism. In Psalm 144:8-9 LXX, the psalmist sings:

The LORD is merciful (οἰκτίρμων), and compassionate;
slow to anger, and abundant in mercy.
The LORD is good (χρηστός) to the whole creation;
and his mercies (οἱ οἰκτιρμοί) are over all his works.

Psalm 144:8 itself closely echoes the fundamental confession of Exodus 34:6 (with the effect of emphasizing God's mercy as shown in the Mosaic covenant), while Psalm 144:9 seemingly expands the scope of God's kindness from his specific graciousness to Israel to encompass the whole of all that God has made. The logic of the psalm seems to anticipate the expansive scope of Jesus' teaching in Luke 6:35-36. Or, to put it the other way around, the Lukan passage echoes the full resonances of the psalm, which, in turn, invokes the story of the revelation of God's name on Sinai.

Thus, the description of God offered in Jesus' teaching strongly affirms continuity with Israel's confessional tradition. The thing that is new here in Luke's Gospel, however, is the explicit call for the hearers to conform their own actions and character to the kind and merciful character of God, an exhortation not found in any of the biblical passages cited above. God's kindness to Israel is meant to call forth a similar responsive kindness in Jesus' hearers. For the most part, however, Luke's allusions to the scriptural narratives of God's kindness do not serve this sort of hortatory purpose in which God's character is proposed as a paradigm for human conduct; instead, they are meant to frame the story of Jesus as the climax of the continuing story of Israel and thereby to evoke faith, praise, and (as we shall see) repentance.

Isaiah's vision of new exodus

Prominent among the past acts through which God's faithfulness to Israel was made known was the miraculous announcement of the end of exile, the return of the people from Babylonian captivity to reinhabit the land of Israel and rebuild the temple in Jerusalem. This return was of such significance in Israel's salvation history that the prophet Isaiah celebrated it in language that portrayed it metaphorically as a new exodus, a second journey through the desert to return to the land of promise.[43] It is therefore significant that Luke heralds the beginning of Jesus' public activity by linking the proclamation of John the Baptist with images taken from Isaiah 40, the pivotal chapter announcing the end of Israel's exile and the promise of return.

> [John the son of Zechariah] went into all the region around the Jordan, proclaiming a baptism of repentance for the forgiveness of sins, as it is written in the book of the words of the prophet Isaiah,
>
>> "The voice of one crying out in the wilderness:
>> 'Prepare the way of the Lord, make his paths straight.
>> Every valley shall be filled, and every mountain and hill
>>   shall be made low,
>> and the crooked shall be made straight, and the rough
>>   ways made smooth;
>> and all flesh shall see the salvation of God.'"
>
> (Luke 3:3-6; citing Isa 40:3-5 LXX)

Luke of course finds the connection between John's preaching and Isaiah 40 already present in Mark 1:2-4, but he has made several significant editorial moves. First, he has disentangled Mark's conflated citation, moving the material from Malachi 3:1/Exodus 23:20 away from this initial account of John's ministry to a later place in the story, where it becomes part of Jesus' own explanation of the meaning of John's prophetic role (Luke 7:24-28).[44] This change not only corrects the apparent inaccuracy of Mark's quotation but, more importantly, in this introductory passage, sharpens the Lukan focus on "the book of the words of the prophet Isaiah" (Luke 3:3). Luke's citation of Isaiah also makes several minor adjustments of the LXX text.[45] But his most important editorial decision is to quote a much lengthier chunk of material from Isaiah 40. Whereas Mark (followed by Matthew) cites only Isaiah 40:3, Luke continues the quotation nearly to the end of Isaiah 40:5 LXX, so that it builds to a climax and concludes with the clause "and all flesh shall see the salvation of God (τὸ σωτήριον τοῦ θεοῦ)."

This artful piece of editing frames the citation as a ringing preview of Luke's overall compositional design.[46] This prominently placed citation of Isaiah 40:3-5, the third and last authorial citation of Scripture in Luke's entire two-volume work, announces in advance that the coming of Jesus will portend not only the end of Israel's exile but also the mission that extends salvation to "all flesh"—that is, to the Gentiles as well as the people of Israel. It is not coincidental that the final words of Paul at the

conclusion of Luke's second volume echo this same passage: "Let it therefore be known to you that this 'salvation of God' (τοῦτο τὸ σωτήριον τοῦ
θεοῦ) has been sent to the Gentiles, and they will listen" (Acts 28:28).[47]
The redundancy of the demonstrative pronoun and definite article in this
phrase has the effect of marking the expression τὸ σωτήριον τοῦ θεοῦ as
a quotation, a quotation of Isaiah 40, already cited in full for the reader
of Luke–Acts in the opening chapters of the Gospel.

Similarly, Luke's account of the presentation of the child Jesus in the
temple has already painted a diptych of witnesses who interpret Jesus'
career as a confirmation of Isaiah's promises to Israel. First, when Luke
introduces the elderly Simeon, he describes him as "righteous and pious,
awaiting the consolation of Israel" (Luke 2:25)—a consolation that he now
declares himself to have witnessed: "for my eyes have seen your salvation (τὸ σωτήριόν σου), which you prepared (ἡτοίμασας) in the presence
of all the peoples, a light for revelation to Gentiles, and for glory to your
people Israel" (2:30-32). The noun σωτήριον directly links this passage
with the passage from Isaiah 40 that appears explicitly in Luke 3:6, and
the verb ἡτοίμασας may be a subtler echo of the same text. These anticipatory ripples of Isaiah 40 in 2:30-32 are instances of the *Vorklang* of an
allusion, faint sympathetic soundings that precede a louder citation later
in the same text.[48] The phrase "light for revelation to Gentiles" (φῶς εἰς
ἀποκάλυψιν ἐθνῶν) also alludes unmistakably to Isaiah, where it is prophesied that God's Servant will be "a light to the nations" (εἰς φῶς ἐθνῶν,
Isa 42:6, 49:6). In the second of these two references, the purpose of that
light is made more explicit: "that my *salvation* may reach to the end of the
earth"—a passage later cited explicitly in Acts 13:47 by Paul and Barnabas
as a prefiguration and warrant for their ministry to Gentiles. Most interesting of all, however, is Luke's statement that Simeon was awaiting "the
consolation (παράκλησιν) of Israel." The theme of *consolation* is the keynote
sounded at the beginning of Isaiah's prophecy of return and restoration:
"Comfort, comfort my people (LXX: Παρακαλεῖτε, παρακαλεῖτε τὸν λαόν
μου), says God" (Isa 40:1). In other words, to say that Simeon was awaiting
"the παράκλησις of Israel" can mean only one thing: he was remembering
Isaiah 40 and awaiting the fulfillment of Isaiah's prophecy that Israel's
time of punishment and exile would come to an end.

This interpretation is further reinforced by the second passage in
Luke's temple diptych (Luke 2:36-38). The prophetess Anna praises God
and speaks about the child Jesus "to all who were awaiting the redemption of Jerusalem" (λύτρωσιν Ἰερουσαλήμ, 2:38).[49] Here Luke's diction
subliminally echoes Isaiah 52:9:

> Break forth together into singing, you ruins of Jerusalem;
> for the Lord has *comforted* his people,
> he has *redeemed Jerusalem.*

So Anna joins Simeon in joyfully declaring that the long story of Israel's exile and hope is at last reaching its dramatic fulfillment in the arrival of the child Jesus. Luke ends his scene at this point, but the reader who knows Isaiah will perceive the metaleptic effect, recalling the way in which this unit of Isaiah's oracle concludes in the verse following the one to which Luke has alluded:

> The Lord has bared his holy arm before the eyes of *all the nations;*
> and all *the ends of the earth shall see the salvation of our God.*

(Isa 52:10)

Once again, the allusion to Isaiah has the effect of joining the redemption of Jerusalem with the motif of proclaiming God's salvation to the whole Gentile world. God's faithfulness to Israel, fully understood in light of these Isaian subtexts, also necessarily entails the mission to the Gentiles that will unfold over the course of Luke's two-volume composition.

The ending of Luke's Gospel signals the reader that the story has not ended with the resurrection of Jesus, but that this mission to the world is only beginning. When the risen Jesus appeared to his disciples, Luke tells us, "he opened their minds to understand the Scriptures." The content of that understanding is summarized under three concise headings: "And he said to them, 'Thus it is written: that the Messiah is to suffer, and to rise from the dead on the third day, *and that repentance and forgiveness of sins is to be proclaimed in his name to all nations* beginning from Jerusalem" (Luke 24:46-47). The narrative unfolding of proclamation to the nations occurs only in Luke's second volume, but it has already been significantly foreshadowed in the first, through echoes of Isaiah. Thus, the Gospel of Luke points readers beyond the self-enclosed world of its own ending, just as the canonical book of Isaiah points to a future not fully realized. Presumably, it is in these Isaian texts that we should look to find where "it is written" that the Gentiles are finally to be included as recipients of the proclamation of forgiveness of sins—a proclamation addressed initially to Israel in Isa 40:1-2.[50]

Judgment, repentance, and forgiveness

At the same time, however, in Luke's story, God's faithfulness to Israel is not a matter of a simple proclamation of amnesty. As Luke 24:47 indicates, the message that is to be preached to all nations includes a summons to *repentance*. Furthermore, the apostolic preaching about Jesus in Acts declares that he has been appointed as the eschatological judge of the world: "He [Jesus] commanded us to preach to the people and to testify that he is the one ordained by God as judge of the living and the dead" (Acts 10:42; cf. 17:31). The fate of individuals in this judgment hangs upon their response to the proclaimed word; those who reject it judge themselves "unworthy of eternal life" (Acts 13:46). As Peter explains in his sermon in Solomon's Portico of the Jerusalem temple, the division of the people between those who respond to the word and those who do not was already foreshadowed in Israel's Scripture:

> Moses said, "The Lord your God will raise up for you from your own people a prophet like me. You will listen to him, whatever he speaks to you." But it will be that everyone who does not listen to that prophet "will be utterly destroyed out of the people." And all the prophets, as many as have spoken, from Samuel and those in sequence after him, also proclaimed these days.
>
> (Acts 3:22-24)

While the reference to a prophet like Moses is clearly a citation of Deuteronomy 18:15, in the Lukan context there is a play on the word ἀναστήσει ("raise up"). Originally in Deuteronomy, it referred to God's causing a prophet to emerge from among the people;[51] however, we have already heard Peter, in his Pentecost sermon, using precisely this same verb to refer to Jesus' resurrection from the dead: "This Jesus God raised up (ἀνέστησεν)" (Acts 2:32). Thus, readers of Acts 3:22 will recognize a double sense in the prophecy that God would "raise up" a prophet like Moses. It is precisely *the resurrection* that marks out Jesus as this prophet. Further, the Deuteronomic admonition to "listen to him" has already been spoken of Jesus by the heavenly voice at the transfiguration (Luke 9:35) in a context where Moses and Jesus are seen together. Thus, the identification of Jesus as the prophet like Moses promised in Deuteronomy is evident.

Our present interest, however, lies in the punishment threatened in Acts 3:23 for those who refuse to listen. The passage in Deuteronomy 18 does mention a dire consequence for those who do not heed God's prophet: "I myself will hold [them] accountable" (Deut 18:19; LXX reads, "I will take vengeance [ἐκδικήσω] on him"). But the wording of Acts 3:23 does not correspond at all to any text of Deuteronomy 18:19, either in the MT or in the LXX. Instead, Acts 3:23 reads, ἐξολεθρευθήσεται ἐκ τοῦ λαοῦ: "he will be utterly destroyed from the people." The NRSV renders Acts 3:22-23 as though it were a single continuous quotation, but it is better to understand it, as in the translation given above, as the consecutive quotation of two *different* passages.

The phrase "will be utterly destroyed from the people" or its close equivalent occurs a number of times in the Pentateuch. Invariably it is the judgment pronounced on persons who are guilty of disregarding God's law and/or desecrating something holy. Such offenses include neglecting the command of circumcision (Gen 17:14), eating leavened bread during the Passover (Exod 12:15, 19) or failing to observe the Passover when on a journey (Num 9:13), using holy oil for ordinary anointing of the body (Exod 30:33), profaning the sabbath (Exod 31:14), failing to bring animals sacrificially slaughtered to the tent of meeting to offer them as sacrifices to the Lord (Lev 17:4, 9), eating blood (Lev 17:14), approaching the consecrated offerings in a state of ritual uncleanness (Lev 22:3) or defiling the sanctuary through corpse impurity (Num 19:20), doing work on the Day of Atonement (Lev 23:29-30), or acting "high-handedly" by despising the word of the Lord (Num 15:30-31). The last of these offenses seems particularly pertinent to the concerns of Acts 3:22-24, but it is probably inappropriate to peg Peter's pronouncement of judgment to any single one of these Old Testament laws. The point is more generally that *on the analogy of these Old Testament sanctions* anyone who fails to listen to Jesus as God's appointed prophet will be guilty of despising and profaning the means provided by God for atonement and for marking the identity of his own people.

For that reason, faith and repentance are the essential elements of right response to the proclaimed word about Jesus, and it is this response that leads to the forgiveness of sins, as definitively articulated in Peter's Pentecost sermon in Acts 2:

> Repent and be baptized every one of you in the name of Jesus Christ so that your sins may be forgiven; and you will receive the gift of the Holy Spirit.[52] For the promise is for you, for your children and for all who are far away [and as we will learn in the unfolding of the narrative, this includes Gentiles], everyone whom the Lord our God calls to him.
>
> (Acts 2:38-39)

That is the summons toward which the plot of Luke's Gospel builds. It is chiefly a word of promise, grounded in the gracious consolatory proclamation of Isaiah that the time of Israel's exile is over, that the time of forgiveness of sins has come near, and that this word of blessing will now extend to all nations. And yet, an ominous undertone remains. Jesus, the one through whom the promise is realized, is set in place by God, as Simeon warns, "for the falling and rising of many in Israel, and as a sign that will be opposed" (Luke 2:34). There is perhaps a distant echo here of Isaiah's prophecy of a stumbling-stone that will cause many to fall (Isa 8:14).

Be that as it may, the story that Luke tells weaves together these complex motifs from Israel's epic narrative. God is a gracious God who is kind, merciful, and patient. He reaches out again and again to deliver and restore Israel when they rebel and fall away. But, as in Exodus 34:6-7, this merciful God "will by no means clear the guilty" if they reject the grace offered to them. This paradoxical dialectic between judgment and grace is carried forward throughout Luke's account. Indeed, the inconclusive ending of Acts serves, among other things, to leave open the question of the church's mission and the world's response to it.[53] If the Gospel of Luke therefore poses a theological conundrum, this result follows from Luke's tenacious adherence to the story of Israel as the hermeneutical matrix for understanding the story of Jesus. Because the God narrated in Luke's Gospel is the same God revealed to Moses and the prophets, and because Luke's unfolding story of the kingdom of God is the fulfillment of that same God's promises, it should come as no surprise that the same mysterious tension between compassion and judgment that we find in Israel's Scripture plays itself out again in the pages of Luke's story. Luke can describe the sacking of Jerusalem by armies as the apocalyptic "days of vengeance, to fulfill all the things that are written" (Luke 21:22). But at the same time, he is confident that the word of the Lord that has come near in Jesus is finally a message for "the consolation of Israel" (2:25). From start to finish in Luke, it is this hopeful word of God's deliverance that predominates and prevails as he patiently and subtly teaches his readers how to read Israel's Scripture with new eyes. And the key to that reading lies in understanding the identity of Jesus as the promised liberator of Israel.

§13 JESUS AS THE REDEEMER OF ISRAEL

In the final chapter of Luke's Gospel, we meet two new characters, Cleopas and his unnamed companion, despondently trudging away from

Jerusalem toward the village of Emmaus (Luke 24:13-35). The crucifixion of their leader Jesus has dashed their dreams. They had dared to believe that he might be the hoped-for messianic figure who would rescue Israel from oppression, but his swift and brutal execution by the Roman imperial forces had doomed that expectation—or so they thought. In a scene of exquisite dramatic irony, the risen Jesus appears and walks with them, unrecognized. He asks what they are discussing, and Cleopas, comically oblivious to the identity of this new traveling companion, asks, "Are you the only stranger visiting Jerusalem who doesn't know what has been happening in these days?" (24:18).

The ironic gap between Cleopas' presumption of superior knowledge and his actual ignorance of Jesus' identity prepares the reader, who has already been informed by the narrator in Luke 24:15-16 that the stranger is Jesus, to interpret the dialogue that follows as a hermeneutical corrective to the preresurrectional understanding of Jesus that the Emmaus pilgrims articulate. The two on the road describe Jesus as "a man, a prophet powerful in deed and word before God and all the people" (24:19; cf. the inadequate understanding of the crowds, as reported in 9:19). Despite his prophetic powers, however, Jesus had been put to death by the chief priests and rulers—hence, the disappointment of these disciples' fervent expectation: "But we had hoped that he was the one who was going to redeem (λυτροῦσθαι) Israel" (24:21).

These poignant words recall precisely the expectation aroused in the glad songs of the Gospel's birth narrative. Zechariah, filled with the Holy Spirit, had declared it in these terms:

> Blessed be the Lord, the God of Israel,
> for he has visited his people and made redemption (λύτρωσιν) for them.
> And he has raised up a horn of salvation for us
> in the house of his servant David.
>
> (Luke 1:68-69)

Consequently, the wistful lament of the Emmaus disciples retraces the experience of the sympathetic reader who has followed the story closely. Why has Israel seemingly not been redeemed? Why has Israel not yet found "salvation from our enemies and from the hand of all who hate us" (Luke 1:71)? The death of Jesus appears to confirm that those enemies still have Israel's fate firmly in their grip. Even the report that some women had found the tomb empty has appeared to Cleopas and friend as a puzzling oddity, the account perhaps of a religious "vision" but nothing like the new messianic kingdom for which they had been hoping (24:22-24).

Much hangs, then, on Jesus' reply:

> And he said to them, "O foolish and slow of heart to trust in all that the prophets spoke! Weren't these things necessary: for the Messiah to suffer and enter into his glory?" And beginning from Moses and from all the prophets, he thoroughly interpreted for them *the things concerning himself in all the Scriptures.*
>
> (Luke 24:25-27)

Luke's sketchy summary is tantalizing, for it does not explain exactly how "all the Scriptures" might be read as testimony to Jesus. The effect of this episode is to bring us up short and send us back to the beginning of the Gospel to reread it, in hopes of discerning more clearly how the identity and mission of Jesus might be prefigured in Israel's Scripture. This second reading of the Gospel will be a retrospective reading in light of the resurrection,[54] seeking to find submerged correspondences between "Moses and the prophets" and the mysterious stranger who chastises us as "slow of heart" for failing to discover such correspondences on our first reading.[55]

The dramatic irony of Luke's Emmaus story implies that if we understand the scriptural witness about the Messiah, we will perceive that he is more than "a prophet powerful in deed and word before God and all the people." That is the true but limited preliminary understanding of Cleopas and his friend, an understanding that the veiled risen Jesus now seeks to correct. Yet—and here we encounter another layer of irony—it has become the conventional view of modern New Testament criticism that the Gospel of Luke represents a "low" or "primitive" Christology. According to this view, Luke portrays Jesus as simply a Spirit-anointed prophet, a teacher of divine wisdom, and a righteous martyr. Lacking, however, are any doctrines of preexistence and incarnation; lacking is any clear assertion of Jesus' identity with God.[56] Sometimes it is suggested that Luke follows his sources closely by keeping references to any superhuman status of Jesus out of his Gospel and reserving all "high" christological affirmations for the Acts of the Apostles, after the resurrection.[57] But, as the Emmaus story suggests, an attentive reading of Luke's Gospel gives us substantial reason to question this characterization of Lukan Christology.

Luke's distinctive portrayal of the identity of Jesus has not always been well understood for at least three closely related but distinguishable reasons. First, the categories of "high" versus "low" Christology are theologically clumsy blunt instruments that fail to reckon with the complexity of the texts.[58] Second, any assessment of Luke's understanding of the identity of Jesus must reckon with the *narrative* mode of the presentation. It will hardly do to extract a list of titles for Jesus that Luke employs in the Gospel and then extrapolate propositional statements about Luke's Christology.[59] Rather, to understand Luke's portrayal of Jesus, our reading must be attuned to Luke's subtle narrative art, for the identity of a character is best understood through the unfolding of events in a story.[60] Third, an important element of that narrative art is the way in which Luke's story evokes echoes of Israel's Scripture and thereby leads readers to a complex, intertextually formed perception of his central character. This is the decisive hermeneutical clue given in the final chapter of Luke's Gospel, as Jesus "opens the Scriptures" to his followers. They had hoped Jesus was "the one to redeem Israel." If, as Luke's ironic tale implies, they were wrong to judge that hope disappointed, then the key to understanding *how* he redeems Israel must be found in a renewed scripturally shaped understanding of Jesus as Israel's redeemer.

If we take our bearings from the Emmaus story, one more important consequence follows: the effort to find a single controlling christological title or motif can only occlude the full range of Luke's presentation of Jesus. The academic penchant for focusing on just one christological category and arguing that it constitutes the central organizing theme for the Christology of an individual New Testament author is no longer a defensible reading strategy. In the case of Luke–Acts, many different categories have been singled out—the Davidic royal Messiah,[61] the prophet like Moses,[62] or the prophets Elijah and Elisha[63]—as the key Old Testament prototypes for Luke's portrayal of Jesus. The very variety of proposals offered testifies against the exclusive centrality of any one of them. Such an approach is particularly ill-suited to account for Luke's narratively shaped christological vision. Luke tells us that the veiled risen Jesus on the road to Emmaus "thoroughly interpreted for them the things concerning himself *in all the Scriptures*" (Luke 24:27). Luke thus implies that Scripture in all its parts *comprehensively* bears witness to the identity of Jesus. If that is so, isolating any one strand out of the interwoven diversity of scriptural witnesses, while of some temporary analytical value, can finally yield only a diminished interpretation of Jesus, if the single extracted strand is taken as sufficient by itself. Instead, following the prompting of Luke 24, we shall identify several of the thicker strands of imagery that Luke weaves together in his account of Jesus. Having identified them, we shall attempt to take the measure of the total integrated portrait that emerges when the strands are seen, as Luke presents them, narratively bound together.

Jesus as the agent of liberation

The Spirit-anointed Servant. The role of Jesus as the agent of Israel's liberation is highlighted dramatically in Luke's distinctive account of Jesus' inauguration of his public ministry (Luke 4:16-30). "Filled with the power of the Spirit," Jesus returns to Nazareth after his wilderness temptation and reads Scripture in the synagogue. The passage that he selects is said to be taken from "the scroll of the prophet Isaiah" (4:17) though it is actually a conflation of two texts, Isaiah 61:1-2 and Isaiah 58:6:

> The Spirit of the Lord is upon me,
> because he has anointed me to announce good news to the poor;
> he has sent me to proclaim release to the prisoners
> and recovery of sight to the blind,
> *to send the broken ones forth in release* (ἀποστεῖλαι τεθραυσμένους ἐν
>   ἀφέσει, Isa 58:6 LXX),
> to proclaim the year of the Lord's favor.
>
> (Luke 4:18-19)

When Jesus follows this reading by declaring, "Today this scripture has been fulfilled in your hearing" (Luke 4:21), the reader of Luke's Gospel has been alerted that Jesus himself is the Spirit-anointed Servant figure whose mission is the liberation of Israel. Luke's citation of Isaiah 61 strongly links Jesus' activity to Isaiah's hope of a restored Israel, brought back from exile. Further, the fragmentary citation of Isaiah 58:6, imbedded within the passage from Isaiah 61, *metaleptically* evokes the prophetic imperative for Israel's authentic worship to be embodied through practices that establish justice:

> Is not this the fast that I choose:
> to loose the bonds of injustice,
> to undo the thongs of the yoke,
> *to let the oppressed go free* (LXX: ἀπόστελλε τεθραυσμένους ἐν ἀφέσει,
>   "send the broken ones forth in release"),
> and to break every yoke?

Is it not to share your bread with the hungry,
and to bring the homeless poor into your house;
when you see the naked, to cover them,
and not to hide yourself from your own kin?
Then your light shall break forth like the dawn,
and your healing shall spring up quickly;
your vindicator shall go before you,
the glory of the LORD shall be your rear guard.
Then you shall call, and the LORD will answer;
you shall cry for help, and he will say, Here I am.

(Isa 58:6-9a)

By invoking this passage about letting the oppressed go free, Luke's story taps into a rich and complex intertextual history. The Isaiah passage is itself intertextually referential; it resonates powerfully with the story of God's action to rescue Israel from slavery in Egypt, as we see particularly in Isaiah's reference to the vindicator going before and the glory of the Lord being the rear guard—an allusion to the pillar of cloud and fire that led Israel in the wilderness and also moved behind the people to protect them from the army of Egypt (Isa 58:8; cf. Exod 13:21-22, 14:19-20; Isa 52:12). Consequently, when Luke inserts the phrase "to let the oppressed go free" into Jesus' sabbath reading in the synagogue, he links Jesus' liberating vocation not only with the Isaianic end of exile but also with its older prototype, the exodus.

In addition to the allusive fusion of these passages, there is also a selective omission in Luke's quotation of Isaiah 61. Jesus' reading breaks off in midsentence, omitting the last part of Isaiah 61:2: "and the day of vengeance of our God; to comfort those who mourn." This sudden silence poses an interesting problem for interpretation. On one reading, Luke deletes "a day of vengeance for our God" because he wants to portray Jesus as offering a graceful word of healing and restoration, not a threat to Israel's enemies.[64] This is of course possible. On the other hand, in view of all we have seen of the Evangelists' effective use of metalepsis as a literary technique, perhaps we should not be quite so quick to suppose that the unquoted material from Isaiah 61:2 is dissonant with Luke's theological views or his narrative program.

The notion of God's punishment of the wicked is hardly absent from Luke's understanding of God's purposes. The Jesus of Luke's Gospel announces woes upon the rich and well fed (Luke 6:20-26, 12:13-21, 16:19-31); Mary's song has already foreshadowed the day when the powerful will be brought down from their thrones (1:51-53). Jesus warns that those who do not repent will perish (13:1-9), just as John the Baptist had declared (3:7-9). Those who do not "enter through the narrow door" will be excluded and left in a place where there is "weeping and gnashing of teeth" (13:22-30). The climax of many such passages in Luke appears in the apocalyptic discourse of Luke 21, in which Jesus prophesies the destruction of Jerusalem by pagan armies and, in words interestingly reminiscent of his earlier closing flourish in the Nazareth synagogue (4:21), declares that "these are the days of vengeance (ἐκδικήσεως), to fulfill all the things that are written" (21:22). In sum, Jesus' spirit-anointed proclamation of good news in Nazareth is *not* good news for the oppressors and those who oppose the work of the Spirit of the Lord. If Jesus is announcing a new exodus of liberation, this very announcement is a two-edged sword, simultaneously announcing judgment on those who resist God's liberating power. Here we see another outworking of the prophecy that Jesus' message will evoke opposition and that he will be the occasion for the falling and rising of many (2:34). On this reading, the incomplete citation of Isaiah 61:2 in Luke 4:18-19 should be heard as a classic instance of *metalepsis*: Jesus announces the acceptable (δεκτός) year of the Lord, but Isaiah's warning of the "day of vengeance" hovers unspoken over the text—and perhaps subtly informs our understanding of the consequences for those in Jesus' own country who do *not* find him "acceptable" (δεκτός, 4:24).

It is not so clear, however, that Luke and his first readers would have understood Isaiah 61:2b as an unambiguous word of negative judgment. The LXX of this verse reads: καὶ ἡμέραν ἀνταποδόσεως παρακαλέσαι πάντας τοὺς πενθοῦντας ("and a day of payback to comfort all those who mourn"). The word ἀνταπόδοσις, like the English word "payback" with which I have translated it here, is multivalent. It can and often does mean "vengeance," as when the once-great hero Samson, now blinded and in chains, prays, "Lord God, remember me and strengthen me only this once so that with this one act of revenge (LXX: ἀνταπόδοσιν) I may pay back (ἀνταποδώσω) the Philistines for my two eyes" (Judg 16:28).[65] On the other hand, "payback" can also, depending on the perspective of the reader, be a matter of joyful restitution, as in Psalm 102:2 LXX (103:2 MT): "Bless the Lord, O my soul, and do not forget all his *benefits* (πάσας τὰς ἀνταποδόσεις αὐτοῦ)." Similarly, in Psalm 18:12 LXX (19:12 MT), the ordinances of God's law are said to be more valuable than gold and sweeter than honey, because "in keeping them there is great *reward* (ἀνταπόδοσις)."[66] In the term's only appearance in the New Testament, coming from the pen of an author roughly contemporary with Luke, ἀνταπόδοσις refers to the reward of an inheritance for those who are obedient (Col 3:24).

It is likely that, despite the negative valence of the term in several other passages in Isaiah, the LXX translator understood ἀνταπόδοσις in Isaiah 61:2 in a positive sense, as shown by the syntactical parallelism of the construction in which it appears:

> The Spirit of the LORD is on me, because he has anointed me.
> He has sent me:
>> to announce good news to the poor,
>> to heal those who are crushed in heart,
>> to proclaim release to the prisoners,
>> to declare the acceptable year of the LORD *and the day of payback*
>>   (ἀνταποδόσεως),
>> to comfort all those who mourn. . . .

In the context of this string of parallel infinitive phrases, the semantic force of ἀνταπόδοσις would almost surely be heard as consolatory, meaning something like "recompense" or "restoration of fortune." Thus, working from the LXX, Luke and his readers almost surely would have understood Isaiah 61:2 in this sense. If so, the metaleptic impact of the fragmentary quotation of Isaiah 61 in Luke 4 would be to strengthen, not undermine, the connotation of gracious promise and fulfillment.

The truth is that both of these readings are possible. By leaving the quotation unfinished, Luke leaves the matter open for the reader, who will come to understand as the story unfolds that the appearance of Jesus on the scene does indeed hold out both possibilities, either destruction for those who stand against God or salvation for those who embrace the announcement of the Lord's spirit-anointed Servant.

In any case, having reflected on what Luke's Jesus does *not* say in his reading from the Isaiah scroll, we return now to the effects created by Luke's addition of the phrase "to send the broken ones forth in release." This extra line from Isaiah 58:6, inserted in this context, creates an emphatic repetition of the noun ἄφεσις ("release") in Jesus' reading of the scriptural text.[67] Jesus' mission includes both proclaiming *release* to the prisoners (Isa 61:1) and sending those who are broken into a condition of *release* (Isa 58:6). This double sounding of ἄφεσις turns up the volume of one more submerged echo in the last line of Jesus' lection: the concluding reference to "the year of the Lord's favor" (ἐνιαυτὸν κυρίου δεκτόν, following Isa 61:2) should be heard as an allusion to the year mandated by Leviticus 25, the "year of release" (25:10 LXX: ἐνιαυτὸς ἀφέσεως) in which all debts are to be cancelled and all slaves set free.[68] Thus, Luke's account of Jesus' reading of Scripture underscores the continuity between Jesus' concern for the poor—a favorite Lukan theme—and the message of the law and the prophets, as represented here by Leviticus and Isaiah.

The density of intertextual interplay in this passage is characteristic of Luke. A single short scriptural quotation, placed on the lips of Jesus at a programmatically crucial moment in the narrative, evokes at least three layers of scriptural memory. As one reads backwards from Luke's citation of Isaiah 61 and 58, they are Israel's new exodus ending the Babylonian exile, the Jubilee Year commanded by Moses, and the first exodus out of Egypt. Readers formed within Israel's encyclopedia of reception will perceive that Luke's Jesus is announcing that the time has come for all three of these prototypes to be brought to fulfillment in their hearing as Jesus performs the reading of Isaiah, both orally and in the acts that follow in the narrative. And Jesus himself takes center stage in the role of the Servant who makes God's liberating power effectual for Israel.

At the same time, however, Jesus encounters rejection in Nazareth. Indeed, he *provokes* rejection by citing biblical stories about the prophets Elijah and Elisha, who extended God's gracious power to non-Israelites such as the widow at Zarephath in Sidon (1 Kgs 17:1-16, a story that finds an important echo in Luke 7:11-17) and Naaman the Syrian (2 Kgs 5:1-14). These references anticipate the expansion of the gospel into the Gentile world—a major theme of Luke's second volume—and hint that the Gentile mission is already prefigured in Israel's Scripture. Thus, Jesus' programmatic preview of his vocation already begins to undercut the assumption that Israel is the exclusive bearer of God's favor. And this makes the people in Nazareth so angry that they want to kill him.

The hostility of the Nazareth villagers to this act of subversive Bible-reading is a clear signal that Jesus (as portrayed in Luke's Gospel) is engaged in *intertextual narration as a countercultural practice*. By bringing together texts from Isaiah about the new exodus and the liberation of Israel with texts from 1 and 2 Kings about prophetic acts of grace toward non-Israelites, Jesus sketches a new and provocative plot line for Israel's story, one in which the role of the Servant as a "light to the nations" takes on new prominence.[69] It is precisely his scriptural argument for denying Israel's exclusive privilege that is so threatening to the crowd in Nazareth.[70] Accordingly, the people's rejection of the Spirit-anointed servant Jesus illustrates the truth of Simeon's earlier prophecy that Jesus would become the catalyst "for the falling and the rising of many in Israel, and . . . a sign that will be opposed so that the inner thoughts of many will be revealed" (Luke 2:34-35).

At one and the same time, then, in Luke 4:16-30, *Jesus announces the fulfillment of the Isaianic hope of national restoration and challenges conventional conceptions of national privilege.* No other story illuminates more clearly the way in which Luke's Jesus carries forward the story of Israel's redemption while at the same time transforming that story into something different and surprising—and thereby arousing opposition and division.

The Davidic royal Messiah. In the Nazareth synagogue sermon Jesus catalyzes a scripturally grounded hope for national restoration but refuses to conform to popular expectations of what such a restoration might entail. Similar patterns of transformative appropriation of Scripture appear throughout Luke's Gospel. We have focused initially on Isaiah's figure of the salvation-bringing Servant, because that is where Luke's narrative focuses our attention at the beginning of Jesus' public activity. We turn now to consider several of the other christological motifs that ramify as the narrative develops.

Already in the Gospel's opening chapters we have encountered the prophetic expectation that Jesus would assume the role of Son of David, the expected royal Messiah who would restore the kingdom of Israel. The angel Gabriel announces to Mary that the child she is to bear will be given "the throne of his father David" and that "he will rule over the house of Jacob forever, and of his kingdom there will be no end" (Luke 1:32-33). Subsequently, this Davidic hope is reinforced by the prophecy of Zechariah, who gives thanks that "the Lord, the God of Israel . . . has raised up for us a horn of salvation *in the house of David his servant*" (1:68-69). The conclusion of this programmatic prophetic speech subtly returns to the same theme by announcing that through God's mercy, "the *Anatolē* from on high will visit us" (1:78). The Greek word ἀνατολή, which literally means "rising" or "that which rises up," conveys a delicate ambiguity. It can refer to the rising of the sun, hence "dawn"; contextually, this seems to be the most obvious meaning in 1:78, for the sentence continues with the image of the ἀνατολή as giving light to those in darkness. Yet the same word can also have a botanical meaning, referring to the "branch" or "shoot" arising from a plant. This is the meaning carried by the word in the LXX's rendering of Jeremiah 23:5 and Zechariah 3:8, 6:12, where it translates the Hebrew צמח, a reference to the hoped-for messianic seed of David: "The days are surely coming, says the LORD, when I will raise up for David a righteous Branch (LXX: ἀνατολή), and he shall reign as king and deal wisely, and shall execute justice and righteousness in the land" (Jer 23:5; cf. Isa 11:1-5). Particularly in view of the titular use of ἀνατολή in Zechariah, the term outgrows the metaphorical sense it had in Jeremiah and flowers into a messianic designation, as clearly seen in Zechariah 6:12 LXX: "Thus says the LORD, the ruler of all: Here is a man whose name is Branch (Ἀνατολή). And he shall rise up (ἀνατελεῖ) from below, and he shall build the temple of the LORD." Thus, in Luke 1:78, when a character also named Zechariah speaks of the coming of an ἀνατολή who will "give light to those who sit in darkness and in the shadow of death" (echoing Isa 9:1) and "guide our feet into the way of peace," Israel's eager hope for the rising of a Davidic ruler—as envisioned in the prophetic book of Zechariah—is not far below the surface.[71] To read the passage well, we need not exclude either possible meaning of ἀνατολή ("dawn" and "branch"); instead, we need to perceive that *both* possible meanings allude to prophetic images (one from Isaiah, the other from Jeremiah and Zechariah) associated with the hope for a future royal Davidic messiah. A sensitive reading of Luke 1:78-79 will hear both of these intertextual echoes.

This Davidic motif is reinforced in Luke's birth story by the explicit description of Bethlehem as "the city of David" (Luke 2:4) and the angelic proclamation to the shepherds that "to you is born this day in the city of David a Savior, who is the Messiah (χριστός), the Lord" (Luke 2:11). The royal messianic significance of χριστός is also presupposed in Luke's authorial remark that Simeon had been promised "he would not see death before he had seen the Lord's Messiah" (τὸν χριστὸν κυρίου, Luke 2:26). By the end of the birth and infancy narrative, then, there can be no doubt of the identification of Jesus as the one destined to assume the Davidic kingship.

Yet this theme seems to recede strangely into the background in the ensuing narrative. This has sometimes been taken as a sign that the royal Davidic material in Luke 1–2 is purely traditional and of little theological importance for Luke. But the prominence given to Davidic categories in the apostolic proclamation in Acts suggests quite the reverse.[72] To mention only the most obvious indicators, both Peter and Paul—in Luke's programmatic accounts of their preaching—explicitly interpret Jesus' resurrection as the fulfillment of David's prophetic words in the Psalms (Acts 2:22-36, 13:32-37). Peter's Pentecost sermon reaches its climax in the declaration that the resurrection of the crucified Jesus proves with certainty that "God has made him both Lord (κύριον) and Messiah (χριστόν)" (Luke 2:36);[73] similarly, Paul's sermon at Pisidian Antioch interprets Jesus' resurrection from the dead as the fulfillment of "the holy and faithful things of David," a somewhat obscure phrase that is closely linked in the sermon with the promise that God's Holy One will not see corruption (Acts 13:34-35; citing Isa 55:3 LXX and Ps 16:10).[74] Further, in the climactic scene of the apostolic council in Jerusalem, James validates the Gentile mission of Paul and Barnabas by quoting a passage from Amos 9:11-12—in a form close to the LXX rendering—that prophesies God will rebuild *the tent of David* that has fallen . . . so that all other peoples may seek the Lord" (Acts 15:16-17).[75] The extension of the gospel to the Gentile world follows upon the "resurrection" of the royal Davidic line. If Luke's rendering of the church's earliest preaching portrays Jesus' resurrection as the fulfillment of promises made to and about a Davidic messiah, and if Luke posits the restoration of the fallen Davidic royal house as a crucial stage in the unfolding plot of salvation history, we can hardly suppose that he has forgotten about these matters throughout the duration of his Gospel account. Surely it is likelier that his account of Jesus is laying the narrative groundwork for a *hermeneutical reshaping* of the Davidic-Messiah tradition.

Indeed, upon closer examination, we see that throughout his story Luke gives occasional prompts to remind us of the importance of the designation χριστός: the crowds speculate (wrongly) whether the fiery John the Baptist might be the Messiah (Luke 3:15), and the demons that Jesus silences are said to know that he is the Messiah (4:41). Perhaps most significantly, Luke retains the Markan scene in which Peter confesses Jesus to be the Messiah (in the Lukan version, τὸν χριστὸν τοῦ θεοῦ; Luke 9:20; cf. Mark 8:29). Here, just as in Mark, this premature confession is promptly silenced with the urgent teaching that the Son of Man must suffer and that those called to follow Jesus must bear the cross[76] and lose their lives for his sake (9:21-27). In light of Luke's repeated positive use of χριστός as a title for Jesus elsewhere, he can hardly regard Peter's confession as mistaken. Instead, the narrative's emphasis on suffering is leading the reader to a reinterpretation of the meaning of χριστός in view of the events in Jerusalem that are still to come; Luke 9:22 points explicitly to the passion narrative (cf. 24:46). Jesus is indeed what Peter affirms, the Messiah of God, but his messianic destiny will necessarily include a redefinition through Jesus' suffering, rejection, death, and finally his resurrection.

After Peter's confession, however, Jesus' injunction to silence appears effective for a time: we hear nothing more of a messiah or of David and his kingdom until near the end of Jesus' journey to Jerusalem, when a blind beggar imploring Jesus' help calls out to him as "Jesus, Son of David" in Luke 18:35-43.[77] From this point onward, as Jesus approaches Jerusalem, royal and Davidic motifs begin emerging more regularly. And, significantly, these messianic themes are foregrounded particularly through Luke's allusive use of the Psalms.

An explicit reference to David[78] occurs in Jesus' controversy discourses with the Jewish authorities in the temple: Jesus poses the question of how the Messiah can be David's son, if David himself (in Ps 110:1) refers to him as "Lord" (Luke 20:41-44). Luke's account follows Mark 12:35-37 closely, with only a few small editorial changes.[79] The most interesting of these alterations appears in the citation formula that introduces the psalm quotation. Where Mark reads, "David himself said in the Holy Spirit," Luke has, "David himself said *in the Book of Psalms*" (Luke 20:42a). This phrasing is one of several Lukan pointers to the Psalms *as texts*, texts that provide a privileged revelatory insight concerning the identity and vocation of Jesus. David's words do not emanate from some undefined location in the spiritual ether; they are to be found in a determinate collection of prophetic writings, the book of Psalms.

Unlike Mark and Matthew, who leave Jesus' riddling question unanswered (though presumably not puzzling to later Christian readers), Luke, in his second volume, provides an explicit solution to the puzzle:

> For David did not ascend into the heavens, but he himself says, "The Lord said to my Lord, 'Sit at my right hand until I set your enemies as a footstool for your feet.'" Let all the house of Israel know assuredly, therefore, that God has appointed him both Lord and Christ, this Jesus whom you crucified.
>
> (Acts 2:34-36)

According to Acts 2, Jesus is indeed David's Son, for Peter's sermon has identified him clearly as the fruit of David's loins (Luke 2:30); yet he is also David's Lord by virtue of his resurrection and ascension to God's right hand, as Psalm 109:1 LXX testifies. Thus, he is *both* "Lord" (κύριον) and "Messiah" (χριστόν). Luke's solution to the riddle posed by Jesus is no different substantively from that adumbrated by Mark and Matthew; the only difference is that Luke's second volume provides a narrative frame for a postresurrectional explication of the riddle's solution. The kingship of David's Son is to be understood, according to Luke, not simply as a role of earthly power; rather, the Psalms point to the heavenly exaltation of the Davidic Messiah.[80]

At the same time, however, to understand Jesus' Davidic sonship through the lens of the Psalms is also to understand another unexpected aspect of the Messiah's story. For Luke, the Davidic figure foreshadowed in the Psalms is not only the exalted bearer of power; he is also *a figure who must undergo suffering*.[81] This startling and offensive interpretation was already foreshadowed in Jesus' response to Peter's confession (Luke 9:20-22), and it lies at the heart of the message that the risen Jesus explains to the two befuddled disciples on the road to Emmaus: "O foolish and slow of heart to trust in all that the prophets spoke! Weren't these things necessary: *for the Messiah to suffer* and enter into his glory?" (Luke 24:25-26). Similarly, the encapsulated story of the Messiah's suffering, death, resurrection, and glory is spelled out a little more fully in Jesus' postresurrectional teaching to the disciples gathered together in Jerusalem:

> And he said to them . . . "[I]t is necessary that all the things written about me in the Law of Moses and the Prophets and the Psalms be fulfilled." Then he opened their minds to understand the Scriptures. And he said to them, "Thus it is written, that *the Messiah is to suffer* and to rise from the dead on the third day, and that repentance for the forgiveness of sins be proclaimed in his name to all the nations."
>
> (Luke 24:44b-47)

Luke's tripartite description of the contents of Scripture ("the Law of Moses, the Prophets, *and the Psalms*") is unusual (in place of the more common "the Law, the Prophets, and the Writings"); whatever other reasons might be given for this formulation, it at least signals the special significance of the Psalter as a medium of revelation of Jesus' identity. Presumably, then, the Psalms may hold particularly important keys to understanding the hermeneutically revolutionary claim that the suffering of the Messiah is scripturally foretold.

In what way might this be so? The answer, once articulated, appears stunningly obvious, if only in retrospect: the "David" who speaks in the psalms is a faithful, righteous figure who undergoes intense suffering, repeatedly appeals to God for deliverance and vindication, and consistently concludes his prayers with praise and thanksgiving. In short, the lament psalms adumbrate the narrative pattern that is both reenacted and newly illuminated in the story of Jesus' crucifixion, resurrection, and exaltation.[82]

Do we find specific evidence in Luke–Acts that Luke did in fact interpret the Psalms in this christological fashion? Close scrutiny of the Lukan passion narrative turns up a few hints. Luke carries over from

Mark several details that allude to the most frequently cited passion psalms: Psalm 22 (dividing garments and casting lots; Luke 23:34) and Psalm 69 (soldiers offering vinegar to drink; Luke 23:36). He also subtly renarrates the Markan reference to the women who watched the crucifixion from afar, to make the wording more audibly echo the lament of the psalmist in Psalm 38:11: "My friends and companions stand aloof from my affliction, and my neighbors *stand far off* (37:11 LXX: οἱ ἔγγιστά μου ἀπὸ μακρόθεν ἔστησαν)." It is perhaps just possible to hear a faint echo of this passage rustling in Mark 15:40: "And there were also women watching from afar (ἀπὸ μακρόθεν)." If Luke has indeed heard such an echo, he amplifies it: "But all his acquaintances stood (Εἱστήκεισαν) far off (ἀπὸ μακρόθεν), along with the women who had followed him from Galilee, watching these things" (Luke 23:49). The otherwise unmotivated introduction of a reference to acquaintances or friends (οἱ γνωστοὶ αὐτῷ) in addition to the women, along with the added observation that they "*stood far off,*" would seem to be details bringing the narrative into subtle but significant coordination with the psalm subtext.[83] Surely, however, the volume of such allusions hardly justifies the strength of Luke's assertion about the scripturally prefigured necessity of Jesus' suffering and death.

The most significant way in which Luke links the psalms of David with the story of Jesus' passion is silently to delete from the Markan account Jesus' dying cry of dereliction ("My God, my God, why have you forsaken me?" Ps 22:1 [21:2 LXX]) and to substitute as Jesus' last words a *different* Davidic psalm text: "Father, into your hands I commit my spirit" (Luke 23:46; citing Ps 30:6 LXX). At the most obvious level, this narrational shift removes a possible source of scandal and portrays Jesus as steadfastly trusting and obedient to God even at the moment of his dying breath. In place of the agonized cry narrated by Mark and Matthew, Luke depicts a Jesus who dies praying for the forgiveness of his enemies (Luke 23:34), assuring the sympathetic thief on the cross of his place in paradise (Luke 23:43), and confidently entrusting his spirit to the heavenly Father. The citation of the key line from Psalm 30 LXX shows Luke's editorial hand at work in the addition of the vocative address of this prayer to the "Father" and, more crucially, in converting the psalm's future tense verb (παραθήσομαι) into a present tense (παρατίθεμαι), thereby making Jesus' words into a performative utterance rather than a mere declaration of intent. Perhaps one of Luke's key reasons for this intertextual substitution was to remove even the hint that God might have *abandoned* the dying Jesus (τί ἐγκατέλιπές με), for we will discover in the speeches in Acts (2:31, 13:35) that Peter and Paul steadfastly insist on God's faithfulness to David's confident prayer in Psalm 15:10 LXX:[84]

> You will not abandon my soul (οὐκ ἐγκαταλείψεις τὴν
>   ψυχήν μου) to Hades,
> nor will you give your Holy One to see corruption.

Thus, Luke finds it highly problematical to portray Jesus as dying in a state of abandonment by God[85] (perhaps this is one of the ways in which he finds Mark's narrative less than "orderly"?), and in Psalm 30 LXX he finds words of the Davidic sufferer that more adequately express his understanding of Jesus' character and destiny.[86]

Yet a more rounded intertextual reading will not lose sight of the fact that Psalm 30 LXX, like Psalm 21 LXX, is also a psalm of lament and petition uttered by a suffering, righteous figure. Both psalms depict the speaker as scorned and distressed, and both, significantly, move finally from lament to thanksgiving and praise. Thus, the different connotative weight of the line Luke chooses to cite should in no way be understood to negate the real suffering of the cross. Indeed, as we have seen, Jesus' suffering is an integral element of Luke's interpretation of the story. Instead, the chief effect of Luke's intertextual renarration is to highlight the *faithfulness* of Jesus to God while also reaffirming God's faithfulness in not abandoning him. Luke is able to achieve this hermeneutical transformation precisely and only because Psalm 30, like Psalm 21, is also a *psalm of David* as a righteous sufferer, and it therefore offers an equally valid and powerful lens through which to read Jesus' death.

The hint that Jesus' messianic identity is prefigured in the psalms of suffering and vindication is developed at much greater length in the apostolic sermons that appear in Luke's second volume. These sermons exemplify precisely the sort of readings that (we may suppose) Luke imagined the risen Jesus to have offered both on the Emmaus Road and in private to his disciples in Jerusalem.[87] We have already briefly noted some instances of these hermeneutical pointers. For example, Peter's Pentecost sermon finds in Psalm 16:8-11 a prefiguration of Jesus' resurrection and in Psalm 110:1 a reference to Jesus' enthronement (Acts 2:22-36). Similarly, Peter's speech before the Jewish council in Acts 4 reads Psalm 118:22 as a prefiguration of Jesus' rejection, death, and vindication: "the stone that was rejected by you, the builders, has become the cornerstone" (Acts 4:8-12).[88] Or to cite one more example that draws on a different Old Testament intertext, Philip, in his encounter with the Ethiopian eunuch, finds "the good news about Jesus" in Isaiah 53's account of the Suffering Servant (Acts 8:26-40).[89]

This last example suggests that Luke is happy to fuse Isaiah's Suffering Servant figure together with the picture of David that he finds in the Psalms.[90] It is noteworthy that in Acts 4:25 and 4:27, both David and Jesus are also referred to as "your servant."[91] Perhaps, to state the point a little more cautiously, Luke finds scriptural prefiguration of Jesus' suffering both in the Isaian Servant and in the figure of David.

In any case, these passages in Acts provide clear models for the reading strategy toward which Luke 24 gestures: a reading strategy that proposes the crucified and risen Jesus as the hermeneutical key to Israel's Scripture, while finding the key to understanding Jesus' messianic vocation in the Davidic psalms. On this reading, the release and redemption of Israel depends not on triumphant conquest through violence but rather on the martyrdom and exaltation of a paradoxical Davidic messiah whose identity is narrated through these scriptural intertexts that sing of lament, suffering, and final vindication by God.

The prophet like (or unlike) Elijah and Elisha. Luke weaves another strand into his narration of Jesus' identity by patterning several episodes in the Gospel on the scriptural stories of the prophets Elijah and Elisha. This is a distinctive element of Luke's telling of the story of Jesus, not significantly paralleled in the other Gospels. We have already noted that in the Nazareth synagogue sermon Jesus arouses the ire of the villagers by making reference to the acts of Elijah and Elisha, who performed prophetic works of power for Gentile outsiders (Luke 4:25-30). In that passage, there is no direct suggestion that these prophets typologically anticipate the figure of Jesus himself; Jesus simply offers their deeds as a comparison to his, providing a precedent to justify his doing miracles elsewhere but not in his hometown.[92] As Luke's narrative unfolds, however, we encounter several other thought-provoking parallels between Jesus and these paradigmatic prophets of old.

One of the most striking of these correspondences appears in the account of Jesus' raising the dead son of a widow (Luke 7:11-17). This story, found only in Luke's Gospel, closely resembles the scriptural tradition of Elijah's raising the son of the widow of Zarephath (1 Kgs 17:17-24), a character of whom readers have already been reminded in Luke 4:26. In both narratives, the only son of a widow has died—a catastrophic situation for a woman left alone without means of support in ancient Middle Eastern culture.[93] In the Elijah narrative, the more detailed of the two, the widow, with whom Elijah has been lodging (1 Kgs 17:19), reproaches Elijah for coming and bringing this disaster upon her by calling her sin to remembrance. Elijah then takes the boy up to his room, lays him on his bed, and "stretched himself upon the child three times" while crying out to God and praying for life to be restored. There is a happy ending, as God hears the prayer, and the boy revives. In Luke 7, the narration is far more compact. Jesus sees a funeral procession coming out of the town of Nain and has compassion on the widow whose son has died. He tells the woman not to weep, touches the bier, and speaks directly to the corpse: "Young man, I say to you, rise!" The dead man immediately sits up and begins to speak, and Jesus presents him again to his mother. It is this last act that most loudly echoes the tale told in 1 Kings. There, after raising the boy, we are told, Elijah took him down from the upper chamber into the main part of the house "and gave him to his mother (καὶ ἔδωκεν αὐτὸν τῇ μητρὶ αὐτοῦ)" (1 Kgs 17:23); Luke's narration of the scene at Nain repeats precisely the same phrase: "The dead man sat up and began to speak, and he [Jesus] gave him to his mother (καὶ ἔδωκεν αὐτὸν τῇ μητρὶ αὐτοῦ)" (Luke 7:15). Through this verbatim repetition of the Elijah story's climactic line, Luke winks at the knowledgeable reader, virtually demanding that the two stories be read together. The townspeople of Nain, who of course know the traditions about Elijah, immediately draw the most obvious conclusion: "A great prophet has been raised up among us!" (7:16)—a new prophet like Elijah.

And yet, when the two stories are juxtaposed, one salient difference looms. Jesus' mighty act requires no stretching himself out on the body, no anguished cries and prayers to God; instead, he speaks a direct word commanding the dead man to rise, just as in the story of the raising of Lazarus in John 11:43-44. A similar contrast appears if Luke 7:11-17 is compared with the analogous story of Elisha's raising the dead son of the Shunammite woman in 2 Kings 4:18-37. There, too, Elisha prays to God and performs a mouth-to-mouth resuscitation of the child. In this respect, the Elijah and Elisha stories are more like each other than either is like the Lukan account of Jesus' raising of the widow's son. In the story of Elijah, we are informed that "the LORD listened to the voice of Elijah" and the life came back into the boy. In the Gospel story, however, it appears that Jesus need not appeal to God; he simply speaks a word of authority, and the miracle happens.[94] Thus, while Jesus' act is reminiscent of Elijah's—so strongly reminiscent that we may speak of a typological relationship between the two figures—the typological link already begins to suggest both likeness and unlikeness. Jesus, the antitype, fulfills the pattern found in the Elijah story but does so in a way that surpasses the type and leads readers to ponder how to interpret this prophetic figure who seems to possess even greater authority than the greatest of Israel's miracle-working prophets.

Nonetheless, Jesus' Elijah-like raising of the dead, along with his other remarkable deeds, understandably provokes popular speculation. Luke tells us a couple of chapters later that Herod the tetrarch has gotten wind of gossip on the street that John the Baptist has been raised from the dead—a rumor at which Herod scoffs—or, more tellingly, "that Elijah had appeared" or "that one of the prophets of ancient times had arisen" (Luke 9:8-10). And in short order, the same whispered speculations are reported to Jesus himself by his disciples (9:18-19). Yet Luke leaves readers in no doubt that these guesses about Jesus' identity, however apparently reasonable they may appear, fall short of grasping the truth. The careful reader has known since Luke 1:17 that it is John, not Jesus, who will go forth "in the spirit and power of Elijah." And the transfiguration scene, which follows almost immediately (9:28-36), portrays Jesus talking with Moses and Elijah; the narrative effect is to associate Jesus *with* them, to reveal them as glorious predecessors, while at the same time distinguishing him *from* them. If Jesus is talking to them, clearly he is not simply the reincarnation of either.

In the events following the transfiguration, as we have already seen, Luke tantalizes us with allusions to the Elijah/Elisha cycle while continuing to mark Jesus' difference from these typological predecessors.[95] Since the great Elijah had summoned fire from heaven to annihilate his adversaries (1 Kgs 18:36-39; 2 Kgs 1:10-12), Jesus' disciples wrongly assume he will do the same. Their question, "Do you want us to call fire to come down from heaven and consume them?" (Luke 9:54), closely echoes the language of 2 Kings 1:10, 12.[96] Firmly rejecting their suggestion, Jesus rebukes them. Some later manuscripts then add an additional word of instruction: "And he said, 'You do not know what Spirit you belong to, for the Son of Man did not come to destroy human lives but to save them'" (Luke 9:55-56). On text-critical grounds, this is almost surely not part of what Luke originally wrote, but it represents an early and theologically astute interpretation of Luke's portrait of Jesus. In this story, he appears as the anti-Elijah, the bearer of salvation rather than violent retribution.

Even the ensuing vignette of Jesus' summoning followers who demur and request permission to tend to family matters first (Luke 9:59-62) produces a similar hermeneutical transposition. The reader immediately recalls Elijah's symbolic act of throwing his mantle on Elisha (1 Kgs 19:19-21), but then realizes with a shock that Jesus' call to discipleship is more imperious and radical than its Old Testament prototype. Elijah had allowed Elisha to leave his twelve yoke of oxen, go back, kiss his father and mother, slaughter the oxen, and throw a feast for his people, before he began to follow and serve. But Jesus greets a similar request with abrupt dismissal: "No one who puts his hand to the plow and looks back is fit for the kingdom of God" (Luke 9:62). After the initial shock subsides a little, the hearer of this story will realize that yet another symbolic reversal has been performed by Jesus' aphorism: the call to follow Elijah required Elisha to *leave* his plowing, while the call to follow Jesus is a call to *begin* plowing and see it through resolutely. Both entail a summons to leave the past, to abandon family and embrace a new vocation of discipleship; yet Jesus' modulation of the metaphor suggests steady, ongoing labor with the prospect of future fruitfulness.

It would be wrong, however, to infer that Luke's use of the Elijah/Elisha typology is entirely dissociative in its effect. Jesus continues throughout the Gospel to behave as a prophet—indeed, he explicitly identifies himself as such (Luke 4:24, 13:33)—and in various ways the significance of his actions is illumined by the many subtle intertextual reminiscences of his prophetic precursors. For example, Jesus' weeping as he contemplates the coming destruction of the city of Jerusalem (19:41-44) evokes memories of Elisha's weeping over the atrocities that he foresees Hazael will perpetrate against the people of Israel (2 Kgs 8:11-12). There is no explicit verbal echo beyond the word "wept" (ἔκλαυσεν), but the two prophetic visions of coming catastrophe are eerily similar, and the portrayal of Jesus as a weeping prophet allies him metaphorically with Elisha.

Or, to take another example, when the Jewish authorities bring the captive Jesus before the Roman governor Pilate, they begin their accusation against him with these words: "We found this man perverting our nation (διαστρέφοντα τὸ ἔθνος ἡμῶν) . . ." (Luke 23:2). Given the numerous earlier associations of Jesus with Elijah, the charge resonates with the accusation made by King Ahab (in the LXX version) when Elijah finally appears before him: "Is it you, the perverter of Israel (ὁ διαστρέφων τὸν Ἰσραηλ)?" (1 Kgs 18:17). This intertextual juxtaposition elegantly illustrates the characteristic Lukan literary technique of projecting a flickering precursor image on a backdrop behind the center-stage action. Those who perceive the connection between the two images will gain a deepened sense of the scene's dramatic complexities. In the case under consideration here, the subtext of the authorities' complaint suggests that Jesus,

like Elijah, is to be characterized as a subversive troublemaker, prophesying against the duly established ruler—in this case Caesar, whose inter-
ests Pilate represents. Surely, however, this allusion is a bit of delicious
Lukan dramatic irony.[97] The speakers cannot intend the echo, for if they
did they would recognize that in 1 Kings 18 it is Elijah who is the true
bearer of God's word, and it is the power-wielding accuser who is the
true perverter. Elijah fires this response back at Ahab: "He answered, 'I
have not perverted Israel (οὐ διαστρέφω τὸν Ισραήλ); but rather you and
the house of your father have perverted it, because you have forsaken the
LORD your God and gone after the Baals'" (1 Kgs 18:18 LXX). In light
of this echo of the Elijah narrative, the authorities' charge against Jesus
boomerangs back on them: *they*, in collaboration with the unjust pagan
powers, are corrupting Israel, and they will ultimately pay the penalty,
as did Ahab and the prophets of Baal. Luke explains none of this, and
hearing the echo is not necessary to follow his story. But the reader who
does hear it will appreciate the narrative irony and the final reversal of
fortunes that it foreshadows.[98]

A final fleeting echo of 2 Kings will stretch our imaginations a bit
further. At the conclusion of the risen Jesus' encounter with the Emmaus
disciples, after Jesus has broken bread with them, the scene reaches its
dramatic climax in a moment of *anagnoresis*: "Then their eyes were
opened (αὐτῶν δὲ διηνοίχθησαν οἱ ὀφθαλμοί), and they recognized him,
and he vanished from their sight" (Luke 24:31). The story stands, and
stands powerfully, on its own, and there is no overt allusion to any Old
Testament precursor. Yet in view of the scene's own thematic emphasis
on the scriptural antecedents of Jesus' career, and in view of the several
allusions elsewhere in the narrative to the Elijah/Elisha cycle, might we
hear a faint rebound of one more such text? In 2 Kings 6, Elisha finds
the city of Dothan surrounded by the hostile army of the king of Aram.
His servant, dismayed, cries, "Alas, master, what shall we do?" Elisha
mysteriously assures the servant that "there are more with us than there
are with them," and then prays for God to open the servant's eyes. "So
the LORD opened his eyes (διήνοιξεν κύριος τοὺς ὀφθαλμοὺς αὐτοῦ) and
he saw, and behold, the mountain was full of horses and chariots of fire
all around Elisha" (2 Kgs 6:17).[99]

This motif of having blind eyes opened to perceive an overwhelmingly
powerful spiritual reality appears very rarely in the Old Testament.[100] If
this reference to the opening of the disciples' eyes in Luke 24:31 is indeed
heard as an echo of the text in 2 Kings, what would such a hearing add to
our reading? It might suggest that the hostility of the "chief priests and

leaders" surrounding and fighting against Jesus—a circumstance perceived by Cleopas and companion as insuperable adversity—was in fact a futile assault against a greater divine power that would ultimately guarantee the deliverance and triumph of Jesus. The chariots of fire of 2 Kings may dimly foreshadow the tongues of fire at Pentecost and perhaps also hint at the reason why the hearts of the disciples *burned* when their eyes were opened by the Lord (Luke 24:32): they were, unbeknownst to them, in the presence of a divine flame.

This proposed reading of a hypothetical faint echo goes far beyond anything that can be ascribed with any degree of confidence to Luke's authorial intention. It may be an instance of "experimental intertextuality," the juxtaposition of texts not obviously or traditionally linked in order to discern new and unexpected senses.[101] Yet in this case, the linkage yields unexpected satisfactions. The plodding Emmaus disciples, like Elisha's servant, are seeing the world through a veil of fear and discouragement. But when their eyes are opened by Jesus, the prophet like Elisha, the veil falls away, and a fiery new world opens before them, disclosing the mighty power of God to save.

If all that be granted, at least as a poetic thought experiment, then we can hardly avoid noticing that the story in 2 Kings continues to a remarkable resolution. In response to Elisha's prayer, the Lord first blinds the Aramaean soldiers so that they are taken captive, then opens their eyes (καὶ διήνοιξεν κύριος τοὺς ὀφθαλμοὺς αὐτῶν[!]) to show them their predicament as prisoners of war. But rather than having them slain, Elisha surprisingly gives orders that they be welcomed at table: "And he set before them a great feast, and they ate and drank: and he dismissed them and they departed to their lord (πρὸς τὸν κύριον αὐτῶν). And the bands of Syria came no longer into the land of Israel" (2 Kgs 6:23). Strange denouement, opening the eyes not only of the enemy soldiers but of readers as well. Those who were enemies are blinded, disarmed, given new sight, welcomed at a feast by the one whom they had sought to kill, and, newly at peace with God's people, sent to their Lord. The semantic ripples run backward and forward from that table in the evening shadows at Emmaus: the strange story of Elisha's nonviolent triumph over his Aramaean enemies now foreshadows the surprising and gracious victory of Jesus over his enemies, and the opening of the soldiers' eyes prefigures not only the opening of the eyes of the Emmaus disciples but also the story of the overthrown enemy Saul/Paul in Acts 9.

This perhaps fanciful intertextual reading indicates how the figural evocation of Elijah and Elisha works in Luke–Acts. Jesus is not Elisha *redivivus*,[102] nor does Luke claim that 2 Kings 6 is some sort of prediction fulfilled by Jesus—nothing so overt and mechanical. Nonetheless, on this reading, 2 Kings 6 may be one source that contains mysteriously hidden "things about [Jesus] himself in all the Scriptures." The intertextual connection consists of fine threads, variously colored and intricately woven. And the interweaving yields a surprising pattern of fresh retrospective readings of Israel's Scripture, readings that in turn reframe and deepen our interpretation of Jesus' identity.

We could continue in this vein for some time, showing how Luke weaves analogous patterns with metaphorical strands likening Jesus to Moses, or to the Suffering Servant of Isaiah, or to the persecuted righteous figure of Wisdom 2:12-20. And even such a demonstration would hardly exhaust the range of intertextual possibilities, for Luke has informed us that there are things about Jesus to be found "in all the Scriptures" (Luke 27:26). Yet we need not belabor the point by exploring these matters further. There have been many capable studies of various christological motifs in Luke–Acts, beyond the representative few that we have traced here.[103] But, as we have suggested, Luke's vision of the identity of Jesus is not comprehended by any one of these motifs, or even by a determinate constellation of the most important of them. Rather, the various scriptural typologies contribute to the construction of a larger epic tapestry; the identity of Jesus is to be found by viewing the intricate portrait woven into Luke's narrative, not by unraveling the different skeins or sources employed in the composition.

Jesus as Lord and God of Israel

There does remain, however, one very important aspect of that composite portrait that we have not yet considered. As we have already seen, both Mark and Matthew draw on scriptural citations and allusions to identify Jesus as the embodiment of the God of Israel. Are there indications of a similar christological claim in Luke's Gospel? I would like to propose that the answer is yes; a careful reading of Luke's narrative, with particular attention to its intertextual relation with the Old Testament, discloses that he does indeed portray Jesus as Israel's Lord and God. This is not simply one more motif among others; rather, it is the narrative foundation for all the others, the one that explains and integrates them all. This interpretation of Jesus' divine identity in Luke has been suggested,[104] but it stands very much in contrast to most readings of Lukan Christology.

It will therefore be necessary to consider the evidence for this reading of Luke at greater length.

In the case of Luke, perhaps even more than with the other Gospels, our interpretation must reckon with the fact that his characterization of Jesus is developed through the medium of *narrative*. It is well, therefore, to remind ourselves again and again of a point already made: we cannot adequately estimate Luke's understanding of Jesus' identity simply by studying christological titles or by isolating direct propositional statements; rather, we come to know Jesus in Luke only as his *narrative identity* is enacted in and through the story. This critical perspective has several implications.

Jesus' identity unfolds *cumulatively* through the Gospel, and a full understanding will therefore require multiple rereadings of the parts in light of the whole—a process of "learning and relearning the identity of Jesus," as Luke posits, qualifies, deconstructs, and elaborates various interpretations of Jesus' personhood and mission.[105] The confessional utterances of characters in the story may turn out to be preliminary, inadequate (e.g., "a prophet mighty in deed and word"), ambiguous, misleading, or even ironically true in a way that the speaker does not yet fully understand ("the one to redeem Israel"). It follows, then, that an integrative understanding of who Jesus is becomes possible only from the story's endpoint, only through a reading that moves from "back to front"—and that includes a retrospective rereading not only of Luke's own narrative but also of Israel's Scripture to which it constantly refers and alludes.[106] Such an approach will not drive a wedge between Luke's "own" Christology and that of his sources; his narrative portrait of Jesus includes not only distinctively Lukan elements but also the traditional elements that he chooses to include in his composition. In the case of Luke's Gospel, such a reading will constantly bear in mind that the Acts of the Apostles, particularly in its accounts of the apostolic preaching, provides an important lens through which the first book's account of "all that Jesus began to do and to teach" must be viewed. With these methodological provisos in hand, we turn now to a rereading of the Gospel that will seek to listen for clues about the way in which Luke understands Jesus' identity in relation to God.

Jesus as the Son of God. Luke makes it clear from the opening scenes of his narrative that his central character Jesus has a divine origin and that he is no ordinary human figure; the angel Gabriel announces to Mary that her child is to be "the Son of the Most High" (Luke 1:32). The careful reader will note the contrast to John, who will be called "*the prophet* of the Most High" (1:76). "Son of the Most High" is not merely an honorific royal title, for Luke carefully informs us that Jesus is to be born to a virgin mother (1:27, 34) and that his conception will occur through the agency of the Holy Spirit, who will "overshadow" Mary. Gabriel's pronouncement then spells out the implications of this miraculous birth: "Therefore the child to be born will also be called holy, God's Son" (1:35).[107] After the trumpet-flourish of this portentous introduction, it is hard to see how any reader could suppose that Luke has a "low" Christology or that the Jesus who will subsequently appear in the story could be rightly interpreted as only a prophet.[108] Jesus enters history through supernatural means, and he is therefore God's Son in some ontological fashion.

The identification of Jesus as Son of God is of course reinforced in Luke's accounts of the baptism of Jesus and the transfiguration. At both of these pivotal dramatic events a voice from heaven speaks, identifying Jesus as "my Son, the beloved" (Luke 3:22) and "my Son, the chosen one" (9:35).[109] Each of these passages in turn evokes a chorus of scriptural echoes. In the case of "my Son, the beloved," the dominant voice in the chorus is the allusion to Isaac in Genesis 22, though when the heavenly voice continues the acclamation by saying "in you I am well pleased," there is an additional echo of God's address to the Servant in Isaiah 42:1: "Here is my servant, whom I uphold, my chosen, in whom my soul delights." This second echo is amplified into a more explicit allusion in the transfiguration passage with its reference to the Son as the "chosen one" (ὁ ἐκλελεγμένος). In the LXX, Isaiah 42:1 is explicitly interpreted as a prophecy concerning Jacob, understood as a corporate designation for "Israel, my chosen one" (ὁ ἐκλεκτός μου). And in both of these passages the royal messianic Psalm 2:7 may reverberate more distantly in the background. While the Old Testament allusions in the baptism and transfiguration texts would seem to identify Jesus with Israel, God's covenant partner rather than God himself, we must recall that Luke regularly weaves together different strands of material and that no one image identifying Jesus should be understood as exclusive of others. Indeed, when these texts are read in narrative sequence with Luke 1:26-38, the effect is to suggest that Jesus' status as Son entails some sort of identity both with God and with Israel/humanity.[110]

The theme of Jesus' sonship surfaces again in the striking prayer of Luke 10:21-22, the so-called *Jubelruf* (joyful shout), in which Jesus suddenly blurts out an expression of intimacy with God the Father that would be immediately at home in John's Gospel.[111]

> At that same hour Jesus rejoiced in the Holy Spirit and said, "I thank you,
> Father, Lord of heaven and earth, because you have hidden these things
> from the wise and the intelligent and have revealed them to infants; yes,
> Father, for such was your gracious will. All things have been handed over
> to me by my Father; and no one knows who the Son is except the Father,
> or who the Father is except the Son and anyone to whom the Son chooses
> to reveal him."

At first glance this effusion appears incongruous with Jesus' manner of speaking in the bulk of the synoptic traditions, though this is in fact one of the double-tradition passages that Luke shares with Matthew (Matt 11:25-27). But on closer reflection, this expression of privileged filial relation to God is entirely consonant with other material in Luke. In addition to the Son of God references in the annunciation, the baptism, and the transfiguration accounts, we might recall the boyhood story in which Jesus replies to the scolding of his anxious parents by shrugging and saying, "Didn't you know that I must be in my Father's house?" (Luke 2:49). Likewise, in the wilderness temptation story, Jesus' successful rebuff of the devil shows that he is truly the Son of God, in a way that rejects the false demonstrations proposed by the tempter (4:1-13). Even Luke's special emphasis on Jesus' intense disciplines of prayer (e.g., 3:21, 6:12, 9:18, 9:28-29) coheres with Jesus' affirmation in Luke 10:22 of a specially intimate and mutual knowledge of God. The claim that "all things have been handed over to me by my Father" serves well as an explanation of Jesus' astonishing power to heal, and his right to confer on his disciples authority over demons, as confirmed by the immediately preceding narrative (10:17-20). This same power to confer divine authority is reiterated at the scene of Jesus' final supper with the disciples, when he says to them: "You are the ones who have remained with me throughout my testings. And I confer upon you, just as my Father has conferred upon me, a kingdom, so that you might eat and drink at my table in my kingdom. And you will sit on thrones, judging the twelve tribes of Israel" (22:28-30). Elsewhere in the story, Jesus has spoken of "the kingdom of God," but now it becomes "*my* kingdom." It is also pertinent to note that Jesus is not himself one of the twelve tribal heads of the new Israel that he envisions; rather, he is the one who appoints the twelve as judges, and so he stands in a position of superior authority.[112] Lastly, even in extremis Jesus continues to pray to his Father and to commit his life into God's hands (23:46).

All of this evidence is consistent with the portrayal of the Father/Son relation in the prayer of Luke 10:21-22: it is a relation of special mutual knowledge that results in Jesus' reception of authority over all things, including the power to reveal the identity of the Father and to confer divine authority upon others. Thus, this interlude in the narrative functions as a dramatic soliloquy, in which Jesus steps from behind a momentarily closed curtain and prays in a way that is meant to be over-heard by the audience. This overheard prayer provides crucial clues that help the audience, in turn, to make sense of the rest of the action on stage both before and after the soliloquy. It is in light of Jesus' special identity as Son of God that the otherwise astounding claims and events of the drama become comprehensible.

Thus, no matter what studies of tradition history might show about the history-of-religions background of "Son of God" as a title,[113] the sig-nificance of this language *within Luke's narrative* cannot be restricted to the realm of royal messianic expectation. Luke certainly does understand Jesus as the heir of David's royal role as son, in the sense of Psalm 2:7. The acclamation of Jesus as God's Son includes this kingly role, but some-thing still greater is here.[114] For Jesus' origins are mysteriously divine, and his personal identity is closely bound with God's own being in a way that transcends the God-relation of any of Israel's past kings or prophets.

Jesus as the Lord of the new exodus. Beyond the passages that identify Jesus as God's Son, we must consider also several texts in Luke's Gospel that ascribe to Jesus roles and actions that are reserved in Israel's Scripture for God alone. Most prominent among these are the passages that announce Jesus' saving activity in imagery drawn from the Isaianic proclamation of a new exodus. We have already given some attention to the way in which Luke's citation of Isaiah 40:3-5 functions as a programmatic intro-duction to the narrative of Jesus' ministry (Luke 3:4-6); it frames his activity in terms of Isaiah's visionary prophecy of the end of Israel's exile, and it thereby serves as a "hermeneutical key for the Lukan program."[115] But our previous examination of this passage did not yet consider what implications this programmatic intertextual reference might have for understanding Jesus' own identity.

In the original prophetic context, there is no question that "the way of the LORD" (דרך יהוה; LXX: τὴν ὁδὸν κυρίου) in Isaiah 40:3 refers to the path through the wilderness of Israel's God, as shown by the follow-ing line, in synonymous parallelism: "Make straight in the desert a high-way for our God." Luke's form of the citation, however, substitutes the pronoun αὐτοῦ for this explicit reference to God in the second line of the couplet: "Make straight *his* paths." This has the effect of leaving "Lord" in the first line ambiguous: when Luke writes, "prepare the way of the Lord," should the reader understand this as a reference to *God's* impending arrival or as an anticipation of the coming of *Jesus*, to whom the narrator has already referred at least twice as "Lord" (Luke 1:43, 2:11)?[116] Both readings are possible; indeed, the ambiguity actually serves Luke's narrative purpose of producing an "overlap" *or* "shared identity" between Jesus the κύριος and the κύριος of Israel.[117]

A similar ambiguity attends the earlier reference in Zechariah's prophecy about his son John: "For you will go before the Lord to prepare his ways" (Luke 1:76). The foregoing reference in Gabriel's announcement of John's birth (1:16-17) would predispose the reader to hear "Lord" as a reference to "the Lord God," but in fact as the plot of the story unfolds, we see that John's role is to be the forerunner of *Jesus*, to whom the narrator refers repeatedly as the κύριος. This role of John as Jesus' predecessor is underscored once again in 7:24-30, this time through the citation of Malachi 3:1/Exodus 23:20: "This is the one about whom it is written, 'Look, I am sending my messenger before your face, who will prepare your way before you.'" In the narrative context of Luke 7, there can be no doubt that the point of the citation is to affirm that John was sent before *Jesus* to prepare *his* way.

The most significant observation here is that in Luke 3:1-6, Luke has taken the keynote passage from Isaiah 40 that declares the salvific coming of Israel's God and worked it narratively into an announcement of the imminent coming of Jesus as the one who would bring "the salvation of God" (Luke 3:6; citing Isa 40:5 LXX). Considering the full content of Isaiah 40, this identification of Jesus as the one in whom "all flesh will see the salvation of God" is hermeneutically momentous, for it is precisely in Isaiah 40 that we find one of the most radical declarations in all of Scripture of the *incomparability* of God:

> To whom, then, will you compare me,
> or who is my equal? says the Holy One.

(Isa 40:25)

It is precisely because God alone possesses all sovereign power that the nations are "like a drop from a bucket" before him (Isa 40:15); that is why he, and he alone, can promise to rescue Israel from captivity. Isaiah's announcement of the new exodus is predicated on the bold claim that the all-powerful God is coming to save his people:

Get you up to a high mountain,
O herald of good tidings to Zion;
lift up your voice with strength,
O herald of good tidings to Jerusalem,
lift it up, do not fear;
say to the cities of Judah,
"Here is your God!"
See, the LORD GOD (LXX: κύριος) *comes* with might,
and his arm rules for him.

(Isa 40:9-10a)

Thus, when Luke 3:4-6 draws on Isaiah 40 to intimate that Jesus is the coming κύριος of whom John speaks, the one whose glorious salvation will be for all flesh, the linkage between this coming figure and the Holy One of Israel can hardly be incidental.[118] This remarkable prefigurative identification also sheds unexpected light on a subsequent text in which Luke again identifies Jesus as "the Coming One."

Jesus as "the Coming One." In Luke 7:18-23, the imprisoned John the Baptist sends messengers to question Jesus about his identity.[119] They ask, as John has instructed them, "Are you ὁ ἐρχόμενος ["the Coming One"], or shall we look for another?" The question is given particular emphasis by its repetition in 7:19 and 7:20 (in contrast to the parallel Matthew 11:3, where the question is posed only once). This is a particularly good example of Luke's emulation of Old Testament narrative style, but it also has the effect of forcing the reader to linger over the question and to ponder its significance, particularly the significance of the key term ὁ ἐρχόμενος. The carefully chosen language of the question evokes Psalm 118:26 (117:26 LXX), which appears in the culminating doxological passage of the cycle of Hallel psalms (Pss 113–118): "Blessed is ὁ ἐρχόμενος in the name of the LORD." The Hallel psalms were sung on the occasion of Israel's great national festivals of Tabernacles and Passover, and both of these festivals were associated with Israel's national liberation from bondage in Egypt and therefore also—in the first-century context—linked with the hope of a future liberation from Roman rule and the coming of a new king.[120] Luke, more clearly than in Mark or Matthew, makes this royal hope fully explicit in his account of Jesus' triumphal entry into Jerusalem, as the crowd chants, using the words of Psalm 118:26, "Blessed is ὁ ἐρχόμενος, *the king* who comes in the name of the Lord" (Luke 19:38). Only Luke here adds ὁ βασιλεὺς as an explanatory gloss on "the Coming One" (cf. Matt 21:9; Mark 11:10). Thus, reading retrospectively in the context of Luke's narrative, we understand that John the Baptist's question in Luke 7:19-20 is a politically loaded query: he is asking whether Jesus intends to proclaim himself Israel's long-awaited ruler who will restore the kingdom of David. The Baptizer is asking, "Are you the Coming One, the coming King?"

In Luke's account (in contrast to Matthew's), Jesus does not answer the question immediately. Instead, he swings into action: "In that hour he healed many from diseases and plagues and evil spirits, and he gave grace to many blind people to see" (Luke 7:21).[121] In one sense, these actions are the answer to the question of John's emissaries. Rather than leaving the actions uninterpreted, however, Jesus does at last supply an answer of sorts. Indeed, his reply speaks volumes without quite answering the question directly: "Go and tell John what you have seen and heard: the blind receive their sight, the lame walk, the lepers are cleansed, the deaf hear, the dead are raised, the poor have good news brought to them. And blessed is anyone who takes no offense at me" (7:23). The reply makes sense as an answer to John's question only when we recognize that it echoes a number of motifs drawn from Isaiah's portrayal of the end of Israel's exile and God's eschatological restoration of the nation. The first and most important echo should remind John's emissaries of Isaiah 35:5-6a:

> Then the eyes of the blind shall be opened,
> and the ears of the deaf unstopped;
> then the lame shall leap like a deer,
> and the tongue of the speechless sing for joy.

These stirring images are part of Isaiah's vision of the exiled Israelites returning on a miraculous highway through the desert to Zion. Isaiah paints a picture of God's healing all that is broken, putting all things right in the eschatological time. Charles Wesley's moving hymn "O for a Thousand Tongues" draws on precisely these images:

> Hear him ye deaf, his praise, ye dumb,
> your loosened tongues employ;
> Ye blind, behold your Savior come,
> and leap, ye lame, for joy.[122]

Thus, by linking Isaiah's images of the eschatological new exodus with Jesus' healing activities, Luke's narrative portrays Jesus as the one whose works are ending the exile and bringing Israel home.

At the same time, Jesus' answer also sounds a second, slightly less prominent, echo in the phrase "the poor have good news proclaimed to them." The Greek expression here, πτωχοὶ εὐαγγελίζονται, reminds us once more of the passage from Isaiah 61 that Jesus had earlier read in the synagogue in Nazareth to inaugurate his public ministry (Luke 4:18):

> The Spirit of the Lord is upon me,
> because he has anointed me to proclaim good news to the poor
>   (εὐαγγελίσασθαι πτωχοῖς).

By connecting these allusions to Isaiah 35 and Isaiah 61, Jesus' reply fuses together the new exodus with the Isaian image of the Spirit-anointed Servant.[123]

Thus, in Luke 7, Jesus' apparently cryptic response to John's disciples is actually a very clear, intertextually coded response.[124] By evoking Isaian texts, Jesus offers a *scriptural* interpretive framework for the miraculous deeds that John's disciples have seen him perform, and he invites John to draw the appropriate conclusions. The passages from Isaiah should signal to John—or to any hearer steeped in Israel's Scripture—that Jesus' activity is indeed to be understood as the inauguration of the coming kingdom of God for which Israel had longed and for which John was waiting.

Yet these passages at the very same time gesture toward a symbolic reshaping of Israel's national hope. In asking whether Jesus was ὁ ἐρχόμενος, John was probably inquiring whether Jesus meant to assume the role of conquering royal Davidic Messiah. But the motifs selected by Jesus in his answer to John's disciples pointedly avoid images of military conquest. They focus instead on actions of healing and restoration.[125] Precisely by doing so, they offer John and his followers a new, nonviolent image of "the Coming One" and teach them to read Israel's Scripture with new eyes. In effect, Jesus' act of teaching John's messengers how to "read" his own ministry in light of Isaiah's words is *in itself* part of his work of opening the eyes of the blind—as we shall see once again in the encounter on the road to Emmaus.

The concluding macarism, "blessed is he who takes no offense at me" (μὴ σκανδαλισθῇ ἐν ἐμοί; literally "is not caused to stumble by me") should perhaps be understood as yet another echo—this time, pointing to Isaiah's image of the stone laid in Zion (Isa 28:16), which will also be a stone of stumbling for Israel (Isa 8:14; cf. the fusion of these two texts in Rom 9:32-33). Isaiah's famous and enigmatic "stone" image draws a sharp contrast between the prophet's trust in God's promise and Israel's faithless reliance on military power as a source of security. Isaiah proclaims that paradoxically it is precisely those who trust in military power who will stumble and be destroyed. The point is that John and his disciples should not "stumble" over Jesus' unexpected *peaceful* way of bringing in God's promised reign.[126] Luke sketches all this with economy of language and literary power through allusion and metalepsis. The reader who knows the Psalter and Isaiah will get the point well enough. In light of the echoes from Psalm 118 and Isaiah, the answer that we as readers are to supply to John's question "Is Jesus the Coming One?" is something like this: "Yes, he is the Coming King to which Psalm 118 points, the eschatological deliverer anticipated every time the Hallel psalms are sung. He is the one for whom we have hoped, but his coming kingdom must be interpreted not in terms of violent or coercive power but in light of Isaiah's images of divine mercy and restoration."

There remains one more important thing to be said about this text. Jesus' answer to John hints at one more, still deeper, truth at the heart of the good news Jesus is proclaiming. The texts from the prophet Isaiah that echo in Jesus' answer once again adumbrate *the return of the Lord to Zion*—just as Luke has already led the reader to expect by placing Isaiah 40:3-5 as the prolegomenon to Jesus' public activity (Luke 3:1-6). According to Isaiah's prophetic vision, Israel is to be saved not by a merely human leader who will bring Israel back from exile; rather, *God himself* will appear on the scene to lead the triumphant procession of returning exiles.[127] As we have already seen, in Luke 7:22 Jesus alludes forcefully to Isaiah 35:5 ("then the eyes of the blind shall be opened, and the ears of the deaf unstopped"). But *how* will these saving acts occur? The answer is given unmistakably in the verse just before this, Isaiah 35:4:

> Say to those who are of a fearful heart,
> "Be strong, do not fear!
> *Behold, your God!*[128]
> Vengeance is coming,
> the payback of God.
> *He will come and save you.*"

In the LXX, the agency of God in bringing salvation in is made even clearer by the translator's decision to include the intensive pronoun in the last line of the verse: αὐτὸς ἥξει καὶ σώσει ἡμᾶς ("He *himself* will come and save us"). Interestingly, in this passage, as in Isaiah 61:2, we find once again a reference to the vengeance or payback associated with

God's restorative coming. If the meaning of "vengeance" is present in Isaiah 35:4, as it almost certainly is in the Hebrew text (נקם), it must be understood to indicate the just punishment of the enemies of the people of God, the divine act of judgment that secures their deliverance from oppression. But the most significant observation is that Jesus' response to John's messengers points their attention to a passage in which *God* will come and save his people by opening the eyes of the blind and the ears of the deaf, enabling the lame to leap and the speechless to break into song. If this prophecy is fulfilled in the healing acts of Jesus himself, should we hear this echo as a metaleptic hint that the identity of this Coming One is something even greater than what John the Baptist envisioned?

Jesus as Kyrios. The suggestion may seem far-fetched until we consider more broadly the way in which the Evangelist Luke subtly narrates the identity of Jesus throughout his Gospel. Luke is the only one of the Gospel writers who regularly uses κύριος as a title for Jesus. Κύριος is, of course, the Greek word used by the Septuagint to translate the holy name of God, the Tetragrammaton. And Luke regularly follows this usage—for example, Luke 1:16: "He will turn many of the people of Israel to *the Lord* their God," where *Lord* clearly refers to the God of Israel. Yet, remarkably, there are also at least fifteen instances in Luke's Gospel where the Evangelist refers to *Jesus* as the κύριος—many of them in Luke's own authorial voice:[129] "And why has this happened to me, that the mother of *my Lord* comes to me?" (Luke 1:43); ". . . to you is born this day in the city of David a Savior, who is Christ *the Lord*" (2:11); "when *the Lord* saw her, he had compassion on her" (7:13); "Mary sat at *the Lord's* feet" (10:39); "*The Lord* turned and looked at Peter" (22:61); "*The Lord* has risen indeed" (24:34). Most appositely, within the very passage we have just considered, we find this: "John summoned two of his disciples, and sent them to *the Lord* to ask . . ." (7:18b-19a). In short, Luke *in his own narration* quite remarkably applies the title κύριος both to the God of Israel and to Jesus of Nazareth—occasionally in a way that suggests a mysterious fusion of divine and human identity in the figure of Jesus.[130] This is not a result of editorial carelessness. Luke has deployed his references to Jesus as κύριος with careful compositional skill to shape the reader's understanding of Jesus' divine identity.[131]

The culmination of Luke's references to Jesus as κύριος appears in the book of Acts, in Peter's address to the Roman centurion Cornelius and his household: "[God] sent the word to the sons of Israel by proclaiming the gospel of peace through Jesus Christ; this one is Lord of all (πάντων κύριος)" (Acts 10:36).[132] This programmatic declaration about Jesus' identity is doubly startling. For the Roman centurion, the ascription of the title "Lord of all" to Jesus can only be heard as a frontal challenge to the imperial propaganda that assigns exactly this honor of universal lordship to Caesar. For example, an imperial inscription from the time of Nero refers to him as ὁ τοῦ παντὸς κόσμου κύριος Νέρων.[133] And Epictetus wryly puts into the mouth of his interlocutor the boast, "But who can put me under compulsion except Caesar, the lord of all (ὁ παντῶν κύριος)?"[134] But at the same time, in a Jewish scriptural context, there is one and only one who can be acclaimed as "Lord of all." The fundamental Deuteronomic confession of Israel's faith declares that there can be only one Lord: ἄκουε Ισραηλ κύριος ὁ θεὸς ἡμῶν κύριος εἷς ἐστιν (Deut 6:4 LXX).

Thus, the hermeneutical effect of Luke's repeated narrative usage of κύριος is not unlike the effect achieved at the end of Paul's Christ-hymn in Philippians 2, which astonishingly ascribes to Jesus the eschatological Lordship that Isaiah 45:23 emphatically reserves for God alone: "so that at the name of Jesus every knee should bend . . . and every tongue should confess that Jesus Christ is *Kyrios*, to the glory of God the Father" (Phil 2:10-11). In that same confession, Luke invites us to join. Consequently, when Jesus says to the messengers of John the Baptist, *"Blessed* is the one who takes no offense in me" (Luke 7:23), his blessing answers in call-and-response fashion the very text to which John's question had alluded, Psalm 118:26: *"Blessed* is the Coming One, the One who comes in the name of the *Kyrios*." It turns out, beyond all possible human power of anticipation, that Jesus is *both* ὁ ἐρχόμενος (the Coming One), *and*, in embodied form, ὁ κύριος (the Lord).

Luke's retention of Markan divine identity motifs. All that we have observed so far about Luke's identification of Jesus with the God of Israel is consistent with the narrative tendencies we have observed in Mark and Matthew. It is therefore unsurprising that Luke, as a reader of Mark, carries over and includes several of the key Markan passages in which Jesus' divine identity is adumbrated. Because we have already considered these passages carefully in a previous chapter, they need not detain us long here, for Luke adopts them with only minor editorial changes.

Luke follows Mark closely in narrating the controversy over Jesus' authority to forgive sins (Luke 5:17-26/Mark 2:1-12). Luke's editorial modifications are chiefly minor stylistic refinements. One of these, however, is of some interest for our topic: in place of Mark's question τίς δύναται ἀφιέναι ἁμαρτίας εἰ μὴ εἷς ὁ θεός, Luke 5:21b reads, τίς δύναται ἁμαρτίας ἀφεῖναι εἰ μὴ μόνος ὁ θεός; this smoothing out of the Greek idiom has the effect of diminishing or eliminating the echo of the Shema that is present in Mark. Nonetheless, the theological force of the question remains the same: the onlookers protest that Jesus is claiming a divine prerogative.[135] And indeed, Luke does not want his readers to miss the point: he repeats and reinforces this theme in his distinctive account of the sinful woman who bathes Jesus' feet with her tears and wipes them with her hair (7:36-50). The conclusion of the tale focuses once again on the offense of Jesus' declaration of forgiveness, leaving the guests at the table of Simon the Pharisee to wonder, "Who is this who even forgives sins?" (7:49).

Similarly, Luke includes the Markan story of the controversy over grain-plucking on the sabbath (Luke 6:1-5/Mark 2:23-28). In this case, Luke's most significant editorial move is to delete the epigrammatic comment that the sabbath was made for humankind, not humankind for the sabbath (Mark 2:27). The effect of this deletion is twofold: it focuses attention more sharply on the christological declaration with which the pericope concludes, and it makes the narrative unambiguously clear in attributing to *Jesus* the words "the Son of Man is Lord of the sabbath."[136] Given Luke's distinctive use of κύριος as an indicator of Jesus' divine identity, the saying assumes particular weight in our assessment of Luke's Christology. Who, after all, can claim for himself authority over the sabbath?

Again, Luke preserves and retells the Markan account of Jesus' stilling of a storm (Luke 8:22-25/Mark 4:35-41). The Lukan editorial touches here are minor, for the most part simply abbreviating and tightening the narrative. The distressed disciples, waking Jesus from sleep, address him not as "teacher" (Mark 4:38) but as "master" (ἐπιστάτα, Luke 8:24)—perhaps a slightly more authoritative title of address, but still well short of the theologically freighted κύριε σῶσον of Matthew 8:25.[137] For Luke, as for Mark, the looming theological question of Jesus' identity is articulated in the disciples' unanswered question at the end: "Who then is this, that he commands even the wind and the waves, and they obey him?" (Luke 8:25).

Finally, in the extended apocalyptic discourse in Luke 21, we hear Jesus saying, "The heaven and the earth will pass away, but my words will never pass away" (Luke 21:33). This astonishing claim, repeated verbatim from Mark 13:31,[138] ascribes to Jesus' teaching the same eternal quality that Isaiah posits of the word of Israel's God: "The grass withers, the flower fades; but the word of our God will stand forever" (Isa 40:8). Here, once again, Luke is following Mark's audacious christological lead. But in incorporating this Markan discourse material, Luke makes one highly significant editorial deletion: he completely omits the following verse, Mark 13:32 (= Matt 24:36), which declares that neither the angels in heaven *nor the Son* knows the day and hour when the prophesied eschatological events will come to pass. Thus Luke tacitly avoids any implication of Jesus' subordinate status or inferior knowledge of the future.

In sum, Luke inherits from Mark narrative traditions that portray Jesus as possessing the authority to forgive sins, to claim sovereignty over sabbath restrictions, and to command the elements of nature. Jesus' word possesses such authority because, according to Luke 21:33, it is none other than the word of God that transcends human mortality and the limitations of the created order. In none of these passages does Luke cite a particular Old Testament text. Yet, given his extensive knowledge of and sensitivity to Israel's Scripture, it would strain credulity to suppose that he was oblivious to the scriptural subtexts of these Markan narrative materials.[139] To the contrary, his decision to include these stories in his own Gospel composition is consistent with the κύριος-Christology that we have seen emerging throughout the narrative. These specific stories reinforce and confirm the Lukan characterization of Jesus as sharing/embodying the identity and presence of Israel's God.

How the divine identity hypothesis illumines other Lukan texts. Once we see this pattern of christological claims taking shape in Luke's Gospel, we can go back through the text and perceive, on a second reading, that a Christology of divine identity also illumines and integrates several other details in Luke's picture that would otherwise seem incongruous, or at best random. The cumulative force of these scattered details is perhaps best appreciated in a broad overview.

In several passages, Luke tells the story in a way that creates a fusion of Jesus' activity with God's. The clearest example appears in Luke's version of the ending of the Gerasene demoniac story (Luke 8:39). Jesus instructs him, "Go back to your house and narrate how much *God* has done for you (ὅσα σοι ἐποίησεν ὁ θεός)." Luke then wraps up the story this way: "And he went away proclaiming through the whole city how much *Jesus* had done for him (ὅσα ἐποίησεν αὐτῷ ὁ Ἰησοῦς)." The parallelism is hardly accidental, and Luke offers no hint that the man's proclamation is either erroneous or disobedient; rather, the reader is left to infer that what Jesus had done *was* in fact what God had done. Similar instances show up several times subsequently in the story. For example, immediately following the transfiguration Jesus heals a demon-afflicted boy and gives him back to his father. Luke concludes the episode by remarking,

"And all were astounded at the greatness of *God*" (Luke 9:43). And again, in Luke's distinctive story of the healing of ten lepers (17:11-19), the one leper who turns back is described as first glorifying God, then falling on his face at Jesus' feet and giving thanks to him—a thoroughly understandable response in the narrative context. The subtle and interesting twist, however, occurs in Jesus' own commentary on the event, which seems to be either a musing to himself or a rhetorical aside addressed to the reader: "Were not the ten cleansed? But where are the nine? Were none of them found returning to give glory *to God* except this foreigner?" (17:17-18). Somehow the leper's action of returning to give thanks to Jesus is closely bound together with—or even identified with—giving praise and glory to God.[140] Taken by themselves, these examples do not prove anything about Jesus' direct identity with God. But read in the context of the other passages we have considered, they are suggestive that something more is here than might meet the eye on a first reading.

A weightier set of texts in this Gospel connects Jesus' mission with the Old Testament theme of God's "visitation" of his people. The paradigmatic precursor text is the scene following the call of Moses in the book of Exodus (Exod 4:27-31). Moses and Aaron assemble the elders of the people; Aaron, the spokesman, explains what God has told Moses and (interestingly) performs signs in the sight of the people. Then, according to the LXX account, "the people believed and rejoiced, because God *visited* (ἐπισκέψατο) the sons of Israel, and because he saw their affliction; and the people bowed down and worshiped" (4:31).[141] It is against this background that we should understand the reaction of the crowd upon witnessing Jesus' raising of the dead son of the widow at Nain: "Great fear seized them all, and they glorified God, saying, 'A great prophet has been raised up among us' and '*God has visited* (ἐπισκέψατο) *his people*'" (Luke 7:16). We are seeing here the narrative outworking of the saving event proleptically announced by Zechariah in the beginning of Luke's story: "God *has visited* (ἐπισκέψατο) *his people* and made redemption for them" (1:68).

Jesus' appearance and powerful acts of grace show that God has at last begun to answer the prayers of the psalmists—particularly in their Septuagintal form. For example, in Psalm 105:4 LXX (106:4 MT), we hear this fervent prayer: "Remember us LORD, in the favor you have for your people; *visit us* with your salvation (ἐπίσκεψαι ἡμᾶς ἐν τῷ σωτηρίῳ σου)." Or again, in Psalm 79 LXX (80 MT), an extended metaphor likens Israel to a vine that God has planted but now left to be consumed and destroyed by invading forces; the psalmist then offers up this appeal: "O

God of mighty acts, turn then, look upon us from heaven and see and *visit* (ἐπίσκεψαι) this vine" (79:15 LXX). Both of these psalms recall God's deliverance of Israel from Egypt and intercede for a similar renewal of God's saving mercy, in which God will hear the cry of the people and come ("visit") to save them again.

This same framework of expectation also informs Zechariah's prophetic hope that "through the tender mercy of our God . . . the dawn (ἀνατολή) from on high will *visit* (ἐπισκέψεται) us" (Luke 1:78). We have already examined the associations of this *anatolē* image with the hope for a new Davidic ruler. Yet the hope that this *anatolē* will come "from on high" suggests that the desired coming Messiah may have a heavenly, more than merely human, origin.[142] And Luke's choice of the verb ἐπισκέψεται in Luke 1:78 reechoes the message of 1:76 that it is the God of Israel who is the one expected to visit and redeem. Thus, Luke leads the reader to perceive that John's vocation to "go before the face of *the Lord* to prepare his way" (1:76) will in fact portend the coming and *visitation* not of some intermediary but of none other than Israel's God.

But there is also an ominous note in the announcement of God's visitation, for as the plot of the Gospel unfolds not all in Israel acknowledge and welcome Jesus as the one who brings deliverance. That is why, when Jesus at last draws near to Jerusalem, he weeps over it and prophesies its destruction, "because you did not recognize the time of your *visitation* (τὸν καιρὸν τῆς ἐπισκοπῆς σου)" (Luke 19:44). The weeping figure in this scene is not merely a distraught prophet who, like Elisha in 2 Kings 8:11-12, foresees a coming catastrophe to be inflicted on Israel; instead, he is the one in whom God's saving visitation is personally enacted. His tears anticipate the rejection that he will suffer at the hands of his own people precisely because they fail to recognize his true identity as the one in whom God is present to them.

The same motif of rejection of the divine presence is subtly foreshadowed in Luke's earlier account of Jesus' healing of a crippled, bent-over woman (Luke 13:10-17). Jesus declares her to be a "daughter of Abraham" who has long been bound by Satan but now "loosed from this bondage on the day of the sabbath" where the reminiscence of Jesus' programmatic description of his mission in 4:18-19 is hardly accidental. As God liberated Israel from bondage in Egypt, so Jesus' liberating act of healing is a sign of God's renewed liberation of his people. But this act of sabbath liberation is opposed by the leader of synagogue, who seeks to turn the crowd against Jesus (13:14). After Jesus' decisive reply in 13:15-16 (once again here Luke describes him tellingly as ὁ κύριος), his detractors back down. The language in which Luke describes their silencing contains a subliminal echo of Isaiah 45:16 LXX:

Luke 13:17a: καὶ ταῦτα λέγοντος αὐτοῦ **κατῃσχύνοντο πάντες οἱ ἀντικείμενοι αὐτῷ**

And when he said this, *all those who opposed him were put to shame*.

Isa 45:16a LXX: αἰσχυνθήσονται καὶ ἐντραπήσονται **πάντες οἱ ἀντικείμενοι αὐτῷ**

All those who oppose him shall be put to shame and disgraced.

If we are justified in hearing this echo, its metaleptic force is considerable in the Lukan narrative. Consider the wider context of the passage in the LXX, which differs here noticeably from the MT:

For you are God, and we did not know you, the God of Israel, the Savior. *All those who oppose him shall be put to shame and disgraced*, and shall walk in shame. You islands, dedicate yourselves to me. Israel is saved by the LORD with an everlasting salvation; forevermore, they shall not be ashamed nor disgraced.

The note explicitly sounded by Luke is the shaming of Jesus' opponents, just as the prophecy of Isaiah foretells that those who oppose the God of Israel will be shamed. But the implicit overtones of the echo also whisper that the κύριος Jesus *is* the God of Israel, the Savior (cf. Luke 2:11), whom these opponents have failed to know. The islands (a frequent Isaian locution for the wider Gentile world) will in due course dedicate themselves to him, and Israel—or at least those in Israel who do come to know him—will indeed receive the promise of everlasting salvation, as symbolized by the liberation of the daughter of Abraham in Luke's story. Thus, if we hear the echo of Isaiah 45 LXX in Luke 13:10-17, we will see that this brief passage hints at Luke's larger plotline *in nuce*.

Another converging hint of Jesus' divine identity is found in the motif of Jesus as the object of worship. As noted in the previous chapter, Luke, unlike Matthew, is notably restrained in his use of the verb προσκυνεῖν. He reserves all reference to the worship of Jesus until the very ending of his Gospel, where we are told that the risen Jesus was carried up into heaven and that the disciples "worshiped him (προσκυνήσαντες αὐτόν) and returned into Jerusalem with great joy" (Luke 24:52). The narrative impact of this concluding description is enhanced by the complete absence of other references to "worship" in this story, save one: in the account of Jesus' temptation in the wilderness, the devil seeks to cajole Jesus into worshiping him, and Jesus emphatically rejects the temptation with a word of Scripture: "It is written, 'The Lord your God you will worship (προσκυνήσεις), and him alone you will serve'" (Luke 4:8; quoting Deut 6:13). Given this single decisive directive, what are we to make of Luke's ending? It seems there are really only three possibilities: the disciples' worship of the risen Jesus is a misguided act of idolatry, or Jesus is in fact the Lord God, or Luke is a confused and careless narrator. It seems that the Gospel of Luke presses us incessantly toward the second of these options.[143]

That is perhaps why, at a couple of junctures in the narrative, Luke's Jesus disconcertingly speaks as though from the divine perspective. The most striking example of this dramatic device appears in Jesus' lament, in the midst of his journey to Jerusalem, over the city in which he knows he will perish: "Jerusalem, Jerusalem, the city that kills the prophets and stones those who are sent to her: how often I have desired to gather your children together as a bird gathers her brood under her wings, and you were not willing" (Luke 13:34). This image derives its particular poignancy from its resonance with several Old Testament passages in which Israel's God is depicted metaphorically as a bird spreading wings to protect Israel. In Deuteronomy 32:10-12, God's care for Israel (here personified as "Jacob") in the wilderness is compared to an eagle's care for its young:

> He sustained him in a desert land, in a howling wilderness waste;
> he shielded him, cared for him, guarded him as the apple of his eye.
> *As an eagle stirs up its nest, and hovers over its young;*
> *as it spreads its wings, takes them up, and bears them aloft on its pinions,*
> the LORD alone guided him; no foreign god was with him.

A similar image appears in the psalmist's confident expression of trust in God as Israel's refuge:

> You who live in the shelter of the Most High,
> who abide in the shadow of the Almighty,
> will say to the LORD, "My refuge and my fortress;
> my God, in whom I trust."
> For he will deliver you from the snare of the fowler
> and from the deadly pestilence;

he will cover you with his pinions,
and under his wings you will find refuge.

(Ps 91:1-4a)

With images such as these shaping Israel's understanding of God's providential care, the hearer of Jesus' lament in Luke 13:34 will immediately
be struck by two remarkable features of his sorrowful words. First, even
though Jesus is facing impending violence and death, he does not appeal
to God to grant the protection of sheltering wings; instead, *he casts himself, at least metaphorically, in the role of the God whose wings seek to shelter
Israel.* Second, his lament portrays Jerusalem as rejecting the protection
he has repeatedly sought to give (even though Luke's narrative makes
no mention of any previous visits by Jesus to Jerusalem!), just as Israel
in Deuteronomy 32 is portrayed as a stubborn people who have forgotten the God who gave them birth (Deut 32:15-18). Who then should we
understand to be the speaker in Luke 13:34? These daring words can
hardly be merely the complaint of a rejected prophet. They are nothing
other than a cry from the heart of Israel's God.

A slightly less dramatic example of Jesus' speech in the persona
of God appears in Luke's apocalyptic discourse, in which Jesus warns
his disciples of coming persecution and admonishes them not to worry
ahead of time about how to speak to the kings and governors who will
arrest them. Why? Because, he assures them, "I will give you a mouth
and a wisdom that none of those who oppose you will be able to stand
against or contradict" (Luke 21:14-15). Since Jesus has already prophesied
his own impending death, this word of assurance seems to presuppose
not only his continuing power beyond death to aid his followers but also
his authority to confer speech and wisdom in a supernatural manner,
just as God promised to give Moses the words to speak before Pharaoh:
"Who gives speech to mortals? Who makes them mute or deaf, seeing
or blind? Is it not I, the LORD? Now go, I will be with your mouth and
teach you what you are to speak" (Exod 4:11-12). This is another illustration of the way in which a consistent Moses typology breaks down under
the logic of Luke's narration: Jesus is cast here not as the Moses figure
who will be given words to testify but rather as the Lord who is the giver
of powerful speech.[144]

The authority claimed here for Jesus belongs to a larger pattern of
Lukan narration in which Jesus is said to confer powers and blessings
that no one but God could confer. How is it that he can appoint disciples
and give them authority over demons and diseases (Luke 9:1-2, 10:19)?

How can he promise, after the resurrection, to send power from on high ("the promise of the Father") upon his followers (24:49) and then, in the dramatic opening scenes of Acts, fulfill that promise by "pouring out" the Holy Spirit (Acts 2:33)? Even more than the power to forgive sins or still storms, surely the power to send the Spirit is a prerogative that belongs exclusively to God.[145] In Peter's Pentecost sermon, the solution to this riddle is made clear: the outpouring of God's Spirit demonstrates that the risen Jesus is seated at God's right hand where he possesses the divine authority that was prefigured in the mysterious words of Psalm 110:1. Simply put, Jesus has the authority to send the Spirit because, as David declared long ago, he is "Lord." The Spirit that Jesus now sends is the same Spirit that God named as "my Spirit" in the prophecy of Joel 3:1 (2:28 ET) and promised to pour out on all flesh (Acts 2:17). While the relations here between Father, Son, and Spirit are complex—I will forbear from any attempt to situate Luke's position in relation to the later controversy over the *filioque* clause—we see that in the giving of the Spirit there is once again the closest possible *Verbindung* of Jesus' identity with the divine identity.

In view of these exegetical findings, I would hazard the following conclusion: *The "low" Christology that much twentieth-century criticism perceived in Luke's Gospel was an artificial construction achieved by excluding the hermeneutical relevance of the wider canonical witness, particularly the Old Testament allusions in Luke's story. It is therefore precisely by attending more fully to the Old Testament allusions in Luke's Gospel that we gain a deeper and firmer grasp of the theological coherence between Luke's testimony and what the church's dogmatic tradition has classically affirmed about the identity of Jesus.*

The Redeemer of Israel

We conclude these reflections on the identity of Jesus in Luke's Gospel by returning to Cleopas and his anonymous companion on the road to Emmaus. "We had hoped," they say dejectedly, "that he was the one who was going to redeem Israel (ὁ μέλλων λυτροῦσθαι τὸν Ἰσραήλ)" (Luke 24:21a). We have seen throughout this chapter that their hope, however ill-informed, was not wrong: Jesus was and is the one who redeems Israel—as promised in the birth and infancy stories and retrospectively explained in the apostolic speeches of Acts. He does so in more ways than the poor sight-impaired Emmaus disciples could have imagined. He redeems Israel as the Spirit-anointed Servant who announces liberation and leads Israel on a new exodus; he redeems Israel as the royal Davidic Messiah who redefines and restores the promised kingdom through his own suffering and vindication; he redeems Israel as the prophet who, like Elijah and Elisha, works healing miracles and unsettles corrupt power. The litany could continue through the many and various ways in which Jesus' actions complete and hermeneutically reshape Israel's complex scriptural story.

But the plaintive words of the Emmaus road trudgers point ironically and unerringly to the deepest truth about Jesus: he is the Redeemer of Israel. And who, according to the scriptural witness, is the Redeemer of Israel? The answer lies in a catena of texts from Isaiah. Let us hear them afresh, recalling that the chief concern of the mysterious stranger on the road was to elucidate the ways in which "the things about himself" were imbedded in Scripture:

> Do not fear, you worm Jacob, you insect Israel!
> I will help you, says the LORD;
> your Redeemer (LXX: ὁ λυτρούμενος σε) is the Holy One of Israel.
>
> (Isa 41:14)[146]

> Thus says the LORD, your Redeemer (LXX: ὁ λυτρούμενος ὑμᾶς), the
>   Holy One of Israel:
> For your sake I will send to Babylon and break down all the bars,
> and the shouting of the Chaldeans will be turned to lamentation.
> I am the LORD, your Holy One, the Creator of Israel, your King.
>
> (Isa 43:14-15)

> Thus says the LORD, your Redeemer (LXX: ὁ λυτρούμενός σε),
> who formed you in the womb:
> I am the LORD, who made all things, who alone stretched
>   out the heavens,
> who by myself spread out the earth;
> . . . who says of Jerusalem, "It shall be inhabited,"
> and of the cities of Judah, "They shall be rebuilt,
> and I will raise up their ruins."
>
> (Isa 44:24, 26b)

> Thus says the LORD, the Redeemer of Israel and his Holy One
>   (LXX: ὁ ῥυσάμενός σε ὁ θεὸς Ισραήλ),
> to one deeply despised, abhorred by the nations, the slave of rulers,
> "Kings shall see and stand up,
> princes, and they shall prostrate themselves,
> because of the LORD, who is faithful,
> the Holy One of Israel, who has chosen you."
>
> (Isa 49:7)

The brilliant dramatic irony of Luke's Emmaus road scene nudges readers inexorably toward a subtle but overwhelming conclusion: the two disciples are wrong to be discouraged but right to have hoped for Jesus to be the one who would redeem Israel. In their puzzled disappointment, they truly name Jesus' identity without realizing what they are saying, for the Redeemer of Israel is none other than Israel's God. And Jesus, in truth, is the embodied, unrecognized, but scripturally attested presence of the One for whom they unwittingly hoped.

§14 LIGHT TO THE NATIONS
The Church's Witness in Luke's Narrative

It is widely acknowledged that Luke, in contrast to the other Evangelists, is a relatively cosmopolitan author who seeks to place his account of Jesus on the map of the broader Mediterranean world. In Luke's second volume, Paul declares in his address to King Agrippa and the Roman governor Festus that the events to which he testifies are, in effect, a matter of public record: "Indeed, the king knows about these things, and to him I speak freely; for I am certain that none of these things has escaped his notice, for this was not done in a corner" (Acts 26:26). The events that Luke describes are framed by the social and political history of the Greco-Roman *oikoumenē*, not just by the local culture of Palestine. The most celebrated instance of this historical framing is of course the much-debated reference in Luke 2:1-2 to the decree of Caesar Augustus mandating a census "when Quirinius was governor of Syria."[147] Similarly, Luke 3:1-2 situates the beginning of John the Baptist's proclamation "in the fifteenth year of the reign of Tiberius Caesar" and also lists other local rulers and officials, including Pontius Pilate. But much of the evidence for Luke's cultural cosmopolitanism actually comes from the second volume of his work rather than from his Gospel. The narrative world of the Gospel sets the stage for the later expansion of "the Way" into the Roman Empire, and one finds in the Gospel a few foreshadowings of this later development; nonetheless, on the whole, Luke is strikingly cautious in reading prefigurations of this subsequent history back into the time of Jesus.

Indeed, at some points Luke actually deletes from his sources material that would trace the roots of the later Gentile mission back to sayings or actions of Jesus of Nazareth. For instance, despite his general interest in positive depictions of female characters, Luke omits Mark's story of Jesus' barrier-breaking encounter with the Syrophoenician woman (Mark 7:24-30). Even more surprisingly, in retelling the story of Jesus' action against the money changers in the temple, he abbreviates Jesus' words: where the Markan Jesus cites a line in full from Isaiah 56:7 ("My house shall be called a house of prayer *for all nations*"), Luke's Jesus says, more crisply, "My house shall be a house of prayer" (Mark 11:17; Luke 19:46). One would think that such details of the Markan narrative would appeal strongly to Luke, given his interest in the gospel's spread to the Gentile world. Why, then, does he omit them? In the case of the Syrophoenician woman, we might conjecture that Luke is nonplussed by a tale in which Jesus is apparently bested and corrected by a witty interlocutor. But it is more difficult to imagine any similar reason for his deletion of "for all nations" from Jesus' words in the temple.[148] It seems likelier that Luke simply regards these elements of the tradition as historically anachronistic: they do not fit his program of narrating the story καθεξῆς, for they project back onto the Jesus-tradition a vision for extending God's grace to Gentiles, a vision that Luke himself regards as a post-Pentecost revelation of the Spirit in the church (Acts 10–15).

When we turn, therefore, to consider the ways in which Luke's *Gospel* draws upon Israel's Scripture to position the community of Jesus' followers in relation to the pagan world, we find a surprising paucity of material. Matthew persistently sprinkles justifications for the Gentile mission throughout his narrative about Jesus. But Luke reserves such justifications for the Acts of the Apostles, so that most of the relevant scriptural texts are to be found there. We shall consider some of this material briefly, because it casts reflected light on certain material in the Gospel. For the most part, however, we must restrict our discussion to the evidence that appears in the Gospel itself.[149] The limited material we do find can be sorted into two general headings: confrontation with the threatening power of empire, and revelation to the Gentile world.

Confronting the power of empire

At a few key junctures in the story, Luke employs Scripture to set his community of readers in a relation of complex countercultural resistance to Roman authority.[150] A stance of resistance is already implied in the politically freighted angelic announcement of Jesus' birth to the shepherds: "to you is born this day in the city of David a Savior (σωτήρ), who is the Messiah (χριστός), the Lord (κύριος)" (Luke 2:11). The titles σωτήρ and κύριος ("Savior" and "Lord") were typically claimed as epithets of the Roman emperor. To cite a single representative instance, a first-century inscription from Asia Minor acclaims "Divine Augustus Caesar, son of a god, imperator of land and sea, the benefactor and savior (σώτηρ) of the whole world."[151] And, as we have noted previously, the birth of Jesus as χριστός in the "city of David" is one of many indicators identifying Jesus as the promised Davidic royal Messiah, the rightful heir of the throne of Israel. Thus, the angel's provocative proclamation alerts Luke's readers that this Jesus is destined to reclaim the sovereignty that Caesar has falsely usurped.

Luke's account of the postbaptismal temptation of Jesus (Luke 4:1-13) offers further insight on this matter. Luke's telling of the tale is similar to Matthew's (Matt 4:1-11), with two salient differences, one well-known, the other too little noted. The well-known difference is that Luke arranges the order of the temptations so that the climactic third temptation occurs on the pinnacle of the temple in Jerusalem; this narrative ordering accords with the centrality of the temple in Luke's theological geography.[152] The little-noted difference, of greater import for our present purposes, is that Luke gives the devil one important extra line to speak, unparalleled in Matthew. After showing Jesus all the kingdoms of the world, he says: "To you I will give their glory and all this authority; *for it has been given over* (παραδέδοται) *to me, and I give it to anyone I please*" (Luke 4:6). In the first-century Mediterranean world, this claim can mean only one thing: the Roman emperor possesses authority because it has been given him by the devil.[153] The kingdoms of the world, which were under the power of the Roman imperium, are said to belong to Satan. Jesus' faithfulness to God entails rejecting the temptation to seize this power for himself, and he overcomes the tempter precisely by clinging to the words of Deuteronomy: "Worship the LORD your God, and serve only him" (Deut 6:13). The message of Scripture, as appropriated by Jesus, serves as an antidote to the idolatrous pretensions of the empire. Because Jesus accepts the role of obedient Israel, quoting Deuteronomy three times (Deut 8:3, 6:13, 6:16) in his responses to the devil, he overcomes idolatry, is filled with "the power of the Spirit" (Luke 4:14), and in the end receives true glory and authority (Acts 2:32-36). In this way, he models the posture that his followers are called to assume in relation to the empire: resisting idolatry and worshiping God alone.

This reading of the temptation narrative stands in sharp contrast to the older, widely influential one that claims Luke–Acts should be interpreted as "political apologetic," seeking to present the church as harmless to the Roman authorities.[154] Much of the evidence for such a view is found in Acts, and even there it relies on a selective reading of the evidence that fails to do full justice to Luke's account of the word of

God as a disturbing force that creates new communities decidedly out of step with Rome's symbolic world. But within the Gospel of Luke itself, it is difficult to sustain the claim that Rome is presented in a favorable light. In his account of the exorcism of the Gerasene demoniac (Luke 8:26-39),[155] Luke retains from his source (Mark 8:9) the provocative detail that in response to Jesus' asking his name, the man replies "'Legion,' for many demons had entered him" (Luke 8:30). In the Roman world, it would be impossible to overlook the political symbolism of this name as a representation of Roman military might or to miss the significance of the detail that Jesus expels the Legion of demons into a herd of swine, unclean pagan animals, who immediately rush into the water and drown. If Luke meant to portray Jesus as innocuous to Roman power, he was certainly an incompetent redactor.

It is also noteworthy that in the Lukan account of Jesus' apocalyptic prophecy of the destruction of Jerusalem, we find this distinctive formulation: "For there will be great distress on the earth and wrath against this people; they will fall by the edge of the sword and be taken away as captives among all nations; and Jerusalem will be trampled on by Gentiles, until the times of the Gentiles are fulfilled" (Luke 21:23b-24). The whole passage is strongly reminiscent of Tobit 14:4-5, which also refers to the people of Israel being taken away as captives, the temple being destroyed, and everything being left desolate until the future fulfillment of "the times of the age." Both in Tobit and in Luke, the primary focus is on God's judgment of Israel, but in neither text are the Gentile forces seen as benign. Jesus' prophecy in Luke 21 unmistakably portrays the trampling Gentile army surrounding Jerusalem (Luke 21:20) as a hostile, destructive force.[156] And the phrase "the times of the Gentiles" designates a limited interval that will, in the history foreordained by God, be superseded by God's kingdom. In Tobit's vision of the future, "Then the nations in the whole world will all be converted and worship God in truth. They will all abandon their idols, which deceitfully have led them into error; and in righteousness they will praise the eternal God" (Tob 14:5). This is the trajectory of Jewish apocalyptic thought to which Luke 21 unmistakably belongs. God's eschatological judgment will not exempt Roman rulers, for the day of judgment "will come upon all who live on the face of the whole earth" (Luke 21:35).

In the meantime, however, Roman might prevails, and Jesus himself falls victim to the Roman punishment of crucifixion. It is not insignificant that Luke's third passion prediction retains the Markan prophecy that the Son of Man "will be handed over to the Gentiles" to suffer mocking, spitting, flogging, and finally execution (Mark 10:33-34/Luke 18:31-33). The centurion's declaration at the foot of the cross that "this man was righteous/innocent" (δίκαιος; Luke 23:47) hardly exculpates the Roman authority; if anything, it underlines their complicity with the Jewish leaders in perpetrating a violent and unjust murder.[157]

This complicity is vividly depicted in a passage in Acts 4 that displays, perhaps more clearly than any other in Luke's two volumes, the way in which the Lukan passion narrative is to be retrospectively interpreted and the way in which the church is called to perceive its position of countercultural resistance to oppressive power, Roman and Jewish alike. Luke gives a remarkable account of the nascent Jerusalem church gathered in corporate prayer. After the release of Peter and John from the custody of the Jewish authorities, the community offers thanksgiving to God by invoking the words of Psalm 2 as a prophetic prefiguration of the events that have taken place:

> [T]hey raised their voices together to God and said, "Sovereign Lord, who made the heaven and the earth, the sea and everything in them, it is you who said by the Holy Spirit through the mouth of our father David, your servant:
>
> > 'Why did the *Gentiles* (ἔθνη) rage,
> > and the *peoples* (λαοί) imagine vain things?
> > The kings of the earth took their stand,
> > and the rulers have gathered together (συνήχθησαν)
> > against the Lord and against his Messiah (χριστοῦ).' [Ps 2:1-2]
>
> For in this city, in fact, both Herod and Pontius Pilate, with the Gentiles (ἔθνεσιν) and the peoples (λαοῖς) of Israel, gathered together (συνήχθησαν) against your holy servant Jesus, whom you anointed (ἔχρισας), to do whatever your hand and your plan had predestined to take place. And now, Lord, look at their threats, and grant to your servants to speak your word with all boldness, while you stretch out your hand to heal, and signs and wonders are performed through the name of your holy servant Jesus."
>
> (Acts 4:24-30)

As the Greek words in parentheses show, the community's prayer produces an exegesis of Psalm 2:1-2, in virtual *pesher* style. God spoke through the mouth of David to declare in advance that the Lord's Anointed would meet unified opposition from both Gentiles and Jews; the harassment now experienced by the community of God's servants is continuing evidence that the rulers of this world are in league against God's designs.

Interestingly, this interpretation is achieved by taking λαοί in Psalm 2:1 LXX, which originally should surely be understood in synonymous parallelism with ἔθνη, as a reference to Israel. This forced exegesis explains the unusual plural form λαοῖς Ἰσραήλ ("*peoples* of Israel") in Acts 4:27. Luke has mapped the church's experience onto Psalm 2, and vice versa. The intertextual fusion proclaims the unholy alliance of Gentile and Jewish forces against God's Messiah and at the same time illuminates Luke's account of God's sovereign plan, which cannot be thwarted by human opposition.

Luke's citation of this psalm, therefore, functions metaleptically to provide assurance and boldness (παρρησία, Acts 4:29, 31) for the community in its stance of countercultural witness. Those who know the psalm will recall that the furious opposition of the kings of the earth is futile: God sits in the heavens and laughs at this pathetic resistance to his plans (Ps 2:4). God will "break them with a rod of iron, and dash them in pieces like a potter's vessel" (2:9). Therefore the community of Jesus' followers is empowered to speak and act peacefully and boldly, knowing that their vindication is in the hand of the God who has already raised Jesus from the dead. This example shows clearly how Luke narrates the church's story (the arrest of Peter and John) intertextually (in relation to Ps 2) in order to encourage the community in its countercultural mission.

But careful attention to the scriptural intertexts in the community's prayer reveals still more. The opening words of the prayer (Acts 4:24) address God as "Sovereign Lord, who made the heaven and the earth, the sea and everything in them" (ὁ ποιήσας τὸν οὐρανὸν καὶ τὴν γῆν καὶ τὴν θάλασσαν καὶ πάντα τὰ ἐν αὐτοῖς). This description of God originates in the Ten Commandments, as formulated in Exodus: because in six days "the Lord made the heaven and the earth and the sea and everything in them" (ἐποίησεν κύριος τὸν οὐρανὸν καὶ τὴν γῆν καὶ τὴν θάλασσαν καὶ πάντα τὰ ἐν αὐτοῖς), the seventh day is to be kept as a sabbath rest (Exod 20:11). Since Luke has already made connections between the sabbath and the proclaiming of release to the captives, this is a singularly appropriate way of addressing God for a community celebrating the release of their leaders from prison. Their new freedom is perhaps to be understood as a sabbath event, a sign of the power of the creator God who made all things.

But a second intertextual layer is perhaps still more significant as a context for the church's celebratory prayer. By addressing God as the one who "made the heaven and the earth, the sea and everything in them," they are invoking another psalm. The one psalm in which this phrase appears is Psalm 146, a psalm already connected to significant prefigurations of Jesus' healing activity. The full force of the allusion can be felt only if we bring to mind the psalm in its entirety (with a few lines particularly pertinent for Luke's narrative context set in italics and the line echoed in the community's prayer in bold):

> Praise the LORD! Praise the LORD, O my soul!
> I will praise the LORD as long as I live; I will sing praises to my God
>   all my life long.
> *Do not put your trust in princes, in mortals, in whom there is no help*
>   (LXX: σωτηρία).
> When their breath departs, they return to the earth; on that very day
>   their plans perish.
> Happy are those whose help is the God of Jacob, whose hope is in the
>   LORD their God,
> **who made heaven and earth, the sea, and all that is in them**
>   (LXX: τὸν ποιήσαντα τὸν οὐρανὸν καὶ τὴν γῆν, τὴν θάλασσαν
>   καὶ πάντα τὰ ἐν αὐτοῖς);
> who keeps faith forever;
> *who executes justice for the oppressed*; who gives food to the hungry.
> *The LORD sets the prisoners free;*
> *the LORD opens the eyes of the blind.*
> *The LORD lifts up those who are bowed down*; the LORD loves the righteous.
> The LORD watches over the strangers; he upholds the
>   orphan and the widow,
> but the way of the wicked he brings to ruin.
> The LORD will reign forever, your God, O Zion, for all generations.
> Praise the LORD!

The resonance of this psalm for the Jerusalem church is striking. Not only does it celebrate the release of prisoners, but it also highlights the futility and mortality of *princes*, thereby nicely introducing Luke's account of the community's meditation on Psalm 2, which speaks of the useless resistance of kings and rulers to the Lord and his Anointed (Acts 4:25-28). With its references to opening the eyes of the blind and lifting up those who are bowed down, this psalm recalls the gracious and powerful actions of Jesus earlier in the story, and it also gestures toward Peter and John's healing of the crippled man in Acts 3, the event that had precipitated their arrest in the first place. Indeed, it is precisely such acts of healing that are recalled in the conclusion of the church's prayer (Acts 4:30). And the overall theme of Psalm 146—praise for God's power, and hope in his setting things right—is precisely apposite for the whole prayer that will follow in Acts 4:25-30.

Thus, both in the Gospel and in Acts, Luke portrays Jesus and his followers as carrying out the inversion prophesied in Mary's song at the beginning of the Gospel: "He has brought down the powerful from their thrones, and lifted up the lowly" (Luke 1:52). This is not to say that they are revolutionaries in the ordinary sense; rather, they are emissaries of a new order of things, in which Jesus transforms kingship and authority. "The kings of the Gentiles lord it over them; and those in authority over them are called benefactors. But not so with you." The disciples are to become servants, just as Jesus himself has become "one who serves" (Luke 22:24-27). Nonetheless, this new order remains deeply threatening to the authorities of the present age. As the Jewish adversaries of Paul and Silas in Thessalonica complain, "These people who have been turning the world upside down have come here also. . . . *They are all acting contrary to the decrees of Caesar* (ἀπέναντι τῶν δογμάτων Καίσαρος), *saying that there is another king named Jesus*" (Acts 17:6-7). Is the charge true? It is indeed, even though with deft dramatic irony Luke enables us to see that the Thessalonian protesters fail to understand the full import of their own words. The world really has been turned upside down by this new king who teaches the poor and hungry to rejoice in hope, and the wealthy to mourn and weep (Luke 6:20-26).

A light for revelation to the Gentiles

In following Luke's retelling of the story of Israel and his portrait of Jesus' identity we have already touched in passing upon a handful of texts that anticipate the church's later mission to the pagan world. Now we foreground the way in which they suggest scriptural warrants for extending the good news about Jesus to the Gentiles.

At the presentation of the infant Jesus in the temple, the aged prophet Simeon, under the inspiration of the Holy Spirit, thanks God and announces that in this child he now can see the dawning of the salvation (σωτήριον) that God has prepared

> . . . before the face of *all the peoples*:
> a light (φῶς) for revelation to the Gentiles (ἐθνῶν),
> and glory to your people Israel.
>
> (Luke 2:30-32)

The parallelism of the last two lines indicates the universal scope of the salvation to be provided in Jesus; it is to be for Gentile and Jew alike.

Simeon's expectation is grounded in the same passages from Isaiah that we have heard echoing elsewhere throughout Luke's narrative. God has appointed his Spirit-anointed Servant to "bring forth justice to the nations" (Isa 42:1) and to be "a light to the nations" (φῶς ἐθνῶν, Isa 42:6 LXX). And again in Isaiah 49, the Servant is told by God:

> It is too light a thing that you should be my servant
> to raise up the tribes of Jacob
> and to restore the survivors of Israel;
> I will give you as a light to the nations (φῶς ἐθνῶν)
> that my salvation (σωτηρίαν) may reach to the end of the earth (ἕως
>   ἐσχάτου τῆς γῆς).
>
> (Isa 49:6)[158]

Thus, in the Lukan infancy narrative, Simeon gratefully prophesies that the infant Jesus is the one who will at last fulfill this Isaianic role of shining a light to the nations.

That Luke has these passages in mind is also suggested in the hinge texts that conclude the Gospel and introduce the Acts of the Apostles. At the conclusion of the risen Lord's appearance to his disciples in Jerusalem in Luke 24, he instructs them that "*it is written* that . . . repentance and forgiveness of sins is to be proclaimed" in the name of the Messiah "*to all nations*, beginning from Jerusalem" (24:47). Here, as throughout Luke 24, we are given a formal claim of scriptural support for the message but no specific indication of the texts where it is to be found. We are required to keep reading in the second volume of the narrative to find the answer. The theme of a mission to the nations is reiterated in Acts 1: "But you will receive power when the Holy Spirit has come upon you; and you will be my witnesses in Jerusalem, in all Judea and Samaria, and to the ends of the earth (ἕως ἐσχάτου τῆς γῆς)." Here the direct echo of Isaiah 49:6 hints that it is through the witness-bearing of Jesus' disciples that the nations are to receive the light of revelation that Isaiah promised, whose first glimmers Simeon saw.

The hint is amply confirmed as the plot unfolds, finally coming to full disclosure when Paul and Barnabas sternly reply to Jewish detractors in Pisidian Antioch:

> Then both Paul and Barnabas spoke out boldly, saying, "It was necessary that the word of God should be spoken first to you. Since you reject it and judge yourselves to be unworthy of eternal life, we are now turning to the Gentiles. For so the Lord has commanded us, saying,

'I have set you to be a light for the Gentiles,
so that you may bring salvation to the ends of the earth.'"

(Acts 13:46-47)

Here at last we find a direct quotation confirming earlier intimations that Luke understands Isaiah 49:6 to portend a mission of proclamation to the whole pagan world.

Passages such as Acts 13:46-47 are sometimes understood to close the door on any possibility of preaching the gospel to Jews, but the logic of Luke's narrative works against such a reading.[159] Much later in the story, we still find Paul speaking of a universal mission of proclamation to Jews and Gentiles alike: "I stand here, testifying to both small and great, saying nothing but what the prophets and Moses said would take place: that the Messiah must suffer, and that, by being the first to rise from the dead, *he would proclaim light both to our people and to the Gentiles*" (26:22-23). This two-pronged mission to Jews and Gentiles alike is, as it were, hardwired into the gospel proclamation by the logic of Isaiah 49, which speaks both of restoring Israel and of sending light to the ends of the earth.[160] Indeed, these two actions of God are different facets of the single reality that Isaiah calls "salvation."

The same Isaianic substratum also grounds Luke's introduction of the public ministry of John the Baptist (Luke 3:1-6), whose work of preparing the way of the Lord is said to correspond to the prophecy of Isaiah 40:3-5. And the climactic line of Luke's quotation from Isaiah is this: "and *all flesh* will see the salvation (σωτήριον) of God" (Luke 3:6). Thus, Luke's stage-setting narration—one of Luke's very rare authorial voiceovers—directs the careful reader back to Isaiah 40, with its visionary hope for a new exodus that will ultimately restore and bless Israel, while also drawing all nations to acknowledge the universal sovereignty of Israel's God. It is possibly this same scriptural image that lies behind Jesus' saying that people will come from east and west, north and south, to feast with Abraham and Isaac and Jacob in the kingdom of God (Luke 13:28-29). There is no specific reference here to Gentiles, but when the saying is read retrospectively within the overall plot of Luke–Acts, this interpretation seems likely.

Even the programmatic episode of Jesus' initial proclamation in the synagogue at Nazareth foreshadows, as we have seen, the message that God's healing grace might embrace non-Israelite outsiders. Jesus provocatively recounts Gentile-inclusive episodes from the stories of Elijah and Elisha (Luke 4:22-30; recalling 1 Kgs 17:1-16 and 2 Kgs 5:1-14), episodes that prefigure the Gentile-inclusion controversies played out subsequently in the pages of Acts.

All things considered, however, the most striking feature of this survey is how little direct scriptural argumentation we find in the Gospel of Luke for an evangelistic outreach to the pagan world. The implied readers of this Gospel are encouraged to understand themselves in direct continuity with Israel's story, as immediate heirs of the tradition. Such readers will encounter a few crucial clues that the eschatological consummation of God's promises to Israel might entail the inclusion of Gentiles to join Israel in worshiping the one true God—as signaled already in Luke 2:30-32. Those readers who perceive the hermeneutical centrality of Isaiah for Luke's account of Israel's eschatological destiny will sense that Gentiles must feature somewhere in the script of God's plan, for surely the "sovereign Lord who made the heaven and the earth, the sea and everything in them" desires that his salvation reach to the ends of the earth. But Luke holds back and does not develop this theme until the second volume of his epic narrative, where it emerges as a central concern of the story, surrounded by numerous scriptural arguments and supports, building momentum in the exasperated speech of Paul and Barnabas at Pisidian Antioch and finally climaxing in James' decision in favor of the Gentile mission at the apostolic council in Acts 15:

> "This agrees with the words of the prophets, as it is written, 'After this I will return, and I will rebuild the dwelling of David, which has fallen; from its ruins I will rebuild it, and I will set it up, so that all other peoples may seek the Lord—*even all the Gentiles over whom my name has been called.* Thus says the Lord, who has been making these things known from long ago.'"
>
> (Acts 15:15-18; quoting [roughly] Amos 9:11-12 LXX)

James' judgment precisely parallels the narrative logic of Isaiah 49:6: the raising up of the tribes of Jacob / the dwelling of David will lead other peoples to seek the Lord, and the Gentiles who come in response to the good news of God's salvation should be welcomed into the eschatological restored community.

In Luke's Gospel, however, we receive only slight prefigurations of this fuller development, and the characters in the story, Jesus' disciples, come to understand these things only after the resurrection, with the guidance of the Holy Spirit and the empirical emergence of Gentile converts. Within the bounds of the first volume of Luke's account, the more characteristic function of Scripture is to shape the community of Jesus' followers as "a people prepared for the Lord" (Luke 1:16), a distinct people living in obedience to God and therefore prepared to resist the world's temptations, to share their resources with the poor, and to do works of love and mercy.

§15 OPENED EYES AND MINDS
Luke's Scriptural Hermeneutics

We have surveyed some representative samples taken from the vast range of material in the Gospel of Luke, as well as in Acts, in which Luke draws upon Scripture to narrate the fulfillment of God's dealing with Israel. From these samples, what can we conclude about Luke's strategies of intertextual narration? We will first offer a few observations about Luke's methods of interpretation, before turning to a summary of some major themes that emerge in his telling of the story.

Luke's manner of engaging Scripture

Luke is above all a storyteller. The mode of his narration is not so didactic as Matthew's; nor is it, like Mark's, mysterious and elusive. Instead, the story that he tells has the character of a *dramatic epic*; it is sweeping in scope and measured in pace. The story's overall message finally emerges with lucidity, but Luke takes his time in allowing the plot to unfold on a grand scale. The tone of the narrative is gracious, patient, and confident, inviting readers to settle back and savor its development, as many different lines and images converge slowly into a complex unity. We might put it this way: Luke's narrative is *symphonic*. It develops long melody lines, plays variations upon them in multiple movements, but finally brings them all together as part of a unified artistic plan—a plan whose composer, Luke insists, is God.

This dramatic epic character of Luke's narrative has several implications for the way in which he weaves Scripture into the composition. The Old Testament texts that appear explicitly in the story are found almost exclusively in the speeches of the characters. Apart from the prologues to each of the two volumes, Luke the narrator almost never steps from behind the curtain to comment on the action.[161] Rather, it is the characters in the drama who cite and interpret the scriptural texts, prompting the reader to consider how the events on stage are linked to earlier events, earlier chapters in the epic. These promptings create a strong sense of historical continuity, an impression that Luke's story belongs integrally to an older series of stories that the reader is expected to recognize, even though the narrator does not pause to explain or retell those older stories. They are treated as *déjà lu*, already read.

For this reason, the Gospel of Luke is fraught with background, thick with scriptural memory. Sometimes Luke will refer in passing to Abraham or Moses or Elijah in a way that requires the hearer of the Gospel to know who these characters are and what they did. More often, however, he will make no explicit reference at all but simply tell the story of Jesus in a way that evocatively echoes the scriptural tales. We have compared this narrative technique to the fleeting projection of shadowy images on a screen behind the action taking place at the front of the stage. For example, Luke ends his narration of Jesus' raising the son of the widow at Nain with the clause, "and he gave him to his mother" (Luke 7:15). The echo of 1 Kings 17:23 will elude the ears of the uninformed reader, but the reader who hears it will pause, smile, and reflect. Luke performs intertextual riffs of this kind again and again. The allusions and echoes accumulate throughout the story. Some of them seem to be explicitly figural, encouraging us to understand Old Testament characters as direct prefigurations of Jesus; others are more indirect, chiefly reminding readers that the God who is scripting the events of Jesus' life is the same God who was known to Israel in the past. And in some cases, the intertextual links between Scripture and Gospel enact ironic reversals: they require readers to mark the distance traveled between (say) Elijah and Jesus, to recognize the reversal of scriptural *topoi*. Jesus will raise the dead son of a widow, but he will not call down fire from heaven to incinerate his opponents.

The effect of this accumulation of scriptural imagery is to encourage the formation of a certain kind of reading community. Luke is *creating* readers, seeking to foster the intertextual competence necessary to appreciate the nuances of the sort of narrative he is spinning. He is not only encouraging his readers to have confident assurance (ἀσφάλεια) about the things they have been taught (Luke 1:4) but also teaching them who they are—the heirs of this story—and how they should therefore read. A story of such complexity and nuance helps to cultivate readers who read patiently, carefully, and subtly. Of course, such cultivation does not happen automatically. It is probably right to see Luke's Gospel as, inter alia, a teaching tool, a story crying out for commentary. The necessary instruction would have been provided by teachers in the early church who expounded the text for their communities of Gentile converts and explained some of its intertextual intricacies.

Yet to describe this gracious, elegant story as a teaching tool is to fall short of appreciating its literary skill and impact. The story does far more than instruct; it creates a world. Those who enter sympathetically into that world will be enchanted, comforted, challenged, even liberated. But one can hardly remain long in Luke's world without seeking to understand more deeply what the risen Lord Jesus means by declaring that "everything written about me in the Law of Moses, the Prophets, and the Psalms must be fulfilled" (Luke 24:44). We turn then to a final summation of the ways in which Luke substantively articulates the implications of reading Israel's Scripture as testimony to Jesus.

The themes of Luke's intertextual narration

Theme 1. Luke's hermeneutical strategy of weaving Old Testament references into his drama produces an insistent and skillful representation of *narrative continuity*: the story of Jesus is joined seamlessly with the much longer narrative of God's promises to Israel, so that it becomes a single story about God's action to gather and redeem "a people prepared for the Lord" (Luke 1:17). The theological effects of this hermeneutical program are of wide-ranging significance. Rather than setting the church against Israel, Luke presents a continuous story of the one people of God. There has always been one elect Israel, and within that Israel, there have always been those who respond to God's redemptive action with faith, and others who turn away and are cut off. Luke sees this pattern continuing in his own time.

Theme 2. Within this story of Israel, Luke's use of Scripture emphatically portrays God as faithful to his covenant promises and gracious in his liberating power. The story has a *plot* scripted by its divine author, and it leads to a triumphant, joyous ending. This is the ground for the *asphaleia* that Luke promises to Theophilus. Readers of this Gospel are meant to come to the final page with a secure sense of the utter reliability of God's plan for Israel and the world. Luke's scriptural references assure us again and again that God's plan is ultimately for the liberation of Israel into a glorious and peaceful destiny.

Theme 3. In the meantime, however, suffering is a real part of present experience, both for Jesus and for his followers. Luke therefore also takes care to affirm that suffering is part of the scripturally disclosed plan of God: it belongs indelibly to the identity of the Messiah. "It is written" that the Messiah must suffer (Luke 24:26-27, 46; reiterated in Acts 26:22-23)—almost surely a reference to the Davidic psalms of lament, as well as to the Isaian Servant—and those who follow Jesus are admonished that they must also take up the cross (Luke 9:23-24, 14:27). Luke's second volume continues to show that the scriptural paradigm of suffering informs the life of Jesus' followers: for example, Stephen (Acts 6:8–8:1), Paul (Acts 9:16, 20:17-24), and James and Peter (Acts 12:1-5), among others (cf. also Acts 8:1b-3). The point is encapsulated in Luke's summary of the message offered by Paul and Barnabas to the disciples in Antioch: "There they strengthened the souls of the disciples and encouraged them to continue in the faith, saying 'It is through many tribulations (θλίψεων) that we must (δεῖ) enter the kingdom of God'" (Acts 14:22). There is no direct citation of Scripture here, but elsewhere for Luke such indications of necessity (δεῖ) invariably point to the providential will of God as disclosed in Scripture. The same biblical texts that foretell the fate of the Messiah also limn the divinely foreordained vocation of those who follow him.

Luke does not explain *why* the cross is part of God's plan. But within Luke's epic drama, readers are encouraged to take the long view. These accounts of persecution and suffering are part of a greater story in which God's just judgment will finally prevail, as signified by the resurrection of Jesus. For that reason, the community can live in patience and even joy in the midst of opposition and adversity.

Theme 4. Luke repeatedly draws upon Scripture to emphasize God's concern for the poor and helpless. The keynote citation of Isaiah 61:1-2 at the beginning of Jesus' ministry (Luke 4:16-19), a distinctive Lukan contribution to the story of Jesus, sets the tone for all that follows: good news to the poor and release to the captives. As we have seen time and again, Luke emphasizes that Moses and the prophets call God's people to share their goods with the poor. Furthermore, Jesus' healings and proclamation of the kingdom already begin to enact the eschatological reversal in which God fills the hungry with good things and sends the rich away empty. Luke emphatically presents this message not as a novelty but as the fulfillment of Israel's Scripture. Or, to put the point the other way around, Moses and the prophets, read retrospectively through the lens of the Jesus story, can be understood even more compellingly as a message of good news for the poor and oppressed.

Theme 5. The scriptural citations and allusions in Luke's narrative also prefigure the extension of the good news to all nations. As we have noted, in the Gospel this theme is foreshadowed but not developed; its full exposition awaits Luke's second book. But the *weight* of Luke's pre-figurative pointers is greater than their number. When in Acts we finally encounter direct references to Isaiah 49:6 (Acts 1:8, 13:47, 26:23), we see that these texts reflect the motif of "light to the Gentiles" back onto the earlier Gospel story. Here again we see the importance of reading the epic drama whole, seeing the way in which developments that emerge fully in later chapters of the narrative provide retrospective illumination of words and events of the earlier chapters.

Theme 6. Luke's use of Scripture places the elect people of God in a sharply countercultural relation to the prevailing structures of the world around them, both in the Jewish world and in the Roman Empire. As the reality of God's promised covenant community takes shape in the world, the world really is turned upside down. Rulers and nations may rage against the Lord, but those who find their identity newly anchored in the Lord's liberating story can speak the word of God with boldness and say, with Peter in Acts 5:29, "We must obey God rather than any human authority."[162] Thus, to read Scripture through Luke's eyes is to gain a firm place to stand against the violent and coercive kingdoms of the world. Those who follow Luke's narration closely may find their tongues loosened, along with Zechariah in Luke 1, to join in the hope-filled intertextual confession:[163]

> By the tender mercy of our God
> The dawn from on high will break upon us,
> to give light to those who sit in darkness and in the shadow of death
> and to guide our feet into the way of peace.

(Luke 1:78-79)

Theme 7. Finally, Luke's narrative exposition of Scripture gradually leads readers to perceive the unity of identity between Israel's *Kyrios* and Christ the *Kyrios*. The One Who Is to Come is not only Israel's true King but also Israel's true God. In a mysterious sense, Jesus is the one through whom the divine liberating action occurs. On a retrospective second reading of the text, we understand Zechariah's Spirit-filled prophecy in a new light:

Blessed be the Lord (κύριος), the God of Israel,
for he has visited (ἐπεσκέψατο) his people and made redemption
(λύτρωσιν) for them.

(Luke 1:68)

In light of Luke's full narrative, we come to understand that Jesus is the κύριος who *visits* and *redeems* Israel.

Thus, Luke's Christology of divine identity requires a fundamental rethinking of our notion of "God." Jesus is the *Kyrios*; the *Kyrios* is Jesus. God is therefore not a *concept* subject to general philosophical elucidation but a "*person*," an agent known through the complex unfolding of his narrative identity—and only so. And precisely for that reason, the "low/high" christological categories collapse completely. God discloses himself to us precisely in lowliness. In Luke's Gospel, the identity of *God* is given specification precisely in and through a narrative account of the human figure Jesus, born in Bethlehem and laid in a manger, sent to proclaim good news to the poor, crucified under Pontius Pilate, risen indeed—and precisely in and through these events revealed as κύριος πάντων: Lord of all.

Chapter 4

THE GOSPEL OF JOHN
The Temple of His Body

"We have found the one about whom Moses wrote in the law,
and also the prophets."

§16 "COME AND SEE"
John as Interpreter of Scripture

In one of the opening scenes of John's Gospel, Jesus abruptly summons a man named Philip to follow him. Philip then seeks out his friend Nathanael and declares, without providing evidence or explanation, "We have found the one about whom Moses wrote in the law, and also the prophets: Jesus, the son of Joseph from Nazareth" (John 1:45). Nathanael understandably expresses a certain sardonic skepticism: Can anything worthwhile come out of an insignificant village like Nazareth? Philip simply replies, "Come and see" (1:46).

That summons, "Come and see," functions also as an invitation to the reader of the Fourth Gospel, an invitation to discern, among other things, whether the Jesus they will meet in this story is in fact prefigured by Moses and the prophets.[1] John has set astonishingly high expectations in the first chapter of his narrative: the opening paragraphs of the story already identify Jesus, a mysterious figure from a small Galilean village, as the *Logos* through whom creation came into being (John 1:1-18), as

281

"the Lamb of God who takes away the sin of the world" (1:29-36), and as Israel's Messiah (1:41). And, for reasons opaque to the reader, Philip now identifies Jesus—who has yet to do anything, at least not anything reported by the narrator—as the true referent to whom Israel's Scriptures point, the law and the prophets alike. It is of course possible that Philip has leaped to a false inference, that he has blurted out an exaggerated and misleading claim, as overeager followers often do. But the solemn opening of John's narrative suggests otherwise: we are given to understand that Philip has somehow intuited a revelatory insight. If so, readers of the text are summoned by Philip's words to come and see *how* this Jesus of Nazareth can be understood as the one about whom Moses and the prophets wrote. But Philip does not actually cite any texts; what passages in Moses and the prophets does he have in mind? And will Jesus accept this portentous description of his identity and somehow fulfill Philip's hermeneutical expectation? To find the answers, we must move deeper into the story.

As the plot unfolds, Jesus comes into conflict with religious authorities who charge him with violating the sabbath: Jesus has healed a lame man and instructed him to stand up and carry his mat (John 5:2-9). The offense lies not in the healing itself but in Jesus' directive to the man to carry his mat, an act that constitutes a technical violation of the commandment that prohibits working on the sabbath (John 5:10-16; cf. Exod 20:8-11; Deut 5:12-15).[2] But the argument quickly escalates from a halakhic dispute to a christological controversy when Jesus justifies what he does by identifying his action with God's own: "But Jesus answered them, 'My Father is working even until now, and I also am working.' Therefore, the Jews sought all the more to kill him, because not only did he relax the sabbath law, but also he was calling God his own Father, thereby making himself equal with God" (John 5:17-18).

Their complaint then becomes the springboard for one of the long self-referential discourses of Jesus that are distinctively characteristic of the Fourth Gospel. And at the climax of this discourse, just about a quarter of the way through John's narrative, we come at last upon the fundamental hermeneutical claim—now stated in Jesus' own words—that illumines John's approach to reading Israel's Scripture. Jesus upbraids his detractors for failing to receive him as the one sent by God:

> "You search the Scriptures, because you think that in them you have eternal life; and *those very Scriptures are the ones that bear witness concerning me.* But you do not want to come to me in order that you might have life. . . .

Do not think that I will accuse you before the Father. But there is one who accuses you: Moses, upon whom you have set your hope. *For if you believed Moses, you would believe me, for he wrote about me.* But if you do not believe the writings of Moses, how will you believe my words?"

(John 5:39-40, 45-47)

So Philip was right. Jesus endorses Philip's eager description of him as "the one whom Moses wrote about in the law." But there is a tragic turn: though Moses wrote about Jesus, the religious teachers of God's people, the ones whose office it is to explicate Moses, now find Jesus unbelievable and reject him. This bitter and paradoxical outcome was foreshadowed already in John's prologue: the Word "came to his own home, and his own people did not receive him" (John 1:11). But only here in John 5 does the *hermeneutical* dimension of this failure come fully into focus.

Jesus does not challenge or denigrate Moses; rather, Moses actually testifies to Jesus. Yet Jesus' adversaries, despite their earnest scrutiny of Moses' writings, lapse into interpretative failure because they reject Jesus' astonishing claim to be the true and ultimate referent to whom Moses' words point. There is a fateful circularity here: reading the writings of Moses should lead to believing in Jesus; but in order to understand Moses' words, one must first come to Jesus to receive life: "You do not have his word (τὸν λόγον αὐτοῦ) remaining in you, because the one he has sent, him you do not believe" (John 5:38). And so those who do not trust Jesus' word remain in incomprehension and death. Only those who enter this hermeneutical loop at the point of believing Jesus can rightly understand what Moses wrote.

And so in John's Gospel, just as in Luke's, there is a call for a retrospective rereading of Israel's Scripture, a *reading backwards* that reinterprets Scripture in light of a new revelation imparted *by* Jesus and focused *on* the person of Jesus himself. Though the narratives of Luke and John are worlds apart stylistically—not least because of John's *polemical* framing of his remarks about the testimony of Scripture—their hermeneutical underpinnings are similar, and the theological distance between Luke 24:27 and John 5:46 is even less than the mere five chapters that would ultimately separate them in the church's fourfold Gospel canon.

Luke 24:27: Then beginning with Moses and all the prophets, he interpreted to them the things about himself in all the Scriptures.

John 5:46: "If you believed Moses, you would believe me, for he wrote about me."

Yet despite this convergence, John's way of handling the biblical texts differs markedly from anything we have seen in the Synoptic Gospels.

John contains relatively few direct citations of the Old Testament. If we tabulate John's Old Testament references in comparison to those of the Synoptics, including allusions, the totals are striking: Matthew, 124; Mark, 70; Luke, 109; and John, 27. While the counting of citations may be slightly skewed, such a tabulation does point to an undeniable feature of John's narrative.[3] Just as he condenses the traditions of Jesus' healing and miracle-working activity down to a few selected episodes that are given more extended development than in the synoptic tradition, so also John focuses on a smaller number of Old Testament quotations. Depending on the criteria employed, studies of John's use of the Old Testament have identified between thirteen and seventeen explicit quotations.[4] Precisely because there are relatively few quotations, each citation that does appear in John's uncluttered narrative assumes proportionately greater gravity as a pointer to Jesus' identity. *If Luke is the master of the deft, fleeting allusion, John is the master of the carefully framed, luminous image that shines brilliantly against a dark canvas and lingers in the imagination.* In this respect, John's narrative technique is analogous to the visual artistry of Rembrandt's portraits. John is not attempting to compile the maximum number of illustrations of how Moses wrote about Jesus. He knows that much more could be said (cf. John 21:25), but he prefers to focus on the artistically selected instance that repays sustained meditation.

That is why, in addition to the smaller number of quotations, there is also a surprisingly low number of obvious verbal allusions to Israel's Scripture in John's Gospel.[5] Or, to put the point more precisely, John's manner of alluding does not depend upon the citation of chains of words and phrases; instead it relies upon evoking *images* and *figures* from Israel's Scripture. For example, when he writes, "And just as Moses lifted up the serpent in the wilderness, so it is necessary for the Son of Man to be lifted up" (John 3:14), John is clearly alluding to the episode narrated in Numbers 21:8-9, but the only explicit *verbal* links between the two passages are the name "Moses" and the word "serpent" (ὄφιν).[6] His intertextual sensibility is more visual than auditory.

To be sure, John does also deal in verbal echoes. The best-known instance is the Gospel's opening sentence, "In the beginning was the word," which both echoes and transforms Genesis 1:1. This is just one of many examples in John's text, some of them very subtle. For example, in John's allusion to Moses and the bronze serpent, the verb "lifted up" (ὕψωσεν/ὑψωθῆναι), which appears nowhere in Numbers 21, may well echo the introductory lines of Isaiah's description of the mysterious Suffering Servant: "Behold, my servant will understand, and will be lifted up (ὑψωθήσεται) and will be glorified exceedingly" (Isa 52:13 LXX). These echoes of Numbers and Isaiah are verbally faint (echoing just a word or two from the scriptural source) but symbolically potent, evoking a rich theological matrix within which the Fourth Gospel's presentation of Jesus is to be understood.

However, John also introduces a substantial number of direct quotations with explicit quotation formulas, often in the form of authorial commentary, in this way resembling Matthew more than Mark or Luke. These formulas follow a pattern that mirrors the structural design of the narrative. From the beginning of the story up until almost the end of chapter 12—that is, throughout the account of Jesus' active public ministry, sometimes designated the "book of signs"—John introduces quotations with "as it is written," "it is written in the prophets," "as Scripture said," or some minor variation on these phrasings (John 1:23; 2:17; 6:31; 6:45; 7:38, 42; 10:34; 12:14). But after Jesus withdraws from public proclamation and activity (12:36b), there is a striking change. After this pivotal point in the plot, almost all the subsequent quotations are introduced with a fulfillment formula employing forms of πληρόω: "in order that the Scripture might be fulfilled."[7]

The only exceptions appear in John 12:39 ("because again Isaiah said") and John 19:37 ("and again another Scripture says"). In both of these instances, the quotation introduced is the second of a pair, as signaled by πάλιν ("again"). It is hardly accidental that these pairs of linked quotations (John 12:38-40, 19:36-37) serve as end punctuation to the two central narrative blocks of the Gospel, the "book of signs" (1:19–12:50) and the "book of the passion" (13:1–19:42).[8] Like the closing cadence at the end of a movement in a symphony, these double fulfillment citations signal that a section of the story is drawing to a close.[9]

What is the significance of this change in the wording of scriptural citation formulas in the latter part of the Gospel? The overall stylistic and theological unity of the Fourth Gospel tells against a simple source-critical explanation; whatever sources may have been employed by the author of this carefully crafted text, he has shaped them into an artistic unity. It is unlikely that a feature so prominent as these fulfillment quotations could have been spliced into the narrative without the author's editorial reflection about the specific wording used to introduce them.

The likeliest explanation for the strong emphasis on "fulfillment" in the latter part of the Gospel is that these citations provide John's theological response to the otherwise incomprehensible adversity that Jesus encounters. The "book of signs" culminates in a grim reflection on the unbelief of the Jewish people in response to Jesus: "But although he did so many signs in their presence they persistently did not believe in him" (John 12:37; cf. 1:11).[10] This sad observation ruefully sums up the outcome of Jesus' public career and functions as a watershed point in the plot. John's shift thereafter to "fulfillment" language in his introductory formulas in the "book of the passion" signals an *apologetic* motivation: the Evangelist is explaining that the suffering and rejection experienced by Jesus in the passion story was not some unforeseen disaster; rather, it was foreordained and played out in fulfillment of God's will, with Jesus' full knowledge and participation.[11] The point may be demonstrated by a list of the events that are said to have happened "in order that the Scripture might be fulfilled."

> John 12:37-40: They did not believe in him (Isa 53:1, 6:10).
>
> John 13:18: One of the disciples will betray Jesus (Ps 41:9).
>
> John 15:24-25: The world has seen and hated both Jesus and his Father (Ps 35:19, 69:5).
>
> John 17:12: One disciple was destined to be lost (no text cited: Ps 41:9?).
>
> John 19:23-24: Soldiers divided Jesus' garments and cast lots for his tunic (Ps 22:19).
>
> John 19:28-29: On the cross, Jesus said, "I thirst" and was offered vinegar to drink (Ps 69:21).
>
> John 19:36-37: In the crucifixion, Jesus' legs were not broken (Exod 12:10, 46; Num 9:12; or Ps 34:21), but his side was pierced (Zech 12:10).

All these events are interpreted, with the aid of the scriptural citations, as the consummation of a divine design that is fully enacted in Jesus' death (John 19:30: τετέλεσται, "it has been brought to completion"). This apologetic motivation also explains why the fulfillment quotations in the Fourth Gospel are clustered toward the end of the story rather than, as in Matthew, at the beginning.

There is a heavy concentration of Psalm texts within the group of Old Testament passages cited by John. More than 60 percent of John's quotations come from the Psalter.[12] Even if this number is slightly inflated, there can be no mistaking the prominence of Psalm passages in the intertextual "genetic code" of the Fourth Gospel. This emphasis on the

Psalter follows almost inevitably from John's concentration on the passion and death of Jesus as the center of gravity in his narrative. Because
the Psalms foreshadow—or, as John might prefer, *express*—the suffering
of the crucified/exalted Jesus, it is understandable that a retrospective
reading of Scripture as witness to Jesus would be drawn to these texts.[13]
It is, however, curious that a Gospel that asserts that *Moses* wrote about
Jesus would make so little effort to explicate the Pentateuch as christological prophecy. Of John's explicit quotations, only one (19:36) can
plausibly be ascribed to the five books of Moses (the instruction not to
break any of the bones of the Passover lamb [Exod 12:46; Num 9:12], and
even in this case the wording of John's citation is actually closer to Psalm
34:20 than to the directive given in Exodus 12, suggesting that even here
"Moses" has been mediated—or filtered—through the Psalter).[14] This
observation about John's explicit Old Testament citations should give us
some pause and lead us to look carefully elsewhere in the narrative for
subtler traces of evidence that might support the curious claim of the
Johannine Jesus that "Moses wrote about me" (John 5:46).

A key hermeneutical test case is the lapidary statement near the end
of the Gospel's prologue: "The law was given through Moses; grace and
truth came through Jesus Christ" (John 1:17). How are these two clauses
related to one another? Does the law given through Moses point to the
grace and truth of Jesus Christ (as 5:46 indicates), so that the latter confirms and completes the testimony of the former? Or does the grace and
truth of Jesus Christ negate and supplant the law?[15] This question hovers
over the Gospel as a whole.

And as it does so, readers may wonder at numerous points whether
John's story is supersessionist: Does it declare Judaism null and void and
replace it with a new and different religion, Christianity, in which Israel's law and Israel's hopes have been radically supplanted by an ethereal
non-Jewish Christ who descends briefly from heaven into the world to
reveal himself and then ascends again to a state of blessed detachment
from the world? This way of formulating the problem already implies the
answer that I think John's Gospel compels us to give: No. If we attend
to the way that Scripture actually functions in John, we will see that the
identity of Jesus is deeply imbedded in Israel's texts and traditions—
especially the traditions centered on the temple and Israel's annual feasts.
This is the world in which John's imagination is immersed; it is impossible to understand John's Jesus apart from the story of Israel and the
liturgical festivals and symbols that recall and re-present that story. It is
not accurate, then, to say that Jesus nullifies or replaces Israel's Torah and

Israel's worship life. Rather, he *assumes* and *transforms* them. But to grasp the way in which this transformation works, we must enter more deeply into John's figural world and consider its hermeneutical logic.

§17 "SALVATION IS FROM THE JEWS"
Israel's Story in John's Narrative

The relative absence of explicit Pentateuchal citations in John, along with the heavy weighting of Psalms, might suggest a focus on liturgical materials and a corresponding lack of interest in the Old Testament narratives of Israel's past. And indeed, as we pose our heuristic question about the way in which the Evangelist uses Scripture to narrate the story of Israel, we will find that John offers fewer signs of interest in narrative continuity than do the Synoptic Gospels. Here in the Fourth Gospel there is no tracing of a genealogical trajectory from Abraham to David to the Exile to the Messiah, as in Matthew (Matt 1:17). There is no celebratory acclamation of a God who "has helped his servant Israel, in remembrance of his mercy, according to the promise he made to our ancestors, to Abraham and to his descendants forever," as in Luke (Luke 1:54-55). It is not easy to see, at least on a first reading, whether the Fourth Gospel has any interest in Israel as such. Furthermore, "the Jews" seem to be the villains of the tale. It is not entirely surprising, then, that this Gospel has sometimes lent itself with alarming ease to anti-Jewish constructions of Christianity[16] or to forms of ahistorical spirituality for which the linear narration of the past history of the people of God plays little role. One outcome of our exploration of John's reading of Scripture will be to interrogate and challenge such anti-Jewish and antihistorically docetic interpretations of the Fourth Gospel. But it is well to recognize in the beginning that the hermeneutical challenge is both significant and grounded in certain troubling features of the text that require close attention.

The difficulty of getting a fix on John's understanding of Israel's story is partly the consequence of his rigorous focus on Christology. If Israel recedes strangely into the background in some readings of John, it is because the figure of Jesus so dominates the attention of the camera. The Evangelist zooms in on Jesus as the figure of central interest and insists that everyone and everything else must find its place in the story's world only in relation to him. For narrative characters and readers alike, the insistent and only question is whether to accept Jesus as the one sent into the world by the Father to reveal the truth and to embody it definitively. All of Israel's past and the totality of the witness of Scripture are absorbed into Jesus' person.

For that reason, in John even more than in the other Gospels, it is hard to distinguish the Evangelist's interpretation of Israel from his interpretation of Jesus. We may do so only in a provisional way, for heuristic purposes. For John, the story of Israel has no independent significance; it finds a place in John's narrative as the symbolic matrix for his portrayal of Jesus. We must hasten to add, however, that this does not mean that Israel plays a minor role, or a negative one. To the contrary, precisely because Israel's Scripture constitutes the network within which John's narrative becomes intelligible—the *encyclopedia* that is presupposed both for the text's production and for its proper reception—Israel's prior life with God becomes seamlessly integrated with the story of Jesus that John tells. We begin then by tracing some of the ways in which John's narrative refers to Israel's scriptural story, always bearing in mind that these fragmentary references find their integrative center in John's account of Jesus, which will accordingly occupy most of our attention in this chapter.

Retrospective references to characters in Israel's story

John's Gospel manifests an unsettling indifference to ordinary perceptions of linear time. Jesus can say, "Before Abraham was, I am" (John 8:58). His interlocutors are shocked, but the reader, prepared by the Gospel's prologue, is meant to believe this startling claim. Similarly, the Evangelist can say that Isaiah witnessed Jesus' glory and spoke about him (John 12:41). Taken in isolation, this statement could be interpreted as a claim about Isaiah's prophetic foresight of future events, but in the context of John's story, which has unambiguously affirmed Jesus' preexistence (1:1-18), John's declaration assumes quite a different meaning: it implies that in Isaiah's vision of the heavenly throne room, the exalted "Lord" that he actually saw was none other than Jesus (Isa 6:1-13).[17] The Jesus who appears in these pages transcends time and is present throughout Israel's past as well as in the present time of the narrative. For that reason, we cannot speak of *Heilsgeschichte* in John, in the sense of a linear chronological development through the history of a people. Nor does John offer a scheme of *promise* and fulfillment. Rather, John summons the reader to recognize the way in which *Israel's Scripture has always been mysteriously suffused with the presence of Jesus*, the figure who steps clearly into the light in the Gospel narrative.

And yet, to put the point that way also suggests that all of Israel's Scripture, rightly understood, can become transparent to the figure of Jesus. For that reason, while John shows little interest in renarrating the scriptural stories, he regularly makes passing allusions to them. The texts we have just mentioned refer to Abraham and Isaiah, expecting readers to know who these figures are and why they are significant. And these are hardly the only scriptural figures named in the Fourth Gospel. It is illuminating to consider some of the several biblical characters named by John and to take note of the features of their stories that his references evoke.

Abraham. In John 8:31-59, Jesus' sharply polemical dialogue with "the Jews" assumes the prior conviction that Abraham is the father of the people of Israel—thus presupposing the whole patriarchal saga of Genesis 12–22, perhaps with particular reference to 12:1-3 and 15:1-6. Both Jesus and his opponents associate Abraham with freedom and with a legitimate place in God's household. The passage shows an interesting similarity to Paul's almost equally polemical argument in Galatians 3 and 4 about who belongs to the true "seed" of Abraham. Recognizing the connection between these texts may help us to understand that John 8:31-59 is not properly understood as anti-Jewish rhetoric; rather, it belongs to the history of intra-Jewish polemic.[18] But none of this is explained by the Evangelist; "our father Abraham" belongs to the text's encyclopedia of production, and a reader ignorant of the story of Abraham will find little explicit help here.

Particularly opaque is Jesus' comment, "If you were children of Abraham, you would do the works of Abraham" (John 8:39). What "works" are indicated by this cryptic comment? An imagination funded by the Genesis stories might supply several interesting possibilities. When he received the word of God, Abraham believed it and left the security of his own people to follow God's call. Likewise, this echo would suggest, those who hear the word of God in Jesus should believe it and abandon the security of their own social position, risking rejection by their own people (cf. 9:22, 12:42-43, 16:2-3). Or perhaps the reference is to Abraham's famous act of hospitality toward his divine visitors (Gen 18:1-15). If so, the contrast with Jesus' interlocutors in John 8 is a devastating one: rather than welcoming their divine visitor, they are seeking to kill him (John 8:40, 59).[19] In any case, the bitter controversy dialogue of John 8 assumes Abraham as a highly significant figure, the father of Israel, one who actually somehow saw Jesus, welcomed God's revelation, and rejoiced (8:56).

Jacob. The story of Jesus' encounter with a Samaritan woman (John 4:4-42) unmistakably evokes the well-known biblical type scene in which a man meets a woman at a well.[20] Lest we miss the allusion, John explicitly names the site of the encounter as "Jacob's well" (4:6). Even though the geographical setting ("a Samaritan city named Sychar, near the plot of ground that Jacob had given to his son Joseph" [4:5]) is different from the location of the story of Jacob's meeting his future wife Rachel at a well (Gen 29:1-20), the Samaritan woman's reference to Jacob's giving the well and allowing flocks to drink (John 4:12) is strongly reminiscent of Genesis 29:10.

The typological echo of the Jacob/Rachel narrative opens the story to various possibilities for figurative interpretation. Jesus has just been described metaphorically as the "bridegroom" (John 3:29-30), and here his encounter with the woman at a well would seem to portend some sort of "marriage"—whether the symbolic inclusion of Samaria as a central feature of the new Israel,[21] or the union of Jesus with the individual believer who receives living water from him (4:10-15) by believing his self-disclosure as the Messiah who proclaims all things (4:25-26). Whichever reading we prefer, there is no question here of a continuation of the physical lineage of Jacob (i.e., Israel) through ordinary marriage and procreation. Rather, in John 4 the story of Jacob and Rachel becomes the figural backdrop for Jesus' self-disclosure and the woman's mission to others[22] previously alienated from Israel who come to know and confess him as "the Savior of the world" (4:39-42). In this case, the narrative of John 4 is intelligible apart from intertextual reference to Jacob, but the narrative takes on an added layer of significance for readers who hear the echoes of Genesis.[23]

Moses. The Fourth Gospel contains repeated references to Moses, some of which we have already noted. Moses' role in John's story is complex and not easily categorized.[24] While in some passages Jesus is contrasted to Moses (John 9:28),[25] in other passages Moses is portrayed as a witness who points to Jesus (as we have seen in 1:45, 5:45-47). The Evangelist's allusions to Moses recall several different aspects of the portrayal of Moses in the Pentateuchal narrative: Moses lifting up the bronze serpent on a pole to ward off the lethal effects of the poisonous serpents that bit the grumbling Israelites (John 3:14/Num 21:4-9); Moses' role in declaring to the Israelites that they would receive manna from heaven (John 6:30-33/Exod 16:1-36); Moses as giver of the law (John 1:17), including the practice of circumcision (John 7:19, 22/Lev 12:3; Gen 17:9-14);[26] Moses as the recipient of revelation, one to whom God spoke directly (John 9:29/Num 12:1-9). In none of these cases does John recount enough of the scriptural story to explicate the reference for readers unfamiliar with these traditions. He simply alludes: ". . . just as Moses lifted up the serpent in the wilderness . . ."; ". . . it was not Moses who gave you the bread from heaven . . ."; "Did not Moses give you the law?"; ". . . God spoke to Moses. . . ." Yet for readers who know these stories by heart, these brief allusions leap off the page and evoke the memory of Moses' role in the whole saga of the exodus. And in each case, the Fourth Gospel's interpretation of Jesus is illumined by these intertextual recollections. It should be noted, however, that Jesus is not portrayed by John as a "new Moses" or as "the prophet like Moses." Instead, he is one far greater. Even in these figurative evocations of the Moses story, Jesus himself is metaphorically equated with the bronze serpent or the bread from heaven, *not* with Moses. Moses plays a more instrumental, preparatory role. Or, to return more precisely to John's description, a witness-bearing role.

Elijah. With regard to witness-bearing, we must also take notice of a few passages in which John refers to Israel's prophets by name. The figure of Elijah is much less prominent in John than in the Synoptic Gospels, but he does put in an appearance, or rather a non-appearance, in John 1:21, 25, where John the Baptist rejects the suggestion that he himself might be Elijah.[27] The question put to John by the priests and Levites presupposes a readership acquainted not only with the scriptural stories about Elijah but also with the expectation in Second Temple Judaism of an eschatological role for a returning Elijah as the harbinger of the Messiah or the messianic age (Mal 4:5-6; Sir 48:4-12).[28] In the same series of interrogations, John also denies that he is either the Messiah or "the prophet"— that is, the prophet like Moses, another anticipated eschatological figure (Deut 18:15-18). It is a striking and surprising fact that John's narrative makes no constructive place for Elijah as a witness to the identity of Jesus. Still, John the Baptist's denials should be understood neither as denigrations of Elijah nor as negations of Israel's future eschatological hope; rather, the denials serve to divert attention from the Baptist. As he goes on to say, he is simply "the voice of one crying in the wilderness," calling God's people to prepare for the coming of the Lord (John 1:23; citing Isa 40:3) and pointing instead to Jesus, the one who must increase as John's own importance decreases (John 3:30). It is Jesus who is the true fulfillment of Israel's eschatological hopes. Perhaps to identify the Baptist directly as Elijah would be to place too much emphasis on his role and, in the mind of John the Evangelist, divert attention from Jesus, who always commands center stage.

Isaiah. The case of Isaiah, however, is different; Isaiah is portrayed by John as standing along with Abraham and Moses as a witness to Jesus. The reference in John 1:23 to Isaiah's prophecy of a voice crying in the wilderness is one of two passages in which John refers to Isaiah by name; the second appears at the conclusion of Jesus' public activity in John 12, where the Evangelist gives back-to-back fulfillment quotations from Isaiah 53:1 and 6:10 and then adds an explanatory remark that "Isaiah said this because he saw his glory and spoke about him" (John 12:36b-41). The passage is significant for present purposes because it refers to "Isaiah" not merely as the source of a prophetic oracle but also as a character in Israel's story, whose prophetic declaration about Jesus is based on a particular event; as suggested above, that event is almost surely the throne vision of Isaiah 6 "in the year that King Uzziah died" (Isa 6:1). If so, the Evangelist expects readers to recall not just the words of a prophetic oracle but also the narrative frame provided by the book of Isaiah: Isaiah's vision and call. It is precisely this narrated incident that explains how Isaiah can be enlisted as a witness to Jesus' divine identity.

David. Finally, we should take note of the figure of David. Only one passage in the Fourth Gospel mentions David by name. In John 7:40-44, the Evangelist narrates a scene in which members of the crowd dispute with one another about whether Jesus might be either "the prophet" or "the Messiah." The latter speculation triggers an objection from some that the Messiah cannot come from Galilee: "Has not the Scripture said that the Messiah comes from the seed of David and from Bethlehem, the village where David was?" (John 7:42). This is a fascinating example not only of Johannine *intertextuality* but of *dramatic irony* as well.

The biblical warrant for expecting the Messiah to come from Bethlehem is Micah 5:2 (5:1 MT and LXX): "But you, O Bethlehem of Ephrathah, who are one of the little clans of Judah, from you shall come forth for me one who is to rule in Israel, whose origin is of old, from ancient days." Matthew cites the passage explicitly (though loosely) as a part of his account of Jesus' birth (Matt 2:3-6).[29] John, however, presupposes this bit of messianic lore as part of his ideal reader's encyclopedia of reception. There is no direct citation of Micah, and the only verbal link between John 7:42 and Micah 5:2 is the place name "Bethlehem." Thus, this is another instance of John's tendency to produce low-volume scriptural allusions. If John does have the Micah passage in mind, however, it is particularly interesting that the ruler who comes from Bethlehem is said to have his origin from of old (the LXX reads ἀπ᾽ ἀρχῆς, "from the beginning"; cf. 1 John 1:1-2). This affirmation resonates intriguingly with the Johannine prologue and John's *logos*-Christology.

But this is only one dimension of the intertextual matrix in which John 7:40-44 is to be interpreted. Because the Gospel of John contains no birth narrative, it has not previously connected Jesus' origins with the village of Bethlehem. Yet readers who know the synoptic tradition can hardly fail to spot the irony in the scene that John has crafted: according to Matthew and Luke, Jesus *does* come from the Davidic line and was born in Bethlehem (Matt 2:1; Luke 2:1-20). So the doubters in the crowd question Jesus' messianic credentials precisely because they do not know where he really comes from—like the Pharisees who say, "We know that God has spoken to Moses, but as for this man, we do not know where he comes from" (John 9:29). And yet, as the controversy in John 9 also ironically suggests, Jesus comes not from any human origin but "from God" (9:33), and he is therefore "above all" (3:31). So those who fail to accept Jesus as Messiah are ignorant of *both* his human Davidic lineage and his heavenly origin. This double-level dramatic irony comes into play, however, only when 7:40-44 is read in its canonical intertextual context. The irony does not require the reader to know Matthew or Luke in specific detail, or even in written form—it is necessary only to know of the tradition of the Messiah's birth in Bethlehem.[30]

In any case, the several references to Jesus as "Messiah" throughout the Fourth Gospel (μεσσίας in John 1:41, 4:25; χριστός in several significant places: 1:17, 7:31, 9:22, 11:27, 17:3, 20:31) strongly imply that Jesus has assumed the mantle of David, Israel's prototypical anointed king. This is perhaps one of the reasons for John's heavy concentration of citations from the Psalms, since David was regarded as author of many of these sacred texts.[31] Further, the Davidic overtones are particularly pronounced in John 10, where Jesus proclaims himself "the good shepherd" (10:11-18) and suggests that he is the one who fulfills the role assigned in the prophecy of Ezekiel to "one shepherd, my servant David" (Ezek 34:23-24). These passages implicitly link Jesus to Israel's hopes and expectations for a Davidic messianic ruler, and they therefore evoke memories of the scriptural stories of David, though once again, as in the other examples we have considered, these stories are presupposed, not renarrated, by John.

"We worship what we know. . . ."

Taken together, John's hints and allusions to major characters in Israel's story suggest a strong positive relation between Israel's past and its fulfillment in the person of Jesus. There is no hint that Israel's story has been a history of futility and error. Rather, the scriptural figures to whom the Fourth Gospel alludes stand as authentic witnesses or prefigurations of Jesus. Especially the figures of Abraham, Moses, and Isaiah are presented as harbingers of the Gospel. Their stories belong to a larger narrative framework that presents Israel as the matrix within which God's saving revelation appears.

Israel's distinctive role in God's dealings with the world is most tellingly disclosed in Jesus' dialogue with the Samaritan woman. In response to her questioning, Jesus favorably contrasts his own kinsfolk to the Samaritans: "You worship what you do not know; we worship what we know, for salvation is from the Jews" (John 4:22). No specific scriptural text is cited here, but Jesus' claim stands in substantive continuity with Israel's prophetic tradition. Isaiah depicts Gentile nations as bowing down before Israel and confessing, "God is with you alone, and there is no other; there is no God besides him" (Isa 45:14). Similarly, Zechariah prophesies that in the time of eschatological fulfillment, "ten men from nations of every language shall take hold of a Jew, grasping his garment and saying, 'Let us go with you, for we have heard that God is with you'" (Zech 8:23). Clearly, John 4 stands in this same prophetic trajectory, according a special salvific role to Israel.

Perhaps the prophetic text most immediately pertinent as context for Jesus' declaration to the Samaritan woman is Isaiah 2:3:

> Many peoples shall come and say,
> "Come, let us go up to the mountain of the LORD,
> to the house of the God of Jacob;
> that he may teach us his ways
> and that we may walk in his paths."
> For out of Zion shall go forth instruction (תורה),
> and the word of the LORD from Jerusalem.

To recall this text, however, is also to recognize that John's Gospel is not only affirming continuity with Israel's scriptural tradition but also performing a hermeneutical transformation. Like Isaiah, Jesus affirms that Israel's God is alone to be worshiped and that Israel has privileged access to the saving knowledge of God, a knowledge that is to be sought and found by other nations. That is what it means to say that "salvation is from the Jews." Neither are the Jews themselves the source of salvation, nor are they to be its only recipients; rather, they are to serve as mediators of saving truth and instruction (*Torah*) about the one God. And yet, in the very same utterance that affirms this Isaianic claim, Jesus also tells the woman that "the hour is coming when you will worship the Father neither on this mountain nor in Jerusalem" (John 4:21), thus revising Isaiah's Zion theology that identifies Mount Zion as the central sacred location where the word of Lord resides and whence it emanates. Whereas the woman had asked whether God was rightly to be worshiped on "this mountain" (Mount Gerizim in Samaria) or in Jerusalem (4:19-20), Jesus explodes the premise that true worship can be localized in this fashion; instead, he teaches that God must be worshiped "in Spirit and in truth" (4:23-24). Thus, Jesus' words simultaneously confirm God's special election of Israel as mediator of salvation to the world and relativize the significance of Jerusalem as a geographical locus of God's presence.

The reason for this shift is simple: John's theology of the incarnate Word will insist that Jesus himself is now the locus of God's presence in the world, the site of true worship and revelation.[32] This is not spelled out explicitly in John 4, but it is symbolically suggested by Jesus' proclamation that he himself is the source of living water that offers eternal life (John 4:10, 13-14).

In any case, John's narrative pervasively presupposes a positive view of the scriptural story of Israel and affirms that God's saving action for the world is mediated through that story as retrospectively interpreted in light of the person of Jesus. The fact that God's revelation in Jesus enacts a hermeneutical transformation of Israel's past does not negate Israel's distinctive place of honor in God's economy. Instead, this hermeneutical transformation brings Israel's past into a new and sharpened focus.

The role of the law in John's Gospel

Something similar can be said about the role of Israel's law in the Fourth Gospel. As we have already observed, John's prologue introduces an enigmatic juxtaposition between the law of Moses and the grace and truth that came through Jesus Christ (John 1:17). Christian interpreters have sometimes read this juxtaposition as an antithesis, setting the grace and truth of Jesus in opposition to the law.[33] But in fact, John's Gospel provides no support for such an antithesis.

Indeed, as we observed at the beginning of this chapter, John explicitly informs readers that Moses actually wrote about Jesus in the law and that the law therefore actually bears witness to the gospel (John 1:45, 5:45-47).[34] Numerous Old Testament passages and images are interpreted in this Gospel as foreshadowing Jesus, and at least one of them is specifically said to come from the "law":

> "If I had not done among them the works that no one else has done, they would not have sin. But now they have seen and hated both me and my Father. But this happened in order that what is written in their law might be fulfilled: 'They hated me gratuitously.'"[35]
>
> (John 15:24-25; loosely quoting a phrase that appears both in Ps 35:19 and Ps 69:5)

So the rejection of Jesus by his own people constitutes a fulfillment and confirmation of Israel's law. This quotation from the Psalms, in company with similar references in John 10:34 and 12:34, shows that John can use the term νόμος ("law") in a broad sense to refer to Scripture as a whole, not just to the Pentateuch, and not just to passages that spell out commandments.[36] It is in this wider sense that the law, according to the Fourth Gospel, can be understood as a witness to Jesus. For example, the Jewish crowd has learned rightly from "the law" that "the Messiah remains forever" (12:34), but John offers no explicit citation in support of this general belief. Certainly this idea does not come from the Pentateuch. Instead, perhaps in the background lies the expectation articulated in Psalm 89 and in 2 Samuel 7:12-14 that God would raise up a successor to David and establish the Davidic kingdom forever. Or perhaps the crowd has some more specific prophecy in mind, such as Ezekiel 37:25: "They shall live in the land that I gave to my servant Jacob, in which your ancestors lived; they and their children and their children's children shall live there forever; *and my servant David shall be their prince forever.*" In any case, regardless of which scriptural texts John may have had in view, he proclaims that the law should be understood as pointing to Jesus.

But on closer examination, we also find a number of references to the law in John that suggest a positive function for the law's prescriptive role in mandating just and merciful practices in the community. In John 7:22-24, Jesus makes a halakhic argument, pointing out that it is accepted practice to perform circumcisions on the sabbath "in order that the law of Moses may not be broken." Thus he observes that there are cases in which the law's regulations may come into conflict and that one commandment may override another.[37] In light of this principle, then, he asks pointedly, "Are you angry at me because I made the whole man well on the sabbath?"[38] This implies that the law's fundamental aim of promoting human wholeness and flourishing can in some instances override its ritual prohibitions.[39] This is certainly not a negation of the law; rather, it is an argument profoundly respectful of the law's own inner logic, an argument that operates within well-established Jewish hermeneutical precedent.

That this is so is underscored by the subtle scriptural allusions in the final thrust of Jesus' rejoinder to his critics: "Do not judge according to appearance, but judge with just judgment" (John 7:24). The unspoken subtexts are 1 Samuel 16:7 ("But the LORD said to Samuel, 'Do not look on his appearance' . . . ; for the LORD does not see as mortals see; they look on the outward appearance, but the LORD looks on the heart") and Isaiah 11:3 ("His delight shall be in the fear of the LORD. He shall not judge by what his eyes see, or decide by what his ears hear; but with righteousness he shall judge the poor, and decide with equity for the meek of the earth"). Interestingly, the first of these passages is taken from the account of Samuel's anointing of David to be Israel's king, and the second describes the hoped-for future Davidic king who will rule righteously over Israel. Perhaps these overtones are not accidental: John is portraying Jesus as the true Messianic king who sees beyond surface appearances to the real substance of the law and who therefore judges with righteousness in a way that brings healing to the poor and downtrodden. Whether this be so or not, it is certainly the case that John's narrative defends Jesus' practice of sabbath-healing as consonant with the law, not contrary to it. Indeed, it is Jesus' *detractors* who in fact fail to "do the law" that was given by Moses (John 7:19).

This paradox plays itself out repeatedly in John's narrative. It is the self-appointed defenders of the law who actually violate it, while Jesus— who stands accused of breaking the law—actually has the law on his side. The Pharisees scornfully hurl the charge that it is only the crowd "which does not know the law" that has been duped into believing in Jesus, and that they are therefore accursed (John 7:45-49). But Nicodemus, a closet sympathizer of Jesus, plaintively protests: "Our law does not judge a man without first hearing from him to find out what he is doing, does it?" (7:50-51). Nicodemus is right, of course. The law of Moses forcefully stipulates that accused members of the community must be given a fair hearing and that the social standing or power of the defendant must not influence judges one way or the other (Deut 1:16-17; cf.

Deut 19:16-18). Thus, by leaping to peremptory judgment against Jesus, as well as by their elitist contempt for the crowd of common people, the Pharisees, as depicted in John, ironically break the very law they suppose themselves to be upholding.[40]

The Fourth Gospel insists repeatedly that the law, far from condemning Jesus, creates the appropriate conditions for the truthful hearing of Jesus' message. The law demands that testimony be confirmed by two witnesses (Deut 17:6, 19:15); therefore, Jesus summons two witnesses in his own defense: himself(!) and "the Father who sent me" (John 8:17-18). Here even a sympathetic reader may feel that the argument strains credulity; it is not without reason that Jesus' interlocutors ask, "Where is your father?" (8:19). But in John's narrative world, this response merely creates another level of dramatic irony; their response proves that the Jewish authorities neither know the Father nor understand the spiritual meaning of Jesus' words.

Or, to take another example, when Jesus scandalously declares, "I and the Father are one" (John 10:30), his opponents accuse him of blasphemy. But Jesus appeals to "the law" once again (in this case Ps 82:6) to justify his claim.

> Jesus answered them, "Is it not written in the law,[41] 'I said, you are gods'? If those to whom the word of God came were called 'gods'—and Scripture cannot be broken—then are you saying to the one whom the Father sanctified and sent into the world, 'you are committing blasphemy,' because I said, 'I am the Son of God'?"
>
> (John 10:34-36)

Jesus here not only claims warrant from the law for his proclamation but also articulates a very high view of Israel's Scripture as unbreakable and unimpeachably true. The argument moves from the lesser to the greater: if other hearers of God's word (whether subordinate ancient deities or earthly rulers) could be called "gods,"[42] how much more so may this be said truly of Jesus, who is the unique heavenly Son sent into the world by the Father? The argument has a certain circularity about it, and we need not render a judgment here on its persuasiveness. The important point is that, rather than challenging Israel's law, Jesus appeals *to* it in defense of his claims.

All of this suggests that there is vivid dramatic irony in the Fourth Gospel's trial scene before the Roman governor, when Pilate says to the Jewish authorities, "Take him and judge him according to your own law" (John 18:31). It has been the consistent testimony of John's story that if they did indeed judge Jesus rightly according to their own law, they would find his testimony to be the truth.[43] And so when they later say to Pilate, "We have a law, and according to that law, he ought to die" (19:7), this is merely one more piece of evidence showing that they have both misjudged Jesus and misinterpreted the very law that actually bears witness to him. And yet, on another reading, might we consider whether this is one more case of exquisitely complex irony? Just as Caiaphas unwittingly prophesies truly that "it is better for you to have one man die for the people than to have the whole nation destroyed" (11:49-52), so also the Jewish leaders before Pilate unwittingly speak the truth: Jesus' death is indeed necessary "according to the law," in the sense that the law prefigures it—as John has told us from the beginning of the story.[44]

In sum, then, there is no suggestion anywhere in the Fourth Gospel that the law is in any respect wrong or deficient. The narrative implies a critique not of the law but of those leaders who abuse the law and fail to keep it (John 7:19). Those whose desire is to do the will of God will recognize the truth and divine origin of Jesus' teaching (7:16-17), and this will enable them to see that the law of Moses points in many and various ways to Jesus as its own fulfillment. John, writing late in the first century, nowhere specifically addresses the controversies that had plagued the Pauline mission churches in an earlier generation, disputes over practices such as circumcision (apparently approved without comment in 7:22-23), food laws, and the observance of special days. Instead, he simply and steadily presupposes the law of Moses and the words of Israel's Scripture as the essential hermeneutical matrix for recognizing and understanding Jesus' testimony.

Israel's festivals

These same affirmations apply *a fortiori* to the great festivals that give shape to Israel's annual cycle of worship and community celebration. More than any of the other Evangelists, John draws attention to these festivals as critical temporal markers in Jesus' story, points of reference around which the plot of the narrative is organized. John's christological interpretation of the symbolism of these festivals will be explored more fully later in this chapter; for now, we note simply that time in John's narrative is structured by the rhythms of Israel's liturgical calendar.[45]

In Deuteronomy 16:16-17, three major pilgrimage festivals are prescribed: the festival of unleavened bread (Passover), the Festival of Weeks

(Pentecost), and the Festival of Booths (*Sukkoth*). On each of these occasions, all the males of Israel were commanded to "appear before the Lord" in Jerusalem.[46] Surprisingly, the Festival of Weeks (Lev 23:15-22) receives no mention in John's narrative,[47] but Passover and the Festival of Booths play prominent roles, along with a fourth observance, the Festival of Dedication. New Testament scholarship has often noted that John, unlike the Synoptic Gospels, narrates Jesus' ministry over a span of time that includes three different Passover festivals (John 2:13, 23; 6:4; 12:1; 13:1). Establishing the chronology of Jesus' public activity or John's relation to the synoptics has proven difficult in light of these references to the festivals. But a critical effect of John's multiple references to the Passover is to anchor Jesus and his followers within the symbolic world of Judaism, portraying them as faithful participants in the pilgrimage festivals that gave shape to Jewish religious practice and identity in the era when the Jerusalem temple still stood.

The Passover, to which John refers repeatedly,[48] of course recalls Israel's deliverance from slavery in Egypt. Thus, the identity-defining Exodus narrative hovers constantly in the background of John's story. The reference to an impending Passover in John 6:4 may appear incidental to the logic of the plot until we recognize that it introduces the episodes of Jesus' miraculous feeding of a crowd (6:5-14) and walking on the sea (6:16-21), incidents that narratively mirror Israel's crossing of the sea (Exod 14:1-31) and reception of manna in the wilderness (Exod 16:1-36).[49] And of course, the final Passover celebration in the Fourth Gospel coincides with Jesus' arrest, crucifixion, and resurrection, giving rise to a wide range of symbolic resonances.

The Feast of Booths (*Sukkoth*; see Lev 23:33-43) also plays a significant role in John's emplotment of incidents. It is mentioned explicitly at John 7:2, and the festival's key symbols of water and light then provide central metaphors in the ensuing discourses, especially in John 7:37-39 and 8:12-20. Because this festival was also associated with Israel's wilderness journey—the temporary booths representing the shelters that the people built during their time in the desert[50]—it was often understood as symbolizing a time of preparation for entry to the land and the fulfillment of God's promises; therefore, it took on messianic overtones.[51] These narrative associations perhaps account for the messianic speculations that John introduces in connection with this festival (7:25-31, 40-44): "But many of the people in the crowd believed in him, and they were saying, 'When the Messiah comes, he won't do more signs than this man has done, will he?'" (7:31).

The third major festival mentioned by John is the Festival of Dedication (τὰ ἐγκαίνια, better: "Inauguration").[52] This holiday commemorated the rededication of the temple by Judas Maccabeus after it had been desecrated by the Seleucid ruler Antiochus IV Epiphanes (1 Macc 4:36-59): "Then Judas and his brothers and all the assembly of Israel determined that every year at that season the days of dedication of the altar should be observed with joy and gladness for eight days, beginning with the twenty-fifth day of the month of Chislev" (1 Macc 4:59). Because this was the celebration of a liberating military victory over a foreign occupying power, messianic/eschatological connotations and hopes inevitably clustered around it. Thus, in John's story the Festival of Dedication once again catalyzes inquiry and speculation about whether Jesus might be the hoped-for Messiah (John 10:24).

Each of these festivals evokes recollections of key narrative moments in Israel's Scripture. As with John's allusions to major characters in Israel's story, so also with his references to the festivals: he does not renarrate the events that the festivals commemorate. But the references presuppose the scriptural narratives, and their significance—including their symbolic import for John's own narration—can be grasped only by readers whose interpretative competence includes knowledge of these liturgical traditions and the stories on which they are based. Likewise, as with John's treatment of the law, so also with the festivals: he does not annul or reject these observances as superstitious or outmoded. Rather, he weaves them into his Gospel as patterns within a larger tapestry, time-shaping patterns that point to Jesus as the one who discloses their true significance. To be sure, he reshapes their traditional meaning in ways that are immediately controversial, as John's story makes abundantly clear. But the reshaping would be impossible and unintelligible apart from the matrix of Israel's narrative and liturgical traditions.

Resistance of the Ioudaioi

It is precisely this reshaping of Israel's tradition, however, that elicits the implacable resistance of the religious authorities in Jerusalem and sets in motion the conflict that leads to Jesus' crucifixion. These hostile religious leaders are variously described in the Fourth Gospel, but most frequently they are simply called οἱ Ἰουδαῖοι ("the Jews"), a term that appears some seventy times in this Gospel. John's puzzling use of this expression has been the object of sustained critical scrutiny.[53] We cannot adequately review the complex debate about this term here,[54] but a few basic observations are in order.

First, John's term "the Jews" should not be understood as a reference to the whole Jewish people in Jesus' time; still less can it apply to all Jews throughout subsequent history. After all, Jesus himself was a Jew, as were all of his original followers. In the Fourth Gospel, the term seems frequently (though not always) to designate a specific group of authorities concentrated in Jerusalem who found Jesus objectionable, opposed his message, and sought to squelch the movement that formed around him. Second, several passages in John seem to equate "the Jews" with the Pharisees.[55] For example, in John 9:13 the blind man healed by Jesus is brought before "the Pharisees" for interrogation, but by 9:18 we find the skeptical interrogators referred to as "the Jews." Further, we are told in 9:22 that the man's parents were "afraid of the Jews" and that "the Jews had already agreed that anyone who confessed Jesus to be the Messiah would be put out of the synagogue." But in 12:42 it is "the Pharisees" to whom this exclusionary power is attributed. Third, these references to expulsion from the synagogue are strange, since neither the Synoptic Gospels nor any other ancient source offers any trace of evidence for such a policy in synagogues during Jesus' lifetime.

John's terminological conflation of "Jews" and "Pharisees" almost surely reflects a historical perspective from the vantage point of the late first century, after the destruction of the temple and after the emergence of the Pharisees as the dominant influences in formative rabbinic Judaism. John's references to exclusion from the synagogue are thinly veiled allusions to the painful state of affairs at the time of the Gospel's composition, near the end of the first century. The apparent anachronism is not a naive mistake by the author but an intentional literary and theological device; John has crafted a "two-level drama" in order to show how events of the author's own time (expulsion of Jesus' followers from the synagogue) belong integrally to the outworking of the story of Jesus.[56] Or, to put the point the other way around: the rejection of Jesus by the religious authorities of his day foreshadows the rejection and ostracism experienced later by the community of those who confess Jesus to be the Messiah.

Sadly, however, John's references to "the Jews" as Jesus' enemies who played an instrumental role in bringing about his death, when read from the perspective of the later Gentile Christian church, seemed to suggest a blanket condemnation of Jews and Judaism, a condemnation that was to have disastrous and violent consequences in later centuries when

Christians found themselves in possession of power. John's terminology also seemed to imply a non-Jewish Jesus with non-Jewish followers, as for example in Jesus' words to Pilate: "If my kingdom were from this world, my servants would have been fighting to keep me from being handed over to the Jews" (John 18:36). But this is a seriously misleading impression, not only as a matter of historical fact but also with regard to the logic of John's own narrative. John's Jesus is deeply imbedded in Jewish Scripture and tradition, and the Gospel affirms rather than negates Israel's story.[57] Therefore, in order to avoid a distorted perspective, throughout the rest of this chapter, I shall adopt the expedient of leaving οἱ Ἰουδαῖοι untranslated, employing the transliterated term *Ioudaioi*. It is my hope that this practice will discourage unreflective identification of John's *Ioudaioi* with the Jewish people as a whole.

If, then, John is not positing a fundamental conflict between Jesus and Judaism, how are we to interpret the narrative's insistent portrayal of Jewish resistance to Jesus and his message? The problem is similar to the one articulated by Apostle Paul in his own agonized deliberations about Israel's failure to accept the gospel message: "They have a zeal for God, but it is not informed by knowledge" (Rom 10:2). That is precisely the plight of Jesus' adversaries in the Fourth Gospel, a plight heightened by John's use of dramatic irony throughout his narrative. The strongest opposition to Jesus comes from the most ardent exponents of obedience to the law, the most devout defenders of God's holiness. They are genuinely convinced that Jesus is a dangerous sinner (John 9:24). They fret that Jesus is encouraging others to break the sabbath (5:10). They are horrified to hear Jesus talking appallingly about consuming human flesh and blood (6:52), making outrageous claims that he existed before Abraham (8:56-59), and, most culpably, committing outright blasphemy (in their view) by claiming to be one with God (5:16-17, 10:30-33). Their concern is that this Jesus, an uneducated but charismatic outsider from obscure origins, is making megalomaniacal claims for his own exalted status, placing himself above the law of Moses, and scorning the authorities who are duly charged with protecting the integrity and sacredness of God's revealed truth.

Worst of all, this Jesus is attracting crowds of enthusiastic followers who are deceived by him into a frenzy of messianic speculation. Such talk is highly dangerous, because the Roman authorities are likely to regard this sort of popular enthusiasm as a potential revolutionary threat to public order. The chief priests and Pharisees anxiously say to one another, "If we let him carry on like this, everyone will believe in him, and the Romans will come and take away what we have, both the holy place and the people" (John 11:48). Their fear is not unfounded. By conspiring to kill Jesus, then, the authorities understand themselves to be acting in good faith, exercising their sacred responsibility to protect the temple and the safety of the people of God. As Jesus will later warn his disciples in his lengthy final discourse, "the hour is coming when anyone who kills you will think he is offering service to God" (16:2). That dire prophecy describes precisely the motivation of the *Ioudaioi* who contrive a way to have Jesus put to death.

That is not to say, of course, that their motives are unmixed. The story strongly suggests that Jesus' adversaries are also envious of his popular influence and protective of their own power. So, John 12:43: "They loved human glory more than the glory of God." Their compromises with Roman authority—compromises that they deem realistic and necessary for the good of the nation—ultimately lead them to grovel before the Roman governor and declare, "We have no king but Caesar" (19:15), a shocking denial of Israel's confession of the unique kingly power of God, a power paradigmatically acclaimed in the Passover festival that celebrates God's sovereign triumph over the royal bluster of Pharaoh.[58] By their acclamation of Caesar as their king, the *Ioudaioi* dissociate themselves de facto from the faithful posture of the prophet Isaiah: "O LORD our God, other lords besides you have ruled over us, but we acknowledge your name alone" (Isa 26:13).[59] All of this is simply to say that the dynamics of betrayal are complex and that John's narrative depicts the way in which devout motives can become entangled with ignoble ones to lead to violence and unwitting apostasy.

At the root of the matter for John, though, is the *inability* of the *Ioudaioi* to recognize Jesus as the one about whom Moses and the prophets wrote. "He came to his own home, and his own people did not receive him" (John 1:11). John's favorite metaphor to describe their condition of incomprehension is the image of blindness. The blind man in John 9 receives sight and comes to believe in Jesus and worship him (9:38), while the leaders who ought to be in the best position to see cannot do so. Jesus encapsulates this paradoxical state of affairs in an aphorism: "For judgment I came into this world, so that the ones who don't see might see, and so that the ones who see might become blind" (9:39).

This reversal of fortunes is not some random irony of history; rather, it is the strange outworking of God's will as foretold in Scripture. At the conclusion of the public phase of Jesus' activity, John pulls back the

curtain and displays key Isaianic prophecies that prefigure the resistance
Jesus encountered:

> Although he had done so many signs in their presence, they did not believe
> in him. This happened so that the word spoken by Isaiah the prophet
> might be fulfilled:
>
>> "Lord, who has believed our message,
>> and the arm of the Lord—to whom has it been revealed?"
>
> That is why they were not able to believe, because again Isaiah said,
>
>> "He blinded their eyes
>> and hardened their hearts
>> so that they would not see with their eyes
>> and understand with their hearts
>> and turn—and I would heal them."
>
> Isaiah said these things, because he saw his glory and spoke about him.
>
> (John 12:37-41; quoting Isa 53:1 and Isa 6:10)

This narrative disclosure is crucial to understanding the failure of the
Ioudaioi to respond to Jesus and his message. Within John's narrative,
their opposition is not a simple matter of self-interested stubbornness;
it is genuinely a case of blindness, and it is God who has "blinded their
eyes." Why? The answer to that question is hidden in mystery. But for
present purposes, here is the important point: *the resistance of the Jewish
authorities to Jesus does not mean that Israel has now been rejected by God or
that their life with God has been annulled*. Rather, this mysterious stubborn
resistance belongs to a pattern that runs throughout Israel's story, from
the grumbling and idolatry of the wilderness generation to the unfaithfulness of kings and people in the days of the prophets, their covenant-
betrayal that finally led to exile. The pattern has not changed. John
sees this pattern clearly displayed in Isaiah, and he contends that it has
replayed itself climactically in the people's rejection of Jesus. Thus, even
the tragic blindness of the *Ioudaioi* in John's narrative is deeply grounded
in the prophetic tradition.

    Unlike Paul, John does not seem to reflect on whether God will ulti-
mately find a way to fulfill his covenant promises by restoring even those
who have been blinded and hardened. Indeed, in some passages he seems
to consign those who fail to believe in Jesus to utter destruction, most
notoriously in John 8, in which Jesus castigates his interlocutors as children of the devil (8:44) and ascribes their unbelief to an ontological dualism: "If I am speaking truth, why don't you believe me? Whoever is from

God hears the words of God. This is why you don't hear, because you are not from God" (8:46b-47). Statements such as this in the Fourth Gospel reflect the bitter conflicts of the late first century, in which at least some Jewish Christians have met with unremitting hostility from synagogue communities that have shunned them. Nonetheless, it is important to recognize that within John's own narrative, the provocative statements of John 8 are finally framed and reinterpreted by the scriptural words of Isaiah cited in John 12 at the end of the book of signs. Here, rather than interpreting Jewish unbelief in Jesus as a sign of cosmic dualism, John places the resistance and unbelief of Jesus' own people under the umbrella of the mysterious sovereign will of the one God of Israel, as proclaimed ahead of time by Isaiah.

And, most tellingly, this section of John's Gospel ends not with a pronouncement of condemnation on the unbelievers but with a hopeful invitation to those who have not accepted the message. The passage, standing structurally at the conclusion of Jesus' public career, should be taken as the hermeneutical frame of reference for all that has gone before. Judgment is still in view, but the mode of discourse is one of *appeal* to the hearers to trust Jesus as the one sent by the Father to offer life. This is an important corrective to the midcourse polemic of John 8:

> Then Jesus cried aloud: "Whoever believes in me believes not in me but in him who sent me. And whoever sees me sees him who sent me. *I have come as light into the world, so that everyone who believes in me should not remain in the darkness. I do not judge anyone who hears my words and does not keep them, for I came not to judge the world, but to save the world.* The one who rejects me and does not receive my word has a judge; on the last day the word that I have spoken will serve as judge, for I have not spoken on my own, but the Father who sent me has himself given me a commandment about what to say and what to speak. And I know that his commandment is eternal life. What I speak, therefore, I speak just as the Father has told me."
>
> (John 12:44-50)

If we read John attentively *as a narrative*, we recognize that this culminating public declaration of Jesus, in combination with the immediately preceding scriptural citations from Isaiah, places Jesus' sharp controversies with the *Ioudaioi* in a more open and hopeful frame of reference. Even though it is somehow God's will to blind the eyes of unbelievers, Jesus declares that he will not judge them, and he continues to hold out the hopeful offer of God's saving word.

Furthermore, we should recall that Isaiah's grim declaration about the blinding and hardening of Israel comes early in the book, at the beginning of Isaiah's prophetic commission. But if we read the entirety of canonical Isaiah, we find the prophet proclaiming a message of restoration, hope, and new creation. An analogous hint may be discovered at the climax of Jesus' public discourse in John 12. Unlike Isaiah, John does not "speak tenderly to Jerusalem" (Isa 40:2) and declare that the time of punishment for unfaithful Israel is at an end. But the intertextual linkage of Jesus' message to Isaiah's may suggest implicitly that redemptive restoration of Israel is not beyond the realm of possibility. If Jesus has come "to save the world" (John 12:47), that mission must surely include God's elect people.

For all these reasons, we cannot close the book on Israel's story when we come to the end of the Fourth Gospel. John has given the story a dramatic new turn, an unexpected resolution in the figure of Jesus. The desired effect of this unexpected fulfillment is to compel readers to understand Jesus by recalling Israel's scriptural story and at the same time to reinterpret its earlier chapters in the clarifying light that Jesus has brought into the world.

§18 JESUS AS THE TEMPLE

Jesus as Word and Wisdom

The opening words of John's Gospel echo the first words of Israel's Scripture: "In the beginning . . ." Although the echo consists of only two words (ἐν ἀρχῇ), its volume is amplified by the placement of these words at the outset of the narrative, corresponding to their placement as the opening words of Genesis. Even more significantly, John's prologue continues to evoke creation themes (John 1:3, 10) and images (light/darkness [John 1:4-5, 7-9; cf. Gen 1:3-5]). A reader conversant with Genesis could hardly fail to hear the echo, as the history of interpretation of John amply demonstrates.[60] And as the prologue unfolds, the reader gradually learns that the mysterious *Logos* who was there "in the beginning" has become flesh and is to be identified directly with Jesus Christ (1:14-18). Thus, the effect of John's introduction is to identify Jesus as a figure present with (or one with) God in the primal act of creation: "All things came into being through him, and apart from him not one thing came into being" (1:3).

This is an astounding claim to make about a human being, a figure of the author's recent historical past. To be sure, the role here ascribed to the *Logos* is not without biblical precedent. Israel's scriptural tradition contains several significant references to a preexistent figure of Wisdom as participant in the creation of the world, most notably in Proverbs 8:22-31. Although Wisdom (חכמה, σοφία) is said to have been created (LXX: κύριος ἔκτισέν με) or, as the Hebrew text has it, "acquired" (קנני) at the beginning of God's works or ways (Prov 8:22), she is described as present with God "before the beginning of the earth" and beside God as a "master worker" (אמון) in the formation of the world.[61] In its original context in Proverbs, this language is almost surely to be understood as poetic personification of God's attribute of wisdom rather than as description of an actual quasidivine *hypostasis*.[62] It is not difficult to see, however, how over time the figure of personified Wisdom could develop into a mythologically conceived personage; indeed, we already see hints of this development in Wisdom of Solomon (see especially Wis 10), though the chief tendency of many later Jewish texts is to identify the figure of Wisdom as a personification of Torah (as in Sir 24:1-23 and Bar 3:35–4:4).

For John, however, the active agent in creation is identified not as the figure of *Sophia* but rather as the Word (*Logos*).[63] John's terminological choice here is perhaps influenced by the narrative of Genesis 1, in which God simply *speaks* all creation into being. John's account also resonates deeply with the language of Psalm 33:6: "*By the word of the LORD the heavens were made* (LXX: τῷ λόγῳ τοῦ κυρίου οἱ οὐρανοὶ ἐστερεώθησαν), and all their host by the breath of his mouth." John's emphasis on the role of the *Logos* in creation finds a parallel in the writings of Philo, who assigns to the quasipersonified figure of the *logos* a unique role of mediation between God and the creation, as in a famous passage from *Quis rerum divinarum heres sit*, 205–6:

> To his *Logos*, His chief messenger, highest in age and honor, the Father of all has given the special prerogative to stand on the border and separate the creature from the Creator. This same *Logos* both pleads with immortal [God] as suppliant for afflicted mortality and acts as ambassador of the Ruler to the subject. . . . [He is] neither uncreated by God, nor created as you, but midway between the two extremes, a surety to both sides.[64]

In Philo, all this seems to have the character of philosophical speculation. The *logos* for Philo, even if quasihypostatized, is a figurative and certainly noncorporeal entity that symbolizes something like God's creative power of reason. But John, in his prologue (John 1:1-18), astonishingly claims that the *Logos* became *flesh*.

The prologue of John's Gospel is best understood as a midrash on Genesis 1, a midrash that links the idea of a preexistent creative divine *logos* to the motif of divine Wisdom seeking a home in the world (e.g., Sir 24:3-8). In contrast, however, to those earlier Jewish traditions that identify the earthly presence of Wisdom among the people Israel or in Israel's law (Sir 24:23; Bar 3:35–4:4), John insists that *Logos*/Wisdom found only rejection in the world, even among God's own people.

> He was in the world, and the world came into being through him; yet the world did not know him. He came to what was his own, and his own people did not accept him.
>
> (John 1:10-11)

This appears very similar to the rather gloomy account offered in 1 Enoch:

> Wisdom could not find a place in which she could dwell; but a place was found for her in the heavens. Then Wisdom went out to dwell with the children of the people, but she found no dwelling place. So Wisdom returned to her place and she settled permanently among the angels.
>
> (1 Enoch 42:1-2)

But the Gospel of John offers a radically different ending to such a tragic tale.[65] Rather than taking up permanent residence among the angels, the divine Word/Wisdom acted to overcome Israel's resistance by becoming flesh in the person of Jesus: "And the Word became flesh and lived (ἐσκήνωσεν) among us, and we have seen his glory, as of a father's only son, full of grace and truth" (John 1:14).[66] Thus, the prologue of the Fourth Gospel immediately situates Jesus in relation to Jewish scriptural traditions about *creation* and *Wisdom*, while at the same time transforming those traditions through the startling claim that the Word/Wisdom through whom everything was made has become enfleshed in Jesus.[67]

The remarkable identification of Jesus as the incarnate Word who was the agent of all creation carries wide-ranging hermeneutical implications for the way that John *reads backwards* to reinterpret Israel's Scripture and Israel's worship traditions: he asserts that Jesus, as the incarnation of God's Word, takes up into himself the significance of all that has gone before in God's dealing with Israel. One of the clearest expressions of this hermeneutical device appears near the beginning of the narrative, after Jesus has driven the sellers and money changers out of the temple.

This passage gives us a crucial point of entry into the scriptural matrix within which we must read John's story of Jesus.

Remembering Scripture and Jesus' word

John emplots his distinctive account of Jesus' dramatic protest against the merchants and money changers in the temple near the beginning of his narrative (John 2:13-22). The placement of the story is freighted with symbolic significance in two ways: it foreshadows the conflict that leads to Jesus' passion and death (signaled by the quotation of Ps 69:9: "Zeal for your house will consume me"),[68] and it points to the figural identification of Jesus' body as a *temple* that will be raised up in the resurrection—as signaled by Jesus' own riddling words: "Destroy this temple, and in three days I will raise it up." Jesus' interlocutors misunderstand his saying because, in the dramatic irony typical of Johannine dialogues, they perceive only the surface literal sense and miss the hidden christological meaning.

John presents both the scriptural text and the word of Jesus as enigmas that become comprehensible only *retrospectively*, only after the resurrection.[69] His emphasis on hermeneutical hindsight is highlighted by the parallelism between John 2:17 and 2:22:

> John 2:17a: His disciples remembered that it was written. . . .
>
> John 2:22a: . . . his disciples remembered that he had said this. . . .

The Greek text in the two formulations is identical: ἐμνήσθησαν οἱ μαθηταὶ αὐτοῦ ὅτι. In both cases, John tells us, the disciples' understanding came only later, only as they read backwards to interpret his actions and words in light of the paradigm-shattering event of his resurrection. That is the point made emphatically in John 2:22: "his disciples remembered . . . and they believed *the Scripture* and *the word that Jesus had spoken*." This is consistent with the Evangelist's overall perspective on the crucial significance of memory and retrospective reading. Later in John's Gospel, in Jesus' farewell discourses, we learn that the disciples' postresurrection remembering is to be aided by the Paraclete, the Holy Spirit, who will recall and interpret Jesus' words for the community (John 14:25-26, 16:12-15). Even more explicitly than the other Gospel writers, then, John champions *reading backwards* as an essential strategy for illuminating Jesus' identity.[70] Only by reading backwards, in light of the resurrection, under the guidance of the Spirit, can we understand both Israel's Scripture and Jesus' words.

This exact same pattern of postresurrection retrospective understanding is described in John's account of Jesus' entry into Jerusalem on a donkey (John 12:12-16). Like the synoptic Evangelists, John portrays the crowd chanting the words of Psalm 118:25-26, and in agreement with Matthew 21:4-5 he observes that the event accords with Scripture: "Jesus found a young donkey and sat on it; as it is written, 'Look, your king is coming, sitting on a donkey's colt'" (12:14-15; quoting Zech 9:9).[71] John then adds a distinctive word of further explanation: "His disciples did not understand these things at *first*; but when Jesus was glorified, then they *remembered* that these things had been written of him and had been done to him" (12:16). This later reemphasis on retrospective imaginative connection between Scripture and Jesus' action reminds the reader of the hermeneutical ground structure that informs John's Gospel from start to finish.

What then, according to John 2:17-22, does a postresurrection reading of Psalm 69 discover in the text? It discloses, among other things, that *Jesus himself is the speaker of Psalm 69:9*, the praying voice who declares, "Zeal for your house will consume me." And that insight in turn opens the window on a fresh appropriation of the entire psalm—indeed, perhaps the entire Psalter—as a proleptic veiled revelation of the identity of Jesus. Indeed, from a range of other evidence we know that the early church did read Psalm 69 in precisely this way: as a passion psalm portraying Jesus as the righteous sufferer.[72] To be sure, in order to read the Psalms this way, it is necessary to cultivate a figural imagination. And so *when John declares that Jesus "was speaking of the temple of his body," a light goes on: the Evangelist, here in the opening chapters of his story, is teaching his readers how to read.* He is teaching us to read *figurally*, teaching us to read Scripture *retrospectively*, in light of the resurrection. Only on such a reading does it make sense to see the Jerusalem temple as *prefiguring* the truth now definitively embodied in the crucified and risen Jesus.[73]

Thus, John 2:13-22 is of great importance. We are informed here that right interpretation of Scripture and of the traditions about Jesus could be done only *retrospectively* after the resurrection; John also instructs his readers to read *figurally*; and the link between the temple and Jesus' body is made explicit, providing a hermeneutical key for John's symbolism throughout the narrative. *Jesus now takes over the temple's function as a place of mediation between God and human beings.*[74]

The hermeneutical revelation offered in 2:21 casts new light on Jesus' earlier enigmatic declaration to Nathanael: "Truly, truly, I say to you, you will see the heaven opened and the angels of God ascending and descending upon the Son of Man" (John 1:51). Jesus has become the nexus between heaven and earth—the role previously ascribed to the temple as the site of God's presence—and thus he fulfills Jacob's naming of the place of his dream vision as *Bethel*: "This is none other than *the house of God*, and this is the gate of heaven" (Gen 28:17).[75] That is also why Jesus can later say to the Samaritan woman, "Woman, believe me, the hour is coming when you will worship the Father neither on this mountain nor in Jerusalem" (John 4:21). True worship is focused not on any geographical location or cultic site; rather, it is focused on the person of Jesus himself, who is both the way to the Father and the place where the presence of God is made known (14:6-7)—indeed, the place where the presence of God dwells.

The symbolism of Jesus as the temple is already foreshadowed in John's prologue, where the Evangelist proclaims that the *Logos* "became flesh and dwelled (ἐσκήνωσεν) among us, and we have seen his glory (δόξαν)" (John 1:14). The verb (σκηνόω), which is etymologically related to the noun σκηνή (tent), almost certainly for John alludes to the tabernacle, where the presence of God was made manifest to Moses and the people of Israel during their wilderness sojourn: "And have them make me a sanctuary, so that I may *dwell* among them. In accordance with all that I show you concerning the pattern of the tabernacle (τῆς σκηνῆς) and of all its furniture, so you shall make it" (Exod 25:8-9). This tabernacle was the precursor and prototype for the Jerusalem temple, the locus of God's presence and glory. In light of this scriptural narrative background, we should certainly read John 1:14 as a subtle anticipation of the theme that will be dramatically unveiled in 2:19-22: Jesus has become the temple, the dwelling place of God's glory in the world.[76] And we should therefore perhaps hear also in John 1:14 an echo of the prophecy of Ezekiel 37:26-27:

> I will make a covenant of peace with them; it shall be an everlasting cove-
> nant with them; and I will bless them and multiply them, and will set *my
> sanctuary* among them forevermore. *My dwelling place* (κατασκήνωσίς) *shall
> be with them*; and I will be their God, and they shall be my people.

Closely linked to this figural correspondence between Jesus and the temple is John's direct allusion to Isaiah's account of his prophetic call through a theophany in the temple (Isa 6:1-5). After quoting Isaiah 53:1 and 6:10, John explains that "Isaiah said these things because he saw [Jesus'] glory and spoke about him" (John 12:37-41). John, reading backwards, interprets Isaiah's temple-centered vision of God's glory as a revelation of Jesus, the rejected Messiah, as the one in whom God's presence is manifest.[77]

Jesus as embodiment of Sukkoth and Passover

An analogous logic applies throughout the Fourth Gospel to Jesus' assumption and transformation of the significance of Israel's religious festivals. Just as Jesus becomes the embodiment of that which the temple had signified, so also he now embodies everything to which Israel's feasts and cultic observances had pointed.

For example, the rituals of *Sukkoth* (the Festival of Booths or Tabernacles)[78] involved outpourings of water and the kindling of lights in the temple, in symbolic anticipation of the fulfillment of Zechariah's apocalyptic vision:

> And there shall be continuous day (it is known to the LORD), not day and not night, *for at evening time there shall be light.* On that day *living waters shall flow out from Jerusalem. . . .*
>
> (Zech 14:7-8)[79]

Therefore, when Jesus cries out[80] on the last day of the festival of Sukkoth, "Let anyone who is thirsty come to me, and let the one who believes in me drink" (John 7:37-38; cf. 7:2) and—on the same occasion[81]—"I am the light of the world" (8:12), he is taking onto himself the symbolism of the occasion, implicitly claiming both to fulfill and to supplant it. The festival's burning torches that symbolize the "continuous day" of God's glorious presence point in fact to Jesus, who is "the true light . . . coming into the world" (1:9). And the abundant water poured out in the festival points to the *living water* that only Jesus can offer, as he has earlier promised to the Samaritan woman (John 4:7-15; cf. Zech 14:8).

When we interpret Jesus' cry in John 7:37-38 in light of the imagery of *Sukkoth* and in light of John's clear identification of Jesus' body as the temple, we find satisfying solutions to a notorious cluster of exegetical problems in the passage.[82]

The structure of John's syntax is ambiguous: Does the substantive participial phrase ὁ πιστεύων εἰς ἐμέ ("the one who believes in me") serve as the subject of the immediately preceding third-person imperative verb πινέτω ("let drink")? This would yield the following translation:

> "If anyone is thirsty, let him come to me, and let the one who believes in me drink. As the Scripture has said, 'out of his belly shall flow rivers of living water.'"

Or does the participial phrase serve as a dangling, grammatically awkward logical antecedent for the pronoun αὐτοῦ ("his") in the last clause of the sentence? This would yield this translation:

> "If anyone is thirsty, let him come to me and drink. The one who believes in me—as Scripture has said—'out of his belly shall flow rivers of living water.'"

Second, does it make sense to imagine that "rivers of living water" will flow *out of the believer*, as almost all English translations have it—or should we understand the sentence to promise that living water will flow *from Jesus*? Third, what could be the source of the apparent quotation of Scripture in John 7:38?

The key to answering all these questions lies in John's emphatic identification of Jesus as the temple. Given the setting of Jesus' words on the last day of the festival, we should recall Zechariah's eschatological image of waters flowing from Jerusalem, the image that is symbolized by the water ritual of *Sukkoth*. This image evokes the earlier prophetic vision of Ezekiel:

> Then he brought me back to the entrance of the temple; there, water was flowing from below the threshold of the temple toward the east (for the temple faced east); and the water was flowing down from below the south end of the threshold of the temple, south of the altar. Then he brought me out by way of the north gate, and led me around on the outside to the outer gate that faces toward the east; and the water was coming out on the south side.
>
> (Ezek 47:1-2)

These images from Ezekiel 47 and Zechariah 14 are the likeliest sources of the "Scripture" to which the Evangelist refers in John 7:38.[83] If so, John's reference to what "Scripture has said" should be understood *not* as the signal of a direct quotation but as a summarizing reference to scriptural texts commonly associated with the festival of *Sukkoth* and with the hope for an eschatological temple in a restored Jerusalem in the promised new age.[84] Accordingly, the source of the superabundant eschatological outpouring of water that Jesus offers is surely not "the believer" (as in most translations) but *Jesus himself as the symbolic temple prefigured in the prophetic texts*. And the reference to Scripture in John 7:38 should be understood not as part of Jesus' cry but as part of the Evangelist's explanatory word to the reader. These interpretative decisions, then, would yield the following translation:

> [Jesus] cried out, "Let anyone who is thirsty come to me, and let the one who believes in me drink." As the Scripture has said, out of his [i.e., Jesus'] belly shall flow rivers of living water. Now he said this about the Spirit, which believers in him were to receive; for as yet there was no Spirit, because Jesus was not yet glorified.
>
> (John 7:37-39)

This interpretation, which accounts for both the syntax and the symbolism of the passage, forcefully suggests that the true meaning of *Sukkoth*—and of the prophetic texts associated with it—is now embodied in Jesus.

Likewise, references to Israel's *Passover* observance appear repeatedly in John's Gospel. These references appear first in relation to Jesus' prophetic action of driving the merchants and money changers out of the temple (John 2:13, 23), next in connection with his multiplication of bread to feed the hungry crowd (6:4), and then in the run-up to his triumphal entrance to Jerusalem (11:55, 12:1).[85] A key dramatic pivot-point occurs in 13:1, following the conclusion of John's narrative of Jesus' public activity (see 12:36b): "Now before the festival of the Passover, Jesus knew that his hour had come to depart from this world and go to the Father." By locating the time of Jesus' "hour" in conjunction with the Passover celebration, John strongly hints at a figural conjunction between the death/glorification of Jesus and the story of Israel's deliverance from bondage in Egypt.

And indeed, John's references to the Passover do come to a climax in the passion narrative, where Jesus' crucifixion takes place on the *day of preparation* for Passover (John 19:14), not on the day of Passover itself as in the Synoptic Gospels. The effect of this chronological shift is to align Jesus' death with the slaughter of the Passover lambs, a point underscored when John tells the reader that the Roman soldiers did not break the legs of Jesus on the cross, thus allowing his death to fulfill the requirement for the preparation of the Passover lamb: "These things occurred so that Scripture might be fulfilled, 'None of his bones shall be

broken'" (19:36). This is certainly an allusion to the divinely given directions for preparing and consuming the Passover lamb: "It shall be eaten
in one house; you shall not take any of the animal outside the house, and
you shall not break any of its bones" (Exod 12:46). The actual wording of
John's quotation, however, appears to be a fusion between the Exodus
narrative and a passage from the Psalms that has no explicit connection
to the Passover festival:

> Many are the afflictions of the righteous,
> but the LORD rescues them from them all.
> He keeps all *their bones*;
> *not one of them will be broken.*
>
>   (Ps 34:19-20)

The relationship among the texts is best displayed by setting the Greek
texts in parallel with one another, with underlining showing the points
from which John has drawn elements of his composite quotation:

John 19:36: ὀστοῦν οὐ συντριβήσεται αὐτοῦ.

Exod 12:46 LXX: καὶ ὀστοῦν οὐ συντρίψετε ἀπ᾽ αὐτοῦ.

Ps 34:20 (33:21 LXX): κύριος φυλάσσει πάντα τὰ ὀστᾶ αὐτῶν ἓν ἐξ αὐτῶν
    οὐ συντριβήσεται.

In John's citation, the singular noun ὀστοῦν ("a bone") agrees with the
Exodus account, but the third-person future passive indicative verb
συντριβήσεται ("will be broken") agrees with the language of the psalm.[86]

If readers with finely tuned ears hear the fusion of these two texts in
John's account, the resulting interpretation will be complex. On the one
hand, the crucifixion of Jesus on the Day of Preparation will represent
a fulfillment of the figural sense of the Passover ordinance and call to
mind God's action of rescuing Israel. And simultaneously, on the other
hand, the metaleptic reminiscence of Psalm 34 suggests not only that
Jesus, the Righteous One par excellence, was to be rescued by God but
that his rescue portends God's ultimate rescue of all the righteous from
all their afflictions (as in Ps 34:19). Both subtexts serve, in different ways,
to shape an interpretation of the crucifixion as a saving event rather than
an ignominious defeat.

Further, John's symbolic linkage of the crucifixion with the Passover
at last explicates the meaning of John the Baptist's mysterious initial

acclamation of Jesus as "the Lamb of God" (John 1:29, 36). The reader who recalls the beginning of the Evangelist's story will now be able to read backwards and interpret this epithet: for John the Evangelist, Jesus, "the Lamb of God who takes away the sin of the world," embodies in his death the true signification of the Passover and Exodus events.

The Good Shepherd at the Feast of Dedication

All of this is fairly familiar to readers of John. But now let us explore in more detail one more festival whose symbolic significance for John is perhaps less widely recognized: the Feast of Dedication. The key text is John 10:22-30. John writes: "At that time the Festival of the Dedication took place in Jerusalem. It was winter, and Jesus was walking in the temple, in the portico of Solomon." It is easy for us to read right over this, but anyone in first-century Israel would immediately have perceived the symbolically fraught character of this setting.

The Festival of Dedication (*Hanukkah*) celebrates the victory of the Maccabean revolt against the oppressive Syrian ruler Antiochus Epiphanes IV. He had occupied the land of Israel and instituted a series of repressive measures designed to force the Jewish people to abandon their observance of Torah. His aim was that they give up the practice of circumcision and their distinctive food laws and so accommodate themselves to Hellenistic culture. Antiochus had even profaned the temple in Jerusalem by setting up an altar within it to the Greek God Zeus. But a group of Jewish resistance fighters led by Judas Maccabeus staged an armed uprising and, against all odds, successfully defeated the imperial power. They reclaimed the temple and rededicated it to the worship of the one God of Israel.[87] Thus, the Festival of Dedication recalled both the renewal of temple worship and the institution of national independence.

But by Jesus' day, the political scene had shifted again. The independent Jewish kingdom established by the Maccabean revolt had not lasted long. In the time of Jesus, Judea was ruled by a Roman governor, Pontius Pilate, and the Jewish people were once again under the thumb of a foreign power. The celebration of *Hanukkah*—the Festival of Dedication— under these circumstances would have been a time when the Jewish people looked back nostalgically to an era of past national glory and, more dangerously, looked forward in hope to Israel's future liberation.

It is on *this* occasion that John describes Jesus walking in the temple—and not just in the temple, but specifically in the Portico of *Solomon*. Solomon, of course, the Son of David, was the king who had most gloriously extended the scope of the ancient Israelite monarchy. And many of the Jewish people were longing for a new "Son of David," a Messiah who would restore the kingdom to Israel.

So as Jesus walks in Solomon's Portico, what words will he speak against this symbolic backdrop? Will he proclaim himself the new Solomon, the new Son of David, the King of Israel? Will he launch a new revolt, like the Maccabean uprising, against the occupying power? That is why the people ask the question they do: "How long will you keep us in suspense? If you are the Messiah, tell us plainly" (John 10:24).

In one sense, Jesus has already answered the crowd's question. Earlier in John 10 he declared, "I am the good shepherd." For the crowd assembled in the Portico of Solomon, the image of the "good shepherd" also carried clear *political* significance, because of a passage they would have known well from the prophecies of Ezekiel 34.[88] The prophet, speaking in the name of God, scolded the leaders of Israel for failing to care properly for God's flock: they were selfish and careless shepherds who had allowed the sheep to be abused and scattered. And then, near the end of the chapter, we find this:

> I will set up over them one shepherd, my servant David, and he shall feed them: he shall feed them and be their shepherd. And I, the LORD, will be their God, and my servant David shall be prince among them; I, the LORD, have spoken.
>
> (Ezek 34:23-24)

It is no wonder, then, that Jesus excited messianic speculation by claiming to be the good shepherd. The "good shepherd" is not simply a consoler who promises to care for the souls of those who believe—as in later sentimental Christian piety. Rather, Jesus is staking symbolic claim to be the new David, the restorer and ruler of Israel. But he has said all this in *figurative* language. And so the crowd presses him for a more explicit declaration of his candidacy for royal office.

But Jesus avoids giving a direct answer. He points simply to the works he has been doing, saying that these testify sufficiently to his identity. John tells us, for example, that Jesus healed a man who had been blind from birth and miraculously fed a hungry crowd. His works are works of *healing* and *feeding*: precisely what the good shepherd of Ezekiel 34 promised to do for the flock. These concrete acts of goodness and mercy should be sufficient proof that he is who he says he is. The passage ends, then, with a word of promise: "No one will snatch them out of my hand." Why? Because, he declares, "I and the Father are one" (John 10:30).

And here Jesus astonishingly claims something that no first-century Jew expected of a messiah: he is one with God. That is why he can make the extravagant promise that no one will be able to snatch the sheep away from him.

How can it be so? The history his people knew was one of failed promises, dashed hopes, ambiguity at best. The Davidic monarchy fell; the Maccabean revolution soured and lost its grip on power. If, as William Butler Yeats prophesied to a much later disillusioned generation, the center cannot hold—if all efforts at creating order collapse into compromise and betrayal, if we continue to walk in the shadow of death—how can Jesus presume to stand in the temple (a temple that was already in ruins by the time John wrote his Gospel) and promise that his sheep will never be snatched away by the blood-dimmed tide of history?

Such an extraordinary promise is valid if and only if Jesus' claim to be one with the Father is also true. The sheep are safe in Jesus' hand only because no one can snatch them out of *God's* hand. Here we must once again recall Ezekiel 34: according to Ezekiel's prophecy, it is not only *David* who will be the shepherd of the sheep but also *God himself*:

> I myself will be shepherd of my sheep, says the Lord GOD. I will seek the lost, and I will bring back the strayed, and I will bind up the injured, and I will strengthen the weak, but the fat and the strong I will destroy. I will feed them with justice.
>
> (Ezek 34:15-16)

So, on that winter day in the temple, Jesus is not talking about politics as usual. He is promising the redemption of the world on the other side of death and resurrection. And in John's narrative world, that promise is valid only because *Jesus is the truth to which the Festival of Dedication points, through a glass darkly*: he is the personal presence of the God of Israel, come at last to rescue his people, to heal and bind up, to feed them with justice.[89]

In light of this sort of figurative hermeneutic, the entirety of the Old Testament becomes figurally available to illumine the identity of Jesus. It is not a matter of locating a few prooftexts that predict events in Jesus' life. Rather, *John sees Israel's Scripture as figurally transparent to the One who became incarnate in Jesus*.

Bread from heaven

Once the realization dawns that the entirety of Israel's Scripture can be transparent to the incarnate Word, we see that it is not just the temple and the festivals that prefigure Jesus; rather, for John, it is the whole narrative of God's gracious dealing with Israel. Consider, for example, the story of the manna in the wilderness of Exodus 16: John insists that it prefigures Jesus, who is the true "bread from heaven" (John 6:31-33).

After Jesus' miraculous feeding of the five thousand in John 6:1-14, John tells an amusing story of the crowd pursuing Jesus around the sea of Tiberias. When they track him down in Capernaum, he rebukes them for seeking the wrong thing:

> "Very truly, I tell you, you are looking for me, not because you saw the signs, but because you ate your fill of the loaves. Do not work for the food that perishes, but for the food that endures for eternal life, which the Son of Man will give you."
>
> (John 6:26-27)

His challenge to the crowd is reminiscent of the urgent call of the prophet Isaiah, who cries out to Israel:

> Ho, everyone who thirsts, come to the waters [cf. John 7:37-38];
> And you that have no money, come, buy and eat!
> Come, buy wine and milk without money and without price.
> Why do you spend your money for that which is not bread,
> And your labor for that which does not satisfy?
> Listen carefully to me, and eat what is good, and delight your-
>   selves in rich food.
> Incline your ear, and come to me; listen, so that you may live.
>
> (Isa 55:1-3a)

There is no direct verbal echo of Isaiah 55 in Jesus' words, but the substantive parallels are intriguing: Like Isaiah, Jesus is counseling his hearers not to waste their labor on insubstantial and unsatisfying desires but to seek after nourishment that is truly life-giving.[90] Jesus is offering something better than perishable fish and barley loaves.

But the crowd fails to understand. They ask, "What sign are you going to give us then, so that we may see it and believe you? . . . Our ancestors ate the manna in the wilderness; as it is written, 'He gave them bread from heaven to eat'" (John 6:30-31). *What sign are you going to give us?* Their question is strange, for just on the previous day Jesus had provided them with food no less remarkable than the manna in the wilderness. What further sign could they possibly need? Their odd question is a symptom of deeper failure to understand what they have already witnessed. They are expecting Jesus to fit the job description of the new prophet like Moses; consequently, their preconceived categories prevent them from seeing what is right before their eyes.

And so Jesus sets them straight. And here we come to the heart of the matter: *Jesus is teaching his hearers how to read Scripture.* The crowd has the right text—they have linked Jesus' feeding of the multitude with Exodus 16, the story of the manna in the wilderness; and the text that they actually cite is Psalm 78:24, which retells and reflects on that story. They have the right text but the wrong reading. They seem to think the story is about Moses as a charismatic wonder-worker. And so Jesus must explain: "Very truly, I tell you, it was not *Moses* who gave you the bread from heaven, but it is *my Father* who gives you the true bread from heaven" (John 6:32). Jesus is simply teaching them basic exegesis: when the text says "he gave them bread from heaven to eat," the subject of the sentence is *God*, not Moses.[91]

But Jesus' instruction in how to read goes beyond this simple corrective. Not only does he insist that it is God the Father who is the true giver, but he also changes the tense of the verb from past to present and suggests that the manna must be interpreted as a *prefiguration* of another, truer bread still to come: "It is my Father who *gives* you the *true bread from heaven.*" Here is the paradigm shift: the manna story is not just about a past event in salvation history; rather, it points forward *figurally* to a different kind of bread altogether. Even though the manna was divinely given, it was still "the food that perishes" (another exegetical allusion: cf. Exod 16:19-21), and those who ate it still died (John 6:49). John is once again teaching his readers how to reread Israel's Scripture; by reading backwards, Jesus reinterprets the manna story as prefiguring *himself.*

The fact that the noun ἄρτος is masculine allows John to craft the artful ambiguity of Jesus' words in John 6:33: the participial phrase ὁ καταβαίνων ἐκ τοῦ οὐρανοῦ can be read either as attributive (thus: "the bread of God is that which comes down from heaven") or as substantive ("the bread of God is the One who comes down from heaven"). We will surely be faithful readers of John's figural hermeneutic if we hear distinct overtones of the latter interpretation. That is the hidden meaning of Jesus' cryptic statement, "For the bread of God is the One that comes down from heaven and gives life to the world" (John 6:33; cf. 1:4, 10:10).

In response to Jesus' declaration, the crowd finally gets beyond the wrong questions and makes the right request: "Sir, give us this bread always." They are like the Samaritan woman a little earlier in the story who asked Jesus, "Sir, give me this water, so that I may never be thirsty" (John 4:15). And Jesus, no longer speaking cryptically, gives them a dramatic answer similar to the answer he gave the woman: "*I am* (ἐγώ εἰμι)—I am the bread of life. Whoever comes to me will never be hungry, and whoever believes in me will never be thirsty" (6:34-35).

So, *by giving himself bodily, Jesus gives life to the world.* Jesus himself is the true bread from heaven, the bread toward which Israel's desire—indeed, the desire of all humanity—should be directed; he is the true meaning of the manna story. Jesus, the one who came down from heaven, is the giver of life, and only when we come to him will we be given the life that endures and overcomes death. According to John's Gospel, that is the true meaning of what Moses wrote.

It would be possible to carry out similar analyses of the subsequent "I am" discourses in John's Gospel, showing how Jesus draws images from Israel's Scripture and declares himself to be the true embodiment of the figurally encoded sense of these images. For example, as John's narrative unfolds, Jesus declares himself to be the Light of the World (8:12, 9:5), the Good Shepherd (10:11, 14), and the true Vine (15:1, 5). Each of these self-designations evokes deep resonances from Scripture, but in distinction from the bread discourse, the Evangelist does not actually specify for the reader the biblical subtexts. Presumably, having explained the necessity and manner of christological figural reading in 2:17-22 (Jesus as the temple) and 6:25-40 (Jesus as the bread that comes down from heaven), he leaves it to his readers to work out the analogous connections in the subsequent ἐγώ εἰμι speeches.[92] Thus the images of light, shepherd, and vine function literarily not as direct allusions but as echoes that beckon the reader to recover their scriptural sources.

Other christological designations

King. In addition to the concrete christological images that John draws out of Israel's Scripture, the Evangelist also employs a number of titular designations for Jesus in his narrative. Prominent among these are King, Messiah, Son of God, and Son of Man. These titles are inextricably interwoven in John's story. Though all of them have roots in the Old Testament, John is surprisingly reserved about tracing them to specific scriptural subtexts. Israel's expectation of a coming messianic figure moves in the depths throughout the narrative, but for the most part it remains submerged at the level of the text's implicit cultural encyclopedia, rather than constituting its explicit argument.

The term βασιλεύς (king) appears at only four places in John's story. The initial instance of the word occurs in Nathanael's abrupt exclamation, "Rabbi, you are the Son of God! You are the King of Israel!" (John 1:49). The synonymous parallelism of these two titles demonstrates that "Son of God" should be heard as a royal honorific designation, as in Psalm 2:7 and 2 Samuel 7:12-14. But there is typical Johannine narrative irony at work in Nathanael's enthusiastic outburst: although what he says is true, he does not fully understand the import of his own utterance. The reader, however, does understand—or will come to understand as the story unfolds—that in the Fourth Gospel "Son of God" is more than an exalted way of acclaiming Israel's expected Davidic king: it carries larger metaphysical implications about Jesus' identity.

The term "king" appears a second time in John's account of Jesus' response to the enthusiastic crowd after his feeding of the five thousand: "When Jesus realized that they were about to come and take him by force to make him king, he withdrew again to the mountain by himself" (John 6:15). Here Jesus' evasive action is not a rejection of the title "king" but an escape from the crowd's ill-timed attempt to force his hand and crown him as their ruler on the basis of a deficient comprehension of his identity and mission;[93] their lack of understanding is clearly portrayed in the dialogical exchange that follows, set in the synagogue in Capernaum (6:25-59).

The third appearance of the term "king" is in the story of Jesus' triumphal entry into Jerusalem (John 12:12-16). In this passage, John, like Matthew in his parallel account (Matt 21:1-9), quotes both Psalm 118:26 and Zechariah 9:9 as scriptural prefigurations of Jesus' symbol-laden entry into the city. In the case of the Psalm citation, however, John adds to the quotation his own interpretative gloss; the crowd chants:

> Blessed is the one who comes in the name of the Lord—
> *Even the King of Israel.*

(John 12:13)

John's specification that the one who comes in the name of the Lord is the *King* parallels Luke's similar explanatory gloss in Luke 19:38, and the full phrase "King of Israel," unparalleled in the synoptic accounts, echoes Nathanael's prophetic outburst in the opening chapter of John's story (John 1:49). The Evangelist then adds the citation of Zechariah 9:9 to indicate that Jesus' action was the fulfillment of Scripture, confirming his identity as the messianic King: "Look, your king is coming, sitting on a donkey's colt" (John 12:15). Characteristically, John appends a hermeneutical clarification, explaining that the disciples' recognition of this figural correspondence with Old Testament texts was a *retrospective* one:

> His disciples did not understand these things at first; but when Jesus was glorified, then they remembered that these things had been written of him and had been done to him.
>
> (John 12:16)

Once again, John is teaching his readers to read backwards.

Strikingly, *John 12:12-16 is the only passage in John's Gospel that explicitly links Jesus' titles as "King" and "Messiah" to specific scriptural subtexts.* In this key text John assures the reader that the ascription of kingship to Jesus is correct, but he also signals that the *character* of this kingship can be understood only by reading backwards to redefine the meaning of "king" in light of the Gospel's revelatory narrative about Jesus.

The ambiguity surrounding the term "king" comes to a thematic climax in a final narrative unit where John employs the word repeatedly: the story of Jesus' interrogation before Pilate (John 18:33-40) and his subsequent torture and crucifixion (19:1-22). Here the Evangelist plays artfully on the various significations of the term as understood or misunderstood by the Roman governor, by the chief priests bringing accusation against Jesus, and by Jesus himself. The key to the dramatic irony of the passage lies in Jesus' rejoinder to Pilate: "My kingdom is not from this world. If my kingdom were from this world, my followers would be fighting to keep me from being handed over to the Jews. But as it is, my kingdom is not from here" (18:36). Jesus implicitly accepts the title of "king" but insists that his kingship is grounded in otherworldly authority and that he exercises kingly power not through military might but through his testimony to the truth (18:37).[94]

Subsequently, in a characteristically Johannine dramatic flourish, the irony of the charge against Jesus is highlighted by the Evangelist's extended account of Pilate's multilingual inscription on the cross and the chief priests' futile objection to it (John 19:19-22). Their complaint reinforces the bitter irony of their fawning declaration to Pilate: "We have no king but Caesar" (19:15).

For the purposes of our present inquiry, however, the salient insight is this: *nowhere in John's fully developed drama of the trial and crucifixion does he make any gesture to explicate his christological redefinition of kingship in light of scriptural warrants.* The redefinition is performed strictly by the authority of Jesus' own words and actions.

John does, however, create an allusive connection between the event of Jesus' crucifixion and his kingship by including within his passion narrative two explicitly marked fulfillment references to royal lament psalms. The first is a direct quotation of Psalm 22:18:

> They divided my clothes among themselves,
> and for my clothing they cast lots [cited in John 19:24].

The second reference is a looser allusion to Psalm 69:21:

> They gave me poison for food,
> And for my thirst they gave me vinegar to drink [cf. John 19:28-29].

Both of these psalms are described in their superscriptions as psalms of David,[95] and both are evoked elsewhere in the New Testament—including prominently, as we have seen, in John 2:17—as prefigurations of Jesus' manner of death.[96] There is an implicit suggestion here that Jesus paradoxically fulfills the role of Davidic kingship precisely through his conformity to the extreme suffering portrayed in these Davidic lament psalms.[97]

Another less often noted Johannine example of Jesus' figural correspondence to the suffering David figure is found in the deliberative meditation ascribed to Jesus near the end of his public activity:

> "*Now my soul is troubled.* And what should I say—'Father, *save me* from this hour'? No, it is for this reason that I have come to this hour."
>
> (John 12:27)

The italicized words in this citation agree closely with Psalm 6:3-4 LXX (6:4-5 ET), as displayed in the words underlined here in the Greek text:

> καὶ ἡ ψυχή μου ἐταράχθη σφόδρα
> καὶ σύ κύριε ἕως πότε
> ἐπίστρεψον κύριε ῥῦσαι τὴν ψυχήν μου
> σῶσόν με ἕνεκεν τοῦ ἐλέους σου
>
> (Ps 6:3-4 LXX)

Νῦν ἡ ψυχή μου τετάρακται, καὶ τί εἴπω;
πάτερ, σῶσόν με ἐκ τῆς ὥρας ταύτης;
ἀλλὰ διὰ τοῦτο ἦλθον εἰς τὴν ὥραν ταύτην.

(John 12:27)[98]

This is an excellent example of an echo that does not rise to the level of overt allusion. But in conjunction with John's allusions in the passion narrative to other Davidic lament psalms, this echo of Psalm 6 reinforces Jesus' inhabiting and reshaping of the role of Davidic king. Jesus echoes David in lamenting that his soul is troubled in a time of trial (Ps 6:3 LXX), but then ponders whether to continue to perform the Davidic script by joining in David's prayer for rescue ("Save me" [Ps 6:4 LXX]). In fact, John's Jesus rejects this option; he chooses instead to embrace the vocation of suffering for which he was sent into the world.[99]

Jesus' figural correspondence to—and fulfillment of—the role of the messianic Davidic king is signaled also by his self-designation as "the Good Shepherd" (John 10:11-18, 27). This image evokes reminiscences not only of Ezekiel 34 but also of Jeremiah 23:1-6, a prominent prophecy of a future faithful shepherd for the people. This passage cries out to be read as an oracle portending a coming king/messiah:

> Then I myself will gather the remnant of my flock out of all the lands where I have driven them, and I will bring them back to their fold, and they shall be fruitful and multiply. I will raise up shepherds over them who will shepherd them, and they shall not fear any longer, or be dismayed, nor shall any be missing,[100] says the LORD. The days are surely coming, says the LORD, when I will raise up for David a righteous Branch, and he shall reign as king and deal wisely, and shall execute justice and righteousness in the land. In his days Judah will be saved and Israel will live in safety. And this is the name by which he will be called: "The LORD is our righteousness."
>
> (Jer 23:3-6)

Once again, however, for John the Evangelist these echoes remain in the background of the story he is telling; nowhere does he quote Ezekiel 34 or Jeremiah 23. The royal messianic meaning of the Good Shepherd image belongs to the hermeneutical potential of the text of John 10, waiting to be activated by those with ears to hear.

Messiah/Christ. John is the only author in the New Testament who uses the Greek word Μεσσίας (Messiah), a "Hellenized transliteration" of the Hebrew מָשִׁיחַ.[101] The term appears just twice in John's Gospel (1:41, 4:25), and both times the Evangelist immediately explains that the term is equivalent to the Greek χριστός (anointed). In the second of these instances, the Samaritan woman, who had initially spoken of the coming Μεσσίας, immediately upon returning to her city, shifts to using the synonymous term ὁ χριστός (4:29). Thereafter, John consistently uses the latter term in his narrative.

It is, however, striking how relatively infrequent are John's usages of these terms. The majority of the instances of "Messiah" and "Christ" are found in the mouths of characters or crowds speculating or wondering about Jesus' identity. One exception is Andrew; having heard John the Baptist's testimony to Jesus (John 1:29-36), he confidently proclaims to his brother Simon, "We have found the Messiah" (1:41). But most of the other instances of this term in John appear not in affirmations or confessions of faith but in various other modes of discourse—invariably using "Messiah" or "Christ" as a title rather than as a proper name:

- *negations*: John the Baptist saying, "I am not the Christ" (John 1:20, 3:28; cf. 1:25);
- *interrogative sentences*: "He cannot be the Christ, can he?" (John 4:29); "When the Christ comes will he do more signs than this man has done?" (John 7:31; cf. 7:26, 27, 40-42);
- *deliberations about messianic expectation*: "We have heard from the law that the Christ remains forever" (John 12:34; cf. 7:40-42);
- *demand for clarification*: "If you are the Christ, tell us plainly" (John 10:24);
- *prohibition of confession*: "The Jews had already agreed that anyone who confessed Jesus to be the Christ would be put out of the synagogue" (John 9:22).

In the entirety of John's Gospel, there are only four unambiguous positive identifications of Jesus as ὁ χριστός. Though the number of these references is small, they are weighty because of their prominent placement within the Gospel's narrative. The first comes at the end of the Gospel's prologue: "The law was given through Moses; grace and truth came through Jesus Christ" (John 1:17). Here it would appear that χριστός is being used either as part of Jesus' proper name or, more likely, as an honorific epithet, similar to the use of ascriptive terms such as Epiphanes or Augustus for other celebrated ancient figures.[102] If so, the best rendering into English would be "grace and truth came through Jesus

Messiah."[103] The same honorific use of χριστός occurs in a curious line in Jesus' "high priestly prayer": "And this is eternal life, that they may know you, the only true God, and Jesus Christ whom you have sent" (17:3). The oddity here is that John's text seems to portray Jesus referring awkwardly to himself in the third person as "Jesus Christ." This anomaly is probably to be explained as an instance in which the line between Jesus' voice and the voice of the narrator becomes blurred, so that the character of Jesus speaks, as it were, from the Evangelist's viewpoint.

The two most determinative occurrences of John's use of χριστός appear at a dramatic climax near the Gospel's midpoint, and in the Evangelist's summary statement about his compositional purpose near the end of the story. In the first of these, Martha of Bethany, imploring Jesus to act to restore the life of her brother Lazarus, speaks out a bold confession: "Yes, Lord, I believe that you are *the Messiah, the Son of God*, the one coming into the world" (ὁ χριστὸς ὁ υἱὸς τοῦ θεοῦ ὁ εἰς τὸν κόσμον ἐρχόμενος, John 11:27).[104] This is exactly the confession that the Evangelist hopes to elicit from his readers: the things in his Gospel have been written "that you may believe that Jesus is the Christ, the Son of God (ὁ χριστὸς ὁ υἱὸς τοῦ θεοῦ); and that believing you may have life in His name" (20:31).

Surveying these passages, we arrive at two important observations. First, nowhere does John attempt to formulate a *scriptural* argument to prove that Jesus is the Christ. John simply proclaims Jesus' messianic identity and promises that those who know and confess him as the Christ will find life. The Evangelist does not, however, set about digging up Old Testament prooftexts to justify his application of this title to Jesus. The terms "Messiah" and "Christ" belong to the broader biblical framework within which John's story unfolds. Second, the climactic confessional formulations of John 11:27 and 20:31 link ὁ χριστὸς directly to ὁ υἱὸς τοῦ θεοῦ. Jesus is both "Christ" and "Son of God," and the two terms appear to be virtually synonymous.

Son of God. This equivalence should come as no surprise, for within Israel's Scripture the royal figure who rules Israel—either in actuality (Ps 2:7) or in future hope (2 Sam 7:12-14; Ps 89:19-37, esp. Ps 89:26) is occasionally given an honorific designation as God's son. This is almost certainly the sense in which Nathanael's acclamation of Jesus as "Son of God" should be understood: "Rabbi, you are the Son of God! [I.e.,] You are the King of Israel!" (John 1:49). In the Fourth Gospel, however, these biblical texts are not cited as warrants for the Evangelist's references to Jesus as Son of God. As with the titles Messiah and Christ, Jesus' identity as "the only[-begotten] Son of God" (3:18; cf. 1:18) is simply posited as a truth that must be acknowledged.[105]

In John's Gospel, the meaning of "Son of God" is greatly expanded to encompass a claim about Jesus' heavenly origin and divine identity (John 3:18, 31-36). This is the basis for his assertion of extraordinary authority: the divine Son of God possesses authority even over the power of death—certainly an authority vastly beyond that of Israel's ordinary human monarchs. It is no accident that when Jesus asserts that he has the power to call the dead out of the tombs (5:25, foreshadowing 11:4) he employs the title "Son of God" for himself; likewise, the dramatic buildup to the story of his raising of Lazarus contains two of John's explicit uses of this title: Jesus' self-designation as the Son of God who will be glorified through Lazarus' death and restoration to life (11:4), and Martha's confession that Jesus can bring her brother back to life because he is "the Messiah, the Son of God" (11:27).

Claims of this kind about Jesus are the basis for the charge pressed by the chief priests[106] that Jesus ought to die for claiming to be the Son of God (John 19:7). If he had merely been claiming to be the new king of Israel, the authorities might regard the claim as ridiculous and politically dangerous (cf. 11:47-48), but there would be no legitimate grounds for seeking capital punishment. They seek Jesus' death because they correctly understand that he actually is claiming divine identity, a claim they regard as self-evidently blasphemous.

Indeed, the one place in John's Gospel where the charge of blasphemy is explicitly leveled at Jesus is John 10:31-39, which is also the *only* passage in this Gospel that adduces a specific Old Testament text to justify or defend the assertion that Jesus can be called God's Son. But the argument offered there will surely strike most readers as bizarre or at best unpersuasive. In response to the accusation of the *Ioudaioi* that "you, though only a human being, are making yourself God," Jesus offers this curious defense:

> "Is it not written in your law, 'I said, you are gods'? If those to whom the word of God came were called 'gods'—and the scripture cannot be annulled—can you say that the one whom the Father has sanctified and sent into the world is blaspheming because I said, 'I am God's Son'?"

> (John 10:34-36; citing Ps 82:6)

The argument is peculiar because the "gods" to which Psalm 82 refers are not, at least on the surface sense of the text, human beings; they are the deities of other ancient Near Eastern nations, as indicated in the psalm's opening verse:

> God has taken his place in the divine council;
> in the midst of the gods he holds judgment.
>
> (Ps 82:1)

God decries their injustice and neglect of the weak and needy, and then, in the passage cited by Jesus, declares that although they are "gods," they will in fact be stripped of their power and "die like mortals" (Ps 82:6-7). The psalm could perhaps be interpreted as a prophetic denunciation of the *rulers* of other nations who may claim divine status or right, but who will in fact be judged by Israel's God and suffer the same fate as all other human beings. But in no event can it reasonably be understood to justify the claim that all human beings—or all Israelites—are in fact "gods." And even if the psalm did mean that, it would not justify Jesus' claim to be the Son of God in the particular unique sense that he claims in John's Gospel.

The only way in which Jesus' argument can be understood as intelligible is to regard it not as a proof of his actual divine identity but as a rather playful gambit that works as an argument *a minori ad maius*. The sense of it would be something like this: "If even these pretentious pagan rulers or phony mythological beings can be addressed by God's (unimpeachably authoritative) word as 'gods,' how much more can I (who really am divine) legitimately call myself God's Son?"[107] It is a rhetorically clever move, but it proves nothing and would actually be persuasive only to a hearer who already accepts the premise that Jesus is in fact who he claims to be. Indeed, as the story continues, we see that his interlocutors are unimpressed, and at the end of this unit they try unsuccessfully to arrest him (John 10:39).

Thus, once again, as with the ascriptions we have examined previously, we see that while the title Son of God has roots in Israel's scriptural traditions, these roots remain entirely subterranean in John's narrative. The term is closely linked with royal acclamations of Israel's king, as well as Israel's hopes for a coming future Messiah. The way in which John uses this language, however, depends not on the evocation of biblical echoes but rather on the naked proclamation of truths that are presented as self-attesting. The whole story is framed by John the Baptist's testimony—

"I myself have seen and have testified that this is the Son of God" (John 1:34)—and by the Evangelist's urgent explanation that he has written his Gospel to elicit from others similar acts of testimony, "so that you may come to believe that Jesus is the Messiah, the Son of God" (20:31). This last summary statement is almost surely meant to express the mystery of Jesus' simultaneous human and divine identity. That same mystery is also encapsulated in the Evangelist's use of the title "Son of Man."

Son of Man. The Fourth Evangelist's distinctive use of the "Son of Man" title (ὁ υἱὸς τοῦ ἀνθρώπου) evokes Old Testament echoes in the service of John's complex and ironic Christology.[108] As we have seen in our reading of the Synoptic Gospels, the expression "Son of Man" alludes to Daniel's vision of an eschatological figure who ascends with the clouds to be enthroned alongside God and to have everlasting dominion over "all peoples, nations, and languages" (Dan 7:13-14). In its original context in Daniel 7, the Son of Man figure symbolizes Israel in its final vindication and triumph over oppressive foreign powers. In the synoptics, Jesus employs the title as an oblique form of self-reference, signifying both his representation of the suffering people Israel and his ultimate vindication and exaltation to a position of cosmic authority, a position from which he will judge the nations.[109]

John presupposes this apocalyptic Son of Man tradition.[110] He applies the title "Son of Man" to Jesus without explanation or argument, and without ever explicitly citing the key source passage in Daniel. Once again, as with his use of royal and messianic titles, he is taking this tradition as already familiar to his readers. But he is also transforming it in several ways.

First of all, while John highlights the imagery of *ascent* in the Danielic Son of Man tradition, he injects the additional complementary imagery of *descent* as an aspect of the Son of Man's action.[111] Both these elements are displayed in Jesus' cryptic dialogue with Nicodemus:

> "If I have told you about earthly things and you do not believe, how can you believe if I tell you about heavenly things? No one has *ascended* into heaven except the one who *descended* from heaven, the Son of Man."
>
> (John 3:12-13)

The bidirectional imagery of the Son of Man's descent from heaven followed by his ascent, which corresponds to John's particular incarnational Christology, is perhaps enabled by the potential ambiguity of the language in Daniel's account of his vision: he reports that "one like a son of man was *coming* (ἤρχετο) with the clouds of heaven" (Dan 7:13 LXX). Does this mean the symbolic figure was coming from heaven to earth or vice versa? Out of context, it could mean either, though the fuller context of the vision makes it clear that the "one like a son of man" was ascending to the heavenly throne room. Nonetheless, John's portrayal of the movement of the Son of Man in both directions exploits the semantic ambiguity of Daniel's word choice.

John employs this figurative scenario to introduce an element not present in Daniel's account: a suggestion that the Son of Man, having first descended to earth, is enabled to be a *revealer* of "heavenly things." Precisely in this role, he can become a bridge or link between the heavenly world and the earthly human world. This is probably the meaning of Jesus' strange promise to Nathanael: "Very truly I tell you, you will see heaven opened and the angels of God *ascending and descending* upon *the Son of Man*" (John 1:51). In this mysterious utterance, the Son of Man is not himself the figure who moves between the two realms; rather, the angels are the heavenly messengers, while Jesus is the intermediary figure who makes the connection possible.

A little later in the story, when Jesus encounters the "murmuring" of the crowd[112] who are offended by his claim to be the true bread that has *come down* from heaven (John 6:33, 41-42, 51, 58), he offers a challenging rejoinder not unlike his earlier rebuke of Nicodemus: "Does this offend you? Then what if you were to see *the Son of Man ascending to where he was before?*" (6:61b-62). Here again we encounter the descent/ascent pattern, this time emphasizing that Jesus has come down to earth to offer himself—even his own flesh (6:27, 51-58)—and hinting that he will offend his hearers even more by his subsequent exaltation and return to his heavenly origin.

John's emphasis on *ascent* carries with it two elements that are consonant with the Danielic and synoptic interpretation of the Son of Man figure. John's Jesus declares that precisely as Son of Man he has received "authority to execute judgment" (John 5:27). But John's Son of Man is also to be *glorified* (12:23, 13:31), as in Daniel 7:14, where the exalted "one like a son of man" is given "dominion and *glory* and kingship." But there is a characteristic Johannine wrinkle in these texts: Jesus speaks as one who has *already* received authority and whose hour of glorification does not await an end-time apocalyptic scenario.

The Evangelist effects this temporal transformation through an artful fusion of Daniel's Son of Man image with two other scriptural echoes, this time from the book of Numbers and from the prophecies of Isaiah. And through these echoes, the Evangelist creates a paradoxical twist: he announces that the "hour" of Jesus' glorification is precisely the hour of his crucifixion. The hermeneutical key to this remarkable move is found in Jesus' words to Nicodemus, immediately after his first full-blown articulation of the descent/ascent pattern:

> "No one has ascended into heaven except the one who descended from heaven, *the Son of Man*. And just as Moses *lifted up* (ὕψωσεν) the serpent in the wilderness, *so must the Son of Man be lifted up* (ὑψωθῆναι), that whoever believes in him may have eternal life."
>
> (John 3:13-15)

In this utterance, Jesus links the "lifting up" of the Son of Man with the strange story of Moses' setting up a bronze serpent in the wilderness to ward off the deadly effects of punitive bites from poisonous snakes (Num 21:4-9). This figural linkage carries two enormously significant theological implications: *it portrays the Son of Man figure as one whose "lifting up" effects atonement from sin*, just as the bronze serpent protected the Israelites from the punishment for their rebellion and complaining against God; and *it transmutes the image of "lifting up" from a picture of the Son of Man's exaltation in the clouds to the gruesome visual image of Jesus impaled on the cross.*

Suddenly, the Son of Man is no longer—or better, not only—a glorious figure enthroned in heavenly splendor and pronouncing judgment on the world; instead, his "exaltation" consists of being nailed to a wooden crossbeam and raised up high as an example of what happens to those who defy the religious and political authorities. Yet John insistently portrays precisely this fate of crucifixion as the moment of Jesus' glorification. How does John produce this symbolic transformation?

One clue lies in John's paradoxical use of the verb "lifted up." A careful reading of the story in Numbers 21 will show that this verb does not appear in the Pentateuchal account. Moses is told by God to "set" the image of a serpent on a pole, and the text says that he "put it upon a pole" (Num 21:9 MT: ויעש משה נחש נחשת וישמהו על הנס; LXX: καὶ ἐποίησεν Μωυσῆς ὄφιν χαλκοῦν καὶ ἔστησεν αὐτὸν ἐπὶ σημείου).[113] Why, then, does John emphasize that Jesus had to be, like the serpent, "lifted up"? The answer lies in hearing another scriptural echo, this time from Isaiah's depiction of the Suffering Servant of the Lord (Isa 52:13–53:12). The account begins with an apparent description of the Servant's exaltation:

the Servant "shall be exalted and lifted up [LXX: ὑψωθήσεται καὶ δοξασθήσεται—"lifted up and glorified"], and shall be very high" (52:13). But Isaiah's prophecy quickly morphs into a portrayal of the Servant as one who undergoes rejection and terrible physical suffering in order to bear the transgressions and iniquities of many. Although the Evangelist does not quote this prophecy in connection with the Son of Man being lifted up like the bronze serpent, he does explicitly cite Isaiah 53:1 later on in the story as a testimony that Isaiah "saw his glory and spoke about him" (John 12:37-41). It therefore seems overwhelmingly likely that John's single word ὑψωθῆναι ("lifted up") echoes and evokes Isaiah's culminating Servant song and that John is hinting that the "glory" Isaiah saw was a vision of the crucified Jesus (Isa 52:13–53:12).[114]

The effect of this complex intertextual overlay is to interpret the story of Jesus' crucifixion as an event that is *simultaneously* a glorious exaltation to power (Dan 7) and a painful vicarious suffering for the sin of others (Num 21:4-9 + Isa 52:13–53:12). The three images of Son of Man, bronze serpent, and Suffering Servant are projected on top of one another and all together interpreted as *prefigurations* of the Gospel story of Jesus' death and resurrection. And in turn, the significance of Jesus' death is reinterpreted by the Evangelist in light of these complex interwoven scriptural images, so that his death is simultaneously a humiliating abasement and a triumph over the world.

This reading is confirmed later on in John's narrative by Jesus' final public interaction with the unbelieving crowd in Jerusalem:

> "Now is the judgment of this world; now the ruler of this world will be driven out. And I, when I am *lifted up* from the earth, will draw all people to myself." *He said this to indicate the kind of death he was to die.*
>
> (John 12:31-33; cf. 8:28)

It would appear that John has performed an astonishing intertextual fusion of Daniel 7:13-14, Numbers 21, and Isaiah 52:13. The intertextual fusion occurs entirely in the hidden realms of allusion and echo, without any explicit quotations of these three Old Testament textual precursors. Yet the theological result of this fusion is explosive: it generates an interpretation of Jesus' death on a cross as the triumphant exaltation of the Son of Man.

§19 THE VINE AND THE BRANCHES
The Church's Oneness in John's Narrative

How does John use Scripture to position the church in relation to the world? When we scan John's Gospel for citations of Israel's Scripture to address this problem, we find that he in fact *never* explicitly cites any biblical text to explicate how Jesus' disciples are to understand their posture in relation to the wider political or cultural world of the Roman Empire in the first century. This fact is surprising, given John's repeated references to "the world" (ὁ κόσμος) as the theater of the incarnation of the Word—mostly as a site of unbelief and hostility to Jesus and his followers. One might expect John to offer some scripturally grounded explanation for the mission of the disciples to the world or for the world's resistance to that mission. But no such explanation is forthcoming from the Evangelist. Or rather, he offers no explanation in the form of direct quotation of Scripture.

John does offer, however, a few tantalizing *echoes* of Scripture that point the church's imagination toward a biblically formed grasp of its place in the wider world. Characteristically for John, these echoes depend less upon sustained repetition of the wording of precursor texts than upon the evocation of *images* from Israel's Scripture. John's imagination, as we have noted, is more visual than verbal; the echoes he creates are, so to speak, visual echoes. They are nonetheless real for that, and in fact perhaps all the more vivid. With regard to envisioning the church's relation to the world, John offers two key evocative images: the vine with its branches, and "other sheep not of this fold." Let us consider each of these in turn.

The vine and the branches

In Jesus' farewell discourse to the disciples, he introduces the image of the vine and the branches (John 15:1-8). This metaphor differs from most of John's other christological images because it explicitly includes Jesus' disciples, who are pictured as the branches (τὰ κλήματα, John 15:5) that must abide in the Vine in order to thrive and bear fruit. This figure summons up echoes from a number of Old Testament texts, chiefly from prophetic oracles, that portray Israel as a vine (ἄμπελος) planted by the Lord (Isa 27:2-6; Jer 2:21; Ezek 15:2, 17:6-10, 19:10-14; Hos 10:1).[115] All of these texts except Isaiah 27:2-6 are judgment oracles, portraying the vine as unfaithful and unfruitful and announcing its imminent destruction.

Particularly in the Ezekiel passages, there is a strong pronouncement that Israel has become a fruitless vine that will wither and be burned up (Ezek 17:9, 19:12-14)—an element of the symbolism that is directly evoked by Jesus' warning: "Whoever does not abide in me is thrown away like a branch and withers; such branches are gathered, thrown into the fire, and burned" (John 15:6; cf. the similar admonition in Isa 27:4-5).

Another pertinent precursor text for John 15, however, is Psalm 80, which takes the vine imagery in a different direction. This poignant prayer is not a judgment oracle but an urgent plea for God, who had planted and cared for the vine, to look down and restore the vine that has now been ravaged by enemies; indeed, it has been cut down and burned with fire (Ps 80:16; cf. John 15:6). Like the prophetic judgment oracles, the psalmist's imagery portrays the "vine" Israel as having fallen on hard times, but here there is a plea for God to restore the nation by raising up and strengthening a "son of man" (Ps 80:18 MT: בֶּן־אָדָם; Ps 79:18 LXX: υἱὸν ἀνθρώπου) who is at God's right hand(!), so that "we will never turn back from you; give us life, and we will call on your name" (Ps 80:17-18). In its original context, this is surely an outcry petitioning God to restore and strengthen Israel's king.[116]

The Evangelist John, however, transforms the image of the vine into a christological symbol. Just as Jesus embodies the true meaning of Israel's temple and its religious festivals, so also he now becomes "the true Vine" (John 15:1), the figural fulfillment of the nation's identity and its hopes. Not incidentally, Jesus also embodies the hope for a king or "son of man" to save the nation, as in Psalm 80:17-18.[117] As with the other Johannine christological symbols we have examined, here also Jesus does not negate or reject Israel's sacred tradition; rather, he reveals the figural meaning latent in the tradition.

The fresh twist in John 15, however, is that within the passage, the focus of attention shifts from Jesus as the true Vine to the role of the *disciples*. Their very life depends on remaining in union with the Vine, and they are promised that those who do abide in union with Jesus will "bear much fruit" (John 15:5). Indeed, Jesus' promise also becomes a description of the vocation to which the disciples are summoned: "You did not choose me but I chose you. And I appointed you to go and bear fruit, fruit that will last, so that the Father will give you whatever you ask him in my name" (15:16). The charge to *go* and bear fruit (ἵνα ὑμεῖς ὑπάγητε καὶ καρπὸν φέρητε) is the language of *mission*; it suggests that this is a commission for the disciples to go out into the world and testify to the words that Jesus brought to them (15:7).[118]

To be sent into the world, however, is to be called to a daunting task. As the discourse continues, Jesus warns his followers—who are now no longer his servants but his friends who are the recipients of all that Jesus has heard from the Father (John 15:15)—that they are destined to encounter the world's hatred and rejection:

> "If the world hates you, be aware that it hated me before it hated you. If you belonged to the world, the world would love you as its own. Because you do not belong to the world, but I have chosen you out of the world— therefore the world hates you. Remember the word that I said to you, 'Servants are not greater than their master.' If they persecuted me, they will persecute you; if they kept my word, they will keep yours also. But they will do all these things to you on account of my name, because they do not know him who sent me."
>
> (John 15:18)

And at this point, we at last encounter a biblical text that indirectly explains, or at least prefigures, the opposition that the disciples can expect to experience. Why has the world hated both Jesus and the Father? Jesus says, "It was to fulfill the word written in their law, 'They hated me without a cause'" (John 15:25). The citation, using the word "law" as a comprehensive descriptor for all of Israel's Scripture,[119] cor- responds loosely to two passages in the Psalms. The most important of these is Psalm 69:4 (68:5 LXX):

> More in number than the hairs of my head
> are those who hate me without cause (LXX: οἱ μισοῦντές με δωρεάν);
> many are those who would destroy me,
> my enemies who accuse me falsely.

There is a similar turn of phrase in Psalm 35:19, but the connection to Psalm 69 is particularly significant, because John has already alerted his readers to interpret this psalm as a prefiguration of Jesus' passion and death (John 2:17-22). The psalm's unremitting account of rejection and suffering, then, points forward to Jesus, as he himself reaffirms in 15:25, but the same text applies by a process of figural transitivity to Jesus' dis- ciples as well. Because they are in organic union with him, as branches are in union with the vine, the world's irrational and vicious response to Jesus and the Father spills over onto them as well—and, we may sup- pose, to the church that later reads this Gospel.

Nevertheless, despite this foreboding picture of the world's hatred, the disciples are sent forth into the world. Their mission was already implied in the charge to "go and bear fruit" (John 15:16), but the reader learns unambiguously of the disciples' difficult calling in the context of Jesus' climactic prayer in John 17, in which he both summarizes his own work as one sent forth from the Father and prays for his disciples as they confront the task he has conferred upon them:

> "I have given them your word, and *the world has hated them because they do not belong to the world, just as I do not belong to the world*. I am not asking you to take them out of the world, but I ask you to protect them from the evil one. They do not belong to the world, just as I do not belong to the world. Sanctify them in the truth; your word is truth. *As you have sent me into the world, so I have sent them into the world*."
>
> (John 17:14-18)

This prayer encapsulates the way in which the Evangelist John positions the church's identity within both the Jewish milieu and the pagan world. The disciples, who represent the church across time, are "branches" bonded in a unity of love and identity with Jesus and with one another. The world is a hostile place where the power of the "evil one"—elsewhere in John called "the ruler of this world"[120]—is a constant danger. Jesus prays for the protection of his followers as he sends them out to continue his mission of revealing the word to an unstilled world that continues to whirl against the Word.

John offers no direct or explicit scriptural warrant for the perilous mission that the disciples are to undertake—no citation, for example, of Isaiah 49:6 ("I will give you as a light to the nations . . ."). Instead, the warrant for their calling is simply Jesus' command, in conjunction with the scripturally inspired figure of the Vine and the branches. Their calling has organic unity with his, including their solidarity in the rejection he experienced. Because they abide in him as the branches abide in the vine, they participate in the christologically defined pattern of giving their lives to proclaim the hope that, precisely because God *loves* the rebellious world, "everyone who believes in him may not perish but may have eternal life" (John 3:16). That is precisely the hope foreshadowed in Psalm 80. There, the vine that God planted "sent out its *branches* (LXX: τὰ κλήματα) to the sea, and its shoots to the River" (80:11 [79:11 LXX]). Thus, even under the conditions of mortality and the world's resistance, the Evangelist persists in hoping that the church can go out to offer the word to the world, while praying along with Israel:

> . . . Give us life, and we will call on your name.
> Restore us, O LORD God of hosts;
> let your face shine, that we may be saved.

(Ps 80:18-19)

Other sheep not of this fold

The question of an apostolic mission to the Gentiles, a significant thematic concern in both Matthew and Luke, recedes into the background in John. There are, however, a few hints in the Fourth Gospel that the Evangelist does envision the extension of the message about Jesus beyond Israel to the wider world. These hints also call forth subtle scriptural reverberations, though John's narrative keeps these reverberations at a very low volume.

A key text for conceptualizing the relationship of the church to its wider environment is Jesus' Good Shepherd discourse in John 10. Jesus presents himself as the Good Shepherd, whose sheep will recognize his voice and follow him, in contrast to the voice of strangers. The discourse is set in the midst of a series of controversial conversations, in which some listeners, such as the man born blind, respond in faith, while others such as the Pharisees refuse to listen and follow (John 9). It is in this narrative context that Jesus declares, "I am the good shepherd. I know my own and my own know me." This may imply that those who refuse to follow are in fact not part of Jesus' own flock—just as Jesus can declare that the unbelieving *Ioudaioi* in the foregoing narrative do not have God as their Father and are "not from God" (8:42-47). Jesus' presence and teaching are producing a division among his Jewish compatriots between those who are and are not his sheep.

It seems, however, that Jesus suddenly transposes his discourse into a new key in John 10:16: "I have other sheep that do not belong to this fold. I must bring them also, and *they* will listen to my voice. So there will be one flock, one shepherd." The promise that there will be "one flock, one shepherd" echoes two passages in Ezekiel that speak of the coming of a Davidic king who will bring justice to the land and care for the people with compassion:

> I will set up over them *one shepherd*, my servant David, and he shall feed
> them: he shall feed them and be their shepherd. And I, the LORD, will
> be their God, and my servant David shall be prince among them; I, the
> LORD, have spoken.
>
> (Ezek 34:23-24)

The same prophetic word appears again just a little later in the book of
Ezekiel: "My servant David shall be king over them; and they shall all
have one shepherd" (Ezek 37:24). This second occurrence of the "one
shepherd" motif appears in the context of prophecies about God's breath-
ing life into the dry bones of the house of Israel (37:1-14) and reuniting
the divided northern and southern kingdoms (37:15-23). It seems clear,
then, that Jesus' use of the image of the good shepherd stakes his claim
to be the hoped-for king who will unite the people of Israel and bring
about eschatological justice. But what then does he mean by speaking of
"other sheep that do not belong to this fold"?

John drops several hints that Jesus has something larger in mind:
the creation of "one flock" that extends beyond the national and ethnic
boundaries of Israel. One crucial hint appears in the heavily ironic passage where the high priest Caiaphas, in a cynical utterance calling for the
judicial murder of Jesus, unwittingly prophesies that Jesus' death will be
of vicarious benefit to the whole nation of Israel. John then injects one of
his hermeneutically illuminating parenthetical voiceovers:

> He did not say this on his own, but being high priest that year he proph-
> esied that Jesus was about to die for the nation, *and not for the nation only,*
> *but to gather into one the dispersed children of God.*
>
> (John 11:51-52)

John's reference to gathering the dispersed children of God who are *not*
part of the nation completely overspills the boundaries of the immediate
narrative setting in Jerusalem, and it suggests a universal dimension to
the saving significance of Jesus' death.[121] In short, it casts light back on
his saying about "other sheep that do not belong to this fold" and suggests that the Evangelist John understands this saying to refer to *Gentiles*
who will hear Jesus' voice and be drawn into his one flock.

This interpretation of John 11:52 is strengthened by one other mysterious piece of John's narrative fabric. Immediately following Jesus' triumphal messianic entry into Jerusalem (12:12-19), some new unidentified

characters appear in the story: "Now among those who went up to worship at the festival were some Greeks. They came to Philip, who was from Bethsaida in Galilee, and said to him, 'Sir, we wish to see Jesus'" (12:20-21). John gives no explanation of who these Greeks might be or why they are coming to worship in Jerusalem at the Passover festival. Perhaps they are among the group of Gentile "godfearers" who are drawn to participation in the life and faith of Jewish communities without undergoing full conversion. But we are left to speculate about their identity and motives, because they immediately disappear entirely from the narrative. When Philip and Andrew go to inform Jesus about the inquiry of the Greeks, he exclaims unexpectedly, "The hour has come for the Son of Man to be glorified" (12:23). This seems like a narrative non sequitur, but Jesus then goes on to speak of his own death, using the metaphor of the grain of wheat that falls into the ground and dies in order to bear much fruit (12:24). As we have already noted, the image of "bearing fruit" may allude to the successful mission of preaching the gospel in the world. If this is what John has in mind, the coded meaning of Jesus' response would be that his own death will be necessary to generate the fruit-bearing mission to the Greeks and "to draw all people to myself" (12:32).

In this context, then, the concluding words of Jesus' response to Philip and Andrew would speak directly of allowing the Greeks/Gentiles access to the community of Jesus' followers: "Whoever serves me must follow me, and where I am, there will my servant be also. *Whoever serves me, the Father will honor*" (John 12:26). If this interpretation is correct, John 12:26 would be the Johannine analog to Paul's proclamation that in Christ there is neither Jew nor Greek (Gal 3:28). For John, the Greeks who seek to follow Jesus would be among the "other sheep" who hear Jesus' voice and follow.

This would produce a hermeneutical transformation and expansion of Ezekiel's vision for "one shepherd" who will preside over one flock. It would suggest that John's ecclesiology is not limited to a vision for a restored ethnic Israel, but that it has universal dimensions. Such a vision would of course be fully consistent with John's depiction of Jesus as the *Logos* through whom all creation came into being and in whom all find life and light.

That this reading is on the right track is confirmed by the conclusion of Jesus' high priestly prayer in John 17. After praying for himself and for his disciples, he strikingly extends the scope of his intercession to include "those who will believe in me through their word, *that they may all be one*" (John 17:20-21a). Their oneness mirrors and participates in the oneness of

Jesus with the Father. And the effect of this oneness is to produce a powerful testimony to the truth of Jesus' word and of his glory. He prays that
all his followers—including the "other sheep," as in 10:16—may become
one, "*so that the world may believe that you have sent me*" and "*so that the
world may know that you have sent me and loved them even as you have loved
me*" (17:21, 23).

According to John's Gospel, then, the power of the church's testimony to the world hinges for John on the oneness of the community
of Jesus' followers, which serves as an outward and visible sign of their
union with Jesus and through him with the Father. All this is conveyed
through two key images: the branches that abide in the Vine, and the
one flock gathered from among the nations to follow the one Good
Shepherd. The power of these images is derived from their grounding
in the earlier scriptural portrayals of God's desire to unify and heal the
nation of Israel through one future just and benevolent king. The Evangelist John, however, draws upon these images to reimagine the church's
position in the world. John is transforming and expanding these biblical
images. Through these transformations, John's Gospel echoes the voice
of the divine Shepherd who seeks to lead his people beyond a gloomy
picture of the church huddled fearfully together, and into a grace-filled
life offered to the whole world.

§20 THE FIGURAL WEB
John's Scriptural Hermeneutics

John's figural hermeneutic allows him to articulate his extraordinary (and
polemical) claim that all of Israel's Scripture actually bears witness to
Jesus: "If you believed Moses, you would believe me, for he wrote about
me" (John 5:46). Thus, even more comprehensively than the other Gospels, John understands the Old Testament as a vast matrix of symbols
prefiguring Jesus. In contrast to Luke's reading of Scripture as a plotted
script showing the outworking of God's promises in time, John understands Scripture as a huge web of christological signifiers generated by
the pretemporal eternal *logos* as intimations of his truth and glory.

Because John engages Israel's Scripture chiefly as a source of *symbols*, he often references the biblical stories not through direct quotation
of texts but through allusions and echoes. He presupposes a significant
knowledge of the characters and stories of the Old Testament, but his
intertextual references tend to focus on vivid visual *images* that evoke the
scriptural background rather than upon the citation and exposition of

chains of words. This hermeneutical strategy—perhaps we should call it a *sensibility* rather than a strategy—imparts to John's narrative a simplicity, immediacy, and remarkable imaginative power.

John reads the entirety of the Old Testament as a web of symbols that must be understood as figural signifiers for Jesus and the life that he offers.[122] In John's narrative, the temple becomes a figural sign for Jesus' body. Consequently, Jesus becomes, in effect, the temple. John writes his Gospel ten or twenty years after the great temple in Jerusalem has been destroyed by the Romans. But in place of Herod's once-impressive stone building, now in ruins, Jesus' *body* is now the place where God dwells, the place where atonement for sin occurs, the place where the division between God and humanity is overcome. John makes this extraordinary claim not by rejecting Israel's Scripture but by *rereading* it to show how it points, if we understand it rightly, to Jesus.

Likewise, the great feasts of Israel's worship are newly seen, in retrospect, to be replete with signs and symbols of Jesus: the pouring of water, the kindling of light, the rededication of the temple, the Passover lamb, the good shepherd who truly feeds and heals God's people. Even the scriptural narrative of Israel's redemption in the exodus becomes a vast figural matrix, a story in which the manna from heaven signifies Jesus' flesh.

In the same way, Israel's hope for a righteous and compassionate king/messiah who will set things right points to the unexpected figure of Jesus, who declares that his kingdom is not of this world (John 18:36) but who is nonetheless the true King of Israel. And the symbolic Son of Man figure, who signifies Israel's eschatological triumph and vindication, paradoxically finds enfleshed fulfillment in Jesus, the Son of Man who is indeed lifted high—but now lifted on the *cross* to draw all people to himself.

Israel had long understood its own identity as a vine lovingly planted and protected by God. Now, in John's Gospel, even Israel itself becomes a figural anticipation of Jesus, who is revealed as the true Vine. He takes into himself all that Israel was called to be, and his followers become the branches whose life flows solely from their union with him.

All this works hermeneutically because, at the beginning and the end of the day, Jesus is the *Logos*, the Word present before creation. All creation breathes with *his* life. He is the divine Wisdom whose very being is the blueprint of all reality. For John the Evangelist, therefore, all of Israel's Scripture is a figural web woven with latent prefigurations of the One without whom not one thing came into being. Thus, to take the example that John sets forth as a hermeneutical key near the beginning of his story, Jesus is not only the temple—the place where we meet God—but also the God who meets us and rescues us by gathering us into union with him. For that reason, reading Scripture figurally—reading backwards in light of the story of Jesus—is an essential means of discerning the anticipatory traces of God the Word in his self-revelation to the world.

CONCLUSION
Did Not Our Hearts Burn within Us?

The four Evangelists as retrospective scriptural interpreters

We began this study of the Evangelists' reading of Israel's Scripture by reflecting on Jesus' words in John 5: "If you believed Moses, you would believe me, for he wrote about me" (John 5:46). This startling assertion provokes a number of serious questions. What could John the Evangelist mean by advancing such an audacious claim? In what sense can Moses be said to have written about Jesus? What would it mean for us to believe that such an assertion might be true? And what sort of hermeneutical landscape might open before us if we learned to read Israel's Scripture not only through the filtering lenses of modern critical methods but also through the eyes of John and the other authors of the canonical Gospels?[1]

Throughout the foregoing chapters we have seen that the hermeneutical key to the Evangelists' engagement with Scripture is their practice of *figural reading*: the discernment of unexpected patterns of correspondence between earlier and later events or persons within a continuous temporal stream. In figural interpretation, the intertextual semantic effects can flow both directions: an earlier text can illuminate a later one, and vice versa. But the temporally ordered sequence of the two poles of a figural correspondence requires that the *comprehension* of the figure—the act of understanding that Erich Auerbach described as the *intellectus spiritualis*—must be retrospective. A figural christological reading of the Old Testament is possible only retrospectively in light of Jesus' life, death, and resurrection. Thus, from the perspective of figural interpretation, it would be an unwarranted hermeneutical presumption to read the Law and the Prophets as deliberately *predicting* events in the life of Jesus. But in light of the unfolding story of Jesus, it is both right and illuminating to *read backwards* and to discover in the Law and the Prophets an unexpected *foreshadowing* of the later story.[2]

In this book, we have considered how each of the four Gospel writers performs the practice of reading backwards. We have sought to listen to the distinctive *voice* of each Evangelist and to delineate the ways in which each one draws upon Scripture—both explicitly and implicitly—in retelling the story of Jesus. I have suggested along the way that each one offers distinctive contributions, as well as distinctive challenges, for theological hermeneutics.

This final chapter, then, will undertake some comparison and assessment. We will ask what might be the advantages and potential pitfalls of seeking to recover and follow the different hermeneutical approaches represented by the four Evangelists. Are there tensions among them? What do they share in common? Can or should we read the texts in the same ways they did? Should we model our understanding of the church's relation to Israel's story, and our picture of the church's mission in the world, on the Evangelists' scripturally shaped vision?

Most significantly, can we share their conviction that a retrospective reading of Israel's Scripture will disclose a mysterious Christology of divine identity? Should we concur with Udo Schnelle that "the OT is silent about Jesus Christ"? Or have we seen sufficient evidence to compel us to follow Martin Luther in seeing the Old Testament as the swaddling cloths in which the Christ child is to be found by those who seek him?

Finally, if Rowan Williams is right to describe the New Testament writings as the earliest stage in a "centuries-long task" of the "reorganization of Israel's religious language," should we regard that task as now finished? Or should we expect that in our century we will continue to participate in the hermeneutical task that the Gospel writers inaugurated?

These are, of course, massive questions. This concluding chapter can hardly hope to settle them definitively. But I will nonetheless set forth some constructive hermeneutical and theological proposals about what we might learn from the four Evangelists as readers of Israel's Scripture. These proposals are intended to invite other readers into a *conversation*—a conversation about matters that are of urgent interest for all who are concerned about the integrity and the future of Christian biblical interpretation.

After the detailed inquiry of the foregoing chapters, it may be helpful to offer a brief overview of our findings in the previous chapters before venturing some synthetic conclusions and constructive hermeneutical reflections.

As we have seen, the Gospels offer us four distinctive voices; they do not speak in unison as interpreters of the Old Testament. Rather, we should hear their testimonies as four distinctive voices singing in *polyphony*. If that is correct, the art of reading the Gospels is like the art of listening to choral singing. Each section in a choir must learn to hear and sing its own part. The choir director does not want everyone gravitating to singing the melody in unison; if that happens, the polyphony and the harmonic texture will be lost. So it is with the fourfold Gospel witness of the New Testament canon. To be sure, in a complex choral work, there may be moments of dissonance between the different parts. Discerning hearers do not want to eliminate the dissonances; rather, the task of appreciation is to develop a nuanced ability to hear how the dissonances belong to a larger artistic design. With that metaphor in mind, then, let us briefly review each of the four parts, each of the four Gospel witnesses, and ask whether they finally cohere in their polyphonic evocations of Israel's Scripture.

Mark: Figuring the mystery of the kingdom of God. Mark delights in veiled, indirect allusion. For him the message of Israel's Scripture is an awesome μυστήριον that comes to its climactic, yet paradoxical, embodiment in the figure of Jesus. Mark reads Scripture in a way that is relentlessly christological, while also insisting that recognition of Jesus' identity cannot be separated from costly discipleship that leads the disciple to take up the cross and follow in the pattern defined by Jesus' death. Those who have ears to hear and eyes to see will recognize that, in Jesus, God's power has broken into the world and Isaiah's promised new exodus is being enacted—yet in a way that thoroughly confounds human expectations. God's counterintuitive inbreaking kingdom encounters blindness and resistance by Israel's leaders, and therefore Jesus and his followers are met with violent opposition.

Mark shows relatively little interest in Scripture as a repository of explicit predictions about the Messiah; rather, for Mark, Scripture provides a rich symbolic vocabulary that enables the Evangelist to adumbrate the astounding truth about Jesus' divine identity. The man Jesus is somehow—in a way that defies understanding—the God of Israel, present among us as the One whom wind and sea obey, and yet at last nailed to a cross. The community of those to whom this apocalyptic secret is given may dare to speak of this awful mystery only in hints, whispers, and scriptural allusions. They are a community living in awe and anticipation, charged to wait and to watch for that which has been hidden to be disclosed (Mark 4:21-25, 13:37). They are the possessors of a secret whose full revelation lies in the future. Mark's hermeneutical strategy, therefore, is to provide cryptic scriptural pointers that draw the discerning reader into the heart of the eschatological mystery. This mysterious aspect of Mark's witness is aptly characterized by the Greek Orthodox tradition, which acclaims him as "the herald of the mystagogy of heaven" (τῆς οὐρανίου μυσταγωγίας τὸν κήρυκα).

What might we say, then, about the advantages and potential pitfalls of Mark's distinctive strategy for engaging the Old Testament in telling the story of Jesus?

The great strength of Markan hermeneutics lies in its fusion of restraint and evocative power. Mark shows a reverent deference to the hiddenness of divine mystery and the paradoxical character of revelation. It is precisely this deference that allows him fully to acknowledge the reality of suffering, the difficulty of discipleship, and the *not yet* pole of eschatology. Mark's Jesus, precisely as the embodiment of Israel's God, fully enters the realm of human suffering and models the costliness of faithfulness in the present age. Mark's sober eschatological reservation also produces a healthy sense of the limits of human language and a strong preference for communicating truth indirectly, through veiled parabolic gesture.

What pitfalls might await the unwary reader who seeks to pattern his or her understanding of the gospel after Mark's artful account of the identity of Jesus? Most importantly, Mark's subtle indirection may allow many readers to miss the message of Jesus' divine identity—as indeed many New Testament critics in the modern era have done. Alongside the danger that veiled communication may leave many in the position of uncomprehending outsiders (Mark 4:10-12), Mark's hermeneutic is also susceptible to the characteristic pitfall of apocalyptic communities: the temptation to an excessive satisfaction in the possession of "insider" knowledge. Mark's full narrative constantly subverts the latter by showing how those to whom it should be given to know the μυστήριον constantly fail and misunderstand, while it is "outsiders" who respond rightly to Jesus. But if we seek to follow Mark's hermeneutical strategy of allusive indirection, vigilance is necessary for us to avoid falling into the trap of smug aesthetic/epistemological superiority. That trap of epistemological smugness is not likely to be a danger for a suffering minority community such as the community of Mark's likely original readers. But for those who stand in more privileged social locations, the warning is not superfluous.

Matthew: Torah transfigured. Matthew, on the other hand, is concerned to demonstrate as explicitly as possible how Jesus' life constituted the fulfillment of the Old Testament. This fulfillment embraces both the coming-true of prophetic utterances (as in the formula quotations) and the narrative enactment of figural correspondences between Jesus and Israel. The latter deserves more attention than it has often been given in the interpretation of Matthew's Gospel; even the formula quotations are often richly allusive, depending for their full force on the device of metalepsis. The quotations are meant to lead the reader back to recover their original contexts. Matthew seeks to show how Jesus reconfigures both Israel and Torah by carrying forward Israel's story—a story sketched in the genealogy as running from Abraham to David, from David to the Babylonian exile, and from the exile to the coming of Messiah Jesus (Matt 1:17). Jesus brings about the end of Israel's exile (depicted metaphorically in the birth and infancy narrative material as a return from Egypt) and creates a new community of disciples who are obedient from the heart to the true intention of the Torah—now disclosed by the sovereign divine authority of Jesus' teaching. Matthew's hermeneutical strategy, therefore, is to elucidate clearly how Jesus interprets and exemplifies Torah—a Torah now reconfigured around Jesus.

At the same time, however, for Matthew, Jesus is more than a messiah and lawgiver. The portrayal of Jesus as the enthroned Son of Man figure who holds authority over heaven and earth (Dan 7) is particularly crucial in Matthew for authorizing Israel's new mission to the nations and the revisionary hermeneutic that justifies it. Matthew's Son of Man Christology places the risen Jesus in the heavenly throne room, with power and authority that extend throughout all time and space.

Finally, at the heart of Matthew's account of the identity of Jesus lies the proclamation that Jesus is Emmanuel, the embodiment of the personal presence of Israel's God; he promises to be present with the gathered community of disciples until the end of the age. Accordingly, he rightly receives the worship of his followers, for he is the locus of God's presence in their midst.

What are the advantages and possible pitfalls of Matthew's hermeneutic? In some ways, they are the flip side of Mark's. In sharp contrast
to Mark, Matthew offers his readers great clarity about how to approach
the reading of Scripture, and he makes his operative hermeneutical fil-
ters explicit on the surface of the text. He draws clear lines of continuity with the story of Israel and overtly portrays Jesus as "God with us,"
the living presence of God who is to be worshiped as the holder of all
authority. At the same time, Matthew also portrays Jesus as a teacher
who both lays down guidelines for community life and frames a forceful scriptural apologetic for the Gentile mission as the logical extension
and fulfillment of Israel's story. Thus, Matthew's robust Christology of
divine identity lays the groundwork for a deep confidence in God's continuing guidance and presence in the church's life.

Are there potential drawbacks to Matthew's narrative portrayal of
Jesus' identity? Three concerns might be mentioned. First, Matthew's
strongly assertive christological position can sometimes bleed over into a
harsh polemical stance toward other Jewish groups who represent different paradigms for interpreting Torah, as seen in the invective aimed at
the scribes and Pharisees in Matthew 23. Second, while Matthew draws
together many different biblical motifs, and while he projects the fulfillment of all of them onto the person of Jesus, it is not always clear that he
has reflected systematically or coherently on how to integrate the resulting picture. How is it possible for Jesus to be simultaneously the figural
fulfillment of Israel returning from exile, the new Moses who expounds
Torah, and the actual embodiment of Israel's God eternally present to his
people? It is not clear that Matthew has thought this through. Finally, in
some cases, Matthew's fondness for overt confessional statement stands
in some tension with Mark's reverent reticence before the divine mystery. Might the unwary reader of Matthew sometimes be tempted to
recapitulate the enthusiastic error of Peter on the mountain of transfiguration (Matt 17:1-8): wanting to construct a fixed dwelling for Jesus,
together with the Law and the Prophets, rather than simply listening
and responding in awe and wonder?

Luke: The story of Israel's redemption. Luke, in contrast to Matthew's
prediction-fulfillment schema, emphasizes *promise* and fulfillment. Israel's Scriptures are read by Luke principally as a treasury of God's promises to the covenant people. The fulfillment of these promises in Jesus is
a demonstration of the faithfulness of Israel's God, a testimony that God
has not forgotten "the promise he made to our ancestors, to Abraham

and to his descendants forever" (Luke 1:55). Therefore, because Israel has languished in oppression, the fulfillment of Scripture entails "good news to the poor," "release to the captives" (Luke 4:18; citing Isa 61:1), and the doom of the rich and powerful. For Luke, the hallmark of right response to the message of Scripture is not so much obedience as *joy*: a glad and grateful reception of the powerful work of salvation performed by God throughout Israel's story; in the events of Jesus' life, death, and resurrection; and in the Spirit's continuing work in the church.

It is crucial to recognize that Luke regards these saving acts as performed *by God*. Luke subtly identifies Jesus as the *Kyrios*, the one who is "Lord of all," the one who fulfills Isaiah's expectation of God as the Redeemer of Israel. His narrative thereby creates in the character of Jesus a paradoxical *Verbindungsidentität* that produces a much richer Christology of divine identity than modern New Testament criticism has tended to perceive.

Luke strongly highlights the continuity of the biblical story and its continuation in the *ekklēsia*. The Spirit is "turning the world upside down" through the church (Acts 17:6) in such a way that the message of the kingdom of God presents a clear and radically *peaceful* alternative to the claims of the empire. God's grace and mercy are not for Israel alone but also for the nations. But the good news for Israel also entails the corollary that those who do not recognize the time of their visitation by the *Kyrios*, those who refuse to listen to Jesus, the prophet like Moses, will be cut off from the people of God (Acts 3:22-23; citing Deut 18:15-20; Lev 23:29; cf. Luke 2:34-35). Luke's hermeneutical strategy, then, is to renarrate the story of Israel in such a way that the story of Jesus and the church can be confidently recognized as the fulfillment of the divine plan for salvation, for Israel and for the whole world. That renarration typically avoids overt assertions about typological equivalences between Jesus and Old Testament precursors; instead, Luke offers subtle echoes of Old Testament motifs and narrative patterns, creating a Scripture-soaked symbolic world for the story of Jesus.

The strengths of Luke's hermeneutical strategy are very considerable. He boldly narrates the historical continuity between Israel's past, present, and future. His vision allows for a comprehensive appropriation of the things about Jesus "in all the scriptures": "the Law of Moses, the Prophets, and the Psalms" (Luke 24:44). He shows Jesus to be precisely the Lord of Israel who passionately seeks the redemption of the poor and downtrodden. And he also shows how the mission to the Gentiles is the outworking of God's longstanding plan for Israel as a light to the nations. His use of

Scripture is characterized by allusive richness and, at the same time, a supple openness that lends itself well to apologetic engagement with outsiders and reasoned debate about the meanings of Israel's Scripture.

Are there potential pitfalls in Luke's hermeneutic? Many twentieth-century German critics suggested that Luke manifests an excessive confidence about the continuity of *Heilsgeschichte*, a potentially triumphalist reading of a smooth linearity that fails to reckon adequately with the disjunctive apocalyptic impact of the cross. I think this is a misguided criticism, an unsympathetic reading of Luke. Luke does, after all, highlight the scripturally prefigured necessity that the Messiah must suffer, and the same theme is carried forward in his narrative of the early church in Acts. Nonetheless, because Luke does so strongly emphasize the expansive power of the Spirit and the providential certainty of God's plan, readers must take care not to fall into the trap of naïve overconfidence. This is one reason why we need Mark alongside Luke in the canon, as a counterweight to any possible triumphalism. In another respect, though, Luke and Mark stand closely together: both narrate the divine identity of Jesus in a way that depends more on subtle intertextual allusion than on the overt confessional claims favored by Matthew and John.

John: Refiguration of Israel's temple and worship. John focuses on fewer scriptural texts than the synoptic authors but develops them in a more artistically rounded way. He frames each scriptural image that he employs with luminous clarity against a dark background, like the figures at the center of Rembrandt's portraits. For John, the Psalms play a dominant role in disclosing the identity of Jesus, while the Pentateuch—despite John's insistence that Moses wrote about Jesus—is not cited frequently. Strikingly, John tells his readers explicitly that Scripture can be understood only retrospectively after the resurrection; readers are instructed to "read backwards" in light of the illumination provided by the Spirit who will come after Jesus' departure. And that retrospective reading will be explicitly *figural* in character.

John reads the entirety of the Old Testament as a vast web of symbols that are to be read as figural signifiers for Jesus and the life that he offers. The temple is a proleptic sign for Jesus' body. Israel's cultic practices and the great feasts of Israel's liturgical calendar encode numerous latent signs and symbols of Jesus: the pouring of water and kindling of lights at the Feast of Tabernacles (*Sukkoth*); the rededication of the temple by the good shepherd who truly feeds and heals God's people; the Passover lamb whose bones are not broken; the bread that comes down from heaven to Israel in the wilderness. All these events and symbols point insistently to Jesus, who embodies that which they signified. When we read the story of Moses lifting up the serpent on a staff in the wilderness, we are to understand that we are reading a prefiguration of the lifting up of the Son of Man on the cross. The words and actions of Moses are to be understood, then, in postresurrectional retrospect as figural foreshadowings of Jesus.

For John, this symbolically transformative hermeneutic is possible for one compelling theological reason: Jesus is the incarnation of the *Logos* who was present before creation, through whom all things were made. He is the divine Wisdom whose being is the ground of the whole created order. That is why he can declare, "I and the Father are one" (John 10:30), both evoking and transforming Israel's *Shema*.[3] So for John, reading Scripture in this figural/symbolic fashion is nothing other than a way of uncovering the preincarnational traces of the Word that has now been gloriously and fully revealed to the world in Jesus.

What are the advantages of John's highly distinctive way of reading Scripture? John offers a profoundly *poetic* reading of the texts, and he is completely straightforward about setting forth his program of retrospective figural interpretation. This sweeping hermeneutical strategy enables a comprehensive reappropriation of Israel's sacred texts—and logically of everything else as well—as metaphorically transparent to the Word that underlies and sustains all creation. Thus, despite the apparent dualism of some passages in John's Gospel, the logic of his scriptural hermeneutic drives toward a mystical affirmation of *incarnation* and of God's mysterious presence in and through the creation. John's hermeneutical strategy may also have profound *apologetic* force in the historical aftermath of the crisis caused for Israel's worship life by the destruction of the temple; the figural reading allows the spiritual reality that the temple had signified to be absorbed into the body of Jesus, who now can offer life and wholeness to the whole world.

What about potential pitfalls or dangers in John's hermeneutical strategy for reading the Old Testament? It appears that his hermeneutic is framed polemically against rival interpreters; those who reject John's readings are characterized in the text as diabolical and ontologically estranged from God (John 8:39-47). This Gospel's approach to Old Testament interpretation can lend itself, therefore, all too readily to anti-Jewish and/or high-handedly supersessionist theologies. The text's apparent dualism can also open the door to forms of ahistorical quasignostic spirituality. It is for that reason that Irenaeus had to contend vigorously for an orthodox, early

Catholic interpretation of John against Valentinian gnostics who found it congenial for their own theological purposes.[4] I have suggested, to the contrary, that John should be read neither as flatly supersessionist nor as hostile to continuity with Israel. The dualistic/gnostic interpretation of John makes the mistake of denying or denigrating the literal sense of Israel's Scripture—whereas the *figural* reading that John practices does not deny the literal sense but completes it by linking it typologically with the narrative of Jesus and disclosing a deeper prefigurative truth within the fleshly, literal historical sense.

The challenge and gift of diversity. While these four different hermeneutical strategies might be in important respects complementary—indeed, their inclusion together in the New Testament canon represents the Christian tradition's judgment that they are so to be understood[5]—they represent distinctly different styles and sensibilities. It is difficult to imagine how any one community of faith could simultaneously embody all four approaches to Scripture with equal emphasis. One function of the church's canon, a diverse collection of writings, is to model a *repertoire* of faithful ways to receive and proclaim God's word. The fourfold Gospel witness is a providential gift to the church; it protects the community against the dangers of rigid monologic discourse and offers a range of theological resources for diverse circumstances. Particular voices within the canon will be more or less useful in different times and places, as the church discerns the points of vital intersection between the Bible and its own immediate cultural situation.[6] And perhaps one consequence of the canonization of such diverse texts is the de facto canonization of a principle of diversity: *the very variety within the fourfold Gospel canon creates a stimulus and encouragement for us to carry on the story in our own voices, working out our own fresh ways of engaging Israel's Scripture.* At the very least, inevitably, some choices have to be made about where the lines of emphasis will finally lie in our own appropriation of the scriptural witness.

But with all due acknowledgment of the hermeneutical diversity of the four Evangelists, another question looms before us: Is it possible still to hear the voices of these four witnesses as a polyphonic chorus singing different parts *in some sort of complex unity?* Or—to shift away from a musical metaphor that may have carried about as much weight as it should—what would *a fourfold-Gospel-shaped hermeneutic* look like? Do the Gospel writers, as interpreters of Scripture, converge and complement each other? What can we learn from reading them together and asking how their *common* fourfold witness might teach us to become better and more faithful readers?

Gospel-shaped hermeneutics?

What would it mean to undertake the task of reading Scripture *along with* the Evangelists? First of all, it would mean cultivating a deep knowledge of the Old Testament texts, getting these texts into our blood and bones. It would mean learning the texts by heart in the fullest sense. The pervasive, complex, and multivalent uses of Scripture that we find in the Gospels could arise only in and for a community immersed in scriptural language and imagery. Scripture provided the "encyclopedia of production" for the Evangelists' narration of the story of Jesus. Their way of pursuing what we call "doing theology" was to produce richly intertextual narrative accounts of the significance of Jesus. Because the language of Scripture was the Evangelists' native medium of expression, their reflection about God was articulated through subtle appropriations and adaptations of that linguistic medium.[7] But alas, many Christian communities have lost touch with the sort of deep primary knowledge of Scripture—especially Israel's Scripture—that would enable them even to perceive the messages conveyed by the Evangelists' biblical allusions and echoes, let alone to employ Scripture with comparable facility in their own preaching and renarration of the gospel story.

How might *we* learn that language? We might do it partly through immersing ourselves in worship, since these texts are constitutive for the church's liturgical traditions; however, for those who are latecomers to those traditions, hard and intentional work may also be required. The playwright Arthur Miller described his own arduous efforts to master the language of Shakespeare:

> You know what I used to do years ago? I would take any of Shakespeare's plays and simply copy them—pretending that I was him, you see. You know, it's a marvelous exercise. Just copy the speeches, and you gradually realize the concision, the packing together of experience, which is hard to do with just your ear. But if you have to work it with a pen or a piece of paper and you see that stuff coming together in the intense inner connection of sound and meaning, it's exhausting, just the thought of it.[8]

Miller's purpose in undertaking this "exhausting" exercise was of course not merely to transcribe Shakespeare's plays but to gain a grasp of the language that would enable him to move on and write his own. Our efforts to learn the Bible by heart, similarly, have as their goal to empower us to speak God's word by renarrating the story of Jesus in our own speaking and writing.

It is precisely at that point that we stand to learn much from the four Evangelists. They provide for us paradigmatic models of how to receive and retell the scriptural story. In light of our study of their elegantly intertextual narratives, I would suggest five ways in which their common witness and example might teach us to embrace a Gospel-shaped hermeneutic, and thereby to become wiser and more insightful readers of Scripture.

Reading backwards. A Gospel-shaped hermeneutic necessarily entails *reading backwards*, reinterpreting Israel's Scripture in light of the story of Jesus. Such a reading is necessarily a *figural reading*, a reading that grasps patterns of correspondence between temporally distinct events, so that these events freshly illuminate each other. This means that for the Evangelists the "meaning" of the Old Testament texts was not confined to the human author's original historical setting or to the meaning that could have been grasped by the original readers. Rather, the Evangelists received Scripture as a complex body of texts given to the community by God, who had scripted the whole biblical drama in such a way that it had multiple senses.[9] Some of these senses are hidden, so that they come into focus only *retrospectively*.

If we follow the example of the Evangelists, we will recognize that Scripture must be reinterpreted in light of the cross and resurrection. The Evangelists were convinced that the events of Jesus' life and death and resurrection were in fact *revelatory*: they held the key to understanding all that had gone before. Of course, the turning of this key opens the door to reassessment and transformation. After the resurrection, the community of Jesus' followers returned to reread Scripture under the guidance of the Spirit and experienced, again and again, an "Aha!" reaction. Their eyes were opened anew to see how Moses and the prophets *prefigure* Jesus. The Gospel of John offers the most explicit account of this hermeneutical reality in its interpretation of Jesus' words about raising up the destroyed temple: "After he was raised from the dead, his disciples remembered that he had said this; and they believed the scripture and the word that Jesus had spoken" (John 2:22). Luke paints a similar picture in his resurrection appearance narratives, where it is only the *risen* Lord who opens the minds of the disciples to understand Scripture. And even Mark, that most restrained of narrators, shows us that it is only after the death of Jesus that any human character—in this case the Roman centurion—first perceives Jesus' true identity as Son of God (Mark 15:39).

Let us be clear about the implication of the Evangelists' example at this point. If we insist—as much modern criticism has done—that the legitimate interpretation of Israel's Scripture must be strictly constrained by the (historically reconstructed) intention of the ancient Hebrew authors, or by the meaning that could have been understood by readers in the original historical settings of the Old Testament texts, we are declaring a priori that the Gospel writers were wrong and misguided and that their claims to revelatory retrospective reading are false. Oddly, both skeptical modern critics and staunch evangelical apologists have typically painted themselves into exactly this same hermeneutical corner, where they then battle over the same narrow turf—whether by debunking the Gospels' interpretations of the Old Testament or by contending desperately that the authors of the Old Testament's narratives and poems actually did intentionally forecast the details of Jesus' life. This misguided debate is generated—on both sides—by the rationalistic historicism of high modernity. But the canonical Evangelists, through their artful narration, offer us a different way to understand the New Testament's transformational reception of the Old as a paradigm-shattering but truthful disclosure of things "hidden from the foundation of the world" (Matt 13:35; freely quoting Ps 78:2). This hermeneutical sensibility locates the deep logic of the intertextual linkage between Israel's Scripture and the Gospels not in human intentionality but in the mysterious providence of God, who is ultimately the author of the correspondences woven into these texts and events, correspondences that could be perceived only in retrospect. In short, *figural interpretation discerns a divinely crafted pattern of coherence within the events and characters of the biblical narratives.* As Auerbach observes, in figural interpretation, "The connection between occurrences is not regarded primarily as a chronological or causal development but as *a oneness within the divine plan*, of which all occurrences are parts and reflections."[10]

Rationalistic criticism either precludes such coherence from the outset or else sees the Gospel stories as prophecy historicized, a fictional mutation that disingenuously manufactures mythical tales by extrapolation from earlier biblical texts. The Evangelists, by contrast, patiently insist that it was precisely the actual teachings and actions of Jesus that lived in the community's memory and subsequently catalyzed a retrospective recognition of unforeseen, divinely scripted, figural linkages with Israel's Scripture.

Conversion of the imagination. Accordingly, the Evangelists' diverse imaginative uses and transformations of the Old Testament texts summon us also to a *conversion of the imagination.* We can hear their proclamation only if we allow their intertextual performances to retrain our sensibilities as readers and to reshape our perception of what is real. If we learn from them how to read, we will approach the reading of Scripture with a heightened awareness of *story, metaphor, prefiguration, allusion, echo, reversal, and irony.* To read Scripture well we must bid farewell to plodding literalism and rationalism in order to embrace *a complex poetic sensibility.*[11] The Gospel writers are trying to teach us to become more interesting people—by teaching us to be more interesting readers. Rather than cutting and pasting the Evangelists' texts into our predetermined categories, we should learn to look where they point—like John the Baptist in the Isenheim altarpiece pointing a long finger toward the crucified Jesus—and to have our minds and hearts remade by what we see. It is not coincidental that Grünewald depicts John pointing to Jesus with his right hand while holding an open Bible in his left.

For the Evangelists, Israel's Scripture told the true *story* of the world. Scripture was not merely a repository of ancient writings containing important laws or ideas or propositions; rather, it traced out a coherent story line that stretched from creation, through the election of Israel, to the *telos* of God's redemption of the world.[12] This story emerges with particular force in Luke's account, but Mark and Matthew share a similar vision. Even John presupposes this narrative framework, as shown by his references to Abraham, Jacob, Moses, Isaiah, and Israel's Passover and wilderness traditions. One significant implication of learning to live in this story-shaped world is that a Gospel-shaped hermeneutic will pay primary attention to large narrative arcs and patterns in the Old Testament, rather than treating Scripture chiefly as a source of oracles, prooftexts, or halakhic regulations. The Evangelists, who are themselves storytellers, are much more interested in the Old Testament as story than as prediction or as law.

Further, because the Evangelists are so deeply immersed in Israel's Scripture, their references and allusions to it are characteristically *metaleptic* in character: that is, they nudge the discerning reader to recognize and recover the context from which their intertextual references are drawn. In many, many instances, a recovery of the fuller original context

The Crucifixion, from the Isenheim Altarpiece, c. 1512–1515 (oil on panel),
Grünewald, Matthias (Mathis Nithart Gothart) (c.1480–1528) / Musee d'Unterlinden,
Colmar, France / Bridgeman Images

will shed light on the story the Evangelists are telling and add important nuance to an otherwise flat surface reading.

To illustrate, let us recall a single example from our reading of the Gospel of Luke: when Luke concludes the story of Jesus' healing of a crippled, bent-over woman, he remarks that "all those who oppose him were put to shame" (Luke 13:17). When we hear in these words the explicit echo of Isaiah 45:16 LXX, Luke's simple narrative explodes with larger christological significance, for in Isaiah it is precisely the enemies of "the God of Israel, the Savior" who are put to shame.

Such evocative hints make a serious demand on the reader-competence of the Gospel's audience, but they also offer serious hermeneutical rewards for those with ears to hear. If we could acquire the single discipline of listening attentively for echoes of Scripture in the

Gospel narratives, it would have an enormous impact on our pastoral imagination and our preaching.

The unity and continuity of Scripture. The Evangelists' retrospective reinterpretation of Israel's story is in no sense a negation or rejection of that story. It is, rather, the story's transfiguration and continuation. This is one of the features that marks the distinction between the canonical Gospels and those later extracanonical writings that either ignore or repudiate Israel and Israel's God.[13] The canonical Evangelists understand themselves to be standing *within* the still-unfolding narrative trajectory of Israel's covenantal relationship with the God of Abraham, Isaac, and Jacob. This means not only that their narratives emphatically exclude the later Marcionite mutation of Christian theology but also that their account of the identity of Jesus must be understood within the framework of Israel's fierce loyalty to the one God of all the earth—a point to which I shall return below.

The Jewishness of the generative matrix for the Gospel narratives must be emphasized because in many sectors of the church there has been a tragic history of overlooking or even severing the gospel's roots in the story of Israel. All too often, neglect of the church's scriptural grounding has diluted Christian preaching into thin, otherworldly abstraction; or worse, it has led to shameful acts of hatred and violence toward the Jewish people. It is my hope that the interpretations offered in this book will encourage Christian readers to reflect more deeply and intentionally on the ways in which, through Jesus Christ, they have been grafted into the story of Israel (cf. Rom 11:11-24). In short, *the findings of this study call for the rejection of naïve Marcionite hermeneutics and for a renewed appreciation of the unity of the Old Testament and New Testament as Christian Scripture.*

The four Gospel writers approach Scripture as a unified whole, but their reading of it is not undifferentiated. Each of the Evangelists seems to operate with a de facto canon within the canon, giving more attention to some parts of Scripture than to others. At one level, this involves a particularly intense focus on certain books: above all the Pentateuch, Isaiah, and the Psalms. Each Gospel writer varies the "mix" of attention given to the different Old Testament witnesses, rather like a recording engineer adjusting the volume of different tracks in the recording studio; for example, Matthew turns up the volume on the prophets, and John puts the Psalms at the forefront of his mix. In some cases, it appears that this sort of intracanonical focus is given not to whole Old Testament books but to briefer selected passages, such as Isaiah 40, the announcement of the end of Israel's exile, or Daniel 7:13-14, the account of the glorified, enthroned Son of Man. Such passages can provide privileged "viewpoints" from which the Evangelists survey the whole of Scripture.

Despite these differences in emphasis, however, all four of the Evangelists are united in their insistent demonstration that the story of Jesus finds its wellsprings in Israel's Scripture. One implication of this common hermeneutical conviction is that the four Gospels stand in closer theological relation to one another than has sometimes been recognized in New Testament scholarship. When we listen carefully to the way that all four Evangelists narrate the story of Jesus through echoes of the Old Testament, we come to understand that the Christologies of the Synoptic Gospels actually have a close affinity to John's Christology of divine identity, though the *poetics* of their articulations of Jesus' scripturally grounded identity differ in interesting ways.

Jesus as the God of Israel. The last observation brings us to the central thesis that surges to the surface when we seek to learn from the Evangelists how to read Scripture. *The more deeply we probe the Jewish and Old Testament roots of the Gospel narratives, the more clearly we see that each of the four Evangelists, in their diverse portrayals, identifies Jesus as the embodiment of the God of Israel.*

This finding runs against the grain of much New Testament scholarship, which has tended to suppose that the earliest and most "Jewish" Christology is a "low" Christology, in which Jesus is a prophet, teacher of wisdom, and proclaimer of the coming kingdom of God, but not a divine figure. The judgment of Bart Ehrman in a recent book expresses this typical position: "The idea that Jesus was divine was a later Christian invention, one found, among our gospels, only in John."[14] At least since the nineteenth century, it has been axiomatic among critical biblical scholars that the "high" Christology of John's Gospel is a late Hellenistic development—and that the more one focuses on the synoptic tradition and locates Jesus within a monotheistic Jewish/Old Testament context, the more improbable it would seem to identify him as divine.[15]

What we have seen in this study, however, is that *it is precisely through drawing on Old Testament images that all four Gospels, in ways both subtle and overt, portray the identity of Jesus as mysteriously fused with the identity of God.* This is true even of Mark and Luke, the two Synoptic Gospels usually thought to have the "lowest" or most "primitive" Christologies. This is not to deny that the Jesus of the Gospels is a human figure. On the contrary, the very same Gospels that identify him as Israel's God simultaneously portray him as a man who hungers, suffers, and dies on a cross. Thereby, they create the stunning paradoxes that the church's later dogmatic controversies sought to address in order to formulate a theological grammar adequate to respect the narrative tensions inescapably posed by the Gospels.

The Gospel narratives, precisely through their reading of the Old Testament to identify Jesus, force us to rethink what we mean when we say the word "God."[16] This point has never been more forcefully expressed than by Karl Barth in part IV/1 of his *Church Dogmatics*:

> We may believe that God can and must only be absolute in contrast to all
> that is relative, exalted in contrast to all that is lowly, active in contrast
> to all suffering, inviolable in contrast to all temptation, transcendent in
> contrast to all immanence, and therefore divine in contrast to everything
> human, in short that He can and must be only the "Wholly Other." But
> such beliefs are shown to be quite untenable, and corrupt and pagan, by
> the fact that God does in fact be and do this in Jesus Christ.[17]

To Barth's declaration, all four canonical Evangelists would say *Amen*: the Gospels narrate the story of how the God of Israel was embodied in Jesus. This means, inter alia, that we should stop using the terms "high" Christology and "low" Christology to characterize the four canonical Gospels. These very categories presuppose an a priori philosophical account of "God" that the Gospel narratives contradict.

The Gospels as testimony and commissioning. Finally, the Evangelists consistently approach Scripture with the presupposition that the God found in the stories of the Old Testament is living and active. It is for that reason—and only for that reason—that the hermeneutic I have been describing can be embraced as *truthful*. It is not an exercise in literary fantasy like, say, trying to live inside the imaginative world of the Lord of the Rings trilogy or the *Star Wars* films. Rather, all of the hermeneutical recommendations I have enumerated here make sense only because God is the primary agent at work in and through the biblical story—and indeed, only because God is in some ultimate sense the author of Israel's story. The one Lord confessed in Israel's *Shema* is the same God actively at work in the death and resurrection of Jesus Christ. Apart from the truth of that claim, any talk of the unity of the Old Testament and the New Testament is simply nonsense.

There is only one reason why the Evangelists' christological interpretation of the Old Testament is not a matter of stealing or twisting Israel's sacred texts:

the God to whom the Gospels bear witness, the God incarnate in Jesus, is the same as the God of Abraham, Isaac, and Jacob. Either that is true, or it is not. If it is not, the Gospels are a delusional and pernicious distortion of Israel's story. If it is true, then the figural literary unity of Scripture, Old Testament and New Testament together, is nothing other than the climactic fruition of that one God's self-revelation. As readers, we are forced to choose which of these hermeneutical forks in the road we will take.

By forcing this choice upon us, the Evangelists compel us to read their Gospels neither as mere sources of historical information nor as entertaining or edifying tales. They compel us instead to read their Gospels as *testimony* to the truth, the sort of testimony that demands a self-involving response. For example, we cannot rightly read Mark's Gospel without hearing Jesus' question to Peter as a question also addressed directly to us: "But you—who do you say that I am?" (Mark 8:29). And we cannot answer that question as Mark desires without understanding how the answer implicates us in the confessional texture woven by the sum of Mark's scriptural allusions and echoes.

But there is more: the testimony of all four Evangelists creates *pressure* on the reader not only to assent intellectually to their confessional claims about Jesus but also to answer the call to discipleship articulated in these four stories. The Evangelists speak to us as Joshua spoke to all the tribes of Israel, narrating the story of God's gracious and mighty acts and then confronting us with an inescapable choice: "Choose this day whom you will serve" (Josh 24:15). If their scripturally formed testimony to Jesus as the embodiment of Israel's God is true, then we cannot avoid the summons that their stories lay—explicitly or implicitly—upon the readers.

> "If any want to become my followers, let them deny themselves and take up their cross and follow me. For those who want to save their life will lose it, and those who lose their life for my sake, and for the sake of the gospel, will save it."
>
> (Mark 8:34-35)

> "Go therefore and make disciples of all nations, baptizing them in the name of the Father and the Son and the Holy Spirit, and teaching them to obey everything that I have commanded you."
>
> (Matt 28:19-20a)

> "[R]epentance and forgiveness of sins is to be proclaimed in his name to all nations beginning from Jerusalem." ". . . [Y]ou will receive power when

the Holy Spirit has come upon you, and you will be my witnesses in Jerusalem, in all Judea and Samaria, and to the ends of the earth."

(Luke 24:47; Acts 1:8)

"Peace be with you. As the Father has sent me, so I send you."

(John 20:21)

The imperative of accepting a *commission* is inescapable for the assenting
reader of all four Gospels.[18]

If the story told by these witnesses is true, we have no alternative but
to see ourselves as caught up within it, participating in the ongoing arc
of the story told by Israel's Scripture, as it is filtered through the prism
of the fourfold Gospel and carried forward through the centuries to us.
The providence of God that binds Israel, Jesus, and the earliest church
into a single grand narrative now embraces us as well. It transforms our
imagination and sends us out also to retell the story.

If we *are* able to follow the Evangelists' guidance on how to read,
we will gain crucial resources for renarrating the story of Jesus in an age
when once again we must articulate the gospel in a fragmented world
urgently seeking coherence and signs of hope. By seeing Israel's Scripture through the eyes of the Gospel writers, may we be encouraged to
read backwards—and empowered to carry forward the story of Jesus
with new freedom and faithfulness. If so, we will find within our own
communities a figural echo of the Emmaus disciples who looked backwards and recalled what Jesus had been trying to teach them while they
were obliviously trudging along the road; like them, perhaps we will say
to one another, "Were not our hearts burning within us . . . while he was
opening the scriptures to us?"

NOTES

Introduction

1   Martin Luther, "Preface to the Old Testament," in vol. 35 of *Luther's Works* (ed. E. Theodore Bachmann; Philadelphia: Muhlenberg, 1960), 235–36. I am indebted to Tucker Ferda for calling my attention to this passage.

2   Erich Auerbach, *Mimesis* (Princeton: Princeton University Press, 1968), 73. See also Auerbach's detailed essay, "Figura," in *Time, History, and Literature: Selected Essays of Erich Auerbach* (ed. James I. Porter; trans. Jane O. Newman; Princeton: Princeton University Press, 2014), 65–113.

3   Another way to put this point is to say that figural reading is a form of inter-textual interpretation that focuses on an intertextuality of *reception* rather than of *production*. For an account of these categories, see Stefan Alkier, "Intertextuality and the Semiotics of Biblical Texts," in *Reading the Bible Intertextually* (ed. Richard B. Hays, Stefan Alkier, and Leroy A. Huizenga; Waco, Tex.: Baylor University Press, 2009, 3–21.

4   Building on Auerbach's work, the most illuminating analysis of figural read-ing in the Christian theological tradition remains that of Hans W. Frei, *The Eclipse of Biblical Narrative: A Study in Eighteenth and Nineteenth Century Hermeneutics* (New Haven: Yale University Press, 1974), esp. 18–37 on fig-ural interpretation in the Protestant Reformers. For a thorough exposition and critical engagement with Auerbach and Frei, see John David Dawson, *Christian Figural Reading and the Fashioning of Identity* (Berkeley: University of California Press, 2002). Dawson places these scholars, alongside Daniel Boyarin, in conversation with Origen of Alexandria and argues that Origen's

approach to figural reading "*extends without supplanting* the former Jewish meanings" of Scripture, for "the spirit does not undermine but instead draws out the fullest meaning of the letter" (217; emphasis added). The distinctive strength of Origen's figural exegesis, according to Dawson's interpretation, lies in "his awareness that classical Christian life is a life of continual transformation of what already is into something different" (214).

5   Frei, *Eclipse*, 33.

6   Udo Schnelle, *Theology of the New Testament* (Grand Rapids: Baker, 2009), 52; emphasis in original. German original: "Eine Biblische Theologie ist nicht möglich, weil 1) das Alte Testament von Jesus Christus *schweigt*, 2) die Auferstehung *eines Gekreuzigten* von den Toten als kontingentes Geschehen sich in keine antike Sinnbildung integrierten lässt," in *Theologie des Neuen Testaments* (Göttingen: Vandenhoeck & Ruprecht, 2007), 40. Schnelle also gives a third reason for the impossibility of a biblical theology: "While the Old Testament can be thought of as the most important cultural and theological context for understanding the New Testament, it is by no means the only one." It is unclear to me why this undeniably true observation should make it *impossible* to articulate a biblical theology.

7   See Richard B. Hays, "Reading Scripture in Light of the Resurrection," in *Art of Reading Scripture* (ed. Ellen F. Davis and Richard B. Hays; Grand Rapids: Eerdmans, 2003), 216–38.

8   My hope, however, is that the present book might encourage many students of Scripture to arrive at home and to know the place for the first time.

9   Rowan Williams, *The Wound of Knowledge: A Theological History from the New Testament to Luther and St. John of the Cross* (Eugene, Ore.: Wipf & Stock, 1998), 1.

10   Williams, *Wound of Knowledge*, 3.

11   Dietrich Bonhoeffer, *Widerstand und Ergebung: Briefe und Aufzeichnungen aus der Haft* (ed. Christian Gremmels, Eberhard Bethge, and Renata Bethge, in collaboration with Ilse Tödt; Gütersloh: Chr. Kaiser, 1998), 226. German original: "Wer zu schnell und zu direkt neutestamentlich sein und empfinden will, ist m. E. kein Christ." I am indebted to Ellen Davis for this reference.

12   For an introductory survey of the question of Jesus' own use of Scripture and of literature on this topic, see Steve Moyise, *Jesus and Scripture: Studying the New Testament Use of the Old Testament* (London: SPCK, 2010; Grand Rapids: Baker Academic, 2010), esp. 79–121.

13   The hypothetical character of historical Jesus research, and its tendency towards self-deceptive methodological circularity, was classically analyzed by Albert Schweitzer, *The Quest of the Historical Jesus* (Minneapolis: Fortress, 2001; German original: *Die Geschichte der Leben-Jesu-Forschung* (Tübingen: Mohr, 1913). The speculative character of the enterprise is most vividly evident in popular attempts to render a portrait of Jesus stripped of his divine aura and messianic pretensions. For illustrations of this sort of reductive "historical Jesus," see, e.g., John Dominic Crossan, *The Historical Jesus: The Life of a Mediterranean Peasant* (San Francisco: HarperCollins, 1991); Bart Ehrman, *How*

Jesus Became God: The Exaltation of a Jewish Preacher from Galilee (New York: HarperOne, 2014); Robert W. Funk, Roy Hoover, et al., *The Five Gospels: The Search for the Authentic Words of Jesus* (New York: Macmillan, 1993). For my critical review of the last of these titles, see Richard B. Hays, "The Corrected Jesus," *First Things* 43 (1994): 43–48. Similar methodological difficulties, however, in principle dog the efforts of scholars who seek to demonstrate that the Gospels are historically factual accounts of what Jesus did and said. For instances of works in this category, see Ben Witherington III, *The Christology of Jesus* (Minneapolis: Fortress, 1990); N. T. Wright, *Jesus and the Victory of God* (London: SPCK, 1996; Minneapolis: Fortress, 1996); idem, *How God Became King: The Forgotten Story of the Gospels* (New York: HarperOne, 2012). Wright's wide-ranging account of Jesus as the one in whom the return of Yahweh to Zion was enacted has provoked much controversy; he has undoubtedly identified a theologically significant theme that appears in the Gospels, particularly Matthew. I do not, however, entirely share his confidence in attributing this self-conception to the hypothesized Jesus of history.

14 See, e.g., Larry Hurtado, *One God, One Lord: Early Christian Devotion and Ancient Jewish Monotheism* (Edinburgh: T&T Clark, 1988); idem, *Lord Jesus Christ: Devotion to Jesus in Earliest Christianity* (Grand Rapids: Eerdmans, 2003). These books have challenged the prevalent older theories of the *Religionsgeschichtliche Schule* about the late date and Hellenistic milieu of the origin of Christian beliefs about the divinity of Jesus. Hurtado has highlighted the evidence for the worship of Jesus in Jewish congregations at an early date; he seeks to explain this phenomenon as a "mutation" or "variant" of earlier Jewish reverence for angels or other "divine agents." The present book does not seek to investigate the question of the etiology of the Gospels' divine identity Christology. I would suggest, however, that Hurtado is certainly correct about the early date and Jewish milieu for this extraordinary development—even though I am not persuaded by his particular hypothesis about the derivation of the confession of Jesus' divine identity from earlier Jewish models of intermediary figures. For an important precursor to Hurtado's work, see Martin Hengel, *Between Jesus and Paul: Studies in the Earliest History of Christianity* (Philadelphia: Fortress, 1983; repr., Waco, Tex.: Baylor University Press, 2013). A number of other scholars have argued along different lines to emphasize the ways in which the canonical Gospels emphasize Jesus' divine identity. See especially Richard Bauckham, *God Crucified: Monotheism and Christology in the New Testament* (Grand Rapids: Eerdmans, 1999); idem, *Jesus and the God of Israel: God Crucified and Other Studies on the New Testament's Christology of Divine Identity* (Grand Rapids: Eerdmans, 2008); C. Kavin Rowe, *Early Narrative Christology: The Lord in the Gospel of Luke* (BZNW 139; Berlin: De Gruyter, 2006; Grand Rapids: Baker Academic, 2009); and, with a number of interesting twists, Daniel Boyarin, *Border Lines: The Partition of Judaeo-Christianity* (Philadelphia: University of Pennsylvania Press, 2004); idem, *The Jewish Gospels: The Story of the Jewish Christ* (New York: The New Press, 2011).

15 Markus Bockmuehl, email correspondence, June 13, 2014; emphasis origi-
    nal. See also his important book *Seeing the Word: Refocusing New Testament
    Study* (Grand Rapids: Baker Academic, 2006). Bockmuehl's concern reso-
    nates with John Calvin's view of figural reading, as interpreted by Hans Frei:
    "Calvin is clearly contending that figural reading is a reading forward of
    the sequence. The meaning pattern of reality is inseparable from its forward
    motion; it is not the product of the wedding of that forward motion with a
    separate backward perpsective on it. . . . The only spiritual act is that of com-
    prehension—an act of mimesis, following the way things really are—rather
    than of creation, if it is to be faithful interpretation" (*Eclipse*, 36).
16 Richard B. Hays, *Echoes of Scripture in the Letters of Paul* (New Haven: Yale
    University Press, 1989), 176–77.
17 For a discussion of critical approaches to the phenomenon of intertextuality,
    see Hays, Alkier, and Huizenga, *Reading the Bible Intertextually*.
18 For a brief account of the role of allusion and echo in scriptural texts, see
    Hays, *Echoes of Scripture in the Letters of Paul*, 14–21. For further development
    and explication, see Richard B. Hays, *The Conversion of the Imagination: Paul
    as Interpreter of Israel's Scripture* (Grand Rapids: Eerdmans, 2005), 27–45.
19 For a full and sophisticated discussion of the trope of metalepsis, see John
    Hollander, *The Figure of Echo: A Mode of Allusion in Milton and After* (Berke-
    ley: University of California Press, 1981).
20 Hollander, *Figure of Echo*, 65.
21 The interculturally pervasive phenomenon of subtle intertextual reference is
    extensively documented by John Miles Foley, *Immanent Art: From Structure
    to Meaning in Traditional Oral Epic* (Bloomington, Ind.: Indiana University
    Press, 1991). Foley is a folklorist who studies traditional oral epics ranging
    from Homer to Beowulf to Serbo-Croatian oral tales. In this material, Foley
    notices something similar to what Hollander observed in the traditions of
    English poetry: sometimes the most important things are left unsaid, and
    the reader or hearer must pick up subtle intertextual clues to interpret what is
    said against the background of previous texts known by heart. The meaning
    effects generated by this device depend upon variations and transpositions of
    the tradition. Foley describes this phenomenon as "metonymic referential-
    ity": the spoken word in the oral epic functions metonymically to suggest or
    refer to other "texts" stored in the memory of the audience.
22 For a broader account of the rhetorical art of Obama's speech, see James
    Wood, "Victory Speech," *New Yorker*, November 17, 2008. For a helpful sim-
    ilar illustration of the way that Martin Luther King Jr., in his famous "I
    Have a Dream" speech, used allusions to Shakespeare, the Bible, the Decla-
    ration of Independence, and the hynm "My Country 'Tis of Thee," see Dale
    C. Allison Jr., *The Intertextual Jesus: Scripture in Q* (Harrisburg, Pa.: Trinity
    International, 2000), 1–2.
23 For a general discussion of intertextual interpretation, see my essay, "'Who
    Has Believed Our Message?' Paul's Reading of Isaiah," in *Conversion of the*

Imagination, 25–49. For a more technical introduction to the issues, see Alkier, "Intertextuality and the Semiotics of Biblical Texts."

24 For close textual study of the linguistic character of the scriptural texts used by Matthew and John, see M. J. J. Menken, *Matthew's Bible: The Old Testament Text of the Evangelist* (BETL 173; Leuven: Peeters, 2004); idem, *Old Testament Quotations in the Fourth Gospel: Studies in Textual Form* (Kampen: Kok Pharos, 1996).

25 See Karen H. Jobes and Moisés Silva, *Invitation to the Septuagint* (2d ed.; Grand Rapids: Baker Academic, 2015); Martin Hengel, *The Septuagint as Christian Scripture: Its Prehistory and the Problem of Its Canon* (OTS; Edinburgh: T&T Clark, 2002); Natalio Fernández Marcos, *The Septuagint in Context: Introduction to the Greek Versions of the Bible* (Leiden: Brill, 2000); Emanuel Tov, *The Text-Critical Use of the Septuagint in Biblical Research* (3d ed.; Winona Lake, Ind.: Eisenbrauns, 2015); J. Ross Wagner, *Reading the Sealed Book: Old Greek Isaiah and the Problem of Septuagint Hermeneutics* (FAT 88; Tübingen: Mohr Siebeck; Waco, Tex.: Baylor University Press, 2013).

26 See Mark Goodacre, *The Case against Q: Studies in Markan Priority and the Synoptic Problem* (Harrisburg, Pa.: Trinity International, 2002).

Chapter 1: Mark

1 For a particularly clear example, see Richard A. Horsley, *Hearing the Whole Story: The Politics of Plot in Mark's Gospel* (Louisville, Ky.: Westminster John Knox, 2001).

2 The significance of the imagery of Israel's continuing exile for the interpretation of the Gospels has been emphasized particularly by N. T. Wright, *Jesus and the Victory of God*; idem, *The New Testament and the People of God* (Christian Origins and the Question of God 1; Minneapolis: Fortress, 1992). Also see James M. Scott, ed., *Exile: Old Testament, Jewish, and Christian Conceptions* (JSJSup 56; Leiden: Brill, 1997). While Wright is certainly correct to draw attention to this motif in the Gospel texts, it would be an exaggeration to suppose that all Jews in the first century C.E. regarded themselves as being literally in exile. Any such claims must be qualified by the unavoidable facts that Israel is in the land (i.e., not literally in Babylon) and that in Jesus' time there was, after all, a functioning temple in Jerusalem. Accordingly, the Evangelists' use of the image of "exile" should be understood as metaphorical in character. Some of Wright's earlier writings might be understood as advocating a literal interpretation of "exile" as the condition of the Jewish people during the Second Temple era, but his most recent major book offers an extensive clarification and defense of his position (*Paul and the Faithfulness of God* [Christian Origins and the Question of God 4; London: SPCK; Minneapolis: Fortress, 2013], 139–63). In one key passage he offers this interpretation: "What then does 'exile' mean, in this continuing sense? Answer: the time of the curse spoken of in Deuteronomy and Leviticus, a curse that lasts

as long as Israel is . . . still subject to the rule, and often the abusive treatment, of foreign nations with their blasphemous and wicked idolatry and immorality, not yet in possession of the promised (if laughably ambitious) global sovereignty" (150). Then, at the conclusion of his careful discussion, he sums up his position as follows: "[I]t is the combination of Deuteronomy [27–30] and Daniel [9], and their regular retrieval in the key sources [i.e., Jewish texts from the Second Temple period] that compels us to go on highlighting *'exile' as the best controlling metaphor* to characterize this continuing moment in the single, though complex, *perceived narrative of a great many Jews*, including Pharisees, in the second-Temple period" (162; emphasis added). Giving due weight to the italicized phrases here will go a long way toward defusing the various objections to Wright's view. In fact, his interpretation of "exile," as he explains it here, is methodologically consistent with his insistence elsewhere that the apocalyptic imagery of the Gospels should for the most part be read metaphorically.

3   Modern biblical criticism conventionally sees the book of Isaiah as a composite work compiled over time. The passage cited here belongs to "Third Isaiah" (Isa 56–66). First-century interpreters such as the author of the Gospel of Mark, however, would have been unaware of such distinctions and subdivisions within canonical Isaiah. By using the name "Isaiah," I do not deny composite authorship; rather, I point to the implied author of the canonical prophetic book, the prophetic voice ("the prophet Isaiah") to which Mark explicitly refers in the Gospel's opening lines. See Christopher R. Seitz, "How Is the Prophet Isaiah Present in the Latter Half of the Book? The Logic of Isaiah 40–66 within the Book of Isaiah," in *Word without End: The Old Testament as Abiding Theological Witness* (Grand Rapids: Eerdmans, 1998; repr., Waco, Tex.: Baylor University Press, 2005), 168–93; repr. from *JBL* 115 (1996): 219–40.

4   Most of the usages of this verb in the Old Testament refer to the tearing of garments, usually as a sign of mourning (e.g., Gen 37:34; Job 1:20). The striking echo of the Hebrew verb in Mark 1:10 is one of several instances that suggest that Mark knew either a Hebrew text of the Old Testament or a Greek version that rendered its Hebrew *Vorlage* more literally than does the LXX.

5   See Ivor S. Buse, "The Markan Account of the Baptism of Jesus and Isaiah LXIII," *JTS* 7 (1956): 74–75. This insight has been further developed by, among others, Joel Marcus, *The Way of the Lord: Christological Exegesis of the Old Testament in the Gospel of Mark* (Louisville, Ky.: Westminster John Knox, 1992), 49–50, 58.

6   See the survey in John J. Collins, *The Apocalyptic Imagination: An Introduction to Jewish Apocalyptic Literature* (2d ed.; The Biblical Resource Series; Grand Rapids: Eerdmans, 1998), esp. 130–31, 153–76, 194–232.

7   Wright, *New Testament and the People of God*, 302–7.

8   Joel Marcus, "The Jewish War and the *Sitz im Leben* of Mark," *JBL* 111 (1992): 441–62; idem, *Mark 1–16: A New Translation with Introduction and Commentary* (AB 27–27A; New York: Doubleday, 2000, 2009), esp. 33–39.

Marcus attempts to determine the date and place of the composition of Mark's Gospel with great specificity on the basis of its allusions to these events. His proposals are ingenious but necessarily speculative.

9   Most modern critics have seen the prophecies of restoration in Amos 9:11-15 as a late secondary addition to the book. In its canonical form, however, the book of Amos manifests the same pattern of judgment, destruction, and restoration that characterizes other prophetic books, particularly canonical Isaiah (see Brevard S. Childs, "Amos," in *Introduction to the Old Testament as Scripture* [Philadelphia: Fortress, 1979], 395–410). For evidence of the importance of Amos' prophecy of restoration in the early church—especially in its LXX form—see Acts 15:13-21.

10 For a useful characterization of Jesus' opponents within the narrative world of Mark, see David Rhoads, Joanna Dewey, and Donald Michie, *Mark as Story: An Introduction to the Narrative of a Gospel* (2d ed.; Philadelphia: Fortress, 1999), esp. 116–22. Their assessment does not adequately grasp the interplay between the demonic forces and the religious authorities in Mark (see below), but the authors do recognize the tension in Mark's plot between Jesus' power to control the demons and his ongoing conflict with human opponents (82–84).

11 See Rendel Harris, *Testimonies* (2 vols.; Cambridge: Cambridge University Press, 1916–1920), 1:49, 2:64–65; Martin C. Albl, *"And Scripture Cannot Be Broken": The Form and Function of the Early Christian "Testimonia" Collections* (NovTSup 96; Leiden: Brill, 1999), 21.

12 As rightly observed by Marcus, *Way of the Lord*, 17.

13 Rikki E. Watts, *Isaiah's New Exodus and Mark* (WUNT 2/88; Tübingen: Mohr Siebeck, 1997), 90. As Watts observes, "This suggests that for Mark the long-awaited coming of Yahweh as King and Warrior has begun, and with it, the inauguration of Israel's eschatological comfort: her deliverance from the hands of the nations, the journey of her exiles to their home and their eventual arriving at Jerusalem, the place of Yahweh's presence." When this explication of the new exodus theme is set alongside the actual events narrated in Mark's Gospel, severe hermeneutical tensions arise, tensions that must be interpreted both in light of Mark's other allusions to Scripture and in light of his open-ended future eschatology.

14 Mark 9:9-13 strengthens the linkage of John to Elijah. On this passage, see Marcus, *Way of the Lord*, 94–110.

15 By contrast, the Jewish arrangement of the scriptural canon places the Writings last, so that the story ends with King Cyrus' decree that the temple in Jerusalem is to be rebuilt and that God's people are to go up to Jerusalem (2 Chr 36:22-23); this arrangement of the material, after the destruction of the Second Temple, imparted a very different kind of open-ended eschatological foreshadowing to the end of the biblical canon.

16 Origen, *Commentary on John* 6.24 (*AEG* 1:279–80); Jerome, *Letters to Pammachius* 57.9 (*NPNF²* 6:116).

17 Marcus (*Way of the Lord*, 12–47) sees strong evidence for the motif of a new exodus in Mark's use of Isa 40:3 but gives relatively little emphasis to Exod 23:20 as a signal of this motif. Richard Schneck (*Isaiah in the Gospel of Mark, I–VII* [Bibal Dissertation Series 1; Vallejo, Calif.: Bibal, 1994], 35–36) recognizes the significance of Exod 23:20, noting that this allusion, together with Mal 3:1 and Isa 40:3, implies the importance of the exodus motif for Mark. He does not, however, adequately hear the overtones of admonition sounded by Mal 3:1. Watts (*Isaiah's New Exodus*, 63–67) attends fully to the Exodus echo but highlights its admonitory function (Exod 23:21) more than its positive promise of protection. He argues further that Mal 3:1 is an ironic reformulation of Exod 23:20 (pp. 71–72) and that the Malachi reference is more influential for Mark (pp. 86–87). Krister Stendahl (*The School of St. Matthew and Its Use of the Old Testament* [2d ed.; ASNU 20; Lund: Gleerup, 1968], 47–54) observes that Exod 23:20 and Mal 3 were linked in the (later) Jewish synagogue lectionary; this fact might suggest the possibility that the linkage of these passages was current already in Judaism prior to Mark's Gospel. On the question of the compilation and dating of this lectionary, see Jacob Mann, *The Bible as Read and Preached in the Old Synagogue: A Study in the Cycles of the Readings from Torah and Prophets, as well as from Psalms, and in the Structure of the Midrashic Homilies* (The Library of Biblical Studies; New York: KTAV, 1971); Ben Zion Wacholder, *Essays on Jewish Chronology and Chronography* (New York: KTAV, 1976).

18 Willard M. Swartley (*Israel's Scripture Traditions and the Synoptic Gospels: Story Shaping Story* [Peabody, Mass.: Hendrickson, 1994]) has acutely observed the linkage of exodus and conquest traditions as a background to the synoptic narratives. See esp. 95–153.

19 See the classic essay of B. W. Anderson, "Exodus Typology in Second Isaiah," in *Israel's Prophetic Heritage: Essays in Honor of James Muilenburg* (ed. Bernhard W. Anderson and Walter Harrelson; New York: Harper, 1962), 177–95.

20 Marcus, *Way of the Lord*; Watts, *Isaiah's New Exodus*.

21 Marcus, *Way of the Lord*, 29; emphasis original.

22 The phrase "prepare the way" (פנה דרך), which appears in the Hebrew texts of Mal 3:1 and Isa 40:3, provides the hook that fastens together the texts in Mark's conflated "Isaiah" citation. Yet, interestingly, the verbal link is present only in the Hebrew text, for the Septuagint employs different Greek verbs in translating these passages.

	MT	LXX
Mal 3:1	ופנה־דרך לפני	καὶ **ἐπιβλέψεται** ὁδὸν πρὸ προσώπου μου
Isa 40:3	פנו דרך יהוה	**ἑτοιμάσατε** τὴν ὁδὸν κυρίου

Since the catchword association between these texts is present only in the Hebrew, it appears that either Mark or the tradition he is using knows the underlying Hebrew of the passages brought together in Mark 1:2-3. Marcus argues (*Way of the Lord*, 15–17), somewhat against the stream of other commentators, that Mark himself is responsible for creating the link between Mal 3:1 and Isa 40:3. Equally significantly, however, it is the *Septuagint's* verb ἑτοιμάζω that provides a catchword link between Exod 23:20 and Isa 40:3, a link absent from the MT.

Exod 23:20: ἵνα φυλάξῃ σε ἐν τῇ ὁδῷ ὅπως εἰσαγάγῃ σε εἰς τὴν γῆν ἣν **ἡτοίμασά** σοι

Isa 40:3: **ἑτοιμάσατε** τὴν ὁδὸν κυρίου εὐθείας ποιεῖτε τὰς τρίβους τοῦ θεοῦ ἡμῶν

In the former text, it is *God* who has "prepared (ἡτοίμασά)" the land that Israel is to enter; in the latter, the hearers of the voice that cries out are admonished to "prepare (ἑτοιμάσατε) the way of the Lord." In both cases, however, it is surely God who is the primary agent, acting to free and restore the people in the land. To prepare the way for God is to acknowledge and await his coming.

23 Watts' study is particularly forceful in its insistence that the mixed quotation in 1:2-3, as Mark's only editorial citation, provides a determinative framework for interpreting the Gospel as a whole (*Isaiah's New Exodus*, esp. 55–90).

24 Again, I do not mean to suggest that Mark has invented this incident. To the contrary, I think it highly likely that the event as Mark narrates it is substantially historical, indeed one of the most secure pieces of information available to us about Jesus' activity (cf. E. P. Sanders, *Jesus and Judaism* [Philadelphia: Fortress, 1985], 61–90, 319–27). For the purposes of the present discussion, however, our interest is in the way in which Mark's narration draws upon Old Testament materials to tell the story.

25 These so-called Markan Sandwiches are characteristic of the Gospel's style. As James Edwards has shown, the literary device often provides clues to the theological purpose of the bracketing narrative (see James R. Edwards, "Markan Sandwiches: The Significance of Interpolations in Mark's Narratives," *NovT* 31 [1989]: 193–216).

26 William R. Telford, *The Barren Temple and the Withered Tree: A Redaction-Critical Analysis of the Cursing of the Fig-Tree Pericope in Mark's Gospel and Its Relation to the Cleansing of the Temple Tradition* (JSNTSup 1; Sheffield: JSOT Press, 1980), 216–18, 231–33, 238–39; Sharyn Echols Dowd, *Prayer, Power, and the Problem of Suffering: Mark 11:22-25 in the Context of Markan Theology* (SBLDS 105; Atlanta: Scholars Press, 1988), 39–55; Sanders, *Jesus and Judaism*, 61–90.

27 I.e., Jesus is not merely seeking to reform current practices and gain minimal access for Gentiles to the outer court of the temple; rather, his symbolic action points more radically to a future in which all nations enter the temple alongside Israel to praise God. This eschatological scenario is rarely sufficiently recognized in commentaries on Mark. The best discussion is to be found in Watts, *Isaiah's New Exodus*, 318–25.

28 If Mark is alluding to Zech 14:21, the reference to "traders" (כנעני) provides further indirect evidence of his knowledge of Hebrew textual traditions, as

against the LXX, which reads: καὶ οὐκ ἔσται Χαναναῖος οὐκέτι ἐν τῷ οἴκῳ κυρίου παντοκράτορος ἐν τῇ ἡμέρᾳ ἐκείνῃ. On the possible allusion to the Hebrew traditions here, see also Joel Marcus, "No More Zealots in the House of the Lord: A Note on the History of Interpretation of Zech 14:21," *NovT* 55 (2013): 22–30.

29   Sanders (*Jesus and Judaism*, 61–76) has forcefully argued the case that Jesus' demonstration in the temple was a prophetic action symbolizing its destruction. Oddly, however, he dismisses the Jeremiah allusion in 11:17 as secondary and inauthentic (66–67). Indeed, he suggests that the Evangelists have used the quotation about the "den of robbers" to cover up the embarrassing historical fact of Jesus' threat of destruction and to "make it appear that Jesus was quite reasonably protesting against dishonesty" (75). He does not consider the possibility that the Jeremiah allusion has precisely the effect of signifying the temple's impending destruction—which is what Jeremiah prophesied to his generation. I think this apparent oversight is to be explained by Sanders' overriding concern to reject anachronistic Protestant interpretations of Jesus' action as a call for reform, "cleansing" the temple of its allegedly disgusting practices of animal sacrifice: "New Testament scholars who write about Jesus' concern for the purity of the temple seem to have in mind a familiar Protestant idea: 'pure' worship consists in the Word, and all external rites should be purged" (67–68). While gratefully accepting Sanders' critique of such readings—and the use to which they have put Mark 11:17—we may also suggest that Sanders' argument for interpreting the temple action as a prophecy of destruction would be supported and strengthened by attending to the wider context of the "den of robbers" allusion. This line of thought would certainly hold good for the analysis of Mark's theology, and I see no reason to deny that the historical figure of Jesus might well have patterned his words and actions after the prophet Jeremiah.

30   Jeremiah 8:13 came to be used as the beginning of the *haftarah* reading for Tishah be-Av, a solemn day commemorating in later rabbinic tradition the destruction of the temple (noted in Telford, *Barren Temple*, 143.)

31   See similar uses of the verb in 1 Kgdms 31:9; 2 Kgdms 1:20; 4:10; 18:19, 20, 26; 3 Kgdms 1:42; 1 Chr 10:9; Ps 67:12 LXX; *Pss. Sol.* 11:1; cf. Ps 39:10 LXX; 95:2 LXX; Jer 20:15.

32   See also Isa 60:6, where the proclamation of good news is associated with the gathering of tribute from the nations, and Isa 61:1, where the good news entails liberation for the oppressed. For similar uses of εὐαγγελίζω, see Joel 2:32 and Nah 1:15.

33   The term εὐαγγέλιον (more characteristically in the plural, εὐαγγέλια) was also significant in Roman imperial propaganda; this point will be discussed in the last part of this chapter.

34   My translation. In the LXX the words "Zion" and "Jerusalem" are not vocatives; in contrast to the MT, the city is not addressed by the imperative verbs "go up" and "lift up." Rather, Zion and Jerusalem are grammatically the indirect objects of the two participles; they are the audience *to* whom the

messenger of good news is to speak. This construction parallels the command "say *to* the cities of Judah" in the last part of the verse. English readers will be immediately familiar with this interpretation because of the KJV's "O thou that tellest good tidings to Zion," set unforgettably to music by Handel. The KJV is following the lead of the LXX and of Jerome's Vulgate: "tu quae evangelizas Sion . . . quae evangelizas Hierusalem."

35 For examples and discussion of this schematization of history, see Collins, *Apocalyptic Imagination*, 63–64, 155–57.

36 The horizon of apocalyptic expectation against which Jesus' message is to be heard is further illumined by texts such as Tob 14:5:

> But God will again have mercy on them, and God will bring them back into the land of Israel; and they will rebuild the temple of God, but not like the first one *until the times of the age shall be fulfilled* (ἕως πληρωθῶσιν καιροὶ τοῦ αἰῶνος). After this they all will return from their exile and will rebuild Jerusalem in splendor; and in it the temple of God will be rebuilt, just as the prophets of Israel have said concerning it.

Of course, in Jesus' time there was a temple in Jerusalem, rebuilt on a grand scale by Herod the Great; nonetheless, as we have seen, Jesus was severely critical of the temple and predicted its destruction. His stance toward the temple bears some affinity to the even more radical attitude of the Qumran covenanters, who regarded the Second Temple and its priesthood as corrupt and may have expected the eventual construction of a new temple under their jurisdiction. Whatever the original provenance of the Temple Scroll, its presence among the Qumran scrolls suggests the covenanters affirmed its depiction of an ideal temple and the critical attitude toward the Second Temple that such a depiction implies (see John J. Collins, *Apocalypticism in the Dead Sea Scrolls* [New York: Routledge, 1997], 58–60).

37 Sanders, *Jesus and Judaism*, 98–106.

38 On Mark's eschatological perspective, see Richard B. Hays, *The Moral Vision of the New Testament: Community, Cross, New Creation: A Contemporary Introduction to New Testament Ethics* (San Francisco: HarperSanFrancisco, 1996), 85–88.

39 On the interpretation of Daniel 7, see Wright, *New Testament and the People of God*, 291–97.

40 Correctly, Wright, *Jesus and the Victory of God*, esp. 339–68, 513–19. Cf. R. T. France, *The Gospel of Mark: A Commentary on the Greek Text* (NIGTC; Grand Rapids: Eerdmans, 2002), esp. 497–501. For a recent defense of the cosmic annihilation view, see Edward Adams, *The Stars Will Fall from Heaven: Cosmic Catastrophe in the New Testament and Its World* (LNTS 347; London: T&T Clark, 2007), 133–66.

41 Elizabeth E. Shively's recent study *Apocalyptic Imagination in the Gospel of Mark: The Literary and Theological Role of Mark 3:22-30* (BZNW 189; Berlin: De Gruyter, 2012) demonstrates the thoroughgoing apocalyptic character of Mark's narrative with particular force and clarity.

42 A theory arose in twentieth-century criticism that Mark's portrayal of the disciples as uncomprehending had a polemical purpose; on this view, Mark, representing a Hellenistic form of Christianity, was seeking to discredit Jesus' original followers, who were the core of the earliest Jewish-Christian community in Jerusalem (Theodore J. Weeden, *Mark–Traditions in Conflict* [Philadelphia: Fortress, 1971]). This hypothesis represents a failure, however, to read the entirety of Mark's narrative, in which the disciples are by no means rejected in the end but included in Jesus' final covenant-sealing supper and summoned, after the resurrection, to rejoin the risen Jesus. It is also hard to resist the impression that readers who insist on interpreting the disciples as "bad guys" in the story have a singularly narrow and simplistic understanding of narrative, in which there can only be heroes and villains. But in fact, one of the distinctive features of narrative is its capacity to disclose complexities of the heart and to lead both characters and readers through development and transformation. For a much more literarily astute reading of the role of the disciples in Mark, see Robert C. Tannehill, "Disciples in Mark: The Function of a Narrative Role," *JR* 57 (1977): 386–405.

43 See also Ps 115:4-8. For discussion of this motif, see G. K. Beale, *We Become What We Worship: A Biblical Theology of Idolatry* (Downers Grove, Ill.: InterVarsity, 2008), 44–47; and Watts, *Isaiah's New Exodus*, 190–93.

44 Watts, *Isaiah's New Exodus*, 183–210.

45 See also the "hardness of heart" of the Pharisees in 3:1-6.

46 Like Jesus' own family (Mark 3:31-35).

47 Note the echoing relationship between 3:29 and 4:12: "whoever blasphemes against the Holy Spirit can never have forgiveness" / "everything comes in parables . . . so that they may not turn again and be forgiven." Cf. Shively, *Apocalyptic Imagination*, 79–80.

48 Watts, *Isaiah's New Exodus*, 208.

49 See, by contrast, Matt 13:11-15.

50 Mark, however, uses ὑπολήνιον for "pit for the wine press" in place of the LXX's προλήνιον.

51 Parenthetically, this example shows that it would hardly have been impossible or even unusual for Jesus to offer interpretations of his own parables. Modernist criticism has generally tended to regard passages such as the interpretation of the parable of the sower (Mark 4:13-20) as later, secondary additions to the tradition. But Isa 5:7 shows that explicit interpretation of a figurative discourse is already clearly attested in Israel's prophetic tradition. This certainly does not *prove* that Mark 4:13-20 preserves authentic dominical tradition, but it does weaken some of the arguments against authenticity.

52 A similar passage in Jer 25:4-7 is particularly interesting, because it portrays the prophets as calling Israel to repentance so that they might *"remain upon the land that the* LORD *has given to you."*

53 Jon D. Levenson, *The Death and Resurrection of the Beloved Son: The Transformation of Child Sacrifice in Judaism and Christianity* (New Haven: Yale University Press, 1993).

54 Shalom Spiegel, *The Last Trial: On the Legends and Lore of the Command to Abraham to Offer Isaac as a Sacrifice: The Akedah* (trans. J. Goldin; New York: Pantheon, 1967). Also, Nils Alstrup Dahl, "Promise and Fulfillment," in *Studies in Paul: Theology for the Early Christian Mission* (Minneapolis: Augsburg, 1977), 131; Donald Juel, *Messianic Exegesis: Christological Interpretation of the Old Testament in Early Christianity* (Philadelphia: Fortress, 1988), 12–13, 80–87.

55 Gary A. Anderson, "Joseph and the Passion of Our Lord," in Davis and Hays, *Art of Reading Scripture*, 198–215. An interesting question would be whether the ultimate fate of Joseph's brothers, restored to relationship with the brother they had sought to kill, might also foreshadow the ultimate fate even of the wicked tenants, Israel's blind leaders.

56 For other christological uses of Ps 118, see Acts 4:11; Eph 2:20; 1 Pet 2:7. See also J. Ross Wagner, "Psalm 118 in Luke–Acts: Tracing a Narrative Thread," in *Early Christian Interpretation of the Scriptures of Israel* (ed. Craig A. Evans and James A. Sanders; JSNTSup 148; Sheffield: Sheffield Academic, 1997), 154–78.

57 Horsley (*Hearing the Whole Story*, 250) inexplicably suggests that 1:1 was not part of the original text of the Gospel but that it was "added later in the manuscript tradition." There is no textual evidence to support this conjecture; the only textual uncertainty in 1:1 concerns the phrase "son of God." The words Ἰησοῦ Χριστοῦ ("Jesus Christ") are present in all extant Greek manuscripts of Mark's Gospel.

58 Wilhelm Wrede, *Das Messiasgeheimnis in Den Evangelien* (Göttingen: Vandenhoeck & Ruprecht, 1901); William Wrede, *The Messianic Secret* (trans. J. C. G. Greig; Cambridge: J. Clarke, 1971).

59 See Marcus, *Mark 1–16*, 525–27.

60 Other images are employed, to be sure, but these four play the largest role in Mark. Richard Horsley has argued that traditions about Moses and Elijah, understood as "popular prophet[s] leading the renewal of Israel against its leaders," provide the primary "prophetic scripts" in relation to which Mark's story of Jesus is to be understood (*Hearing the Whole Story*, 231–53; quotation on 235). Certainly the Gospel of Mark does contain several passages that connect Jesus typologically to Moses and Elijah. For Moses, see Mark 6:30-44, 9:38-41; for Elijah, see Mark 5:21-43, 6:15. Both figures appear with Jesus in the transfiguration account (9:2-8). While the Moses typology is a significant secondary motif in Mark's Christology (a motif that Matthew will later develop more fully), Horsley fails to reckon sufficiently with Mark's explicit indications that the identification of Jesus with Elijah is mistaken, or at least inadequate (Mark 6:14-16, 8:27-30). For Mark, the Elijah figure is John the Baptist (Mark 9:9-13), who prepares the way for the coming of Jesus.

61 The one other case is Mark 9:41, in which the titular interpretation is possible but not certain.

62 For other examples of this royal use of *Christos* in the LXX Psalms, see Ps 2:2; 19:7; 83:10; 88:39, 52; 131:10, 17. Psalms 89 and 132 (LXX: 88 and 131) are

particularly significant because the title *Christos* is applied to the king precisely in contexts where the promise of an eternal Davidic line is reiterated. Significant also is the designation of the hoped-for Davidic ruler as *Christos* in *Pss. Sol.* 17:32; 18:1, 3, 5 (see John J. Collins, *The Scepter and the Star: The Messiahs of the Dead Sea Scrolls and Other Ancient Literature* [ABRL; New York: Doubleday, 1995], 53–56).

63   The assignment of titles to particular psalms suggests that some of them were being read during the Second Temple period in eschatological terms. See Brevard S. Childs, "Psalm Titles and Midrashic Exegesis," *JSemS* 16 (1971): 137–50; Martin Rösel, "Die Psalmüberschriften des Septuaginta-Psalters," in *Der Septuaginta Psalter: Sprachliche und theologische Aspekte* (ed. Erich Zenger; HBS 32; Freiburg: Herder, 2001), 125–48, here 137–39.

64   See also Ps 89:3-4, 132:11-12.

65   4QFlor 1.10–13, cited according to the translation of Florentino García Martínez, *The Dead Sea Scrolls Translated* (2d ed.; Leiden: Brill; Grand Rapids: Eerdmans [jointly published], 1996), 136. The other text cited here alongside 2 Sam 7:12-14 is Amos 9:11—a passage that also turns up, interestingly, as a key prooftext in Acts 15:15-17.

66   On the text-critical problem, see Bruce M. Metzger, *A Textual Commentary on the Greek New Testament* (4th ed.; Stuttgart: Deutsche Bibelgesellschaft, 1994), 62; Bart D. Ehrman, *The Orthodox Corruption of Scripture: The Effect of Early Christological Controversies on the Text of the New Testament* (New York: Oxford University Press, 1993), 72–75; Marcus, *Mark 1–16*, 141.

67   For detailed demonstration that Mark 1:11 echoes Isa 42:1, see Marcus, *Way of the Lord*, 48–56, 72–75. If Mark 1:11 alludes to this text, it is another case where Mark seems to presuppose a Hebrew textual tradition, for the phrase "I am well pleased" corresponds more closely to the Hebrew רצתה נפשי ("my soul delights") than to the LXX. Isa 42:1 LXX reads προσεδέξατο αὐτὸν ἡ ψυχή μου ("my soul has accepted him"). Mark's phrase ἐν σοὶ εὐδόκησα ("in you I am well pleased") looks like an independent rendering of a Hebrew *Vorlage*, or at least the reflection of a Greek translation closer in form to the MT.

68   The Isaianic servant is also said to be "anointed" by God in another of the servant passages: "The spirit of the Lord is upon me *because he has anointed me*" (Isa 61:1). Perhaps even more interestingly, both in Ps 89:38-39 and 89:50-51, the terms "anointed one" and "servant" are used in synonymous parallelism. Although Mark does not cite these passages, they demonstrate how easily the proposed linkage between the messianic imagery and servant imagery could be made.

69   While Mark does not develop a sustained analogy between Moses and Jesus, it is worth noting that the ideas of Moses as king and shepherd, especially during the exodus, can be found among Second Temple and later rabbinic texts (see Wayne A. Meeks, *The Prophet-King: Moses Traditions and the Johannine Christology* [NovTSup 14; Leiden: Brill, 1967]).

70 Dennis C. Duling ("Solomon, Exorcism, and the Son of David," *HTR* 68 [1975]: 235–52) and Bruce D. Chilton ("Jesus Ben David: Reflection on the Davidssohnfrage," *JSNT* 14 [1982]: 88–112) have argued that "Son of David" language is not messianic in Mark but rather links Jesus with Solomon, whom some traditions identify as a healer and exorcist. Yet, the messianic elements of the language, particularly in view of the larger context, are difficult to deny (see esp. Marcus, *Way of the Lord*, 151–52). If elements of a tradition about Solomon are in play here, they are not pitted against the messianic overtones called up by the title (so Stephen P. Ahearne-Kroll, *The Psalms of Lament in Mark's Passion: Jesus' Davidic Suffering* [SNTSMS 142; Cambridge: Cambridge University Press, 2007], 138–44).

71 Paul J. Achtemeier, *Mark* (Proclamation Commentaries; Philadelphia: Fortress, 1986), 56–58; Rudolf Bultmann, *The History of the Synoptic Tradition* (trans. John Marsh; rev. ed.; New York: Harper & Row, 1968), 136–37; Horsley, *Hearing the Whole Story*, 20.

72 An analogous but distinguishable motif appears in the exorcism stories, where the demons recognize and rightly identify Jesus (Mark 1:21-28, 3:10-11, 5:1-20).

73 Several features of the description appear to belong to the Festival of Tabernacles rather than Passover. Charles W. F. Smith ("No Time for Figs," *JBL* 79 [1960]: 315–27) notes features such as the cries of "Hosanna"; the presence of branches, which are reminiscent of the *lûlābîm* carried by worshipers during tabernacles; and the influence of Ps 118, a text associated with tabernacles, though not exclusively. It is sometimes proposed that Jesus' entry into the city really occurred during this fall festival (see T. W. Manson, "The Cleansing of the Temple," *BJRL* 33 [1951]: 271–82, here 276–82; Smith, "No Time for Figs"). If this is correct, the close collocation of tabernacles and Passover that results from Mark's narrative has a striking symbolic effect: the themes of national restoration associated with tabernacles are superimposed upon Passover, which celebrates Israel's escape from bondage in Egypt—and the combined significance of these narratives is concentrated on the figure of Jesus, entering the city as the peaceful king of Zech 9:9.

74 E.g., Morna D. Hooker, *The Gospel according to Saint Mark* (BNTC; London: A&C Black, 1991), 256.

75 Cf. the citation of Ps 18:50 above.

76 Hooker, *Gospel according to Saint Mark*, 292.

77 Translation by R. B. Wright, in James H. Charlesworth, ed., *The Old Testament Pseudepigrapha* (2 vols.; Garden City, N.Y.: Doubleday, 1983–1985), 2:667.

78 Cf. Stephen H. Smith, "The Function of the Son of David Tradition in Mark's Gospel," *NTS* 42 (1996): 523–39.

79 Marcus, *Way of the Lord*, 149–50.

80 Donald H. Juel, *Messiah and Temple: The Trial of Jesus in the Gospel of Mark* (SBLDS 31; Missoula, Mont.: Scholars Press, 1977), esp. 81–83, 107, 212; Frank J. Matera, *The Kingship of Jesus: Composition and Theology in Mark 15* (SBLDS 66; Chico, Calif.: Scholars Press, 1982); Marcus, *Way of the Lord*, 150.

81 Rowan Williams, *Christ on Trial: How the Gospel Unsettles Our Judgment* (London: Fount, 2000), 6–7.

82 Marcus, *Way of the Lord*, 137.

83 For a concise and judicious survey of the issues, see Marcus, *Mark 1–16*, 528–32. See also Delbert Burkett, *The Son of Man Debate: A History and Evaluation* (SNTSMS 107; Cambridge: Cambridge University Press, 1999); Simon J. Gathercole, *The Pre-existent Son: Recovering the Christologies of Matthew, Mark, and Luke* (Grand Rapids: Eerdmans, 2006), 253–71.

84 In Daniel, the allusion is a thinly veiled reference to the action of Antiochus IV Epiphanes, who set up an altar to Zeus in the Jerusalem temple in 168 B.C.E. (see 1 Macc 1:54-61). Mark now takes this event as a prophetic foreshadowing of some final desecration of the temple.

85 See also Joel 2:31; Ezek 32:7-8; Amos 8:9.

86 Bultmann, *History of the Synoptic Tradition*, 15–16, 120–25, 136–37, 150–63.

87 Richard Horsley rewrites Mark's story at this point by harmonizing Mark 14:62 with the more noncommittal parallels in Matthew and Luke and proposing that a hypothetical "earlier version of Mark . . . almost certainly had Jesus reply 'You say so' to the high priest as well as to Pilate" (*Hearing the Whole Story*, 252). A few later manuscripts (Θ, f^{13}, 565, 700, 2542[s]) do read in 14:62, "You say that I am," which is almost certainly a harmonizing conflation. Apparently realizing the weakness of this evidence, Horsley does not mention these manuscripts and proffers instead the textually unattested hypothesis of a precanonical Mark followed by the other synoptics but later altered by a redactor. This speculative suggestion abruptly abandons Horsley's own announced program of reading Mark as a "whole story" without contamination from other canonical sources. In this one instance, Horsley treats Matthew and Luke as reliable guides to the interpretation of Mark— more reliable, in fact, than the strikingly distinctive text that has come down to us as Mark's story. This strange methodological lapse is driven by Horsley's programmatic agenda of denying that Mark portrays Jesus as the Davidic Messiah. In fact, Mark 14:62 is the rock on which Horsley's reading runs aground. (I cannot resist observing that this example well illustrates the accuracy of Horsley's own description of himself as "literarily challenged" [vii]: he fails to appreciate the overwhelming dramatic impact of Jesus' overt declaration of his identity after such long narrative deferral.) For a much more literarily deft appraisal, see Williams, *Christ on Trial*, 5–9.

88 *Ta'anit* 68d. Collins, *Scepter and the Star*, 63.

89 Wright, *New Testament and the People of God*, 291–97.

90 See Daniel Boyarin, *The Jewish Gospels: The Story of the Jewish Christ* (New York: New Press, 2012), 56–59.

91 Alan F. Segal (*Two Powers in Heaven: Early Rabbinic Reports about Christianity and Gnosticism* [Leiden: Brill, 2002; repr., Waco, Tex.: Baylor University Press, 2012]) has shown how the later rabbinic polemic against "two powers in heaven" was directed against various Jewish traditions that included, inter alia, the New Testament writers' application of apocalyptic passages

such as Dan 7:13-14 to Jesus. Daniel Boyarin ("The Gospel of the *Memra*: Jewish Binitarianism and the Prologue to John," *HTR* 94 [2001]: 243–84) has contended provocatively that, despite the rabbinic effort to suppress this "heresy," some form of "binitarianism" was "the religious Koine of Jews in Palestine and the Diaspora" (260). The traditions described by these studies provide a background against which Mark's narrative portrayal of Jesus can be plausibly understood.

92   Bauckham (*God Crucified*, esp. 25–42) has made the compelling argument that the earliest Christology identified Jesus' actions and character with those of the one unique God of Israel. This divine-identity Christology takes seriously Jewish monotheism's understanding of God. Jewish monotheism, that is, was more concerned with *who* God is than with abstract qualities of divinity. Such a perspective allows one to see how the actions and character that the New Testament authors attribute to Jesus (e.g., accepting worship, offering forgiveness, exercising control over creation, sharing God's throne) include him within the identity of the unique God of Israel.

93   Watts, *Isaiah's New Exodus*, 80.

94   Marcus, *Way of the Lord*, 38–39.

95   For an instructive contrast, see John 20:28, where Thomas addresses the risen Jesus as ὁ κύριός μου καὶ ὁ θεός μου ("My Lord and my God").

96   Interestingly, the fifth-century uncial manuscript W continues the citation of Isa 40 to include the entirety of Isa 40:3-8. This certainly does not reflect the original text of Mark's Gospel, but it does show that some early readers of the text were acutely interested in the fuller Isaian framework of Mark's citation.

97   In his recent study *The Pre-existent Son* (249–52), Simon Gathercole cautiously advances the suggestion, following the lead of several significant German scholars, that the scriptural citation in Mark 1:2 ("See, I am sending my messenger ahead of *you*, who will prepare *your* way. . . .") should be interpreted as a heavenly court utterance, evoking an imagined "prehistoric scene" in which God the Father addresses the Son about the preparation for his impending mission of being sent into the world. We of course have ample analogies for this sort of reading of Scripture in the Letter to the Hebrews (e.g., Heb 1:5-14). Even within Mark's own narrative, there is one very clear example in 12:35-37, in which we hear in the words of Ps 110:1: "the one Kyrios speaking in heaven to the other" (Gathercole, *Pre-existent Son*, 251; citing Johannes Schreiber, *Die Markuspassion: Eine Redaktionsgeschichtliche Untersuchung* [BZNW 68; Berlin: De Gruyter, 1993], 238). Interestingly, Ps 110:1 also appears in Heb 1:13, explicitly interpreted as God's address to Jesus. Gathercole, whose discussion focuses on the question of Jesus' *pre-existence* rather than the question of his *divine identity*, is uncertain whether to accept this interpretation in relation to Mark 1:2-3. Reading the text as a reference to divine identity seems, on the whole, the likeliest interpretation of the text, even though Mark, yet again, leaves significant ambiguity in his spare narration.

98   See Bultmann, *History of the Synoptic Tradition*, 14–16.

99   Marcus (*Mark 1–16*, 222) rightly suggests that the phrasing of the question (τίς δύναται ἀφιέναι ἁμαρτίας εἰ μὴ εἷς ὁ θεός, literally, "Who is able to forgive sins except One, i.e., God") recalls the *Shema* (Deut 6:4). The same phrasing is echoed in Jesus' encounter with the rich inquirer (Mark 10:18): τί με λέγεις ἀγαθόν; οὐδεὶς ἀγαθὸς εἰ μὴ εἷς ὁ θεός ("Why do you call me good? No one is good except One, i.e., God"). The discerning reader will recognize that—in light of other evidence in the Gospel—the rich inquirer has spoken more truly than he realizes.

100 For other similar accounts of divine forgiveness of sins, see Isa 44:22; Ps 103:3, 130:3-4.

101 Marcus, *Mark 1–16*, 222-23.

102 "Thus, for Mark, the heavenly God remains the ultimate forgiver, but at the climax of history he has delegated his power of absolution to a 'Son of Man' who carries out his gracious will in the earthly sphere." Marcus, *Mark 1–16*, 223. Also Rudolf Pesch, *Das Markusevangelium* (2 vols.; HTKNT 2; Freiburg: Herder, 1976), 1:160–61; Hans-Josef Klauck, "Die Frage der Sündenvergebung in der Perikope von der Heilung des Gelähmten (Mk 2, 1–12 Parr)," *BZ* 25 (1981): 243.

103 Mark's verb ἐπετίμησεν is the same word that he employs repeatedly in exorcism stories to describe Jesus' rebuking of demonic powers (e.g., Mark 1:25, 3:12, 9:25; cf. 8:32-33). Thus, the storm is treated as though it were a manifestation of hostile demonic power. Consequently, the storm-stilling passage further accentuates the motif of cosmic conflict that characterizes Mark's apocalyptic narrative throughout (Shively, *Apocalyptic Imagination*, 161, 175, 181).

104 Cf. also Ps 114.

105 Marcus, *Mark 1–16*, 338. It is sometimes suggested (e.g., O. Lamar Cope, *Matthew, a Scribe Trained for the Kingdom of Heaven* [CBQMS 5; Washington, D.C.: Catholic Biblical Association, 1976], 96–97) that the portrayal of Jesus asleep during a storm recalls Jonah 1:4-16. In this case, the parallelism between Jesus and Jonah is interesting but misleading: Jesus is not running away from God, the storm signifies not God's anger but the hostile powers that God subdues, and the storm is calmed not by throwing the offender overboard but by the sovereign command of Jesus. Marcus—following Pesch, *Das Markusevangelium*, 1:269—correctly observes that, in Mark, Jesus is "in an essential way more like God than like Jonah."

106 Marcus (*Mark 1–16*, 338) notes that "because of their daily recitation of [Ps 44:23], the Levites were called 'the wakers' (cf. *b. Soṭ.* 48a)."

107 E.g., Hooker, *Gospel according to Saint Mark*, 169. Ps 77:19-20 would provide a particularly nice link to the feeding of the five thousand, since it speaks of God leading his people "like a flock."

108 The LXX's περιπατῶν . . . ἐπὶ θαλάσσης (Job 9:8) may be compared to Mark's ἐπὶ τῆς θαλάσσης περιπατοῦντα (Mark 6:49).

109 Augustine, *Cons.* 2.47, as translated by T. C. Oden and C. A. Hall, *Mark* (ACCS; Downers Grove, Ill.: InterVarsity, 1995), 95. This explanation is

particularly unsatisfactory, because according to the story the disciples do not cry out to Jesus for help; they are terrified of him because they think he is a ghost.

110 The Hebrew text of Job 9:11 reads: הן יעבר עלי ולא אראה ויחלף ולא אבין לו. The last clause could well be translated as "and I do not understand him," a rendering that would make the citation even more telling as an intertextual counterpoint to Mark 6:45-52. The verb עבר ("pass by") is often translated in the LXX by παρελθεῖν (as in Exod 33:19, 22; 34:6). The LXX translator of Job, however, has used παρελθεῖν in the second clause of 9:11 (to render חלף) rather than the first.

111 Commentators regularly note the possibility of an allusion to Job 9:8 in Mark 6:45-52. Only a few of the ones I have consulted note the possible significance of Job 9:11 for understanding Mark's reference to Jesus' intent to "pass by" the disciples (e.g., Eugene Boring, *Mark: A Commentary* [NTL; Louisville, Ky.: Westminster John Knox, 2006], 190; William L. Lane, *The Gospel according to Mark: The English Text with Introduction, Exposition, and Notes* [NICNT; Grand Rapids: Eerdmans, 1974], 236; and France, *Gospel of Mark*, 272n68).

112 Pesch, *Das Markusevangelium*, 1:361; John Paul Heil, *Jesus Walking on the Sea: Meaning and Gospel Functions of Matt. 14:22-33, Mark 6:45-52, and John 6:15b-21* (AnBib 87; Rome: Biblical Institute, 1981), 69–72; Marcus, *Mark 1–16*, 426. See also 1 Kings 19:11-13.

113 Marcus, *Mark 1–16*, 462; similarly, Heil, *Jesus Walking on the Sea*, 70.

114 Oden and Hall, *Mark*, 104. Marcus (*Mark 1–16*, 480–81) independently offers a similar reading.

115 Lane, *Gospel according to Mark*, 268; Marcus, *Mark 1–16*, 480–81. In this way, Mark 7:37 parallels the independent tradition found in Matt 11:2-6 and Luke 7:18-23, where the reference to Isa 35:5-6 is even more overt. Surprisingly, Watts (*Isaiah's New Exodus*) offers no extended discussion of Mark 7:37 as another indicator of the significance of the Isaianic new exodus motif in Mark.

116 As noted particularly by Marcus, *Mark 1–16*, 481.

117 The subtle ascription of divine status to Jesus in Mark 7:37 would be strengthened even further if we follow the suggestion (Pesch, *Das Markusevangelium*, 1:398; Marcus, *Mark 1–16*, 480–81) that the phrase καλῶς πάντα πεποίηκεν ("he has done all things well") should be heard as an echo of Gen 1:31, in which God pronounces all the things that he has made good (LXX: καὶ εἶδεν ὁ θεὸς τὰ πάντα ὅσα ἐποίησεν καὶ ἰδοὺ καλὰ λίαν). The echo is certainly stronger in the Greek than is apparent in most English translations.

118 The last line of Isa 35:4 LXX reads αὐτὸς ἥξει καὶ σώσει ἡμᾶς. In view of the emphatic αὐτὸς, this should be translated "He *himself* will come and save us."

119 Note the close parallelism between Isa 35:4 and Isa 40:9-10. Pesch (*Das Markusevangelium*, 1:398) points out the allusion to Isa 35:4 and comments, "In Jesus ist Gott gekommen, der den Menschen Heil bringt."

120 Isa 35:4 LXX has ὁ θεὸς ἡμῶν ("*our* God") rather than ὁ θεὸς ὑμῶν ("*your* God").

121   The image of the barren or devastated fig tree occurs also in several other Old Testament passages as a symbol for the fate of the people. See, e.g., Mic 7:1; Joel 1:7; Hos 9:10, 16-17. For full discussion, see Telford, *Barren Temple*, 133–63.

122   For a complex analysis of the problem of Jesus' divine identity in this passage, see Robert Jenson, "Jesus, Identity, and Exegesis," in *Seeking the Identity of Jesus: A Pilgrimage* (ed. Beverly Roberts Gaventa and Richard B. Hays; Grand Rapids: Eerdmans, 2008), 43–59, esp. 51–59.

123   For an evocative discussion of this theme, see Joel Marcus, "Identity and Ambiguity in Markan Christology," in Gaventa and Hays, *Seeking the Identity of Jesus*, 133–47.

124   Juel (*Messiah and Temple*, 83) has made the intriguing suggestion that the centurion's cry does not function as a confession about Jesus at the surface level of the story—the centurion could not know the deeper meaning of his statement. Rather, at this level, the centurion, as one of Jesus' enemies, utters a sarcastic taunt: "Sure, this man was God's son" (Donald H. Juel, *A Master of Surprise: Mark Interpreted* [Minneapolis: Fortress, 1994], 74n7; cf. Robert M. Fowler, *Let the Reader Understand: Reader-Response Criticism and the Gospel of Mark* [Minneapolis: Fortress, 1991], 22–24, 205–9). On this view, the dramatic irony of the sneering comment consists in the recognition that the centurion's words are profoundly true at the deeper level of the meaning of the narrative. I must, however, demur. As interesting as this proposal is, it does not adequately account for the revelatory significance of Jesus' death in Mark's Gospel. The irony of the centurion's statement is to be found precisely in the fact that at the moment of Jesus' death someone (a Gentile soldier at that!) finally perceives an important element of the truth of Jesus' identity—Jesus is the Son of God. Mark tips his hand here. Mark's subtle reconfiguration of christological categories and identification of Jesus with the God of Israel are most clearly revealed at the cross.

125   At Mark 14:49, the marginal notation in Nestle-Aland[28] offers a suggested reference to Isa 53:7. This seems to be pulled out of thin air (or, more charitably, out of later Christian interpretative tradition). Not only is there nothing in the immediate context to suggest an allusion to Isa 53, but 53:7 is a particularly doubtful text to adduce here, since it speaks of the servant's remaining silent and not opening his mouth. But here in Mark 14:49, Jesus is represented as speaking and chiding his captors.

126   David C. Steinmetz ("Uncovering a Second Narrative: Detective Fiction and the Construction of Historical Method," in Davis and Hays, *Art of Reading Scripture*, 54–65) has drawn illuminating analogies between reading mystery fiction and historical reflection. Steinmetz speaks of a second narrative—a rereading that reconfigures the evidence in the original narrative in a way that makes sense in terms of the end of the story. This "reading backwards" is suggestive for conceptualizing our exegesis of Mark. Mark's narrative reads differently when retrospectively reconfigured in light of Jesus' crucifixion and resurrection at the end of the story. From this perspective, subtle aspects of the

story emerge more clearly upon rereading. But this is also true of the Psalms (indeed, of the Old Testament in general). The Psalms will read differently in the light of texts such as Mark's narrative that reconfigure the story and hopes of Israel in light of Jesus.

127 Some LXX manuscripts (B, ℵ*, W) render the imperative as a second person plural (πατάξατε). The second-person singular found in A, Q, ℵᶜ, L, and C agrees with the reading found in the MT and makes better sense contextually. Mark differs significantly from LXX. But the first-person singular future indicative πατάξω is distinctive to Mark. No other extant text of Zechariah supports such a reading. Marcus, *Way of the Lord*, 154n9. Also, see J. de Waard, *A Comparative Study of the Old Testament Text in the Dead Sea Scrolls and in the New Testament* (STDJ 4; Leiden: Brill, 1965), 37–38.

128 Mark's form of the citation also changes the second verb to a third-person plural future passive indicative: διασκορπισθήσονται ("will be scattered"). The LXX reading, by contrast, offers not only a different verb but also a second-person plural aorist imperative form: ἐκσπάσατε ("scatter").

129 See Carol L. Meyers and Eric M. Meyers, *Zechariah 9–14: A New Translation with Introduction and Commentary* (AB 25C; New York: Doubleday, 1993), 397–406.

130 Joel Marcus (*Way of the Lord*, 154–58) has expertly summarized a body of rabbinic commentary on Zech 14 that finds in this prophecy a foretelling of the resurrection of the dead (see *Ruth Rab.* 2; *Eccl. Rab.* 1.11; *Cant. Rab.* 4.11). The key passage is Zech 14:4-6, which declares that the Lord's feet "shall stand on the Mount of Olives" and that on that day "the LORD my God will come, *and all the holy ones with him.*" An awareness of this rabbinic tradition presents the interpreter of Mark with a problem: Should we suppose that Mark already knew traditions of this kind and meant to use Zech 13:7 as a striking metaleptic citation that beckons the reader to see Jesus' death as prefatory to the day of the Lord's coming and the general resurrection? Or, alternatively, should we note that Mark offers no explicit citations of Zech 14 and conclude that the later rabbinic traditions cited by Marcus were not part of his field of vision? In favor of the former view is that Mark seems to include other veiled allusions to Zech 9–14 (Jesus' triumphal entry hinting at 9:9 and his action in the temple pointing to 14:20-21).

131 This is an instance of Mark's vivid use of the present tense (σταυροῦσουσιν) for historical narration. It is worth noticing the circumspect restraint of Mark's manner of telling the story, in contrast to some later Christian effusive meditations on the physical suffering of the crucifixion, as reflected, for example, in Mel Gibson's Hollywood film *The Passion of the Christ*.

132 John D. Crossan, "Form for Absence: The Markan Creation of Gospel," *Semeia* 12 (1978): 41–55.

133 This is a good illustration of the kind of "recurrence" or "clustering" of allusions that helps to confirm the presence of an intertextual echo. See Hays, *Conversion of the Imagination*, 104–7.

134   The MT text of this verse places the affirmation in the third person rather than the first: "he did not hide his face from *him* but heard when *he* cried to him." Interestingly, the NRSV chooses here to follow the LXX rather than the MT.

135   This way of speaking of Mark's readership does not presuppose any particular hypothesis about "the Markan community"—a highly elusive scholarly construct (see the useful discussion and critique of modern hypotheses by Dwight N. Peterson, *The Origins of Mark: The Markan Community in Current Debate* [BibInt 48; Leiden: Brill, 2000]). Mark may well have been writing broadly for readers in many different locations in the ancient Mediterranean world. (See Richard Bauckham, ed., *The Gospels for All Christians: Rethinking the Gospel Audiences* [Grand Rapids: Eerdmans, 1998]; as well as the critical rejoinder by Margaret M. Mitchell, "Patristic Counter-evidence to the Claim that 'The Gospels Were Written for All Christians,'" *NTS* 51 [2005]: 36–79.) But to refer to such readers as "the church," as I shall do, is to affirm that they are followers of Jesus who have come to believe in the message of his death and resurrection as decisive saving events and who therefore understand themselves as called to a confessional identity and mission that distinguish them from others in their immediate social environment.

136   It was once widely believed that Mark was written in Rome and reflected the church's situation under the Neronian persecution in the decade of the 60s. See C. E. B. Cranfield, *The Gospel according to Saint Mark: An Introduction and Commentary by C.E.B. Cranfield* (CGTC; Cambridge: Cambridge University Press, 1959 [1974 printing]), 8–9; Walter Grundmann, *Das Evangelium Des Markus: Includes Bibliographical References and Index* (3d ed.; THKNT 7; Berlin: Evangelische Verlagsanstalt, 1977), 18–20; Vincent Taylor, *The Gospel according to St. Mark: The Greek Text with Introduction, Notes, and Indexes* (2d ed.; Grand Rapids: Baker, 1966), 32; Lane, *Gospel according to Mark*, 24–25; Rudolf Pesch, *Das Markusevangelium*, 1:12–14; Joachim Gnilka, *Das Evangelium nach Markus* (2 vols.; EKKNT 2; Zürich: Benziger, Neukirchen Neukirchener Verlag, 1978–1979), 1:34; Martin Hengel, *Studies in the Gospel of Mark* (trans. John Bowden; Philadelphia: Fortress, 1985), 28–30. More recently, Joel Marcus has argued for a Palestinian setting in the time immediately around the Roman destruction of the temple in Jerusalem (Marcus, "Jewish War"; idem, *Mark 1–16*, 37–39). In my judgment, these attempts to locate Mark's reading community with historical precision remain necessarily speculative, because the text itself simply does not provide enough specific information to permit any degree of certainty. For present purposes, however, the precise historical setting of the Gospel is not a matter of crucial importance. What does matter is that Mark portrays the followers of Jesus as living in a situation of danger and persecution, wherever that might be.

137   Interestingly, this reference to the Spirit's role in empowering the testimony of persecuted Christians is one of only three places where Mark uses the name "the Holy Spirit" (see also 3:29, 12:36; cf. 1:10, 12).

138   There is an even more striking parallel in 2 Esd 6:25, an apocalyptic text nearly contemporary with Mark: "It shall be that whoever remains after all that I have foretold to you shall be saved and shall see my salvation and the end of my world."

139   See esp. Marcus, *Mark 1–16*, 889–91.

140   For a thorough review of the main positions on the meaning of "abomination," see esp. Adela Yarbro Collins, *Mark: A Commentary* (Hermeneia; Minneapolis: Fortress, 2007), 607–10.

141   See also Joel 2:31; Ezek 32:7-8; Amos 8:9.

142   The situation is a little more complicated in Joel, where the darkening of the sun and moon and stars is associated both with the disastrous invasion of Jerusalem by a foreign army (Joel 2:10) and with God's ultimate judgment of the invading powers (3:15) on the day "when I restore the fortunes of Judah and Jerusalem" (3:1).

143   Joel Marcus, "Crucifixion as Parodic Exaltation," *JBL* 125 (2006): 73–87.

144   See Craig A. Evans, "The Beginning of the Good News and the Fulfillment of Scripture in the Gospel of Mark," in *Hearing the Old Testment in the New Testament* (ed. Stanley E. Porter; McMaster New Testament Studies; Grand Rapids: Eerdmans, 2006), 93. On assessing the state of discussion concerning the worship of the Roman emperor, see C. Kavin Rowe, "Luke–Acts and the Imperial Cult: A Way through the Conundrum?" *JSNT* 27 (2005): 279–300; and N. T. Wright, *Paul and the Faithfulness of God* (Christian Origins and the Question of God 4; Minneapolis: Fortress, 2013), 311–43.

145   Evans, "Beginning of the Good News," 93–94, 97.

146   Evans, "Beginning of the Good News," 87.

147   For a survey of Jewish political resistance inspired by exegesis of Isa 40, see Evans, "Beginning of the Good News," 97–103.

148   Ched Myers, *Binding the Strong Man: A Political Reading of Mark's Story of Jesus* (repr.; Maryknoll, N.Y.: Orbis Books, 2008), 190–94. The fact that the "sea" in the story is the Sea of Galilee rather than the Mediterranean is beside the point, since on this reading the political symbolism, not the literal geography, is the primary thrust of the story.

149   On this theme see Willard M. Swartley, *Mark: The Way for All Nations* (Scottdale, Pa.: Herald, 1979); and more recently, Kelley R. Iverson, *Gentiles in the Gospel of Mark: "Even the Dogs under the Table Eat the Children's Crumbs"* (LNTS 339; London: T&T Clark, 2007).

150   Parenthetically, it might be asked why, if such a vision is found prominently in Isaiah, it would have been impossible for Jesus of Nazareth to have read and embraced it. But such a line of thought would take us beyond our immediate concerns and into the realm of reconstructing the history *behind* the Gospels. To anticipate the argument, the improbability of Jesus' advocacy for such a view would be suggested by the lack of clear corroborating evidence in other Gospel traditions (i.e., applying the criterion of coherence) and the abundant evidence that the early Christian movement found inclusion of Gentiles a highly controversial issue and, according to the evidence of Paul's

letters and Acts, never seemed to resolve it on the basis of appeals to the teachings of Jesus.

151 E.g., Iverson, *Gentiles*, 67–82.

152 Living beneath this text could well be Mal 3:1.

153 Alfred Suhl, *Die Funktion der alttestamentliche Zitate und Anspielungen im Markusevangelium* (Gütersloh: Gütersloher Verlagshaus Gerd Mohn, 1965). In his *Vorwort*, Suhl indicates that he began his study with the intention of opposing Marxsen's interpretation of Mark but found himself, in the course of the work, increasingly convinced by Marxsen's position. Since Marxsen was Suhl's dissertation supervisor, this is perhaps not an entirely surprising outcome.

154 Horsley, *Hearing the Whole Story*, 232.

155 E.g., Howard Clark Kee, "The Function of Scriptural Quotations and Allusions in Mark 11–16," in *Jesus und Paulus: Festschrift f. Werner Georg Kümmel z. 70. Geburstag* (ed. E. Earle Ellis and Erich Grässer; Göttingen: Vandenhoeck & Ruprecht, 1975), 165–85; Morna D. Hooker, *Jesus and the Servant: The Influence of the Servant Concept of Deutero-Isaiah in the New Testament* (London: SPCK, 1959); Marcus, *Way of the Lord*; Watts, *Isaiah's New Exodus*; Schneck, *Isaiah in the Gospel of Mark*; Thomas R. Hatina, *In Search of a Context: The Function of Scripture in Mark's Narrative* (JSNTSup 232; London: Sheffield Academic, 2002); Ahearne-Kroll, *Psalms of Lament*.

156 Zvi Ben-Porat, "The Poetics of Allusion," *Poetics and Theory of Literature* 1 (1976): 105–28.

157 For the full implications of my use of this phrase, see Umberto Eco, *A Theory of Semiotics* (Bloomington: Indiana University Press, 1979), 98–114.

158 The same emphasis on intentionality is found in the purpose clauses (with ἵνα) of Mark 4:21.

159 Several ancient scribes obviously felt similar unease about the sentence as Mark wrote it: several manuscripts (D it sa[mss] bo[pt]) support the reading ἅπτεται ("Is a lamp *lit* . . . ?"), but the more difficult reading ἔρχεται is clearly original. Interestingly, both Matthew and Luke also ameliorate the construction in different ways.

160 On this reading of the text, see Gathercole, *Pre-existent Son*, 171–72. Also, Eduard Schweizer, *Das Evangelium nach Markus* (NTD; Göttingen: Vandenhoeck & Ruprecht, 1967), 55; G. Schneider, "Das Bildwort von der Lampe," *ZNW* 61 (1970): 183–209; Pesch, *Das Markusevangelium*, 1:249 (following Schneider); Cranfield, *Gospel according to Saint Mark*, 164; M. J. Lagrange, *Evangile Selon Saint Marc* (Etudes Bibliques; Paris: J. Gabalda, 1911), 113; Grundmann, *Das Evangelium des Markus*, 96; Lane, *Gospel according to Mark*, 165–67.

161 Notice that in Matthew, the component sentences of Mark 4:21-25 are strewn about in different places in the narrative: Matt 5:15, 10:26, 7:2, and 13:12. Needless to say, this passage creates complicated questions for source theories about the Synoptic Gospels.

162 The fuller context of the quotation is illuminating with regard to the present argument: "Poetry provides the one permissible way of saying one thing and meaning another. People say, 'Why don't you say what you mean?' We never

do that, do we, being all of us too much poets. We like to talk in parables and in hints and in indirections—whether from diffidence or some other instinct" (Robert Frost, "Education by Poetry," speech delivered at Amherst College and subsequently revised for publication in the *Amherst Graduates' Quarterly* [February 1931]).

163 Frank Kermode, *The Genesis of Secrecy: On the Interpretation of Narrative* (Cambridge, Mass.: Harvard University Press, 1979), 47.

164 Williams, *Christ on Trial*, 6; emphasis original. Williams' imbedded quotation is from Anita Mason, *The Illusionist* (London: Abacus, 1983), 127.

165 The fear of the women is, of course, in response to the message of the resurrection of Jesus the crucified One. I would suggest that a similar response of reticent fear and trembling is equally appropriate when we read the story of the crucifixion, if we have rightly followed Mark's narrative clues about the identity of the one on the cross.

166 Doxastikon at the "Lord, I Have Cried," Vespers of St. Mark the Evangelist (April 25), with Greek text in TO MHNAION TOU APRILOU (Athens: Saliberos, 1904), 102. I am grateful to John Chryssavgis for drawing this tradition to my attention and to George Parsenios for assistance with identifying the citation.

Chapter 2: Matthew

1 Williams, *Wound of Knowledge*, 11.

2 Paul S. Minear, *The Good News according to Matthew: A Training Manual for Prophets* (St. Louis: Chalice, 2000).

3 On the development and significance of the fourfold Gospel canon, see Graham N. Stanton, "The Fourfold Gospel," *NTS* 43 (1997): 317–46; idem, *The Gospels and Jesus* (2d ed.; Oxford Bible Series; Oxford: Oxford University Press, 2002).

4 For an extensive bibliography of commentaries on Matthew prior to 1800, see Ulrich Luz, *Matthew: A Commentary* (trans. Wilhelm C. Linss; 3 vols.; Hermeneia; Minneapolis: Augsburg, 1989–2005), 1:19–22. By comparison, there are virtually no patristic commentaries on Mark.

5 Another quotation in this format appears in some late manuscripts at Matt 27:35, but this has apparently been interpolated by later scribes, under the influence of John 19:24. It is perhaps noteworthy that all ten authentic Matthean formula quotations cite texts from the prophets, whereas the text cited in 27:35 is Ps 22:19, making the formulaic τὸ ῥηθὲν διὰ τοῦ προφήτου not strictly appropriate, unless the psalmist should be regarded as a prophet. For discussion of these passages, see George M. Soares Prabhu, *The Formula Quotations in the Infancy Narrative of Matthew: An Enquiry into the Tradition History of Mt 1–2* (AnBib 63; Rome: Biblical Institute, 1976). The most detailed discussion of the text-form of Matthew's citations is Menken, *Matthew's Bible*.

6   In two of these three instances, Matthew breaks the formal pattern by placing the citation on the lips of characters in the story, and in the third (3:3) he
avoids the verb πληρωθῇ because the citation points to John the Baptist rather
than to Jesus himself; the language of "fulfillment" is reserved by Matthew
for quotations that prefigure Jesus.

7   Contra Matthew P. Knowles, "Scripture, History, Messiah: Scriptural Fulfillment and the Fullness of Time in Matthew's Gospel," in Porter, *Hearing
the Old Testament in the New Testament*, 59–82.

8   See, e.g., Luz, *Matthew*, 1:79–93; Graham N. Stanton, *A Gospel for a New
People: Studies in Matthew* (Louisville, Ky.: Westminster John Knox, 1993);
J. Andrew Overman, *Matthew's Gospel and Formative Judaism: The Social
World of the Matthean Community* (Minneapolis: Fortress, 1990); J. Andrew
Overman, *Church and Community in Crisis: The Gospel according to Matthew*
(The New Testament in Context; Valley Forge, Pa.: Trinity International,
1996); Anthony J. Saldarini, *Matthew's Christian-Jewish Community* (Chicago
Studies in the History of Judaism; Chicago: University of Chicago Press,
1994); David C. Sim, *The Gospel of Matthew and Christian Judaism: The History
and Social Setting of the Matthean Community* (Studies of the New Testament
and Its World; Edinburgh: T&T Clark, 1998).

9   Stendahl, *School of St. Matthew*. The second edition of Stendahl's monograph
qualifies this claim somewhat more cautiously than the original 1954 edition.

10   See Knowles, "Scripture, History, Messiah," 59–82.

11   Georg Strecker, *Der Weg der Gerechtigkeit: Untersuchung Zur Theologie
Des Matthäus* (Göttingen: Vandenhoeck & Ruprecht, 1966); S. Vernon
McCasland, "Matthew Twists the Scriptures," *JBL* 80 (1961): 143–48.

12   See especially Stanton, *Gospel for a New People*, 346–63; Menken, *Matthew's
Bible*, 15–199.

13   Donald Senior, "The Lure of the Formula Quotations: Re-assessing Matthew's Use of the Old Testament with the Passion Narrative as a Test Case,"
in *Scriptures in the Gospels* (ed. Christopher M. Tuckett; BETL 131; Leuven:
Leuven University Press, 1997), 89–115. Also, Knowles, "Scripture, History,
Messiah," 66.

14   Senior, "Lure," 90.

15   Senior ("Lure," 89) counts 61 quotations and points out that "The Nestle-
Aland appendix lists 294 implicit citations or allusions in Matthew."

16   Senior, "Lure," 115.

17   For the most detailed and methodologically elegant study of one of these
narrative typologies, see Dale C. Allison Jr., *The New Moses: A Matthean
Typology* (Minneapolis: Fortress, 1993). Leroy Huizenga (*The New Isaac:
Tradition and Intertextuality in the Gospel of Matthew* [NovTSup 131; Leiden:
Brill, 2009]) argues that the Matthean Jesus should also be understood in
typological relation to the figure of Isaac in the *Akedah* tradition.

18   This impression is heightened if one reads the KJV, whose use of the Elizabe-
than active verb "begat" more accurately reproduces the syntax of Matthew's
Greek than does the NRSV's periphrastic "was the father of." So, in KJV:

"Jechonias begat Salathiel, and Salathiel begat Zorobabel. And Zorobabel begat Abiud, and Abiud begat Eliakim, and Eliakim begat Azor . . ." (Matt 1:12b-13), and so on through forty-two generations. The cultural sensibilities of our time would prefer a more engaging or elegant opening.

19 This point holds despite the odd fact that the genealogy traces Jesus' lineage through Joseph (1:16), who, according to Matt 1:18-25, is not Jesus' biological father.

20 The phrase βίβλος γενέσεως appears both in Gen 2:4 LXX, where it introduces the account of the creation of man and woman, and in 5:1 LXX, where it introduces a list of Adam's descendants.

21 W. D. Davies and Dale C. Allison Jr., *A Critical and Exegetical Commentary on the Gospel according to Saint Matthew: In Three Volumes* (ICC; Edinburgh: T&T Clark, 1988–1997), 1:149–54.

22 Stefan Alkier, "Zeichen der Erinnerung—Die Genealogie in Mt 1 als intertextuelle Disposition" (paper presented at the annual meeting of the SNTS, Durham, England, 2002), 18–19. Published as Stefan Alkier, "From Text to Intertext: Intertextuality as a Paradigm for Reading Matthew," *HvTSt* 61 (2005): 1–18. Cf. Jason B. Hood (*The Messiah, His Brothers, and the Nations: Matthew 1.1-17* [LNTS 441; New York: T&T Clark, 2011]) arguing that the genealogy is a summary of Israel's story and legitimation of Jesus' messianic vocation both to save Israel (the "and his brothers" addition to "Judah") and to "transform" the Gentiles (the four righteous Gentile women) into faithful followers of the Messiah.

23 See Stephen C. Carlson, "The Davidic Key for Counting the Generations in Matthew 1:17," *CBQ* 76 (2014): 665–83.

24 On the importance of Abrahamic covenant traditions in Matthew, see Robert L. Brawley, "Evocative Allusions in Matthew: Matthew 5:5 as a Test Case," in *Literary Encounters with the Reign of God* (ed. Sharon H. Ringe and H. C. Paul Kim; New York: T&T Clark, 2004), 127–48.

25 Alkier, "From Text to Intertext," 12.

26 Boris Repschinski, "'For He Will Save His People from Their Sins' (Mt 1:21): A Christology for Christian Jews," *CBQ* 68 (2006): 248–67.

27 Wright, *Jesus and the Victory of God*. Wright contends that the Jesus of history understood his own mission in these terms; whether that is so or not, *Matthew* certainly understood Jesus' work in that way.

28 For further discussion, see Luz, *Matthew*, 1:83–85; and Jane Schaberg, "Feminist Interpretations of the Infancy Narrative of Matthew," in *A Feminist Companion to Mariology* (ed. Amy-Jill Levine and Maria Mayo Robbins; Feminist Companion to the New Testament and Early Christian Writings; London: T&T Clark, 2005), 15–36.

29 Davies and Allison, *Matthew*, 1:171.

30 The superscription to Ps 51, by giving the psalm a narrative context in the account of David's taking of Bathsheba, shows that Israel's later interpretative tradition continued to understand David, not Bathsheba, as the sinner in the story.

31 In this way, they prefigure the Canaanite woman of Matt 15:21-28. See Amy-
    Jill Levine, "Matthew's Advice to a Divided Readership," in *The Gospel of
    Matthew in Current Study: Studies in Memory of William G. Thompson, S.J.* (ed.
    David E. Aune; Grand Rapids: Eerdmans, 2001), 22–41.

32 Richard Bauckham ("Tamar's Ancestry and Rahab's Marriage: Two Problems
    in the Matthean Genealogy," *NovT* 37 [1995]: 313–29) shows that references
    to Tamar as "daughter of Aram" in *Jub.* 41:1 and *T. Jud.* 10:1 should not be
    understood to mean that she was an Aramaean. As Bauckham demonstrates,
    however, the biblical account in Gen 38 is ambiguous on the question of her
    ancestry, and Philo (*Virt.* 220–22) refers to her as a Syrian Palestinian—i.e., a
    Canaanite—who converted to worship the one true God. The text of *b. Sot.* 10
    provides evidence for a rabbinic tradition that she was a proselyte.

33 This does not necessarily mean that she was herself a Hittite, but Matthew
    might have inferred that she was.

34 This observation is also directly pertinent, of course, to the question of
    how Matthew uses Scripture to define the identity of Jesus. I would like to
    acknowledge that my reflections about Matthew's identification of Jesus with
    Israel have been independently reinforced by an unpublished essay by Gaylen
    Leverett, "Jesus as Israel: A Matthean Analogy." See also Dale C. Allison Jr.,
    "The Son of God as Israel," *IBS* 9 (1987): 74–81.

35 On the details of the textual differences, see Menken, *Matthew's Bible*, 133–
    42. For purposes of the present discussion, it makes little difference whether
    Matthew was translating the Hebrew independently or following an extant
    Greek translation closer in wording to the MT. Davies and Allison (*Mat-
    thew*, 1:262n8) mention that a scribal note in the margin of ℵ ascribes Mat-
    thew's quotation to Num 24:8, which reads, in the LXX, "God led him out
    of Egypt." Given the widespread use of the oracle of Balaam as a messianic
    testimony (esp. Num 24:17), it is not surprising that early Christian readers,
    finding that the LXX of Hos 11:1 gave no support to Matthew's citation,
    would be drawn to Num 24:8 instead. Note also that Num 24:7 LXX reads,
    "A man shall come forth out of his [Israel's] seed, and he shall rule many
    nations." There is no evidence, however, that Matthew was aware of any of
    this. The suggestion of Davies and Allison (*Matthew*, 1:262) that Matthew's
    attention was drawn first to Num 24 and then secondarily to Hos 11:1 is purely
    speculative.

36 Does this pattern of deliverance also prefigure the story of Jesus' death and
    resurrection? Matthew offers no explicit indication to that effect, but the
    symbolic inference lies readily at hand. In the subsequent liturgical tradition
    of the church, the story of Israel's crossing of the sea (Exod 14) is incorpo-
    rated into the lections for the Easter Vigil.

37 Davies and Allison (*Matthew*, 1:263–64) rightly identify this figural dimen-
    sion of the story and see here a connection to other ancient Jewish sources
    that envision a new "eschatological exodus and return to the land."

38 Thus, this citation reinforces the earlier quotation of Isa 7:14 as a word spoken
    "by the LORD" identifying Jesus as a "son" through whom God is present to

the people (Matt 1:21-23). These are the only two Matthean fulfillment quotations in which the words ὑπὸ κυρίου appear in the citation formula. For the classic defense of this interpretation, see Rudolf Pesch, "Der Gottessohn im matthäischen Evangelienprolog (1-2)," *Biblica* 48 (1967): 395–420.

39 These two identical divine proclamations echo several other scriptural texts: Gen 22:2; Ps 2:7; Isa 42:1. Matthew 17:5 adds ἀκούετε αὐτοῦ, probably also evoking Deut 18:15.

40 Menken (*Matthew's Bible*, 146–48) discusses the geographical problem of Rachel's place of burial, traditionally near Bethlehem (Gen 35:19-20, 48:7), and its relation to Ramah in the territory of Benjamin. Menken seems more concerned about this issue than is Matthew, for whom the crucial points are Rachel's symbolic role as mother of the nation, and the link between "Ramah" and Israel's exile.

41 Rightly noted by Christine Ritter, *Rachels Klage Im Antiken Judentum und Frühen Christentum: Eine Auslegungsgeschichtliche Studie* (AGJU 52; Leiden: Brill, 2003), 121. See also Menken (*Matthew's Bible*, 146), who cites several rabbinic passages that give a similar reading of Jer 31:15. See, e.g., *Gen. Rab.* 82.10: "We find Israel called after Rachel, as it says, Rachel weeping for her children."

42 Ritter (*Rachels Klage*, 122–23) cautiously puts forward this suggestion.

43 What I am claiming here about Matthew is formally analogous to the finding of recent studies of Paul's readings of Israel's Scripture: Matthew, like Paul, sees a coherent *plot* in the Old Testament texts that he cites. For Paul, see J. Ross Wagner, *Heralds of the Good News: Isaiah and Paul "in Concert" in the Letter to the Romans* (NovTSup 101; Leiden: Brill, 2002); Francis Watson, *Paul and the Hermeneutics of Faith* (London: T&T Clark, 2004).

44 Davies and Allison, *Matthew*, 1:262–64; Luz, *Matthew*, 1:120–21.

45 Mark 1:13 simply reports, "He was in the wilderness forty days, tempted by Satan."

46 Allison, *New Moses*, 165–72.

47 Jeremy S. Begbie, *Music, Modernity and God* (Oxford: Oxford University Press, 2013), ch. 6 and p. 168n75.

48 On the theme of Jesus' obedience as a key element of Matthean Christology, see R. W. L. Moberly, *The Bible, Theology, and Faith: A Study of Abraham and Jesus* (Cambridge Studies in Christian Doctrine; Cambridge: Cambridge University Press, 2000).

49 Should we interpret ὁ ἄνθρωπος here as an implicit christological title, akin to ὁ υἱὸς τοῦ ἀνθρώπου?

50 Moberly, *Bible, Theology, and Faith*, 198–205; Birger Gerhardsson, *The Testing of God's Son: (Matt. 4: 1–11 & par.): An Analysis of an Early Christian Midrash* (ConBNT 2:1; Lund: Gleerup, 1966).

51 The place name Massah means "test" in Hebrew; the full story is found in Exod 17:1-7. A parallel story appears in Num 20:1-13, with interesting differences. The tradition preserved in Numbers refers to the place only as Meribah, while Exod 17:7 gives both names, Massah and Meribah. The use of the

name Massah in Deut 6:16 suggests that the Exodus account is the one in view in that passage.

52 The wording of this quotation differs slightly from both MT and LXX. Where both of these traditions read, "The LORD your God you shall *fear* (MT: תירא, LXX: φοβηθήσῃ) and him you shall serve," Matthew changes "fear" to "worship" (προσκυνήσεις) and in the second clause adds "only" (μόνῳ). Both of these readings appear in Deut 6:13 LXX^A, but this is probably to be explained as scribal assimilation to the text of Matt 4:10 and Luke 4:8. The close agreement between Matthew and Luke is often taken as evidence that both are following a text-form found in Q (Menken, *Matthew's Bible*, 239). As I explained in the introduction, however, I am not assuming the Q hypothesis. In this case, it seems probable to me that Matthew himself is the likely source of the quotation's wording. He is particularly fond of the verb προσκυνέω, which appears thirteen times in his gospel (vs. twice in Mark and three times in Luke), and, apart from the present passage, he regularly uses it to show that the act or posture of worship is directed toward Jesus. Particularly telling are the instances in 2:2, 8, 11 (the Magi worship the infant Jesus), 14:33 (the disciples worship Jesus after he has walked on water), and 28:9, 17 (women and disciples worship the risen Jesus in resurrection appearance stories). If I am correct in assuming that Matthew is responsible for the rendering of Deut 6:13 found in Matt 4:10, there is a delicate irony here fraught with theological import: in Matthew's telling of the story, the devil seeks to lure Jesus to *worship* him, but this would be a disastrous reversal of the true order of reality, in which Jesus himself is the proper object of worship—as demonstrated by Matthew's other uses of προσκυνεῖν. It follows, of course, that if only God is to be worshiped—as the quotation affirms—Jesus himself must be God.

53 Deuteronomy 10:20, which contains the same wording, is another possible source of the quotation. For reasons that will emerge in our discussion of the passage, there is good reason to think of Deut 6:13 as the primary source. See also Maarten J. J. Menken, "Deuteronomy in Matthew's Gospel," in *Deuteronomy in the New Testament* (ed. Maarten J. J. Menken and Steve Moyise; LNTS 358; London: T&T Clark, 2007), 46n21.

54 Gerhardsson, *Testing of God's Son*, 62–66.

55 There is no trace of such an idea in Mark.

56 For a discussion of transformation of the heart in Matthew, see Hays, *Moral Vision*, 96–99.

57 This feature of Matthew's Gospel has led some interpreters to propose that Matthew represents a community that has remained fully within the bounds of first-century Judaism, that Matthew represents not "Jewish Christianity" but "Christian Judaism." See esp. Sim, *Gospel of Matthew and Christian Judaism*. For the opposing view that Matthew's vision places him outside the perimeter of Jewish belief and practice, see Stanton, *Gospel for a New People*; and John Riches, *Conflicting Mythologies: Identity Formation in the Gospels of Mark and Matthew* (Edinburgh: T&T Clark, 2000), esp. 316–24.

58 Matthew is following Mark 7:17-23 closely here, but, with characteristic diplomacy, he silently deletes 7:19b, "declaring all foods clean." The Markan formulation is notoriously ambiguous. Literally, the participial phrase reads "cleansing all foods." English translations that say "Thus he declared all foods clean" (NRSV) are broadly interpretative, resolving the ambiguity in favor of a categorical declaration. The other possibility is that the Markan sentence simply means, "Whatever goes into a man is not able to defile him, because it does not go into the heart but into the stomach, and then goes out into the sewer, [thereby] cleansing all foods [by excreting them]." It is possible that Matthew deletes the last phrase simply because he finds it crude and in poor taste. Alternatively, he may fear that it leaves the door open to a radical antinomianism that he finds objectionable.

59 The precise wording of the *Shema* as cited in the Gospels is an enormously complex problem, on both text-critical and source-critical grounds. Matthew's version ("You shall love the Lord your God with all your heart [καρδίᾳ] and all your soul [ψυχῇ] and all your mind [διανοίᾳ]") does not agree exactly with the MT or with any of the LXX manuscripts or with the parallels in Mark and Luke. For a helpful, detailed discussion of the issues, see Paul Foster, "Why Did Matthew Get the Shema Wrong? A Study of Matthew 22:37," *JBL* 122 (2003): 309–33. Matthew's divergence from other known versions of the *Shema* has sometimes been used to argue that Matthew must have been a Gentile not deeply familiar with Jewish liturgical practices. Foster's essay refutes this argument, not least because we lack clear evidence of a fixed liturgical practice of recitation of the *Shema* in Jewish synagogues in the first century C.E. For our present purposes, the intricate debates about this problem are not terribly crucial. Given the narrative context, it is abundantly clear that Matthew's Jesus is quoting Deut 6:5. If there is some issue at stake in Matthew's use of διανοία rather than δύναμις as the third element in the formula, it is not evident what it might be. See also a critique of Foster's argument by Christopher M. Tuckett, "Matthew: The Social and Historical Context—Jewish Christian and/or Gentile?" in *The Gospel of Matthew at the Crossroads of Early Christianity* (ed. Donald Senior; BETL 243; Leuven: Uitgeverig Peeters, 2011), 99–129, esp. 108–16.

60 Victor Paul Furnish, *The Love Command in the New Testament* (Nashville: Abingdon, 1972).

61 Perhaps surprisingly, Luz writes very little about this in his "history of interpretation" section (both in vol. 1 regarding Matt 7:12 and in vol. 3 regarding Matt 22:40). On whether the "two basic commandments provide a critical principle for the interpretation of Torah," he writes, "The church's precritical tradition showed scarcely any interest in this question" (3:80).

62 Davies and Allison, *Matthew*, 610. Surprisingly, Ben Witherington III (*Matthew* [Smyth & Helwys Bible Commentary; Macon, Ga.: Smyth & Helwys, 2006]), who seeks at every turn to emphasize wisdom motifs in Matthew, seems to overlook this striking parallel. Even the marginal apparatus in the

Nestle-Aland takes note only of Sir 28:2 as a parallel to Matt 6:12, overlooking the significance of the wider context in Sirach.

63   The most significant changes in Matt 9:9-12 are in the name of the tax collector whom Jesus summons to follow him (Mark calls him "Levi," while Matthew calls him "Matthew") and in Matthew's correction of the odd Markan phrase "the scribes of the Pharisees."

64   Modern critical readers may find in Hos 6:1-3 a depiction of an insincere or inadequate repentance, but it is doubtful that the text would have been so understood by ancient readers. Certainly Matthew offers no hint of understanding the passage that way.

65   Matthew corrects Mark by omitting the erroneous phrase "when Abiathar was high priest" (Mark 2:26). This is one of many editorial nuances that show how carefully Matthew was reading his sources. He does not merely take over scriptural references from Mark; he cross-checks them, either directly against the Old Testament text or against his comprehensive knowledge of that text.

66   Matthew deletes the saying that "the sabbath was made for man, and not man for the sabbath"; in its place, he adds vv. 6-7, which assert a precedent for the disciples' grain-plucking actions in the labors of the priests in the temple on the sabbath.

67   Once again, it should be observed that Matthew's focus on the practice of mercy is rooted deeply in Jewish tradition. The depth of those roots may be seen, for example, in Jesus' great parable of the final judgment, in which those who "inherit the kingdom" are those who have cared for the hungry, the thirsty, the strangers, the naked, the sick, and the prisoners (Matt 25:35-36). Jesus' teaching here is a distillation of admonitions such as Isa 58:6-7 ("Is not this the fast that I choose: . . . Is it not to share your bread with the hungry and bring the homeless poor into your house; when you see the naked to cover them, and not to hide yourself from your own kin?"), Tob 4:15 ("Give some of your food to the hungry, and some of your clothing to the naked"), and Sir 7:32-35 ("Stretch out your hand to the poor, so that your blessing may be complete. . . . Do not hesitate to visit the sick, because for such deeds you will be loved").

68   Matthew's apparent conflation of Law and Prophets is anticipated by Paul in 1 Cor 14:21, where he introduces a quotation of Isa 28:11-12 with the formula ἐν τῷ νόμῳ γέγραπται ὅτι.

69   ʾAbot de Rabbi Nathan 4, cited according to the translation of *The Fathers according to Rabbi Nathan* (trans. J. Goldin; Yale Judaica Series 10; New Haven: Yale University Press, 1955), 34.

70   Alongside Hos 6:6 could be placed other prophetic texts that similarly highlight *mercy* as a central theme. Consider Mic 6:8 LXX: "Or what does the LORD seek from you except to do justice and to love *mercy* (ἔλεον) and to be ready to go with the LORD your God?" Or again, Zech 7:9 LXX: "Thus says the LORD, the ruler of all: Judge with just judgment, do *mercy* (ἔλεος) and kindness each to his brother, and do not oppress the widow and the orphan

and the proselyte and the poor. . . ." Matthew does not quote these texts, but they hover in the background, implicitly informing and supporting his insistence on mercy as hermeneutical key to the law.

71   For a detailed study of these passages, see Amy-Jill Levine, *The Social and Ethnic Dimensions of Matthean Salvation History* (Studies in the Bible and Early Christianity 14; Lewiston, N.Y.: Edwin Mellen, 1988).

72   Of course, in view of the story's ending, Matt 15:21-28 has precisely the opposite effect: it is one of several Matthean foreshadowings of the mission to the Gentiles.

73   See also Matt 18:12-14.

74   Kermode, *Genesis of Secrecy*, 30.

75   Surprisingly, a number of commentators regard vv. 14-15 as a post-Matthean insertion. For a concise summary of the arguments for this proposal, see Menken, *Matthew's Bible*, 230–31. Against this view, four strong counterarguments may be suggested: (1) no manuscript of Matthew lacks these verses; (2) the formal difference from Matthew's usual "fulfillment" formula is satisfactorily explained by the fact that this prophecy is not a messianic oracle about Jesus but rather a characterization of the people's blindness, in Isaiah's time as well as Matthew's own; (3) it is entirely consistent with Matthew's redactional technique to supply explicitly an extended explanatory scriptural quotation where Mark offers only an allusion; and (4) the addition of the explicit quotation neatly serves Matthew's purpose of casting blame on the people for their rejection of God's word, while at the same time reaffirming God's intention to redeem and heal them.

76   In this case, Matthew follows Mark 7:1-23 very closely. He rearranges the order of the elements in the story, but his content and wording are substantially identical to Mark's, except for his telling omission of Mark 7:19b, which might be interpreted as an explicit abrogation of the laws about unclean food. The quotation of Isa 29:13 in Matt 15:8-9 is identical to the wording of Mark 7:6-7. The only difference is that Mark places the quotation at the beginning of Jesus' response, whereas Matthew defers it to follow the charge that the Pharisees and scribes nullify the commandment of God by failing to honor father and mother.

77   A significant and difficult textual variant occurs in 15:6. Instead of reading "the word of God" (τὸν λόγον τοῦ θεοῦ), Sinaiticus originally read "the law of God" (τὸν νόμον τοῦ θεοῦ). The latter was corrected by a scribe to read "word" but then corrected again by a second scribe to read "law"! Further, "the word of God" in Matt 15:6 could well be an assimilation to Mark 7:13. It is tempting to read "law" as original, since it would fit nicely with the prophetic transposition of the "law" we have been tracing in Matthew's narrative. Nonetheless, the external textual evidence for "word" outweighs that of "law," and one should not make too much of this uncertain variant (see Metzger, *Textual Commentary*, 31).

78   Isaiah 29, a prophetic indictment of Judah's blindness, played an important role in the early church's attempts to explain the Jewish rejection of the gospel.

Paul cites bits of the passage twice in his extended discussion of Israel's blindness in Rom 9–11 (Isa 29:16 in Rom 9:20, and Isa 29:10 in Rom 11:8), and in
1 Cor 1:19 he quotes Isa 29:14 as a reproach to those at Corinth who boasted in
their "wisdom." There is also an echo of Isa 29:13 in Col 2:22. These recurrent
references suggest that Paul had meditated on Isa 29 as a prefiguration of the
resistance to the gospel that he encountered in his missionary work—from Jews
and Gentiles alike. But the Pauline texts give no hint that this reading of the
passage found its source in a tradition of Jesus' sayings. Nonetheless, the use of
this text in the controversy discourse narrated in Mark 7:1-23 and Matt 15:1-20
bears a striking resemblance to Paul's appeal to Isa 29 in his reflections on the
hardening of Israel in Rom 9:20 and 11:8.

79   Wolfgang Trilling, *Das wahre Israel: Studien zur Theologie des Matthäusevan-
     geliums* (Erfurter Theologische Studien 7; Leipzig: St. Benno-Verlag, 1959).

80   See Dorothy Jean Weaver ("'Thus You Will Know Them by Their Fruits': The
     Roman Characters of the Gospel of Matthew," in *The Gospel of Matthew in Its
     Roman Imperial Context* [ed. John Riches and David C. Sim; JSNTSup 276;
     London: T&T Clark, 2005], 107–27).

81   Possibly a false tale? Cf. 1 Sam 31:3-6.

82   Ulrich Luz, "Der Antijudaismus im Matthäusevangelium als historisches
     und theologisches Problem: Eine Skizze," *EvTh* 53 (1993): 310–27; reprinted
     as "Anti-Judaism in Matthew," in *Studies in Matthew* (trans. Rosemary Selle;
     Grand Rapids: Eerdmans, 2005), 243–61.

83   See Hays, *Moral Vision*, 97–99, 319–29.

84   It is tempting here to correlate the twelve at the last supper with the "twelve
     pillars, corresponding to the twelve tribes of Israel" that Moses set up around
     the altar at the foot of Mount Sinai (Exod 24:4)—but this is to press the
     typology further than Matthew takes it. Whether or not the link is made
     between disciples and pillars (as in Gal 2:9), the symbolism of the twelve as
     representing the twelve tribes is obvious and widely recognized.

85   Commentators sometimes also suggest a third echo here, a reminiscence of
     the Suffering Servant of Isa 52:13–53:12. This proposed link depends on the
     words *"which is poured out for many"* (Matt 26:28). This is a possible reminis-
     cence of Isa 53:12, which says (in the MT) that the servant "poured himself
     out to death" (the LXX here, however, reads: παρεδόθη εἰς θάνατον ἡ ψυχὴ
     αὐτοῦ). The possible echo of Isaiah is strengthened by the words περὶ πολλῶν,
     perhaps recalling the clause later in Isa 53:12 that say, "he bore the sin of
     many" (LXX: πολλῶν). If we hear this third echo, it would have the effect of
     emphasizing still further the vicarious effect of Jesus' suffering and death as
     part of the covenant-sealing act. But the echo remains faint.

86   There are a number of important—though not the most reliable—ancient
     manuscripts that include "new" (καινῆς) before "covenant" in Matt 26:28.
     Although probably an assimilation to Luke 22:20, the textual variant none-
     theless points us in the right direction, viz., to Jeremiah's new covenant lan-
     guage (Jer 31:31; see Metzger, *Textual Commentary*, 54). Moreover, Matthew,
     unlike Mark and Luke, makes explicit the connection between the (new)

covenant and "the forgiveness of sins," thereby evoking further the new covenant language of Jer 31 (Matt 26:28; Jer 31:43).

87 Catherine Sider Hamilton, "'His Blood Be Upon Us': Innocent Blood and the Death of Jesus in Matthew," *CBQ* 70 (2008): 82–100; T. B. Cargal, "'His Blood Be Upon Us and Upon Our Children': A Matthean Double Entendre?" *NTS* 37 (1991): 101–12.

88 For a concise survey of the extensive allusions to Scripture in Matthew's passion narrative, see Senior, "Lure," 108–14.

89 See, as possible evidence for this, his highly uncomplimentary characterization of the false account of the empty tomb that "is still told among the Jews to this day" (28:15). But even here, the false story is the responsibility of the chief priests and elders, who conspire to mislead the people by devising a conspiracy to cover up the truth. If the people are deceived about the empty tomb, it is not so much their own fault as the fault of the bad shepherds.

90 Sanders, *Jesus and Judaism*, 103–4. Sanders is concerned to argue that Matt 19:28 is an authentic saying of the Jesus of history and that it provides insight into his proclamation of Jewish restoration eschatology. I find Sanders' argument persuasive, but my point here is the relatively simpler and more certain one that, whatever may have been true of Jesus of Nazareth, *Matthew* was certainly expecting such a restoration. See also the insightful discussion in Bockmuehl, *Seeing the Word*, 189–228, esp. 211–28.

91 This statement represents a change of position from the interpretation that I put forward earlier in *Moral Vision*, 423–24.

92 Again, see Levine, *Social and Ethnic Dimensions*, 206–15; cf. Bockmuehl, *Seeing the Word*, 218–19.

93 On Jesus' obedience as a key theme in Matthew, see Dale C. Allison Jr., "The Embodiment of God's Will: Jesus in Matthew," in Gaventa and Hays, *Seeking the Identity of Jesus*, 117–32.

94 A recent study by Leroy Huizenga (*New Isaac*) contends that this allusion is part of a larger Matthean typology linking Jesus with Isaac: Jesus is the obedient son who takes the role of atoning sacrifice but nonetheless subsequently becomes the heir who embodies God's promise.

95 See Joel Marcus, "The Old Testament and the Death of Jesus: The Role of Scripture in the Gospel Passion Narratives," in *The Death of Jesus in Early Christianity* (ed. John T. Carroll et al.; Peabody, Mass.: Hendrickson, 1995), 226–27.

96 David M. Moffitt, "Righteous Bloodshed, Matthew's Passion Narrative, and the Temple's Destruction: Lamentations as a Matthean Intertext," *JBL* 125 (2006): 299–320. On Matt 27:39 and Lam 2:15, see esp. 310–12.

97 See Matthew Black, "The Throne-theophany Prophetic Commission and the 'Son of Man': A Study in Tradition-History," in *Jews, Greeks and Christians: Religious Cultures in Late Antiquity: Essays in Honor of William David Davies* (ed. Robert Hamerton-Kelly and Robin Scroggs; Leiden: Brill, 1976), 57–73.

98   As Dale Allison summarizes, "Jesus is the Moses-like Messiah who proclaims the eschatological will of God on a mountain typologically equated with Sinai" (*New Moses*, 185).

99   For a summary of the evidence and a skeptical conclusion, see Allison, *New Moses*, 293–98.

100   Allison, *New Moses*, 264.

101   This brief sketch has highlighted only a few of the most striking ways in which Matthew develops his portrait of Jesus through overlaying Jesus-traditions on Mosaic prototypes. Allison's learned study traces out many more intriguing correspondences beyond the ones mentioned here. Not every example is equally persuasive, but cumulatively the weight of evidence is compelling. Of course, this is not to say that the Moses typology comprehensively explains Matthew's interpretation of Jesus. There is far more to say about Jesus than can be expressed in any one scriptural correspondence. Allison's summary judgment provides a balanced assessment: "The Moses typology is no more the trunk of Matthew's christology than it is only a distal twig. It is somewhere in between: I should liken it to a main branch" (*New Moses*, 268).

102   Verse numbering in the MT differs slightly from the NRSV. The citation is actually a loose paraphrase of the Micah passage, not agreeing in detail with either the MT or the LXX. Micah's prophecy identifies Bethlehem of Ephrathah as "one of the little clans of Judah," but Matthew transforms this into "*by no means least* among the *rulers* of Judah.*" Also, while the prophecy does refer to a ruler who is to shepherd his flock, the sentence in Micah does not explicitly describe the flock as "my people Israel," though there is a reference to the "sons of Israel" in the previous verse. On the textual complexities of this passage, see Menken, *Matthew's Bible*, 255–63.

103   For a helpful survey of critical discussion on the question of Jewish traditions that understood Solomon, the Son of David, as an exorcist, see Duling, "Solomon," 235–52.

104   For the whole story, see 2 Sam 5:6-10. It is sometimes suggested that this (proverbial?) prohibition of the blind and the lame from the temple refers to Lev 21:16-24, but this reference is not really apposite, for the Leviticus passage is concerned explicitly with restrictions on the selection of *priests* who are allowed to approach the altar to make offerings. It is not a general ban intended to keep unfortunate lame and blind persons out of the temple. (Rightly observed by Luz, *Matthew*, 3:13n78.) The whole passage in 2 Sam 5:6-10 is full of difficult problems for interpretation. For further discussion, see S. R. Driver, *Notes on the Hebrew Text and the Topography of the Books of Samuel: With an Introduction on Hebrew Palaeography and the Ancient Versions and Facsimiles of Inscriptions and Maps* (Oxford: Clarendon, 1960), 258–62; A. A. Anderson, *2 Samuel* (WBC; Dallas, Tex.: Word Books, 1989), 79–88.

105   4Q521 2.ii.1, 5–8, 11–13, as translated in Collins, *Scepter and the Star*, 117.

106   See Florentino García Martínez, "Messianic Hopes in the Qumran Writings," in *The People of the Dead Sea Scrolls: Their Writings, Beliefs, and Practices*

(ed. Florentino García Martínez and Julio Trebolle Barrera; trans. Wilfred G. E. Watson; Leiden: E. J. Brill, 1993), 168.

107 Rightly noted by Collins, *Scepter and the Star*, 118. For the full text of the Eighteen Benedictions, see David Instone-Brewer, "The Eighteen Benedictions and the Minim Before 70 CE," *JTS* 54 (2003) 25–44.

108 It is well known that here Matthew silently corrects a Markan mistake by omitting Mark's phrase "when Abiathar was high priest" (Mark 2:26).

109 E.g., Matthew explicitly identifies the interlocutors as a group of Pharisees; Jesus frames the debate by prompting the Pharisees to answer the question "whose son is he?" and places the answer ("of David") in their mouths; Matthew frames the quotation of Ps 110:1 with two affirmations that "David calls (καλεῖ) him Lord." For Matthew, the pericope also is placed as the conclusion of the controversies in the temple, and it leads directly into the extended prophetic denunciation of the scribes and Pharisees in Matt 23.

110 See Menken, *Matthew's Bible*, 105–16.

111 Menken (*Matthew's Bible*, 108–9) offers a different explanation for the editorial substitution of Isa 62:11: because the city of Jerusalem is depicted as hostile to Jesus, the acclamation of the "crowds" (as distinguished from the "city") in Matt 21:9 must be understood not as a word of *consolation* to Jerusalem (as in Zech 9:9) but as an *announcement* that the city is being commanded to acknowledge Jesus as the messianic king. Therefore, the wording of Isa 62:11 is more appropriate to Matthew's narrative context than the wording of Zechariah. Even if this explanation be accepted, it overlooks the metaleptic impact of drawing Isa 62:11 into conjunction with Jesus' entry into the city. Matthew's interweaving of two texts can produce multiple simultaneous literary effects.

112 So also Menken, *Matthew's Bible*, 110.

113 For the most thorough attempt to develop this interpretation in a full-length commentary, see Witherington, *Matthew*.

114 M. Jack Suggs, *Wisdom, Christology, and Law in Matthew's Gospel* (Cambridge, Mass.: Harvard University Press, 1970). Well before Suggs' work, it had been observed that there was a parallel between this distinctively Matthean *Heilandsruf* and the wisdom tradition, esp. Sir 51:23-27 (cf. also Sir 6:28). Recognition of the parallel goes back at least to D. F. Strauss (see H. D. Betz, "The Logion of the Easy Yoke and of Rest [Matt 11:28-30]," *JBL* 86 [1967]: 10–24).

115 Helmut Koester and James M. Robinson, *Trajectories through Early Christianity* (Philadelphia: Fortress, 1971). Of course, this linkage of Jesus with a feminine divine hypostasis has proven irresistible to feminist theologians and biblical scholars (e.g., Elisabeth Schüssler Fiorenza, *Jesus: Miriam's Child, Sophia's Prophet: Critical Issues in Feminist Christology* [New York: Continuum, 1994]). Even among scholars who do not subscribe to the Robinson-Koester model of early doctrinal development or espouse feminist projects of christological reconstruction, the interpretation of Matt 11:28-30 in terms of wisdom Christology has proven widely influential (e.g., Ben Witherington III,

Jesus the Sage: The Pilgrimage of Wisdom [Minneapolis: Fortress, 1994], 205–8; his views are further developed in his Matthew commentary [Witherington, *Matthew*, 239–40]; see also Celia Deutsch, *Hidden Wisdom and the Easy Yoke: Wisdom, Torah, and Discipleship in Matthew 11.25–30* [Sheffield: JSOT Press, 1987]).

116   Davies and Allison, *Matthew* 2:287–93. For other interpretations that minimize the construct of wisdom Christology, see also Luz, *Matthew* 2:172; Gathercole, *Pre-existent Son*, 119–23.

117   The strongest challenge was posed by Stanton, *Gospel for a New People*, 368–70. See also Grant Macaskill, *Revealed Wisdom and Inaugurated Eschatology in Ancient Judaism and Early Christianity* (JSOTSup 115; Leiden: Brill, 2007), 144–52; see also the often-overlooked work by Frances Taylor Gench, *Wisdom in the Christology of Matthew* (Lanham, Md.: University Press of America, 1997).

118   As is often noted, Matthew may create a subtle linkage between "the works of the Christ" in 11:2 (τὰ ἔργα τοῦ Χριστοῦ) and the "works of Wisdom" in 11:19 (καὶ ἐδικαιώθη ἡ σοφία ἀπὸ τῶν ἔργων αὐτῆς). Compare the rather different phraseology in Luke's version (7:18, 35).

119   This perspective comes into view only when we read Matthew as a continuous narrative, rather than form-critically isolating 11:25-30 from its narrative context, as is so often done in New Testament criticism.

120   The phrase in Matthew corresponds exactly to the Hebrew wording attested in the MT: ומצאו מרגוע לנפשכם. The LXX, oddly, reads, "you will find *purification* for your souls" (εὑρήσετε ἁγνισμὸν ταῖς ψυχαῖς ὑμῶν). While Davies and Allison (*Matthew*, 2:272) suggest that "the promise of rest in Matt 11:28 is modeled upon Exod 33:14," the wording of that passage is not even remotely as close to Matt 11:28 as is Jer 6:16.

121   Macaskill (*Revealed Wisdom and Inaugurated Eschatology*, 145) speaks of "an inversion of Wisdom thinking" and points out the strongly apocalyptic character of the claim that God has hidden the truth from "the wise and learned" (11:25) and revealed it to an elect group.

122   Therefore, Graham Stanton is quite right to question whether Jesus' words are in fact "comfortable" (*Gospel for a New People*, 373–77).

123   The paucity of such references in the New Testament as a whole was noted forcefully by Hooker, *Jesus and the Servant*. For additional comment on the absence of the Servant from Matthew's narrative, see now Huizenga, *New Isaac*, 189–208.

124   The idea of a cycle of "Servant Songs" in Isaiah that would link this passage to Isa 53 is a modern critical construction; ancient evidence for such readings of Isaiah appears to be lacking.

125   For exposition of a similar phenomenon in the Pauline letters, see Richard B. Hays, "Christ Prays the Psalms: Israel's Psalter as Matrix of Early Christology," in *Conversion of the Imagination*, 101–18.

126   For a detailed study of this aspect of Matthean Christology, see David D. Kupp, *Matthew's Emmanuel: Divine Presence and God's People in the First*

Gospel (SNTSMS 90; Cambridge: Cambridge University Press, 1996), 49–108.

127 This makes particularly good sense if the promised child is understood as a son of Ahaz who will signify the continuation of the Davidic dynasty. For this interpretation, see, e.g., Hans Wildberger, *Isaiah: A Continental Commentary* (trans. Thomas H. Trapp; Continental Commentaries; Minneapolis: Fortress, 1991 [c2002]), 306–14; Stuart A. Irvine, *Isaiah, Ahaz, and the Syro-Ephraimitic Crisis* (SBLDS 123; Atlanta: Scholars Press, 1990), 159–71. For the alternative view that the child will be a son of the prophet himself, see R. E. Clements, *Isaiah 1–39* (NCBC; Grand Rapids: Eerdmans, 1980), 85–88.

128 See Warren Carter, "Evoking Isaiah: Matthean Soteriology and an Intertextual Reading of Isaiah 7–9 and Matthew 1:23 and 4:15–16," *JBL* 119 (2000): 503–20. As Warren Carter asks and then answers, "How, then, does evoking and elaborating the Isaianic context help the Gospel's audience? His name [Emmanuel] is double-edged, promising salvation from imperial power, but also delivering judgment if God's action is rejected."

129 See Larry W. Hurtado, *Lord Jesus Christ: Devotion to Jesus in Earliest Christianity* (Grand Rapids: Eerdmans, 2003), 338.

130 On the various possible uses of προσκυνεῖν, see Larry W. Hurtado, "The Binitarian Shape of Early Christian Worship," in *The Jewish Roots of Christological Monotheism: Papers from the St. Andrews Conference on the Historical Origins of the Worship of Jesus* (ed. Carey C. Newman et al.; Leiden: Brill, 1999), 187–213.

131 For a full treatment of προσκυνεῖν in Matthew, see now Joshua E. Leim, *Matthew's Theological Grammar: The Father and The Son* (WUNT 2/402; Tübingen: Mohr Siebeck, 2015); idem, "Worshiping the Father, Worshiping the Son: Cultic Language and the Identity of God in the Gospel of Matthew," *JTI* 9 (2015): 65–84. Leim reaches conclusions very similar to those I have argued here.

132 The inference that Jesus is the "something greater" is strongly reinforced by the closely analogous assertions later in the same chapter that Jesus (along with his message?) is something greater than either Jonah or Solomon (Matt 12:41-42).

133 Jesus' presence as supplanting the temple as the locus of God's presence is explored extensively by Kupp, *Matthew's Emmanuel*, 224–28.

134 For a full discussion, see Joseph Sievers, "'Where Two or Three . . .': The Rabbinic Concept of Shekhinah and Matthew 18:20," in *The Jewish Roots of Christian Liturgy* (ed. Eugene J. Fisher; New York: Paulist, 1990), 47–61.

135 For further discussion, see Kupp, *Matthew's Emmanuel*, 192–96. Without arguing for any literary dependence on *m.Aboth* 3:2, Kupp suggests that the correspondence between the rabbinic saying and Matt 18:20 demonstrates a concern about God's presence that predates the Matthean saying. Davies and Allison (*Matthew*, 2:790) argue that the rabbinic parallels of Matt 18:20 were produced independent from the early Christian tradition. Above all, see Segal, *Two Powers in Heaven*.

136 Kupp, *Matthew's Emmanuel*, 139.

137 Key parallels between Matthew and the LXX text are noted where appropriate.

138 Kupp, *Matthew's Emmanuel*, 226–27.

139 The notion that the magi were "kings" comes not from Matthew but from this intertextual collocation with Isaiah. See esp. Isa 60:3: "Nations shall come to your light, and kings to the brightness of your dawn."

140 The MT reads הֹלְכִים (LXX: πορευόμενος). On Matthew's different text (καθήμενος), see Stendahl, *School of St. Matthew*, 105; Davies and Allison, *Critical and Exegetical Commentary*, 1:385; Menken, *Matthew's Bible*, 15–19.

141 This expression does *not* signify that Galilee was predominantly Gentile in population and culture in Matthew's time. On this question, see Mark A. Chancey, *The Myth of a Gentile Galilee* (SNTSMS 118; Cambridge: Cambridge University Press, 2002). Warren Carter suggests that the construction "Galilee of the Gentiles" is a genitive of possession and means that Galilee is under the rule of Gentiles ("Evoking Isaiah," 516–17). This is certainly a possible reading of the phrase. But in view of the link that Matthew elsewhere makes between the rising of the light and the Gentile mission, it seems preferable to understand 4:16 in similar terms.

142 See also the closely related Servant passage in Isa 49:6: "It is too light a thing that you should be my servant to raise up the tribes of Jacob and to restore the survivors of Israel; I will give you as a light to the nations, that my salvation may reach to the end of the earth." Matthew does not quote this text, but in view of his interest in Isaiah and explicit citation of Isa 42 later in Matt 12, it can hardly be far from his field of vision.

143 The link between Matt 4:16 and the visit of the magi is strengthened by the fact that Matthew repeats ἀνατολή three times in the latter passage (2:1, 2, 9).

144 Interestingly, Luz (*Matthew*, 195) cites Christian traditions of interpretation that parse Isa 9:1 as referring separately in its two clauses to Jews (the people sitting in darkness) and to Gentiles (those who are sitting in the land and shadow of death). This is a distinctly different approach from the reading I have offered here, in which *both* phrases designate the original Jewish beneficiaries of Jesus' revelation and, at the same time, *both* phrases metaphorically point forward to the inclusion of Gentile converts.

145 Davies and Allison, *Matthew*, 1:385.

146 This is a good example of the way in which recurrence of references to a text can enhance our confidence about the discernment of other echoes of passages found prominently in the same context. Matthew 12:15-21 proves unmistakably that the Evangelist was interested in Isa 42 and saw in it a significant prefiguration of the events he narrates in his Gospel.

147 See, e.g., Richard Beaton, *Isaiah's Christ in Matthew's Gospel* (SNTSMS 123; Cambridge: Cambridge University Press, 2002), 194: "On a linear, or narrative, level the citation seems to validate Jesus' withdrawal, command to secrecy and/or the healings, all of which occur in the preceding narrative of Matt 12:14-16. As was observed, however, this level of reference cannot

account for the copious amount of superfluous content in this extended quotation. . . . Matthew, a careful but creative redactor/author, appears to have intentionally included the extra content to buttress his portrait of Jesus." See also Menken, *Matthew's Bible*, 51–65.

148 Menken (*Matthew's Bible*, 80) observes that this minor difference is probably a Matthean stylistic correction: "The use of ἐλπίζειν with the prepositions ἐπί, εἰς and ἐν is unusual or rare in Greek, which normally has the dative to indicate the basis of hope."

149 Rightly suggested by Beaton, *Isaiah's Christ*, 153: "As Jesus ('he will save his people from their sins') and Emmanuel ('God with us') are the only names explicitly given to Jesus in Matthew, an alert reader should have remembered these names from early on."

150 Beaton, *Isaiah's Christ*, 195–96.

151 One might also note that the very next person to identify Jesus as the "son of David" after the crowd's question in 12:23 (μήτι οὗτός ἐστιν ὁ υἱὸς Δαυίδ;) is the *Canaanite* woman (15:22). She may proleptically fulfill the vision of Isa 42:4 cited in Matt 12:21.

152 Luke's editorial placement of a similar logion in Luke 13:28-29 lacks the reference to "sons of the kingdom" and makes it far less clear that the people who come from all directions to eat in the kingdom of God will be Gentiles. Luke's narrative shaping of the material may reflect his compositional intention to reserve the message of Gentile inclusion for the second volume of his work, rather than attributing it to Jesus' preresurrection teachings.

153 Interestingly, Matthew uses two different verbs: ἄνδρες Νινευῖται ἀναστήσονται . . . βασίλισσα νότου ἐγερθήσεται. Both verbs are of course used in the New Testament in reference to resurrection, but the latter, a passive form, makes the reference especially clear.

154 There is longstanding dispute about whether the passage concerns only the judgment of Gentile nations or whether "all the nations" should be taken to include Israel as well. This question is closely tied to the question of whether "the least of these my brothers" in the text refers only to Jesus' followers or to the needy of the world more generally. For literature on this question, see Luz, *Matthew*, 3:279–82. We need not resolve these issues in order to make the point being developed here: on any reading, Gentiles are included in the group being judged, and the distinction between "sheep" and "goats" seems to have nothing to do with Israelite vs. non-Israelite identity.

155 Another parallel is that in Dan 7:14 the nations are said to "serve/worship" (λατρεύουσα) the Son of Man. Conceptually, this resembles the disciples' action in 28:17: they "worship" (προσεκύνησαν) the risen Jesus who now has all authority (28:18).

156 This reading is considered but rejected by Terence L. Donaldson (*Jesus on the Mountain: A Study in Matthean Theology* [JSNTSup 8; Sheffield: JSOT Press, 1985], 176–78: ". . . while Matthew may have made some use of Danielic language, he did not intend his closing pericope to be a fulfillment of Dan 7.13f, so that the Daniel passage was not the controlling factor in its construction. . . .

So while Dan 7.13f may have had some influence on Matthew's choice of vocabulary in 28.16-20, it is of no real help in discovering the theological core of the passage. And what is true of Dan 7.13 is true of other suggested Old Testament texts as well. No single Old Testament passage has yet been found which provides a unifying principle for all features of 28.16-20" (177). This passage, published thirty years ago, interestingly illustrates the distance our discipline has moved in the intervening time. Methodologically, Donaldson is looking for a source that explains or controls the Matthean passage. But an intertextual methodology asks the very different question of how Matthew is creatively reconfiguring the Old Testament language, and what effects the reconfiguration achieves.

157   We might add to this list the Canaanite woman (15:21-28), though her story is strikingly lacking in scriptural echoes or antecedents.

158   For a detailed analysis of an analogous narrative technique in Pseudo-Philo's *Liber Antiquitatum Biblicarum*, see Bruce N. Fisk, *Do You Not Remember? Scripture Story, and Exegesis in the Rewritten Bible of Pseudo-Philo* (JSPSup 37; Sheffield: Sheffield Academic, 2001).

159   A similar citation technique may be found in Matt 3:17 and 17:5, where the words spoken by the heavenly voice at Jesus' Baptism and transfiguration seem to combine echoes of Gen 22:2, 12; Ps 2:7; and Isa 42:11. A related but distinguishable phenomenon appears in Matt 26:28, where the single phrase "my blood of the covenant" evokes hermeneutically significant echoes of two different scriptural intertexts: Exod 24:8 and Zech 9:11.

Chapter 3: Luke

1   Nils Alstrup Dahl, *Jesus in the Memory of the Early Church* (Minneapolis: Augsburg, 1976), 84.

2   The name Θεόφιλος means "Godlover," or "friend of God." For discussion, see Joseph A. Fitzmyer, *The Gospel according to Luke: Introduction, Translation, and Notes* (2 vols.; AB 28–28A; Garden City, N.Y.: Doubleday, 1981–1985), 1:299–300.

3   Kenneth Duncan Litwak (*Echoes of Scripture in Luke–Acts: Telling the History of God's People Intertextually* [JSNTSup 285; London: T&T Clark, 2005]) rightly emphasizes the ecclesiological dimensions of Luke's scriptural allusions. His study, however, sometimes argues in an unnecessarily one-sided manner against interpreters who have focused on christological themes in Luke–Acts.

4   Exceptions: Luke 2:23-24, 3:4-6.

5   Robert L. Brawley, *Text to Text Pours Forth Speech: Voices of Scripture in Luke–Acts* (Bloomington: Indiana University Press, 1995), 3.

6   For different ways of construing the way Luke's "fulfillment" language works, see Rebecca I. Denova, *The Things Accomplished among Us: Prophetic Tradition in the Structural Pattern of Luke–Acts* (JSNTSup 141; Sheffield:

Sheffield Academic, 1997); and Darrell L. Bock, *Proclamation from Prophecy and Pattern: Lucan Old Testament Christology* (JSNTSup 12; Sheffield: JSOT Press, 1987).

7 C. Kavin Rowe, "History, Hermeneutics, and the Unity of Luke–Acts," *JSNT* 28 (2005): 131–57. See also the responses by Luke Timothy Johnson, "Literary Criticism of Luke–Acts: Is Reception-History Pertinent?" *JSNT* 28 (2005): 159–62; and Markus Bockmuehl, "Why Not Let Acts Be Acts? In Conversation with C. Kavin Rowe," *JSNT* 28 (2005): 163–66. "Luke–Acts" as a unified literary work is an interpretative convention of modernity. For recent discussion from a variety of perspectives see the essays in Andrew F. Gregory and C. Kavin Rowe, eds., *Rethinking the Unity and Reception of Luke and Acts* (Columbia: University of South Carolina Press, 2010).

8 For a detailed treatment of this theme, see Mark Strauss, *The Davidic Messiah in Luke–Acts: The Promise and Its Fulfillment in Lukan Christology* (JSNTSup 110; Sheffield: Sheffield Academic, 1995), 76–129.

9 This description of the reader refers, of course, to the "ideal reader" of the text. To the extent that Luke's actual audiences did not have such knowledge as part of their cultural repertoire, it would have been the task of preachers and teachers in the early communities that read this Gospel to explicate the text by filling in whatever background was necessary.

10 That this passage was read as a messianic text by at least some non-Christian Jews is confirmed by the discovery among the Dead Sea Scrolls of a fragmentary anthology of messianic texts, 4Q174 (also known as 4QFlorilegium): "*The Lord declares to you that He will build you a House* (2 Sam. vii, 11c). *I will raise up your seed after you* (2 Sam. vii, 12). *I will establish the throne of his kingdom [for ever]* (2 Sam. vii, 13). *[I will be] his father and he shall be my son* (2 Sam. vii, 14). He is the Branch of David who shall arise with the Interpreter of the law [to rule] in Zion [at the end] of time. As it is written, *I will raise up the tent of David that is fallen* (Amos ix, 11). That is to say, the fallen *tent of David* is he who shall arise to save Israel" (4QFlor 1.10–13, cited in Geza Vermes, *The Dead Sea Scrolls in English* [4th ed.; Sheffield: Sheffield Academic, 1995], 354).

11 David W. Pao and Eckhard J. Schnabel, "Luke," in *Commentary on the New Testament Use of the Old Testament* (ed. G. K. Beale and D. A. Carson; Grand Rapids: Baker Academic, 2007), 255.

12 For detailed discussion of Hannah's song and other Old Testament texts as background to Mary's song, see Ulrike Mittmann-Richert, *Magnifikat und Benediktus: Die Ältesten Zeugnisse der Judenchristlichen Tradition von der Geburt Des Messias* (WUNT 2/90; Tübingen: Mohr Siebeck, 1996), 7–28.

13 Cf. Luke 1:69: καὶ ἤγειρεν κέρας σωτηρίας ἡμῖν ἐν οἴκῳ Δαυὶδ παιδὸς αὐτοῦ.

14 For a detailed study, see Marianne Grohmann, "Psalm 113 and the Song of Hannah (1 Samuel 2:1-10): A Paradigm for Intertextual Reading?" in Hays, Alkier, and Huizenga, *Reading the Bible Intertextually*, 119–35.

15 Nils Alstrup Dahl, "Story of Abraham in Luke–Acts," in *Jesus in the Memory of the Early Church*, 66–86.

16 The *topos* of God's providing sons for previously barren women—for whom Sarah is the archetype—is repeated numerous times in Israel's canonical stories: Rebekah, Rachel, Hannah, and the unnamed mother of Samson all exemplify the pattern. For extended discussion, see Mary Callaway, *Sing, O Barren One: A Study in Comparative Midrash* (SBLDS 91; Atlanta: Scholars Press, 1986). Elizabeth's glad words in Luke 1:25 closely echo the declaration of Rachel in Gen 30:23 LXX: ἀφεῖλεν ὁ θεός μου τὸ ὄνειδος ("God has taken away my reproach").

17 Pao and Schnabel, "Luke," in Beale and Carson, *Commentary*, 257. For a full discussion, see David W. Pao, *Acts and the Isaianic New Exodus* (WUNT 2/130; Tübingen: Mohr Siebeck, 2000), 217–48.

18 Joel Green, "The Problem of a Beginning: Israel's Scriptures in Luke 1–2," *BBR* 4 (1994): 61–85.

19 In Hans Conzelmann, *Die Mitte der Zeit: Studien Zur Theologie Des Lukas* (BHT 17; Tübingen: Mohr Siebeck, 1954; ET: *The Theology of St. Luke* [trans. Geoffrey Buswell; New York: Harper, 1961]), for example, these opening chapters of Luke's Gospel hardly appear at all, and they are given no significant place in determining the contours of Lukan theology. Consider, for example, the following observation from Conzelmann's widely influential study: "Im Gegensatz zum Tempel werden bestimmte Gestalten und Ereignisse der alttestamentlichen Geschichte *nicht* in die historische Reflexion einbezogen. Dass Abraham bei Lukas stärker hervortritt als bei Mc ist durch die Vorlagen bedingt" (143).

20 As correctly observed by Dietrich Rusam, *Das Alte Testament bei Lukas* (BZNW 112; Berlin: De Gruyter, 2003), 40–89. Rusam writes, "Die beiden ersten Kapitel des Lk Doppelwerks haben—literarisch gesehen—dabei Brückenfunktion: Sie gehören zur Heilsgeschichte und stellen zugleich die Verbindung her zwischen der voraufgegangenen und der nachfolgend geschilderten Heilsgeschichte" (88).

21 The close verbal similarities between the passages are more apparent in the Greek than in many English translations.

22 It is widely recognized that Luke gives the reader a strong prompt to read the story of Jesus in typological correspondence to the story of Israel's exodus. For a study of a similar use of "new exodus" typology also in Luke's second volume, see Pao, *Acts and the Isaianic New Exodus.*

23 I say this despite my respect for the work of David P. Moessner, *Lord of the Banquet: The Literary and Theological Significance of the Lukan Travel Narrative* (Minneapolis: Fortress, 1989), who seeks to demonstrate a comprehensive pattern of correspondence between Luke's "travel narrative" material and the narrative sequence of Deuteronomy.

24 On these intertextual links, see Thomas L. Brodie, *The Crucial Bridge: The Elijah-Elisha Narrative as an Interpretive Synthesis of Genesis-Kings and a Literary Model for the Gospels* (Collegeville, Minn.: Liturgical, 2000); idem, "Towards Unravelling Luke's Use of the Old Testament: Luke 7:11–17 as an Imitatio of 1 Kings 17:17–24," *NTS* 32 (1986): 247–67. Unfortunately, the same

judgment that applies to Moessner's work on Deuteronomic correspondences applies to Brodie's arguments: it seems to me that he presses too hard to privilege a single intertextual precursor as the "explanation" for Luke's narrative.

25 On the rhetorical figure of dissimile and its effects, see Hays, *Echoes of Scripture in the Letters of Paul*, 140–42. The aptness of the category to Luke's implicit contrast between Jesus and Elijah may be illustrated by recalling George deForest Lord's description of its effects in *Paradise Lost*: dissimile is "a trope developed from Homer in which characters and places, often of exotic and legendary power, are invoked only to be discarded as false or inferior by comparison with Milton's true mythical vision" (*Classical Presences in Seventeenth-Century English Poetry* [New Haven: Yale University Press, 1987], 40). Luke's rhetorical strategy differs from Milton's, however, in that the contrast is implicit rather than explicit: he does not directly state that Jesus is "not like Elijah."

26 On the "volume" of intertextual echoes, see Hays, *Conversion of the Imagination*, 36–37.

27 Christian readers might consider, by way of comparison, how a simple phrase such as "swaddling clothes" would automatically evoke recollection of Luke's nativity story.

28 It might be asked whether this passage reflects a specifically Lukan theology, or whether it simply preserves a historical tradition about the teaching of Jesus. Despite the fact that this passage is not multiply attested, I would be inclined to think that it very likely does preserve authentic Jesus-tradition. Nonetheless, the question of the historical origin of the material is not really pertinent for the present analysis. The fact is that the material appears only in Luke's Gospel, and it clearly furthers his compositional purposes: it coheres with Luke's literary emphasis on Jesus' liberating activity as a continuation of the biblical story.

29 Bob Dylan interprets this aspect of the Gospel narrative well: the reason why "the first ones now will later be last" is because "the times, they are a-changin'."

30 Again, Luke 14:7-11 consists of special Lukan material, not paralleled in Mark or Matthew.

31 The standard commentaries do not usually discuss this phrase. See, for example, Fitzmyer, *Luke*, 2:1132; I. Howard Marshall, *The Gospel of Luke: A Commentary on the Greek Text* (NIGTC; Grand Rapids: Eerdmans, 1978), 636.

32 The only other instance appears in Luke 3:3-6.

33 This small narrative detail illustrates the way in which close attention to Old Testament precursor texts can yield theologically provocative results. If Luke identifies Jesus as Israel's Lord, how are we to assess theologically the significance of his birth and upbringing in a *poor* family (cf. 2 Cor 8:9)? The christological and ethical implications are considerable, but our recognition of them depends on recovering Luke's allusion to Lev 12:8.

34 It should be noted also that in Acts, Luke portrays Paul in a similar light as a devoutly observant Jew—indeed, as one who undertakes a Nazirite vow

(Acts 16:3, 18:18, and esp. 21:20-26). Jacob Jervell, *The Unknown Paul: Essays on Luke–Acts and Early Christian History* (Minneapolis: Augsburg, 1984), 68–76, esp. 71.

35 This is a piece of triple-tradition material, which Luke preserves intact from his Markan source (Mark 1:44). While the pericope is not distinctively Lukan, it meshes smoothly with Luke's interest in Jesus' harmonious obedience to Torah.

36 Crispin H. T. Fletcher-Louis, "Jesus Inspects His Priestly War Party (Luke 14:25-35)," in *The Old Testament in the New Testament: Essays in Honour of J.L. North* (ed. Steve Moyise; JSNT 189; Sheffield: Sheffield Academic, 2000), 126–43, esp. 138–40.

37 The omission of the verse in some manuscripts is readily explicable as a later Christian editorial revision after the hardening of the division between church and synagogue. On balance, 23:34 should be understood as part of the original form of Luke's story. See Eldon Jay Epp, "The 'Ignorance Motif' in Acts and Anti-Judaic Tendencies in Codex Bezae," *HTR* 55 (1962): 51–62; Nathan Eubank, "A Disconcerting Prayer: On the Originality of Luke 23:34a," *JBL* 129 (2010): 521–36. Jesus' appeal for forgiveness on the ground of ignorance is thoroughly consistent with Luke's overall narrative and theological program (cf. Luke Timothy Johnson, *The Gospel of Luke* [SP 3; Collegeville, Minn.: Liturgical, 1991], 376).

38 On this narrative detail, Luke also stands in agreement with Mark and Matthew.

39 Beverly Roberts Gaventa, *The Acts of the Apostles* (ANTC; Nashville: Abingdon, 2003); idem, "Learning and Relearning the Identity of Jesus from Luke–Acts," in Gaventa and Hays, *Seeking the Identity of Jesus*, 148–65.

40 Rather than "Be merciful, just as your Father is merciful," Matt 5:48 reads, "You will be perfect (τέλειοι), just as your heavenly Father is perfect (τέλειος)," echoing a different confluence of Old Testament precursors, Deut 18:13 and Lev 19:2. It is speculative to ask whether Luke knew Matthew's version of this saying or vice versa. It is equally difficult to determine whether one or the other is closer to what Jesus actually taught. It is far more fruitful to explore the way in which the two different forms of the saying draw upon different Old Testament sources and suggest, within the context of the Gospel in which they appear, interestingly different visions of discipleship and of the character of God.

41 Interestingly, the Vulgate renders it with *benignus*, suggesting the same shade of meaning to which I am drawing attention here.

42 See, e.g., Neh 9:17; Ps 86:15 (85:15 LXX), 103:8 (102:8 LXX), 111:4 (110:4 LXX); Joel 2:13; Jonah 4:2; Sir 2:11; cf. similar formulations in Deut 4:31; 2 Chr 30:9; Neh 9:31; Ps 78:38 (77:38 LXX); and Jas 1:5.

43 Anderson, "Exodus Typology in Second Isaiah," 177–95.

44 This is a good example of Luke's general preference for placing Old Testament citations in the mouths of his characters.

45 For a concise examination of the textual issues, see Pao, *Acts and the Isaianic New Exodus*, 38–39.

46 Pao, *Acts and the Isaianic New Exodus*, 37–69.

47 Rightly noted by Pao (*Acts and the Isaianic New Exodus*, 40), who observes also that in Luke–Acts "the neuter form of the noun σωτήριον" appears only in Luke 2:30, 3:5, and Acts 28:28, thus strengthening the connection between these passages. (Elsewhere Luke prefers the feminine σωτηρία, which appears ten times in Luke–Acts.) The neuter σωτήριον appears only one other time in the New Testament, in Eph 6:17, where it also occurs in an allusion to Isaiah (Isa 59:17).

48 On the phenomenon of *Vorklang*, see Hollander, *Figure of Echo*, 50, 100.

49 The reading "awaiting redemption *in* Jerusalem," found in a large number of manuscripts (A D L Θ Ψ 0130 *f*¹³ 33 M syʰ), probably represents a later stage of transmission of the tradition in which Christian scribes, knowing that Jerusalem has been destroyed, no longer expect the redemption of the city or its people. On the other hand, the reading "awaiting the redemption *of* Jerusalem" (found in ℵ B W Ξ 1. 565* lat syˢ·ᵖ co, and attested in the Latin text of Irenaeus) reflects an earlier stage of the tradition, and it is consistent with Luke's own eschatological perspective.

50 Pao (*Acts and the Isaianic New Exodus*, 84–86) perceptively suggests that in Luke 24:46-47 the unexplained reference to scriptural warrant for proclamation to all nations should be understood, in light of Acts 1:8 and 13:47, as a specific allusion to Isa 49:6. I would suggest, however, that the absence of a specific textual reference suggests that Luke is thinking not of a single verse but more broadly of Isaiah 40–66 as a whole, read as a prophetic anticipation of the extension of God's salvation to the world.

51 Richard D. Nelson, *Deuteronomy: A Commentary* (OTL; Louisville, Ky.: Westminster John Knox, 2002), 235; Duane L. Christensen, *Deuteronomy* (WBC 6, rev.; Nashville: Thomas Nelson, 2001), 409.

52 Peter's announcement recapitulates what Jesus had told the disciples at the end of Luke's Gospel, esp. Luke 24:47, 49. Indeed, the whole sermon in Acts 2 can be read as an expansion and elaboration of Luke 24:44-49.

53 On the narrative function of "incomplete closure" in Luke and Acts, see Mikeal C. Parsons, "Narrative Closure and Openness in the Plot of the Third Gospel: The Sense of an Ending in Luke 24:50–53," in *SBL Seminar Papers, 1986* (ed. K. H. Richards; SBLSP 25; Atlanta: Scholars Press, 1986), 201–23.

54 See Richard B. Hays, "Reading Scripture in Light of the Resurrection," in Davis and Hays, *Art of Reading Scripture*, 216–38.

55 Fitzmyer (*Luke*, 2:1558) comments, "The Lucan Christ catechizes the disciples, setting their hearts afire with his interpretation of Old Testament Scriptures. He gives no specific references to the *Tôrāh* or to the *Nĕbî'im*, and the modern reader will look in vain for the Passages in the Old Testament to which the Lucan Christ refers when he speaks of 'what pertained to himself in every part of Scripture' (v 27), especially to himself as 'the Messiah' who

was 'bound to suffer' (v 26)." Precisely for that reason, Fitzmyer's "modern reader" needs to be converted and taught by Luke's entire story.

56 See Conzelmann, *Theology of St. Luke*, 170–206. For a representative view, see, e.g., John Drury, "Luke, Gospel of," in *A Dictionary of Biblical Interpretation* (ed. R. J. Coggins and J. L. Houlden; London: SCM Press, 1990), 410–13: "It has long been noticed that [Luke] has a 'lower' christology than the other Evangelists, and a much lower one than John." Similarly, Christopher M. Tuckett observes, "Many have argued that, insofar as Luke's views can be discerned, the picture is fundamentally a 'subordinationist' one: Jesus is presented as above all a human being who is subordinate to God" ("The Christology of Luke–Acts," in *The Unity of Luke–Acts* [ed. Joseph Verheyden; Leuven: Leuven University Press, 1999], 133–64, quotation from 148–49). To be sure, there have been major monographs arguing instead for a "higher" Lukan Christology (notably Bock, *Proclamation from Prophecy*; H. Douglas Buckwalter, *The Character and Purpose of Luke's Christology* [SNTSMS 89; Cambridge: Cambridge University Press, 1996]). But, as Tuckett observes, these have on the whole failed to tip the scales of critical opinion in the field.

57 The classic influential statement of this view is C. F. D. Moule, "The Christology of Acts," in *Studies in Luke–Acts: Essays Presented in Honor of Paul Schubert* (ed. J. Louis Martyn and Leander E. Keck; Nashville: Abingdon, 1966), 159–85.

58 This may be seen by a moment's reflection on the classic Chalcedonian formulation that Jesus was both truly divine and truly human. Is that a "high" or a "low" Christology? It is, of course, both at the same time. To be sure, the Chalcedonian formula might be classified as a "high" Christology, because it fully affirms Jesus' divinity. At the same time, however, it also safeguards Jesus' full humanity and thus includes within its purview the narrative features that are characteristically thought to demonstrate a "low" Christology.

59 As cogently articulated by Leander E. Keck, "Toward the Renewal of New Testament Christology," *NTS* 32 (1986): 362–77 (repr., in Keck, *Why Christ Matters: Toward a New Testament Christology* [Waco, Tex.: Baylor University Press, 2015], 1–18).

60 On narrative identity, see Paul Ricoeur, *Oneself as Another* (Chicago: University of Chicago Press, 1995). Also Hans W. Frei, *The Identity of Jesus Christ: The Hermeneutical Bases of Dogmatic Theology* (Philadelphia: Fortress, 1975). Approaches of this kind have been helpfully applied in Lukan studies by Rowe, *Early Narrative Christology*; Gaventa, "Learning and Relearning," 148–65.

61 See Strauss, *Davidic Messiah in Luke–Acts*.

62 See Johnson, *Gospel of Luke*, esp. 18–21.

63 See Thomas L. Brodie, "Towards Unravelling Luke's Use of the Old Testament: Luke 7:11–17 as an Imitatio of 1 Kings 17:17–24," *NTS* 32 (1986): 247–67; and idem, *Crucial Bridge*.

64 E.g., Joseph Fitzmyer writes, "The last part of 61:2 is omitted, 'the day of vengeance of our God,' since it is scarcely suited to the salvific period now being inaugurated." Fitzmyer, *Luke*, 1:533.

65 For similar uses of the word in the LXX, see Ps 68:23, 90:8, 93:2; Jer 28:56; and Hos 9:7. Particularly pertinent for the interpretation of Isa 61:2 are the instances in Isa 34:8, 59:18, and 66:6, where the term appears in judgment oracles.

66 For similar positive uses, see also Judg 9:16 and 2 Sam 19:37.

67 Noted rightly by Joel B. Green, *The Gospel of Luke* (NICNT; Grand Rapids: Eerdmans, 1997), 210.

68 Many commentators note that לקרא שנת רצון ליהוה ("to proclaim the year of the LORD's favor") in Isa 61:2 is a reference to the Year of Jubilee as described in Lev 25 (Brevard S. Childs, *Isaiah* [OTL; Louisville, Ky.: Westminster John Knox, 2001], 505; John D. W. Watts, *Isaiah 34–66* [WBC 25; Waco, Tex.: Word Books, 1987], 873). This allusion to Lev 25:10 is strongly suggested by the phrase לקרא לשבוים דרור ("to proclaim liberty") in the previous verse (Isa 61:1), which is often used in association with the Jubilee Year (Lev 25:10; Jer 34:8; Ezek 46:17). In Isa 61, the Jubilee is being recast as a symbol for God's action to release Israel from exile and to reverse the status (including economic status) of God's people. Thus, the reference to Lev 25:10 in Isa 61:1-2 is shaped by Isaiah's proclamation of good news in Isa 40:1-10. See also Sharon H. Ringe, *Jesus, Liberation, and the Biblical Jubilee: Images for Ethics and Christology* (Philadelphia: Fortress, 1985); John Howard Yoder, *The Politics of Jesus: Vicit Agnus Noster* (2d ed.; Grand Rapids: Eerdmans, 1994), 60–75.

69 Peter Mallen (*The Reading and Transformation of Isaiah in Luke–Acts* [LNTS 367; London: T&T Clark, 2008], 108–13) has argued that Luke's emphasis on the extension of salvation to the nations is one of his most important hermeneutical transformations of Isaiah.

70 As James A. Sanders explains, "No prophet is *dektos* ["acceptable"] to his own people when he applies their precious, authoritative traditions in such a way as to challenge the thinking of the people and their corruption of consciousness." "Isaiah in Luke," in *Luke and Scripture: The Function of Sacred Tradition in Luke-Acts* (ed. Craig A. Evans and James A. Sanders; Minneapolis: Fortress, 1993), 14–25, citation on 23.

71 Mittmann-Richert (*Magnifikat und Benediktus*, 121–27) interprets Luke 1:78 as a reference to a "(Davids)spross aus der Höhe" and interprets this as an "Ausdruck eines ganz bestimmten, traditionell geprägten Messiasverständnisses" that highlights the Messiah's physical descent from David. This meaning, she contends, would have been "unmittelbar verständlich" for "in der Tradition geschulter Ohren" (citations on 127).

72 For the most thoroughgoing study of the prominence of Davidic messiahship in Luke–Acts, see Strauss, *Davidic Messiah in Luke–Acts*. Cf. also P. Doble, "Luke 24.26, 44—Songs of God's Servant: David and His Psalms in Luke–Acts," *JSNT* 28 (2006): 267–83; David P. Moessner, "*Two* Lords 'at the Right Hand'? The Psalms and an Intertextual Reading of Peter's Pentecost Speech (Acts 2:14-36)," in *Literary Studies in Luke–Acts: Essays in Honor of Joseph B.*

Tyson (ed. Richard P. Thompson and Thomas E. Phillips; Macon, Ga.: Mercer University Press, 1998), 215–32; idem, "The 'Script' of the Scriptures in Acts: Suffering as God's 'Plan' (βουλή) for the World for the 'Release of Sins,'" in *History, Literature, and Society in the Book of Acts* (ed. Ben Witherington III; Cambridge: Cambridge University Press, 1996), 218–50.

73   This formulation shows clearly that for Luke, χριστός is not a proper name but a title that means "Messiah"; in the following discussion of royal Davidic imagery, it will be translated accordingly.

74   On this difficult passage, see especially the helpful analysis of Luke Timothy Johnson, *Septuagintal Midrash in the Speeches of Acts* (The Père Marquette Lecture in Theology; Milwaukee: Marquette University Press, 2002), 36–40.

75   Here again, cf. 4Q174, which cites precisely the same text as part of a florilegium of Messianic texts.

76   Luke adds "daily" (9:23) to emphasize the ongoing character of discipleship.

77   Here again, of course, Luke is drawing on Markan source material (Mark 10:46-52).

78   For discussion of the messianic acclamation of Jesus as king in the triumphal entry to Jerusalem (19:28-40), see the discussion of Jesus as "the Coming One," below.

79   E.g., Luke's citation of the psalm replaces Mark's ὑποκάτω with ὑποπόδιον, thus agreeing more precisely with the text of Ps 109:1 LXX and producing the reading "until I put your enemies as a footstool under your feet."

80   On this passage, see C. Kavin Rowe, "Acts 2:36 and the Continuity of Lukan Christology," *NTS* 53 (2007): 37–56.

81   On this theme as a key to Luke's Christology and soteriology, see Moessner, "The 'Script' of the Scriptures."

82   On the importance of this lament psalm pattern for the earliest formation of New Testament Christology, including the Pauline traditions, see Richard B. Hays, "Christ Prays the Psalms," in *Conversion of the Imagination*, 101–18.

83   The Nestle-Aland apparatus suggests also a possible allusion to Ps 88:9. The LXX at this verse (Ps 87:9 LXX) does refer to the sufferer's acquaintances (τοε γνωστούς μου), but otherwise, in comparison to Ps 37:11 LXX, the wording is more distant from Luke 23:49. Doble ("The Psalms in Luke–Acts," in *The Psalms in the New Testament* [ed. Steve Moyise and Maarten J. J. Menken; London: T&T Clark, 2004], 116) treats the Lukan narrative as an allusion to Ps 87 LXX and suggests that the wider context of vv. 4-13 in the psalm is immediately relevant to Luke's passion account. Against this proposal, it should be observed that Ps 37 LXX is a psalm of David, whereas Ps 87 LXX is not.

84   On the importance of this psalm for Luke's narrative construal of Jesus' fulfillment of Scripture, see Moessner, "*Two* Lords 'at the Right Hand'?" 215–32.

85   Rightly noted by Doble, "Psalms in Luke–Acts," 113.

86   Reading the psalm as a whole, we may wonder whether perhaps Ps 30:22 could be heard as a metaleptic reply to Mark's citation of Ps 21:2 LXX?

87 As noted also by Charles H. Talbert, *Reading Acts: A Literary and Theological Commentary on the Acts of the Apostles* (rev. ed.; Reading the New Testament; Macon, Ga.: Smyth & Helwys, 2005), 77–78.

88 Notice that once again here we find the climactic Hallel psalm playing a crucial role in Luke's narrative. For studies of the importance of Ps 118 in Luke–Acts, see James A. Sanders, "A Hermeneutic Fabric: Psalm 118 in Luke's Entrance Narrative," in Evans and Sanders, *Luke and Scripture*, 140–53; Wagner, "Psalm 118 in Luke–Acts," 154–78.

89 For an illuminating exposition of Acts 8:26-40 in light of Luke's resurrection themes, see Joel B. Green, "Witnesses of His Resurrection: Resurrection, Salvation, Discipleship, and Mission in the Acts of the Apostles," in *Life in the Face of Death: The Resurrection Message of the New Testament* (ed. Richard N. Longenecker; Grand Rapids: Eerdmans, 1998), 227–46, esp. 233–35.

90 See the study of these themes in Strauss (*Davidic Messiah in Luke–Acts*, 324–33), who helpfully notes the thematic links that are made among the Psalms, the Suffering Servant, and Luke's passion narrative by Luke's characterization of Jesus as "innocent" or "righteous" (see, e.g., Luke 23:4, 14, 15, 22, 47; cf. Acts 13:28).

91 Acts 4:25: "It is you who said by the Holy Spirit through the mouth of our father David, your *servant* (Δαυὶδ παιδός σου). . . ." Acts 4:27: "For truly, in this city, both Herod and Pontius Pilate gathered together with the nations and peoples of Israel against your holy *servant* Jesus, whom you *anointed* (τὸν ἅγιον παῖδά σου Ιησοῦν ὅν ἔκρισας). . . ." The reference to the anointed servant of course recalls Luke's evocation of the Servant figure of Isa 61:1 in Luke 4:18. At the same time, in this context, where Jesus is linked with David as God's servant, the verb ἔχρισας certainly has messianic overtones: Jesus is the Messiah (χριστός) because he is God's anointed one, who endures, just as David did, the hostility of his adversaries and triumphs over them.

92 At the same time, of course, this conflict prefigures the controversy over extension of the gospel to the Gentiles, as narrated in extenso in Acts.

93 As noted by Green, *Luke*, 289–92, with references cited there.

94 Rightly observed by Brodie, "Towards Unravelling," 256: "Unlike Elijah, who is described as calling on the Lord to restore the boy's life (1 Kgs 17.21b), Jesus is depicted as the Lord who issues a sovereign command that the boy be raised."

95 Brodie remarks, "Just as *imitatio* was almost invariably shadowed by *emulatio*, by a desire to rival and, if possible, surpass the ancient text, so . . . there is a considerable ambiguity in [Luke's] general treatment of the Elijah theme: in Luke's text, Jesus is both identified with and differentiated from Elijah" ("Towards Unravelling," 260).

96 Many manuscripts add: "as Elijah did." This reading is found in A C D W Θ Ψ *f*¹·¹³ 33 M et al. Manuscripts that lack these words include p45 p75 ℵ B L Ξ 579 700* and 1241. This is probably a later gloss on the original text that makes explicit what would already have been obvious to earlier readers sharing with Luke a cultural encyclopedia that included the tales of Elijah.

97 On dramatic irony as a chief Lukan theological medium, see Rowe, *Early Narrative Christology*; and William S. Kurz, S.J., *Reading Luke–Acts: Dynamics of Biblical Narrative* (Louisville, Ky.: Westminster John Knox, 1993), 64–66, 138–44.

98 In this case, there is a possible secondary echo as well, of one more scene in which the true spokesmen of Israel's God are accused by a wicked ruler of perverting the people. In Exod 5:4 LXX, Egypt's Pharaoh dismisses the request of Moses and Aaron to let the people go into the wilderness to worship: "Why, Moses and Aaron, do you turn my [!] people away (διαστρέφετε τὸν λαόν μου) from their works?" If indeed we hear this secondary echo in the scene of Jesus' arraignment before Pilate, we see once again an intricate metaleptic foreshadowing of a coming reversal of power, in which the mighty will be put down from their thrones and the people of God vindicated and set free.

99 The image of "chariots of fire," which also occurs in 2 Kgs 2:11, was employed by William Blake in his poem "Jerusalem." The poem was subsequently used as the text of a hymn, which in turn served as the inspiration for the title of the 1981 film *Chariots of Fire.*

100 Genesis 3:5, 7, of course, tells of the opening of the human creature's eyes to the reality of evil/sin and its consequences. In this case, the opening of the eyes corresponds to the knowledge of deep damage.

101 See Alkier, "Intertextuality," 3–21, esp. 9–11.

102 Contra Fitzmyer, *Luke*, 1:213–15.

103 On Moses, Luke T. Johnson, *Luke–Acts: A Story of Prophet and People* (Chicago: Franciscan Herald, 1981); Moessner, *Lord of the Banquet*. On wisdom, Lothar Ruppert, *Jesus Als der Leidende Gerechte? Der Weg Jesu Im Lichte Eines Alt- und Zwischentestamentlichen Motivs* (SBS; Stuttgart: KBW Verlag, 1972). For a survey of various christological motifs in Luke, see Fitzmyer, *Luke*, 1:192–219.

104 Buckwalter, *Character and Purpose*; Max Turner, "'Trinitarian' Pneumatology in the New Testament? Towards an Explanation of the Worship of Jesus," *AsTJ* 57–58 (2003): 167–86; Rowe, *Early Narrative Christology*; Stanley E. Porter, "Scripture Justifies Mission: The Use of the Old Testament in Luke–Acts," in Porter, *Hearing the Old Testament in the New Testament*, 114–18.

105 Gaventa, "Learning and Relearning," 148–65.

106 See Steinmetz, "Uncovering a Second Narrative," 54–65.

107 Modern English translations (RSV, NRSV, NIV) characteristically overlook the force of the καί in the last line of 1:35. I would suggest that here it means "also" and that it logically connects ἅγιον in this line to πνεῦμα ἅγιον at the beginning of the quotation from Gabriel. Thus: "The *Holy* Spirit will come upon you . . . therefore also (καί) the child to be born will be called *holy* . . ."

108 At this point, it would seem that the interpretative instincts of untutored Christian readers have usually been better than those of learned Lukan scholars who have bracketed this scene out as somehow less than definitive for understanding Luke's Christology.

109 In Luke 9:35, the textual tradition is divided between ὁ υἱός μου ὁ ἐκλελεγμένος and ὁ υἱός μου ὁ ἀγαπητός. The latter reading almost surely reflects scribal assimilation of the text to 3:22 as well as to the synoptic parallels in Mark 9:7 and Matt 17:5.

110 We should note also the climactic reference in Luke's genealogy to Adam as "son of God" (3:38). It is not just coincidental that the very next words in Luke are "But Jesus, full of the Holy Spirit . . ." (4:1), and that the scene thus introduced is one in which the devil taunts Jesus with a challenge to prove that he is the Son of God. The effect of this narrative technique is to link Jesus associatively with Adam. Adam is son of God because he is God's direct sovereign creation and has no human parents. It is possible that Luke is obliquely suggesting a christological identification of Jesus as the new Adam (cf. Rom 5:12-21). If so, however, this is not a theme he develops elsewhere.

111 On this passage as a key indicator of Jesus' identity, see the interesting treatment in Joseph Ratzinger (Pope Benedict XVI), *Jesus of Nazareth: From the Baptism in the Jordan to the Transfiguration* (trans. Adrian J. Walker; New York: Doubleday, 2007), 339–45.

112 This is a point emphasized by Sanders, *Jesus and Judaism*, 95–106.

113 Werner Kramer, *Christ, Lord, Son of God* (trans. Brian Hardy; SBT 50; London: SCM Press, 1966); Wilhelm Bousset, *Kyrios Christos: Geschichte des Christusglaubens von den Anfängen des Christentums bis Irenaeus* (Göttingen: Vandenhoeck & Ruprecht, 1913); ET: *Kyrios Christos: A History of the Belief in Christ from the Beginnings of Christianity to Irenaeus* (Nashville: Abingdon, 1970; repr., Waco, Tex.: Baylor University Press, 2013). History of religions studies often shed much light on the ancient world, but they are typically rather naïve about the hermeneutic substitution of meaning-determining-context. This approach substitutes the "background" to Luke for the meaning of Luke's words. At the most, the background can sensitize us to wider assumptions about the way the narrative would have been construed. But the meaning of the words in the story will be that given by the story itself.

114 We should also observe that to proclaim Jesus as Son of God could well be heard as a politically provocative challenge to the authority of the Roman emperor, who also claimed precisely the title of υἱός θεοῦ.

115 Pao, *Acts and the Isaianic New Exodus*, 38. Pao actually describes it as "*the* hermeneutical key" (emphasis added). For reasons that should be clear by now, I think it is methodologically mistaken to look for a single theme or image as the one key to Luke's narrative design. Nonetheless, my discussion of the passage is significantly indebted to Pao's insightful exegetical work.

116 Rowe, *Early Narrative Christology*, 70–77.

117 Rowe, *Early Narrative Christology*, 74–77.

118 Pao's analysis (*Acts and the Isaianic New Exodus*, 147–80) argues that in the Acts of the Apostles the "Agent" of the new exodus is the word of God. But Pao does not focus the meaning of "word of God" in christological terms (as in the Johannine prologue). Rather, in terms of the Acts narrative, the word of God is the proclaimed message. But Luke 3:1-6 would suggest that

however much the proclaimed message may have an instrumental role in implementing the new exodus, the true *agent* of the new exodus is Jesus the Lord himself. (This is also the implication of Acts 1:1.)

119   A nearly identical account appears in Matt 11:2-6. This passage therefore belongs to material sometimes designated as coming from the hypothetical Q source. Our chief concern here, however, is not with source-critical issues. Because the story functions in slightly different ways within Luke and Matthew, our particular focus here will be on exegesis of the passage in its *Lukan* setting.

120   On the importance of the festivals and their link to political hope, see E. P. Sanders, *Judaism: Practice and Belief, 63 BCE–66 CE* (Philadelphia: Trinity International, 1992), 135, 140, et passim.

121   The NRSV renders this verse in a way that suggests the healing actions had preceded the question of John's disciples: "Jesus had just then cured many people of diseases. . . ." But this pluperfect verbal construction forces an unnatural sense upon the simple aorist ἐθεράπευσεν. The more natural interpretation of Luke's Greek is that Jesus performed the healings *following* the question posed to him.

122   Charles Wesley, "O for a Thousand Tongues," in *The United Methodist Hymnal* (Nashville: United Methodist Publishing House, 1989), 57.

123   Further, Isa 35 and 61 are not the only passages evoked by Jesus' description of the miraculous deeds he is performing. For other possible echoes, see Isa 26:19, 29:18, 42:18; and Ps 146:7-9; cf. also 4Q521. For a full listing of the allusive parallels, see Dale C. Allison Jr., *The Intertextual Jesus: Scripture in Q* (Harrisburg, Pa.: Trinity International, 2000), 109–14. The multiplicity of echoes suggests that Luke 7:22 is not an allusion to a single text but rather a richly suggestive evocation of a cloud of texts that characterized Israel's expectation of restoration and healing.

124   The following paragraphs draw on my "Reading the Bible with Eyes of Faith."

125   The Dead Sea Scrolls have now yielded up evidence that other Jewish interpreters of this era drew upon precisely these same Isaianic texts as a description of the Lord's saving actions in the eschatological age. See particularly 4Q521.

126   The writer of the nineteenth-century hymn "Lead on, O King Eternal" gets the point just right:

> For not with swords loud clashing, nor roll of stirring drums;
> with deeds of love and mercy the heavenly kingdom comes.

E. W. Shurtleff, "Lead On, O King Eternal," in *United Methodist Hymnal*, 580.

127   This theme is of course crucially important in Wright, *Jesus and the Victory*, esp. 615–24.

128   The correctness of this construal of the syntax is confirmed by the closely parallel Isa 40:9: "Say to the cities of Judah, 'Behold, your God.'"

129   This tally does not count the vocative κύριε and other ambiguous instances.

130   For a thorough, theologically sophisticated analysis of this striking phenomenon in Lukan narrative Christology, see C. Kavin Rowe, *Early Narrative*

Christology. For an earlier concise preview of his observations, see idem, "Luke and the Trinity: An Essay in Ecclesial Biblical Theology," *SJT* 56 (2003): 1–26.

131   For this reason, we cannot suppose that Acts 2:36 articulates an adoptionist Christology in which Jesus is "appointed" κύριος only at the time of the resurrection. Jesus has already been named as κύριος from the beginning of Luke's two-volume work. The climactic declaration of Peter's Pentecost sermon in Acts 2:36 should be understood to mean that as a result of the resurrection and the outpouring of the Spirit, all Israel should now *know* that God has appointed Jesus both Lord and Christ. The change effected by the resurrection is an epistemological one for the audience, not an ontological transformation or a change of status for Jesus himself. On the whole question, see Rowe, "Acts 2:36 and the Continuity of Lukan Christology."

132   The manuscript evidence is divided on the inclusion or omission of the relative pronoun ὅν in this verse. With the inclusion of the relative pronoun in the text, the main verb of the clause would have to be οἴδατε in Acts 10:37. The translation given here, however, follows א¹ A B 81 614 1739 and a few other manuscripts in reading the verse without the pronoun; this has the effect of strengthening the affirmations in both clauses of Acts 10:37. The reading with the pronoun requires that οὗτός ἐστιν πάντων κύριος be read as a parenthetical interjection. For purposes of the present argument, the sense of this clause is not materially affected. But narratively, it is hard to understand why Peter should (even rhetorically) treat the affirmations of Acts 10:36 as something already known to his Gentile audience, and it is easy to see how the addition of ON could have arisen through dittography: ΤΟΝΛΟΓΟΝΟΝ.

133   Wilhelm Dittenberger, *Sylloge Inscriptionum Graecarum, a Guilelmo Dittenbergero Condita et Aucta, Nunc Tertium Edita* (Lipsiae: Apud S. Hirzelium, 1915–1924), 1:376.31.

134   Epictetus, *Discourses* 4.1.12.

135   See Rowe, *Early Narrative Christology*, 92–104.

136   In the Markan version of the story, it would be possible to understand Jesus' words as those spoken in 2:27 and to read 2:28, introduced by ὥστε, as the narrator's summary comment. See, e.g., Lane, *Gospel according to Mark*, 117–20.

137   Rowe (*Early Narrative Christology*, 84) contends that "ἐπιστάτης is actually used by Luke to convey in the speaker some distance from Jesus and his purposes." Rowe suggests that in Luke's five other uses of the term, "it conveys either misunderstanding or insufficient faith."

138   With perhaps the addition of μή, which would make the saying still more emphatic. A few manuscripts of Mark (B, D*) lack this word in 13:31.

139   For specific identification of these subtexts, see discussion of the relevant Markan passages.

140   See also Luke 18:41-43, for a similar response by a healed blind man. All of these examples are briefly noted by Rowe, *Early Narrative Christology*, 120–21n129.

141   Here, as elsewhere, the verb ἐπισκέπτομαι translates the Hebrew פקד, which has a wide range of meanings including "look after, take care of."

142 Rightly Gathercole, *Pre-existent Son*, esp. 231–42; cf. also William Horbury, *Jewish Messianism and the Cult of Christ* (London: SCM Press, 1998), 86–108.

143 In the Acts of the Apostles, the pressure of the text continues to move the reader in a similar direction. There, in Peter's Pentecost sermon we encounter a citation of Joel 3:5 (2:32 ET): "everyone who calls on the name of the Lord will be saved" (Acts 2:21). As Luke's account unfolds, we learn in no uncertain terms that "the Lord" is Jesus (2:36; cf. "the Lord our God" in 2:39), that those who believe Peter's message are to be baptized in the name of Jesus (2:38), and that there is "no other name" given by which human beings can be saved (4:12). The reader who connects the dots can hardly avoid the implication of the divine identity of Jesus as Lord.

144 Note that in the very similar commissioning promise of Luke 12:11-12, it is the Holy Spirit who will teach the disciples what to say when they are hauled up before hostile authorities.

145 Turner, "'Trinitarian' Pneumatology," 167–86.

146 These passages are cited as translated from the MT by the NRSV. The LXX renderings differ in significant respects, but all agree in referring to God as the Redeemer of Israel. I have parenthetically cited the relevant divine titles as they appear in the LXX.

147 My point here is not to assert any claims for the factual accuracy of details of Luke's story; rather, I am drawing attention to the way he sets his narrative within the symbolic world of political affairs. For discussion of the difficulties surrounding the historical reference of Luke 2:1-2, see, e.g., Raymond E. Brown, *The Birth of the Messiah: A Commentary on the Infancy Narratives in the Gospels of Matthew and Luke* (rev. ed.; New York: Doubleday, 1993), 395–96, 412–18, 547–55, 666–68. Also see Fitzmyer, *Luke*, 1:392–94, 399–405; Marshall, *Gospel of Luke*, 98–104; François Bovon, *Luke 1: A Commentary on the Gospel of Luke 1:1–9:50* (trans. Christine M. Thomas; Hermeneia; Minneapolis: Fortress, 2002), 84.

148 It is possible that Luke, with his strong sense of style, might have savored the sharper rhetorical contrast produced by this deletion: "It is written: 'My house shall be a house of prayer,' but you have made it 'a den of robbers.'" If this explanation is to be preferred, then the Isaiah citation should probably be understood as carrying metaleptic force, *hinting* at a concern for the nations without articulating it.

149 One possible indicator of Luke's broader field of vision may be found in his version of the genealogy of Jesus, which traces the line back not just to Abraham, the progenitor of Israel, but to Adam, the first human being (3:23-38). Might we infer that Luke is identifying Jesus as the culmination not just of Israel's national destiny but of all world history? Of course, as in the case of the Matthean genealogy, some of the names in Luke's list evoke memories of scriptural stories. However, in contrast to Matthew's three-part periodization of the genealogy, which imparts a clear narrative structure to the past, Luke simply gives us a continuous patrilineal stream extending backwards to Adam. This unbroken continuity may in itself be suggestive of Luke's interest in portraying

the continuity of the Gospel with the universal plan of God. (For more on "the plan of God" in Luke–Acts, see John T. Squires, *The Plan of God in Luke–Acts* [SNTSMS 76; Cambridge: Cambridge University Press, 1993].)

150 For a comprehensive study of this phenomenon in Acts, see C. Kavin Rowe, *World Upside Down: Reading Acts in the Graeco-Roman Age* (New York: Oxford University Press, 2009).

151 Cited in David C. Braund, *Augustus to Nero: A Sourcebook on Roman History, 31 BC–AD 68* (London: Crook Helm, 1985), 40 (no. 66).

152 Whether Luke knew Matthew's account (as I am inclined to suspect), or whether he was drawing on a Q source for this temptation material, it seems likely that Luke is responsible for reordering the material to place the temple temptation as the culminating one. The Matthean narrative sequence (Matt 4:1-11), building up to a final scene on a high mountain where Jesus is offered "all the kingdoms of the world," is perhaps the more natural one.

153 A highly pertinent comparison is found in Rev 13:3b-4: "In amazement the whole earth followed the beast. They worshiped the dragon, *for he had given his authority to the beast*, and they worshiped the beast, saying, 'Who is like the beast, and who can fight against it?'"

154 Conzelmann, *Mitte der Zeit*, 117–28. On Luke–Acts as "political apologetic," see Paul W. Walaskay, *And So We Came to Rome: The Political Perspective of St. Luke* (SNTSMS 49; Cambridge: Cambridge University Press, 1983). Ernst Haenchen's commentary on Acts is the most learned and well-known commentary that takes this position (*The Acts of the Apostles: A Commentary* [Louisville, Ky.: Westminster John Knox, 1971]). Richard J. Cassidy, *Jesus, Politics, and Society: A Study of Luke's Gospel* (Maryknoll, N.Y.: Orbis Books, 1978) argues against it. These one-sided views of Acts have now been superseded by Rowe, *World Upside Down*.

155 Luke gives an editorially abbreviated account of Mark 5:1-20.

156 It is likely that Luke's specific articulation of the prophecy in 21:20-24 owes something to his post-70 historical perspective, for he and his readers know well that the temple has in fact been destroyed by the Romans.

157 Noteworthy in this respect is the Lukan portrayal of an emergent friendship between Herod and Pilate (Luke 23:12), a motif reflected again in Acts 4:27.

158 The translation given here is the NRSV; the parenthetical Greek phrases show the corresponding language in the LXX rendering of the verse.

159 For a reading that would close the door on preaching to Jews, see Jack T. Sanders, *The Jews in Luke–Acts* (Philadelphia: Fortress, 1987). For a reading that attends to the way Luke sees the church's mission as continuing toward Jews, see Jervell, *Luke and the People of God*; idem, *Theology of the Acts*.

160 Cf. Rom 1:16: the gospel is "the power of God for salvation to everyone who trusts God, to the Jew first and also to the Greek."

161 Of course, we hear the voice of Luke the omniscient narrator throughout the text, and his evaluative perspective comprehensively shapes the reader's perception of the narrated events. The distinction I am drawing here is between narration and commentary. Luke gives us very little of the latter.

162   This is the NRSV translation.

163   The Old Testament echoes in this passage include at least the following: Ps 106:10, 14 LXX; Isa 9:1, 42:7, 59:8, 60:1-2.

Chapter 4: John

1   For a recent overview of various issues concerning John's use of Scripture, with helpful bibliography, see Alicia D. Myers, "Abiding Words: An Introduction to Perspectives on John's Use of Scripture," in *Abiding Words: The Use of Scripture in the Gospel of John* (Alicia D. Myers and Bruce G. Schuchard; Atlanta: SBL Press, 2015), 1–20.

2   Jeremiah 17:21-22 specifically prohibits carrying a burden or bringing it into Jerusalem on the sabbath. Mishnah *Šabb.* 7.2 lists thirty-nine classes of work prohibited on the sabbath. The last item in the list is "taking out aught from one domain to another." John P. Meier ("The Historical Jesus and the Historical Sabbath," in *Redefining First-Century Jewish and Christian Identities: Essays in Honor of Ed Parish Sanders* [ed. Fabian E. Udoh et al.; Notre Dame: University of Notre Dame Press, 2008], 297–307), on form-critical grounds, dismisses this story, as well as the healing story in John 9, as valid *historical* evidence about controversy surrounding Jesus' healing on the sabbath (302–3). He then notes, almost as an afterthought, that John 5 focuses the controversy not on the act of healing but on the prohibited carrying of a burden, but he regards this as a late, secondary addendum to the tradition that "tries to make the sabbath disputes more plausible" (307n15). To the contrary, the possibility should at least be considered that 5:9-10 preserves an early tradition that explains why Jesus' sabbath healing activity was controversial in the first place, despite the absence of a scriptural basis for prohibition of healing on the sabbath. In any case, the historical antiquity and reliability of the tradition behind John's narrative is immaterial for the questions at hand in my discussion. Within the narrative world of John 5 the controversy focuses on the prohibited carrying of a burden, and it morphs into a larger dispute and discourse about Jesus' relation to the Father.

3   The numbers cited were complied by C. K. Barrett, who simply counted the references (including allusions) listed in the Westcott and Hort critical edition of the New Testament. C. K. Barrett, "The Old Testament in the Fourth Gospel," *JTS* 48 (1947): 155–69; the reference to Westcott and Hort is on p. 155.

4   See, e.g., Bruce G. Schuchard, *Scripture within Scripture: The Interrelationship of Form and Function in the Explicit Old Testament Citations in the Gospel of John* (SBLDS 133; Atlanta: Scholars Press, 1992), xiii–xiv (thirteen quotations); Andreas J. Köstenberger, "John," in Beale and Carson, *Commentary*, 415–21 (fourteen quotations); Margaret Daly-Denton, *David in the Fourth Gospel: The Johannine Reception of the Psalms* (AGJU 47; Leiden: Brill, 2000), 33–34 (sixteen quotations); Menken, *Old Testament Quotations*, 11–12 (seventeen quotations).

5   Margaret Daly-Denton (*David in the Fourth Gospel*, 30) describes overt allusions in the Fourth Gospel as "quite rare" and suggests there are only two that would meet strict criteria for identifying allusions: "the reference to the angels ascending and descending on the Son of Man (2:51 [*sic*, read 1:51 instead], alluding to Gen 28:12) and the speculation of the crowd that the Christ is to be of the seed of David and is to come from Bethlehem (7:42, alluding to 2 Sam 7:12 and Ps [88]89:3-4)." This judgment surely results from an excessively stringent definition of what constitutes an allusion. By contrast, Andreas Köstenberger ("John," 419–20) lists more than sixty "Old Testament allusions and verbal parallels" in the Gospel, in addition to the explicit quotations. Daly-Denton is of course aware of the much richer intertextual character of John's Gospel. She goes on to say that "the apparent infrequency of Scripture reference in the Fourth Gospel is quite deceptive" and to speak of the "highly allusive quality of [John's] writing."

6   The phrase "in the wilderness" also appears earlier in the Numbers passage, not in relation to Moses' action of lifting up the serpent but as part of the people's complaint: "Why have you brought us out of Egypt to kill us in the wilderness?" (Num 21:5 LXX).

7   In John 19:28, the formula ἵνα τελειωθῇ ἡ γραφή ("in order that the scripture might be brought to completion") introduces a word of Jesus but not a direct scriptural quotation. John's poetic purpose in selecting this distinctive wording in just this place in the story will be discussed below.

8   The latter designation requires comment. The titles "book of signs" and "book of glory" were proposed by Raymond Brown in his excellent and highly influential Anchor Bible commentary on the Fourth Gospel (*The Gospel according to John* [AB 29–29A; Garden City, N.Y.: Doubleday, 1966–1970]). Brown's analysis included chap. 20 as part of the book of glory (13:1–20:31), with chap. 21 seen as an epilogue added at a later redactional stage. The term "book of the passion," adopted above, was suggested earlier by C. H. Dodd (*The Interpretation of the Fourth Gospel* [Cambridge: Cambridge University Press, 1953]); this terminology is preferred, rightly in my judgment, by Marianne Meye Thompson ("'They Bear Witness to Me': The Psalms in the Passion Narrative of the Gospel of John," in *The Word Leaps the Gap: Essays on Scripture and Theology in Honor of Richard B. Hays* [ed. J. Ross Wagner, C. Kavin Rowe, and A. Katherine Grieb; Grand Rapids: Eerdmans, 2008], 267–83), to whom I owe the important observation of the structural role of the paired quotations in 12:38-40 and 19:36-37; for additional discussion, see Martin Hengel, "The Old Testament in the Fourth Gospel," in *The Gospels and the Scriptures of Israel* (ed. Craig A. Evans and W. Richard Stegner; JSNTSup 104; Sheffield: Sheffield Academic, 1994), 380–95. If we follow these pairings as structural clues to the narrative, we will then see the second major section ending at the end of chap. 19, with chaps. 20–21 constituting a final separate narrative unit (a "book of resurrection"?). For a strong argument that John 21 belongs to the original narrative design of the Gospel, see Paul S. Minear, "The Original Functions of John 21," *JBL* 102 (1983): 85–98. Other supporters

of this view are cited in Beverly Roberts Gaventa, "The Archive of Excess: John 21 and the Problem of Narrative Closure," in *Exploring the Gospel of John: In Honor of D. Moody Smith* (ed. R. Alan Culpepper and C. Clifton Black; Louisville, Ky.: Westminster John Knox, 1996), 240–53. For a very different argument in favor of seeing John 21 as part of the Gospel's design, based on a complex theory of numerical composition, see now Richard Bauckham, *The Testimony of the Beloved Disciple: Narrative, History, and Theology in the Gospel of John* (Grand Rapids: Baker Academic, 2007), 271–84.

9　Interestingly, there are no direct scriptural quotations in the Gospel's well-developed account of the resurrection (chaps. 20 and 21).

10　My translation *"persistently* did not believe" seeks to emphasize the force of the imperfect tense verb ἐπίστευον.

11　Thompson comments: "[T]aken together, the scriptures cited in 12:38–19:42 bear witness . . . to Jesus' rejection, as do the quotations from Isaiah that summarize the predominantly negative response to Jesus' signs. The belief that Scripture testifies to Jesus' identity as Israel's Messiah lies behind those texts, but the actual quotations foreground the negative response to him. It is Israel's unbelief, the rejection of Jesus by 'his own' (1:11), that particularly troubles the evangelist and demands a scriptural explanation" ("'They Bear Witness,'" 268).

12　Daly-Denton actually says 76%, but this appears to be a computational error, because her immediately preceding text states that "the Psalter is the source for ten of the sixteen quotations found in the Fourth Gospel." Her contrasting figures for the synoptics are Mark, 21%; Matthew, 18%; Luke, 31% (Daly-Denton, *David in the Fourth Gospel*, 34). I would conjecture that the figure of 76% is derived in the following way: Daly-Denton notes that John has thirteen "readily identifiable" Scripture quotations, of which seven derive from the Psalms. She then notes that there are three more citations that do not fully correspond to any known Scripture passages, all of which she regards as "non literal quotations from the psalms." It would seem that for the purposes of her statistical analysis, she has added these three quotations to the numerator but not the denominator of her tabulation of Johannine quotations: this would yield ten out of thirteen, or 76.9%. All these percentages, of course, might vary with different ways of counting and attributing the quotations. But on any reckoning of the statistics, it is difficult to quarrel with Köstenberger's judgment that for John "[t]he OT theological center, at least as far as explicit OT quotations are concerned, is clearly the Psalter" ("John," 419).

13　See Hays, "Christ Prays the Psalms," 101–18. I have proposed that the psalms of suffering and vindication were the generative matrix for the early Christian conviction that the death and resurrection of Jesus occurred "according to the Scriptures." The evidence of John's Gospel is entirely consistent with this thesis.

14　For discussion of the textual source of this quotation, see Menken, *Old Testament Quotations*, 147–66. Menken concludes that Ps 33:21 LXX provides "the basic text" and that the Pentateuchal texts "supplied the material for changes in it" (165).

15 For discussion, see Brown, *John*, 1:16.

16 See Adele Reinhartz, "The Gospel of John: How the 'Jews' Became Part of the Plot," in *Jesus, Judaism and Christian Anti-Judaism: Reading the New Testament after the Holocaust* (ed. Paula Fredriksen and Adele Reinhartz; Louisville, Ky.: Westminster John Knox, 2002), 99–116.

17 For further discussion, and for the argument that "he saw his glory" refers to the manifestation of divine glory in the earthly Jesus, see Catrin H. Williams, "Isaiah in John's Gospel," in *Isaiah in the New Testament* (ed. Steve Moyise and Maarten J. J. Menken; London: T&T Clark, 2005), 101–2.

18 On the interpretation of Gal 3 and 4 as an intra-Jewish debate about scriptural interpretation, see Richard B. Hays, "Galatians," in *New Interpreter's Bible* (vol. 11, Second Corinthians–Philemon; ed. Leander E. Keck; Nashville: Abingdon, 2000). On ancient Jewish polemical discourse, see Luke Timothy Johnson, "The New Testament's Anti-Jewish Slander and Conventions of Ancient Rhetoric," *JBL* 108 (1989): 419–41. For a discussion of John's ambivalent portrayal of the Jews and Jewishness vis-à-vis the scriptural figures of Moses and Abraham, see Raimo Hakola, *Identity Matters: John, the Jews and Jewishness* (NovTSup 118; Boston: Brill, 2005).

19 Precisely in this attempt, however, they may be ironically echoing in the wrong way another of the works of Abraham: his attempt to sacrifice his own son (Gen 22). If so, by the end of the story, they actually carry out the act of killing Abraham's one true son, the very thing that Abraham was divinely prevented from doing (Gen 22:11-12). This proposed reading may be particularly fanciful, however, since John nowhere else refers to the *Akedah* tradition. And indeed, he never refers to Jesus himself as Abraham's son or Abraham's σπέρμα. This is perhaps the most striking difference between John 8 and Galatians.

20 See, e.g., Gen 24:10-61, 29:1-20; Exod 2:16-22. On biblical type scenes, including betrothal type scenes, see Robert Alter, *The Art of Biblical Narrative* (New York: Basic Books, 1981), 55–78; on betrothal imagery in John 4, see Sandra M. Schneiders, *The Revelatory Text: Interpreting the New Testament as Sacred Scripture* (San Francisco: HarperCollins, 1991), 180–99.

21 See Schneiders, *Revelatory Text*, 187–89.

22 The Samaritan woman's action of returning to the city to tell her people about Jesus mirrors Rachel's running home to tell her father about Jacob (Gen 29:12).

23 There is also another important allusion to the story of Jacob in John 1:51, where the image of "angels ascending and descending upon the Son of Man" recalls the account of Jacob's dream in Gen 28:10-17, and see esp. v. 12. For further discussion of Jacob traditions in John 4, see Jerome H. Neyrey, "Jacob Traditions and the Interpretation of John 4:10-26," *CBQ* 41 (1979): 419–37.

24 For a wide-ranging study of the significance of traditions about Moses in the Fourth Gospel, see Meeks, *Prophet-King*; see also John Lierman, "The

Mosaic Pattern of John's Christology," in *Challenging Perspectives on the Gospel of John* (ed. John Lierman; WUNT 2/219; Tübingen: Mohr Siebeck, 2006): 210–34.

25 It should be noted, however, that the opposition here between Moses and Jesus is placed in the mouth of "the Pharisees" (9:13-17) or, apparently synonymously, "the Jews" (9:18-22). The contrast is probably meant to be ironic and materially mistaken, in view of the Evangelist's earlier presentation of Moses as witness to Jesus.

26 Genesis 17:9-14 is included here because of the conventional belief that Moses was the author of the Pentateuch. Thus, even though Gen 17 describes the institution of the covenant of circumcision with Abraham, the Evangelist may have nonetheless thought of circumcision as "given" by Moses in the sense that Moses was author of this text, which communicated the commandment of circumcision to subsequent generations.

27 J. Louis Martyn, "We Have Found Elijah," in *The Gospel of John in Christian History: Essays for Interpreters* (Eugene, Ore.: Wipf & Stock, 2004), 9–54, proposes that the signs source used by John explicitly identified Jesus as Elijah, an identification that may still be detected in John the Baptist's denial that he himself is Elijah (because Jesus is).

28 Cf. Mark 9:11-13, in which Jesus does apparently identify the Baptist as Elijah, an identification made explicit by Matthew—with his typical concern for clarity—in Matt 17:10-13. The contrast to John 1:21 is striking.

29 Matthew characteristically alters the citation by fusing it with 2 Sam 5:2.

30 The alternative to this reading would be to suppose that John does not know, or rejects, the tradition of Jesus' Davidic descent or birth in Bethlehem. In that case, the point would be that some members of the crowd are looking for a messiah of fleshly Davidic origin, in contrast to Jesus' real origin in heaven. On this reading, the crowd would simply be wrong, and John would in effect be promulgating a radically non-Davidic interpretation of Jesus' messiahship. So D. Moody Smith, *John* (Abingdon New Testament Commentaries; Nashville: Abingdon, 1999), 175, who alleges that either John is ignorant of these traditions of Jesus' birth or deems them inadequate to warrant Jesus' claim to messiahship; C. K. Barrett, *The Gospel according to St. John: An Introduction with Commentary and Notes on the Greek Text* (2d ed.; Philadelphia: Westminster, 1978), 330–31, allows that John knows these traditions but contends that Johannine irony judges the place of Jesus' birth a trivial matter in light of his heavenly origins. Andrew T. Lincoln, *The Gospel according to Saint John* (Black's New Testament Commentaries; New York: Continuum, 2005), 258, aptly notes that it is unlikely that John would have raised an objection from Scripture if he did not think it could be answered; cf. Brown, *John*, 1:330. In view of the evidence, it appears that John does think of Jesus as the Davidic Messiah. If so, the more complex ironic reading given above—which is in any case more characteristic of Johannine sensibilities—is to be preferred.

31 For full discussion, see Daly-Denton, *David in the Fourth Gospel*.

32 Often John is understood to present Jesus as the *replacement* of the temple, as well as of Jewish feasts, institutions, and even the entire sacrificial system. For various accounts of John's "replacement theology," see Brown, *John*, 1:104; Barrett, *John*, 191; James D. G. Dunn, *The Partings of the Ways: Between Christianity and Judaism and Their Significance for the Character of Christianity* (2d ed.; London: SCM Press, 2006), 93–95; Charles Talbert, *Reading John: A Literary and Theological Commentary on the Fourth Gospel and the Johannine Epistles* (New York: Crossroad, 1992), 92–93; and for a discussion of some problems with this reading, see Marianne Meye Thompson, *John: A Commentary* (NTL; Louisville, Ky.: Westminster John Knox, 2015), 62–63. But the terms *assume* and *transform*, even *embody*, are more apt to John's incarnational theology and his figural reading of Scripture that points to that which is brought to fruition in Jesus.

33 E.g., see Rudolf Bultmann, *The Gospel of John: A Commentary* (Philadelphia: Westminster, 1971), 78–79; E. C. Hoskyns, *The Fourth Gospel* (ed. Francis N. Davey; London: Faber & Faber, 1947), 152.

34 Cf. Rom 3:21.

35 This is my translation, which attempts to capture the etymology of the adverb δωρεάν.

36 For a similar use of νόμος in Paul, see also Rom 3:19; 1 Cor 14:21; Gal 4:21.

37 As acknowledged in *m.Ned.* 3:11: "R. Jose says, 'Great is circumcision since it overrides the stringent Sabbath.'"

38 "This is an argument *a minori ad maius* (from the lesser to the greater), quite common in rabbinic logic. Circumcision affects only a part of the body; if that is permitted, an action affecting the good of the whole body should be permitted" (Brown, *John*, 1:313).

39 For a similar argument, more extensively developed, see Luke 13:10-17.

40 I hasten to note that this sentence is a narrative-critical observation about the situation narrated by the Fourth Gospel, not an assertion about the actual opinions or practices of first-century Pharisees.

41 Nestle-Aland[27] follows the reading of manuscripts that read ἐν τῷ νόμῳ ὑμῶν ("in *your* law"). Actually, however, there is fairly strong external support in the manuscript tradition for a text that lacks the second-person plural pronoun (P[45] ℵ* D Θ as well as some versions), as in the translation given here. The fact that similar distancing pronouns appear in 8:17 and 15:25, with no manuscript evidence for their omission, suggests that the absence of the pronoun at 10:34 is not the result of intentional scribal correction in the manuscripts that lack it. Surely it is likelier that later Gentile Christian scribes would have added ὑμῶν, perhaps on the analogy of 8:17 and 15:25, rather than that they would have deleted it.

42 For present purposes, we need not explore the history-of-religions background of this psalm, which probably evokes a mythological picture of a heavenly council of the gods, here depicted as judged by the sovereign authority of the one God of Israel for failing to promote justice; so Patrick D. Miller, *Interpreting the Psalms* (Philadelphia: Fortress, 1987), 120–24; James

Luther Mays, *Psalms* (Interpretation; Louisville, Ky.: Westminster John Knox, 1994), 269–70. In the context of the argument in John 10, the psalm is understood to refer to mortal human beings (cf. Ps 82:7), probably human kings and rulers, whose status provides precedent for the royal "Son of God" title to be applied nonblasphemously to Jesus.

43 Lincoln, *John*, 460–61, puts the point negatively: the law was not able to do what "the Jews" want it to do: condemn Jesus.

44 Hoskyns, *John*, 523; and C. S. Keener, *The Gospel of John: A Commentary* (Peabody, Mass.: Hendrickson, 2003), 2:1125, suggest in passing this double meaning in John's statement.

45 On this point, see Gale A. Yee, *Jewish Feasts and the Gospel of John* (Wilmington, Del.: Michael Glazier, 1989); and Michael A. Daise, *Feasts in John: Jewish Festivals and Jesus' "Hour" in the Fourth Gospel* (WUNT 2/229; Tübingen: Mohr Siebeck, 2007). Most commentaries typically acknowledge and discuss the importance of the Jewish feasts as the backdrop for John's presentation of Jesus; some take Israel's liturgical calendar as providing the structure of John's narrative (see Brown, *John*; Thompson, *John*).

46 Sanders, *Judaism*, 130, guesses that the average person probably attended one of these three festivals a year.

47 There is an unspecified "festival of the Jews" in John 5:1. It is sometimes suggested that this might be the Festival of Weeks (see the discussion in Brown, *John*, 1:206), but the text offers no links to any particular feast. In this case, the mention of the feast seems simply to serve the narrative function of explaining the occasion for Jesus to go up to Jerusalem.

48 At least in the following references: 2:13, 23; 4:45; 6:4; 11:55; 12:1, 12, 20; 13:1, 29; 18:28, 39; 19:14.

49 John's narrative explicitly thematizes the second of these parallels but only faintly echoes the first. While commentators typically elaborate the connections between Passover, the reception of manna, and the feeding of the five thousand and Jesus' subsequent discourse (6:35-58), fewer call attention to the connections between Israel's sea crossing and Jesus' walking on the sea. Those who do, detect parallels between God's path through the sea in the course of delivering Israel from Egypt (Ps 77:19-20) and Jesus' own walking on the sea, and not between Israel's and Jesus' safe crossing (e.g., Brown, *John*, 1:255–56; Keener, *John*, 1:673; Lincoln, *John*, 218). But for a fuller study of allusions and echoes of Exodus traditions in John, see Andrew C. Brunson, *Psalm 118 in the Gospel of John: An Intertextual Study on the New Exodus Pattern in the Theology of John* (WUNT 2/158; Tübingen: Mohr Siebeck, 2003); for specific discussion of Passover and Exodus typology, including the sea crossing, see 156–59.

50 "You shall live in booths for seven days; all that are citizens in Israel shall live in booths, so that your generations may know that I made the people of Israel live in booths when I brought them out of the land of Egypt. I am the LORD your God" (Lev 23:42-43).

51 See Francis J. Moloney, S.D.B., *Signs and Shadows: Reading John 5–12* (Minneapolis: Fortress, 1996), 66–70; Thompson, *John*, 166–68; Seth Klayman, "Sukkoth from the Tanakh to Tannaitic Texts: Exegetical Traditions, Emergent Rituals, and Eschatological Associations" (Ph.D. diss., Duke University, 2008).

52 On the terminology, see Bauckham, *Testimony of the Beloved Disciple*, 258–60. This is the festival generally known today by its Hebrew name, *Hanukkah*.

53 E.g., Reimund Bieringer, Didier Pollefeyt, and Frederique Vandecasteele-Vanneuville, eds., *Anti-Judaism and the Fourth Gospel* (Louisville, Ky.: Westminster John Knox, 2000).

54 For extensive discussion, see Shaye J. D. Cohen, *The Beginnings of Jewishness: Boundaries, Varieties, Uncertainties* (Berkeley: University of California Press, 2001); Daniel Boyarin, "The *Ioudaioi* in John and the Prehistory of 'Judaism,'" in *Pauline Conversations in Context: Essays in Honor of Calvin J. Roetzel* (ed. Janice Capel Anderson, Philip Sellew, and Claudia Setzer; JSNTSup 221; London: Sheffield Academic, 2002), 216–39; Steve Mason, "Jews, Judaeans, Judaizing, Judaism: Problems of Categorization in Ancient History," *JSJ* 38 (2007): 457–512.

55 See on this point, D. Moody Smith, *The Fourth Gospel in Four Dimensions: Judaism and Jesus, the Gospels and Scripture* (Columbia: University of South Carolina Press, 2008), 5.

56 This was the highly influential thesis of J. Louis Martyn, *History and Theology in the Fourth Gospel* (3d ed.; Louisville, Ky.: Westminster John Knox, 2003), first published in 1968. Martyn's thesis and supporting historical arguments have come under repeated criticism; for discussion with appreciative appraisals, see D. Moody Smith, "The Contribution of J. Louis Martyn to the Understanding of the Gospel of John," in *The Conversation Continues: Studies in Paul and John in Honor of J. Louis Martyn* (ed. Robert T. Fortna and Beverly R. Gaventa; Nashville: Abingdon, 1990), 275–94; and Joel Marcus, "*Birkat Ha-Minim* Revisited," *NTS* 55 (2009): 523–51.

57 A summary sentence from D. Moody Smith gets the evidence just right: "Since John knows and affirms biblical history, Jewish Scriptures, messianic hopes, and eschatological expectation—while reinterpreting them—it should not surprise us to find that he takes a similar stance with respect to temple and cult" (Smith, *Fourth Gospel in Four Dimensions*, 23).

58 In the Passover Haggadah, the blessing after the Great Hallel acknowledges God's sole sovereignty: "From everlasting to everlasting thou art God; Beside thee we have no king, redeemer, or savior; No liberator, deliverer, provider; None who takes pity in every time of distress and trouble. We have no king but thee." But the date at which this refrain became part of the Passover liturgy is uncertain. The blessing or song may be alluded to in *b. Pesaḥ* 118a.

59 The Isaiah citation is noted by Brown, *John*, 2:895.

60 See, e.g., discussions in Brown, *John*, 1:4; Lincoln, *John*, 94–95; J. Ramsey Michaels, *The Gospel of John* (NICNT; Grand Rapids: Eerdmans, 2010), 46–57; Thompson, *John*, 27; and Keener, *John*, 1:365, with ample documentation.

Peder Borgen views John 1:1-18 as a homily on the beginning of Genesis ("Observations on the Targumic Character of the Prologue of John," *NTS* 16 [1969]: 288–95; and "Logos Was the True Light: Contributions to the Interpretation of the Prologue of John," *NovT* 14 [1972]: 115–30); so also Boyarin, "Gospel of the *Memra*," 243–84.

61   Cf. Wis 8:4: "She is an initiate in the knowledge of God, and an associate in his works." Or again, 9:9: "With you is Wisdom, she who knows your works and was present when you made the world."

62   In his study of Jewish "divine agent" figures, Larry Hurtado discusses both Wisdom and Word under the heading "personified divine attributes as divine agents" (*One God, One Lord*, 41–50). Michael Willett, *Wisdom Christology in the Fourth Gospel* (San Francisco: Mellen, 1992), 23–26, reviews the various interpretative proposals. See also Craig A. Evans, *Word and Glory: On the Exegetical and Theological Background of John's Prologue* (JSNTSup 89; Sheffield: Sheffield Academic, 1993).

63   Peter Phillips proposes that the links between the wisdom traditions and the opening verses of John are intertextual rather than propositional, drawing on the contexts and ideas surrounding *sophia* rather than on the lexeme itself (*The Prologue of the Fourth Gospel: A Sequential Reading* [LNTS 294; London: T&T Clark, 2006], 119).

64   Translation from F. H. Colson and G. H. Whittaker, *Philo: Volume 4* (LCL; London: Heinemann, 1932), 385. I have taken the liberty of replacing the English "Word" with the transliterated Greek word "*Logos*."

65   The motif of rejected Wisdom withdrawing from the stubborn people and returning to the heavens does, however, find a parallel elsewhere in John's Gospel. In John 7:34, Jesus reacts to the resistance of the Pharisees, who have sent temple guards to arrest him, by declaring, "I will be with you a little while longer, and then I am going to him who sent me. *You will search for me, but you will not find me*; and where I am, you cannot come." This is strikingly reminiscent of the words of personified Wisdom in Proverbs:

> I will pour out my thoughts to you;
> I will make my words known to you.
> Because I have called and you refused,
> Have stretched out my hand and no one heeded,
> And because you have ignored all my counsel
> And would have none of my reproof,
> I also will laugh at your calamity;
> I will mock when panic strikes you. . . .
> Then they will call upon me, but I will not answer;
> *They will seek me diligently but will not find me.*

(Prov 1:23b-26, 28)

Martin Scott, *Sophia and the Johannine Jesus* (JSNTSup 71; Sheffield: JSOT Press, 1992), 137–39; and Ben Witherington III, *John's Wisdom: A Commentary on the Fourth Gospel* (Louisville, Ky.: Westminster John Knox, 1995), 54, argue that John appropriates wisdom traditions in part because of the elements of judgment and rejection inherent within them. But John Ashton, *Studying John: Approaches to the Fourth Gospel* (Oxford: Clarendon, 1998), 16–17, contends that John counters the pessimistic views of Wisdom's inability to find a dwelling place on earth: Wisdom is now available in or as Jesus of Nazareth, rather than inaccessible.

66 On this analysis of the Johannine prologue, see Boyarin, "Gospel of the *Memra*," 89–111. Boyarin's incisive interpretation informs the reading I have offered in these paragraphs on the prologue.

67 Richard Bauckham has emphasized that within Israel's Scripture the work of creation of the world is solely to be attributed to the action of the one God of Israel (*Jesus and the God of Israel*, 7–11). Within this theological framework, references to the role of Wisdom in creation of the world must be understood as the poetic personification of a divine attribute, not as the name of a created entity.

68 John's citation of Ps 69:9 (68:10 LXX) has shifted the verb tense from the aorist form in the LXX (κατέφαγεν) to the future tense form (καταφάγεται), thus facilitating its interpretation as a prefiguration of Jesus' action.

69 The observations on John 2 summarized here were developed more fully in my earlier essay "Reading Scripture in Light of the Resurrection," in Davis and Hays, *Art of Reading Scripture*, 216–38; see esp. 221–24.

70 See Marianne Meye Thompson, "Learning the Identity of Jesus from the Gospel of John," in Gaventa and Hays, *Seeking the Identity of Jesus*, 166–79.

71 John does not, however, identify Zechariah as the source of the quotation.

72 John's christological reading of the Psalms, particularly the psalms of lament, is entirely consonant with other important streams of tradition in early Christianity. For other readings of Ps 69 as speech of the Messiah, see Rom 15:3; Matt 27:48; Mark 15:36; Luke 23:36; John 19:29. C. H. Dodd (*According to the Scriptures: The Sub-structure of New Testament Theology* [London: Nisbet, 1952], 57–60, 96–97) observes the wide range of different citations of this psalm by various New Testament writers and concludes as follows: "The intention of the New Testament writers is clearly to apply the whole [of Ps 69] to the sufferings and ultimate triumph of Christ" (97). On the whole question, see Hays, "Christ Prays the Psalms," 101–18. For wider reflections on this topic, see Brian E. Daley, "Is Patristic Exegesis Still Usable? Reflections on Early Christian Interpretation of the Psalms," in Davis and Hays, *Art of Reading Scripture*, 69–88.

73 Once again, I would insist that the retrospective interpretation of an Old Testament text as a figural precursor of a subsequent person or event does not deny or negate the historical reality of the precursor. Both the Old Testament type and the New Testament antitype stand together as concrete disclosures of God's activity in the world. Therefore, the hermeneutical current flows in both directions, and the "meaning" of each pole in the typological correlation is enhanced by its relation to the other.

74 For an exposition of the pervasive allusions to the temple motif in John, see Ulrich Busse, "Die Tempelmetaphorik als ein Beispiel von implizitem Rekurs auf die biblische Tradition im Johannesevangelium," in Tuckett, *Scriptures in the Gospels*, 395–428.

75 For this reading, see Knut Backhaus, "'Before Abraham was, I am': The Book of Genesis and the Genesis of Christology," in *Genesis and Christian Theology* (ed. Nathan MacDonald, Mark W. Elliott, and Grant Macaskill; Grand Rapids: Eerdmans, 2012), 74–84, 78; Witherington, *John's Wisdom*, 72–73; Mary L. Coloe, *God Dwells with Us: Temple Symbolism in the Fourth Gospel* (Collegeville, Minn.: Liturgical, 2001), 73, 215; John F. McHugh, *John 1–4* (ICC; London: T&T Clark, 2009), 169; Lincoln, *John*, 122; Keener, *John*, 1:489; for more extensive discussion of the links between the narrative of Jacob's dream, John 1:51, and Jesus' identification as the temple, see Alan R. Kerr, *The Temple of Jesus' Body: The Temple Theme in the Gospel of John* (JSNTSup 220; Sheffield: Sheffield Academic, 2002), 150–56.

76 For an extended exposition of this theme, see Coloe, *God Dwells with Us*, 23–27, 31–63.

77 See also Larry W. Hurtado, "Remembering and Revelation: The Historic and Glorified Jesus in the Gospel of John," in *Israel's God and Rebecca's Children: Christology and Community in Early Judaism and Christianity, Essays in Honor of Larry W. Hurtado and Alan F. Segal* (ed. David B. Capes, April D. DeConick, Helen K. Bond, and Troy Miller; Waco, Tex.: Baylor University Press, 2007), 195–213.

78 For a careful study of these ritual practices, see Klayman, "Sukkoth from the Tanakh to Tannaitic Texts"; as well as Jeffrey L. Rubenstein, *The History of Sukkot in the Second Temple and Rabbinic Periods* (BJS 302; Atlanta: Scholars Press, 1995); Håkan Ulfgard, *The Story of Sukkoth* (BGBE 34; Tübingen: Mohr Siebeck, 1998).

79 On the use of Zechariah in John, see William Randolph Bynum, "Quotations of Zechariah in the Fourth Gospel," in Myers and Schuchard, *Abiding Words*, 47–74.

80 The vivid verb ἔκραξεν draws the reader's attention to the dramatic public character of Jesus' declaration.

81 This reading presupposes the consensus text-critical judgment that the story of Jesus' gracious response to the woman caught in adultery (John 7:53–8:11) is a later addition to the text of John's Gospel. Originally, Jesus' claim to be the light of the world and the objection of the Pharisees (8:12-20) would have followed directly upon the controversies described in 7:40-52, making it clear that the declaration of 8:12, which is explicitly situated "in the treasury of the temple" (8:20), belongs to John's account of Jesus' activity at the Festival of Booths, a narrative unit that began back in 7:2.

82 For a detailed treatment of the syntactical and source-critical challenges associated with this text, see Menken, *Old Testament Quotations*, 187–203.

83 For a full discussion of Johannine allusions to Ezekiel, see Gary T. Manning, *Echoes of a Prophet: The Use of Ezekiel in the Gospel of John and in Literature of the Second Temple Period* (JSNTSup 270; London: T&T Clark, 2004).

84 Possibly also relevant here is Zech 13:1: "On that day a fountain shall be opened for the house of David and the inhabitants of Jerusalem, to cleanse them from sin and impurity." Cf. also Jer 2:13: "For my people have committed two evils: they have forsaken me, the fountain of living water, and dug out cisterns for themselves, cracked cisterns that can hold no water."

85 It is interesting, however, that in none of these passages does John hint at any direct symbolic connection between the Passover festival and the actions of Jesus that take place in conjunction with it. The feeding of the crowd of course echoes the story of God's provision of manna in the wilderness, a major event in the Exodus story, but John makes no discernible attempt to link the manna story of Exod 16 specifically to the *Passover* narrative of Exod 12.

86 For more detailed analysis of the textual form of the citation, see Menken, *Old Testament Quotations*, 147–66.

87 For a detailed account, see Josephus, *Ant.* 12.316–26.

88 See Manning, *Echoes of a Prophet*, 100–135.

89 It is sometimes thought that the Gospel of John lacks any concern for justice. On the contrary, this concern is powerfully present for those who have ears to hear the scriptural resonances of John's words and images.

90 See Diana Swancutt, "Hungers Assuaged by the Bread from Heaven: 'Eating Jesus' as Isaian Call to Belief: The Confluence of Isaiah 55 and Psalm 78(77) in John 6:22–71," in Evans and Sanders, *Early Christian Interpretation*, 218–51.

91 Peder Borgen, *Bread from Heaven: An Exegetical Study in the Concept of Manna in the Gospel of John and the Writings of Philo* (NovTSup 10; Leiden: Brill, 1965), 61–67, shows that the instruction on how to read the Scripture follows the rabbinic pattern of instruction: "Do not read *x*, but rather read *y*." But whereas Borgen emphasizes the *contrast* between Jesus and the manna that such reading produces, Susan Hylen emphasizes the *continuity* between them (*Allusion and Meaning in John 6* [BZNW 137; Berlin: De Gruyter, 2005]); so also Thompson, *John*, 148. John's rereading of Israel's story and its Scripture does not constitute a rejection of Israel's past or its formative narratives; rather, in John's view these are both *assumed* and *transformed*.

92 John's Gospel also includes several other prominent ἐγώ εἰμι statements on the lips of Jesus, notably "I am the Resurrection and the Life" (11:25) and "I am the Way, the Truth, and the Life" (14:6). While these dramatic claims are highly significant expressions of John's Christology, they are not as clearly evocative of specific scriptural subtexts as are the images of Temple, Bread, Light, Shepherd, and Vine.

93 Rightly noted by Wayne Meeks, *Prophet-King*, 87–91. Meeks' study as a whole emphasizes the connection between the titles "Prophet" and "King" in John, and it demonstrates that these offices were held closely together in Jewish traditions about Moses.

94 See here especially Andrew Lincoln, *Truth on Trial: The Lawsuit Motif in the Fourth Gospel* (Peabody, Mass.: Hendrickson, 2000).

95 While the date of these superscriptions remains disputed, Davidic authorship of the psalms was a "given" (see Daly-Denton, *David in the Fourth Gospel*, 318).

96 In addition to John 2:17, see also John 15:25; Rom 11:9-10, 15:3; and the offering of sour wine to Jesus on the cross in all three synoptic passion narratives (Matt 27:48; Mark 15:36; Luke 23:36). Cf. also the citation of the same psalm in Acts 1:20.

97 For the argument that the psalms in the passion narratives evoke the suffering and death of the king (or Messiah), see Martin Hengel, *The Atonement: The Origins of the Doctrine in the New Testament* (Philadelphia: Fortress, 1981); Juel, *Messianic Exegesis*, 102–3; Daly-Denton, *David in the Fourth Gospel*, 238–39; Thompson, "'They Bear Witness.'" The view that John employs these psalms to portray Jesus as the king who suffers and dies need not be construed as in conflict with the interpretation that these psalms are laments of the paradigmatic "righteous sufferer."

98 John's citation changes the LXX's aorist verb ἐταράχθη to the perfect tense τετάρακται to suit the narrative context into which he has placed the echo.

99 Another rarely observed Johannine instance of Jesus' echoing the Psalter appears in the staged public prayer that Jesus prays just before calling Lazarus out of the tomb. The prayer begins, "I thank you that you have heard me . . ." (πάτερ, εὐχαριστῶ σοι ὅτι ἤκουσάς μου [John 11:41]). This closely echoes the victorious prayer of Ps 118:21: "I thank you that you have answered me (ἐξομολογήσομαί σοι ὅτι ἐπήκουσάς μου) and have become my salvation" (Ps 118:21 [117:21 LXX]). The verbal agreement between Jesus' prayer and the psalmist's celebratory prayer is not exact, but the echo is especially intriguing in light of the New Testament's frequent citation of this same psalm (including in John 12:13) and in light of the fact that the immediately following verses declare, "The stone that the builders rejected has become the chief cornerstone; this is the LORD's doing, and it is marvelous in our eyes" (Ps 118:22-23 [117:22-23 LXX])—a passage that is cited in the synoptic triple tradition as a foreshadowing of the resurrection of Jesus (Matt 21:42; Mark 12:10-11; Luke 20:17), a function parallel to the raising of Lazarus in John. I am indebted to my student Hans Arneson for calling this echo to my attention. For a thorough discussion of Psalm 118 in its Jewish setting and its role in the festivals, see Brunson, *Psalm 118 in the Gospel of John*.

100 Jeremiah's prophecy that none of the sheep will be missing may also be the text that lies behind Jesus' later statement that "I protected them in your name that you have given me. I guarded them and not one of them was lost . . . so that the Scripture might be fulfilled" (John 17:12).

101 BDAG, 635.

102 For an illuminating discussion of this sort of honorific use of χριστός in Paul's letters, see Matthew V. Novenson, *Christ among the Messiahs: Christ Language*

in Paul and Messiah Language in Ancient Judaism (Oxford: Oxford University Press, 2012).

103   It is possible, though far from certain, that the expression "grace and truth" echoes the attributes proclaimed in God's self-revelation to Moses in Exod 34:6, which declares that the Lord abounds in "steadfast love and faithfulness." The problem, however, is that the language of the LXX in this passage does not correspond very closely to John's choice of words. To argue that John is alluding to Exod 34:6, one would have to hypothesize that John's phrase ἡ χάρις καὶ ἡ ἀλήθεια represents an independent translation from the Hebrew text, which reads חסד ואמת.

104   On ὁ ἐρχόμενος as a messianic designation, see Hays, *Conversion of the Imagination*, 119–42.

105   The exegesis of John 1:18 is a notoriously difficult and debated topic, as is the larger question of the meaning of John's Father-Son language. (For a detailed exegesis of this verse and presentation of its challenges, see McHugh, *John 1–4*, 69–77, 97–103.) On the possible sources of John's Father-Son language, see John Ashton, *Understanding the Fourth Gospel* (2d ed.; Oxford: Oxford University Press, 2007), esp. 211–32; and on the broader theological implications of the language, see C. K. Barrett, "Christocentric or Theocentric? Observations on the Theological Method of the Fourth Gospel," in *Essays on John* (Philadelphia: Westminster, 1982), 1–18; and Marianne Meye Thompson, *The God of the Gospel of John* (Grand Rapids: Eerdmans, 2001). These issues extend beyond the scope of the present study, which focuses on John's interpretation of *Scripture* rather than on his Christology more generally. Likewise, it should be acknowledged that the acclamation "son of [a] god" was employed in Roman imperial propaganda as a title for the Roman emperors, beginning with Augustus Caesar. (On this, see Hans-Josef Klauck, *The Religious Context of Early Christianity: A Guide to Graeco-Roman Religions* [Edinburgh: T&T Clark, 2000], 250–330.) The symbolic clash between Jesus and imperial authority underlies Jesus' tense dialogue with Pilate in 18:33-38, but the issue of *divine sonship* is not thematized in John's narrative at that point. In the passion narrative, it is the chief priests who complain that Jesus' claim to be Son of God is a violation of *Jewish* law (19:7; perhaps looking back to 10:33-38), not Roman authority.

106   The text of John 19:7 attributes this charge to "the Jews," but the context shows that it is the chief priests and their guards who are the instigators of the complaint (19:6). This is one of the passages that shows how problematic it is to interpret John's *Ioudaioi* as signifying the Jewish people as a whole.

107   For a consideration of this passage in Jewish midrash, and the possibility that "gods" refers to the Israelites when they received the law at Sinai and so qualify as "those to whom the word of God came," see Jerome H. Neyrey, "'I Said: You Are Gods': Psalm 82:6 and John 10," *JBL* 108 (1989): 647–63; Thompson, *John*, 235–37; and Anthony Tyrrell Hanson, *The Prophetic Gospel: A Study of John and the Old Testament* (Edinburgh: T&T Clark, 1991), 144–49, who catalogs a variety of other interpretations. Even so, the argument works

a minori ad maius, especially for readers not conversant with Jewish interpretative traditions.

108 For a survey of interpretative proposals regarding Son of Man, see the essays in *"Who Is This Son of Man?": The Latest Scholarship on a Puzzling Expression of the Historical Jesus* (ed. Larry W. Hurtado and Paul L. Owen; Edinburgh: T&T Clark, 2011).

109 In John, the promise that Jesus will be "lifted up" always applies to him as Son of Man (John 3:14, 8:28, 12:34); it is as the Son of Man that he has all power to judge (John 5:27).

110 Ben Reynolds, in *The Apocalyptic Son of Man in the Gospel of John* (WUNT 2/249; Tübingen: Mohr Siebeck, 2008), defends this reading of the Johannine Son of Man.

111 Francis J. Moloney, *The Johannine Son of Man* (2d ed.; BSRel 14; Rome: Libreria Ateneo Salesiano, 1978) insists that "Son of Man" refers to Jesus' humanity and that the applicability of the designation to Jesus depends upon the incarnation. Joel Marcus draws upon Jewish speculation about Adam as a figure of great glory, even godlikeness, in his argument that "[i]n 'the Son of Man' the godlike one is human; the title, in its implied union of these two aspects, is intrinsically incarnational" ("Son of Man as Son of Adam," *RB* 110 [2003]: 38–61, 370–86, citation from 384).

112 Another Old Testament echo: the "murmuring" of the crowd (John 6:61) in response to Jesus' bread of life discourse echoes the murmuring of God's people in the wilderness (Exod 16).

113 Parenthetically, one might ask whether the Greek text's association of the bronze serpent with the noun σημεῖον ("signal pole" or "sign") might have encouraged John's figural reading of the story.

114 See esp. Bauckham, *Jesus and the God of Israel*, 46–50; Lincoln, *John*, 153, suggests that the threefold reference to the Son of Man's being "lifted up" in John (John 3:14, 8:28, and 12:32-34) corresponds to the threefold passion predictions regarding the Son of Man in Mark; see also Craig A. Evans, "Obduracy and the Lord's Servant: Some Observations on the Use of the Old Testament in the Fourth Gospel," in *Early Jewish and Christian Exegesis: Studies in Memory of William Hugh Brownlee* (ed. Craig A. Evans and William F. Stinespring; Atlanta: Scholars Press, 1987), 221–36; and most recently, Daniel J. Brendsel, *"Isaiah Saw His Glory": The Use of Isaiah 52–53 in John 12* (BZNW 208; Boston: De Gruyter, 2014), 123–34.

115 A closely related passage is Isa 5:1-7, which uses the symbol of Israel as a vineyard (ἀμπελὼν, Isa 5:7), also in a judgment oracle.

116 Regrettably, the NRSV translates Ps 80:17 in a way that weakens the reference to a kingly figure and completely erases the hermeneutically interesting reference to a "son of man."

117 For a helpful exposition of the christological symbolism of Ps 80 in John 15, see particularly Andrew Streett, *The Vine and the Son of Man: Eschatological Interpretation of Psalm 80 in Early Judaism* (Minneapolis: Fortress, 2014), 209–22.

118 For the image of bearing fruit as a metaphor for the results of apostolic preaching, see Rom 1:13, 15:28; Phil 1:22.

119 For a similar expansive use of "law," see also John 10:34, 12:34; Rom 3:19; cf. 1 Cor 14:21; Gal 4:21.

120 John 12:31, 14:30, 16:11. Despite Jesus' verbal sparring with Pilate in John 18, there is no indication in this Gospel that "the ruler of this world" could allude to the Roman emperor.

121 Ezekiel's image of God as the shepherd who seeks out and rescues sheep that have been scattered among the peoples in other countries (Ezek 34:11-16) probably refers not to Gentiles but to the people of Israel who have been scattered in exile in the diaspora. John does not quote this text, but given his general affinity for the imagery of Ezek 34, it might well be heard as an intertext for John's statement that the purpose of Jesus' death will be "to gather into one the dispersed children of God."

122 The relentless christological focus of John's hermeneutic stands in fascinating juxtaposition to Paul's strongly ecclesiocentric hermeneutic. Paul tends to evoke Scripture primarily to interpret the identity and vocation of the *church*. (See Hays, *Echoes of Scripture*) For John, by contrast, the accent of scriptural interpretation falls heavily on the imaginative representation of the identity of Jesus himself.

Conclusion

1 The reader should take careful note of the construction of this sentence: "not only . . . but also." I am proposing not the rejection of modern critical readings but a corrective and enrichment.

2 For a brief exposition of Auerbach's understanding of figural interpretation, see the introduction to this volume. In *Christian Figural Reading*, John David Dawson carefully explicates the way in which Hans Frei, drawing on John Calvin, attempts to reinterpret Auerbach's analysis of *figura* to imply that "the glance backward can only be gained by a prior reading forward, *from* figure *toward* fulfillment." This would mean that "in order to read the Bible figurally, the Christian must reenact in his or her own reading the progression *from* ancient figure *to* subsequent fulfillment, just as though he or she were an ancient Israelite attempting to discern the figural dimension of persons and events" (Dawson, *Christian Figural Reading and the Fashioning of Identity* [Berkeley: University of California Press, 2001], 155–56; emphasis original). It seems to me that at this point Frei has superimposed Calvin's theology on Auerbach. Our reading of the Gospels, however, has shown that the Evangelists urge upon their readers a different sort of imaginative identification with characters in the story: we are to read as though we were among Jesus' early followers, discovering with surprise *after* his death and resurrection how our memories of him awaken unexpected echoes of Israel's Scripture.

3 On John 10:30 as a transformative allusion to the *Shema*, see Lori Ann Robinson Baron, "The Shema in John's Gospel against Its Backgrounds in Second Temple Judaism" (Ph.D. diss., Duke University, 2015), 348–52.

4 See Irenaeus, *Against Heresies* I.viii.5; I.ix.1–3; III.xi.7.

5 The triennial lectionary cycle represents one discipline of interpretation that would attempt to do justice to each synoptic witness.

6 As I am in the final days of drafting this conclusion during the visit of Pope Francis to the United States in September 2015, one illustration comes to mind: Pope Francis, with his emphasis on generosity, peace, and God's love for the poor, embodies a distinctly Lukan sensibility, in contrast to his predecessor in the papacy, Benedict XVI, who embodied a more Matthean concern for clarity of teaching, moral order, and the authoritative message entrusted to the church. Surely both of these emphases are necessary for the *bene esse* of the church across time. But each of these Popes spoke the word that he discerned as most needful for his particular historical moment. It would be an interesting exercise, beyond the scope of this book, to analyze whether these different sensibilities might be reflected in the specific scriptural texts actually cited by these two Popes in their respective writings and public addresses.

7 For an analogy from a more recent time, consider the hymns of Charles Wesley: many of them are patchwork quilts of scriptural references and allusions.

8 Arthur Miller, quoted by Richard Eyre in his director's notes for the *Playbill* for the Broadway production of *The Crucible*, 2001.

9 See thesis number four in Davis and Hays, "Nine Theses on the Interpretation of Scripture," in *Art of Reading Scripture*, 2–3: "Texts of Scripture do not have a single meaning limited to the intent of the original author. In accord with Jewish and Christian traditions, we affirm that Scripture has multiple complex senses given by God, the author of the whole drama."

10 Auerbach, *Mimesis*, 555; emphasis added. Dawson helpfully elaborates: "Auerbach observes that, for the Christian figural reader of the biblical text, God is both enactor and interpreter of the events depicted by the text. They have meaning and significance because they are the idiom in which God acts and speaks. Although one may refer to a figure 'announcing' its fulfillment, it is ultimately God who does the announcing, for a person or an event is a *figura* precisely because it begins an extended divine utterance that embraces subsequent persons and events. . . . If, then, Jesus is the fulfillment of Joshua, that is because both Joshua and Jesus help enact a single divine performative intention" (*Christian Figural Reading*, 85).

11 The Gospels are full of what Rowan Williams has called "language under pressure," which works "by insisting on developing certain sorts of pattern . . . by coupling what is not normally coupled (metaphor, paradox), by undermining surface meanings (irony) or by forcing us to relearn speaking or perceiving (fractured and chaotic language, alienating or puzzling description)" (*The Edge of Words: God and the Habits of Language* [London: Bloomsbury, 2014], 150).

12 See Richard Bauckham, "Reading Scripture as a Coherent Story," in Davis and Hays, *Art of Reading Scripture*, 38–53.

13 For an illustration, see my presentation of the contrast between Mark's scripturally inflected telling of the parable of the wicked tenants (Mark 12:1-12) and the secondary retelling of the same story in the Gospel of Thomas, which strips out the scriptural allusions (Richard B. Hays, *Reading Backwards: Figural Christology and the Fourfold Gospel Witness* [Waco, Tex.: Baylor University Press, 2014], 9–12).

14 Bart D. Ehrman, *Jesus, Interrupted: Revealing the Hidden Contradictions in the Bible (and Why We Don't Know about Them)* (New York: HarperCollins, 2009), 249. See also his most recent popularization of this familiar claim: Ehrman, *How Jesus Became God*.

15 One classic statement of such a view is Bousset, *Kyrios Christos*. For a concise critique of some of the problems with Bousset's account, see Hurtado, *Lord Jesus Christ*, 19–24.

16 Once again, I would draw the reader's attention to the important work of Bauckham, *Jesus and the God of Israel*.

17 Barth, *Church Dogmatics* IV/1, 186.

18 As Auerbach—writing strictly as a literary critic—observes about the Gospel of Mark, "[T]he story speaks to everybody; everybody is urged and indeed required to take sides for or against it. Even ignoring it implies taking sides" (*Mimesis*, 48).

BIBLIOGRAPHY

Aboth de-Rabbi Nathan. English. *The Fathers According to Rabbi Nathan.* Translated by J. Goldin. Yale Judaica Series 10. New Haven: Yale University Press, 1955.

Achtemeier, Paul J. *Mark.* Proclamation Commentaries. Philadelphia: Fortress, 1986.

Adams, Edward. *The Stars Will Fall from Heaven: Cosmic Catastrophe in the New Testament and Its World.* LNTS 347. London: T&T Clark, 2007.

Ahearne-Kroll, Stephen P. *The Psalms of Lament in Mark's Passion: Jesus' Davidic Suffering.* SNTSMS 142. Cambridge: Cambridge University Press, 2007.

Albl, Martin C. *"And Scripture Cannot Be Broken": The Form and Function of the Early Christian "Testimonia" Collections.* NovTSup 96. Leiden: Brill, 1999.

Alkier, Stefan. "Intertextuality and the Semiotics of Biblical Texts." Pages 3–21 in Hays, Alkier, and Huizenga, *Reading the Bible Intertextually.*

———. "Zeichen der Erinnerung—Die Genealogie in Mt 1 als intertextuelle Disposition." Paper presented at the annual meeting of the SNTS. Durham, England, 2002. Published as Stefan Alkier,

"From Text to Intertext: Intertextuality as a Paradigm for Reading Matthew." *HvTSt* 61 (2005): 1–18.

Allison, Dale C., Jr. "The Embodiment of God's Will: Jesus in Matthew." Pages 117–32 in Gaventa and Hays, *Seeking the Identity of Jesus.*

———. *The Intertextual Jesus: Scripture in Q.* Harrisburg, Pa.: Trinity Press International, 2000.

———. *The New Moses: A Matthean Typology.* Minneapolis: Fortress, 1993.

———. "The Son of God as Israel." *IBS* 9 (1987): 74–81.

Alter, Robert. *The Art of Biblical Narrative.* New York: Basic Books, 1981.

Anderson, A. A. *2 Samuel.* WBC. Dallas: Word Books, 1989.

Anderson, Bernard W. "Exodus Typology in Second Isaiah." Pages 177–95 in *Israel's Prophetic Heritage: Essays in Honor of James Muilenburg.* Edited by Bernhard W. Anderson and Walter Harrelson. New York: Harper, 1962.

Anderson, Gary A. "Joseph and the Passion of Our Lord." Pages 198–215 in Davis and Hays, *Art of Reading Scripture.*

Ashton, John. *Studying John: Approaches to the Fourth Gospel.* Oxford: Clarendon, 1998.

———. *Understanding the Fourth Gospel.* 2d ed. Oxford: Oxford University Press, 2007.

Auerbach, Erich. "Figura." Pages 65–113 in *Time, History, and Literature: Selected Essays of Erich Auerbach.* Edited by James I. Porter. Translated by Jane O. Newman. Princeton: Princeton University Press, 2014).

———. *Mimesis: The Representation of Reality in Western Literature.* Translated by Willard R. Trask. Princeton: Princeton University Press, 2013.

Backhaus, Knut. "'Before Abraham was, I am': The Book of Genesis and the Genesis of Christology." Pages 74–84 in *Genesis and Christian Theology.* Edited by Nathan MacDonald, Mark W. Elliott, and Grant Macaskill. Grand Rapids: Eerdmans, 2012.

Bacon, Benjamin W. *Studies in Matthew.* London: Constable, 1930.

Baron, Lori Ann Robinson. "The Shema in John's Gospel against Its Backgrounds in Second Temple Judaism." Ph.D. diss., Duke University, 2015

Barrett, C. K. *Essays on John.* Philadelphia: Westminster, 1982.

———. *The Gospel according to St. John: An Introduction with Commentary and Notes on the Greek Text.* 2d ed. Philadelphia: Westminster, 1978.

———. "The Old Testament in the Fourth Gospel." *JTS* 48 (1947): 155–69.

Barth, Karl. *Church Dogmatics* IV/1. Edited by G. W. Bromiley and T. F. Torrance. Translated by G. W. Bromiley. Edinburgh: T&T Clark, 1975.

Bauckham, Richard. *God Crucified: Monotheism and Christology in the New Testament*. Grand Rapids: Eerdmans, 1999.

———. *The Gospels for All Christians: Rethinking the Gospel Audiences*. Grand Rapids: Eerdmans, 1998.

———. *Jesus and the God of Israel: God Crucified and Other Studies on the New Testament's Christology of Divine Identity*. Grand Rapids: Eerdmans, 2009.

———. "Reading Scripture as a Coherent Story." Pages 38–53 in Davis and Hays, *Art of Reading Scripture*.

———. "Tamar's Ancestry and Rahab's Marriage: Two Problems in the Matthean Genealogy." *NovT* 37 (1995): 313–29.

———. *The Testimony of the Beloved Disciple: Narrative, History, and Theology in the Gospel of John*. Grand Rapids: Baker Academic, 2007.

Bauer, W., F. W. Danker, W. F. Arndt, and F. W. Gingrich, eds. *Greek-English Lexicon of the New Testament and Other Early Christian Literature*. 3d ed. Chicago: University of Chicago Press, 1999. [= BDAG]

Beale, G. K. *We Become What We Worship: A Biblical Theology of Idolatry*. Downers Grove, Ill.: InterVarsity, 2008.

Beale, G. K., and D. A. Carson, ed. *Commentary on the New Testament Use of the Old Testament*. Grand Rapids: Baker Academic, 2007.

Beaton, Richard. *Isaiah's Christ in Matthew's Gospel*. SNTSMS 123. Cambridge: Cambridge University Press, 2002.

Begbie, Jeremy S. *Music, Modernity and God*. Oxford: Oxford University Press, 2013.

Ben-Porat, Zvi. "The Poetics of Allusion." *Poetics and Theory of Literature* 1 (1976): 105–28.

Betz, H. D. "Logion of the Easy Yoke and of Rest (Matt 11:28-30)." *JBL* 86 (1967): 10–24.

Bieringer, Reimund, Didier Pollefeyt, and Frederique Vandecasteele-Vanneuville, eds. *Anti-Judaism and the Fourth Gospel*. Louisville, Ky.: Westminster John Knox, 2000.

Black, Matthew. "The Throne-theophany Prophetic Commission and the 'Son of Man': A Study in Tradition-History." Pages 57–73 in *Jews, Greeks and Christians: Religious Cultures in Late Antiquity: Essays in*

Honor of William David Davies. Edited by Robert Hamerton-Kelly and Robin Scroggs. Leiden: Brill, 1976.

Bloom, Harold. *The Anxiety of Influence: A Theory of Poetry*. New York: Oxford University Press, 1973.

Bock, Darrell L. *Proclamation from Prophecy and Pattern: Lucan Old Testament Christology*. JSNTSup 12. Sheffield: JSOT Press, 1987.

Bockmuehl, Marcus. *Seeing the Word: Refocusing New Testament Study*. Studies in Theological Interpretation. Grand Rapids: Baker Academic, 2006.

———. "Why Not Let Acts Be Acts? In Conversation with C. Kavin Rowe." *JSNT* 28 (2005): 163–66.

Bonhoeffer, Dietrich. *Widerstand und Ergebung: Briefe und Aufzeichnungen aus der Haft*. Edited by Christian Gremmels, Eberhard Bethge, and Renata Bethge, in collaboration with Ilse Tödt. Gütersloh: Chr. Kaiser, 1998.

Borgen, Peder. *Bread from Heaven: An Exegetical Study in the Concept of Manna in the Gospel of John and the Writings of Philo*. NovTSup 10. Leiden: Brill, 1965.

———. "Logos Was the True Light: Contributions to the Interpretation of the Prologue of John." *NovT* 14 (1972): 115–30.

———. "Observations on the Targumic Character of the Prologue of John." *NTS* 16 (1969): 288–95.

Boring, Eugene. *Mark: A Commentary*. NTL. Louisville, Ky.: Westminster John Knox, 2006.

Bousset, Wilhelm. *Kyrios Christos: Geschichte des Christusglaubens von den Anfängen des Christentums bis Irenaeus*. Göttingen: Vandenhoeck & Ruprecht, 1913; rev. ed., 1921. ET: *Kyrios Christos: A History of the Belief in Christ from the Beginnings of Christianity to Irenaeus*. Nashville: Abingdon, 1970. Repr., Waco, Tex.: Baylor University Press, 2013.

Bovon, François. *Luke 1: A Commentary on the Gospel of Luke 1:1–9:50*. Translated by Christine M. Thomas. Hermeneia. Minneapolis: Fortress, 2002.

Boyarin, Daniel. *Border Lines: The Partition of Judaeo-Christianity*. Philadelphia: University of Pennsylvania Press, 2004.

———. "The Gospel of the *Memra*: Jewish Binitarianism and the Prologue to John." *HTR* 94 (2001): 243–84.

———. "The *Ioudaioi* in John and the Prehistory of 'Judaism.'" Pages 216–39 in *Pauline Conversations in Context: Essays in Honor of Calvin*

J. Roetzel. Edited by Janice Capel Anderson, Philip Sellew, and Claudia Setzer. JSNTSup 221. London: Sheffield Academic, 2002.

———. *The Jewish Gospels: The Story of the Jewish Christ.* New York: New Press, 2012.

Braund, David C. *Augustus to Nero: A Sourcebook on Roman History, 31 BC–AD 68.* London: Crook Helm, 1985.

Brawley, Robert L. "Evocative Allusions in Matthew: Matthew 5:5 as a Test Case." Pages 127–48 in *Literary Encounters with the Reign of God.* Edited by Sharon H. Ringe and H. C. Paul Kim. New York: T&T Clark, 2004.

———. *Text to Text Pours Forth Speech: Voices of Scripture in Luke–Acts.* Bloomington: Indiana University Press, 1995.

Brendsel, Daniel J. *"Isaiah Saw His Glory": The Use of Isaiah 52–53 in John 12.* BZNW 208. Boston: De Gruyter, 2014.

Brodie, Thomas L. *The Crucial Bridge: The Elijah-Elisha Narrative as an Interpretive Synthesis of Genesis-Kings and a Literary Model for the Gospels.* Collegeville, Minn.: Liturgical, 2000.

———. "Towards Unravelling Luke's Use of the Old Testament: Luke 7:11–17 as an Imitatio of 1 Kings 17:17–24." *NTS* 32 (1986): 247–67.

Brown, Raymond E. *The Birth of the Messiah: A Commentary on the Infancy Narratives in the Gospels of Matthew and Luke.* Rev. ed. New York: Doubleday, 1993.

———. *The Gospel according to John.* AB 29–29A. Garden City, N.Y.: Doubleday, 1966–1970.

Brueggemann, Walter. *Isaiah.* WBC. Louisville, Ky.: Westminster John Knox, 1998.

Brunson, Andrew C. *Psalm 118 in the Gospel of John: An Intertextual Study on the New Exodus Pattern in the Theology of John.* WUNT 2/158. Tübingen: Mohr Siebeck, 2003.

Buckwalter, H. Douglas. *The Character and Purpose of Luke's Christology.* SNTSMS 89. Cambridge: Cambridge University Press, 1996.

Bultmann, Rudolf. *The Gospel of John: A Commentary.* Philadelphia: Westminster, 1971.

———. *The History of the Synoptic Tradition.* Translated by John Marsh. Rev. ed. New York: Harper & Row, 1968.

Burkett, Delbert. *The Son of Man Debate: A History and Evaluation.* SNTSMS 107. Cambridge: Cambridge University Press, 1999.

Buse, Ivor S. "The Markan Account of the Baptism of Jesus and Isaiah LXIII." *JTS* 7 (1956): 74–75.

Busse, Ulrich. "Die Tempelmetaphorik als ein Beispiel von implizitem Rekurs auf die biblische Tradition im Johannesevangelium." Pages 395–428 in Tuckett, *Scriptures in the Gospels*.

Bynum, William Randolph. "Quotations of Zechariah in the Fourth Gospel." Pages 47–74 in Myers and Schuchard, *Abiding Words*.

Callaway, Mary. *Sing, O Barren One: A Study in Comparative Midrash*. SBLDS 91. Atlanta: Scholars Press, 1986.

Cargal, T. B. "'His Blood Be Upon Us and Upon Our Children': A Matthean Double Entendre?" *NTS* 37 (1991): 101–12.

Carlson, Stephen C. "The Davidic Key for Counting the Generations in Matthew 1:17." *CBQ* 76 (2014): 665–83.

Carter, Warren. "Evoking Isaiah: Matthean Soteriology and an Intertextual Reading of Isaiah 7–9 and Matthew 1:23 and 4:15–16." *JBL* 119 (2000): 503–20.

Cassidy, Richard J. *Jesus, Politics, and Society: A Study of Luke's Gospel*. Maryknoll, N.Y.: Orbis Books, 1978.

Chancey, Mark A. *The Myth of a Gentile Galilee*. SNTSMS 118. Cambridge: Cambridge University Press, 2002.

Charlesworth, James H., ed. *The Old Testament Pseudepigrapha*. 2 vols. Garden City, N.Y.: Doubleday, 1983–1985.

Childs, Brevard S. *Introduction to the Old Testament as Scripture*. Philadelphia: Fortress, 1979.

———. *Isaiah*. OTL. Louisville, Ky.: Westminster John Knox, 2001.

———. "Psalm Titles and Midrashic Exegesis." *JSemS* 16 (1971): 137–50.

Chilton, Bruce D. "Jesus Ben David: Reflection on the Davidssohn-frage." *JSNT* 14 (1982): 88–112.

Christensen, Duane L. *Deuteronomy*. WBC 6, revised. Nashville: Thomas Nelson, 2001.

Clements, R. E. *Isaiah 1–39*. NCBC. Grand Rapids: Eerdmans, 1980.

Coggins, R. J., and J. L. Houlden, eds. *A Dictionary of Biblical Interpretation*. London: SCM Press, 1990.

Cohen, Shaye J. D. *The Beginnings of Jewishness: Boundaries, Varieties, Uncertainties*. Berkeley: University of California Press, 2001.

Collins, Adela Yarbro. *Mark: A Commentary*. Hermeneia. Minneapolis: Fortress, 2007.

Collins, John J. *The Apocalyptic Imagination: An Introduction to Jewish Apocalyptic Literature*. 2d ed. The Biblical Resource Series. Grand Rapids: Eerdmans, 1998.

———. *Apocalypticism in the Dead Sea Scrolls*. New York: Routledge, 1997.

———. *The Scepter and the Star: The Messiahs of the Dead Sea Scrolls and Other Ancient Literature.* ABRL. New York: Doubleday, 1995.

Coloe, Mary L. *God Dwells with Us: Temple Symbolism in the Fourth Gospel.* Collegeville, Minn.: Liturgical, 2001.

Colson, F. H., and G. H. Whittaker. *Philo: Volume 4.* LCL. London: Heinemann, 1932.

Conzelmann, Hans. *Die Mitte der Zeit: Studien Zur Theologie Des Lukas.* BHT 17. Tübingen: Mohr Siebeck, 1954. ET: *The Theology of St. Luke.* Translated by Geoffrey Buswell. New York: Harper, 1961.

Cope, O. Lamar. *Matthew, a Scribe Trained for the Kingdom of Heaven.* CBQMS 5. Washington, D.C.: Catholic Biblical Association, 1976.

Cranfield, C. E. B. *The Gospel according to Saint Mark: An Introduction and Commentary by C.E.B. Cranfield.* CGTC. Cambridge: Cambridge University Press, 1959 (1974 printing).

Crossan, John Dominic. "Form for Absence: The Markan Creation of Gospel." *Semeia* 12 (1978): 41–55.

———. *The Historical Jesus: The Life of a Mediterranean Peasant.* San Francisco: HarperCollins, 1991.

Dahl, Nils Alstrup. *Jesus in the Memory of the Early Church.* Minneapolis: Augsburg, 1976.

———. *Studies in Paul: Theology for the Early Christian Mission.* Minneapolis: Augsburg, 1977.

Daise, Michael A. *Feasts in John: Jewish Festivals and Jesus' "Hour" in the Fourth Gospel.* WUNT 2/229. Tübingen: Mohr Siebeck, 2007.

Daley, Brian E. "Is Patristic Exegesis Still Usable? Reflections on Early Christian Interpretation of the Psalms." Pages 69–88 in Davis and Hays, *Art of Reading Scripture.*

Daly-Denton, Margaret. *David in the Fourth Gospel: The Johannine Reception of the Psalms.* AGJU 47. Leiden: Brill, 2000.

Davies, W. D., and Dale C. Allison, Jr. *A Critical and Exegetical Commentary on the Gospel according to Saint Matthew: In Three Volumes.* ICC. Edinburgh: T&T Clark, 1988–1997.

Davis, Ellen F., and Richard B. Hays, eds. *The Art of Reading Scripture.* Grand Rapids: Eerdmans, 2003.

———. "Nine Theses on the Interpretation of Scripture." Pages 1–8 in Davis and Hays, *Art of Reading Scripture.*

Dawson, John David. *Christian Figural Reading and the Fashioning of Identity.* Berkeley: University of California Press, 2001.

Denova, Rebecca I. *The Things Accomplished among Us: Prophetic Tradition in the Structural Pattern of Luke–Acts.* JSNT 141. Sheffield: Sheffield Academic, 1997.

Deutsch, Celia. *Hidden Wisdom and the Easy Yoke: Wisdom, Torah, and Discipleship in Matthew 11.25–30.* Sheffield: JSOT Press, 1987.

Dittenberger, Wilhelm. *Sylloge Inscriptionum Graecarum, a Guilelmo Dittenbergero Condita et Aucta, Nunc Tertium Edita.* Lipsiae: Apud S. Hirzelium, 1915–1924.

Doble, Peter. "Luke 24. 26, 44—Songs of God's Servant: David and His Psalms in Luke–Acts." *JSNT* 28 (2006): 267–83.

———. "The Psalms in Luke–Acts." Pages 83–117 in *The Psalms in the New Testament.* Edited by Steve Moyise and Maarten J. J. Menken. London: T&T Clark, 2004.

Dodd, C. H. *According to the Scriptures: The Sub-structure of New Testament Theology.* London: Nisbet, 1952.

———. *The Interpretation of the Fourth Gospel.* Cambridge: Cambridge University Press, 1953.

Donaldson, Terence L. *Jesus on the Mountain: A Study in Matthean Theology.* JSNTSup 8. Sheffield: JSOT Press, 1985.

Dowd, Sharyn Echols. *Prayer, Power, and the Problem of Suffering: Mark 11:22–25 in the Context of Markan Theology.* SBLDS 105. Atlanta: Scholars Press, 1988.

Driver, S. R. *Notes on the Hebrew Text and the Topography of the Books of Samuel: With an Introduction on Hebrew Palaeography and the Ancient Versions and Facsimiles of Inscriptions and Maps.* Oxford: Clarendon, 1960.

Drury, John. "Luke, Gospel of." In *A Dictionary of Biblical Interpretation.* Edited by R. J. Goggins and J. L. Houlden. London: SCM Press, 1990.

Duling, Dennis C. "Solomon, Exorcism, and the Son of David." *HTR* 68 (1975): 235–52.

Dunn, James D. G. *The Partings of the Ways: Between Christianity and Judaism and Their Significance for the Character of Christianity.* 2d ed. London: SCM Press, 2006.

Eco, Umberto. *A Theory of Semiotics.* Bloomington: Indiana University Press, 1979.

Edwards, James R. "Markan Sandwiches: The Significance of Interpolations in Mark's Narratives." *NovT* 31 (1989): 193–216.

Ehrman, Bart D. *How Jesus Became God: The Exaltation of a Jewish Preacher from Galilee.* New York: HarperOne, 2014.

———. *Jesus, Interrupted: Revealing the Hidden Contradictions in the Bible (and Why We Don't Know about Them)*. New York: Harper-Collins, 2009.

———. *The Orthodox Corruption of Scripture: The Effect of Early Christological Controversies on the Text of the New Testament*. New York: Oxford University Press, 1993.

Eliot, T. S. "The Dry Salvages." In *The Complete Poems and Plays*. New York: Harcourt, Brace & World, 1962.

Epp, Eldon Jay. "The 'Ignorance Motif' in Acts and Anti-Judaic Tendencies in Codex Bezae." *HTR* 55 (1962): 51–62.

Eubank, Nathan. "A Disconcerting Prayer: On the Originality of Luke 23:34a." *JBL* 129 (2010): 521–36.

Evans, Craig A. "The Beginning of the Good News and the Fulfillment of Scripture in the Gospel of Mark." Pages 83–103 in Porter, *Hearing the Old Testament in the New Testament*.

———. "Obduracy and the Lord's Servant: Some Observations on the Use of the Old Testament in the Fourth Gospel." Pages 221–36 in *Early Jewish and Christian Exegesis: Studies in Memory of William Hugh Brownlee*. Edited by Craig A. Evans and William F. Stinespring. Atlanta: Scholars Press, 1987.

———. *Word and Glory: On the Exegetical and Theological Background of John's Prologue*. JSNTSup 89. Sheffield: Sheffield Academic, 1993.

Evans, Craig A., and James A. Sanders, eds. *Early Christian Interpretation of the Scriptures of Israel*. JSNTSup 148. Sheffield: Sheffield Academic, 1997.

———. *Luke and Scripture: The Function of Sacred Tradition in Luke–Acts*. Minneapolis: Fortress, 1993.

Fernández Marcos, Natalio. *The Septuagint in Context: Introduction to the Greek Versions of the Bible*. Translated by Wilfred G. E. Watson. Leiden: Brill, 2000.

Fitzmyer, Joseph A. *The Gospel according to Luke: Introduction, Translation, and Notes*. AB 28–28A. Garden City, N.Y.: Doubleday, 1981–1985.

Fletcher-Louis, Crispin H. T. "Jesus Inspects His Priestly War Party (Luke 14:25-35)." Pages 126–43 in *The Old Testament in the New Testament: Essays in Honour of J.L. North*. Edited by Steve Moyise. JSNT 189. Sheffield: Sheffield Academic, 2000.

Foley, John Miles. *Immanent Art: From Structure to Meaning in Traditional Oral Epic*. Bloomington: Indiana University Press, 1991.

Foster, P. "Why Did Matthew Get the Shema Wrong? A Study of Matthew 22:37." *JBL* 122 (2003): 309–33.

Fowler, Robert M. *Let the Reader Understand: Reader-Response Criticism and the Gospel of Mark*. Minneapolis: Fortress, 1991.

France, R. T. *The Gospel of Mark: A Commentary on the Greek Text*. NIGTC. Grand Rapids: Eerdmans, 2002.

Frei, Hans W. *The Eclipse of Biblical Narrative: A Study in Eighteenth and Nineteenth Century Hermeneutics*. New Haven: Yale University Press, 1974.

———. *The Identity of Jesus Christ: The Hermeneutical Bases of Dogmatic Theology*. Philadelphia: Fortress, 1975.

Frost, Robert. "Education by Poetry." Speech delivered at Amherst College and subsequently revised for publication in the *Amherst Graduates' Quarterly* (February 1931).

Funk, Robert W., Roy Hoover, et al. *The Five Gospels: The Search for the Authentic Words of Jesus*. New York: Macmillan, 1993.

Furnish, Victor Paul. *The Love Command in the New Testament*. Nashville: Abingdon, 1972.

García Martínez, Florentino. "Messianic Hopes in the Qumran Writings." Pages 159–89 in *The People of the Dead Sea Scrolls: Their Writings, Beliefs, and Practices*. Edited by Florentino García Martínez and Julio Trebolle Barrera. Translated by Wilfred G. E. Watson. Leiden: E. J. Brill, 1993.

Gathercole, Simon J. *The Pre-existent Son: Recovering the Christologies of Matthew, Mark, and Luke*. Grand Rapids: Eerdmans, 2006.

Gaventa, Beverly Roberts. *The Acts of the Apostles*. ANTC. Nashville: Abingdon, 2003.

———. "The Archive of Excess: John 21 and the Problem of Narrative Closure." Pages 240–53 in *Exploring the Gospel of John: In Honor of D. Moody Smith*. Edited by R. Alan Culpepper and C. Clifton Black. Louisville, Ky.: Westminster John Knox, 1996.

———. "Learning and Relearning the Identity of Jesus from Luke–Acts." Pages 148–65 in Gaventa and Hays, *Seeking the Identity of Jesus*.

Gaventa, Beverly Roberts, and Richard B. Hays, eds. *Seeking the Identity of Jesus: A Pilgrimage*. Grand Rapids: Eerdmans, 2008.

Gench, Frances Taylor. *Wisdom in the Christology of Matthew*. Lanham, Md.: University Press of America, 1997.

Gerhardsson, Birger. *The Testing of God's Son: (Matt. 4: 1–11 & par.): An Analysis of an Early Christian Midrash.* ConBNT 2:1. Lund: Gleerup, 1966.

Gnilka, Joachim. *Das Evangelium nach Markus.* 2 vols. EKKNT 2. Zürich: Benziger, Neukirchen Neukirchener Verlag, 1978–1979.

Goodacre, Mark. *The Case against Q: Studies in Markan Priority and the Synoptic Problem.* Harrisburg, Pa.: Trinity International, 2002.

Gray, Timothy C. *The Temple in the Gospel of Mark: A Study in Its Narrative Role.* WUNT 2/242. Tübingen: Mohr Siebeck, 2008.

Green, Joel B. *The Gospel of Luke.* NICNT. Grand Rapids: Eerdmans, 1997.

———. "The Problem of a Beginning: Israel's Scriptures in Luke 1–2." *BBR* 4 (1994): 61–85.

———. "Witnesses of His Resurrection: Resurrection, Salvation, Discipleship, and Mission in the Acts of the Apostles." Pages 227–46 in *Life in the Face of Death: The Resurrection Message of the New Testament.* Edited by Richard N. Longenecker. Grand Rapids: Eerdmans, 1998.

Gregory, Andrew F., and C. Kavin Rowe, eds. *Rethinking the Unity and Reception of Luke and Acts.* Columbia: University of South Carolina Press, 2010.

Grohmann, Marianne. "Psalm 113 and the Song of Hannah (1 Samuel 2:1-10): A Paradigm for Intertextual Reading?" Pages 119–35 in Hays, Alkier, and Huizenga, *Reading the Bible Intertextually.*

Grundmann, Walter. *Das Evangelium Des Markus: Includes Bibliographical References and Index.* 3d ed. THKNT 7. Aufl. Berlin: Evangelische Verlagsanstalt, 1977.

Haenchen, Ernst. *The Acts of the Apostles: A Commentary.* Louisville, Ky.: Westminster John Knox, 1971.

Hakola, Raimo. *Identity Matters: John, the Jews and Jewishness.* NovTSup 118. Boston: Brill, 2005.

Hamerton-Kelly, R. G. *Pre-existence, Wisdom, and the Son of Man: A Study of the Idea of Pre-existence in the New Testament.* SNTSMS 21. Cambridge: Cambridge University Press, 1973.

Hamilton, Catherine Sider. "'His Blood Be Upon Us': Innocent Blood and the Death of Jesus in Matthew." *CBQ* 70 (2008): 82–100.

Hanson, Anthony Tyrrell. *The Prophetic Gospel: A Study of John and the Old Testament.* Edinburgh: T&T Clark, 1991.

Harris, Rendel. *Testimonies.* 2 vols. Cambridge: Cambridge University Press, 1916–1920.

Hatina, Thomas R. *In Search of a Context: The Function of Scripture in Mark's Narrative.* JSNTSup 232. London: Sheffield Academic, 2002.

Hays, Richard B. "Christ Prays the Psalms: Israel's Psalter as Matrix of Early Christology." Pages 101–18 in Hays, *Conversion of the Imagination.*

———. *The Conversion of the Imagination: Paul as Interpreter of Israel's Scripture.* Grand Rapids: Eerdmans, 2005.

———. "The Corrected Jesus." *First Things* 43 (1994): 43–48.

———. *Echoes of Scripture in the Letters of Paul.* New Haven: Yale University Press, 1989.

———. "Galatians." Pages 181–348 in *Second Corinthians–Philemon.* Vol. 11 of *New Interpreter's Bible.* Edited by Leander E. Keck. Nashville: Abingdon, 2000.

———. *The Moral Vision of the New Testament: Community, Cross, New Creation: A Contemporary Introduction to New Testament Ethics.* San Francisco: HarperSanFrancisco, 1996.

———. *Reading Backwards: Figural Christology and the Fourfold Gospel Witness.* Waco, Tex.: Baylor University Press, 2014.

———. "Reading the Bible with Eyes of Faith: Theological Exegesis from the Perspective of Biblical Studies." Pages 82–101 in *Sharper than a Two-Edged Sword: Preaching, Teaching, and Living the Bible.* Edited by Michael Root and James J. Buckley. Grand Rapids: Eerdmans, 2008.

———. "Reading Scripture in Light of the Resurrection." Pages 216–38 in Davis and Hays, *Art of Reading Scripture.*

———. "'Who Has Believed Our Message?' Paul's Reading of Isaiah." Pages 25–49 in Hays, *Conversion of the Imagination.*

Hays, Richard B., Stefan Alkier, and Leroy A. Huizenga, eds. *Reading the Bible Intertextually.* Waco, Tex.: Baylor University Press, 2009. Translation of *Die Bibel Im Dialog der Schriften: Konzepte Intertextueller Bibellektüre.* Tübingen: Francke, 2005.

Heil, John Paul. *Jesus Walking on the Sea: Meaning and Gospel Functions of Matt. 14:22-33, Mark 6:45-52, and John 6:15b-21.* AnBib 87. Rome: Biblical Institute, 1981.

Hengel, Martin. *The Atonement: The Origins of the Doctrine in the New Testament.* Philadelphia: Fortress, 1981.

———. *Between Jesus and Paul: Studies in the Earliest History of Christianity.* Philadelphia: Fortress, 1983. Repr., Waco, Tex.: Baylor University Press, 2013.

————. "The Old Testament in the Fourth Gospel." Pages 380–95 in *The Gospels and the Scriptures of Israel*. Edited by Craig A. Evans and W. Richard Stegner. JSNTSup 104. Sheffield: Sheffield Academic, 1994.

————. *The Septuagint as Christian Scripture: Its Prehistory and the Problem of Its Canon*. OTS. Edinburgh: T&T Clark, 2002.

Hoffman, Lawrence A., ed. *The Amidah*. Vol 2, *My People's Prayer Book: Traditional Prayers, Modern Commentaries*. Woodstock, Vt.: Jewish Lights, 1997.

————. *Studies in the Gospel of Mark*. Translated by John Bowden. Philadelphia: Fortress, 1985.

Hollander, John. *The Figure of Echo: A Mode of Allusion in Milton and After*. Berkeley: University of California Press, 1981.

Hood, Jason B. *The Messiah, His Brothers, and the Nations: Matthew 1.1–17* LNTS 441. New York: T&T Clark, 2011.

Hooker, Morna D. *The Gospel according to Saint Mark*. BNTC. London: A&C Black, 1991.

————. *Jesus and the Servant: The Influence of the Servant Concept of Deutero-Isaiah in the New Testament*. London: SPCK, 1959.

Horbury, William. *Jewish Messianism and the Cult of Christ*. London: SCM Press, 1998.

Horsley, Richard A. *Hearing the Whole Story: The Politics of Plot in Mark's Gospel*. Louisville, Ky.: Westminster John Knox, 2001.

Hoskyns, E. C. *The Fourth Gospel*. Edited by Francis N. Davey. London: Faber & Faber, 1947.

Huizenga, Leroy. *The New Isaac: Tradition and Intertextuality in the Gospel of Matthew*. NovTSup 131. Leiden: Brill, 2009.

Hurtado, Larry W. "The Binitarian Shape of Early Christian Worship." Pages 187–213 in *The Jewish Roots of Christological Monotheism: Papers from the St. Andrews Conference on the Historical Origins of the Worship of Jesus*. Edited by Carey C. Newman et al. Leiden: Brill, 1999.

————. *Lord Jesus Christ: Devotion to Jesus in Earliest Christianity*. Grand Rapids: Eerdmans, 2003.

————. *One God, One Lord: Early Christian Devotion and Ancient Jewish Monotheism*. 2d ed. London: T&T Clark, 2003.

————. "Remembering and Revelation: The Historic and Glorified Jesus in the Gospel of John." Pages 195–213 in *Israel's God and Rebecca's Children: Christology and Community in Early Judaism and Christianity, Essays in Honor of Larry W. Hurtado and Alan F. Segal*. Edited by David B. Capes, April D. DeConick, Helen K. Bond, and Troy Miller. Waco, Tex.: Baylor University Press, 2007.

Hurtado, Larry W., and Paul L. Owen, eds. *"Who Is This Son of Man?":* *The Latest Scholarship on a Puzzling Expression of the Historical Jesus.* Edinburgh: T&T Clark, 2011.

Hylen, Susan. *Allusion and Meaning in John 6.* BZNW 137. Berlin: De Gruyter, 2005.

Instone-Brewer, David. "The Eighteen Benedictions and the Minim before 70 CE." *JTS* 54 (2003) 25–44.

Irvine, Stuart A. *Isaiah, Ahaz, and the Syro-Ephraimitic Crisis.* SBLDS 123. Atlanta: Scholars Press, 1990.

Iverson, Kelley R. *Gentiles in the Gospel of Mark: "Even the Dogs under the Table Eat the Children's Crumbs."* LNTS 339. London: T&T Clark, 2007.

Jervell, Jacob. *Luke and the People of God.* Minneapolis: Augsburg, 1972.

———. *The Theology of the Acts of the Apostles.* Cambridge: Cambridge University Press, 1996.

———. *The Unknown Paul: Essays on Luke–Acts and Early Christian History.* Minneapolis: Augsburg, 1984.

Jobes, Karen H., and Moisés Silva. *Invitation to the Septuagint.* 2d ed. Grand Rapids: Baker Academic, 2015.

Johnson, Luke Timothy. *The Gospel of Luke.* SP 3. Collegeville, Minn.: Liturgical, 1991.

———. "Literary Criticism of Luke–Acts: Is Reception-History Pertinent?" *JSNT* 28 (2005): 159–62.

———. *Luke–Acts: A Story of Prophet and People.* Chicago: Franciscan Herald, 1981.

———. "The New Testament's Anti-Jewish Slander and Conventions of Ancient Rhetoric." *JBL* 108 (1989): 419–41.

———. *Septuagintal Midrash in the Speeches of Acts.* The Père Marquette Lecture in Theology. Milwaukee: Marquette University Press, 2002.

Juel, Donald. *A Master of Surprise: Mark Interpreted.* Minneapolis: Fortress, 1994.

———. *Messiah and Temple: The Trial of Jesus in the Gospel of Mark.* SBLDS 31. Missoula, Mont.: Scholars Press, 1977.

———. *Messianic Exegesis: Christological Interpretation of the Old Testament in Early Christianity.* Philadelphia: Fortress, 1988.

Keck, Leander E. "Toward the Renewal of New Testament Christology." *NTS* 3 (1986): 362–77. Reprinted in Leander E. Keck, *Why Christ Matters: Toward a New Testament Christology.* Waco, Tex.: Baylor University Press, 2015.

Kee, Howard Clark. "The Function of Scriptural Quotations and Allusions in Mark 11–16." Pages 165–85 in *Jesus und Paulus: Festschrift f. Werner Georg Kümmel z. 70. Geburstag.* Edited by E. Earle Ellis and Erich Grässer. Göttingen: Vandenhoeck & Ruprecht, 1975.

Keener, C. S. *The Gospel of John: A Commentary.* 2 vols. Peabody, Mass.: Hendrickson, 2003.

Kermode, Frank. *The Genesis of Secrecy: On the Interpretation of Narrative.* The Charles Eliot Norton Lectures. Cambridge, Mass.: Harvard University Press, 1979.

Kerr, Alan R. *The Temple of Jesus' Body: The Temple Theme in the Gospel of John.* JSNTSup 220. Sheffield: Sheffield Academic, 2002.

Klayman, Seth. "Sukkoth from the Tanakh to Tannaitic Texts: Exegetical Traditions, Emergent Rituals, and Eschatological Associations." Ph.D. diss., Duke University, 2008.

Klauck, Hans-Josef. "Die Frage der Sündenvergebung in der Perikope von der Heilung Des Gelälhmten (Mk 2, 1-12 Parr)." *BZ* 25 (1981): 223–48.

———. *The Religious Context of Early Christianity: A Guide to Graeco-Roman Religions.* Edinburgh: T&T Clark, 2000.

Knowles, Matthew P. "Scripture, History, Messiah: Scriptural Fulfillment and the Fullness of Time in Matthew's Gospel." Pages 59–92 in Porter, *Hearing the Old Testament in the New Testament.*

Köstenberger, Andreas J. "John." Pages 415–512 in Beale and Carson, *Commentary.*

Kramer, Werner. *Christ, Lord, Son of God.* Translated by Brian Hardy. SBT 50. London: SCM Press, 1966.

Kupp, David D. *Matthew's Emmanuel: Divine Presence and God's People in the First Gospel.* SNTSMS 90. Cambridge: Cambridge University Press, 1996.

Kurz, William S., S.J. *Reading Luke–Acts: Dynamics of Biblical Narrative.* Louisville, Ky.: Westminster John Knox, 1993.

Lagrange, M. J. *Evangile Selon Saint Marc.* Etudes Bibliques. Paris: J. Gabalda, 1911.

Lane, William L. *The Gospel according to Mark: The English Text with Introduction, Exposition, and Notes.* NICNT. Grand Rapids: Eerdmans, 1974.

Leim, Joshua E. *Matthew's Theological Grammar: The Father and the Son.* WUNT 2/402. Tübingen: Mohr Siebeck, 2015.

———. "Worshiping the Father, Worshiping the Son: Cultic Language and the Identity of God in the Gospel of Matthew." *JTI* 9 (2015): 65–84.

Levenson, Jon D. *The Death and Resurrection of the Beloved Son: The Transformation of Child Sacrifice in Judaism and Christianity.* New Haven: Yale University Press, 1993.

Levine, Amy-Jill. "Matthew's Advice to a Divided Readership." Pages 22–41 in *The Gospel of Matthew in Current Study: Studies in Memory of William G. Thompson, S.J.* Edited by David E. Aune. Grand Rapids: Eerdmans, 2001.

———. *The Social and Ethnic Dimensions of Matthean Salvation History.* Studies in the Bible and Early Christianity 14. Lewiston, N.Y.: Edwin Mellen, 1988.

Lierman, John. "The Mosaic Pattern of John's Christology." Pages 210–34 in *Challenging Perspectives on the Gospel of John.* Edited by John Lierman. WUNT 2/219. Tübingen: Mohr Siebeck, 2006.

Lincoln, Andrew T. *The Gospel according to Saint John.* Black's New Testament Commentaries. New York: Continuum, 2005.

———. *Truth on Trial: The Lawsuit Motif in the Fourth Gospel.* Peabody, Mass.: Hendrickson, 2000.

Lindbeck, George A. *The Church in a Postliberal Age.* Edited by James J. Buckley. Radical Traditions. London: SCM Press, 2002.

Litwak, Kenneth Duncan. *Echoes of Scripture in Luke–Acts: Telling the History of God's People Intertextually.* JSNTSup 285. London: T&T Clark, 2005.

Lord, George deForest. *Classical Presences in Seventeenth-Century English Poetry.* New Haven: Yale University Press, 1987.

Luther, Martin. "Preface to the Old Testament." In vol. 35 of *Luther's Works.* Edited by E. Theodore Bachmann. Philadelphia: Muhlenberg, 1960.

Luz, Ulrich. "Der Antijudaismus im Matthäusevangelium als historisches und theologisches Problem: Eine Skizze." *EvTh* 53 (1993): 310–27. Reprinted as Ulrich Luz, "Anti-Judaism in Matthew." Pages 243–61 in *Studies in Matthew.* Translated by Rosemary Selle. Grand Rapids: Eerdmans, 2005.

———. *Matthew: A Commentary.* Translated by Wilhelm C. Linss. 3 vols. Hermeneia. Minneapolis: Augsburg, 1989–2005.

Macaskill, Grant. *Revealed Wisdom and Inaugurated Eschatology in Ancient Judaism and Early Christianity*. JSOTSup 115. Leiden: Brill, 2007.

Mallen, Peter. *The Reading and Transformation of Isaiah in Luke–Acts*. LNTS 367. London: T&T Clark, 2008.

Mann, Jacob. *The Bible as Read and Preached in the Old Synagogue: A Study in the Cycles of the Readings from Torah and Prophets, as well as from Psalms, and in the Structure of the Midrashic Homilies*. The Library of Biblical Studies. New York: KTAV, 1971.

Manning, Gary T. *Echoes of a Prophet: The Use of Ezekiel in the Gospel of John and in Literature of the Second Temple Period*. JSNTSup 270. London: T&T Clark, 2004.

Manson, T. W. "The Cleansing of the Temple." *BJRL* 33 (1951): 271–82.

Marcus, Joel. "*Birkat Ha-Minim* Revisited." *NTS* 55 (2009): 523–51.

———. "Crucifixion as Parodic Exaltation." *JBL* 125 (2006): 73–87.

———. "Identity and Ambiguity in Markan Christology." Pages 133–47 in Gaventa and Hays, *Seeking the Identity of Jesus*.

———. "The Jewish War and the *Sitz im Leben* of Mark." *JBL* 111 (1992): 441–62.

———. *Mark 1–16: A New Translation with Introduction and Commentary*. 2 vols. AB 27–27A. New York: Doubleday, 2000, 2009.

———. "No More Zealots in the House of the Lord: A Note on the History of Interpretation of Zech 14:21." *NovT* 55 (2013): 22–30.

———. "The Old Testament and the Death of Jesus: The Role of Scripture in the Gospel Passion Narratives." Pages 204–33 in *The Death of Jesus in Early Christianity*. Edited by John T. Carroll et al. Peabody, Mass.: Hendrickson, 1995.

———. "Son of Man as Son of Adam." *RB* 110 (2003): 38–61, 370–86.

———. *The Way of the Lord: Christological Exegesis of the Old Testament in the Gospel of Mark*. Louisville, Ky.: Westminster John Knox, 1992.

Marshall, I. Howard. *The Gospel of Luke: A Commentary on the Greek Text*. NIGTC. Grand Rapids: Eerdmans, 1978.

Martyn, J. Louis. *History and Theology in the Fourth Gospel*. 3d ed. Louisville, Ky.: Westminster John Knox, 2003.

———. "We Have Found Elijah." Pages 9–54 in *The Gospel of John in Christian History: Essays for Interpreters*. Eugene, Ore.: Wipf & Stock, 2004.

Mason, Steve. "Jews, Judaeans, Judaizing, Judaism: Problems of Categorization in Ancient History." *JSJ* 38 (2007): 457–512.

Matera, Frank J. *The Kingship of Jesus: Composition and Theology in Mark 15*. SBLDS 66. Chico, Calif.: Scholars Press, 1982.

Mays, James Luther. *Psalms*. Interpretation. Louisville, Ky.: Westminster John Knox, 1994.

McCasland, S. Vernon. "Matthew Twists the Scriptures." *JBL* 80 (1961): 143–48.

McHugh, John F. *John 1–4: A Critical and Exegetical Commentary*. ICC. London: T&T Clark, 2009.

Meeks, Wayne A. *The Prophet-King: Moses Traditions and the Johannine Christology*. NovTSup 14. Leiden: Brill, 1967.

Meier, John P. "The Historical Jesus and the Historical Sabbath." Pages 297–307 in *Redefining First-Century Jewish and Christian Identities: Essays in Honor of Ed Parish Sanders*. Edited by Fabian E. Udoh et al. Notre Dame: University of Notre Dame Press, 2008.

Menken, Maarten J. J. "Deuteronomy in Matthew's Gospel." Pages 42–62 in *Deuteronomy in the New Testament*. Edited by Maarten J. J. Menken and Steve Moyise. LNTS 358. London: T&T Clark, 2007.

———. *Matthew's Bible: The Old Testament Text of the Evangelist*. BETL 173. Leuven: Leuven University Press, 2004.

———. *Old Testament Quotations in the Fourth Gospel: Studies in Textual Form*. Kampen: Kok Pharos, 1996.

Metzger, Bruce M. *A Textual Commentary on the Greek New Testament*. 2d ed. Stuttgart: German Bible Society, 1994.

Meyers, Carol L., and Eric M. Meyers. *Zechariah 9–14: A New Translation with Introduction and Commentary*. AB 25C. New York: Doubleday, 1993.

Michaels, Ramsey. *The Gospel of John*. NICNT. Grand Rapids: Eerdmans, 2010.

Miller, Patrick D. *Interpreting the Psalms*. Philadelphia: Fortress, 1987.

Minear, Paul S. *The Good News according to Matthew: A Training Manual for Prophets*. St. Louis: Chalice, 2000.

———. "The Original Functions of John 21." *JBL* 102 (1983): 85–98.

Mitchell, Margaret M. "Patristic Counter-evidence to the Claim that 'The Gospels Were Written for All Christians.'" *NTS* 51 (2005): 36–79.

Mittmann-Richert, Ulrike. *Magnifikat und Benediktus: Die Ältesten Zeugnisse der Judenchristlichen Tradition von der Geburt Des Messias*. WUNT 2/90. Tübingen: Mohr Siebeck, 1996.

Moberly, R. W. L. *The Bible, Theology, and Faith: A Study of Abraham and Jesus*. Cambridge Studies in Christian Doctrine. Cambridge: Cambridge University Press, 2000.

Moessner, David P. *Lord of the Banquet: The Literary and Theological Significance of the Lukan Travel Narrative*. Minneapolis: Fortress, 1989.

———. "The 'Script' of the Scriptures in Acts: Suffering as God's 'Plan' (βουλή) for the World for the 'Release of Sins.'" Pages 218–50 in *History, Literature, and Society in the Book of Acts*. Edited by Ben Witherington III. Cambridge: Cambridge University Press, 1996.

———. "*Two* Lords 'at the Right Hand'? The Psalms and an Intertextual Reading of Peter's Pentecost Speech (Acts 2:14-36)." Pages 215–32 in *Literary Studies in Luke–Acts: Essays in Honor of Joseph B. Tyson*. Edited by Richard P. Thompson and Thomas E. Phillips. Macon, Ga.: Mercer University Press, 1998.

Moffitt, David M. "Righteous Bloodshed, Matthew's Passion Narrative, and the Temple's Destruction: Lamentations as a Matthean Intertext." *JBL* 125 (2006): 299–320.

Moloney, Francis J., S.D.B. *The Johannine Son of Man*. 2d ed. BSRel 14. Rome: Libreria Ateneo Salesiano, 1978.

———. *Signs and Shadows: Reading John 5–12*. Minneapolis: Fortress, 1996.

Moule, C. F. D. "The Christology of Acts." Pages 159–85 in *Studies in Luke–Acts: Essays Presented in Honor of Paul Schubert*. Edited by J. Louis Martyn and Leander E. Keck. Nashville: Abingdon, 1966.

Moyise, Steve. *Jesus and Scripture: Studying the New Testament Use of the Old Testament*. London: SPCK; Grand Rapids: Baker Academic, 2010.

Myers, Alicia D. "Abiding Words: An Introduction to Perspectives on John's Use of Scripture." Pages 1–20 in Myers and Schuchard, *Abiding Words*.

Myers, Alicia D., and Bruce G. Schuchard. *Abiding Words: The Use of Scripture in the Gospel of John*. Atlanta: SBL Press, 2015.

Myers, Ched. *Binding the Strong Man: A Political Reading of Mark's Story of Jesus*. Repr., Maryknoll, N.Y.: Orbis Books, 2008.

Nelson, Richard D. *Deuteronomy: A Commentary*. OTL. Louisville, Ky.: Westminster John Knox, 2002.

Newman, Carey C. *Paul's Glory-Christology: Tradition and Rhetoric*. NovTSupp 69. Leiden: Brill, 1992.

Neyrey, Jerome H. "'I Said: You Are Gods': Psalm 82:6 and John 10." *JBL* 108 (1989): 647–63.

————. "Jacob Traditions and the Interpretation of John 4:10-26." *CBQ* 41 (1979): 419–37.

Novenson, Matthew V. *Christ among the Messiahs: Christ Language in Paul and Messiah Language in Ancient Judaism*. Oxford: Oxford University Press, 2012.

Overman, J. Andrew. *Church and Community in Crisis: The Gospel according to Matthew*. The New Testament in Context. Valley Forge, Pa.: Trinity International, 1996.

————. *Matthew's Gospel and Formative Judaism: The Social World of the Matthean Community*. Minneapolis: Fortress, 1990.

Pao, David W. *Acts and the Isaianic New Exodus*. WUNT 2/130. Tübingen: Mohr Siebeck, 2000.

Pao, David W., and Eckhard J. Schnabel. "Luke." Pages 251–414 in Beale and Carson, *Commentary*.

Parry, Donald W., Emanuel Tov, et al., eds. *The Dead Sea Scrolls Reader*. Leiden: Brill, 2004–2005.

Parsons, Mikeal C. "Narrative Closure and Openness in the Plot of the Third Gospel: The Sense of an Ending in Luke 24:50–53." Pages 201–23 in *SBL Seminar Papers, 1986*. Edited by K. H. Richards. SBLSP 25. Atlanta: Scholars Press, 1986.

Pesch, Rudolf. *Das Markusevangelium*. 2 vols. HTKNT 2. Freiburg: Herder, 1976.

————. "Der Gottessohn im matthäischen Evangelienprolog (1-2)." *Biblica* 48 (1967): 395–420.

Peterson, Dwight N. *The Origins of Mark: The Markan Community in Current Debate*. BibInt 48. Leiden: Brill, 2000.

Phillips, Peter. *The Prologue of the Fourth Gospel: A Sequential Reading*. LNTS 294. London: T&T Clark, 2006.

Porter, Stanley E., ed. *Hearing the Old Testment in the New Testament*. McMaster New Testament Studies. Grand Rapids: Eerdmans, 2006.

————. "Scripture Justifies Mission: The Use of the Old Testament in Luke–Acts." Pages 104–26 in Porter, *Hearing the Old Testament in the New Testament*.

Prabhu, George M. Soares. *The Formula Quotations in the Infancy Narrative of Matthew: An Enquiry into the Tradition History of Mt 1–2*. AnBib 63. Rome: Biblical Institute, 1976.

Ratzinger, Joseph (Pope Benedict XVI). *Jesus of Nazareth: From the Baptism in the Jordan to the Transfiguration*. Translated by Adrian J. Walker. New York: Doubleday, 2007.

Reinhartz, Adele. "The Gospel of John: How the 'Jews' Became Part of the Plot." Pages 99–116 in *Jesus, Judaism and Christian Anti-Judaism: Reading the New Testament after the Holocaust*. Edited by Paula Fredriksen and Adele Reinhartz. Louisville, Ky.: Westminster John Knox, 2002.

Repschinski, Boris. "'For He Will Save His People from Their Sins' (Mt 1:21): A Christology for Christian Jews." *CBQ* 68 (2006): 248–67.

Reynolds, Ben. *The Apocalyptic Son of Man in the Gospel of John*. WUNT 2/249. Tübingen: Mohr Siebeck, 2008.

Rhoads, David, Joanna Dewey, and Donald Michie. *Mark as Story: An Introduction to the Narrative of a Gospel*. 2d ed. Philadelphia: Fortress, 1999.

Riches, John. *Conflicting Mythologies: Identity Formation in the Gospels of Mark and Matthew*. Edinburgh: T&T Clark, 2000.

Ricoeur, Paul. *Oneself as Another*. Chicago: University of Chicago Press, 1995.

Ringe, Sharon H. *Jesus, Liberation, and the Biblical Jubilee: Images for Ethics and Christology*. Philadelphia: Fortress, 1985.

Ritter, Christine. *Rachels Klage Im Antiken Judentum und Frühen Christentum: Eine Auslegungsgeschichtliche Studie*. AGJU 52. Leiden: Brill, 2003.

Robinson, James M., and Helmut Koester. *Trajectories through Early Christianity*. Philadelphia: Fortress, 1971.

Rösel, Martin. "Die Psalmüberschriften des Septuaginta-Psalters." Pages 124–48 in *Der Septuaginta Psalter: Sprachliche und theologische Aspekte*. Edited by Erich Zenger. HBS 32. Freiburg: Herder, 2001.

Rowe, C. Kavin. "Acts 2:36 and the Continuity of Lukan Christology." *NTS* 53 (2007): 37–56.

———. *Early Narrative Christology: The Lord in the Gospel of Luke*. BZNW 139. Berlin: De Gruyter, 2006.

———. "History, Hermeneutics, and the Unity of Luke–Acts." *JSNT* 28 (2005): 131–57.

———. "Luke and the Trinity: An Essay in Ecclesial Biblical Theology." *SJT* 56 (2003): 1–26.

———. "Luke–Acts and the Imperial Cult: A Way through the Conundrum?" *JSNT* 27 (2005): 279–300.

———. *World Upside Down: Reading Acts in the Graeco-Roman Age*. New York: Oxford University Press, 2009.

Rubenstein, Jeffrey L. *The History of Sukkot in the Second Temple and Rabbinic Periods*. BJS 302. Atlanta: Scholars Press, 1995.

Ruppert, Lothar. *Jesus Als der Leidende Gerechte? Der Weg Jesu Im Lichte Eines Alt- und Zwischentestamentlichen Motivs*. SBS. Stuttgart: KBW Verlag, 1972.

Rusam, Dietrich. *Das Alte Testament bei Lukas*. BZNW 112. Berlin: De Gruyter, 2003.

Saldarini, Anthony U. *Matthew's Christian-Jewish Community*. Chicago Studies in the History of Judaism. Chicago: University of Chicago Press, 1994.

Sanders, E. P. *Jesus and Judaism*. Philadelphia: Fortress, 1985.

———. *Judaism: Practice and Belief, 63 BCE–66 CE*. Philadelphia: Trinity International, 1992.

Sanders, Jack T. *The Jews in Luke–Acts*. Philadelphia: Fortress, 1987.

Sanders, James A. "A Hermeneutic Fabric: Psalm 118 in Luke's Entrance Narrative." Pages 140–53 in Evans and Sanders, *Luke and Scripture*.

———. "Isaiah in Luke." Pages 14–25 in Evans and Sanders, *Luke and Scripture*.

Schaberg, Jane. "Feminist Interpretations of the Infancy Narrative of Matthew." Pages 15–36 in *A Feminist Companion to Mariology*. Edited by Amy-Jill Levine and Maria Mayo Robbins. Feminist Companion to the New Testament and Early Christian Writings. London: T&T Clark, 2005.

Schneck, Richard. *Isaiah in the Gospel of Mark, I–VIII*. Bibal Dissertation Series 1. Vallejo, Calif.: Bibal, 1994.

Schneider, G. "Das Bildwort von der Lampe." *ZNW* 61 (1970): 183–209.

Schneiders, Sandra M. *The Revelatory Text: Interpreting the New Testament as Sacred Scripture*. San Francisco: HarperCollins, 1991.

Schnelle, Udo. *Theology of the New Testament*. Grand Rapids: Baker, 2009.

Schuchard, Bruce G. *Scripture within Scripture: The Interrelationship of Form and Function in the Explicit Old Testament Citations in the Gospel of John*. SBLDS 133. Atlanta: Scholars Press, 1992.

Schüssler Fiorenza, Elisabeth. *Jesus: Miriam's Child, Sophia's Prophet: Critical Issues in Feminist Christology*. New York: Continuum, 1994.

Schweizer, Eduard. *Das Evangelium nach Markus*. NTD. Göttingen: Vandenhoeck & Ruprecht, 1967.

Scott, James M., ed. *Exile: Old Testament, Jewish, and Christian Conceptions*. JSJSup 56. Leiden: Brill, 1997.

Scott, Martin. *Sophia and the Johannine Jesus*. JSNTSup 71. Sheffield: JSOT Press, 1992.

Segal, Alan F. *Two Powers in Heaven: Early Rabbinic Reports about Christianity and Gnosticism*. Leiden: Brill, 2002. Repr., Waco, Tex.: Baylor University Press, 2012.

Seitz, Christopher R. *Word without End: The Old Testament as Abiding Theological Witness*. Grand Rapids: Eerdmans, 1998. Repr., Waco, Tex.: Baylor University Press, 2005.

Senior, Donald. "The Lure of the Formula Quotations: Re-assessing Matthew's Use of the Old Testament with the Passion Narrative as a Test Case." Pages 89–115 in Tuckett, *Scriptures in the Gospels*.

Shively, Elizabeth E. *Apocalyptic Imagination in the Gospel of Mark: The Literary and Theological Role of Mark 3:22–30*. BZNW 189. Berlin: De Gruyter, 2012.

Sievers, Joseph. "'Where Two or Three . . .': The Rabbinic Concept of Shekhinah and Matthew 18:20." Pages 47–61 in *The Jewish Roots of Christian Liturgy*. Edited by Eugene J. Fisher. New York: Paulist, 1990.

Sim, David C. *The Gospel of Matthew and Christian Judaism: The History and Social Setting of the Matthean Community*. Studies of the New Testament and Its World. Edinburgh: T&T Clark, 1998.

Smith, Charles W. F. "No Time for Figs." *JBL* 79 (1960): 315–27.

Smith, D. Moody. "The Contribution of J. Louis Martyn to the Understanding of the Gospel of John." Pages 275–94 in *The Conversation Continues: Studies in Paul and John in Honor of J. Louis Martyn*. Edited by Robert T. Fortna and Beverly R. Gaventa. Nashville: Abingdon, 1990.

———. *The Fourth Gospel in Four Dimensions: Judaism and Jesus, the Gospels and Scripture*. Columbia: University of South Carolina Press, 2008.

———. *John*. Abingdon New Testament Commentaries. Nashville: Abingdon, 1999.

Smith, Stephen H. "The Function of the Son of David Tradition in Mark's Gospel." *NTS* 42 (1996): 523–39.

Spiegel, Shalom. *The Last Trial: On the Legends and Lore of the Command to Abraham to Offer Isaac as a Sacrifice: The Akedah*. Translated by J. Goldin. New York: Pantheon, 1967.

Squires, John T. *The Plan of God in Luke–Acts*. SNTSMS 76. Cambridge: Cambridge University Press, 1993.

Stanton, Graham N. "The Fourfold Gospel." *NTS* 43 (1997): 317–46.

———. *A Gospel for a New People: Studies in Matthew*. Louisville, Ky.: Westminster John Knox, 1993.

———. *The Gospels and Jesus.* 2d ed. Oxford Bible Series. Oxford: Oxford University Press, 2002.

Steinmetz, David C. "Uncovering a Second Narrative: Detective Fiction and the Construction of Historical Method." Pages 54–65 in Davis and Hays, *Art of Reading Scripture.*

Stendahl, Krister. *The School of St. Matthew and Its Use of the Old Testament.* 2d ed. ASNU 20. Lund: Gleerup, 1968.

Strauss, Mark. *The Davidic Messiah in Luke–Acts: The Promise and Its Fulfillment in Lukan Christology.* JSNTSup 110. Sheffield: Sheffield Academic, 1995.

Strecker, Georg. *Der Weg der Gerechtigkeit: Untersuchung Zur Theologie Des Matthäus.* Göttingen: Vandenhoeck & Ruprecht, 1966.

Streett, Andrew. *The Vine and the Son of Man: Eschatological Interpretation of Psalm 80 in Early Judaism.* Minneapolis: Fortress, 2014.

Suggs, M. Jack. *Wisdom, Christology, and Law in Matthew's Gospel.* Cambridge, Mass.: Harvard University Press, 1970.

Suhl, Alfred. *Die Funktion der alttestamentliche Zitate und Anspielungen im Markusevangelium.* Gütersloh: Gütersloher Verlagshaus Gerd Mohn, 1965.

Swancutt, Diana. "Hungers Assuaged by the Bread from Heaven: 'Eating Jesus' as Isaian Call to Belief: The Confluence of Isaiah 55 and Psalm 78(77) in John 6:22-71." Pages 218–51 in Evans and Sanders, *Early Christian Interpretation.*

Swartley, Willard M. *Israel's Scripture Traditions and the Synoptic Gospels: Story Shaping Story.* Peabody, Mass.: Hendrickson, 1994.

———. *Mark: The Way for All Nations.* Scottdale, Pa.: Herald, 1979.

Schweitzer, Albert. *The Quest of the Historical Jesus.* Minneapolis: Fortress, 2001. German original: *Die Geschichte der Leben—Jesu—Forschung.* Tübingen: Mohr, 1913.

Talbert, Charles H. *Reading Acts: A Literary and Theological Commentary on the Acts of the Apostles.* Rev. ed. Reading the New Testament. Macon, Ga.: Smyth & Helwys, 2005.

———. *Reading John: A Literary and Theological Commentary on the Fourth Gospel and the Johannine Epistles.* New York: Crossroad, 1992.

Tannehill, Robert C. "Disciples in Mark: The Function of a Narrative Role." *JR* 57 (1977): 386–405.

Taylor, Vincent. *The Gospel according to St. Mark: The Greek Text with Introduction, Notes, and Indexes.* 2d ed. Grand Rapids: Baker, 1966.

Telford, William R. *The Barren Temple and the Withered Tree: A Redaction-Critical Analysis of the Cursing of the Fig-Tree Pericope in Mark's Gospel and Its Relation to the Cleansing of the Temple Tradition.* JSNTSup 1. Sheffield: JSOT Press, 1980.

Thompson, Marianne Meye. *The God of the Gospel of John.* Grand Rapids: Eerdmans, 2001.

———. *John: A Commentary.* NTL. Louisville, Ky.: Westminster John Knox, 2015.

———. "Learning the Identity of Jesus from the Gospel of John." Pages 166–79 in Gaventa and Hays, *Seeking the Identity of Jesus.*

———. "'They Bear Witness to Me': The Psalms in the Passion Narrative of the Gospel of John." Pages 267–83 in *The Word Leaps the Gap: Essays on Scripture and Theology in Honor of Richard B. Hays.* Edited by J. Ross Wagner, C. Kavin Rowe, and A. Katherine Grieb. Grand Rapids: Eerdmans, 2008.

Tov, Emanuel. *The Text-Critical Use of the Septuagint in Biblical Research.* 3d ed. Winona Lake, Ind.: Eisenbrauns, 2015.

Trilling, Wolfgang. *Das wahre Israel: Studien zur Theologie des Matthäusevangeliums.* Erfurter Theologische Studien 7. Leipzig: St. Benno-Verlag, 1959.

Tuckett, Christopher M. "The Christology of Luke–Acts." Pages 133–64 in *The Unity of Luke–Acts.* Edited by Joseph Verheyden. Leuven: Leuven University Press, 1999.

———. "Matthew: The Social and Historical Context—Jewish Christian and/or Gentile?" Pages 99–129 in *The Gospel of Matthew at the Crossroads of Early Christianity.* Edited by Donald Senior. BETL 243. Leuven: Uitgeverig Peeters, 2011.

———, ed. *The Scriptures in the Gospels.* BETL 131. Leuven: Leuven University Press, 1997.

Turner, Max. "'Trinitarian' Pneumatology in the New Testament? Towards an Explanation of the Worship of Jesus." *AsTJ* 57–58 (2003): 167–86.

Ulfgard, Håkan. *The Story of Sukkoth.* BGBE 34. Tübingen: Mohr Siebeck, 1998.

The United Methodist Hymnal. Nashville: United Methodist Publishing House, 1989.

Vermes, Geza. *The Dead Sea Scrolls in English.* 4th ed. Sheffield: Sheffield Academic, 1995.

Waard, J. de. *A Comparative Study of the Old Testament Text in the Dead Sea Scrolls and in the New Testament.* STDJ 4. Leiden: Brill, 1965.

Wacholder, Ben Zion. *Essays on Jewish Chronology and Chronography.* New York: KTAV, 1976.

Wagner, J. Ross. *Heralds of the Good News: Isaiah and Paul "in Concert" in the Letter to the Romans.* NovTSup 101. Leiden: Brill, 2002.

———. "Psalm 118 in Luke–Acts: Tracing a Narrative Thread." Pages 154–78 in Evans and Sanders, *Early Christian Interpretation.*

———. *Reading the Sealed Book: Old Greek Isaiah and the Problem of Septuagint Hermeneutics.* FAT 88. Tübingen: Mohr Siebeck; Waco, Tex.: Baylor University Press, 2013.

Walaskay, Paul W. *And So We Came to Rome: The Political Perspective of St. Luke.* SNTSMS 49. Cambridge: Cambridge University Press, 1983.

Watson, Francis. *Paul and the Hermeneutics of Faith.* London: T&T Clark, 2004.

Watts, John D. W. *Isaiah 34–66.* WBC 25. Waco, Tex.: Word Books, 1987.

Watts, Rikki E. *Isaiah's New Exodus and Mark.* WUNT 2/88. Tübingen: Mohr Siebeck, 1997.

Weaver, Dorothy Jean. "'Thus You Will Know Them by Their Fruits': The Roman Characters of the Gospel of Matthew." Pages 107–27 in *The Gospel of Matthew in Its Roman Imperial Context.* Edited by John Riches and David C. Sim. JSNTSup 276. London: T&T Clark, 2005.

Weeden, Theodore J. *Mark-Traditions in Conflict.* Philadelphia: Fortress, 1971.

Wildberger, Hans. *Isaiah: A Continental Commentary.* Translated by Thomas H. Trapp. Continental Commentaries. Minneapolis: Fortress, 1991 (c2002).

Willett, Michael. *Wisdom Christology in the Fourth Gospel.* San Francisco: Mellen, 1992.

Williams, Catrin H. "Isaiah in John's Gospel." Pages 101–16 in *Isaiah in the New Testament.* Edited by Steve Moyise and Maarten J. J. Menken. London: T&T Clark, 2005.

Williams, Rowan. *Christ on Trial: How the Gospel Unsettles Our Judgment.* London: Fount, 2000.

———. *The Edge of Words: God and the Habits of Language.* London: Bloomsbury, 2014.

———. *The Wound of Knowledge: A Theological History from the New Testament to Luther and St. John of the Cross.* Eugene, Ore.: Wipf & Stock, 1998.

Witherington, Ben, III. *The Christology of Jesus*. Minneapolis: Fortress, 1990.

————. *Jesus the Sage: The Pilgrimage of Wisdom*. Minneapolis: Fortress, 1994.

————. *John's Wisdom: A Commentary on the Fourth Gospel*. Louisville, Ky.: Westminster John Knox, 1995.

————. *Matthew*. Smyth & Helwys Bible Commentary. Macon, Ga.: Smyth & Helwys, 2006.

Wood, James. "Victory Speech." *New Yorker*, November 17, 2008.

Wrede, Wilhelm. *Das Messiasgeheimnis in Den Evangelien*. Göttingen: Vandernhoeck & Ruprecht. 1901. ET: *The Messianic Secret*. Translated by J. C. G. Greig. Cambridge: J. Clarke, 1971.

Wright, N. T. *How God Became King: The Forgotten Story of the Gospels*. New York: HarperOne, 2012.

————. *Jesus and the Victory of God*. Christian Origins and the Question of God 2. Minneapolis: Fortress, 1996.

————. *The New Testament and the People of God*. Christian Origins and the Question of God 1. Minneapolis: Fortress, 1992.

————. *Paul and the Faithfulness of God*. Christian Origins and the Question of God 4. Minneapolis: Fortress, 2013.

Yee, Gale A. *Jewish Feasts and the Gospel of John*. Wilmington, Del.: Michael Glazier, 1989.

Yoder, John Howard. *The Politics of Jesus: Vicit Agnus Noster*. 2d ed. Grand Rapids: Eerdmans, 1994.

Index of Scripture and Ancient Sources

Index of Names

Lane, William L., 385n111, 385n115, 388n136, 390n160, 421n136
Leim, Joshua E., 405n131
Levenson, Jon D., 378n53
Leverett, Gaylen, 394n34
Levine, Amy-Jill, 393n28, 394n31, 399n71, 401n92
Lierman, John, 427n24
Lincoln, Andrew T., 428n30, 430n43, 430n49, 431n60, 434n75, 436n94, 438n114
Linss, Wilhelm C., 391n4
Litwak, Kenneth Duncan, 408n3
Longenecker, Richard N., 417n89
Lord, George deforest, 411n25
Luther, Martin, 1–4, 348, 367n1
Luz, Ulrich, 391n4, 392n8, 393n28, 395n44, 397n61, 400n82, 402n104, 404n116, 406n144, 407n154

Macaskill, Grant, 404n117, 404n121, 434n75
MacDonald, Nathan, 434n75
Mallen, Peter, 415n69
Mann, Jacob, 374n17
Manning, Gary T., 435n83, 435n88
Manson, T. W., 381n73
Marcus, Joel, 98, 372n5, 372n8, 373n12, 373n14, 374n17, 374n20, 374n21, 374n22, 376n28, 379n59, 380n66, 380n67, 381n70, 381n79, 381n80, 382n82, 382n83, 383n94, 384n99, 384n101, 384n102, 384n105, 384n105, 384n106, 385n112, 385n113, 385n114, 385n115, 385n116, 385n117, 386n123, 387n127, 387n130, 388n136, 389n139, 389n143, 390n155, 401n95, 431n56, 438n111
Marsh, John, 381n71

Marshall, I. Howard, 411n31, 422n147
Martyn, J. Louis, 414n57, 428n27, 431n56
Marxsen, Willi, 97, 390n153
Mason, Anita, 391n164
Mason, Steve, 431n54
Matera, Frank J., 381n80
Mays, James Luther, 429n42
McCasland, S. Vernon, 392n11
McHugh, John F., 434n75, 437n105
Meeks, Wayne A., 380n69, 427n24, 435n93
Meier, John P., 424n2
Menken, Maarten J. J., 371n24, 391n5, 392n12, 394n35, 395n40, 395n41, 396n52–53, 399n75, 402n102, 403n110, 403n111, 403n112, 406n140, 406n147, 407n148, 416n83, 424n4, 426n14, 427n17, 434n82
Metzger, Bruce M., 380n66, 399n77, 400n86
Meyers, Carol L., 387n129
Meyers, Eric M., 387n129
Michaels, J. Ramsey, 431n60
Michie, Donald, 373n10
Miller, Arthur, 357, 440n8
Miller, Patrick D., 429n42
Miller, Troy, 434n77
Milton, John, 370n19, 411n25
Minear, Paul S., 391n2, 425n8
Mitchell, Margaret M., 388n135
Mittmann-Richert, Ulrike, 409n12, 415n71
Moberly, R. W. L., 395n48, 395n50
Moessner, David P., 410n23, 410n24, 415n72, 416n81, 416n84, 418n103
Moffitt, David M., 401n96
Moloney, Francis J., S.D.B., 431n51, 438n111